The Wines of California

Born in London, Stephen Brook studied English and philosophy at Trinity College, Cambridge. After many years as a publisher's editor, he became a freelance writer in 1982, specializing in travel and wine. His *Liquid Gold: Dessert Wines of the World* won the André Simon Award in 1987. Other awards include the Wines of France award in 1995 and the Bunch Award for wine writer of the year in 1996. He is the author of *Sauvignon Blanc and Sémillon* and *Pauillac*; his *Sauternes and the Other Sweet Wines of Bordeaux* published by Faber in 1995 is now the standard work on the subject. His many travel books – including *New York Days, New York Nights, The Double Eagle*, and *L.A. Lore* – have won wide acclaim, and *The Club: The Jews of Modern Britain* was a best seller. He has contributed travel articles to many newspapers and magazines and writes regularly on wine for *Decanter*, of which he is a Contributing Editor, and *Condé Nast Traveller*.

THE WINES OF CALIFORNIA

STEPHEN BROOK

faber and faber

LONDON · NEW YORK

First published in 1999
by Faber and Faber Limited
3 Queen Square London WC1N 3AU

Published in the United States by
Faber and Faber, Inc.,
a division of Farrar, Straus and Giroux, Inc., New York

Phototypeset by Intype London Ltd
Printed in England by Clays Ltd, St Ives plc

A CIP record for this book
is available from the British Library

ISBN 0–571–19030–8

2 4 6 8 10 9 7 5 3 1

Contents

CONTENTS

Maps

Acknowledgments

I would like to thank the Wine Institute of California for their assistance both with travel and with itineraries, and for organizing tastings and other practical help. In San Francisco, Jennifer Sangiuliano organized my travels to perfection, and I also appreciated the assistance of Joe Rollo, Wendell Lee, and Gladys Horiuchi. In London John McLaren and Venla Freeman kindly acted as a liaison between San Francisco and myself. Brent Shortridge and Kate Jones of the Napa Valley Vintners Association organized tastings and practical assistance in California, and Corwyn Lovin of the International Visitors Program at UC Davis was an enthusiastic and knowledgeable companion on tours of the Sierra Foothills and elsewhere. I also wish to thank, for their time and attention and general helpfulness, Bernadette Byrne in Mendocino, Robyn Rauh of A Taste of Monterey, and Mark Chandler of the Lodi-Woodbridge Winegrape Commission.

The wine country is well known for its openness and hospitality, but I do need to single out and thank the following individuals, who lodged me, fed me, and talked to me: Justin and Deborah Baldwin, Bo Barrett, Davis Bynum, Eileen Crane, Paul Draper, Gary Eberle, Randall Grahm, Tim Hanni MW, John and Steven Kautz, Mike Lee, Doug Meador, Sir Peter Michael, Lisa Ota of Wente, Jeff Patterson, Alan and Lesley Pierson, Tony Soter, Philip and Brigitta Togni, Marimar Torres; Randy Ullom, Jenny Williamson and Judy Groverman Walker, all of Kendall-Jackson; Bill Vyenielo and Richard Ward. In Britain, Neville Blech, K.D. Abigail, Bibendum, Thorman Hunt, Vinceremos and Joseph Berkmann were generous with tastings and samples, and I wish to thank Jancis Robinson for allowing me to ransack her wine library.

Introduction

I have sometimes been asked what it is about California wines that appeals to me so strongly. The answer is brief: generosity. Blessed with a climate as close to ideal as one could imagine for grape growing, most California wine regions routinely succeed in offering rich, full-bodied, fleshy, opulent wines that make an immediate sensory appeal. California wine offers instantaneous pleasure. Of course, there is more to a great wine than its opening invitation to the senses, but it makes for a terrific start.

I first got to know and drink good California wines in the late 1970s. Working in those days for an academic publisher in London, I would occasionally find myself on the West Coast visiting authors at the major universities. Sometimes I would be invited to their homes for dinner and I would throw out the mildly offensive remark that the wines of California were scarcely a match for their European models. Since many of my professorial friends were also wine buffs, my dismissive statement nearly always had the desired effect of goading them to descend into their cellars, or wherever their wines were hoarded, to prise out a distinguished bottle – a Martha's Vineyard or a Chalone or a Stony Hill – just to prove me wrong. It was a lousy trick to play on them, but at least we all got to drink and enjoy good wine.

Meanwhile back in London I was attending tastings, often organized by the late Geoffrey Roberts, who did so much to persuade a conservative drinking public that California had something special to offer complacent palates. There I got to know wines such as Ridge Monte Bello and Mayacamas Cabernets, and was able to compare Napa Cabernets from the great 1974 vintage. Some years later, living for three months in New York, I roamed the wine stores, plucking interesting-sounding bottles from the shelves. This too contributed, in a pleasingly haphazard way, to my education in California wine. Most memorable were the Fumé Blanc bottlings from Chateau St Jean. These were vineyard-designated bottlings made by Richard Arrowood. Very high in alcohol and lavishly oaked, they bore no resemblance to either white Graves or racy Sancerre. They were generous to a fault; big brash wines that, at the time, I adored. I'm not sure that I would still like such wines – the style has long been out of fashion – but they bowled me over.

Ever since I have been a regular visitor to California, and whenever chance or a commission took me to the West Coast, I made time to visit estates and learn more about their wines. I was impressed then, as I am impressed now, by the welcome accorded me. I recall hours spent in the spring sunshine at Mayacamas and Mount Eden, enjoying the view and a glass of something splendid in the company of the winemaker or owner. There were no secrets, no mystique about wine. My questions, whether about viticulture or winemaking techniques, were readily answered. All that mattered, finally, was the liquid in the glass, that distillation of soil and sunshine, those heady aromas of vibrant fruit, the persistence of flavour at the back of the palate. Wine, all my days in California persuaded me, was about pleasure.

It is, of course, all very well my professing a deep affection for these wines. It is another matter to write about them. It may seem a trifle perverse for an Englishman to survey the Californian scene, but I hope that the fact that I am very much an outsider may be seen in some respects as advantageous. I have no intention of using my familiarity with European vineyards and wines to make direct comparisons between them and their Californian counterparts. Californian winemakers keep insisting, and rightly so, that they are not trying to make Gevrey-Chambertin or Volnay when they produce Pinot Noir. Instead they are trying to produce Carneros Pinot Noir, or Santa Maria Valley Pinot Noir, or whatever.

Fair enough. But what does that mean in practice? What it means is a summation of everything that makes California distinctive: its climate, its viticultural practices, choices made during vinification, and indeed a wine culture that differs considerably from its European opposite number. It is the purpose of this book, arguably an unrealizable one, to establish what those differences are and why they matter.

At the same time I hope this book will have some value as a

work of reference. The wine industry in California changes so rapidly that any book is bound to be at least partly out of date even while fingers are tapping at keyboards. Nonetheless there is a wealth of information – about wine regions, grape varieties, individual vineyard sites, fads, fashions, and scientific developments in vineyard and winery – that will round out any wine enthusiast's appreciation of Californian wine, yet this information is not always easy to find. The first sections of this book deal with the many wine regions within California. I regret to say they will not make for racy reading, but I hope they will help the reader sort out whether Green Valley is part of Russian River Valley or vice versa, and where on earth Cucamonga is. I also hope that some readers will find the lists of single vineyards useful: more and more 'vineyard-designated' wines are appearing from California, but it is often difficult to work out where these vineyards are and what is supposed to be so special about them.

In the following sections I look at issues in viticulture and winemaking, assuming a certain basic knowledge but not requiring technical expertise on the part of the reader. Those who find such matters boring can skip these chapters, but I believe they are crucial to an understanding of the basic preoccupation at the core of this book: what is it that makes Californian wines distinctive?

One peculiar feature of this book is the final section on wineries. With so many wineries in California, a complete and exhaustive discussion of each and every one of them would have resulted in a book that weighed as much as a case of magnums. In the cases of Napa and Sonoma, I have made a series of selections. Each of these regions has two chapters. In the first I have selected wineries that seem of exceptional interest or quality or importance and dealt with them at some length; the second deals, more briefly, with other properties within the region.

I have, in my study, thousands of tasting notes devoted to California wines. The reader will be relieved to know that I do not propose to present them here. The books by James Laube and Robert Parker are stuffed with tasting notes, so anyone desperate to know what a 1992 Monteviña Barbera tasted like can flick through those immense tomes. Most California wines are consumed young, are indeed intended to be consumed young. There seems little point in my reprinting, at enormous length, my reflections on wines that only the smallest fraction of the readers are likely to experience. Some exceptions have crept in here and there, but they are not a central feature of this book.

On the other hand, I hope that anyone perusing this book will, at the end of a very long day, have enough information to know how to approach the buying and drinking of California wines. I make clear my personal preferences among wineries, among wine regions, among vintages. I believe that is what is required of a wine writer as opposed to a wine critic. I do not see it, at least not in the context of this book, as my primary role to assess individual wines. That task I am happy to leave to my *confrères*, many of whom have tasted more exhaustively than I would ever wish to do. My goal is different: to come to grips with a relatively new and fascinating wine culture. Of course I have fallen short, but the exploration has been absorbing and infinitely rewarding, and I hope some of my own enthusiasm will be communicated through the pages that follow.

I

From the Beginning

In the beginning there was coast and ocean. California is climate. Its history is interesting but in a sense irrelevant, so dominant is the particularity of the Californian climate. The briefest visit to the West Coast can persuade the visitor that there are few places on earth so climatically benign as California. Agoston Haraszthy, the Hungarian entrepreneur who is known as the 'Father of California Wine', noted in 1862: 'The California climate, with the exception of the sea-coast, especially where the prevailing western winds drive the fogs over the locality, is eminently adapted for the culture of grape-vines, and it is proved conclusively that no European locality can equal within 200 per cent its productiveness. The oldest inhabitants have no recollection of a failure in the crops of grapes.'[1] From spring until autumn rain is almost unheard of. Sunshine, rarely tainted by worrisome humidity, pours from the skies. The natural aridity of the land has long been countered by irrigation. Citrus groves, orchards, and vineyards flourish where once there was sand and scrub. Unnaturally, California has been made fertile.

Yet sunshine alone is insufficient to produce great wine. Otherwise the most celebrated growths in the Old World would come from Algeria and Morocco, which is hardly the case. California has another factor to toss into the climatic pot: the ocean. The Pacific is cold, and its collision with the warm land mass of the California coast generates the morning fogs that make an August holiday in San Francisco so frustrating. The cold water rippling along the surface of the ocean condenses the warmer air above, thus creating billowing fog. While inland California, or even Berkeley across the Bay, is basking in 80-degree sunshine, it can be a chilly 60 degrees in San Francisco until, later in the morning, the fog at last burns off. A similar phenomenon occurs in numerous places along the coast. That is why there are virtually no vineyards close to the ocean. The terraced vineyards of Bandol or the Ligurian coast look out on to the balmy Mediterranean, but there is no equivalent in California. It is simply too cold to ripen grapes along the shoreline.

Inland, meanwhile, as the day wears on the heat begins to rise, and cooler air rushes through the coastal gaps, cooling those inland valleys and tempering a heat that would otherwise bake the vines. The further one moves northwards (in the north-south oriented valleys of the North Coast) or eastwards (in the east-west oriented valleys of the Central Coast), the less pronounced is the maritime influence and the higher the temperature. California's largest grape-growing region, the San Joaquin Valley, is too far inland to experience any maritime influence, and consequently the region is poorly suited to the production of good-quality wine. But in Napa, Mendocino, or Santa Barbara, those fogs and breezes help to moderate the summer heat and prolong the growing season; they help to conserve acidity in the grapes and give the fruit a natural balance that favours the potential for fine wine production.

In some areas, grapes are grown above the fog line: Sonoma Mountain, Howell Mountain, the Mendocino Ridges. Here elevation compensates for the absence of cooling fog, but the climatic variation among the mountain vineyards, as well as their more impoverished soils, gives a completely different structure to the growing season and hence to the quality of the fruit produced, which tends to be more dense and tannic. Nonetheless, the great majority of high-quality wine regions are subject to maritime influence. It is not only the mountain regions that experience the cool nights that help retain acidity in the grapes; chilly nights are common in most wine regions except for the Central Valley.

In 1938 two professors at the Davis campus of the University of California (hereafter referred to as UC Davis), Maynard Amerine and Albert Winkler, devised the 'heat summation system' which was adopted as the best, or at least the most convenient, way to assess the suitability of a region to specific varietals and viticultural practices. The system was to prove of immense importance. What Amerine and Winkler did was measure the average daily temperature from April to October within various wine regions. A 'degree day' was the number of days the temperature exceeded 50 degrees Fahrenheit. If the average temperature was 65 degrees, then the

degree day was expressed as 15. The lower the total number
of degree days, the cooler the region. Amerine and Winkler, on
this basis, divided California into five regions. Region I has fewer
than 2,500 degree days (for the sake of European comparison,
Trier in the Mosel has 1,730, Beaune 2,400). Region II has 2,501
to 3,000 (Bordeaux is a low Region II, Piedmont a high one).
Region III has 3,001 to 3,500, Region IV 3,501 to 4,000, and
Region V over 4,001. Most wine regions associated with high
quality fall within Regions I and II.

The system was widely used, and still is, but today its deficiencies
are openly acknowledged. Temperature is, after all, just one of
many ways to measure climate. The system ignored such factors
as rainfall, cloud cover, fog, latitude, and wind, which can affect
ripening patterns. Moreover, the mean temperature was calculated
by adding together the minimum and maximum temperatures for
a day and dividing by two, which may have the merit of simplicity
but not of accuracy. James Halliday has pointed out the short-
comings persuasively: 'The distinction between mean and true
average temperature becomes important when considering the difference between (say) the climate of the Napa floor and the adjacent
mountain tops or between the North Coast and the Central Coast.
Thus if St Helena has a daily range of 95°F and 50°F, but with fog
in the morning, sea breezes in the afternoon, and only a short
period of temperature above 85°F, it will nonetheless have a higher
mean temperature than the mountaintop which has a lower
maximum, a similar minimum but – because of the absence of fog
– more effective heat during the day.'[2] It was miscalculations such
as this which persuaded growers, on the advice of Davis professors,
that the Salinas Valley in Monterey was a suitable place to grow
Cabernet Sauvignon. They were to be proved wrong.

Today there are far more sophisticated ways of measuring climatic variations. The broad weather patterns in the principal
regions are now well understood, if only after long and not always
happy experience, and today the focus has switched to microclimates. The Adcon system, for instance, is a weather station
implanted in the vineyard; it yields a great deal of data on not just
weather but soil moisture, and permits easy comparison with
similar data acquired from other weather stations. Such systems
help vineyard managers not only to assess the maturation of their
ripening fruit, but also to see how suitable certain sites are for

specific varietals or clones. In some cases, the information collected by the Adcon system can crucially affect the decision whether or not to plant vines in a particular spot.

It is not clear whether the first people to plant vines in California were all that conscious of climate, the feature since recognized as paramount. They were Spanish missionaries eager to produce wine primarily for sacramental purposes. Indeed the first vines were planted not in northern California but at Mission San Francisco Xavier on the southern California peninsula, now part of Mexico, where a Jesuit priest, Father Juan Ugarte, planted vines in 1697. The first mission in what is now California was established by Father Junipero Serra in 1769 at San Diego, but there is no conclusive evidence that wines were planted there.

Over the next few decades twenty-one missions were established further north, and where a mission was established, a vineyard was bound to follow (with the exception of two missions along the coast where the climate was too foggy for viticulture). By far the largest was the Mission San Gabriel at Los Angeles. The variety planted was either Criolla, a variety long cultivated in Mexico but unknown in Europe, or a variety closely related to the Chilean one known as Pais.[3] Once established in California, it was given, for obvious reasons, the American name of Mission. Since Mission is still grown, it is possible to sample wines that may be akin to those made in the eighteenth century. Mission makes a rather miserable table wine, but takes well to fortification.

In 1833 the missions were secularized by the Mexican government, and from this point on the production of wine, hitherto a preserve of a conservative church, became open to entrepreneurial immigrants. Foremost among them was a Bordelais with the encouraging name of Jean Louis Vignes. He came to Los Angeles in 1833 and planted *Vitis vinifera* vines within the city limits. Vignes had the vines shipped from France to Boston and then to California via Cape Horn. The Union Station in downtown Los Angeles was built above the petrifying roots of those early *vinifera* vines. Although the location does not strike one as ideal for grape growing, Vignes's business flourished for decades. Most of his wines were fortified, so deficiencies in quality could be more easily disguised. Vignes was also a cooper, so he was able to introduce the practical option of making barrels from local species of oak.

4

By 1850 there were about a dozen grape growers in the Los Angeles area. More vine roots are probably buried beneath Disneyland, since a pair of German musicians in Anaheim, south of Los Angeles, also planted vines here in the 1850s and formed the Los Angeles Vineyard Society, selling 20–acre blocks of irrigated planted land to German settlers. These vineyards succumbed to a terminal bacterial infection in the 1880s, however, and were never replanted.

It would be some time before vines were planted in northern California. Father Pablo Mugartegui is credited with the first plantings, which took place in 1779 at Mission San Juan Capistrano in present-day Orange County; the first northern California wine was produced a few years later in 1782. Vineyards crept closer to the present-day heartland of quality wine production when in 1817 they were established in San Rafael. Seven years on, vines were planted at the most northerly of the California missions, San Francisco Solano at Sonoma, which flourished for over a decade. Although it did not survive long into the 1840s, it had by then fulfilled its primary purpose of providing a source for other plantings, not only in Sonoma but also in Napa Valley. Meanwhile Russian immigrants, drawn to northern California by the prospect of good fur trapping, had been planting vines further north.[4]

The expansion of the northern California vineyards became possible thanks to the distribution of land grants. In 1834 General Mariano Guadalupe Vallejo was appointed by the Mexican government to administer its northern territories and secularize the missions. The padres were predictably unhappy about this, and many vineyards and other mission possessions were deliberately destroyed. By way of reward Vallejo was given a huge ranch in Petaluma, which he chose to keep for himself, but he handed out other land grants such as the 11,800–acre Rancho Caymus, which was awarded to an early settler, George Yount of Missouri, in 1836. Within the boundaries of Rancho Caymus were almost all the portions of Napa Valley that are today most prized as a source of outstanding grapes. By 1838 Yount had planted his first vineyard, with Mission grapes. There was more to follow. In 1844 Yount received the 4,400–acre Ranch La Jota on Howell Mountain. All this occurred some four years before the foundation of the town of Napa. By the end of the 1840s vineyards were established in many parts of the state: in Santa Clara, Alameda, Sacramento, and Contra Costa counties, all east of the San Francisco Bay, as well as in Napa and Sonoma.

These land grants did not establish grape growing as a major industry in Sonoma and Napa. They were handed out mainly to the friends and relatives of General Vallejo. Nonetheless, they laid the foundations for stable land ownership, which in turn led to viticultural development as one form of agricultural exploitation. However, the suitability of Sonoma and Napa valleys for grape growing was becoming well understood, and in 1852 a certain J. W. Osborne brought from Massachusetts cuttings that formed the basis of a nursery in Napa Valley, located at Oak Knoll not far from the present-day Trefethen vineyards. *Vitis vinifera* varieties such as Muscat of Alexandria and Zinfandel were among the cuttings installed. Within a few years Osborne's vineyard, with almost 60 acres under vine, was the largest in Napa Valley, and grape growers in northern California now had numerous alternatives to the Mission grape.[5] Planting of new vineyards was also stimulated by a four-year exemption from taxes passed in 1859 by the California state legislature.[6]

Important though these developments were, they were overshadowed by the plantings in Sonoma Valley, which was separated from Napa by the Mayacamas Mountains, and elsewhere in the state. Gus Sebastiani, interviewed in 1975, recalled – though not from memory! – that in the late nineteenth century there were about sixty wineries in Sonoma Valley: 'The whole valley was a blanket of vines. They'd make wine, then sell it to the bigger firms with facilities for filtering and bottling.'[7] In the 1860s, areas today considered marginal, such as El Dorado County in the Sierra Foothills and Los Angeles, had a far higher acreage than Napa. However by the late 1860s Napa was beginning to catch up, with over 2,000 acres under cultivation. Los Angeles, which in the 1880s had about 10,000 acres under vine and some fifty wineries in operation, vanished from the scene with remarkable suddenness after Pierce's Disease attacked the vineyards. As we shall see later, this disease still threatens many California vineyards.

J. W. Osborne had set a useful precedent, and French immigrants such as Charles Lefranc began to bring in other *vinifera* varieties. Although Mission was still ubiquitous, varieties such as Riesling, Palomino (called Golden Chasselas in California), and Cinsault (then known as Black Malvoisie) were increasingly encountered.

Nor were the French the only newcomers to plant vines in California. Germans such as Jacob Bundschu were doing the same and it was they, rather than the French, who would dominate Californian wine production during the late nineteenth century.[8]

Gradually the immigrants who were to give their names to Napa's most celebrated wineries began to settle in the area. In 1861 Charles Krug arrived, and during the following decade established his own winery, which by 1876 was turning out 500,000 gallons. Jacob Schram, another German, followed in 1862, and chose to plant vines on less fertile hillside slopes. The same phenomenon occurred in the Santa Cruz Mountains south of San Francisco, where many vineyards were planted at elevations of about 2,000 feet. Schram's vineyard was on slopes near Calistoga. His winery would flourish for some fifty years until Prohibition dealt it a death blow. Beringer was founded in 1876, Inglenook in 1879, Greystone in 1888.

The name of H. W. Crabb does not resonate in the same way as those of Schram, Krug, or Beringer, but he had the foresight to plant his 360-acre vineyard in Oakville. It too flourished and he began producing wines, many from good-quality *vinifera* varieties, in the early 1870s. He named his vineyard To-Kalon (Greek for 'the highest good') and although the stone winery he built has long been in ruins, the vineyard, obviously replanted, lives on as one of the most treasured sites in the Mondavi portfolio. By 1880 To-Kalon was the largest vineyard in the Valley and was planted with hundreds of experimental varieties. A contemporary development was the establishment in Rutherford of the Inglenook vineyard, initially planted with Cinsault by a banker called William Watson.[9]

Under the subsequent proprietorship of Gustav Niebaum, a Finnish sea captain who bought the 1,000-acre estate in 1879, Inglenook would become the most quality-conscious of all the Napa estates. Niebaum, who was born in 1842, took his second career very seriously, undertaking studies in oenology. He planted the best varieties from the classic French and German wine regions, as well as some of the more rustic and generous-yielding varieties encountered throughout the California wine regions at this time. Moreover, Niebaum was the first to bottle his wines under his own label, which promoted the recognition of Napa as an outstanding wine region. After Niebaum died in 1908 his widow Suzanne took over, and then asked the husband of her niece, John Daniel, to look after the property.

Sonoma was developing at an equally rapid pace. In 1857 a Hungarian by the name of Agoston Haraszthy began planting vineyards at Buena Vista. The flamboyant Haraszthy has become a figure of legend, and he did make a huge impact on the nascent California wine industry. He claimed to be a count and a colonel, but was neither, although he was born into the minor Hungarian nobility in 1812. He emigrated to Wisconsin in 1842; there he founded a town he named after himself, and came out to California during the Gold Rush in 1848, becoming sheriff of San Diego and an importer of vine cuttings. He planted a few vineyards near San Diego and in San Mateo County, none of which flourished, before coming to Sonoma, where in 1856 he bought a vineyard which belonged to the brother of General Vallejo and which he named Buena Vista. He advocated dry-farmed viticulture, and his own wines received numerous medals at local fairs. He employed Chinese labourers to build tunnels in which he could age his wines, and had casks fashioned from redwood trees. From his nurseries he sold cuttings to growers throughout the state. He was not averse to arranging useful dynastic marriages, and two of his sons were married to the twin daughters of General Vallejo.

Of greater importance, he persuaded Governor Downey of California to send him back to Europe in 1861 to become acquainted with current thinking on viticulture. Haraszthy did not waste his time: he returned from Malaga, Heidelberg, Genoa and Bordeaux with 100,000 cuttings from some 1,400 different varieties.[10] It would have been more helpful had Haraszthy kept better records of what these varieties were, but unfortunately they were catalogued under about 500 different names. Often propagated without correct identification and then sold to grape growers, they led to tremendous confusion which has continued to the present day. Only in the 1990s have the techniques of DNA testing been harnessed to identify the more obscure varieties still extant in vineyards established at the turn of the century. With financial backing from banker William Ralston, Haraszthy expanded Buena Vista, but soon became financially overstretched. Ralston withdrew his support and in 1866 Haraszthy was ousted. He left for Nicaragua to develop a sugar cane plantation, and in 1869 he vanished while, it was claimed, trying to cross an alligator-infested stream.

It was not until the 1940s that the Buena Vista estate was redis-covered and redeveloped.

In 1859 a German immigrant from Geisenheim, Emil Dresel, was planting varieties such as Silvaner and Traminer in his Rhinefarm vineyard.[11] Despite the later dominance of Napa Valley, for much of the nineteenth century Sonoma was far more important in terms of volume. By 1875 it was producing 40 per cent of all California wine, more than any other county in the state, with Napa lagging behind in fourth position, and Los Angeles still claiming second place. Vast vineyards such as one planted in 1886 on the Sonoma side of the Mayacamas Mountains consolidated the county's reputation: it still survives under the name of Monte Rosso, and is owned by the Martini winery. Another celebrated vineyard was Fountain Grove north of Santa Rosa, which was also the headquarters of Thomas Lake Harris's Brotherhood of the New Life (New Age quackery being nothing new in California). After Harris moved to England in 1892 the estate was run by a Japanese disciple, who kept the property going and released many fine wines before Prohibition. The estate was finally wound up in 1951.

Beginning with the mission at Sonoma itself, vineyard develop-ment in the county took place largely in the south, until in the 1880s sites near Healdsburg and further north were planted with vines. The future Italian-Swiss Colony at Asti, which by the 1930s was the largest American winery, was first established during this decade. It was founded as an act of charity by San Francisco banker Andrea Sbarboro, so that impoverished immigrants from Switzerland and Italy could earn some money by growing grapes. Before too long it lost its charitable status and became a commer-cial venture, which thrived. In 1897 the winemaker, Pietro Rosso, constructed a 300,000-gallon underground tank that was the largest in the world, and remained in use until 1982. The Colony's best-known wine was a Chianti-style red. The Colony was bought by Heublein after World War II, but in 1982 the company closed the facility down and sold it to ISC Wines.

Korbel sparkling wine cellars were founded by Bohemian immi-grants in Russian River Valley in 1886. The Foppiano winery near Healdsburg was established in 1896, twenty years after the Simi winery was built by two brothers from Piedmont on the outskirts of Healdsburg, where it still stands. Meanwhile, in southern Cali-fornia, the vanished vineyards of Los Angeles were replaced in the early twentieth century by large ranches to the east, notably in Cucamonga, where some immense wineries, many specializing in fortified styles, were established. By 1919 the acreage here was 20,000: double the size of Napa Valley. However, Prohibition and urban sprawl would see these vineyards replaced by airports and housing tracts.[12]

In northern California red Bordeaux varieties remained scarce until the 1880s, and it is believed that the first varietal wine produced in Sonoma was a Cabernet Sauvignon made as recently as 1882 at Dunfillan Vineyard, when a British army captain, James Drummond, made wines from cuttings he had supposedly imported from Châteaux Lafite and Margaux.[13]

Despite the high reputation in Napa of vintages such as 1878 and 1879, one wonders how good the wines were, since they were mostly made from varieties such as Cinsault, although the substantial proportion of Zinfandel would have given good if uneven wines. Moreover, white wine production would have been problematical. Without temperature control, and with the must fermented at least partially on the skins, the white wines must have had an oxidative character akin to the old-fashioned whites that can still be encountered in such relatively isolated wine regions as Portugal and Georgia. However good the best wines may have been, they had to compete against a subculture of fraudulent and mislabelled wines that inflicted such severe damage on the overall reputation of the Californian wine industry that the state legislature was provoked into passing the Pure Wine Law in 1880 to outlaw the most reprehensible practices.[14]

Nonetheless, by the late 1870s Napa Valley was beginning to enjoy the kind of recognition for the quality of its wines that sustains it today. With a transcontinental railway network in place by 1869, transportation from the West Coast to other parts of the country presented few problems. The economic depression that affected other parts of the nation had little impact on the expansion of vineyards and wineries. The stone wineries – Liparita, Bryn & Chaix (now Chateau Woltner), and La Jota – that still dot the slopes of Howell Mountain, Mount Veeder, and other elevated spots are relics of the expansion that took place in the 1880s. Immigrant growers in particular sought out mountain sites both because their native traditions encouraged them to do so, and, as Bob Travers of Mayacamas suggested to me, because such sites were usually free from the frosts that could damage vineyards on the valley floor. Within a decade Howell Mountain in particular, with 600 acres under vine, would be acclaimed as the source of some of California's most outstanding red wines. Zinfandels from St Helena and Oakville fetched considerably higher prices than those from Sonoma, for instance. And despite the relatively primitive conditions of most wineries, there were proprietors who took great pains to ensure decent quality. Gustav Niebaum at Inglenook during the rainy 1882 harvest separated leaves and other matter from the grapes, a measure that his neighbours regarded as peculiar.[15] He also installed concrete floors and steam-cleaning devices purely to improve sanitation, to which most wineries paid insufficient regard.

Nor was he entirely alone. Charles Krug, who was Napa Valley's leading grower in the 1870s, employed the latest technology and initiated the California tradition of helping his competitors. He assisted young men such as Jacob Beringer who trained with him and subsequently established their own, highly successful wineries. Frederick and Jacob Beringer began planting their 97 acres of vineyards in 1875 and built the splendid Rhine House in 1884. Chinese labourers gouged tunnels into the rock behind the house, and these are still in use, since their mean temperature is an ideal 58 degrees. By the late nineteenth century the Napa Valley floor was dotted with the immense stone wineries – Greystone, Far Niente, Inglenook – that remain as evidence of Napa's economic success as a wine region. Nor was the market for the wines restricted to the United States. Wines were routinely shipped in barrel to Europe, Central America, Australia, and the Far East.

But the euphoria would prove short-lived. Already the phylloxera louse was creeping along Napa Valley, even though acreage was expanding at a phenomenal rate. In 1881 alone, for instance, 4,000 acres were planted, and by 1885 there were over 100 wineries in operation. Nor was this the end of expansion: some eight years later there were 140 wineries in the valley.[16] In 1887 there were 16,611 acres under vine, of which about one third was planted with Zinfandel; the Bordeaux red varieties accounted for a mere 779 acres. Both the Riesling family and Mission accounted for over 2,000 acres each.[17] It was not until the 1970s that Napa would return to this level of plantation.

Foreshadowing a similar miscalculation a century later, agricultural specialists recommended that growers should use a supposedly resistant rootstock called *V. Californica*. By the time the error of this advice was acknowledged, it was too late. The infestation by the deadly louse was rapid. By 1893 half the vineyards in Napa Valley were showing signs of infection. Thousands of acres were terminally diseased. Many growers were ruined. Jacob Schram, for example, could not afford the costs of replanting. The agriculturalist Arthur Hayne, after visiting France to see how the French were coping with the same problem, recommended, for once correctly, that St George should be chosen as a resistant rootstock. Just as in Europe, many sites were abandoned during the phase of replanting. Carneros in particular, now a highly regarded zone for cool-climate viticulture, was not replanted in the early years of this century.[18]

Despite the disaster of phylloxera and the blighting of all but 3,000 acres by 1900, the California wine industry was far from destroyed. Quantities may have been reduced, but demand remained high and so did prices. The replanting required after the devastation of phylloxera led, as it would in the 1980s and 1990s, to considerable viticultural improvements. The spacing patterns (6 feet by 12 feet) that would soon become ubiquitous in California became established, and although head-pruning was retained for many varieties, the Bordeaux system of training along wires was increasingly adopted, on the grounds that such training led to more generous crops.[19]

Historians such as Charles Sullivan have shed some light on winemaking practices at the turn of the century. Their lack of sophistication must have led to many spoilt wines, as well as to others that were robust and long-lived. Grapes were picked late, giving ripe fruit and high alcohol but low acidities. The lack of temperature control must certainly have been a major problem, especially for white wines, but was moderated by the construction of stone wineries with relatively cool interiors, an important factor in regions where harvesting often took place in hot conditions. The inability to control fermentation temperatures must inevitably have led to stuck fermentations, and high levels of volatile acidity must have resulted in wines of doubtful stability and bacterial spoilage. However, in an age when such problems were considered unavoidable, the wines were highly regarded.[20] It seems that many of the acclaimed wines were based on single varieties, but as in Australia, wines were marketed according to style rather than variety. Wines labelled as claret or burgundy bore little relation to their French models, but they denoted styles of varying body and strength.

Although the damage done by phylloxera diminished the acreage in Napa to some 3,000 acres by the turn of the century, recovery was swift; by 1910 the acreage under vine had been restored to the levels of the early 1890s. A relative newcomer to the valley also began to make a strong impact. Georges de Latour had emigrated from the Périgord in 1883 and came to Napa in 1899, where he planted 128 acres of French cuttings he imported for that purpose. The first vines to go into the ground were workhorse grapes such as Alicante Bouschet, Aramon, and Grenache, but over the next few years he planted better varieties such as Sauvignon Blanc, Sémillon, Cabernet Sauvignon, and Pinot Noir. Gradually he expanded his holdings, but only started producing wines in 1909. Soon his estate, Beaulieu, became one of the most celebrated in California.

The recovery was fleeting. This time it was not disease but a fit of morality that was to inflict enormous damage on California's wine industry. During the second decade of the twentieth century Prohibition was in the air, although it did not take effect until 1919. However, by 1914 some thirty-three American states were already 'dry'. Between 1914 and 1920 the acreage of vineyards declined by 30 per cent, both because of the threat of Prohibition and because other crops, notably prunes and walnuts, offered a more attractive return on investment.[21]

It would be wrong to think that Prohibition was a total disaster in California. Although commercial wine production was forbidden and many of the 700 wineries then in existence were forced to close their doors, grape growing was still permitted, which explains why even in 1920 some 1,000 acres were newly planted in Napa, a trend that continued until 1923. Tens of thousands of acres were planted in other parts of California, notably the Central Valley, during the same period. Home winemaking for purely domestic consumption was also permitted. The Volstead National Prohibition Act included a clause, Section 29, that allowed the householder to make 'nonintoxicating cider and fruit juices exclusively for use in his home', the maximum annual production permitted being 200 gallons. Italian families in particular brought traditions of domestic production with them from the homeland.

I well recall an elderly gentleman in suburban Boston whom I encountered in the mid-1970s. He still made and enjoyed his own wine. It probably wasn't very good, but it fulfilled his expectations and was cheap to produce.

Because many of these home winemakers lived on the East Coast, the grapes shipped had to be capable of surviving the journey. Thick-skinned, deeply coloured varieties such as Carignan, Alicante Bouschet, and Petite Sirah were ideal for such purposes, and canny California growers favoured such varieties over the better quality Pinots, Rieslings, and Cabernets as they sought to survive the economic problems posed by Prohibition. Many vineyard owners profited greatly from the demand for grapes by home winemakers and grape production actually increased during the Prohibition years. By 1927 the acreage occupied by vineyards in California was an astonishing 635,000, about 100,000 acres more than in 1975.[22] These figures include table and raisin grapes. As Charles Sullivan points out: 'One of the negative outcomes of Prohibition in California was the virtual disappearance of almost all first-rate wine grape vines.'[23] A similar point has been made very succinctly by Philip Wagner: 'Prohibition proved merely to be a ban on superior wines.'[24] However, grape prices went through the roof, increasing tenfold in some instances. It has been estimated that the production of 'nonintoxicating' wine for domestic consumption in the 1920s exceeded that produced by commercial wineries before Prohibition.[25] Leon Adams recounts how packages of pressed grapes called wine bricks were shipped to home winemakers, accompanied by a yeast pill, which the purchaser was begged not to use 'because if you do this, this will turn into wine, which would be illegal.' Quite so.[26] Alternatively you could purchase a product called 'Vine-Glo', a concentrate delivered to your home by a man who added something to the juice and was even kind enough to return two months later with a few cartons of empty bottles, which he would fill with the liquid that had been quietly bubbling away in the meantime.[27]

There was a similar boom in sacramental wine, which was also permitted under the Volstead Act. This allowed many Italian and Irish wineries, such as Concannon in Livermore Valley and indeed the Beaulieu winery, which enjoyed useful connections among the Roman Catholic hierarchy in the United States, to continue production right through the Prohibition period. However, priests administering Holy Communion were outnumbered by rabbis, and Beaulieu had a profitable sideline in kosher wines. Leon Adams has described the wonderful revival of religious faith that took place during the 1920s: 'The Jewish faith requires the religious use of wine in the home. Anybody could call himself a rabbi and get a permit to buy wine legally, merely by presenting a list of his congregation. Millions of all faiths and no faith became members of fake synagogues, some without their knowledge when the lists were copied from telephone directories. (My next-door neighbor in San Francisco bought port and sherry at $4 a gallon from a rabbi whose synagogue was a hall bedroom, which he called "Congregation L'Chayim".)'[28] Since it was also legal to sell and consume wine for 'medicinal' purposes, there was an astonishing increase in ailments that demanded treatment with such products as Paul Masson's 'Medicinal Champagne'.[29]

Despite the popularity of home winemaking and the amazing resurgence in the production of sacramental wines, Prohibition did eventually have a harsh economic impact on the California wine industry. By 1925 the supply of grapes exceeded even the considerable demand, and prices plummeted. By the late 1920s the planting of vines had ground to a halt, and within Napa Valley prices reached an all-time low in 1932.[30]

Repeal, when it eventually came on 5 December 1933, caught the surviving wineries off guard. With hindsight it should have been obvious that demand for wine of decent quality, as opposed to the rot-gut brewed up on the East Coast, would be strong. However, laying aside stocks of wine for the long-awaited day of Repeal was a costly business that hardly any wineries could afford. Only Beaulieu, Napa's most prestigious estate, had succeeded in doing so and had been quietly increasing wine production since 1930. When Repeal eventually came, Beaulieu had substantial stocks of mature bottled wines to sell. Other large estates, such as Inglenook and Martini (technically the best equipped of the Napa wineries and the first to invest in temperature control), were soon ready to resume production. Carl Bundschu became the winemaker at Inglenook, and in 1936 John Daniel and his sister inherited the property. From 1935 to 1963 the wines at Inglenook were made by George Deuer. John Daniel maintained the estate's high standards by selecting the best casks each year and releasing them separately as Special Cask bottlings. Other wineries had disappeared for ever. Despite the demand for wine prices were not that high, and many landowners were discouraged from resuming viticulture for the simple reason that for an entire decade after Repeal it remained more profitable to grow plums than grapes.

Despite the economic opportunities offered by Repeal, the wine industry remained in desperate straits for many years. As has already been mentioned, low-quality but durable varieties such as Carignan and Alicante Bouschet were widely planted, and the sought-after white varieties such as Riesling and Silvaner were thin on the ground. In 1934 the *California Wine Review* calculated that of Napa's 11,000 acres of vines, 40 per cent were composed of Petite Sirah, 25 per cent of Alicante, 15 per cent of Zinfandel, and 11 per cent of Carignane. It was not an analysis to reassure those who aspired to the production of high-quality wines. As Leon Adams succinctly put it: the American wine industry 'was making the wrong kinds of wine from the wrong kinds of grapes for the wrong kinds of consumers in a whiskey-drinking nation with guilt feelings about imbibing in general and a confused attitude toward wine in particular.'[31]

Moreover, the prolonged closure of so many wineries meant that even those that reopened for business after 1933 were, for the most part, poorly equipped. Cooperage was antiquated if not moribund; equipment was rusty and contaminated with disuse. Inevitably wine quality suffered and ailments such as protein instability and refermentation in bottle were common. Moreover, the national palate, such as it was, had suffered. Thirteen years of exposure to home-made wine, moonshine, and soft drinks had not exactly enhanced connoisseurship. Many people, grown accustomed to their home brews after many years of legitimate 'home wine-making', saw little reason to spend good money on bottled wines often no better, and sometimes far worse, than their own products. The appreciation of good-quality red wines nurtured by the Niebaums and other leading wine families of California had atrophied. Before Prohibition dry wine had outsold sweet; by 1934 sweet wine, often fortified, outsold dry wine threefold.[32] The statistics for 1953 show the desperate plight of table wine producers. In that year 9 million gallons of white table wine were produced, and 19 million gallons of red; but 82 million gallons of dessert wine, mostly cheap Muscats and port- and sherry-style wines, were also produced.[33] It was not until 1968 that this trend was reversed.

The market for fine wine which should have been vibrant was in fact close to dead, and easily satisfied by the stocks available from wineries such as Beaulieu. Louis Martini and Inglenook were just about the only Napa wineries to specialize in varietally labelled wines. (Martin Ray claimed to have been the first winemaker to release varietally labelled wines after Prohibition.[34]) James Lapsley has summarized the dire position of the wine industry as follows: 'The cold reality at Repeal was that winemaking in California was a poorly organized, highly competitive, and undercapitalized industry attempting to meet the unknown demand of a fragmented national market from an oversupply of low-quality grapes, all in the depths of the depression.'[35] After Repeal there was a rush to revive former wineries and to establish new ones, but of the 800 wineries open for business in 1934, only 212 were still functioning four years later.[36] By 1938 the situation was so desperate, with an unusable surplus of grapes, that the California state legislature passed an emergency measure requiring every grower to consign 45 per cent of his crop for brandy production.

Despite the gradual increase in varietally labelled wines, they were in fact loosely defined, since the legal requirement for a 'varietal' wine was a paltry 51 per cent. Martini, supposedly pioneers of varietally labelled wines, frequently blended in up to 30 per cent of other varieties. Louis P. Martini, interviewed as recently as 1976, took a view that today seems wildly old-fashioned, not to say patronizing: 'The most important thing on the label is the brand name, the name of the winery that's putting it out. Everything else is of minimal importance. Vintage doesn't mean that much, variety doesn't mean that much because it depends on where it's grown, appellation of origin doesn't mean that much because you can make a lousy wine even out of Napa grapes if you don't know what you're doing, "estate bottled" and all that junk doesn't mean anything at all.' At this time the principal Martini wines were 'Mountain Red', which was mostly Zinfandel, 'and the balance is whatever we've got left over of other varieties'. Their Burgundy was 60 per cent Petite Sirah, the rest being Gamay and Pinot Noir, the aim being to produce 'a heavy bodied red wine'.[37]

By the end of the 1930s replanting was at last taking place in Napa Valley. It was mostly the old standby varieties such Zinfandel and Petite Sirah that were being planted, but Cabernet Sauvignon, which at Repeal had only survived at Inglenook, Beaulieu, and at one or two small vineyards, was also going into the ground. The science of oenology, so underdeveloped at the time Prohibition was introduced, was on firmer ground by the 1940s, and authorities such as Professor Maynard Amerine became more influential, recommending the planting of noble varieties and urging the use of temperature control and selected yeasts in the wineries. He joined the Department of Viticulture and Enology at Davis in 1936 and remained there for thirty-eight years, devising the famous heat summation system in collaboration with Albert Winkler, and writing sixteen books and innumerable articles. He died in 1998 at the age of 86.

André Tchelitscheff, a newcomer to Napa Valley who was lured from his native France to the quality-conscious Beaulieu estate, was to have a vast influence on Napa as a whole, since he instantly recognized the deficiencies of the region, both in the vineyards and the wineries. At Beaulieu he created one of the outstanding wines of the valley, the Georges de Latour Private Reserve. This was a selection of the estate's best Rutherford Cabernet Sauvignon, aged in barrels for two years and for a further two in bottle before release. The first vintage was 1936.

Tchelitscheff had been born in Russia in 1901, fought in the civil war, emigrated to the future Yugoslavia, and studied viticulture at Brno in Moravia before going to France to work at viticultural research institutes. He came to California in 1938 and died there at a ripe old age in 1994. With him he brought his French training and an instinctive understanding of winemaking that was evidently lacking in post-Prohibition California. He understood the importance of temperature control during fermentation and the significance of malolactic fermentation. When he came to Beaulieu in 1938 he was appalled by the condition of the winery, with rusty crushers and pumps, corroded filters, and dangerous metals infusing the wine. Although techniques for cooling the must and wine had been devised forty years earlier in Australia, Tchelitscheff still had to resort to blocks of ice when he came to Beaulieu. The land of the future was still in the Dark Ages when it came to winemaking technology. Fortunately Latour agreed to Tchelitscheff's demands for new investment. Latour died in 1940 and his widow Fernande, and then her daughter Hélène de Pins, kept the winery running. By the mid-1960s it was producing 150,000 cases per year. After his retirement from Beaulieu in 1973 Tchelitscheff did not retreat to a verandah and rocking chair. Way back in 1947 he had established the Oenological Research Centre of Napa Valley, which grew to give technical advice to eighty wineries. He also began to act as a freelance consultant to wineries throughout California, and it is to his further credit that he encouraged the development of wine regions far away from his beloved Napa Valley. He was a consultant to the Sonoma wineries of Jordan, Buena Vista, and Simi, but also assisted the Hoffman Ranch in Paso Robles and the new Firestone operation in Santa Ynez, not to mention wineries in Washington and Oregon. It is hard to think of a single individual, other than Robert Mondavi, who had a more profound influence on the quality of wine in America.

To return to the time when Tchelitscheff was beginning the American phase of his long career, it is worth recalling that the influential wine writer and importer Frank Schoonmaker was a firm advocate of varietal and regional labelling. It is interesting to see which were the wineries that he singled out for distribution in 1939, having sampled over 500 wines. The selection may not have been as arduous as it sounds, since at this time about 80 per cent of all Californian wine production left the state in bulk to be bottled elsewhere. The favoured wineries were Wente of Livermore Valley, Fountain Grove of Santa Rosa, Paul Masson of Saratoga, Inglenook, and Larkmead, a Napa winery that became defunct in the 1950s. In 1940 Schoonmaker added to the roster Louis Martini and the sparkling wine house of Korbell.

World War II did no harm to the California wine and grape industry. Raisins, that useful by-product of the grape industry, were in strong demand, and the conflict in Europe meant that wine imports to the United States had virtually ground to a halt, leaving the field wide open to California producers. Nonetheless the late 1940s and 1950s were not a period of great distinction for the wine industry. Many wineries remained moribund. A few newcomers, such as Cesare Mondavi, who, having been previously based in Lodi, acquired the Sunny St Helena winery and subsequently the Charles Krug winery, made a major impact on the industry, and large producers such as Louis Martini and the Christian Brothers set up operations in Napa Valley. But the most revered names of the period were, in economic terms, small-timers: the McCreas at Stony Hill, Lee Stewart at Souverain, the Taylors at Mayacamas.

One should not forget Martin Ray, the iconoclastic, quarrelsome winemaker who bought the Paul Masson winery in 1936, sold it to Seagrams in 1943, and then installed himself at Mount Eden, 2,000 feet up in the Santa Cruz Mountains, where for over thirty years he produced a series of superlative wines. Ray was fanatical about quality and always believed a wine labelled as a varietal should be 100 per cent varietal. Indeed in the 1940s he claimed to be the only producer whose wines were purely varietal. At that time it was possible to label a wine as, say, Cabernet Sauvignon, and blend in 49 per cent of other varieties. That clearly was no formula for quality wine production, and was easily open to abuse; Ray's articulate opposition to such a lax rule did not make him popular with the major players of the California wine industry. He also opposed any use of additives, such as chemicals, sugar, or concentrated grape juice. In an interview shortly before his death in the mid-1970s he declared: 'It's hard to buy even a California Cabernet today that is not a bit on the sweet side from concentrate. If you could see the circularization we are subjected to, offering us tankcar loads of concentrate! You know they're selling it somewhere!'[38]

Despite the efforts of men such as Ray and Tchelitscheff, California as a whole, even the prestigious Napa Valley, was still backward in terms of the grape varieties planted. Today's fashionable varieties were only minimally represented: in 1961 a mere 6 per cent of the total surface was planted with Cabernet Sauvignon, Pinot Noir, and Chardonnay, a figure that rose to 66 per cent thirty years later. Exactly the same was true in other New World countries at this time, where the now ubiquitous Chardonnay was virtually unheard of. However, in Napa Valley it was equally true that the most undistinguished and least suitable varieties for fine wine production were on the wane: the old standbys, such as Alicante, Mission, and Grand Noir, were by 1961 reduced to 9 per cent of the total. The varieties dominant at this time – Zinfandel and Petite Sirah among the reds and Sauvignon and French Colombard among the whites – were by no means contemptible.[39] However, many wines were made in a sweet style, which would have disguised whatever intrinsic quality the grapes may have had. Sweetness also ironed out vintage as well as varietal distinctions, and this suited admirably the men who ran the large drinks corporations such as Heublein as well as the bulk wineries of the

Central Valley, allowing them to establish brands that would offer bland consistency rather than the nuances that make wine a more interesting drink than Seven-Up.

Today anyone growing grapes in Napa Valley would be foolish not to label the resulting wine with the Napa appellation, but that was not the case in the 1930s and 1940s and beyond. Cooperatives had been founded after Repeal, and they found a ready market among bulk wine producers in other parts of California. Gallo, no doubt looking for economies of scale, made the simple decision in 1952 to purchase the entire production of the Napa Cooperative Winery. What's more, this arrangement was maintained for thirty-four years, ensuring the mighty Gallos a steady supply of good-quality blending wines. This supply was immense: in 1956 the co-operative vinified 40 per cent of the total production of Napa Valley.

Of course if Napa had a future, it lay at the top end of the market, since it was evident that the Valley was capable of producing outstanding and long-lived wines. Gradually new winemakers appeared on the scene. Men such as Lee Stewart, James Zellerbach at Hanzell in Sonoma (who pioneered the use of French oak barrels) and Fred McCrea produced some remarkable wines, which found an avid following, and yet California was still not universally recognized as one of the world's major wine regions. All that began to change when this handful of individuals was joined in the course of the 1960s by a spate of new (or revived) wineries that swiftly made their mark: Heitz, Spring Mountain, Chateau Montelena, Freemark Abbey, Sterling, and, later in the decade, Robert Mondavi. By now the decline in Napa vineyard acreage had been reversed. By the early 1970s 20,000 acres were under vine, compared to a mere 10,000 in 1963, and the varieties being planted tended to be noble ones. It is hard to imagine, as one trawls the length of Highway 29 up the valley, that in 1960 there were only twenty-five wineries here. By 1967 the figure had risen slightly, while in California as a whole there were 227 bonded wineries in existence in that year. Large corporations such as Heublein acquired historic wineries, and famous old names such as Beringer were bought up by companies well aware of the investment potential of Napa's vineyards.

In 1969 Beaulieu, after years of under-investment, was sold for $8.4 million to Heublein. The Latour family, now cash-rich, was happy enough, but it was an ominous sign. Those who feared that the growing presence of corporations such as Heublein could be detrimental to wine quality had reason to be anxious. According to one account, one Heublein executive proposed replanting the entire Beaulieu estate to Gamay.[40] Dr Richard Peterson, who became the winemaker after Andre Tchelitscheff's retirement, recalls the puzzlement of a Heublein executive who could not understand why, given the fact that Chardonnay grapes cost $900 per ton and Thompson Seedless a mere $50, Beaulieu were not using the latter to produce their sparkling wine. Peterson adds, however, 'In the five years I worked for Heublein at Beaulieu Vineyards they *never* ordered me to do anything that lessened the quality of any Beaulieu Vineyards wine.'[41]

There was another cloud on the horizon. The valley's proximity to San Francisco, and its natural beauty, were gaining it a reputation as a tourist destination. Ultimately the two land uses would be incompatible: unrestrained expansion of tourist-related facilities as well as suburban housing would lead to the shrinking of the area consecrated to vineyards. Many grape growers, for whom agriculture was a business, were tempted to sell out to property developers. A great political battle was fought through the 1960s to designate the valley as an Agricultural Preserve which would place severe restrictions on urbanization and protect the interests of vineyard owners. In 1968 the preservationists, led by, among others, the late Jack Davies of Schramsberg, were victorious.

Although the rural character of Napa Valley was protected to a degree, expansion continued. By 1990 there would be 200 Napa wineries and the figure continues to rise. A similar process took place in Sonoma, but was delayed by about a decade. Prestigious and well-financed estates such as Chateau St Jean, Jordan, and Matanzas Creek were founded as recently as the mid-1970s. If these and other estates were mostly the hobbies of rich folk seeking a lifestyle replete with epicurean associations, other new vineyards were no more than tax shelters. Especially in the untested expanses of Monterey, planting a vineyard could give a return on investment of 165 per cent. Doug Meador of Ventana Vineyards in Monterey recalls: 'Investors were drawn here both because of the financial return and because the glamour of the wine industry appealed to them. But people weren't farming grapes, they were farming the tax man. So they planted where they shouldn't have. It was a case of the ignorant leading the ignorant.' Many of those early plantings, especially of Cabernet Sauvignon that never ripened properly in the cool, wind-swept expanses of Monterey, no longer exist, or not in their original form.

Napa was a safer bet, as its vineyards were, relatively speaking, a known quantity. Moreover, Napa continued to enjoy the limelight thanks in large part to Steven Spurrier's inspired if serendipitous decision to organize, in Paris in 1976, a tasting that would pit recent Napa vintages against the finest wines of France. The result is the stuff of legend: in terms of ranking, the Americans cleaned up, even though the differences in scores between the wines were not in fact that great. The reported arrogance and misplaced self-confidence of the French tasters – who included Pierre Tari of Château Giscours, Aubert de Villaine, co-owner of the Domaine de la Romanée-Conti, the journalist Michel Dovaz, and a sprinkling of top sommeliers and restaurateurs – provided wonderful copy for journalists and only magnified the propaganda victory of the Californians.

Although it is possible to explain why the fleshier, more overtly fruity American wines should have been more impressive to the tasters than their more reserved French counterparts, the tasting established beyond doubt that Napa Valley was capable of producing world-class wines. Bo Barrett, now winemaker at one of the triumphant estates, Chateau Montelena, told me: 'Beating the French is like beating your dad at tennis. It's a bittersweet experience.' Although winemakers such as André Tchelitscheff and Martin Ray had been producing world-class wines for decades, it wasn't until the early 1970s that superb wines became common rather than exceptional. Warren Winiarski of Stag's Leap Wine Cellars, when asked to explain this sudden development, answered: 'Capital was infused in vineyards and in small operations which could give the continuity of attention to detail that's necessary to produce really outstanding wines. The stage was set, the potential was there, but economic underpinning was necessary to actualize the potential.'[42] Attention to detail, in the case of Stag's Leap, included such practices as cluster-thinning to limit the size of the crop and harvesting block by block to ensure all the fruit is picked at its peak of ripeness.

Nonetheless the morale-boosting outcome of the Paris tasting was no guarantee of easy times in the wine industry. A slump in 1973, sparked by the nationwide energy crisis and high inflation, led to a virtual freeze on new plantations in Napa Valley, which continued until the early 1980s. The vineyards, unregulated by any system comparable to the French *appellation contrôlée*, were subject to the swings of fashion. In 1974 63 per cent of Napa vineyards were planted with red grapes. The short-lived trend towards white wines meant that by 1981 red grapes accounted for only half the plantings, which by then consisted of 22,000 acres.[43]

In the mid-1970s the largest winery by far in Napa Valley was that of the Christian Brothers, where the wines had been made for decades by the legendary Brother Timothy. Its production of Napa wines, still and sparkling, was about one million cases. In addition its vineyards and wineries in other parts of the state, including the Central Valley, concentrated on sweet and fortified wines. The Brothers had begun making wine in 1882 in Martinez near Suisun Bay (between Lodi and San Francisco) and expanded into Napa in 1932, using the name Mont La Salle. Even in the 1970s there was something distinctly old-fashioned about this monastic operation. Wines were first vintage-dated in 1976. Brother Timothy was very keen on the idea of blending, and red wines were stored in large casks for an average of four years. Yet standards were surprisingly high given the size of the operation. All the Napa grapes were picked by hand and I recall some late harvest wines from this now defunct winery that were of outstanding quality. Their Napa Valley showcase had been the magnificent Greystone cellar, which the Christian Brothers bought in 1950 and which is now the West Coast headquarters of the Culinary Institute of America and houses a restaurant as well as other facilities.

Gradually the structure of vineyard ownership began to change. Many growers were the descendants of the German and Italian settlers who had established vineyards here in the late nineteenth century. They were farmers, not winemakers, but many of them delivered excellent grapes to the wineries that purchased from them. Many of the families that subsequently became well known as winery owners started out as growers. However, the larger wineries tried to secure sources of grapes that would be more secure than the vagaries of contractual purchase. This gave rise to the development of very large holdings in the hands of a single proprietor or winery.

The most obvious example of this kind of entrepreneurship is that of Andy Beckstoffer. A Southerner with no background in wine and little taste for it in his early years, Beckstoffer was a business school graduate, who in the 1960s was working for Heublein. He helped them to acquire the prize wineries in Napa: Inglenook and Beaulieu. In 1964 Inglenook had been sold by John Daniel to United Vintners, part of the Allied Grape Growers group, for $1.2 million. Reassurances from United Vintners that they would maintain the winery's high quality proved worthless. The winery became a showcase for tourists, but the wines were made elsewhere. New ranges were introduced to promote, under the Inglenook Navalle label, mediocre wines produced from Central Valley fruit. Daniel retired as a consultant in 1966, and in 1969 Heublein bought United Vintners, thus acquiring Inglenook as part of the package. Daniel died in 1970, and there is evidence to suggest he committed suicide. Heublein continued the policy of mass-market expansion. In Daniel's day Inglenook had produced 5,000 cases. Heublein took production up to a few million cases, much of which was sold as estate-bottled even though the fruit had not come from the Inglenook estate.[44] In the 1980s Inglenook realized it needed to revamp its image and improve the quality of its wines if it were to remain competitive, but the attempt failed commercially, and the winery was sold in 1993 to the Canandaigua group.

Meanwhile, Beckstoffer had persuaded Heublein to purchase 800 acres of vineyard land in Napa and Mendocino counties to ensure a supply of good-quality grapes grown to meet the requirements of the company's wineries. Beckstoffer oversaw this operation, setting up a separate vineyard company; when in 1972, Heublein decided to unload its vineyards, Beckstoffer volunteered to take them off their hands if they could supply some initial financing. This they agreed to do, and overnight Beckstoffer became one of the largest owners of vineyards in the state. Some rough times followed, with Beckstoffer finding himself $7 million in debt by 1978 and obliged to sell some of his holdings and refinance his company. He managed to hang on, and prospered. Not even phylloxera slowed him down significantly, as replanting allowed him to introduce the innovative vineyard practices, such as denser spacing, that he had long championed.

Beckstoffer's holdings have grown, and in 1993 he managed to acquire one of the most superlative vineyards in California, the Beaulieu No. 4 block, one of the sources of Beaulieu's Private

Reserve Cabernet Sauvignon. In total he now owns 2,200 acres in the North Coast area (1,200 in Napa alone) and supplies twenty-five wineries, including Spottswoode and Duckhorn. Given the current valuation of Californian vineyards at anything up to $75,000 per acre, this makes Beckstoffer a very rich man. Like Doug Meador in Monterey County, Beckstoffer has no fetish about low yields. Closer spacing, clonal and rootstock selection, and irrigation have allowed him to achieve generous yields in certain sites without, he feels, sacrificing fruit quality.[45]

Andy Beckstoffer is by no means the only major proprietor of vineyards in California. More and more, however, it is the large wineries that are acquiring land and developing it. John Shafer of Stags Leap District has estimated that 70 per cent of all Napa vineyards are owned and controlled by wineries. Gallo owns thousands of acres in Sonoma, and Mondavi, Beringer, and Kendall-Jackson own vast ranches throughout the coastal regions.

The growth in both vineyards and wineries throughout the state required a qualified workforce to run them. There were two colleges that specialized in training viticulturalists and winemakers – UC Davis and Fresno – and the majority of the young men and women who were running the state's wineries were graduates of one or the other. It has become fashionable to pour scorn on the kind of training that these graduates received. Both colleges, detractors claimed, were geared to industrial grape and wine production, recommending practices that led to large crops but paid scant attention to the quality of the fruit. At Davis, it is said, students were taught not to screw up. Nothing was to be left to chance: oenology was the mastering of natural processes, not a working in harmony with them. Indigenous yeasts were unreliable; better then to work solely with more predictable cultivated yeasts. Barrel-fermentation was difficult to monitor and expensive to boot; better to ferment in temperature-controlled stainless steel, and then employ barrel ageing to give the wine its desired oakiness and structure.

There may well be some truth in these strictures, but the defenders of Davis insist that the instruction was essentially technical and never pretended to be otherwise. The primary object of that training was to keep wines free of faults. 'Davis is not a cooking school,' Professor Carole Meredith told me. 'We're not here to teach artistry. We teach technical principles to enable our graduates to gain control over the viticultural and oenological processes.'

Davis today is a highly sophisticated institution, but one does get the impression that this was not the case thirty years ago. Famously, it gave the wrong advice when in the 1960s it advocated the use of a rootstock, AXR-1, that was not completely resistant to phylloxera. Along came a variant of phylloxera a decade or so later, and tens of thousands of acres had to be grubbed up and replanted at vast expense. Gary Eberle, a pioneering winemaker in Paso Robles, recalls: 'I was one of the class of 1973 at Davis and the truth is that we all became winemakers without any kind of apprenticeship. When we got our first jobs, we were flying by the seat of our pants. At Davis we had never made wine in anything larger than a garbage can. But since the class of 1973 included people such as Andrew Quady, Brian Croser from Australia, and Merry Edwards, they must have taught us something.'

It should also be remembered that in 1951 Davis set up a programme to import clones of the major grape varieties and to heat-treat them so as to eliminate viruses, which had bedevilled Californian vineyards over the previous decade. No doubt many of those clones were chosen for their generous yields rather than for their intrinsic merit, but nonetheless Davis did much to ensure that cuttings propagated and planted throughout the state would at least be healthy. It also made available cuttings of good-quality varieties that had previously been hard to obtain.

There were a plethora of other developments too. Over the last twenty years there has been intense and often bitter debate between conservative growers and more entrepreneurial wine producers. The debate focused on the extent to which the narrow and increasingly crowded and urbanized Napa Valley should allow further development. Additional elements of controversy were introduced when some growers sought to limit the extent to which Napa wineries could vinify grapes from outside the region. Newcomers to the region found it almost impossible to secure permits for new wineries and tasting rooms, as conservationists sought to put the brakes on ruinous development. There were strong arguments on both sides, and it must have been obvious to everyone that a *laissez-faire* approach would result in the long-term destruction of Napa's vineyards.

Wine fashions changed too. With the distinguished exception of

Schramsberg and Domaine Chandon, high-quality sparkling wines were hard to find in California. Then in the late 1980s there was a rash of development, as Mumm, Taittinger, Deutz, Roederer, and the Spanish cava producers Cordoniu and Freixenet, all established sparkling wine facilities. In the 1980s the anti-alcohol movement gained ground, obliging wineries to post alarmist warning labels not only throughout their wineries and tasting rooms but on the bottles themselves. The return of phylloxera in the late 1980s necessitated extensive replanting throughout the affected regions. Most growers and wineries with vineyards played safe, planting the fashionable French varieties, now including Merlot, but there were also patches of varieties such as Syrah, Viognier, and San-giovese that showed considerable promise.

California has remained conscious of its relative inexperience. It is still a youthful wine region. To be sure, wines have been produced here for 150 years, but the double blow of phylloxera and Prohib-ition turned the clock back. Wine producers who began their careers in the 1960s or earlier, men such as Robert Mondavi, Philip Togni and Paul Draper, are still there and still restless. They know that in terms of the correct identification of vineyard sites by microclimate and variety, in terms of making the right choices in spacing, pruning, and training that would achieve a desirable level of maturity in the vineyard without producing overripe fruit, and countless other matters in vineyard and winery alike, California remains in its infancy. It enjoys, on the other hand, the incompar-able gift of climate, an appreciative market for its wines even at alarmingly high prices, and, above all, the continuing dedication of its winemakers. The likes of Robert Mondavi, Warren Winiarski, Paul Draper, and Randall Grahm are well known, but the more discreet efforts of such winemakers as Eileen Crane, Randy Dunn, Mike Lee, Tom Rinaldi, John Thacher, Joel Peterson, Craig Williams, Jim Clendenen, David Bruce, Gary Eberle, Ric Forman, and countless others, all of long experience and all still in place, are of equal importance.

NOTES

1 Agoston Haraszthy, *Grape Culture, Wines, and Winemaking*, p. 11
2 James Halliday, *Wine Atlas of California*, p. 14

3 Jancis Robinson, *Vines, Grapes and Wines*, p. 227
4 Charles L. Sullivan, *Napa Wine*, pp. 4–8
5 Ibid, pp. 11, 18–19, 24
6 Leon D. Adams, *The Wines of America*, p. 19
7 Robert Benson, *Great Winemakers of California*, p. 255
8 Ibid., pp. 27–8, 32
9 Ibid., pp. 34–5, 50–51
10 Haraszthy, p. xx
11 Ibid., p. 139
12 Halliday, pp. 370–1
13 Berger and Hinkle, *Beyond the Grapes: An Inside Look at Sonoma County*,
   pp. 8–11
14 Philip Wagner, *American Wines and Wine-Making*, p. 46
15 James Conaway, *Napa*, p. 71
16 Sullivan, pp. 89, 103
17 James T. Lapsley, *Bottled Poetry*, p. 42
18 Sullivan, pp. 85–6, 110, 123
19 Ibid., p. 145
20 Ibid., pp. 145–7
21 Ibid., p. 178
22 Adams, p. 230
23 Sullivan, p. 193
24 Wagner, p. 51
25 Adams, p. 23
26 Ibid., p. 25
27 Hugh Johnson, *The Story of Wine*, p. 445
28 Adams, pp. 24–5
29 Johnson, p. 443
30 Adams, pp. 196, 204
31 Ibid., p. 29
32 Lapsley, p. 68
33 Wagner, p. 57
34 Benson, p. 28
35 Lapsley, p. 24
36 Adams, p. 231
37 Benson, pp. 212–4
38 Benson, pp. 24–5
39 Sullivan, p. 246
40 Conaway, p. 141
41 Benson, pp. 99–100
42 Ibid., p. 136
43 Ibid., p. 308
44 Sullivan, p. 277
45 Jeff Morgan, *Wine Spectator*, 31 March 1997

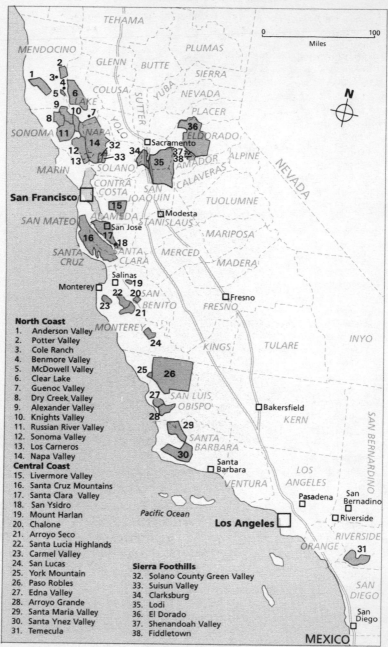

THE WINES OF CALIFORNIA

North Coast
1. Anderson Valley
2. Potter Valley
3. Cole Ranch
4. Benmore Valley
5. McDowell Valley
6. Clear Lake
7. Guenoc Valley
8. Dry Creek Valley
9. Alexander Valley
10. Knights Valley
11. Russian River Valley
12. Sonoma Valley
13. Los Carneros
14. Napa Valley

Central Coast
15. Livermore Valley
16. Santa Cruz Mountains
17. Santa Clara Valley
18. San Ysidro
19. Mount Harlan
20. Chalone
21. Arroyo Seco
22. Santa Lucia Highlands
23. Carmel Valley
24. San Lucas
25. York Mountain
26. Paso Robles
27. Edna Valley
28. Arroyo Grande
29. Santa Maria Valley
30. Santa Ynez Valley
31. Temecula

Sierra Foothills
32. Solano County Green Valley
33. Suisun Valley
34. Clarksburg
35. Lodi
36. El Dorado
37. Shenandoah Valley
38. Fiddletown

General map of California

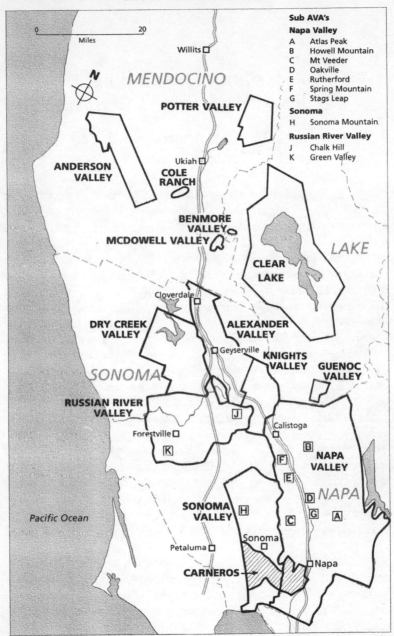

0   20
Miles

Sub AVA's

Napa Valley

A   Atlas Peak
B   Howell Mountain
C   Mt Veeder
D   Oakville
E   Rutherford
F   Spring Mountain
G   Stags Leap

Sonoma

H   Sonoma Mountain

Russian River Valley

J   Chalk Hill
K   Green Valley

MENDOCINO

Willits

POTTER VALLEY

ANDERSON
VALLEY

Ukiah

COLE
RANCH

BENMORE
VALLEY
MCDOWELL VALLEY

LAKE

CLEAR
LAKE

Cloverdale

DRY CREEK
VALLEY

ALEXANDER
VALLEY

Geyserville

KNIGHTS
VALLEY

GUENOC
VALLEY

SONOMA

RUSSIAN RIVER
VALLEY

J

Forestville

K

Calistoga

B

NAPA
VALLEY

F

NAPA

E

D

SONOMA
VALLEY

H

C

G

A

Pacific Ocean

Petaluma

Sonoma

CARNEROS

Napa

North Coast

2
Acres and Appellations: The Rules of the Game

California is responsible for producing 94 per cent of all the wine produced in the United States, and if it were considered as a nation, it would be the world's fourth largest producer after Italy, France, and Spain. Vineyards can be found in forty-five of California's fifty-eight counties. By 1998 there were 407,231 acres planted with vineyards throughout California, and of those, about 80,000 are non-bearing. There has been a steady increase in acreage during the last decade. In 1986 there were 332,600 acres planted (20,600 non-bearing); in 1990 there were 335,200 planted (44,200 non-bearing). The striking increase in non-bearing acreage no doubt reflects the major replanting that took place after the onslaught of phylloxera in the late 1980s and early 1990s. It is important to bear in mind that almost half the grapes grown in California are table or raisin grapes.

Hugh Thatcher, a wine merchant in California, is slightly uneasy about the expansion in vineyards during the 1990s: 'As the American economy has bounced back, huge plantings have been taking place, and the likely outcome is that there will be a glut of wine which will sort out the men from the boys. What I always find astonishing is that winery owners often ask me, a mere salesman, what they should plant. The consequence will surely be that a lot of varieties will be planted in sites that they're not suited to.'

A breakdown of acreage in 1997 according to grape varieties is most revealing, especially when one considers the growth, or decline, since 1986, which is represented by the figure in parentheses: Cabernet Sauvignon 45,307 (23,149), Zinfandel 50,498 (25,797), Merlot 38,522 (13,417), Grenache 11,699 (14,669), Barbera 11,137 (13,417), Pinot Noir 11,158 (7,667), Petite Sirah

2,692 (4,983), Syrah 4,277 (119), and Sangiovese 2,498. Among white grapes: Chardonnay 88,517 (29,319), French Colombard 46,076 (69,713), Chenin Blanc 21,647 (40,088), Sauvignon Blanc 11,312 (15,193), Riesling 2,522 (8,449), Gewürztraminer 1,715 (3,350), and Viognier 1,117. Grape varieties will be looked at in far greater detail in later chapters.

What should be a fairly straightforward task – outlining the different regions in which grapes are grown and wines are produced – is in fact needlessly complicated. At the most basic level, that of counties, it is simple enough. We know where Santa Barbara County is located, and the same goes for Napa, Mendocino and the others. However, within, and indeed across, certain counties, a system of appellations has been devised that complicates the issue. It is important to note that the Californian appellation system has little in common with those of Europe. The French AOC, the Italian DOC or (even better) DOCG, are supposed to relate to quality as well as typicity. In California, quality is not an issue. Veteran winemakers such as Gus Sebastiani in Sonoma were vehemently opposed to setting up an appellation system that was not tied into a quality control standard. The appellation system that eventually prevailed was purely geographical: a wine labelled Sonoma Mountain or Edna Valley merely has to have been pro duced mostly within a particular geographic zone. But it's not that simple. Zones overlap, giving producers in some regions, notably Sonoma, the option of using a variety of different appellations, all equally legal. There are, in effect, sub-appellations within appellations.

Place the blame at the door of the Bureau of Alcohol, Tobacco and Firearms. Any single federal agency empowered to regulate such disparate vices is bound to get its knickers in a twist and generate such absurdities as viticultural zones that don't contain a single winery. In the elaborations that follow, I shall do my best to untangle some of the confusion.

The creation of appellations is partly, I suspect, an attempt to secure credibility for certain California regions. John Shafer admits that part of the reason for pressing for an appellation for Stags Leap was the advantage to be gained from cooperative marketing. It is by no means clear to me that the characteristics claimed for certain appellations – Stags Leap District in Napa, for example – are as distinctive as the guidelines would suggest. In blind tastings

33

of various Napa sub-appellations, only Carneros and Rutherford have struck me as truly distinctive. But this should not cause any heartache. I know I would have great difficulty distinguishing certain Pauillacs from St Juliens within the Médoc, and I would be hard pressed to single out, on the basis of a blind tasting, a Clos Vougeot. Appellation is an inexact science, wherever it is applied.

The system of AVAs (American Viticultural Areas) was created in 1978 by the BATF. Napa Valley was the first AVA to be officially recognized, in 1981, but even such a seemingly simple matter as defining its boundaries proved enormously complicated. Clearly all the vineyards on the valley floor, from Napa up to Calistoga, were within Napa Valley, and there was a strong case for including the mountain districts such as Spring Mountain, Howell Mountain, and Mount Veeder. But what of the side valleys – Chiles Valley, Pope Valley – that had historically been considered part of Napa Valley even though they were geographically and climatically distinct? It was to the clear commercial advantage of those with vineyards in the outer regions of Napa County to have their ranches included within the Napa Valley AVA, and they fought hard, and in the end successfully, to be included.

Sub-appellations also tend to become political issues. California is full of small AVAs essentially created to benefit a single estate. Thus Sonoma's Chalk Hill, a sub-appellation of Russian River Valley, itself a sub-appellation of Sonoma County, largely benefits Chalk Hill Winery, and the same is true of Atlas Peak within Napa Valley.

An AVA is defined by the BATF as 'a delimited grape growing region distinguished by geographic features, the boundaries of which have been recognized and defined.' If only that were as easy as it sounds. Moreover, an AVA is not created by the BATF, which has no role of *institut national* as embodied in the French INAO. Anyone can petition to have an AVA created, which is why a number of special-interest AVAs have come into being, despite the absence of 'defined geographical features'.

There is, as Randall Grahm has observed, no chalk at Chalk Hill. Of course, if you are the only winery proposing an AVA for your district, it is by definition hard for anyone to object, and many meaningless AVAs have been created on the nod.

Visiting the Au Bon Climat winery in Santa Barbara County one day, my chat with Jim Clendenen was interrupted by an official lugging a briefcase filled with papers relating to a new AVA that was under consideration: Coastal California. Opinions, such as that of Mr Clendenen, were being sounded out, and petitions were being organized. It was by no means clear to me what purpose, in terms of service to the wine-buying consumer, would be served by a Coastal California appellation, and it came as no surprise to discover that the moving force behind it was Kendall-Jackson, a large-volume group of wineries all located in coastal counties. If the application succeeded, Kendall-Jackson could give up the bland-sounding California appellation for its large-volume blends and substitute for it the classier-sounding Coastal California appellation. Meanwhile some of its competitors, still relying on fruit from Lodi or Livermore, would be stuck with the lowly California appellation.

At last count there were about seventy AVAs in California, though I suspect the figure has risen. If an AVA is cited on the label, then 85 per cent of the grapes used in that wine must have come from that district. This too seems a fudge. I know of at least one winery with a prestigious AVA at its disposal that buys Chardonnay from Lodi. As long as these grapes don't make up more than 15 per cent of the blend, it remains perfectly legal to label and market the wine as Carneros Chardonnay.

The BATF is at pains to point out that an AVA carries with it no implication that the wine produced in it is of higher quality than that from, say, a county appellation. The Bureau states: 'BATF does not wish to give the impression by approving a Viticultural Area that it is approving or endorsing the quality of wine from this area . . . BATF approves a viticultural area by finding that the area is distinct from surrounding areas, but no better than other areas.' Thus the definition of an AVA can single out its soil, elevation and other features as distinctive without suggesting that they add up to a capacity to produce excellent wine. Although certain AVAs have acquired cachet – thus Santa Maria Valley for Pinot Noir – others, such as North Coast or Central Coast, are so broadly defined that they are virtually meaningless.

There is considerable scepticism about AVAs within the higher echelons of the wine industry. The bitter experience of defining the boundaries of the Stags Leap District AVA seems to have persuaded many growers that the political battles with neighbours are scarcely worth the time and trouble entailed. Bo Barrett, whose Chateau Montelena is located within Calistoga, points out that there is no great demand for a Calistoga AVA to partner those that already exist for, say, Rutherford or Oakville. Creating an AVA is, in his view, 'a dilution of effort. We know we can produce great wine in Calistoga, and having our own AVA won't change that, since the AVA on the label is no guarantee of quality.' A legal adviser to the Wine Institute of California told me that in practice almost all the work regarding definition of boundaries and the other criteria for a new AVA is completed before the BATF is petitioned. The more agreement between affected wineries that can be achieved before the application is submitted, the more likely it is to be granted without the spun-out complications of formal hearings. Submitting a petition can be an expensive business, as lengthy reports are commissioned from historians and geologists to back up any application and lend it weight.

Other wine regulations relating to labelling are just as confusing, and, some would say, misleading. Take, for example, the seemingly unambiguous term 'estate-bottled'. As long as a vineyard, even if not actually owned by a winery, is controlled by a winery in terms of viticultural decisions on, for example, irrigation, pruning, and harvesting, then the production from that vineyard can be used in an 'estate-bottled' wine. However, the winery and the vineyard have to be in the same viticultural area. Thus Wente, located in Livermore Valley, can have a long-term contract with a vineyard within the region and bottle its production as 'estate-bottled', but it is forbidden to use the term for the production of the vineyards it does indeed own in Sonoma. On the other hand, it is doubtful whether many consumers, in the United States or abroad, place a great deal of value on the words 'estate-bottled' on a bottle of California wine.

Further regulations worth knowing about include the ruling that a varietally labelled wine must contain 75 per cent of that variety, an AVA-labelled wine 85 per cent of that variety, and a vintage wine 95 per cent of wine from the specified vintage. If a wine bears a county appellation, then it must contain at least 75 per cent of wine originating in that county; however, if the label reads Napa Valley, then 85 per cent of the wine must have come from that region. If a single vineyard is named on the label, then 95 per cent of the fruit must have come from that site. Until 1983, a 'varietal' wine only needed to contain a minimum of 51 per cent of that variety, which was clearly an absurdity.

There are also modern-day absurdities that the authorities seem powerless to prevent. One of the Beringer brands is Napa Ridge. The impression given by such a name is that it has something to do with Napa Valley. In fact, the wines are not even made in Napa, and they are labelled with the California appellation, which strongly suggests they contain virtually no Napa wine at all. Almadén have released a wine called Chardonnay 'with natural juices'. This is probably a fruit juice with a dash of wine in it, but the impression given is that it is a wine with a dash of fruit juice in it – a cooler. Legally, a wine thus labelled need contain no more than 10 per cent wine. Furthermore, since the rules stipulate that any wine labelled Chardonnay must contain at least 75 per cent of that variety, then the quantity of Chardonnay in a wine 'with natural juices' need be no more than 7.5 per cent. This is legal, but deceptive.

By and large California wineries are not keen to dupe the consumer, although the overall laxity of the regulations often makes it easy for an element of deception to creep in.

The Wine Regions

3
Napa

The Napa Valley extends some thirty miles from the mouth of the Napa River as it empties into San Pablo Bay northwards to Calistoga and Mount St Helena. From an elevation of 250–350 feet at Calistoga, the valley slopes gently down to sea level in a southerly direction. The valley is hemmed in by hills on either side and only five miles wide at its broadest point. At the southern end of the valley Mount Veeder and Atlas Peak frame the valley floor; further north Spring Mountain and Howell Mountain face each other, with the valley below.

Geologically speaking, the Napa Valley is an uplifted seabed; along its seams volcanic activity deposited rock and ash on to its surface. Fluctuating sea levels led to repeated layerings of sedimentary material over millions of years. Not surprisingly the soil composition of Napa Valley is exceedingly complex. Indeed, it remains an unstable region of volcanic mountains, seismic activity, and hot springs.

Although a drive up the valley suggests a high degree of uniformity, that is far from true. The northern part is considerably hotter than the southern, on average 10 degrees Fahrenheit warmer than the city of Napa and, to use the Californians' favourite heat summation system, a warm Region III. However, nights can be cool, thanks to Calistoga's elevation and the cold air passing from Russian River through Knights Valley to Calistoga, and in spring frosts can be a problem. There are marked differences in soil types and microclimates between the western and eastern slopes of the flanking mountains. Spring and Diamond Mountains to the west are thickly wooded and wetter than the slopes of Howell Mountain, which is craggier and drier. Although generalizations are dangerous in Napa Valley, the southern part of the valley has

41

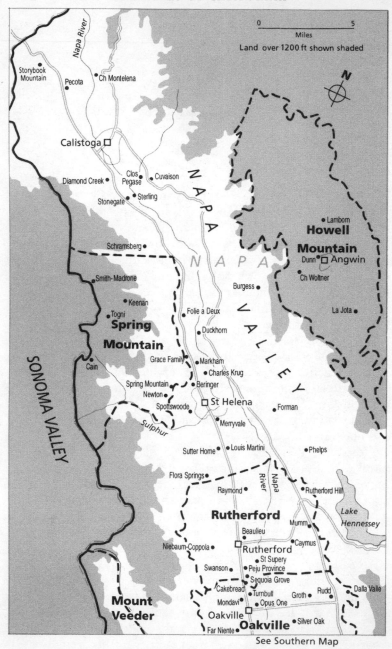

Northern Napa Valley

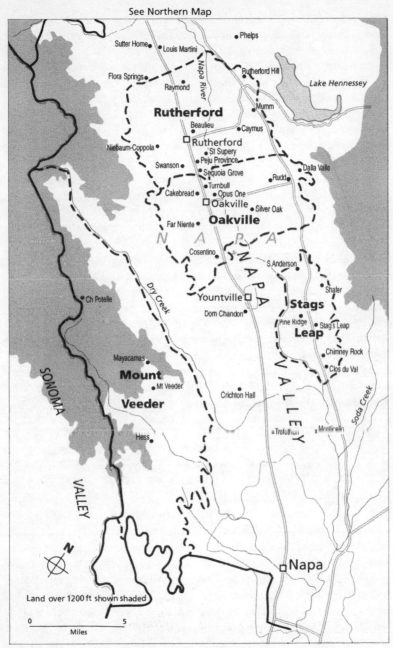

Southern Napa Valley

firm, slow-draining clay soils which tend to give wines lighter in structure than those produced from the northern part, where the soils are more gravelly, deep, and porous.

The most celebrated feature of the valley's soil structure is the presence of at least ten alluvial fans, each contributing its own blend of soil, texture, and structure. These fans have been created by creeks descending towards the Napa River. The most celebrated of these is the Rutherford Bench, and ambitious local growers have been seeking to identify and define others, most notably the Oakville Bench.

Maritime influence is, of course, crucial. As in summer the temperature rises in the valley, the warm air mass also rises, allowing cooler air to rush in, from San Pablo Bay in southern Napa, and via the Russian River in northern Napa. Marine influence is of less importance among the mountain vineyards. Their elevation at up to 2,400 feet means that daytime temperatures during the summer are on average 3 to 10 degrees lower than on the valley floor. However, since these vineyards are above the fog line, the grapes have longer exposure to sunlight and thus a more uniform ripening cycle. The relative coolness also helps to preserve acidity. Rainfall levels tend to be higher than on the valley floor, but afternoon breezes help reduce the risk of mildew and rot. Whereas the valley floor soils are quite rich and deep, those on the mountainsides tend to be thin and infertile, naturally reducing yields. Berries are often smaller with thick skins, giving fruit rich in tannin.

Each of the valley's main growing regions likes to claim that its fruit has specific characteristics, a Californian version of *terroir*. In some cases this is clearly discernible. Cabernet Sauvignon from Oak Knoll, a cool region, is quite different in flavour and structure from a typical Cabernet from Calistoga or Howell Mountain. I am not sure that it is so easy to distinguish between, for example, Spring Mountain and Mount Veeder, or Oakville and Rutherford. There are undeniable differences in soil structure and microclimate, but other factors – such as trellising, canopy management, yield, and harvesting date, as well as winemaking practices such as cultivated yeasts, maceration, and oak treatment – all play their part too and are not site-specific. I have undertaken a number of tastings to try to discern differences between the subregions within Napa, and although it is often possible to distinguish valley wine from mountain wine, or Calistoga from Oak Knoll, it is by no means easy to taste a Napa Cabernet or Merlot blind and declare, with any confidence, that this has to be a Stags Leap or an Oakville. Nonetheless it is a welcome trend that more and more wineries are identifying subregions on their labels. Pine Ridge was a pioneer in this respect, producing over the years four different cuvées of Cabernet (Diamond Mountain, Howell Mountain, Stags Leap, and Rutherford); and Mondavi has followed suit, with separate Stags Leap and Oakville bottlings.

Gary Andrus, the owner of Pine Ridge, has had a great deal of experience making wines from different subregions and feels there is a distinctive character to each. In a magazine interview, he said he preferred 'the finesse of Diamond Mountain to the intensity of Howell Mountain.' And he's not provincial when it comes to Stags Leap. 'In great years, Rutherford Bench makes better wines; in good years it's Stags Leap.'[1]

Napa Valley's 36,650 acres of vines account for 11 per cent of California's total acreage. 10,600 acres are planted with Cabernet Sauvignon, with Chardonnay the other leading variety (9,330 acres). There are about 230 wineries in operation but many are 'boutique' wineries producing well under 1,000 cases annually.

The prestige of the region and the high price of land (in 1996, about $50,000 per acre plus development costs) has encouraged the proliferation of these tiny wineries. Throw in a celebrity wine-maker such as Heidi Peterson Barrett or Helen Turley, and such wineries feel justified in charging $50 upwards for a bottle of red. In some cases the costs of a multi-million-dollar winery must also be recouped.

An absurd and deplorable competitiveness between these micro-wineries has led to spiralling attention-seeking prices, sustained by the razzmatazz of auctions and special bottlings. In June 1998, 1994 Colgin Cabernet was fetching $1,342 at auction (it had been released a year earlier at $50), and 1994 Screaming Eagle also fetched over $1,000 per bottle. This trend, which I will discuss more fully elsewhere, plays a part in narrowing the range of wines available from Napa. Cabernet, admittedly the ideal variety for the region, is increasingly dominating all other varieties, and grapes such as Sauvignon Blanc and Muscat Canelli are no longer planted since they generate insufficient income for both growers and wineries. No doubt the cult of the super-Cabernet presents no problems while the American economy is going through a golden age, with

45

bottles of wine becoming little more than fashion accessories in some circles, but it will be interesting to see how long this particular madness will be sustained.

Atlas Peak

This AVA to the east of the Stags Leap District was created in 1992. The soil is volcanic, not fertile but well drained. Rainfall is low, making this an arid region. Elevation means that it is also a cool region, officially Region II, but cooler and wetter than this would suggest. Daytime temperatures can be up to 15 degrees Fahrenheit cooler than on the valley floor. Nights are cold, and the growing season prolonged.

There is only one winery here, Atlas Peak. Its vineyard was developed originally by William Hill, and the investors in Atlas Peak Winery were convinced that the region was well suited to the growing not only of Cabernet, Merlot, and Zinfandel, but Sangiovese, which has become the speciality of the winery. About 150 acres of Sangiovese have been planted out of a total of 900 in the AVA.

Many vintages from Atlas Peak have been disappointing, but it is probably too early to say whether this is due to the deficiencies of the AVA region or to other factors.

Calistoga

Not an AVA, and unlikely ever to become one, the Calistoga region in northern Napa has a strong character of its own. Fogs burn off faster here in the north of the valley, so the region heats up more rapidly during the day. But the vineyards also lie at a slightly higher elevation than elsewhere along the valley floor. Nights can be quite cool, as air slides down from the surrounding mountains, so the rating of Calistoga as a high Region III is not quite as alarming as it sounds. The soils are rocky or gravelly, and deep and well drained, and the source of some superb grapes, such as the Cabernet Sauvignon from Eisele Vineyard. The lack of vigour in the soils keeps yields at sensible levels and results in red wines of considerable concentration and power.

Chiles Valley

This region to the east of Napa Valley has little in common with the rest of Napa and owes its inclusion within the appellation to its long historic associations with the valley. Chiles Valley is a hot region, and the growing season is relatively short. Many of the 1,000 acres of vineyards are planted on the valley floor at an elevation of about 900 feet. Nichelini is one of the major vineyard owners here. It is not an area known for the distinction of its wines. After petitioning from the valley's principal grower, Volker Eisele, AVA status was approved in 1999.

Diamond Mountain

Although not an AVA, Diamond Mountain, part of the Mayacamas range, has acquired an identity of its own thanks to the presence of Diamond Mountain Ranch, a 120-acre vineyard now owned by Sterling, and the highly regarded Diamond Creek estate which produces some very long-lived Cabernet Sauvignons. The vineyards are located at between 600 and 1,700 feet. Yields are low and quality high. Soils are very varied, as the four different Cabernets from Diamond Creek illustrate each year.

Howell Mountain

On the opposite side of the valley from Diamond Mountain lies Howell Mountain, which in the nineteenth century was already acclaimed for the quality of its wines. Angwin, the little town in the heart of the region, is a stronghold of the Seventh Day Adventists, for whom wine has few positive connotations. Their presence on Howell Mountain may have contributed to the fact that only in the last fifteen to twenty years has there been a serious revival of viticulture. The appellation was approved in 1983.

Howell Mountain vineyards are situated at an elevation that varies from 1,400 to 2,200 feet. The soils are essentially volcanic and well-drained, although not especially deep. Yields can be very low, and irrigation is widespread, since dry-farmed vineyards tend to yield no more than 1 ton per acre. Exposures are very varied, so microclimatic conditions are diverse. As is the case with most mountain vineyards, the growing season is longer than on the valley floor and the heat patterns are more regular. Moreover, night-time temperatures can be surprisingly warm given the elevation, balancing the somewhat lower daytime temperature. The average mean temperature in Angwin is 56.8 degrees Fahrenheit, compared to 58.6 in St Helena. Randy Dunn in Angwin reports night-time temperatures as being up to 20 degrees higher. What seems to happen is a temperature inversion: the warm air from the valley rises at night, while the colder mountain air descends. One advantage of the relatively even temperatures is that frost is rare. The good drainage, the absence of fog and the frequent breeziness help to keep rot at bay.

Around Angwin, where many vineyards are located on a high plateau, the soil is reddish and stony. Elsewhere on the mountain the soils have a high volcanic ash (or tufa) content. There has been considerable vineyard expansion here over recent years, and current acreage stands at around 700. Above all, this is red-wine country – both Cabernet and Zinfandel achieve splendid results – and Chardonnay, which is also grown here, tends to be on the lean and austere side of the spectrum. The reds are often big, brawny wines, deep in colour and rich in tannin, and the best winemakers seek to retain the intrinsic character of this mountain fruit while moderating the potential astringency and toughness of the wines. Of the numerous winemakers who use Howell Mountain fruit, the best known and longest established include Dunn, La Jota, and Summit Lake. The Bancroft Vineyard supplies outstanding Merlot to Beringer. Other large Napa wineries have been busy acquiring or leasing vineyards here.

Mount Veeder

This AVA, created in 1990 and amended in 1993, lies on the southwest side of Napa Valley at an elevation of 1,000 to 2,400 feet. Here too the vineyards, which mostly face east and are on quite steep slopes, are above the fog line. Frost is very rare, but rainfall is relatively high. Soils are very varied, and include sandstone, light clay, volcanic ash, and shale. They are deeper than those on Howell Mountain, and drainage is excellent. Generalizations about soil are dangerous, as at Mayacamas the soil is only between 18 and 36 inches deep before you hit the rock. Bob Travers of Mayacamas believed the top of Mount Veeder was probably on the borderline between Regions I and II, but found that although winters could be cold, with occasional snow, in summer there was less variation in temperature than on the valley floor. This is tough land to farm, and growers such as Donald Hess have made intense studies of their vineyards to ensure that each parcel is correctly cultivated in terms of canopy management and irrigation.

There are about 1,000 acres planted, and the dominant varieties are Cabernet and Chardonnay, followed by Zinfandel and Merlot. The red wines tend to be less brawny and spicy than those from Howell Mountain, but there is no shortage of tannin, intensity, and richness with Mount Veeder fruit. The principal wineries here are Hess, Mayacamas, Mount Veeder Winery, and Chateau Potelle.

Oak Knoll District

A leading candidate for promotion to AVA status, this relatively cool area of southern Napa lies south of Yountville and west of Stags Leap. Trefethen is the leading winery here, and Mondavi own a large vineyard.

Oakville

The large Oakville region, an AVA since 1993, with approximately 5,800 acres under vine, is dominated by the Mondavi winery, and its creation Opus One. Oakville is best known for its Cabernet Sauvignon, although the cool mornings beneath their blanket of fog also make it suitable for Chardonnay and Sauvignon Blanc. H. W. Crabb's celebrated To-Kalon vineyard was established in Oakville, and was acquired in the 1960s by Robert Mondavi. This winery's highly regarded Fumé Blanc Reserve comes from here. Phelps's Backus Vineyard is another outstanding Oakville site.

Oakville is fairly warm, though cooler than Rutherford, and is classified as a Region III. It is not unusual for the harvest of white grapes to begin in mid or late August. The soils are varied. There is benchland, comparable to that of neighbouring Rutherford, formed by six streams that flow down from the Mayacamas Mountains. These gentle gravelly northeast-facing slopes are well drained, but as one moves eastward towards the Napa River the soil becomes more alluvial, with a higher content of silt and clay. There have been moves to establish a separate Oakville Bench AVA, but disagreements about the extent, or even the existence, of the Bench have seen the proposal shelved.

Oakville regularly delivers ripe, beautifully balanced Cabernet. Although the grapes are bought by wineries all over Napa Valley, the best-known estates located within the region are Mondavi, Opus One, Far Niente, Groth, Swanson, Harlan, Plumpjack, Dalla Valle, Paradigm and Franciscan. The renowned Martha's Vineyard is also located in Oakville.

Pope Valley

Pope Valley is not an AVA, but has been included within Napa Valley for historic reasons. Rather like Chiles Valley it lies to the east, and has a shorter, drier growing season. Fog is unknown. The best-known vineyard here is St Supéry's Dollarhide Ranch. Flora Springs owns the Cypress Ranch, where Sangiovese is grown. Hess have also bought substantial acreage here, intending to plant Cabernet Sauvignon, Merlot, and Zinfandel. Days can be very hot and nights very cool (10 degrees Fahrenheit warmer by day and 10 degrees cooler by night than at Rutherford), which, in the experience of St Supéry, gives softer tannins but wines that age well.

Rutherford

If any portion of Napa Valley has a claim to unique distinction, it is surely Rutherford. This is the historic heartland of the Valley, the home of Inglenook and Beaulieu, and the source of Napa's most noble and long-lived red wines. Slightly warmer than Oakville, it is not ideally suited to the cultivation of white grapes such as Chardonnay. The magnificence of Rutherford Cabernet and other Bordeaux varieties is usually attributed to the presence of its benchland, the alluvial fans of gravelly loam deposited by creeks descending from the Mayacamas Mountains. These soils retain moisture admirably. However the AVA, which was created in 1993, includes the whole of Rutherford and not just the benchland. Of the 6,650 acres in Rutherford, only about 2,800 are located on the Bench.

The Rutherford Bench is visible to the west of Highway 29: a succession of gently sloping, well-drained vineyards, rising to the west to a height of 500 feet, sheltered yet well exposed. Here and there the benchland crosses the highway and slopes towards the Napa River. The tell-tale character of the soil and of the Cabernet grapes grown here is a quality identified as 'Rutherford Dust'. So varied are the descriptions of this fruit character that it is hard to know what is meant by most of them. In my own tastings of Rutherford wines alongside those from other valley floor AVAs, I do discern a character that is rich and earthy without ever seeming coarse or astringent. There also seems to be a tad more aromatic complexity than on, say, Oakville Cabernet, which often has a more pure cassis character. But so many other variables come into play – vintage, yields, winemaking practices, oak-ageing, and so forth – that it would be rash to attribute a specific *terroir* character to Rutherford wines, although they are clearly distinctive.

Numerous wineries buy fruit from Rutherford, although only a few, notably Niebaum-Coppola, Frog's Leap, and Staglin, are actually located here. Other wineries using Rutherford fruit include Grgich Hills, Heitz (Bella Oaks Vineyard), Flora Springs, Far Niente, Pine Ridge, Freemark Abbey (Sycamore and Bosché Vineyards), and Swanson.

St Helena

Like Rutherford and Oakville, St Helena is best adapted to the growing of red grapes, notably the Bordeaux varieties. Its northerly location up the valley means that the overall climate is quite hot, and rainfall is higher than further south. The soils are very varied, being both gravelly and rich in sandy loam. Despite the warmth of the region, it is capable of producing Cabernets of remarkable elegance, of which Spottswoode is the classic example. The AVA is recent, having only been approved in 1995.

Spring Mountain District

Another mountain appellation, this lies south of Diamond Mountain, and the 400 acres of vineyards stretch far back into the Mayacamas Mountains, rising from 500 feet to 2,100 feet. The steepness of the terrain means that some of the vineyards are terraced and, incidentally, exceptionally beautiful. Higher up, there are thin volcanic soils that give wines similar in tannic structure to those from Howell Mountain on the opposite side of the valley, while on the lower slopes deeper soils give more overtly fruity wines. Spring Mountain enjoys a long growing season, with harvests up to three weeks later than those on the valley floor. The absence of fog leads to long sun-filled summer days, although the average summer temperature is about 10 degrees lower than on the valley floor.

The grape variety blend is more diverse than on the valley floor, and Chardonnay, Sauvignon Blanc, and even Riesling do well here, as do most of the Bordeaux varieties, including Petit Verdot and Zinfandel. Recent plantings of Syrah also show great promise. Not all is well among the exquisite vineyards: Pierce's Disease has posed major problems at a number of estates.

Although the AVA was approved in 1993, few wineries use the appellation. The reason seems to be that the association with Spring Mountain winery, glorified as Falcon Crest in the television series of that name, is regarded as somewhat vulgar. So the classy estates in these hills – Newton, Cain, Stony Hill, Togni – would rather keep their distance, even though Spring Mountain winery is making excellent wines under new ownership.

Stags Leap District

After a tremendous four-year debate about the northern boundaries of this viticultural area, the AVA was finally approved in 1989. The BATF adopted a fairly generous view by accepting the claims of certain outlying estates and vineyards – Mondavi and Silverado, among others – to be included. This decision put some distinguished noses out of joint, notably those of Warren Winiarski and John Shafer, who would have preferred a more purist approach. Indeed, the original proposals would have limited the appellation to a couple of hundred acres. Today the AVA consists of about 2,700 acres, of which half are planted, bordered to the east by the rocky 200-foot-high palisades from which the district derives its name, and to the west by the Napa River. The northern boundary lies at the Yountville Cross Road. Cabernet Sauvignon and Merlot dominate the slopes east of the Silverado Trail, while to the west, between the road and the Napa River, one can find other grapes such as Sauvignon Blanc.

Stags Leap was the last of the prestigious valley floor districts to be developed as vineyards. It's true that the Stags' Leap Winery had been active here in the last decade of the nineteenth century, but that was a fairly isolated development. The first significant vineyard planted here in modern times was laid out in 1961 by Nathan Fay, whose Cabernet Sauvignon vineyard was purchased by Stag's Leap Wine Cellars in 1986. The revived Stags' Leap Winery and Warren Winiarski's Stag's Leap Wine Cellars were established in 1972, along with Clos du Val. Pine Ridge and Shafer started up in 1978. For some years it was not clear whether 'Stags Leap' was a name attached to two wineries or whether it referred to a geographical entity. The matter was put to the test when Pine Ridge released a wine with 'Stag's Leap Vineyard' on the label. Both Stag's Leap Wine Cellars and Stags' Leap Winery claimed the name was a trademark and took Pine Ridge to court. An out-of-court settlement veered in Pine Ridge's favour by declaring that 'Stags Leap' was a geographical term and not a commercial trademark. Ironically, it was this decision that paved the way towards the eventual designation of the region as an AVA.

The distinguishing characteristics of Stags Leap are the reddish, gravelly soil – mostly volcanic and well drained but with a tougher subsoil of bedrock that moderates the vigour of the vines – and the jagged basalt rocks of the palisades. By day the palisades reflect heat back on to the vineyards – or at least on to those that lie east of the Silverado Trail – while at night cooling breezes from the San Pablo Bay waft over the vines, giving relatively low night-time temperatures and helping to conserve acidity in the grapes. The presence of knolls to the west of the Trail and the higher palisades to the east create a kind of funnel, which focuses the action of the breezes. Although midday temperatures can be considerably higher than in the centre of the valley, the overall heat summation is Region II, thanks to the cooling effect of those breezes in the early morning and late afternoon. This coolness is compensated for by a longer growing season than other valley floor districts.

The consequence, in terms of the wine's structure, is a lush, supple quality that makes the Cabernet Sauvignons accessible when young without seeming to compromise their capacity to age. These are the most overtly charming, silky, and seductive of Napa Cabernets. Merlot from Stags Leap also shows abundant charm. The wines are naturally elegant and their tannins, while present, are subdued. Many tasters identify a black-cherry fruit character as well as cassis. For John Shafer, the overriding character of the wines is texture, a velvetiness and suppleness that is instantly accessible but does not imply an inability to age in bottle, as his own 1978 Cabernet testifies.

There used to be quite a lot of Chardonnay, Riesling, and Chenin Blanc planted in Stags Leap, but replanting after phylloxera has tended to favour the Bordeaux varieties that perform so gracefully here. Replantings by forward-looking proprietors such as Mondavi and others tend to be attentive to such factors as rootstock, clone, and trellising, and it is probable that the wines of the future will be even finer than those that emerged from the district in the 1970s and 1980s. The original Fay Vineyard was almost entirely replanted by Winiarski. More sophisticated vineyard management throughout the district should give rise to a preponderance of red wines of greater density and structure without, it is hoped, sacrificing the elegance and fleshiness which are the hallmarks of Stags Leap wines.

The best-known winery is Stag's Leap Wine Cellars, and others of comparable stature include Shafer, Clos du Val, and Pine Ridge. Other wineries to look out for include Chimney Rock, Hartwell, and Silverado.

Wild Horse Valley

This is the most obscure of Napa AVAs, with only about 100 acres under vine. Birkmeyer is probably the best known vineyard. It is located to the east of Carneros on well-drained reddish volcanic soils occupying a kind of plateau about 1,000 feet up. Constant breezes delay the ripening, and the region is best suited to grapes such as Pinot Noir, Chardonnay, Riesling and Viognier. No wineries operate within Wild Horse Valley. The AVA was approved in 1988.

Yountville

It is typical of the impenetrable politics of appellation in California that Wild Horse Valley, home to just three smallish vineyards, should enjoy its own appellation, while Yountville, the district in which grapes were first planted in Napa Valley, should have none. (However, it seemed likely by late 1998 that approval of a Yountville AVA was imminent.) Located in the southern part of the valley, it benefits directly from the fogs and winds coming off the San

Pablo Bay. The soils are mostly gravelly loam and tend, especially when close to the Napa River, to be worryingly vigorous. There are 3,500 acres of vineyards.

Although one would imagine that Yountville is a touch too cool for Cabernet Sauvignon, vineyards such as Napanook, now part of the Dominus estate, do deliver Cabernet of outstanding quality. Chardonnay does well here, and also flourishes in hillside appendages to Yountville such as American Canyon and Coombsville, where vineyards and new housing developments compete for space. Silverado is one of a number of estates that has bought vineyard land here.

SINGLE VINEYARDS

A substantial portion of vineyards in Napa Valley is still owned by individual growers rather than by wineries. Some of the more prestigious vineyards – such as Martha's Vineyard or Backus – appear on the label; others do not. The following is not a complete list of grower-owned vineyards in Napa Valley, and mostly excludes those owned by and supplying a single winery, but a selection of those most frequently encountered or referred to. In some cases the vineyards are leased by wineries or have contracts to supply wineries with the bulk or even the whole of their production.

Aida. Owned since 1996 by Oliver Caldwell. 18 acres of Petite Sirah, Zinfandel and Cabernet Sauvignon. Supplies Zinfandel and Petite Sirah to Turley as well as to Caldwell's new winery.

Armstrong Ranch. Diamond Mountain. 13 acres planted at 1,150 feet. Sells Cabernet Sauvignon to Rombauer.

Atlas Peak. Atlas Peak. 120 acres of Sangiovese, some of which is sold to Signorello.

Backus. Oakville. 45 acres planted in 1975, leased by Phelps from 1977 until 1996, when Phelps bought the vineyard. Located along Silverado Trail south of Oakville Crossroad.

Banca Dorada. Rutherford Bench. Bought by Phelps in 1983. 35 acres of Cabernet Sauvignon.

Bancroft. Howell Mountain. 90 acres. Owned by Jim Bancroft, who also makes some wine from these grapes. Planted in 1983 at 1,800 feet with Cabernet Sauvignon, Merlot, Cabernet Franc, and Chardonnay. Volcanic ash soil. Chardonnay originally sold to Stony Hill but later budded over to Merlot, which is sold to Beringer.

Beatty Ranch. Howell Mountain. 40 acres. Planted with Cabernet Sauvignon and Zinfandel. The oldest Zinfandel vineyard on Howell Mountain, planted in early twentieth century. Dry-farmed. Mostly sold to Dunn, Cornerstone, Deer Park, and Howell Mountain Vineyard, which is co-owned by Mike Beatty.

Bella Oaks. On southwest side of Rutherford, along Bella Oaks Lane. Planted in 1971 by Bernard (Barney) and Belle Rhodes. 16 acres of Cabernet Sauvignon, regularly bought by Heitz since 1976. Much replanted after eutypiose damaged the vines, so no wine produced in 1991–92. Located 3 miles north of Martha's Vineyard and gives a leaner, lighter wine.

Birkmeyer. Wild Horse Valley. 18 acres planted since 1964 at 1,500 feet on rocky soil with Riesling and Chardonnay. Very low-yielding. Has supplied Riesling to Stag's Leap Wine Cellars.

Michael Black. Sells Merlot to Paul Hobbs.

Black-Sears. Howell Mountain. Owned by Joyce and Jerre Sears. 2,400 feet high and thus highest vineyard on Howell Mountain. Organic and dry-farmed. Sells 30-year-old Zinfandel to Elyse, Cornerstone, Turley, and Howell Mountain Vineyard, of which the Searses are co-owners.

Bosché. Rutherford. 19 acres of Cabernet Sauvignon and 2 of Merlot, originally planted in 1964. Silty clay loam with some sand. Originally owned by John and Lorraine Bosché and fruit sold since 1970 to its present owners, Freemark Abbey.

Brandlin Ranch. Mount Veeder. Sells Zinfandel to Rosenblum. Bought by Peter Franus in 1997.

Caldwell. Coombsville. 25 acres planted from 1980 with Cabernet Sauvignon, Cabernet Franc, Merlot, Malbec, Petit Verdot, Syrah, and Chardonnay. Spaced at 2,400 vines per acre. Grapes sold to Pahlmeyer, Jade Mountain, Selene, and Dunn.

Canard. Calistoga. 24 acres that include 3 acres of 100-year-old Zinfandel, bought by Ravenswood. Also Napa Gamay, Cabernet Franc, and Merlot.

Carpy Ranch. Rutherford Cross Road. 89 acres of Chardonnay sold to Freemark Abbey.

Carr. Mount Veeder. Owned by Norman Carr. 1,200 feet. Sells Chardonnay to Patz & Hall.

Casanova. Owned by Frank Casanova. Sells Zinfandel to Tulocay.

Chabot. St Helena. Planted in 1962 as the Lemmon Vineyard on a site originally planted in the nineteenth century. 35 acres. Farmed by Beringer, who use much of the fruit for their Private Reserve Cabernet Sauvignon.

Richard Chambers. Stags Leap. Planted with Cabernet Sauvignon, Cabernet Franc and Merlot, mostly sold to S. Anderson.

Cliff. Owned by Ron Cliff. Sells Cabernet Sauvignon to Tulocay.

La Cuesta. Pope Valley. Contains some Petite Sirah claimed to be 150 years old. Supplies Rosenblum with Petite Sirah.

Diamond Mountain Ranch. 199 acres. Planted with Cabernet Sauvignon, Chardonnay, Cabernet Franc and Merlot at 1,500–1,700 feet. Owned since 1978 by Sterling.

Dickerson. Owned by William Dickerson. 10 acres of Zinfandel planted in 1910 and sold to Ravenswood.

Eisele. Calistoga. Sold to Araujo estate (see p. 345) in 1990. Previously used for a single-vineyard Cabernet Sauvignon from Phelps from 1975 to 1991.

Volker Eisele. Chiles Valley. 60 acres planted at about 1,000 feet with Cabernet Sauvignon, Cabernet Franc, Zinfandel, Chardonnay, Sémillon, and Sauvignon Blanc. Sells grapes to Page Mill and other wineries.

Fay. Stags Leap. Founded by Nathan Fay and planted with Cabernet Sauvignon. Bought by Stags Leap Wine Cellars in 1986.

Fortuna. Rutherford. Sells Cabernet Sauvignon to Page Mill.

Glen Oaks. Chiles Valley. Owned by Louis Martini. 185 acres

planted at 700 feet with Cabernet Sauvignon, Merlot, Petite Sirah, and Cabernet Franc. Shallow clay loam soils.

Hayne. St Helena. Supplies Zinfandel and Petite Sirah to Turley.

Haynes. Coombsville. Owned by Duncan Haynes. 40 acres, planted in 1968 with Pinot Noir and Chardonnay. Sells fruit to Tulocay, Whitford, and others.

Heinemann. Spring Mountain. Planted with Pinot Noir in 1971 at 600 feet, and grapes sold to Schug. Grafted over to Cabernet Sauvignon in mid-1990s.

George Hendry. 80 acres planted in early 1970s with Cabernet Sauvignon, Chardonnay, Pinot Noir and Zinfandel. Sells Zinfandel to Rosenblum, Franus, and others.

Herrick. 350 acres south of Yountville, planted with Cabernet Sauvignon, Merlot, Sauvignon and Sémillon.

Inglewood. Planted in 1968 with Merlot, Cabernet Sauvignon, and Cabernet Franc. Formerly sold to Freemark Abbey and Rutherford Hill, but Merlot bottled under the label of owner Bill Jaeger. Up for sale in late 1990s.

Juliana. Pope Valley. Owned by Tucker Catlin. Planted with Sangiovese, Sauvignon Blanc, and Merlot, some of which is sold to La Sirena and Judd's Hill.

Lamborn. Howell Mountain. 9 acres of Zinfandel, Sangiovese, and Nebbiolo. Used by Lamborn Family winery and sells Zinfandel to Rocking Horse.

Leonardini. Rutherford. Planted with Cabernet Sauvignon, Merlot, and Zinfandel. Sells to Whitehall Lane and Galleron.

Liparita. Howell Mountain. Owned since 1996 by Kendall-Jackson. 80 acres planted from 1985–88 at 1,700–1,850 feet, with Cabernet Sauvignon, Chardonnay, Merlot and Sauvignon Blanc. Grapes formerly sold to Peter Michael, Hobbs, and Liparita Cellars.

Madrona Ranch. St Helena. Owned by vineyard manager David Abreu. Sells Bordeaux varieties to Etude, Selene, and Pahlmeyer. Minute quantities are vinified for Abreu by Ric Forman.

Marston. Spring Mountain. 35 acres planted with Cabernet Sauvignon, Merlot, and Syrah. Includes some 80-year-old dry-farmed Petite Sirah vines that used to be sold to Thackrey, until Beringer took a long-term lease on the vineyard.

Martha's Vineyard. Oakville. Planted in 1961 by Bernard and Belle Rhodes, and sold in 1963 to Tom and Martha May. 34 acres. Planted with Cabernet Sauvignon on a gravelly bench and dry-farmed. None made from 1993–95 because of disease and replanting.

Mast. Between Napa and Yountville. 19 acres of Cabernet Sauvignon planted in 1975.

Holbrook Mitchell. Yountville. Sells Cabernet Sauvignon, Cabernet Franc, and Merlot to Rosenblum.

Moore. Sells Zinfandel to Turley.

Morisoli. Rutherford. Owned by Gary Morisoli. 22 acres of Cabernet Sauvignon planted in 1980, and 2 acres of mixed varieties including Zinfandel planted in 1915. Grapes sold to Whitehall Lane and Elyse.

Napanook. Yountville. 41 acres of Cabernet Sauvignon. Formerly the property of Inglenook's John Daniel and his daughters, and now the core of the Dominus estate.

Oakville Ranch. Supplies Cabernet Sauvignon and Chardonnay to Lewis Cellars.

O'Shaughnessy. Rutherford. Planted only with Merlot. Sells grapes to Page Mill.

Pallisades. Calistoga. 42 acres owned by Clos Pegase, and planted with Cabernet Sauvignon and Petite Sirah.

Park Muscadine. Howell Mountain. Supplied Zinfandel to Ridge and Elyse. Bought by Randy Dunn, renamed, and replanted with Cabernet Sauvignon, some of which is sold to Cornerstone.

Penny Lane. Oakville. Owned by Marc Cruciger. Sells Sangiovese to Saddleback.

Pershing. 25 acres in Mayacamas Mountains planted from

1979–85 at 750–1,000 feet, with Cabernet Franc, Cabernet Sauvignon, and Merlot. Sells grapes to Stonegate.

Pickle Canyon. Mount Veeder. Planted in 1973 at 900 feet with 20 acres of Cabernet Sauvignon, Chardonnay, Merlot, Pinot Noir and Zinfandel.

Preston. Rutherford. Owned by Dick Preston. 12 acres planted in 1973 with 12 acres of Cabernet Sauvignon. Sold only to V. Sattui.

Priest Ranch. Chiles Valley. 100 acres planted at 2,200 feet with Cabernet Sauvignon, Chenin Blanc, Riesling and Zinfandel.

Rancho Chimiles. Chiles Valley. Owned by Terry Wilson. Sells Sauvignon Blanc to Stag's Leap Wine Cellars.

Robinson. Stags Leap. Owned by Norm Robinson. Sells Cabernet Sauvignon to Cronin and Rocking Horse.

Las Rocas. Stags Leap. Bought by Phelps in 1983 and replanted in 1990s after phylloxera. 40 acres planted with Cabernet Sauvignon and Merlot on clay loam soil.

Rossi. St Helena. Planted with very old Syrah sold to Sean Thackrey.

Salleri. Calistoga. Tiny 1-acre Zinfandel vineyard planted in 1920s. Fruit sold to Biale.

Schmidt. Yountville. Owned since 1991 by Swanson. Best known for old-vine Syrah, previously sold to Thackrey.

Spaulding. Diamond Mountain. 17 acres planted in early 1970s at 600–1,000 feet, with Cabernet Sauvignon, Chardonnay, and Merlot. Grapes sold to Stonegate.

State Lane. Yountville. 25 acres planted with Cabernet Sauvignon and sold to Beringer.

Sycamore. Rutherford. Owned by John Bryan. Set against western slopes and planted in 1979 with 22 acres of Cabernet Sauvignon, Cabernet Franc, and Sauvignon Blanc. Supplies Freemark Abbey.

Tench. Oakville. 12 acres planted in late 1960s on Silverado Trail at Oakville Cross Road. Planted with Cabernet Sauvignon, Malbec, Merlot, and Sauvignon Blanc.

Three Palms. Calistoga. 75 acres, owned by John Upton. But replanted from 1992–99 after phylloxera. Grapes sold to Sterling and Duckhorn. The new Duckhorn block will be 15 acres planted with Merlot, Cabernet Sauvignon, Cabernet Franc, and Petit Verdot. Rocky, gravelly soils, low-yielding.

To-Kalon. Oakville. Originally planted in H. W. Crabb in 1866. Owned since 1966 by Robert Mondavi and planted with Cabernet Sauvignon and Sauvignon Blanc.

Vine Hill Ranch. Oakville. 135 acres owned by Bob Phillips and planted from 1978–91 with Cabernet Sauvignon, Chardonnay, Merlot, and Sauvignon Blanc. Grapes sold to Duckhorn, Kendall-Jackson, and Etude.

Waters Ranch. Atlas Peak. Owned by Pahlmeyer. 80 acres at 1,700–2,200 feet. In 1999 will be planted with all 5 Bordeaux varieties, as well as Sémillon and Sauvignon Blanc.

White Cottage Ranch. Howell Mountain. Owned by winemaker Dennis Johns. Some Cabernet Sauvignon sold to Robert Craig.

Whitney 'Tennessee' Vineyard. 104-year-old Zinfandel sold to Turley, until sale of vineyard to Grgich in 1996.

York Creek. Spring Mountain. Owned by Fritz Maytag. 200 acres planted at 1,200–1,950 feet, with Cabernet Sauvignon, Zinfandel, Merlot, and Petite Sirah. Grapes used to be sold to Ridge and Belvedere.

NOTE

1 Kim Marcus, *Wine Spectator*, 31 August 1990

4

Sonoma

Sonoma County today has its fair share of imposing and prestigious wineries – Chateau St Jean, Ferrari-Carano, Sebastiani, and Jordan are a match for any grand estate in Napa Valley – but it was not always thus. Despite its long history, beginning with the early missions and then with the dynamism of Agoston Haraszthy, Sonoma remained steeped in rusticity until twenty-five years ago. It was hard to think of estates with a comparable prestige to, say, Inglenook or Beaulieu. Whereas Napa was developed in the late nineteenth century by German growers such as Krug, Schram, and Beringer, who formed large estates with imposing stone wineries, Sonoma remained the preserve of Italian farmers, who cultivated grapes on a much smaller scale. Philip Wagner, writing in the 1950s, took his readers through the county, pointing out the names of wineries (some of which still exist) such as Seghesio, Mazzoni, Pastori, Pedroncelli, Nervo, Frei, Oneto, Cambiaso, Foppiano, Sodini, and so forth.

It remained that way until about 1970. Before then much of what is today valuable vineyard land was given over to walnuts, pears, almonds and prunes. Doug Nalle recalls how in 1975 Dry Creek Valley was still filled with prune trees on the flat land. The good vineyards were planted at the turn of the century on the slopes; vines planted on the flat land were intended to produce bulk wines. The varieties planted were the old standbys of Carignane, Petite Sirah and Zinfandel, rich, dark, heavy, powerful, and rustic. French Colombard was the dominant white variety. The great majority of the fruit and wines produced made their way into bulk wines or jug wines. Grapes were a commodity and yields were generous. It is reasonable to suppose that given the climate, the hillside location of the best vineyards, and an abundance of sound grape varieties, even those jug wines, if not diluted with lesser quality fruit from other regions, may have been of decent quality: robust and heartwarming.

In the old days much of the wine was dispatched to vast vinification and blending plants at Asti or in the Central Valley, but today the Central Valley has come to Sonoma. Gallo has been a major investor in vineyard land, bringing in bulldozers acquired

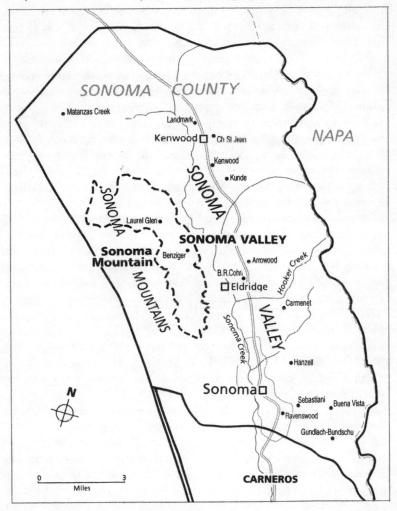

Sonoma Valley

cheaply after the completion of the Alaskan Pipeline project and employing them to move mountains – or at least hillsides. No longer are those grapes shipped out of county. Sonoma now features proudly on the labels of the upper echelons of many Gallo wines. Yet for the most part Sonoma remains a region of small vineyards and small wineries. The great names of Sonoma – Kistler, Williams-Selyem, Rochioli, Hanzell, Arrowood, Laurel Glen, Rafanelli – remain modest in size. A few wineries that started out that way – Ravenswood, Sonoma-Cutrer – have expanded, but they are the exception rather than the rule.

There are about 40,000 acres under vine in Sonoma County, and over 150 wineries in operation. Exact figures are hard to come by, but the acreage of the major varieties is approximately as follows: Cabernet Sauvignon (7,500), Zinfandel (4,250), Pinot Noir (4,150), Merlot (5,500); and among whites, Chardonnay (13,300), Sauvignon Blanc (1,700), French Colombard (600), and Gewürztraminer (300). Given the size of the county it is dangerous to generalize, but Sonoma overall must be a trifle cooler than Napa, giving elegant, medium-bodied wines and succeeding extremely well with such delicate varieties as Pinot Noir.

Sonoma is divided into very distinctive climatic zones. The south, focused around the towns of Sonoma and Glen Ellen and not far from Carneros and San Pablo Bay, is relatively cool. Northwest of Sonoma lies the city of Santa Rosa. To the north of Santa Rosa is the small Chalk Hill appellation, and to the west the very cool Green Valley. Northwest of Santa Rosa is the well-known Russian River Valley, which has a well-deserved reputation for its Pinot Noir. To the north lies Healdsburg, a pretty little place and the ideal base for exploring the county. North of Healdsburg, Dry Creek stretches north towards Lake Sonoma. This is quite a warm region and best known for its excellent Zinfandels. Northeast of Healdsburg is Alexander Valley, which can be quite hot on the valley floor though there are some excellent vineyards along the west-facing slopes of the Mayacamas Mountains. Alexander Valley is linked to Calistoga and Napa Valley by the narrow Knights Valley, where there are only a few wineries. In short, Sonoma is a very diverse region, delivering a variety of styles and offering wines to please most tastes.

Alexander Valley

The valley, which became an AVA in 1988, is named after Captain Cyrus Alexander, a fur trapper from Pennsylvania who in the 1840s was awarded a land grant of 48,000 acres by General Vallejo. Captain Alexander planted the first grapes here in 1846 and managed the land until his death in 1872. The valley is some twenty miles long, beginning just south of Healdsburg and continuing north, following the Russian River, as far as Cloverdale and the border with Mendocino County. It is a warm region, classified as Region III; it has limited maritime influence and few fogs, and the further north one goes the hotter it gets. The heart of the region is around Geyserville, between Cloverdale and Healdsburg, and here the steady heat is extremely favourable to the cultivation of Zinfandel. Ridge produces one of its most outstanding Zinfandels from Geyserville fruit. Yet surprisingly it is possible to grow white grapes, such as Chardonnay and Sauvignon, with considerable success. Famous vineyards such as the Gauer Ranch (now owned by Kendall-Jackson and renamed the Alexander Mountain Estate), Robert Young, and Belle Terre are all located in the Alexander Valley. Chateau St Jean was a pioneer of Alexander Valley Sauvignon Blanc, and Murphy-Goode is among the leading producers of the variety today.

The drawback of the valley is its fertility. Its 7,000 acres of mostly sandy loam and gravelly loam soils are generously productive, and firm measures need to be taken to prevent the vines from overcropping. Not surprisingly, hillside and benchland sites tend to give lower yields and better quality fruit than the valley floor. At its best, Alexander Valley fruit is rich, soft, powerful, and packed with flavour. Silver Oak, although based in Napa Valley, has long made a celebrated Cabernet from the valley, as have Clos du Bois, Simi, Geyser Peak, and other wineries. Alexander Valley reds that taste mean and lean have acquired those characteristics from overcropped and thus underripe fruit. Chardonnays vary greatly in style, but the consensus now seems to be that the valley is better suited to red varieties than to Chardonnay and other whites. Cabernet Sauvignon can, indeed, perform exceptionally well here. In general the wines of Alexander Valley are best enjoyed relatively young, though bottlings from Simi and other wineries have shown that the reds are capable of ageing if yields are kept to reasonable levels.

Carneros

As it is wedded to Napa County, this region is considered separately.

Chalk Hill

This sub-appellation is in fact part of the Russian River Valley. Best known for its Chardonnay, it encompasses about 1,000 acres to the east of Windsor. Despite its name, there is no chalk here: the whiteness of the soil is derived from volcanic ash rather than limestone. It differs from the rest of Russian River Valley in the absence of coastal fog, since the hilly terrain impedes such incursions. Thus it is warmer than Russian River, while at the same the presence of ocean breezes means it is cooler than Alexander and Knights valleys, both of which lie to the immediate north. For what it's worth, Chalk Hill is notched up as a Region II.

The veteran winemaker Rodney Strong first used Chalk Hill on the label of some of the Chardonnays he grew here in the 1970s. Naturally it is the Chalk Hill winery that benefits most from the existence of the sub-appellation. Although Chardonnay is easily the dominant variety, a good deal of Merlot has been planted in recent years.

I leave the last word to Randall Grahm, who in a series of brilliant parodies of haikus by Basho, penned the following:

> Climbing the chalk hill
> The whiteness is blinding.
> No lime in sight!

Dry Creek Valley

While Alexander Valley heads north from Healdsburg, Dry Creek Valley veers to the northwest for about sixteen miles in the direction of Lake Sonoma. It seems that a certain A. J. Galloway planted vines here in 1864, but the first commercial vineyard was developed by a Frenchman, Georges Bloch, who originally planted vines in

Dry Creek Valley in 1870. A winery was established two years later. By 1890 about 800 acres were in production, most of them planted by Italian immigrants. At this time Zinfandel was the leading variety, as well as Riesling and Mission, although most vineyards would have contained a field blend combining numerous varieties in the same parcel. A few of those ancient vineyards are still in production. The region expanded rapidly and by the last decade of the nineteenth century some thirteen wineries were in operation. Today there are twenty-three.

The region covers at least 6,000 acres and does have a fairly distinctive climate. The narrowness of the valley – which is two miles wide at its broadest point – and the coastal mountains to the west protect it from the fog that keeps the Russian River Valley so cool. The fog that does intrude into Dry Creek tends to burn off quickly, and in summer the valley can be quite warm, although the heat diminishes earlier in the day than it does in neighbouring Alexander Valley. The southern end of the valley is cooler than the north, and the valley as a whole crosses from Region II into Region III as one moves north. It is also slightly wetter than the regions to the east such as Alexander Valley and Knights Valley, a factor that probably encouraged the development of the region in the nineteenth century, since it was well suited to dry-farming.

Soil types are varied, but the benchlands are distinguished by the presence of a rare gravel compound known as Dry Creek Conglomerate. This is a reddish, rocky, well-drained soil, in contrast to the deeper, more alluvial soils of the valley floor. A profusion of microclimates allows a large number of grape varieties to be cultivated with considerable success, although the region has become best known for well-structured and concentrated Zinfandel and delicately herbaceous Sauvignon Blanc. Cabernet Sauvignon is also grown here, but does not always attain satisfactory ripeness levels, and Merlot has proved a better bet. Fans of the grassier, bell-pepper strain of Cabernet will find Dry Creek versions highly acceptable. Chardonnay is also not an ideal variety in Dry Creek, although it can do well in the more southerly parts of the valley. However, plantings of Rhône varieties have proved very successful, especially from Preston, which first planted Syrah about twenty years ago.

Green Valley

This western sub-appellation within Russian River Valley is becoming increasingly fashionable now that cool-climate wines have come into vogue. The Pacific Ocean is only ten miles to the west, though of course some fairly rugged mountains intervene. 'Cool', of course, is a relative term, especially now that even growers in Lodi like to claim their area shares that virtue. Laurence Sterling of Iron Horse admits that it sometimes soars to 102 degrees in summer, but the heat is moderated by distinctly cool nights, when the temperature can fall to about 48. Overall, Green Valley qualifies as a Region I growing area.

The soil is sandier than in other parts of Russian River and phylloxera has been less widespread than in most other parts of the county. Climate rather than soil gives the wines their character-istic high acidity, which makes the region so propitious for sparkling wines, of which Iron Horse is the leading producer. The Burgundian varieties thrive here too, which is why Marimar Torres decided to locate her vineyard and winery here.

About 1,000 acres are in production, and half are planted with Chardonnay. Local growers and winemakers like to claim that Chardonnay made from Green Valley fruit has a Chablis-like character. This is not really so, since Green Valley Chardonnay does not have the mineral bite of good Chablis, but the fruit does have a marked acidity, and an appley freshness which sets it apart from Chardonnay grown in warmer parts of the North Coast.

Knights Valley

This narrow valley links Alexander Valley with the top end of Napa Valley. It's a hot region, especially on the valley floor where Beringer have planted large vineyards with Cabernet Sauvignon and Sauvignon Blanc. However, nights can be quite cool, or at any rate cooler than Napa Valley to the southeast. About 1,000 acres are now in production throughout the valley. The Peter Michael winery, which has planted vineyards at high hillside locations on volcanic soils, has been demonstrating the region's potential for complex and well-structured wines. Peter Michael have planted red varieties at 1,000 feet and whites at 1,800, and the grapes ripen about three weeks later than those grown on the valley floor.

Northern Sonoma

This catch-all appellation, approved in 1990, embraces Chalk Hill, Alexander Valley, Knights Valley, Dry Creek Valley, Russian River Valley, and parts of Green Valley and Sonoma Coast. It is rarely encountered on a label, except by Gallo, who petitioned to have the appellation created in the first place. If appellations are supposed to provide consumers with relevant information, then Northern Sonoma seems among the most pointless of them all.

Russian River Valley

This is the most celebrated of Sonoma regions, first exploited in 1886 when the sparkling wine producer Korbel established a winery here. It takes its name from the river, itself named after the Russian fur traders who settled along the Sonoma coast. The region was recognized as a prime grape growing region by Italian immigrants in the mid to late nineteenth century. Almost 200 wineries were active at the turn of the century, but Prohibition soon drove the vast majority out of business. Korbel helped sustain the region, since it required considerable quantities of Chardonnay and Pinot Noir during its heyday in the 1960s. Foppiano was another major player in the valley long before it became fashionable. Today there are about fifty wineries based here, and about 200 growers.

Russian River Valley has about 10,000 acres under vine. The region includes not only the slopes above the riverbanks, but the floodplains too, approaching Santa Rosa to the east and Sebastopol to the south. It became an AVA in 1983, although Louis Foppiano had already been using the name on his labels for about ten years. The valley has a distinctly cool climate, sustained by morning fogs rolling in from the Pacific; it falls into Region I, although the northern third of the region is warmer than the rest. Close to the river banks the soil is alluvial and rich, whereas the slopes, which are gentle and east-facing, have a far higher gravel content. The gravel can be very deep, giving excellent drainage. The alluvial soils, with their rich sandy loams, are in general better suited to white varieties than red. In the southern part of the valley you can also find soils based on decomposed sandstone and loam. Rainfall is relatively high, averaging 75 centimetres, although it can be considerably higher. The growing season is prolonged, allowing a slow, even ripening, but rot can be a problem when rain falls in late summer or autumn. Persistent fog can also promote mildew, so growing grapes here is not without its risks.

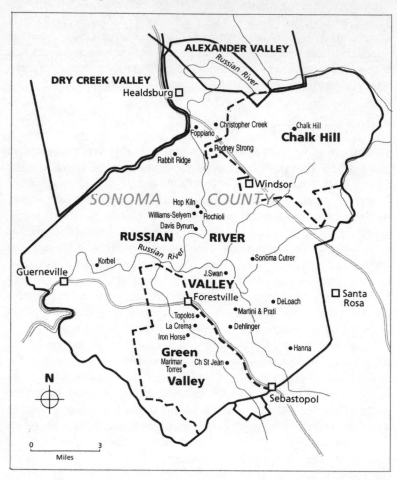

Russian River

Russian River has become known for the high quality of its Pinot Noirs, which are among the most prized in California, even though varieties such as Pinot Noir, Chardonnay, and Riesling were only planted in the early 1970s. Pinot Noir in particular benefits greatly from the cool winds that come through the Petaluma Gap and swing northwards through the valley. The most highly regarded sector of the valley lies along Westside Road to the west of Windsor. Here the Allen and Rochioli vineyards were among the first to demonstrate the tremendous potential for complex Pinot Noir, and winemakers such as Gary Farrell, Tom Dehlinger, and the Williams-Selyem duo were quick to show how exciting the wines produced from them could be, pure in varietal character but with a touch of opulence too. The cool climate also benefits varieties such as Sauvignon Blanc, and some attractive Chardonnay is grown here as well. More surprisingly, Zinfandel can succeed here too, especially in the eastern part of Russian River Valley, which is slightly warmer and tends to give fruit with lower acidity. Although this was never thought of as a good area for Bordeaux reds, producers such as DeLoach and Dehlinger have shown that they can do well here.

Parts of Russian River – Green Valley to the west, Chalk Hill to the east – have sub-appellations of their own. For the most part Russian River is a region of small to medium-sized vineyards, although Gallo have ruffled some local feathers by planting 800 acres here, notably at its Laguna Ranch. Kendall-Jackson is another large winery that has been developing vineyards in the valley.

In addition to the wineries already mentioned, the leading estates include DeLoach, Rabbit Ridge, Hop Kiln, Davis Bynum, and Rutz.

Sonoma Coast

This immense AVA was created in 1987 at the behest of the Sonoma-Cutrer winery. It was always designed to be a cool-climate zone, predominantly Region I. It stretches all the way from the boundary with Marin County in the south up to Mendocino in the north. It encompasses some 12,000 acres, but almost all those vineyards have the right to use other appellations. Only in the north is there no overlap. I am not sure that there is any legal sanction for the practice, but I have seen Occidental cited on labels as a zone of production, and many top vineyards do seem to be located in this area just to the west of Green Valley. It is all very confusing.

Nonetheless there can be no doubt that the vineyards planted on ridgetops are capable of producing superlative Chardonnay and

Pinot Noir. Proximity to the Pacific ensures a plethora of cooling breezes and sweeps of fog, and sometimes this can be too much of a good thing. At one of the top vineyards, Camp Meeting Ridge, the summer temperature ranges from 72 to 84 degrees Fahrenheit, which is decidedly cool, encouraging a long slow maturation. Growers claim that these vineyards offer the longest hang-time of any region in California. The finest vineyards here, many of which are not far from the town of Fort Ross, are truly marginal, and there are years when it is a struggle for the grapes to ripen fully. The Summa Vineyard reports that its grapes ripen fully in only one year out of four, which makes viticulture an expensive proposition. The ridges are studded with small vineyards, planted at heights ranging from 800 to 1,800 feet, which is usually just above the fog line at 900–1,000 feet. These vineyards sell first-rate (and very expensive) fruit to demanding wineries such as Kistler, Williams-Selyem and Littorai, but the big boys are also moving in. Kendall-Jackson are persuaded that the region can be the source of excellent Pinot Noir, and are planting 182 acres here. Caymus are also developing vineyards, and Jayson Pahlmeyer has bought 70 acres.

Among the most highly regarded vineyards here are Camp Meeting Ridge, Hirsch, Hellenthal, Charles Ranch, Summa, and Bohan Ranch. Among the wineries using fruit from these vineyards are Kistler, Littorai, Marcassin, Williams-Selyem, Hartford Court, and Whitcraft.

Sonoma Mountain

This is a sub-appellation within the very heart of Sonoma Valley. It was originally developed, according to Ray Kaufman of Laurel Glen, by German growers in the late nineteenth century, who planted Zinfandel and Pinot Noir. As the name suggests, the vineyards are planted high up, the lowest at 400 feet, the majority at between 1,100 and 1,600 feet. The zone lies around the village of Glen Ellen, which is located closer to the valley floor. Being above the fog line, the region is a warm one, best suited to the growing of red varieties such as Cabernet Sauvignon and Zinfandel. Temperatures tend to be surprisingly even, rarely plummeting during the night. Ripening is slow and steady, giving rich, well-structured fruit. Rainfall is about one-third higher than in Sonoma Valley. There are about 650 acres under vine, usually on east-facing slopes.

The soil is generally volcanic, with tufa and ash, as well as some gravel. Laurel Glen is the best known estate. Benziger also use a good deal of Sonoma Mountain fruit, which can be of superlative quality.

Sonoma Valley

This is the historic heartland of Sonoma County, at least as far as viticulture is concerned. The Sonoma Mission was located here, and the Buena Vista estate was established here in 1857 by Agoston Haraszthy. The valley used be known by the dramatic name of the Valley of the Moon, a description derived from its crescent shape rather than from any lunar features of the landscape. Despite its long history, the region did not have any great reputation for outstanding wines, since it was dominated by families such as the Sebastianis, who were content to supply the market for cheap and cheerful jug wines. Only in the 1970s did the area begin to realize its potential for high-quality wines in a variety of styles. It was granted AVA status in 1981.

It is a thoroughly diverse area, with a clear distinction between the north and the south. As is often the case in North Coast regions, the north is hotter, although wetter, than the south. To the south it abuts the Carneros region and is consequently influenced by the maritime climate of San Pablo Bay. The valley continues northward for some twenty-five miles, through Sonoma itself, past Glen Ellen and Kenwood, to the fringes of Santa Rosa. At its broadest point, the valley is some eight miles wide. To the east lie the Mayacamas Mountains, to the west the Sonoma Mountains. The north is also not without maritime influence, with cooling air flowing through the Petaluma Gap. Glen Ellen and Kenwood, being the least affected by maritime influence, whether from north or south, tend to be the hottest areas. In general the valley is very dry, with an average rainfall of 20 inches. As a consequence the familiar hazards of viticulture, such as mildew and botrytis, are rare.

Not only is the climate varied, but soils and elevations differ too. The soils, which can be quite fertile, are a blend of sandstone, shale, and oceanic sediment, as well as the commonly encountered sand and gravel. The cooler south is best suited to Chardonnay, Pinot Noir, Gewürztraminer, and Merlot, whereas Cabernet Sauvignon and Zinfandel (and Merlot too) thrive in the warmer areas around Glen Ellen and Kenwood, especially on hillside vineyards. Some very old parcels of Zinfandel are still in production, notably the vines planted in 1882 that are now vinified by Kunde. Ravenswood sources some of its most outstanding single-vineyard Zinfandels from long-established vineyards such as Old Hill.

There has been a remarkable expansion over the past decade, and the vineyard area has now risen to about 13,000 acres. Sebastiani is the largest winery, but other wineries as well as individual farmers have developed substantial vineyards here. Kenwood manage the 110-acre Jack London Ranch, and Martini, although based in Napa Valley, own the excellent 200-acre Monte Rosso. Other fine sites include Los Chamizal, McCrea (which supplies superb Chardonnay to Kistler), and Beltane.

There are a number of wineries based in the valley that manage to combine quite high production levels with excellent quality. Among them are Benziger, Chateau St Jean, Kenwood, Gundlach-Bundschu, and Ravenswood. Kunde, having been major grape growers for decades, have now transformed themselves into a winery as well. Another relative newcomer, Arrowood, was founded by the winemaker who put Chateau St Jean on the map: Richard Arrowood. Matanzas Creek, located in the far north of the region and only a short distance from Santa Rosa, has established an enviable reputation for Sauvignon Blanc, Chardonnay, and Merlot.

SINGLE VINEYARDS

As in the previous chapter, the following is a selection of some of the better-known vineyards and is not intended to be a complete listing of the roughly 200 individual sites now in production.

Alegria. Russian River Valley. Owned by Bill Nachbaur. Sells Syrah to Wellington and Hamel.

Allen. Russian River Valley. Owned by Howard Allen. Planted in 1973 with 58 acres of Chardonnay and Pinot Noir. The source of outstanding grapes for wineries such as Davis Bynum, Gary Farrell, Rochioli, Chateau Souverain, and Williams-Selyem.

Arrendell. Green Valley. Owned by Kendall-Jackson. Supplies Pinot Noir and Chardonnay to Hartford Court.

Ash Creek. Alexander Valley. Sells Cabernet Sauvignon to Benziger.

Bacigalupi. Russian River Valley. Owned by Roger Bacigalupi, a Healdsburg dentist. On Westside Road, 60 acres of Chardonnay and Pinot Noir. Sold to Gary Farrell, Belvedere, and others.

Barricia. Sonoma Valley. Owned by Pat Herron. Sells Merlot and Zinfandel to Ravenswood and Kenwood.

Belle Terre. Alexander Valley. Owned by Henry Dick. Planted with 1,200 acres of Chardonnay in the mid-1960s at 500 feet on gravelly soil above the Russian River. Mostly sold to Chateau St Jean. The 1973 Chardonnay from Chateau Montelena that triumphed in the Paris tasting organized by Steven Spurrier was partly made from Belle Terre fruit. Also sells Malbec to Arrowood.

Belloni. Russian River Valley. Owned by Riccardo Belloni. Sells Zinfandel to Ravenswood.

Beltane. Sonoma Valley, just north of Glen Ellen. Owned by Alexa Wood. 80 acres of Chardonnay, Sauvignon Blanc, Zinfandel, Cabernet Sauvignon and Merlot. Sold exclusively to Kenwood.

Black Mountain. Alexander Valley. Owned by Ken Toth and planted with 115 acres of Zinfandel, Cabernet Sauvignon, Petite Sirah, Sauvignon Blanc, and Chardonnay.

Blue Rock. Alexander Valley. Owned by Ken Kahn. Sells Cabernet Franc, Malbec and Petit Verdot to Benziger.

Buckeye. Alexander Valley. Terraced and south-facing vineyards. The Cabernet Sauvignon is planted at an elevation of 2,000 feet and is sold to Kendall-Jackson.

Raymond Burr. Dry Creek Valley. Established by the late actor in the 1980s. South-facing terraced vineyards, planted with Cabernet Sauvignon and Cabernet Franc. Sold to Pedroncelli and others.

Camp Meeting Ridge. Sonoma Coast. Owned by Walt and Joan Flowers, who supply Chardonnay and Pinot Noir to Kistler and other wineries, as well as vinifying some of their own production of closely planted Chardonnay and Pinot Noir. 32 acres at 1,200–1,400 feet, a mile inland from the Pacific.

Los Chamizal. Sonoma Valley. Sells Zinfandel to Haywood and others.

Charles Ranch. Sonoma Coast. Sells Chardonnay to Martinelli.

Collins. Russian River Valley. 30 acres of Zinfandel planted from 1910–30. Sold to Limerick Lane and Farrell.

Cooke. Sonoma Valley. Owned by Charles Cooke. 22 acres. Sells Zinfandel to Ravenswood.

Danielik. Supplies Merlot to Farrell.

Diamond Oaks. Alexander Valley. Sells Malbec to Arrowood.

Richard Dinner. Sonoma Mountain. Sells Chardonnay to Paul Hobbs.

Dorothy's. Dry Creek. Sells Chardonnay to Alderbrook.

Dutton Ranch. Green Valley. 950 acres. Widely dispersed vineyards owned by Warren Dutton. Grapes sold to Kistler, J. Fritz, Hartford Court, and other wineries.

Elissa. Dry Creek Valley. Owned by Bill and Sally Hambrecht. Planted mostly with Zinfandel.

Fay. Alexander Valley. Owned by John Fay. Sells Cabernet Sauvignon to Pedroncelli.

Francisco's Vineyard. Sonoma Valley. 34 acres planted with Zinfandel, Chardonnay and Pinot Noir.

Frati. Russian River Valley. Owned by Angelo Frati. Sells Zinfandel to Swan.

Gamba. Russian River Valley. Zinfandel. Sells to Alderbrook.

Gauer Ranch. Alexander Valley. 557 acres. In 1972 Ed Gauer planted the vineyards at 400 to 2,400 feet. Gauer sold the estate to Chevron in 1992, and it was bought in 1995 by Kendall-Jackson and renamed the Alexander Mountain Estate. The most sought-after section is the Upper Barn. Chardonnay sold to Marcassin, Peter Michael, and Mueller.

Gregory. Sonoma Valley. Owned by Dick Gregory. Sells Cabernet Sauvignon to Ravenswood.

Grist. Sells Zinfandel to Turley.

Hafner. Alexander Valley. 98 acres of Chardonnay and Cabernet Sauvignon, increasingly vinified by the family's own winery.

Hartford. Owned by Donald Hartford. Provides grapes from 80-year-old Zinfandel vines to Hartford Court.

Hedin. Russian River Valley. Owned by Roger Hedin. Supplies Davis Bynum with Cabernet Sauvignon and Rabbit Ridge with Zinfandel.

Heintz Ranch. Sonoma Coast. Planted in 1983. Sells Chardonnay to Littorai.

Hellenthal. Sonoma Coast. Sells Pinot Noir to La Jota.

Hillcrest. Sonoma Coast. Planted in 1973. Sells Chardonnay to Littorai.

Hirsch. Sonoma Coast. Owned by David Hirsch. 1,200–1,550 feet. Planted in 1990. Sold Pinot Noir to Sea Ridge, before its closure in 1995, and other wineries, including Littorai, Williams-Selyem, Whitcraft, Siduri, and Kistler.

Jessandra Vittoria. Owned by Robert Mark Kamen. 40 acres of Cabernet Franc and Sangiovese. 20 per cent of the vineyard was damaged by fire in 1996.

Jimtown Ranch. Alexander Valley. 200 acres. Supplied Ridge until acquired by Bill and Sally Hambrecht in 1988. Planted on the valley floor, mostly with Chardonnay, Merlot, and Sauvignon Blanc. Supplies Belvedere with Chardonnay.

Frank Johnson. Russian River Valley. Supplies Chardonnay and Pinot Noir to Pedroncelli.

Kunde. Planted with many varieties, including Muscat and Merlot. Sells to numerous wineries as well as supplying own winery.

Ladi's. Owned by Ladi Danielik. Sells Cabernet Sauvignon and Merlot to Farrell.

Jack London. Sonoma Valley. 110 acres. Owned by Milo Shepard, but Kenwood have exclusive rights to manage the vineyard and market its wines. Red lava soil. Originally planted in the 1880s, but current plantings of Chardonnay, Pinot Noir, Merlot, Cabernet Franc, Cabernet Sauvignon, and Zinfandel date from 1972 onwards.

Lorenzo. Sonoma Coast. 10 acres. Sells Chardonnay to Marcassin.

Mays Canyon. Russian River Valley. Planted in 1983. Sells Pinot Noir to Littorai.

McCrea. Sonoma Mountain. Owned by Kistler. 30 acres of Chardonnay.

McIlroy. Russian River Valley. Sells Gewürztraminer to Alderbrook, and Chardonnay to Davis Bynum.

Martinelli. Russian River Valley. Sells Pinot Noir to Signorello.

Mazzoni. Sells Zinfandel to Kenwood.

Monte Rosso. Founded in the 1880s by Emanuel Goldstein, and owned since 1938 by Louis Martini. Planted at 900–1,200 feet. 200 acres, including 65 of Cabernet Sauvignon, 60 of Zinfandel (originally planted in the 1890s), as well as Cabernet Franc, Petit Verdot, Sémillon, Riesling, and Muscat. Mostly vinified by Martini, but some grapes sold to Villa Mount Eden; Zinfandel sold to Biale, Saddleback, and Ravenswood.

Moshin. Russian River Valley. Supplies Pinot Noir to Davis Bynum and Gary Farrell.

Nun's Canyon. Sonoma Valley. 115 acres including 8 acres of 90-year-old Zinfandel planted at 1,200 feet. Supplied Kenwood, until bought in 1996 by St Francis.

Oakridge. Alexander Valley. Planted at 2,000 feet. Sells Cabernet Sauvignon to Chateau Souverain.

Old Hill. Sonoma Valley. Owned by Otto Teller. 18 acres of Zinfandel planted in 1890s. Grapes sold to Ravenswood and Topolos.

Olivet Lane. 80 acres of Chardonnay and Pinot Noir planted in 1976. Owned by Pellegrini, but fruit is also sold to Kenwood, Whitcraft, Farrell, and Williams-Selyem.

Olsen. Russian River Valley. Sells Zinfandel to Rabbit Ridge.

Pagani Ranch. Sonoma Valley. Planted with Zinfandel, Mourvèdre, and Petite Sirah. Sells to Ridge and St Francis.

Pedroni-Bushell. Supplies Zinfandel to Pedroncelli.

Petite Etoile. Russian River Valley. 40 acres. Supplies Sauvignon Blanc to Chateau St Jean, who bought the vineyard in 1989.

Pickberry. Sonoma Mountain. Owned by Chris Strotz. Planted with Cabernet Sauvignon, Cabernet Franc and Merlot. Supplies Ravenswood.

Poplar. Russian River Valley. Owned by Donna and Kent Ritchie. Sell Chardonnay to J. Fritz and White Oak.

Preston Ranch. Russian River Valley. Supplies Arrowood with Riesling.

Rhinefarm. Sonoma Valley. 125 acres. Owned by Gundlach-Bundschu.

Rochioli. Russian River Valley. 100 acres of Pinot Noir, Chardonnay, Zinfandel, Cabernet Sauvignon, and Sauvignon Blanc. Partly vinified by Rochioli, but fruit also sold to Williams-Selyem, Farrell, Castalia, Chateau Souverain, and Davis Bynum.

Rockaway Creek Ranch. Alexander Valley. 130 acres, owned since 1992 by Bill and Sally Hambrecht. Terraced hillsides planted with Merlot, Cabernet Sauvignon, Zinfandel, Syrah, Petite Sirah and Sangiovese. Supplies Belvedere.

Rockpile. Dry Creek Valley. Sells Zinfandel to Rosenblum.

Rossi. Sonoma Valley. Owned by Val Rossi. Established in 1910. Planted with Zinfandel, Petite Sirah, and Alicante. Sells to Topolos.

Samsel. Sonoma Valley. Owned by William Samsel. Zinfandel planted in 1910. Sells grapes to Rosenblum.

Sanchietti. Russian River Valley. Sells Pinot Noir to Hartford Court.

Saralee's Vineyard. Russian River. Owned by Richard and Saralee Kunde. Planted with Pinot Noir, Pinot Blanc, Syrah, Viognier, Gewürztraminer and Pinot Gris. Fruit sold to Arrowood, Swan, Patz & Hall, Alderbrook, and others.

Scherrer. Alexander Valley. 28 acres. 75-year-old Zinfandel, vinified by Fred Scherrer's winery and also sold to Greenwood Ridge in Mendocino.

Shiloh Hill. Russian River Valley. Owned by Howard Bracker. Sells Syrah to Alderbrook.

Shone. Russian River Valley. Owned by Santa Rosa Junior College. Sells Sauvignon Blanc to Davis Bynum.

Sodini. Russian River Valley. Planted with Zinfandel in 1905. Supplies Rochioli and others.

Steiner. Sonoma Mountain. Owned by Dave Steiner. Planted in 1970s with 25 acres of Cabernet Sauvignon, as well as smaller parcels of Pinot Noir and Cabernet Franc. Fruit sold to Swan, Kenwood, and others.

Stuhlmuller. Alexander Valley. Owned by Roger Stuhlmuller. 130 acres, with Chardonnay and Cabernet Sauvignon. Sells to Cronin, Chateau Souverain, Fetzer, Page Mill, and Clos du Val. Also used by the family's own winery since 1996.

Summa. Sonoma Coast. Owned by Scott Zeller. 1,200 feet high. Sells Pinot Noir to Williams-Selyem.

Summers Ranch. Knights Valley. Owned by Jim Summers. Sells Merlot to Ravenswood and Judd's Hill.

Tarman. Dry Creek Valley. Owned by Bill and Sally Hambrecht. Planted at 800 feet with Cabernet Sauvignon and Merlot.

Teldeschi. Dry Creek. Owned by Dan Teldeschi. 80 acres. Zinfandel and Petite Sirah to Carlisle Cellars and Duxoup, as well as to the new Teldeschi winery.

Trentadue. 250 acres. Partly vinified at the Trentadue Winery, but also supplies Ridge with the grapes for its Geyserville Zinfandel.

Valsecchi. Sonoma Valley. Sells Zinfandel to Biale.

Van der Kamp. Sonoma Mountain. Sells Pinot Noir to Siduri.

Los Vinedos del Rio. 172 acres: 74 Merlot, 26 Chardonnay, also

Gewürztraminer and Sémillon. South of Healdsburg. Owned since 1962 by Louis Martini and the source of America's first varietal Merlot in the late 1960s.

Vine Hill. Russian River Valley. Chardonnay. Owned by Kistler.

Westside. Russian River Valley. Farmed by Rochioli. Sells Chardonnay to Chateau Souverain.

Westside Farms. Russian River Valley. Owned by Ron Kaiser. Sells Pinot Noir to Chateau Souverain.

Wildwood. Sonoma Valley. Planted on volcanic soil at 1,500 feet with Chardonnay and other varieties. One of the suppliers of Chateau St Jean and also used by Kunde estate, which owns the vineyard. Sells Barbera to Benziger.

Wine Creek. Dry Creek Valley. Planted with Cabernet Sauvignon, Merlot and Zinfandel at 1,000 feet. Owned by Bill and Sally Hambrecht. Deep red volcanic soils.

Wolfspierre. Sonoma Mountain. Sells Pinot Noir to Swan.

Wood Road. Russian River Valley. Sells Zinfandel to Ravenswood.

Robert Young. Alexander Valley. 425 acres. Supplies Chardonnay, Pinot Blanc, Sauvignon Blanc and Sémillon to Chateau St Jean, Belvedere, and others.

5
Carneros

Although Carneros was thought of as grassy ranchland until the 1970s, the tradition of grape growing goes back a long time. The region had its origin in the land grants handed out by General Vallejo in the 1836. They were rapidly subdivided and smaller ranches were acquired by land-hungry settlers in the 1840s. It was primarily farming and ranching country, enjoying the advantage of easy transportation of its produce to San Francisco. Orchards and vineyards were also planted here, and the first recorded vineyard is that of Jacob Leese, in the late 1830s. Leese was Vallejo's son-in-law, and had been granted the 18,000-acre Rancho Huichica. Another land grant in the area was known as Rincon de Los Carneros, *carneros* being Spanish for ram. The first Carneros winery was founded by William H. Winter in 1870, and its primary source of fruit was the vineyard planted by Winter on the former Rancho Huichica. In 1881 the winery changed hands, and the new owner was James Simonton, who changed its name to Talcoa Vineyards. The best known of the early Carneros vineyards was the Stanly Ranch, which was established towards the end of the century on over 300 acres. In 1899 the Garetto winery was set up, and although it fell into disuse, was later revived by Bouchaine as its principal winery.

Phylloxera wiped out viticulture in Carneros, and, as elsewhere, Prohibition impeded any revival. After Repeal, two of the leading winemakers of Napa Valley, André Tchelitscheff and Louis M. Martini, recognized the quality of Carneros fruit and began purchasing grapes from what remained of the Stanly Ranch. Two hundred acres belonging to the ranch were bought by Martini in 1942 and renamed the La Loma Vineyard. In the late 1940s Martini was the first to plant a number of clones of Pinot Noir and Chardonnay, but it would not be until the 1960s that vineyard development began in any major way. In 1961 Tchelitscheff persuaded Beaulieu to develop 142 acres of vineyards, mostly planted with Chardonnay, in the region. Rene di Rosa established his Winery Lake Vineyard in 1960, and other growers such as the Sangiacomo family, the Lees, the Bartoluccis, and the St Clairs, laid out vineyards. Buena Vista Winery made enormous land purchases and initiated vineyard development of 1,365 acres from 1969 onwards. The Carneros Creek Winery was founded in 1972 as the first of the modern Carneros wineries, and in 1980 Bouchaine took over the former Garetto winery. Wine producers such

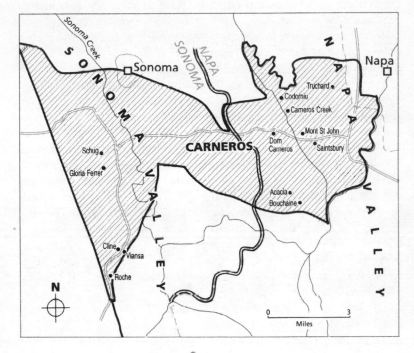

Carneros

as ZD, Burgess, and Veedercrest began using the Carneros appellation on their labels.[1] This did not mean that Carneros fruit was regarded as anything special at this time, and property values remained low. It was only in the 1970s that the merits and typicity of Carneros fruit began to be appreciated. By the 1980s vineyard expansion was rapid, with the arrival of sparkling wine facilities such as Domaine Carneros, Cordoníu, and Gloria Ferrer, and the purchase of land by Mondavi, Clos Pegase, Cuvaison, and other wineries.

It has long been recognized that the Carneros region enjoys a very distinctive microclimate, thanks to its proximity to San Pablo Bay. Administratively, 55 per cent of the region lies within Napa County and 45 per cent within Sonoma County, which is why I have decided to devote a separate section to Carneros. The climate is quite distinct, and not only because of its relative coolness. Carneros is also drier than other parts of Sonoma and Napa, with an average of 22.5 inches of rain. Rain is virtually unheard of between May and October, and in 1997, for instance, there was also no rain between January and May. Enthusiasts for the region believe all these factors are responsible in varying degrees for the quality of the fruit grown here.

The topography is one of gently rolling hills, and signs of human habitation are rare. Variations in exposure and elevation are in general less important than the common factors of the region, notably fog, wind, and lack of rainfall. Fog from the bay reaches a height of 400 feet or so, and evenings and nights are cool, thus helping to conserve acidity in the grapes. In summer, Carneros is often the first Napa region to be swathed in the swirling fog, and the last to be freed from its chilly grip. Frost is infrequent. Budbreak occurs early in Carneros, and this too prolongs the growing season and hang-time, which also promotes the accumulation of flavour in the grapes. The region veers in its heat summation between Region I and a very cool Region II. Robert Sinskey likes to point out that this is still considerably warmer than St Emilion or Pomerol.

The low rainfall and the poor soils make drip irrigation essential; only about 5 per cent of Carneros land is dry-farmed. The soil is quite shallow, essentially a dense layer of clay no more than 2 or 3 feet deep. This shallowness and infertility of the soil help to restrict the vigour of the vines. There are two principal soil types. The first is the so-called Haire series, which is yellowish-brown in colour and rich in fossils, which contribute calcium to the soil and give it a high pH. The second is known as Diablo clay, which is blacker in colour and derived from more profound marine sediments; it is less rich in fossils than the Haire series but high in

manganese. Diablo is usually founded at a higher elevation than
Haire.

The region is not only more exposed to maritime influences than
the areas to the north; it is also windier, although the precise effect
of strong, steady winds on viticulture is not entirely clear. Persistent
strong winds clearly reduce risks of mildew and rot, but they can
also shut down the vines, and in early summer they can be responsible for uneven setting.[2] I have read that wind thickens the skins
of grapes in order to stave off evaporation, and this in turn results,
though I do not understand how, in greater spiciness in the fruit.
Carneros Chardonnay does have a marked acidity, and the Pinot
Noir can have a strawberry-tinged spiciness, but these are subjec-
tive assessments that fail to take into account the variables of
microclimate, vintage, clonal selection and wine-makings styles.

The Carneros AVA was created in 1983, and by 1993 some
6,500 acres had been planted. Precise figures are hard to come by,
but Richard Ward of Saintsbury estimates that about 8,000 acres
were planted by the late 1990s. Although the plantable acreage is
over 15,000, further expansion is likely to be slow, since land has
become very expensive and there is a lack of water for irrigation
in certain areas without wells or reservoirs. The varietal mix is as
follows: Chardonnay 3,900 acres, Pinot Noir 2,800 acres, Cabernet
Sauvignon 320 acres, Merlot 720 acres.

Merlot – which in some vineyards is replacing Pinot Noir when
parcels affected by phylloxera are replanted – is better suited to
the conditions of Carneros than Cabernet Sauvignon. Quite apart
from the fact that the degree days are slightly higher than on the
Right Bank of Bordeaux, ensuring ripe grapes, the clay soils are
also well suited to the cultivation of Merlot, which is handy, given
the current obsession with the variety in California. Some dis-
passionate observers, however, are not convinced that Carneros is
suitable for Bordeaux varieties, and suspect that economic rather
than qualitative criteria have swung the balance in their flavour.

The coolness of Carneros, and the marked citrus and apple
flavours of the Chardonnay grown there, make it one of the leading
areas for the production of grapes for sparkling wine. It is no
coincidence that French and Spanish companies specializing in
sparkling wine, notably Taittinger at Domaine Carneros, Gloria
Ferrer, and Cordoníu, have set up their California operations in
Carneros. It is estimated that about one-third of all the Chardonnay

and Pinot Noir grown here is used for sparkling wine. Wineries in Napa Valley such as Mumm and Domaine Chandon also buy a good deal of Carneros fruit.

Although the overall heat patterns may give a climate more benign than that of Bordeaux, other factors – such as fog, very low rainfall, and wind – conspire against the optimal development of the vines and their fruit. It is hardly surprising that the growers cultivating vineyards in Carneros have undertaken viticultural research, intently studying such matters as trellising, row orientation, spacing and density, in order to ensure both that the potential of the region is exploited to the full and that costly mistakes are not made.

Research was also undertaken here in 1987 to establish the flavour spectrum of Carneros fruit. Pinot Noir from two vintages was compared with Pinots from other parts of Napa and Sonoma; the experiment was repeated with Chardonnay. The upshot of these tastings was not exactly surprising. Tasters were asked to devise 'descriptors' to match the discerned fruit quality. Carneros Pinot Noir was deemed to have intense cherry/berry character, while Chardonnay gave citrussy, Muscat-like fruit, and had delicacy without any loss of structure and body. Some years ago the Australian wine writer (and winemaker) James Halliday confirmed these descriptors for Carneros Pinot Noir, but also found 'something virginal' in the wines: 'consistently correct, pure and delicate, yet that wildness – an animal scent – and velvety textural opulence of the very greatest Pinot Noirs are (with the odd exception) still to manifest themselves.'[3] This judgment still strikes me as essentially correct. While the purity of flavour of a fine Carneros Pinot Noir is alluring, they can lack complexity. Chardonnay, on the other hand, benefits from that purity, which can be such a refreshing contrast to the buttery oiliness of so much heavy-handed Chardonnay from warmer regions.

Relatively few wineries are based in the Carneros region. The best known is probably Saintsbury, which has for many years produced consistently high-quality bottlings of Chardonnay and Pinot Noir. Acacia, part of the Chalone Group, used to do the same, but the decimations of phylloxera and corporate streamlining seem to have resulted in the elimination of the single-vineyard wines which established its reputation. Walter Schug, who used to make the wines for Phelps, has built a winery within the Sonoma sector of Carneros, though his performance to date has been patchy. Much the same is true of Bouchaine.

Carneros Creek belongs to Francis Mahoney, one of the pioneers of California Pinot Noir. Like Dick Ward at Saintsbury, he releases wines at three quality levels, but I find it hard to get excited at anything below the Signature Reserve level. Mont St John remains an old-fashioned Italian winery; the Bertolucci family are better known, however, as organic grape growers. Their own wines are somewhat rustic. Truchard, also better known as growers than as winemakers, are expanding, and are good sources for Carneros Syrah and Merlot as well as for the Burgundian varieties.

On the other hand, a large number of wineries routinely make use of Carneros fruit. Robert Mondavi has been bottling Carneros-appellation Chardonnay and Pinot Noir for some years. Robert Sinskey, although located in Stags Leap District, is a Carneros Pinot Noir specialist. Other wineries with regular Carneros bottlings include Buena Vista, Cuvaison, Etude, Kent Rasmussen, and ZD.

VINEYARDS

Abbott's. 22 acres planted with Chardonnay and Pinot Noir. Bought by St Clement winery in the late 1980s.

Las Amigas. 138 acres. Owned by the Louis Martini Winery until 1993, when it was sold to the Beckstoffer family, who replanted entirely with Chardonnay, Pinot Noir and Merlot. Sells Pinot Noir to Signorello.

Beckstoffer. Owned by Andy Beckstoffer. Sells Pinot Noir and Chardonnay to Schug and other wineries.

Durell. 66 acres in northern Carneros planted on clay and clay loam soils. Average age of vines 15 years. Planted with 59 acres Chardonnay, 5.5 Syrah, and 3 Zinfandel, sold to Kistler, Kendall-Jackson, Steele, and Edmunds St John (Syrah) until acquired by Kendall-Jackson in 1994.

Hudson. Owned by Lee Hudson. Planted with Chardonnay, Syrah, Cabernet Franc, Merlot, and Pinot Noir. Grapes sold to Saintsbury,

Duxoup, Havens, Macrostie, Kongsgaard, Marcassin, Kistler, and Jade Mountain.

Hyde. Owned by Larry Hyde. 150 acres of Pinot Noir, Chardonnay, Sauvignon Blanc, and Bordeaux varieties. Known for its wide selection of Chardonnay and Pinot Noir clones, and for Musqué clone Sauvignon. Sells grapes to Long, Patz & Hall, Selene, Kistler, Hobbs, Spottswoode, Ramey and other wineries.

Madonna. Owned by Buck Bertolucci. Dry-farmed, organic, 74-acre vineyard founded in 1970. Planted with Chardonnay and Pinot Noir. Formerly sold to Acacia, now used by Mont St John.

Marina. 50 acres of Chardonnay developed by Acacia winery.

St Clair. Owned by Jim St Clair, who used to sell his grapes to Acacia until 1992.

Sangiacomo. Owned by Angelo Sangiacomo. Originally planted in 1969. Now 900 acres of Chardonnay, Pinot Noir, Sauvignon Blanc, and Merlot, supplying about 40 wineries, including Steele, Macrostie, Fetzer, Bernardus, Ravenswood, Matanzas Creek, Phelps, Gundlach-Bundschu, and Carmenet.

Stanly Ranch. Supplies Pinot Noir to Beringer.

Truchard. The most northerly vineyard in Carneros. 169 acres of Merlot, Cabernet Franc, Cabernet Sauvignon, Chardonnay, Pinot Noir, Syrah and Zinfandel. Partly vinified by the Truchard winery. Also sells to Havens and Cornerstone.

Willow Lake. Planted with Pinot Noir, Merlot and Chardonnay. Fruit sold to Charles Krug.

Winery Lake. Celebrated 175-acre vineyard planted by Rene di Rosa in 1966. 7 soil types, including fossilized shells and volcanic rocks. Originally planted with Riesling, Pinot Noir, Gewürztraminer, and Merlot. Now planted with 100 acres Chardonnay, 60 Pinot Noir, 15 Merlot. Sold in 1986 to Seagram. Supplies Sterling and Mumm.

NOTES

1 Roy Andries De Groot, *The Wines of California*, pp. 86–7
2 James Halliday, *Wines Atlas of California*, p. 49
3 Halliday, p. 51

6

Mendocino and Lake Counties

Mendocino is archetypal northern California terrain, with redwood forests and a rugged coastline that attract tourists in their thousands. Roughly parallel to the shore are a number of valleys where grapes are grown. The county's southern border is some ninety miles north of San Francisco. Microclimates vary considerably, but the majority of those vineyards are warm, and slot neatly into Region III. However, the Anderson Valley, which is closest to the Pacific, is distinctly cool and parts of Redwood Valley are Region II.

Until well into the nineteenth century Mendocino County was quite isolated. Access was hindered by the mountains separating it from Sonoma, and although from 1910 onwards railway lines connected Ukiah with the counties to the south, roads were few and inadequate. In contrast, Napa and Sonoma had easy access to the ports and rail depots of San Francisco and Oakland. The 1860s saw the first major wave of migrants, the majority of them Italian, into Mendocino. 'My ancestors settled here,' says Greg Graziano, 'because Mendocino reminded them of Italy.' They established farms modelled on those they had known in Europe, planting olives and vines and orchards as well as other crops. Many of the original cuttings were brought here from the Italian-Swiss Colony in Asti, Sonoma, and Mendocino in effect became a colony of the colony, supplying it with grapes. It is estimated that half of all the grape production from Mendocino was dispatched to the Colony. This hardly encouraged Mendocino to develop its own stylistic identity. The varieties planted were the familiar standbys, Carignane and French Colombard. Expansion was rapid, and by 1910 almost 6,000 acres were planted.

Prohibition had the same lamentable effect in Mendocino as elsewhere along the North Coast. Some of the old hillside vineyards remained intact, but the wineries were virtually wiped out. When Fetzer was created in 1968 it was only the second operational winery in the county, the other being Parducci. Fetzer's growth, and its consequent demand for grapes, ensured the survival of many vineyards that might otherwise have been grubbed up. Another factor that helped preserve the old vineyards that are now so highly prized was the vogue in the 1980s for White Zinfandel. Wineries seeking new sources of Zinfandel bought up Mendocino fruit, even though it seems faintly shocking that such venerable vines should have been put to such abject use.

Parducci's history is typical of the way in which immigrants created and sustained the Californian wine business. Adolfo Parducci was born in southern California, but spent his teenage years working in Italy. Returning to California at 16, he settled in San Francisco and ran a business buying grapes and selling them to home winemakers. After marrying a girl from Cloverdale in Sonoma, he built a winery there to produce sacramental wines, and then moved north to the Ukiah Valley, where the present winery was built in the 1930s. The grape-selling business continued, but Adolfo Parducci also set up a winemaking cooperative. John became the winemaker after the end of World War II, and in 1964 he and his brother George bought the business from their father and other members of the family and concentrated on producing varietal wines and developing their 400 acres of vineyards. Parducci, in the 1960s, was the first Mendocino estate to plant prestigious varietals such as Chardonnay and Cabernet Sauvignon.

Mendocino remains a region of small growers (some of whom notoriously farm marijuana rather than vines) and some 160 grape farmers cultivate about 300 vineyards today. Quite a few of them are direct descendants of the families who planted the first vines over a century ago. Despite the county's reputation for powerful Cabernet Sauvignon, Petite Sirah, and Zinfandel, Chardonnay is now the dominant variety, accounting for about 4,500 acres out of the current total of 15,000. In 1998 there were 1,900 acres of Zinfandel, 1,460 of Cabernet Sauvignon, 1,360 of Merlot and, surprisingly, 760 of Carignane. Although there are a few large concerns – vineyards such as Beckstoffer's and Fetzer's – Mendocino has until recently been spared the corporate vineyard development that took place along the Central Coast. Nonetheless, this is beginning to change and in the mid-1990s wineries such as

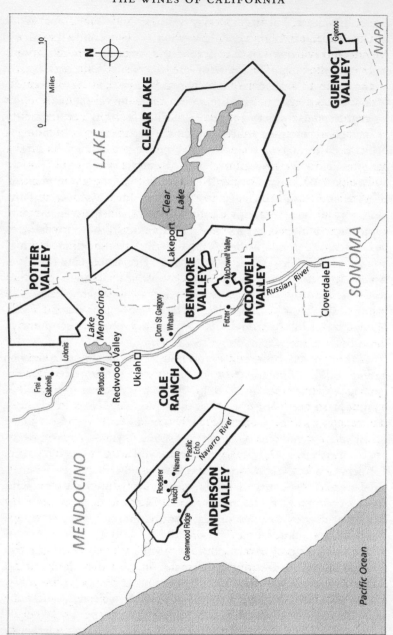

Mendocino

Kendall-Jackson, Beringer, Mondavi, Gallo, and Duckhorn had all bought substantial acreage in Mendocino. The average size of a Mendocino vineyard is 20 acres, and organic viticulture has a strong following. The Fetzers were pioneers in this regard, and today some 25 per cent of all vineyards are certified as organic. Mendocino's secret weapon has been the survival of many older vineyards, and about 3,500 acres of vineyards planted over fifty years ago remain in production. Yet the region still retains its colonial culture, as it were, since about 70 per cent of its grapes are vinified outside the county, mostly by larger wineries in Sonoma and Napa.[1] Within the county there are only thirty-seven wineries. If Mendocino's grapes used to be cheap, that is no longer the case, and in 1996 prices were approaching those from Sonoma. Chardonnay, indeed, was priced at $1,600 per ton. However, as more vineyards replanted after phylloxera in Napa, Sonoma and elsewhere come into production, the spot-market demand for Mendocino fruit may decrease. Nonetheless it seems likely that within the next decade some areas to the north of Redwood Valley will begin to be developed for wine production – Fetzer have already planted some vineyards up here – even though high rainfall makes the climate marginal.

The climate is continental, especially in the eastern parts of the county, and bud-break is usually about two weeks later than in Napa and Sonoma. The average rainfall in Ukiah is 37 inches, making it somewhat wetter than Sonoma. The cold winters have the benefit of killing off Pierce's Disease, which cannot survive below 26 degrees Fahrenheit. Diseases such as mildew and botrytis are rare, which also favours organic viticulture. Phylloxera, however, has become widespread in areas such as Anderson Valley. Winters may be severe, but the summers in these inland valleys can be very hot, although it cools down a great deal at night. In general, the uncertainties of the climate lead to greater vintage variation than in Sonoma or Napa.

The soils are very diverse, but essentially alluvial, with gravelly loams, and certain locations, especially on the valley floor, can be rather too fertile for high-quality viticulture. The best vineyards, not surprisingly, are located on the slopes and ridgetops, where the soils are more shallow and it is less likely that the vines will be overcropped. Benchland and ridgetop soils tend to be quite rocky and well drained.

It is impossible to discern a unifying characteristic of Mendocino fruit, given the size and diversity of the vineyard areas within the county, but many winemakers remark on the fruit's clear definition, a focus that derives from the high tartaric acidity of many of the grapes. Chardonnay in particular is characterized by good acidity and low pH, even after the wine has completed malolactic fermentation. Although the naturally crisp and lean style of Mendocino Chardonnay does not find favour with most American consumers, larger wineries find it a useful blending component, since it can moderate the tropical-fruit character often encountered in Chardonnay from the Central Coast and other regions.

There is a tradition of experimentation in Mendocino, which is less enslaved by the overall American worship of Cabernet and Chardonnay. McDowell Valley Vineyards have been producing Rhône varieties since the late 1970s, and in the 1990s the winery decided to concentrate on them to the exclusion of other varieties. Greg Graziano is a winemaker whose label Monte Volpe is devoted to Italian varieties, including such relatively obscure ones as Arneis and Tocai Friulano. Graziano is convinced that the Mendocino climate is ideally suited to these varieties and now has his eye on Greco, Fiano, and Cortese.

In Anderson Valley you can find Alsatian-style Gewürztraminer and Riesling. Jeff Hinchcliffe at Gabrielli has been vinifying Sangiovese since 1994, as well as a white blend that includes Tocai and Chenin Blanc. Hinchcliffe is also using local Mendocino oak for some of his wines. Deborah Cahn of Navarro echoes a widely held view in the county when she says, 'We're still discovering what the possibilities are up here. That's true of California as a whole, but especially of Mendocino. For instance, we have a hunch that Pinot Gris will do well in Anderson Valley, although that proposition will take years to test. That makes a grower's life risky but exciting.' The difficulty that the more adventurous growers will undoubtedly face is that it is impossible to demand high prices for wines that can be quite expensive to produce. Gewürztraminer, for example, is low-yielding in Mendocino, rarely giving more than 3 tons per acre, and it can be tricky to harvest. Yet the finished wine has to be priced well below a Chardonnay picked at double the yield. As a consequence, some growers are replacing Gewürztraminer with the more fashionable Pinot Noir. Joseph Phelps in

Napa continues to produce an off-dry Gewürztraminer from Anderson Valley fruit.

Anderson Valley

This narrow valley follows the Navarro River as it flows towards the Pacific. About twenty-five miles long, it is two miles wide at it broadest point but mostly far more hemmed in by the mountains. It remains a deeply rural area, with forests, orchards and walnut plantations as well as about 1,400 acres of vineyards. The two principal villages are Boonville and Philo, which offer simple accommodation, decent food at renovated inns, and a microbrewery at which serious summer thirst can be quenched.

The northwest part of Anderson Valley, stretching up to Navarro, can be cool and foggy, so much so that at times this part of the valley must seem almost marginal for grape growing. Spring frosts can be a major problem, and morning fogs rather too persistent for comfort. The most successful grape varieties here are Gewürztraminer and Pinot Noir, and both Pinot Noir and Chardonnay provide base wines for sparkling wines. Riesling can also do well. A bit further south, around Boonville, the climate is less demanding, and varieties such as Merlot and Sauvignon Blanc can be successfully cultivated. The further east one goes, the higher and warmer the land, favouring the growing of Cabernet Sauvignon, Merlot, and Zinfandel. In recent years it has been recognized that Cabernet and Merlot were planted in locations where the grapes do not always ripen, and these plantations are being replaced with more appropriate varieties. The most distinctive vineyards in Anderson Valley are the ridgetop sites high above the fog line. They have recently been granted their own AVA of Mendocino Ridge. Anderson Valley as a whole became an AVA in 1983.

The Italian-Swiss Colony planted a large vineyard here in 1946, but the grapes rarely ripened sufficiently, and the valley-floor vineyard was abandoned about ten years later. The first successful attempt to establish vineyards in the valley was made in 1964 by Dr Donald Edmeades, who planted 11 acres, followed by Husch in 1969 and Pepperwood Springs in 1974. The major vineyard expansion took place in the 1980s and certain viticultural 'errors' are gradually being corrected. Navarro have been experimenting with different clones and trellising systems and Greenwood Ridge has doubled the density of its plantations since the early 1990s.

This is a Region I in terms of heat summation, and the soil on the river benchlands is mostly clay and gravel. It may sound like classic grape growing country, but it's not all beer and skittles up here. 'This is a horrible place to grow grapes,' admits Jim Klein, the winemaker at Navarro. 'We get rain in summer as well as winter, and rot can be a major problem. And acidity. Sheep knock over your fences, and bears and mountain lions can come wandering down the slopes. Every season brings its own problems, and the job of the winemaker is to turn them to his advantage. When we look at the fruit we're growing, the factors that most interest us are not ripeness as such, but tartaric acid and pH. It can be very tricky to get the wines into proper balance.'

Anderson Valley fruit can have a very distinct character. The Chardonnay is usually crisp and quite high in acidity, with flavours of apple and especially pear. Pinot Noir can be very successful, but shows the lack of consistency one would expect from a region of constant climatic variation. The high acidity of Anderson Valley grapes does make them eminently suitable for sparkling wines, and it is no coincidence that Roederer has chosen the valley for its American operation; Pacific Echo (formerly Scharffenberger), in which LVMH of France is a major shareholder, is also based here, and other wineries offer sparkling wines as part of their range. The acidity can be more troubling for table wines, however, and some growers refer to the area as Acid Valley. However, uncomfortable levels of acidity are more common with valley-floor fruit than with grapes grown on benchland and ridges.

Cole Valley

A minute AVA, consisting of a single 61-acre farm (Cole Ranch) located between Ukiah and Boonville at 1,400–1,600 feet. Forty-eight acres are planted with Cabernet Sauvignon, the remainder with Chardonnay and Riesling; most of the fruit is bought by Fetzer. There are no wineries.

McDowell Valley

This AVA, created in 1982, lies east of the town of Hopland. 750 acres of vines are planted on benchland sloping towards the Russian River at 850 to 1,000 feet. The reddish soil is gravelly with volcanic elements. The majority of the vineyards are owned by the McDowell Valley Winery, but there are also four independent growers. The winery specializes in Rhône varietals, but Chardonnay, Cabernet Sauvignon, and Sauvignon Blanc are also grown here. The climate is somewhat cooler than its northern neighbour, Redwood Valley, and registers as Region II.

Mendocino Ridge

A recently approved AVA (1997) with exciting potential. The regulations stipulate that only vineyards above 1,200 feet, with exposure towards the Pacific Ocean, qualify for inclusion. These sites tend to be located within pockets of redwood and Douglas fir forests on high ridgetops. Being above the fog line, they enjoy long warm summer days refreshed by ocean breezes. At present there are 75 acres of such vineyards, planted mostly with Zinfandel, but also with Syrah, Merlot, Chardonnay, and Cabernet Sauvignon. Among them are three old Italian vineyards with a high reputation: Ciapusci, Zeni and DuPratt.

There is only one winery within the AVA: Greenwood Ridge. Its owner, Allan Green, confesses to mixed feelings about the new appellation. For twenty years he has worked to promote the reputation of Anderson Valley. It would still be legal for him to use the Anderson Valley appellation on his labels, as Mendocino Ridge is only a sub-appellation. He accepts that his Mendocino Ridge vineyards have a different character which justifies the sub-appellation, but his tasting room is within Anderson Valley, which could confuse customers further. Certainly the Greenwood Ridge vineyards are of high quality. Jed Steele buys some Cabernet Sauvignon here for use in the Signature Series for Villa Mt Eden, where he is the consultant winemaker.

Potter Valley

The most northerly of Mendocino regions, Potter Valley, which became an AVA in 1983, lies northeast of Redwood Valley. Being northerly and thirty miles inland, it is a region of cold winters, not helped by the elevation of 1,000–1,200 feet. Frost is frequent, and fogs common in spring, although the valley is too far inland for maritime influence to be a major factor. Nights are cold, but daytime temperatures can soar. The soils are quite rich. This is primarily white-grape country, with Sauvignon Blanc, Sémillon, Chardonnay and Riesling doing well, and there is also some Pinot Noir, most of which is used for sparkling wine. In certain years, when it rains close to harvest time, varieties such as Sémillon and Riesling are benignly affected by botrytis.

There are no wineries here, so the fruit is sold off to various wineries, including Robert Mondavi and the sparkling wine producers Domaine Chandon and Pacific Echo. With 1,300 acres under vine there are plenty of grapes available. Mondavi is one of the wineries hoping to acquire land here.

Redwood Valley

This important region became an AVA in 1997. The valley runs north from Ukiah for about twelve miles, following the course of the Russian River. Grapes were already being grown here in the nineteenth century. Being an inland valley, it is warmer than Anderson Valley but cooler than Ukiah and counts as a Region II. Fog is infrequent, but the climate is moderated by Pacific breezes. There are 2,500 acres under vine, and about two-thirds of the grapes are red. The most common varieties grown on its red-clay soils are Zinfandel, Cabernet Sauvignon, Petite Sirah, Pinot Noir and Sangiovese. There is every reason to suppose that Syrah will flourish here too. Some wine producers, such as Jeff Hinchcliffe of Gabrielli, believe Redwood Valley is too warm to give ideal Pinot Noir. One interesting development here has been the replanting of Zinfandel as head-pruned, dry-farmed vines, thus perpetuating Mendocino's finest viticultural tradition. Indeed, it was the presence of old Zinfandel vineyards in the valley that helped draw attention to Mendocino in the 1970s. White grapes, notably Sauvignon Blanc and Chardonnay, can also be of fine quality.

Sanel Valley

Not an AVA at present, but the region hopes soon to become one. It consists of the area just south of the Ukiah Valley, focused on the town of Hopland. This is the warmest region of Mendocino. Red varieties are planted on the slopes above the river, Chardonnay and Sauvignon Blanc are grown lower down and closer to the Russian River itself.

Ukiah Valley

Like Sanel Valley, this region, the largest in the county, has not yet been granted its own AVA. It stretches for about twenty miles between Hopland and Ukiah, and thus south of Redwood Valley. This is a warm region with fairly deep soils, essentially Region III and thus well suited to the red grapes grown on the benchlands here: mostly Cabernet Sauvignon and Zinfandel, although some old Carignane and Petite Sirah also survive. Sauvignon Blanc and Chardonnay can also be of good quality, although they tend to be more full-bodied than those grown in Anderson Valley. There is a good deal of experimentation going on here, with Italian and Rhône varieties being planted at higher elevations, especially around Talmage. Some of the largest wineries in the county, especially Fetzer and Parducci, own substantial vineyards here. Mondavi is hoping to buy and develop some 300 acres in the northern part of the valley.

Yorkville Highlands

This region lies in southern Mendocino, close to the north end of Sonoma's Alexander Valley. Mostly given over to sheep ranches, it's a warm area, but cooled by afternoon breezes. Sauvignon Blanc and Cabernet Sauvignon are the most successful varieties here, but Merlot, Pinot Noir and Petit Verdot have also done well. At present only about 100 acres are in production, but it seems probable that more vineyards will be planted here in the future.

VINEYARDS

Alder Springs. 2,000 feet high. Planted with Chardonnay and Pinot Noir. Sells grapes to Patz & Hall.

BJL. Potter Valley. 100 acres, planted with 30 each of Chardonnay and Pinot Noir, as well as Sauvignon Blanc, Sémillon and Riesling. Grapes sold to Hidden Cellars and Kalin.

Ciapusci. Mendocino Ridge. Owned by Nick Ciapusci. A Zinfandel vineyard originally planted in 1900 on thin, rocky soil 7 miles from the Pacific coast. Sells to Edmeades and others.

Dennison. Anderson Valley. Sells Chardonnay, Riesling, and Pinot Noir to Gabrielli, Edmeades, and Steele.

DuPratt. Mendocino Ridge. Owned by Tom Krig. 15 acres of Pinot Noir, Zinfandel, and Chardonnay. Sells to Steele, Greenwood Ridge, and others.

Eaglepoint Ranch. Owned by John Scharffenberger since 1974. On Red Mountain above Ukiah Valley. 75 acres. Planted with head-pruned Zinfandel, Sangiovese, and Syrah on rocky soils. Sells to numerous wineries, including Lonetree, Edmeades, Navarro, Fetzer, and Jeff Cohn.

Ferrington. Anderson Valley. Owned by Richard Ferrington. Sells Sauvignon Blanc to Greenwood Ridge and Pinot Noir to Williams-Selyem.

Floodgate. Anderson Valley. Owned by Bill and Sally Hambrecht. 62 acres, 3 acres from Pacific Ocean. Planted with Pinot Noir, Chardonnay, and Gewürztraminer. Sells to Belvedere and Gabrielli.

Goforth. Redwood Valley. Owned by Ted Goforth. Planted in 1972 with dry-farmed, head-pruned Zinfandel. Sells to Gabrielli.

Lolonis. Redwood Valley. 300 acres northeast of Ukiah. Planted with Cabernet Sauvignon, Chardonnay, Merlot, Petite Sirah, Sauvignon Blanc and Zinfandel. Vineyard founded in 1920. The fruit is used by the Lolonis winery and also sold to Fetzer, Parducci, Steele, and Kendall-Jackson.

McNab Ranch. Ukiah Valley. Sells Riesling to Gabrielli.

Nelson Ranch. 200 acres planted between Ukiah and Hopland from the 1940s onwards. Cabernet Sauvignon, Carignane, Chardonnay, Riesling, Merlot, Pinot Noir and Zinfandel.

One Acre. Anderson Valley. 1,600 feet. Planted in 1986. Sells Pinot Noir to Littorai.

Pacini. Redwood Valley. Owned by Larry Pacini. 28 acres near Talmage. Planted with dry-farmed Zinfandel and Petite Sirah. Average age of vines 50 years, the oldest vines 90 years old. Sold to Hidden Cellars, Steele, Claudia Springs, and others.

Rhodes. Redwood Valley. Supplies Zinfandel to Rosenblum and Jeff Cohn.

Rose. Anderson Valley. Sells Pinot Noir to Siduri and Kendall-Jackson.

Savoy. Anderson Valley. Planted in 1991. Sells Pinot Noir to Littorai.

Weir. Yorkville Highlands. Owned by Bill Weir. Sells Pinot Noir to Rutz and Gabrielli.

Zeni. Mendocino Ridge. Owned by George Zeni. Planted with Zinfandel. Sells to Edmeades.

LAKE COUNTY

Lake County lies to the east of Mendocino County, and its most important growing region is around Clear Lake, about fifteen miles east of Hopland. The county didn't even formally exist until 1861, as it was considered an extension of Napa County. It was quite an important wine-producing region in the late nineteenth century. There were 600 acres under vine in the 1880s and by the turn of the century over thirty wineries were in operation. Prohibition dealt a death blow to wine production, but vineyards were replanted in the 1970s. In 1965 only 300 acres remained out of the 1,000 in production before Prohibition, but a few years later large areas were being planted with vines. By 1983 there were 3,000 acres in production, but by 1998 this had only risen to 3,900. According to James Halliday, UC Davis at first advised growers to plant red grapes by the shores of the lake and white grapes on cooler sites on the hillsides. This advice turned out to be completely wrong 'largely because of soil conditions but also because of inadequacies in the heat summation method.'[2] Outbreaks of phylloxera in the county have stimulated various growers to revise their patterns of planting.

The climate is quite distinctive. Being an inland region, it is largely free of maritime influence, which is also blocked by the intervention of the Mayacamas Mountains to the west of the county. The large expanse of Clear Lake helps to stabilize the temperature. In general summers are very hot, but the elevation of roughly 1,300 feet ensures that nights are fairly cool. Soils are both volcanic and alluvial clay loams and can be quite rich and heavy, especially around the shore.

About half the vineyards are planted with white varieties, including 700 acres each of Sauvignon Blanc and Chardonnay. There are 900 acres of Cabernet Sauvignon, 435 of Zinfandel, and 470 of Merlot. Riesling, once important here, is in sharp decline. If any single variety was associated with Lake County, it had to be Sauvignon Blanc. Kendall-Jackson's Clear Lake winery specialized in Sauvignon in the 1980s, even producing some impressive botry-tized versions. Konocti was the other major winery here until its purchase by Jed Steele in 1996, and Guenoc is a major force in the AVA which takes its name. A number of large wineries from outside the county have been major purchasers of grapes or are acquiring vineyards here. Fetzer, Beringer, Louis Martini, Sutter Home, and Parducci are all major players. Martini own the Perini Springs Ranch, planted at a height of 2,000 feet with 23 acres of Cabernet Sauvignon and 5 acres of Barbera, a variety for which Martini have long been famous. The Lake County climate is far from ideal for red varieties such as Merlot and Cabernet Sauvignon, but Jed Steele and others suspect that it could prove ideal for Syrah.

Benmore Valley

This small 170-acre AVA on the western border with Mendocino County is very high up at 2,400 feet. It is a cool Region I and Chardonnay is the principal grape grown here. It is essentially the domain of Geyser Peak in Sonoma, and a little Syrah as well as Chardonnay has been planted.

Clear Lake

Clear Lake contains 90 per cent of all the vineyard area in Lake County, making it by far the largest AVA in the region. The vines are planted at elevations ranging from 1,300 to 1,800 feet. Rainfall is very low, so there is no dry-farming here. Late bud-break gives a relatively short growing season.

Guenoc Valley

This region in the southern part of the county, just fifteen miles north of Calistoga, is one of those AVAs created to match the aspirations of its only winery. The AVA was established in 1981 at the behest of winery owner Orville Magoon. The vineyards are fairly high at 1,000–1,400 feet, and spring frosts can be troublesome. Nonetheless the area is quite warm overall, and registers as a cool Region III. There is little maritime influence and fogs are infrequent. Rainfall can be as high as 50 inches per year. The varieties planted on its 400 acres are Cabernet Sauvignon, Chardonnay, and a little Sauvignon Blanc. The soil is mostly alluvial, with gravel, sand, and silt.

VINEYARDS

Catfish. Owned by Howard Strickler. 7 acres, with 100-year-old Zinfandel. Sells to Jed Steele.

NOTES

1 Article by Jennifer Burns, *Wine Business Monthly*, July 1996
2 James Halliday, *Wine Atlas of California*, p. 214

7
Around the Bay

Although California wine has become so closely identified with the Napa and Sonoma valleys, there are some important vineyard sites considerably closer to San Francisco, both in the counties south of the city, and to the east of San Francisco Bay.

South of San Francisco lies the laid-back town of Santa Cruz, separated from the city by a range of mountains just inland from the coastline. On the eastern side of those mountains is present-day Silicon Valley, taking in the university town of Palo Alto and the sprawling city of San Jose. You can drive all the way from San Francisco to San Jose without glimpsing a single vine. The vineyards are tucked into the mountains to the west of Santa Clara Valley, which lies between San Jose and Gilroy to the southeast. Both the Santa Cruz Mountains and the Santa Clara Valley, which share a boundary, were important wine regions in the nineteenth century, but urban sprawl has taken its toll on both. Santa Clara County contains two AVAs: Santa Clara Valley and Hecker Pass.

Alameda County

Although the substantial Livermore vineyards are within the county, few wineries remain in a county that is now so encroached upon by urban and suburban development. Elliston Vineyards in Sunol is one historic property that, despite many changes of ownership, is still producing wine, much of it with grapes from other regions.

Contra Costa County

Before Prohibition there were 6,000 acres under vine here, and some twenty-seven wineries. Indeed, this was one of the first areas in northern California to be planted with vines, as Dr John Marsh put in vineyards at the foot of Mount Diablo in 1846.[1] Inevitably, urban sprawl pushing eastwards from San Francisco and the Oakland area has had a devastating effect on the vineyards. There were vineyards here in the 1840s, and this was where the vast Christian Brothers operation had its origins. The Italian-Swiss Colony also owned sites here. A few vineyards remain, including some extremely old and much sought after acreage of Mourvedre and Zinfandel. The best-known vineyard here is Bridgehead in Oakley, owned by Cline.

Livermore Valley

The most important region and AVA (approved 1982) within Alameda County is Livermore, where Wente has long been based. The valley is about fifteen miles long and some ten miles wide. The soil here at the base of the coastal ranges is quite rocky and very gravelly, and probably best suited to Bordeaux varieties. Despite the remarkable quality of these deep gravel soils, the wines of Livermore have failed to exhibit a strong personality of their own. James Concannon described them as follows: 'Our red wines are lighter bodied than those from Napa but they have complexity to them. The whites have fruit and full bodiedness you might not find in other areas. They don't have as high acid as Monterey and the cooler areas.'[2] Karl Wente also remarked on the full body achieved by Livermore's whites wines, especially Sauvignon Blanc.[3]

The first vineyards were laid out here in 1881, when J. F. Crabb of Napa sold thousands of Zinfandel cuttings to J. F. Black in Pleasanton.[4] Indeed in the 1880s many vineyards were planted here: Olivina, Chateau Bellevue, Ruby Hill, Giersburg, and a number of others, most of which have vanished beneath the neatly laid out tract housing. Three other enterprises in the early 1880s proved of more lasting significance: Charles Wetmore established his Cresta Blanca estate here in 1882, and the following year Carl Wente planted 40 acres in the valley and James Concannon followed suit. Wente plausibly claim to be the oldest family-owned

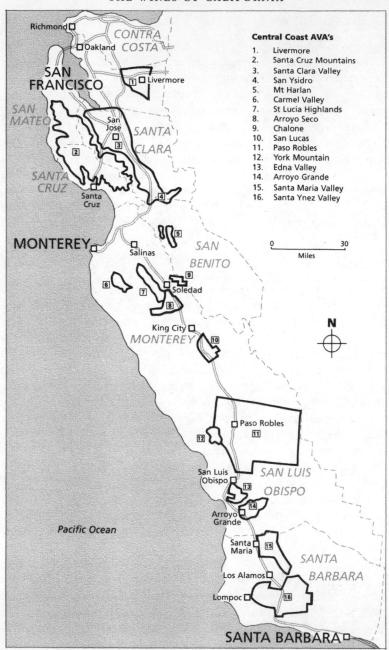

Central Coast AVA's

1. Livermore
2. Santa Cruz Mountains
3. Santa Clara Valley
4. San Ysidro
5. Mt Harlan
6. Carmel Valley
7. St Lucia Highlands
8. Arroyo Seco
9. Chalone
10. San Lucas
11. Paso Robles
12. York Mountain
13. Edna Valley
14. Arroyo Grande
15. Santa Maria Valley
16. Santa Ynez Valley

Central Coast

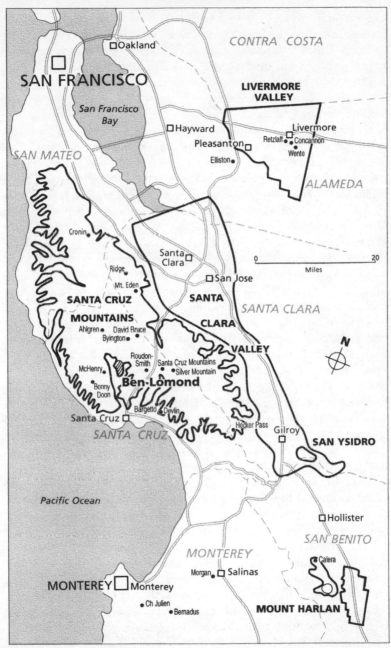

Santa Cruz to Monterey

estate and winery in the United States. Carl Wente had emigrated to the United States from Germany and worked for Charles Krug in Napa Valley before coming out to Livermore. He was attracted by the gravelly soil that seemed reminiscent of that of the Graves, although the climate is warmer here than in Bordeaux.

Charles Wetmore imported cuttings of Sauvignon Blanc and Sémillon from Château d'Yquem in the 1880s, and shared them with his neighbour Carl Wente, who used them as the basis for what became known as the Wente clones of these varieties. Carl Wente was succeeded by his sons Herman and Ernest. Ernest's son Karl ran the business until 1977, when he succumbed to a heart attack at the age of 49 and was replaced by his widow Jean. Today the next generation is in control: Eric, Philip, and Carolyn. In 1981 Wente purchased the site of the Cresta Blanca winery, thus uniting the pioneering properties of Livermore Valley, and replanted the Charles Wetmore Vineyard. There was further consolidation in 1992 when Wente acquired the one other large winery in Livermore, Concannon. Today Wente own 1,392 acres in Livermore, and even more in Monterey County.

Concannon, which was founded in 1883 by an Irishman who had emigrated to Boston before crossing the continent, managed to survive Prohibition by producing altar wines. This was no mere opportunism, as Concannon had been producing them more or less from the start. It established a reputation with its Petite Sirah, believed to be the first varietally labelled example of this grape. The Wentes, being a Lutheran family, were less well situated to enter the altar-wine market, and survived Prohibition by shipping grapes and producing sweet wines for Beaulieu, who were well connected with the Catholic Church.

Most of the valleys in northern California have a north/south orientation, and Livermore is unusual in having an east/west orientation, exposing it directly to cool maritime air in the late afternoon during the summer months. This has, of course, a beneficial cooling effect, as do occasional foggy mornings. Nonetheless, Livermore is not quite as cool as its promoters like to suggest, and according to the heat summation system the valley is low Region III. The valley is fringed by mountains on all sides, so maritime influences are modified by these natural barriers. The county has been losing vineyards, recently at the rate of about 20 per cent every decade. Tract housing has taken the place of vines. The cities of Livermore and Pleasanton, which are joined at the hip, have expanded greatly as a result of university installations and new electronics industries. In 1968 the major vineyard owners, Wente and Concannon, signed agreements with the county that allowed their vineyards to be taxable as farms, thus ensuring their long-term survival.[5] Today the area under vine is roughly 1,600 acres. In Livermore 700 acres are planted with Chardonnay, 200 with Sauvignon Blanc, and 200 with Cabernet Sauvignon.

San Francisco Bay

This new AVA, approved in 1999, takes in five counties – San Francisco, San Mateo, Santa Clara, Alameda, Contra Costa – and parts of two others, Santa Cruz and San Benito. The new AVA has 5,800 acres of vineyards and thirty-nine wineries. Its usefulness is questionable, given the size and diversity of the area.

Santa Clara Valley

There were vines planted at Mission Santa Clara as long ago as 1780, and a century later the valley was more significant viticulturally than Napa Valley to the north. Good-quality French vine cuttings had been imported in 1854 by Antoine Delmas, and the prevailing Mission vines began to give way to European varieties. It was Paul Masson and Charles Lefranc who transformed Santa Clara into a major wine region.

Masson was born in Beaune in 1859. When phylloxera destroyed his family vineyards in Burgundy, he came to California, where he married the daughter of another French immigrant, Charles Lefranc, who was already producing wines in Santa Clara. The two men became partners until 1892, when Masson set up his own sparkling wine company. At the turn of the century he planted his famous La Cresta vineyard and constructed his winery there. He sold the business to Martin Ray in 1936 and died four years later at the ripe age of 81. In 1942 Ray sold the property to Sam Bronfman of Seagram, and under his direction Masson was expanded into an immense wine business with 4,500 acres of vineyards.

By 1900 there were about 8,500 acres under vine, with over 100 wineries, mostly to the north and east of San Jose. Curiously many of these wineries and vineyards survived Prohibition, and when Repeal came there were still sixty-four wineries in operation.[6] It wasn't puritanism so much as the technological revolution that spelt doom to so many vineyards. The valley had little renown as a tourist destination, so there was little of the pressure that enabled Napa to survive as an agricultural preserve. Indeed, the Santa Clara Valley is a dreadful reminder of what might have happened to Napa Valley had the preserve not come into being. By 1970 the 8,000 acres still planted in 1948 had been reduced to 2,000; by 1982 there were still 1,500 acres left under vine, prompting the creation of the AVA in 1990, and indeed by the early 1990s there had been a slight revival. Today there are some 1,100 acres in production; no longer in the original sites, which long ago were paved with concrete and tarmac, but south of San Jose and around Gilroy. Almost half are planted with Chardonnay, and Cabernet Sauvignon is also commonly grown. The climate is designated as Region II overall, and maritime influence is quite strong.

There are two large wineries still based in San Jose, but neither relies greatly on grapes from Santa Clara County. Mirassou owns some 200 acres in the county, but this is overshadowed by the 600 they own in Monterey County to the south. Similarly J. Lohr relies on grapes from its 1,000 acres of vineyards in Paso Robles and Monterey. That it remains based in San Jose is more or less an accident of history.

Hecker Pass

This small region lies just west of Gilroy. Despite its name, the region is not in the mountains and the vineyards are planted either on the valley floor or on gentle slopes. Its vineyards and small wineries no longer have a reputation for exceptional quality. Sarah's Vineyard is the leading winery here. Hecker Pass has no strong identity of its own, a situation not helped by the fact that it is absorbed by two separate though clearly overlapping AVAs: Santa Clara Valley and Santa Cruz Mountains. Some of its surviving wineries still specialize in inexpensive jug wines.

San Ysidro District

Although Hecker Pass is not an AVA, San Ysidro, which lies just east of Gilroy, does enjoy that dubious distinction. Thanks to occasional fogs and maritime air currents in the afternoon, it is considerably cooler here than in Gilroy itself. Chardonnay is the principal variety planted on its 520 acres.

Santa Cruz Mountains

Vineyards were first established in these rugged mountains in 1854 by Lyman Burrell alongside what is now Summit Road. Today this is home to the Burrell School Vineyards. In the 1860s vines were also planted by the Jarvis Brothers. This vineyard, in the Vine Hill district, is now the site of the Santa Cruz Mountain Vineyard. La Questa Vineyard at Woodside was laid out in 1883 by Emmett Rixford and produced some notable Cabernets until the property was subdivided after Repeal. Only one acre remains, but it still produces Cabernet. The famous Monte Bello Vineyard was planted by Dr Osea Perrone in 1892. Dr Perrone operated the winery until his death in 1912. Nearby the Pichetti family built a winery in 1896, and at one time, Paul Draper of Ridge estimates, there were ten wineries functioning on the Monte Bello Ridge.

The most famous winery of the region was the Novitiate facility in Los Gatos, southwest of San Jose, although it mostly supplied altar wines. Almadén was founded east of Los Gatos in 1852, but only a few acres of its original vineyards survive. By the mid-1980s the company had increased its holdings to 6,000 acres, but most were in San Benito and Monterey counties. The name Almadén, meaning 'mine' in Moorish, was conceived in 1887.

Some of the region's vineyards were located around Woodside, which lies between San Francisco and San Jose at the top end of the valley, while other vineyards were scattered along the slopes and ridges of the Santa Cruz Mountains themselves. By the time Prohibition was introduced, there were 1,600 acres of vineyards and almost forty wineries in production. Santa Clara Valley survived Prohibition relatively unscathed, but the same was not true of the more isolated Santa Cruz vineyards, most of which disappeared. Today there are about 700 acres in production, of which just over 100 are actually within Santa Cruz County, and most of the twenty or so wineries within the county purchase grapes from outside it.

The revival of Santa Cruz Mountains began when Martin Ray bought the former Masson winery and then in 1943 set up his own winery at Mount Eden. He developed a formidable reputation both for being difficult to get along with and for his exceptional Pinot Noirs, Chardonnays, and Cabernets. Ray was meticulous with his harvesting, crushing the grapes at five in the morning. He refused to use sugar or chemical additives or grape juice concentrate, all of which were common practices at that time. He used only French oak, and new oak to ferment his white wines. The Chardonnays were bottled relatively young, but his red wines were aged, without racking, for up to 3 years.[7] These long-lived wines persuaded many growers as well as consumers of the outstanding quality of Santa Cruz Mountains fruit. Martin Ray kept going until 1972, when legal action from his investors forced him to relinquish the property, which new owners transformed into the Mount Eden Vineyards. In 1982 Santa Cruz Mountains was awarded its AVA, which somewhat confusingly also includes parts of southern San Mateo County. The minimum height is about 1,000 feet, thus ensuring that the vineyards are located above the fog line.

Another major player up in these mountains, who is still very much with us, is Dr David Bruce, who was trained by Martin Ray and set up his own winery in 1961. Two years earlier David Bennion had founded Ridge Vineyards, but for the past thirty years it has been Paul Draper who has maintained the very high reputation of this estate. Bruce's wines have been inconsistent, with many superlative vintages of Pinot Noir and Chardonnay both from local grapes and from outside the county, but also many puzzling failures. Ridge, on the other hand, has been a model of consistency despite the fact that in the 1970s it made a fetish of single-vineyard wines, especially Zinfandel. Nowadays Ridge plays to its strengths, producing magnificent Cabernet, Merlot and Chardonnay from its own mountain vineyards, and buying in Zinfandel and Petite Sirah from sites with a proven track record, whether in Paso Robles or Sonoma.

This is a hard region to characterize, as its microclimates, expositions, and soils, although predominantly Franciscan shale, are so varied. Franciscan shale, Martin Ray once explained, 'is almost like rotten rock. When it's wet, fracture a piece in your hands. It always fractures more or less horizontally and vertically at a right angle. It's just like a first class, authentic Parmesan cheese: it breaks up. So every time you work that land those little particles become smaller, and, ultimately, after twenty or thirty years, it gets so it's almost chalk.'[8]

In addition, the vineyards are dispersed among the numerous ridges of the region, some facing towards the ocean, others facing inland towards the Santa Clara Valley, the latter usually enjoying a warmer climate than the former. Being, for the most part, high in the mountains, many vineyards are classified as Region I, and rainfall, although variable, can be quite high. David Bruce's vineyards, which are over 2,000 feet high, get between 40 and 80 inches of rain annually. Since they are above the fog line, the vines benefit from long sunny days. The principal varieties cultivated are Chardonnay, Pinot Noir, and Cabernet Sauvignon. Towards the north of the region, around Woodside, winemaker Robert Mullen finds that only Chardonnay and Pinot Noir are certain to ripen each year, whereas Cabernet Sauvignon is marginal.

There is no doubt, however, that the settlers who first planted vineyards here knew what they were doing. The best wines from these mountains rank among the finest in California. No one would dispute that Ridge's Monte Bello Cabernet Sauvignon is one of the state's 'first growths', and the Burgundian wines from Martin Ray and his successors at Mount Eden are also of legendary quality, both for their concentration of flavour and for their remarkable longevity. David Bruce believes that in the 1960s no region in California was producing better wines than those produced by Martin Ray. How long the region will survive, it is hard to say. Isolated and remote, planted on difficult and rocky terrain, these vineyards, with the exception of Monte Bello, can scarcely be a profitable proposition, and despite the established quality of the best wines over a century or more, the Santa Cruz Mountains appellation has never enjoyed the cachet of some of the other coastal appellations.

Ben Lomond Mountain

Established in 1988, this is the only AVA within the Santa Cruz Mountains AVA, located a few miles northwest of the town of Santa Cruz. 800 feet high, it's a wet region, receiving about 60 inches of rainfall annually. With only 100 acres planted, it is very difficult to say what the distinguishing characteristics of Ben Lomond wines are. I have never seen the appellation identified on a label, and am not sure why it exists at all.

VINEYARDS

Arata. Santa Cruz. Sells Cabernet Sauvignon to Sunrise.

Aptos. Santa Cruz. Sells Chardonnay to Cronin.

Bald Mountain. Santa Cruz. 36 acres planted at 1,500 feet. Sells Chardonnay to Thunder Mountain and Byington.

Bates Ranch. Santa Cruz. Owned by John Bates. 24 dry-farmed acres planted in 1972 at 600–900 feet. Cabernet Sauvignon, Cabernet Franc, and other grapes sold to Ahlgren, Cronin, Bargetto, Byington, Thunder Mountain, and Santa Cruz Mountain Vineyard.

Beauregard Ranch. Santa Cruz. Owned by Jim Beauregard. An old vineyard originally established in the nineteenth century and replanted in the 1972 near Bonny Doon. 4.4 acres planted at 1,600 feet with Cabernet Sauvignon, Chardonnay, and Zinfandel, which are sold to Ahlgren, Devlin, Page Mill, Hallcrest, Thunder Mountain, and Storrs.

Beyers Ranch. Livermore. Owned by Wente. Sells Zinfandel to Tamás and Chardonnay to Sunrise.

Blanches Vineyard. Livermore. Owned by Ault family. 14 acres of Chardonnay and Cabernet Sauvignon planted at 750 feet. Fruit used for their Cedar Mountain winery and sold to other wineries.

Bridgehead. Oakley, Contra Costa County. Planted in late nineteenth century. Dry-farmed. Owned by Cline. Zinfandel and Mourvèdre. Also sells to Ridge.

Christie. Santa Cruz. Sells Chardonnay to Storrs.

Cinnabar. Santa Cruz. Grapes used by Cinnabar winery and Cabernet Sauvignon sold to Santa Cruz Mountain Vineyard.

Dirk. Santa Cruz. Owned by Dirk Reed. Sells Chardonnay to Byington and Storrs.

Dreyer. Santa Cruz. Sells Chardonnay and Cabernet Sauvignon to Cronin.

Duarte. Oakley, Contra Costa County. Zinfandel. Sells to Turley.

Figoni Ranch. Livermore. Owned by Wente. Sells Sauvignon Blanc to Tamás.

Garbett. Santa Clara. Owned by Elizabeth Garbett. Provides Chardonnay to Page Mill.

Hayes Ranch. Livermore. Owned by Wente. Sells Chardonnay to Tamás.

Jimsomare Ranch. Santa Cruz. Owned by James Schwabacher. 40 acres planted at 1,300–2,000 feet with Cabernet Sauvignon and Chardonnay. Sells to Ridge and others.

Karla's Vineyard. Contra Costa County. Sells Zinfandel to Rosenblum.

Longridge. Santa Cruz. Sells Pinot Noir to Silver Mountain.

Matteson. Santa Cruz. Owned by Mike Matteson. 14 acres planted in 1980 near Watsonville. Sells Chardonnay, Pinot Noir, and Cabernet Sauvignon to Santa Cruz Mountain Vineyard, Cronin, Salamandre, and Thunder Mountain.

Mayers. Santa Cruz. Owned by Ed Mayers. Sells Chardonnay to Ahlgren.

Meyley. Santa Cruz. Owned by Redtree Properties. Planted in 1984 at 1,700 feet. 7 acres of Chardonnay.

Miller. Santa Cruz. Sells Chardonnay to Santa Cruz Mountain Vineyard.

Mistral. Santa Clara Valley. Owned by John Dyson. 300 acres close to San Ysidro. Planted with Chardonnay, Pinot Blanc, Pinot Noir, Sauvignon Blanc and Merlot. Sells to Concannon, Au Bon Climat (until 1997), and other wineries.

Pato. Contra Costa County. Sells Zinfandel to Neyers and Mourvedre to Rosenblum.

Picchetti. Santa Cruz. 3 acres of 100-year-old Zinfandel. Sells to Sunrise.

Portola Valley. Santa Cruz. Sells Chardonnay to Cronin.

La Questa. Santa Cruz. Owned by Woodside Vineyards. 1 acre of old Cabernet Sauvignon.

Raboli. Livermore. 98 acres, including Zinfandel, planted in 1922. Grapes are sold to Wente and Murrieta's Well.

Peter Martin Ray Vineyard. Santa Cruz. 15 acres planted in 1961 and replanted in 1982 at 1,800 feet, with Cabernet Sauvignon, Pinot Noir, and Chardonnay. Grapes sold to Cronin.

Redwood Hill. Santa Cruz. Owned by Joanne Barber. Sells Chardonnay to Byington.

Saint Charles. Santa Cruz. Owned by Hong Kong Metro Realty. 32 acres planted at 1,500 feet, from 1938 onwards, with Sauvignon Blanc, Chenin Blanc, Sémillon , Pinot Blanc, and Pinot Noir. Grapes sold to Ahlgren, Sunrise, and Byington.

San Ysidro Vineyard. Santa Clara Valley. 150 acres of Chardonnay, Pinot Noir, and Merlot.

Saratoga. Santa Cruz. Owned by Tom Mudd. Sells Chardonnay to Cinnabar.

Toy. Livermore Valley. Owned by Art Toy. Sells Cabernet Sauvignon and Chardonnay to Fenestra and Livermore Valley Cellars.

Vanumanutagi. Santa Cruz. Owned by Leonard Ware. 10 acres of Chardonnay near Watsonville at 600–900 feet. Grapes sold to Storrs and Cronin.

Vista Verde. Santa Clara. Sells Arneis to Au Bon Climat and Wild Horse.

NOTES

1 James Laube, *California Wine*, p. 6
2 Robert Benson, *Great Winemakers of California*, p. 63
3 Ibid., p. 70
4 Charles L. Sullivan, *Napa Wine*, p. 81
5 Leon D. Adams, The *Wines of America*, p. 346
6 Ibid., p. 363
7 Benson, p. 27
8 Ibid., p. 24

8

Monterey

With just under 40,000 acres planted throughout the county by late 1998, Monterey has become a major player in California wine production. Yet this is a comparatively recent development, and for many years arguments raged about the suitability of Monterey for grape growing. Certainly, grave mistakes were made in the past, but it does seem that after a few decades of trial and much error, growers have now got the measure of Monterey. It was the experts from UC Davis, Maynard Amerine and A. J. Winkler, who from 1935 onwards opined that Monterey had the makings of a good Region I vineyard area, but they found few people prepared to take their advice. The consensus was that Monterey was too chilly and blustery for grape production. When they reiterated their recommendation in 1960, some wine producers began to take notice.

Vineyards had been planted in the Salinas Valley by the friars based at the Spanish mission in Soledad, but no trace of them remains. Thereafter viticulture ceased for a century and a half. Thirty-five years ago there were few vines in the county, at least not in the Salinas Valley, where the majority of vineyards are now planted. High above the valley were the Chalone vineyards, originally planted in 1919. In 1962 Paul Masson planted 1,000 acres of vineyards near Greenfield, and Mirassou followed suit with 1,200 acres. In 1963 Wente was drawn here by lack of local vineyard land in Livermore Valley, and planted 700 acres in Arroyo Seco.

Mirassou, one of the pioneers in Monterey, had in fact been founded in 1854 and is one of the oldest wine companies in California. It was created by a French immigrant called Pierre Pellier who brought cuttings with him. The name Mirassou comes from

Pellier's son-in-law, who succeeded him in the business, which was based in San Jose. Only bulk wines were made until 1942. As the company expanded, it needed to look elsewhere for vineyard holdings, and Monterey County represented the ideal solution. In 1961 they planted 300 acres on the west side of the valley near Soledad. One problem with Central Coast valley floor sites was that they were prone to frosts. But a major breakthrough took place when in the 1960s overhead sprinklers were developed, replacing the polluting smudge pots that had been the most widely practised method of frost protection until that time. Nor was lack of water a problem: the underground Salinas River provided abundant water for irrigation. If it was good enough for the lettuces grown in the valley, it would be good enough for the vines.

Both Mirassou and Masson were pleased with the early results from their new vineyards, and planted more: Mirassou added 600 acres, and Masson planted an astonishing 4,500 acres near Greenfield and Soledad. In the early 1970s the frenzy of planting continued, fuelled not only by studies that seemed to confirm the suitability of Monterey for grape farming, but by tax shelter incentives. Almadén established a 2,000-acre vineyard just south of King City.[1] It was at this time that the world's largest single vineyard, the 7,500-acre San Bernabe, was planted near King City, having been funded by the Prudential Insurance Company. The vineyard is now owned by Delicato Vineyards, based in the Central Valley, and it has expanded to a potential area of 8,500 acres. Another vast enterprise was the 9,600-acre collection of vineyards assembled by Myron McFarland and his brother in 1972. It was the mouth-watering prospect of nearly 10,000 acres of varietals freshly planted in a promising Region I that persuaded Dr Richard Peterson to give up his prestigious job at Beaulieu and set up The Monterey Vineyard in collaboration with the McFarlands. A few years later the excessive ambition of the scheme became apparent when Peterson and the McFarlands went their separate ways. The Monterey Vineyard simply could not cope with the volume of fruit, of varying quality, that the McFarlands delivered.[2]

By 1975 there were about 35,000 acres of vineyards in the county, although that figure diminished slightly during the 1980s. By 1982 there were fewer than 20,000 acres. However, there was another spurt in new plantings in the late 1980s, which accelerated in the early 1990s, when large wineries, afflicted by phylloxera in

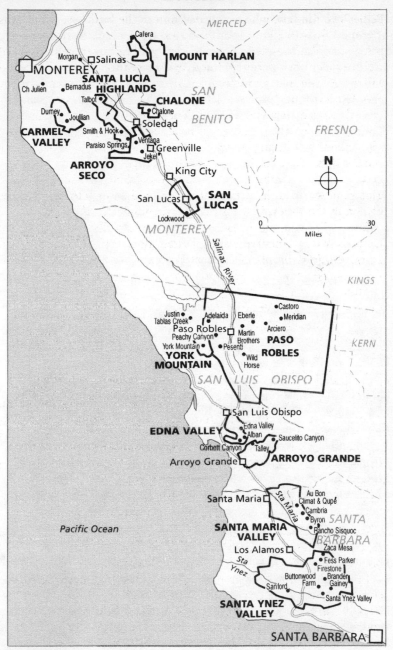

Monterey to Santa Barbara

their North Coast vineyards, were anxious to secure new sources of grapes. In 1996 alone about 6,000 acres were planted, and only slightly less the following year. Not only were new vineyards laid out, but older ones were replanted, and red varieties often replaced with more suitable white ones. The major players in this love affair with Monterey were Kendall-Jackson (who have planted 2,500 acres), Mondavi with 1,350, Raymond with 300 acres planted south of Gonzalez, and Hess with 350, as well as Phelps, Villa Mount Eden, and Caymus.

The Salinas Valley is flanked by the Santa Lucia Mountains to the west and the Gavilan Mountains to the east. The soils are meagre and not remarkable, being composed of silty loam and sand, but they do drain well, which is an advantage given the necessity for irrigation. In some areas around Arroyo Seco there is more rock and gravel in the soil, which is quite deep. It was correctly perceived that this was essentially a cool-climate region, pierced by cold Pacific winds in the summer afternoons which slowed down the growing cycle of the vines. As the day wears on, the hot air rises, drawing in cooler air and fog during the summer afternoons; this fog is later displaced by the strong winds that blast down the valley. Moreover, the climate was even and dry, and the lack of rainfall – it ranges from 6 to 10 inches annually – was compensated for by the ease of irrigation, which had turned the Salinas Valley into one of America's primary sources of vegetables and lettuce. Driving up the valley from Salinas, one soon notices that vineyards are planted up to 1,000 feet on the slopes and benchlands, while the flat valley floor is coated with intensively farmed vegetables. Water for irrigation is drawn from the under-ground Salinas River, which originates in San Luis Obispo County to the south. In the early days some growers irrigated excessively, which contributed to over-vigorous growth and the resulting vegetal flavours of much of the fruit. Dr Richard Peterson noted that the sandiness of the soil provided a natural break on the vine's vigour, so that it was very difficult to obtain more than 3 tons per acre (although much higher tonnage has been achieved by some growers), which gives the wines great intensity of flavour, especially Cabernet Sauvignon. However, in the same interview[3] Peterson went on to say, 'Cabernet to me tastes like green peppers', so I suspect that what he was really saying was that the growing conditions of the Salinas Valley only accentuated the vegetal character of (unripe) Cabernet.

It would be a mistake to think of the Salinas Valley as a uniform growing region. The valley is over eighty miles long and up to five miles wide, and the climate grows steadily warmer as one moves towards the southeast. Consequently, red grapes tend to be planted only in the southern third of the valley, a Region III, whereas the northern sectors, around Gonzalez, are Region I. Indeed among the valley's southernmost vineyards, in the San Lucas area, the heat summation crosses over into a very warm Region IV. Phylloxera is certainly present in the Salinas Valley, though it seems that the sandier soils have slowed its growth.

In the excitement of the early days of grape growing in Salinas Valley, Edmund Mirassou declared that before too long 100,000 acres would be planted here. It was not to be, since the climate has proved far from ideal for some grape varieties. A study published by Professor Winkler in 1960 had argued that the potential for Cabernet was even greater than in Napa Valley.[4] Vines were duly planted, but it soon became apparent that Cabernet Sauvignon from here exhibited vegetal characteristics – aromas of bell pepper and asparagus – that suggested the grapes were not ripening fully, despite the considerable length of Monterey's growing season. The harvest often stretches into October or even November, which is all the more remarkable given that bud-break can be as early as February. The combination of heat, cold winds, and irrigation made it difficult for growers to keep the vines balanced in terms of sugar and acidity production. As in Carneros, high winds can inhibit maturation and sustain high levels of acidity, which is fine for most white varieties, but not so desirable for reds. And when winds are as strong as they can be here, leaves can shut down so as to protect their moisture content from desiccation. This in turn brings photosynthesis to a temporary halt and delays maturation. Although new trellising and wind protection measures have been introduced to ensure healthier growth, success has been limited and the acreage of Cabernet Sauvignon has diminished significantly. Of the 4,250 acres of Cabernet now planted, almost all are on benchlands in southern Monterey, in the Santa Lucia Highlands, or in Carmel Valley, where Durney first planted the variety in 1968.

It wasn't just the howling wind that caused problems with

ripening. The Amerine/Winkler forecast that the Salinas Valley was a Region I neglected to take into account that the days were shorter here. Richard Peterson consulted thermographs he installed in the vineyards and it soon became apparent to him that the heat peaks were brief, and dropped rapidly once the wind picked up. 'The vineyards north of the winery are doing best,' he observed. 'They're elevated 400 feet or so and protected from that afternoon breeze; we may get 2,100 degree days up there, and only 1,600 here at the winery. The vineyard area around Gonzalez is the *coolest in California*! Some of the sections wouldn't even make Region I.'[5]

White grapes dominate Monterey, especially in the cooler northern sections of the Salinas Valley. The most recent estimates suggest that about two-thirds of all plantations are of white varieties, with 16,200 acres of Chardonnay, 1,600 of Riesling, 2,100 of Pinot Noir, 3,700 of Merlot, and 600 of Pinot Blanc. There are also a few hundred acres of Chenin Blanc and Sauvignon Blanc. Monterey has established a good reputation for Riesling from wineries such as Jekel, Wente, J. Lohr, and Lockwood, and 40 per cent of California's Riesling vines are planted here, especially around Greenfield. Furthermore, about half of all California's Pinot Blanc is grown in Monterey County. Despite the unsurprising dominance of Chardonnay, it is not a variety that seems to perform especially well in Monterey, at least not in the Salinas Valley. However, it is only fair to point out that certain Monterey Chardonnays, such as Mer & Soleil, have met with great acclaim, although more fastidious palates, including my own, find its fruit-salady character cloying. Where Monterey does do well is with varieties such as Riesling, Sauvignon Blanc, and Gewürztraminer. Pinot Noir, which one might expect to do well here, has not proved exceptional as yet.

Growers such as Doug Meador of Ventana Vineyards are convinced that Monterey has turned the corner in terms of adapting viticulture to the peculiarities of the local climate. He does not deny that quality used to be very patchy but insists that nowadays it is possible to combine high-quality fruit with generous yields. Techniques such as leaf-pulling and closer vine spacing have helped achieve this. The great attractions for the large wine companies that have invested heavily in the region are the quality of the fruit, the relatively high yields that can be obtained, and the suitability of the vineyards for mechanical harvesting, which was pioneered in the region by Mirassou. Mechanical night harvesting has proved very successful, bringing in fresh clean juice with a low pH that is well suited to the production of sparkling wine, which has become a speciality at Wente and other wineries. It does seem that the vegetal character – once so widespread that it was commonly described as the 'Monterey veggies' – is no longer a problem. With the moderation of bulk farming practices such as excessive irrigation and fertilization, sprawl trellising, and overcropping, the quality of the fruit has improved beyond measure.

Doug Meador does not believe one should give up on red varieties in the Salinas Valley. Except in the south, Cabernet Sauvignon will always have to struggle to reach full maturity, and he believes Merlot is a better prospect, 'although Pétrus needn't quake in its boots'. It may, he thinks, be possible to produce leaner, claret-like reds here with lower pH than Napa Valley Cabernets and Meritages. Both Malbec and Tempranillo show promise here, says Meador.

Monterey County appears on many labels as a region though not an AVA. Within it are five AVAs: Arroyo Seco, Carmel Valley, Chalone, Santa Lucia Highlands, and San Lucas. Monterey has in effect been dealt with above. In addition there is a cluster of tiny AVAs all within San Benito County, which will be dealt with under the latter heading.

Arroyo Seco

This AVA, approved in 1983, is approximately midway down the Salinas Valley. From just south of Soledad it encircles the town of Greenfield. A tongue of land flickers westwards for a few miles along the course of Arroyo Seco itself. Here Jekel's Sanctuary Vineyard is sheltered from the Monterey wind, allowing red grapes to be grown with success. It lies west of the town and south of Soledad. Wente and Mirassou planted vineyards here in the 1960s and today just under 5,000 acres are cultivated. Wente remains the principal owner, with 680 acres, followed by Mirassou with 600, J. Lohr with 335, Jekel with 325, and Ventana with 300. Hess have also acquired vineyards here. The soils tend to be sandier and rockier here than in other parts of the valley. The vineyards are planted on gently sloping benchlands close to the canyon-like mouth of the Arroyo Seco river, and since the contours of the land

and the canyon rim offer some protection against the Monterey winds, it is possible to ripen Cabernet Sauvignon and other red varieties here, as well as the ubiquitous Chardonnay.

Riesling is also very successful and in some years has produced exceptional late harvest wines. Jeff Meier, the winemaker at J. Lohr, finds that the Chardonnay they grow here has higher extract than the same variety grown in Napa or Sonoma, but he is at a loss to explain why. Less surprisingly, given the windy and cool climate, the pH is also lower.

Here and there within Arroyo Seco you can see rows of cypress trees that have been planted to protect the vines from the winds. J. Lohr have been particularly keen on this kind of wind-break. Experienced growers such as Doug Meador are sceptical, however. 'Winds have a way of getting round them or under them, and then they emerge with even greater velocity than before.' Bill Jekel took a different approach at his Sanctuary Vineyard by planting the vines beneath a cliff rim, thus protecting them quite effectively from the winds.

Carmel Valley

The valley, which became an AVA in 1983, runs southeast from Monterey itself, and thus lies east of the Pacific and west of the Salinas Valley, being separated from both by chains of mountains. Beginning at Carmel Valley Village, the region, which is shaped like a rugby ball, continues southeast as far as Cachagua. Many of the vineyards are planted quite high up, some as high as 2,000 feet, so they are less susceptible to fog influence and to the powerful winds of the Salinas Valley; rainfall, however, is relatively high during the winter months. The soils tend to be well-drained sandy loam, and in some areas there is a subsoil of clay or decomposed sandstone.

Unlike most of Monterey County this is red wine territory, with both Cabernet Sauvignon and Merlot giving good results. Durney was the first estate to plant red varieties here back in 1968. Only 12 per cent of the 300 acres here are planted with Chardonnay. Warm autumn days and cool nights always bring the grapes to full ripeness. As is the case elsewhere in the county, many vines are planted on their own roots.

Ridge Watson, the winemaker at Joullian, has over the years

noted the deep colour of the valley's red wines, which he attributes to the wide swings in temperature, which can vary up to 50 degrees on a single day. The only drawback in the red wines can be a certain astringency, as the berries are smaller than those grown in Salinas Valley or the Napa Valley floor, and thus there is a tighter ratio of skins to juice during fermentation. He finds Carmel Valley Cabernet comparable in structure to Napa mountain fruit. As for the white wines, he finds the Chardonnay from Carmel Valley has a stronger lemon/lime component than North Coast Chardonnays.

Chalone

Chalone is an example of an AVA created (in 1982) to accommodate a single winery. In this case, it makes sense. The Chalone estate lies within Monterey County, but has little in common, climatically, with the Salinas Valley. Chalone lies high up in the Gavilan Mountains, about five miles from Soledad as the crow flies, and just two miles from the jagged rockscape of the Pinnacles National Monument. From Soledad a narrow road climbs east, high into the hills through a desolate landscape until at last vineyards are spotted; at the very end of the road lies the winery, 2,000 feet above the valley floor.

The vineyards are between 1,800 and 2,000 feet and any morning fog burns off by ten. The daily temperature can fluctuate considerably in summer. Despite the elevation Chalone is consistently warmer than the Salinas Valley, being relatively immune from the cooling wind that roars down the valley below, and the heat summation system places it as a Region II. Annual rainfall however, averaging 12 inches, is only slightly higher than in the valley.

The soil is volcanic: limestone deposits interspersed with reddish, decomposed granite and moderate amounts of clay. It is low in nutrients but has excellent drainage. The topsoil is thin, in some places no more than a foot deep, and beneath lies a layer of limestone.

Some 187 acres are in production at Chalone, and 67 per cent of that is Chardonnay. The surface area will increase by the end of the century, as 50 acres of Pinot Noir as well as 50 acres of other varieties were planted here in 1997. The original vineyard was planted by a Frenchman called Tamm in the late nineteenth century, presumably because its limestone soil, a rarity in California, reminded him of Burgundy. Some of the vines planted here in 1919 still survive and are the oldest Chardonnay and Chenin Blanc still in production in Monterey County. More vines were planted in 1946: Chardonnay, Chenin Blanc, Pinot Blanc, and Pinot Noir. In 1965 Richard Graff bought the estate and planted more vineyards, putting Chalone on the map both as a winery and as a *terroir*. The poverty of the soil and the lack of rainfall means that yields here are very low, often no more than one ton per acre. The younger vines can achieve up to 3 tons per acre. Graff always argued that it was the limestone soil, above all, that gave his wines, especially the Pinot Noir, their typicity, quality, and longevity.

San Benito County

This county lies along the northeastern flank of the Salinas Valley. Cross the Gavilan Mountains to the east of Salinas and Gonzalez and you will find yourself in the San Benito Valley, which is parallel to the Salinas Valley. The valley slopes southeastwards for some sixty miles from Hollister, and the AVAs occupy some of the western flanks of the mountains dividing the valley from Salinas. There were probably vineyards here in the late eighteenth century, when Franciscan missionaries established mission San Juan Bautista. In the mid-nineteenth century Théophile Vaché planted vineyards south of the mission. By the 1880s there were 400 acres of vines in the county. Prohibition forced many of the wineries to close, but 2,000 acres of vineyards continued to supply grapes for home winemakers.

In past decades the county provided grapes for the Almadén winery that was located nearby. Louis Benoist of Almadén first came here in 1954. He bought the Cienega vineyard and winery, and then planted vineyards around Paicines. By 1967 Almadén owned 4,500 acres in the valley, installed with overhead sprinklers for frost protection.[6] After the winery was sold in 1987, operations moved to Madera in the Central Valley. Current acreage figures vary according to the source and range between 1,700 and 2,500. The climate is Region II, rainfall averages about 15 inches annually, and the soils are well-drained loams with rocky subsoils.

The AVAs within the county are Mount Harlan, Paicines, Cienega, Lime Kiln, and Pacheco Pass. The one with the best claim to fame is Mount Harlan, designated as an AVA in 1990 and containing a single winery, the adventurous Burgundian-modelled Calera, planted high up in the Gavilan Mountains. There are 47 acres under vine and an elevation of about 2,200 feet. Almadén owned most of the vineyards in Paicines until the winery was sold.

San Lucas

Located at the southernmost point of the Salinas Valley, San Lucas, an AVA since 1987, is the area located between King City and San Ardo. It was first developed by Almadén in the 1970s and it rapidly became a region of industrial-scale viticulture. The soil is a deep shale loam and sand, and on the alluvial terraces the drainage is good. This is a hot area, oppressively so in summer, and parts of the region are classified as Region IV, although nights can be quite cool. Winds are less ardent than further north in the valley. The wines tend to be fairly soft and broad, and the principal varieties are Cabernet Sauvignon, Merlot, and Chardonnay, which, surprisingly, accounts for half the 8,000 acres of vines. Lockwood is the only winery located here, and the estate owns 1,650 acres of vineyards, followed by Monterey Vineyard with 1,100 at their Paris Valley vineyard.

Santa Lucia Highlands

The Highlands, which became an AVA in 1992, follow the benchlands along the western side of the Salinas Valley, snuggling up against Arroyo Seco to the south. The Highlands are separated from the valley floor by a clearly visible fault line, northwards from Arroyo Seco to just beyond Gonzalez. Most of the 2,300 acres of vineyards are planted on alluvial fans that lie above the fog line and can benefit from the sunny southeast exposure. Half the grapes planted are Chardonnay, but Cabernet Sauvignon and Merlot are also present. At its best, Santa Lucia Highlands fruit can show both great richness and a cleansing acidity. A multiplicity of exposures and elevations means that many varieties were planted in the wrong places. There were many trials and almost as many errors.

Smith & Hook and, more recently, Mer & Soleil and Paraiso Spring Vineyards use a good deal of Santa Lucia Highlands fruit.

VINEYARDS

Chalone. Gavilan Mountains. Fruit mostly used by Chalone Winery, but also sold to David Bruce, Testarossa, Wild Horse, and Bernardus.

Cobblestone. Arroyo Seco. Owned by Sal Levine. Sells Pinot Blanc to Monterey Peninsula.

Gemelli. Cienega Valley. Sells Negrette, Grenache and Trousseau to Wild Horse.

Hacienda. Arroyo Seco. Sandy loam. 369 acres of Chardonnay, 17 Merlot, 2 Sémillon. Acquired by Kendall-Jackson in 1990 and supplies Kendall-Jackson and Camelot.

Los Lobos. Sells Syrah and Cabernet Sauvignon to Salamandre.

Lockwood. 1,650 acres in San Lucas. Planted in 1981 with Chardonnay, Cabernet Sauvignon, Riesling, Sauvignon Blanc, Sémillon, Pinot Blanc, Merlot, Cabernet Franc, Pinot Noir, Chenin Blanc, and Muscat Canelli. Sells to Bonny Doon, Mondavi, Estancia.

Michaud. San Benito. 18 acres. Owned by Michael Michaud. Sells Chardonnay and Pinot Blanc to Testarossa.

Paradise. Planted on benchlands at the mouth of the Arroyo Seco river near Soledad. Acquired by Kendall-Jackson in 1990. 657 acres of Chardonnay, with another 500 acres to be planted. Well-drained gravelly loam and a southwest exposition. Supplies Kendall-Jackson and Camelot.

Paraiso Springs. 400 acres in the Santa Lucia Highlands. Planted in 1973 by Rich Smith with Pinot Blanc, Pinot Noir, and other varieties. Fruit goes to the Paraiso Springs winery and to Fetzer, Mondavi, and Pavona.

Pinnacles. 900 acres originally planted by Paul Masson and now owned by Estancia. Mostly Chardonnay and Pinot Noir.

Pisoni. Santa Lucia Highlands. Sells Pinot Noir and Chardonnay to Patz & Hall, Siduri, and Testarossa.

Quinn. Carmel Valley. Sells Cabernet Sauvignon to Cloninger.

La Reina. Santa Lucia Highlands. Sells Chardonnay to Joullian.

San Bernabe. 7,500 acres near King City, and another 1,000 acres within the 11-mile-long vineyard are not yet in production. Divided into 188 blocks. Originally planted for McCarthy Farming from 1972 to 1974 with financing from Prudential Insurance, but sections have been replanted since, as they have succumbed to various diseases. Bought by Delicato in 1988. Originally two-thirds red grapes, but now only one-third. Delicato have grafted over 1,200 acres to Chardonnay and restored Merlot at the expense of Chenin Blanc. French Colombard, Grey Riesling, and Silvaner are also being phased out or greatly reduced. Formerly 23 varieties were grown here, now reduced to 17. Sells to Bonny Doon and Wild Horse.

Siletto Ranch. San Benito. Sells Trousseau to Wild Horse.

Sleepy Hollow. At the north end of the Salinas Valley near Chular. 400 acres planted in the early 1970s with Chardonnay, Pinot Noir and Riesling. Bought by Talbott in 1995. Supplies Caymus, Joullian, Testarossa, Monterey Peninsula, and other wineries.

Smith and Hook. Sells Cabernet Sauvignon to Fenestra.

Ventana. 300 acres in Arroyo Seco. Pioneering vineyards established by Doug Meador in 1972, and planted with Riesling, Gewürztraminer, Chardonnay, Sauvignon Blanc, Pinot Noir, Cabernet Sauvignon, Merlot, and Syrah. Sells to Ahlgren, Cain, River Run, Woodside, Fogarty, Geyser Peak, Cronin, and Bernardus.

NOTES

1 Leon D. Adams, *The Wines of America*, pp. 383–4
2 Robert Benson, *Great Winemakers of California*, pp. 101–3
3 Ibid., p. 105
4 Dan Berger, 'The Trouble with Monterey', *Los Angeles Times*, January 1998
5 Benson, pp. 103–4
6 Adams, pp. 380–81

9
San Luis Obispo County

This chapter looks at two regions within San Luis Obispo County: Paso Robles and Edna Valley. It is hard to imagine a greater contrast than that between the decidedly warm Paso Robles region and the decidedly cool Edna Valley.

PASO ROBLES

The Paso Robles region, an AVA created in 1983, is divided by the north-south Highway 101. The name is a contraction of 'El Paso de Robles', the pass of the oaks. The western side is hilly, the eastern side more of a plateau. Grapes were probably planted here in the late eighteenth century, as there were two Spanish missions in the area, the Mission San Miguel and the Mission San Luis. It is believed that the first vineyard was planted in 1797. As was the case at other missions, viticulture eventually came to a halt, until it was revived by Andrew York at Ascension Winery (now York Mountain Winery), who planted Mission, Zinfandel, and Alicante Bouschet. He was followed by Gerd Klintworth in 1886 and by the Frenchman Adolf Siot in 1890. In the 1920s the Polish musician and statesman Ignace Paderewski bought 2,000 acres in the Adelaida Hills, planting Petite Sirah and Zinfandel at his Rancho San Ignacio. He intended to start up a winery but was understandably deterred by Prohibition. The vines were neglected after his death in 1941.[1]

Although the mountainous stretches between Highway 101 and the Pacific have very diverse microclimates, Paso Robles as a whole is a warm region, designated as a high Region II or Region III, and thus comparable to Alexander Valley in Sonoma County. As one moves further east from the highway, the hotter the climate becomes. Like Alexander Valley, it is best suited to red varieties, including the Bordeaux favourites, although a little of everything tends to be grown here. However, the structure of the red wines coming out of Paso Robles tends to be soft and fleshy, with gentle tannins and a more overt fruit character. The vegetal character that used to mar Monterey reds is virtually unknown here. Anyone who has had the opportunity to taste side by side the Sonoma and Paso Robles Zinfandels produced by Ridge will surely have noticed that the Paso Robles bottling is always more charming, more luscious than its counterparts from Lytton Springs or Geyserville. If Paso Robles reds lack the power of the best of the North Coast reds, they make up for it with charm and approachability. They are wines that give intense pleasure, even though they may lack the awesome qualities that appeal to reviewers and collectors.

West of Highway 101 the terrain rises as one follows any of the roads – Chimney Rock, Peachy Canyon, Adelaida – that wind into the mountains. This is a surprisingly wild region, where many wineries are fenced in to keep out deer and mountain lions. Most of these roads come to a dead end, and at various spots along them you will find the wineries whose vineyards are located at an elevation of up to 2,000 feet. Of the subregions within the Santa Lucia Mountains, Adelaida is the most likely candidate to be granted its own AVA in the near future. This valley lies sixteen miles west of the town of Paso Robles. A Region II, it benefits from cooling ocean breezes, and the summer temperature rarely exceeds 95 degrees. The soil is dominated by miocene sea deposits, and is rich in calcium and minerals. The hilly terrain means that soils, exposures, and microclimates are extremely varied, and wineries such as Justin are engaged in long-term research to get to know their *terroir*. With rainfall of 25 to 50 inches annually irrigation is unnecessary, but yields often average only 2 tons per acre.

The Santa Lucia Mountains effectively block the maritime influence of the Pacific, although some cool air comes though the Templeton Gap, which roughly follows Highway 46 from Cambria to Templeton. It would seem, however, that elevation and exposure have more to do with the relative coolness of the mountain vineyards. Nonetheless the majority of these vineyards, with the exception of York Mountain, being a Region II, are still distinctly warmer than Edna Valley or the Salinas Valley. Rainfall, however, is higher, at about 35 inches and in some spots as much as 50 inches, as compared to 8–13 inches east of Paso Robles. On the lower slopes, where many vineyards are laid out, you can find alluvial terraces and occasional outcrops of limestone. These soils are well drained and surprisingly fertile thanks to the relatively high rainfall, so overcropping can be a real risk unless curtailed by pruning and canopy management. Spring frost can be a problem.

There is one AVA within the Santa Lucia Mountains: York Mountain (see below). There have also been other adjustments within the Paso Robles AVA, which in recent years has been extended to embrace wineries of obvious quality such as Justin and Tablas Creek. This, says Ken Volk of Wild Horse, is one of the few instances where expansion of an appellation has been clearly beneficial. One of the best-known vineyards in this area was planted in the 1960s by Dr Stanley Hoffman in the Adelaida Hills, with enthusiastic advice from André Tchelitscheff.

Most of the older vineyards are located around Templeton, just south of Paso Robles. Here the old-timers knew the vines would benefit from the cool air that flows in through the Templeton Gap. They were also attracted here by the accessibility provided after 1886 by the construction of the Southern Pacific Railway. Many of the early settlers were Swiss and Italians – Martinelli, Dusi, Bianchi, and many others – who established vineyards in the 1920s and 1930s, some of which still survive. Not all of them produce wine of particularly good quality, but now and again one encounters a full-bodied Zinfandel or other red made from old vineyards established fifty years ago or more. These settlers and their families provided their neighbours with good-quality Zinfandel grapes for home winemaking during Prohibition, thus helping to keep some of the old vineyards in production.

The 'east side' began to be planted in the early 1970s. This is a plateau about 1,200 feet high, which explains why the nights are cool, sometimes dropping to the low 50s in summer, which can be a relief after the 100-degree days that are by no means uncommon here. A second moderating influence is the Templeton Gap, which brings Pacific breezes in from the Cambria area. The soils are mostly decomposed granite and shale, with sandy loams on the terraces near the Salinas and Estrella rivers.

Bob Young planted a vineyard now known as Rancho Dos Amigos, and Herman Schwartz established the Rancho Tierra

Rejada here in 1973. In 1977 Gary Eberle planted the 500-acre Estrella River vineyards which now belong to Meridian and constructed the Estrella River winery for his relative Cliff Giacobine. Eberle's plantings included 35 acres of Syrah, which at that time was quite a novelty. In the early 1980s, when Estrella River's production had grown to 200,000 cases, Gary Eberle left to set up his own winery. The Estrella River vineyards were planted on the Estrella Bench just east of Paso Robles, a warmer area than either Templeton or the Santa Lucia Mountains. The soil is relatively infertile and the microclimate fairly uniform. Irrigation is essential, as rain only falls between November and April. Gary Eberle points out that they rarely experience the damp cool weather that would be commonplace in Bordeaux. This means that afflictions such as downy mildew are unknown, and there is no need to spray routinely with Bordeaux mixture. The level nature of the land and its low cost, compared to many other California wine regions, has encouraged the planting of large vineyards by wineries such as Arciero and Meridian. Many of these are laid out on either side of Highway 46 East.

Paso Robles has not been subjected to the vast vineyard development that characterized Monterey. Nonetheless a few large wineries have gained a foothold in the region. The Southcorp corporation of Australia, which owns Penfolds and Lindemans, has acquired about 600 acres, much of which will be marketed under its Seven Peaks label. Other wineries that have purchased vineyards here include Gallo (700 acres), Kendall-Jackson, Mondavi, Beringer, Chateau Potelle, and Rabbit Ridge. For many of these outsiders, the primary attraction of Paso Robles is the quality of its supple, deep-coloured Cabernet Sauvignons. A particularly interesting development has been the decision by the Perrin family of France, proprietors of, among other estates, Beaucastel in Châteauneuf-du-Pape, to develop a large vineyard in the Santa Lucia Mountains. Known as Tablas Creek, it is planted with Rhône varieties propagated from clones planted in their own vineyards in France. It is now supplying many other vineyards, such as the Rideau Vineyard in Santa Ynez Valley, with high-quality plant material.

The strength of Paso Robles undoubtedly lies with red grapes, notably Cabernet Sauvignon and Zinfandel. The old Zinfandel vineyards planted by the Italians and their descendants have been

yielding wonderful fruit for decades, and winemakers such as Gary
Eberle have demonstrated the excellence of the region's Cabernet.

By the end of 1998 the total acreage in Paso Robles and Edna
Valley was 13,400, divided among the following varietals: Cabernet
Sauvignon (3,650), Chardonnay (3,600), Merlot (2,000), Zinfandel
(1,730), Sauvignon Blanc (620), Syrah (390), Muscat Canelli (164),
Petite Sirah (129), Cabernet Franc (108), Sangiovese (160). There
are also small areas (fewer than 100 acres each) of Chenin Blanc,
Barbera, Gewürztraminer, Grenache, Riesling, Malbec, Marsanne,
Roussanne, Mourvèdre, Nebbiolo, Petit Verdot, Pinot Blanc, Pinot
Gris, Pinot Noir, Sémillon, and Viognier.

The region is blessed with many outstanding wineries. Meridian,
despite its size, offers some excellent wines at sensible prices.
Smaller producers with a good record for high-quality wines
include Eberle, Peachy Canyon, Adelaida Cellars, Castoro, Wild
Horse, and York Mountain.

However, there is considerable debate within the region about
whether to promote Paso Robles as a region or whether to create
and focus on subregions. At present the only subregional AVA is
York Mountain, but there is pressure from growers who own other
westside vineyards to create additional AVAs in Adelaida, Peachy
Canyon, and Templeton Gap. Essentially this is a debate between
eastsiders and westsiders. Enthusiasts for new AVAs, such as Doug
Beckett of Peachy Canyon and John Munch of Adelaida, argue
that it would help rather than denigrate the Paso Robles appellation
if high-quality sub-appellations were created. Other producers,
such as Ken Volk of Wild Horse, are opposed: 'Once Paso Robles
is firmly established, then we can go on from there. Fracturing this
AVA now would dilute the integrity of the area. It's too confusing
for people.' Tony Shumrick of Tobin James winery is even more
forthright: 'What makes Highway 101 the dividing line? It's pretty
crazy. The east-west issue is real simple; no one on the Eastside
has old vines, but the Eastside grows grapes every bit as good.
Each side has its great wines, but there's more room for growth
here on the Eastside.'[2] Clearly this is an argument that is going to
run for a long time.

York Mountain

This AVA, dating from 1983, embraces one of the oldest commercial wineries in the region, which bears the same name. It was established in 1882 by Andrew York under the name of Ascension Winery nine miles west of Templeton. These are high vineyards, planted at 1,600 to 1,800 feet. As it is only seven miles inland from the ocean, maritime influence is marked and fogs are not uncommon. Rainfall is high, usually about 45 inches annually. Elevation and ocean influences combine to put York Mountain firmly into Region I. Red varieties predominate, led by Pinot Noir and Zinfandel. Only about 30 acres are planted, and the occasional underripe flavours in the fruit may deter further expansion.

EDNA VALLEY

If maritime influence infiltrates Paso Robles only sporadically, it is a major factor in Edna Valley, a region that lies a few miles southeast of the town of San Luis Obispo. At its warmest, Edna Valley achieves a low Region II, enjoying cool summers but fairly warm springs. The terrain is fairly flat, so there is little variation between one part of the valley and another. Morning fogs are common and can be quite slow to burn off. Early afternoons can be very hot, but before too long breezes emanating from Morro Bay, fifteen miles to the northwest, cool things down. The region is sheltered by the Santa Lucia Mountains that form a border to the northeast, while to the southwest it is hemmed in by the San Luis Range. These hills form a pocket that contains the cool air once it flows into Edna Valley. However, there is nothing to impede ocean breezes from entering the valley. While Paso Robles, at least on the east side of the highway, is a very dry area, Edna Valley has fairly high humidity. Rainfall is modest, at 20 inches per year, and it mostly falls between December and March. Frost is rare, but not unknown. Ailments such as downy mildew that are absent from Paso Robles do occur here and spraying is a common safeguard. Botrytis can occur during the harvest. Chardonnay, occupying 69 per cent of the vineyards, is by far the most widely planted variety.

The soil is composed of marine sediments, a legacy from the time when this was an estuary, but there is also a good deal of volcanic soil in the form of decomposed granite and tufa as well as clay, which differentiates it from the other east-west valleys further south, such as Santa Maria and Santa Ynez, which are much sandier.

The growing season is a long one, with early bud-break and the harvest not usually beginning until late in September and often continuing into late October. Leaf removal is practised in many vineyards as a precaution against botrytis, but more often than not it does settle on some of the fruit during the autumn. A dash of botrytis is not necessarily detrimental, giving a certain honeyed richness and viscosity to fruit that is already laced through with exotic fruit aromas and flavours. Nonetheless, an outbreak of botrytis is usually a signal that harvesting should begin, and be completed as soon as possible. A style of Chardonnay that could otherwise be cloying is redeemed by the natural low pH of the grapes and a sturdy acidity that is usually retained in the wine.

Some years ago a fair amount of Pinot Noir was planted here, with the intention of using it as a component in sparkling wine. This never proved particularly successful, so acreage has diminished. However, Pinot Noir does very well in the Arroyo Grande region, where Talley have had particular success with the variety.

Although Edna Valley is thought of as a very new wine region, there were vineyards here in the nineteenth century. Vines had been planted by the San Luis Obispo mission, and the vineyards were revived in the 1860s by a Frenchman called Pierre Dallidet. Some vines survived phylloxera, but Prohibition finished them off. Like Monterey, it was recommended as a grape growing area by Amerine and Winkler back in the 1930s, but no one took up the challenge until 1968, when the county farm adviser planted an experimental vineyard. The results were thought promising once the grapes were vinified a few years later at Davis. Commercial vineyard development began in the 1970s, when the Niven family planted their Paragon Vineyard in 1973.[3] Today Paragon Vineyards, spread among seven sites, accounts for two-thirds of all Edna Valley grapes. In those days it was by no means clear which varieties would do best in Edna Valley, so there was a tendency to plant half a dozen and see what worked best. It was not long before the answer became clear: Chardonnay. Andy MacGregor followed the Nivens' example in 1975. In 1979 the Nivens, in collaboration with Richard Graff of Chalone, built a winery, Edna

Valley Vineyard, to which they supplied the grapes, which were vinified and marketed by the Chalone group. The first vintage was 1980. Edna Valley became an AVA as long ago as 1982. By 1997 there were just over 2,000 acres of vineyards in Edna Valley and Arroyo Grande, of which 459 were not yet in production.

Arroyo Grande

This subregion, which became an AVA in 1990, lies southeast from Edna Valley and their boundaries touch close to Alban vineyard. It has a more even temperature, being less windy and less subject to maritime influences, even though fog does penetrate the region. Both Laetitia and Talley have vineyards here, and some exceptional Chardonnay and Pinot Noir is produced. Further inland, in the very hot Saucelito Canyon, the eponymous winery produces some extremely robust Zinfandel. The soils are lighter than those of Edna Valley, since they contain far less clay. There are about 450 acres under vine.

VINEYARDS

Alban. Edna Valley. 53 acres of mostly Rhône varieties. Mostly used by John Alban's own winery but grapes also sold to Thackrey, Qupé, Au Bon Climat, and Sine Qua Non.

James Berry. Paso Robles. Terraced vineyards in Santa Lucia Mountains on rocky, chalky soil. Planted with Rhône varieties and Chardonnay. Grapes sold to Wild Horse and Fetzer.

Chamisal. Edna Valley. Planted in late 1970s. 30 acres Chardonnay, 30 Pinot Noir.

Corbett Canyon. Edna Valley. About 1,000 acres, mostly Chardonnay and a little Pinot Noir.

Davenport Creek. Edna Valley. Owned by Meridian. 95 acres of Chardonnay.

Dusi Ranch. Paso Robles. South of the town on the east side of Highway 101. Planted with 40 acres of Zinfandel in 1923. Grapes sold to Ridge and Peachy Canyon.

Edna Ranch. Edna Valley. Planted with 325 acres Chardonnay, 129 Pinot Noir, 17 Syrah.

Fralich. Paso Robles. Owned by Harry Fralich. Supplies Syrah and Viognier to Eberle.

French Camp. Paso Robles. Owned by Hank Ashby. Sells Sauvignon Blanc, Chardonnay and Muscat Canelli to Fess Parker, Pesenti, and Page Mill.

Hoffman Mountain Ranch (HMR). Paso Robles. Planted in Santa Lucia Mountains at 1,500 feet by Dr Stanley Hoffman. 63 acres, including 24 of Pinot Noir. Sold by Hoffman family in 1982 and the current owner is the Van Steenwyck family of Adelaida winery.

Lewis. Edna Valley. 7 acres Chardonnay.

MacGregor. Edna Valley. 62 acres Chardonnay and 1 Pinot Noir. The grapes are sold to Mount Eden, Leeward, Karly, Morgan, Windermere, Hart's Desire, and Piedra Creek.

Mission View. Paso Robles. 40 acres planted 1981–83. 11 acres Chardonnay, 10 Zinfandel, 7 Cabernet Sauvignon, 5 Sauvignon Blanc, 3 Muscat Canelli, and 2 each of Merlot and Cabernet Franc. Clay loam soil. Grapes used by Mission View winery and sold to Adelaida, York Mountain, and Castoro.

Paragon. Edna Valley. Owned by the Niven family. Planted from 1973 onwards with 553 acres Chardonnay, 50 Sauvignon Blanc, 106 Cabernet Sauvignon, 115 Pinot Noir, 15 Pinot Gris, 5 Sémillon, and 11 Syrah. Now 1,000 acres. Much of the crop went to Edna Valley Vineyards, and in 1996 a partnership was formed with the Southcorp corporation of Australia. Sells Chardonnay to Rosenblum and Pinot Noir to Wild Horse as well as supplying fruit to Southcorp's Seven Peaks range.

Perata. Paso Robles, west of Highway 101. Planted with Cabernet Sauvignon and Merlot. Grapes sold to Wild Horse.

Piccho. Arroyo Grande. Owned by Laetitia. 67 acres Chardonnay, 48 Pinot Blanc, 65 Pinot Noir.

Ranchita Canyon. Paso Robles. Sells Zinfandel and Petite Sirah to David Bruce.

Salaal. Edna Valley. Planted with 18 acres Chardonnay, 6 Pinot Noir.

Saucelito Canyon. Arroyo Grande. Planted with 8 acres Zinfandel, 1 acre Cabernet Sauvignon.

Richard Sauret. Paso Robles. 5 acres of Zinfandel planted in 1972. Grapes sold to Byington, Rosenblum and Eberle.

Steinbeck. Paso Robles. Supplies Syrah to Eberle.

Talley. Arroyo Grande. Divided between the 77-acre Rincon Vineyard, and the slightly cooler 15-acre Rosemary's Vineyard. Planted mostly with Pinot Noir and Chardonnay. Most fruit used in the Talley winery but also sells to Au Bon Climat, Ojai, and Babcock.

Twin Hills. Paso Robles. Sells Zinfandel to Pavona.

Weir Ranch. Edna Valley. Planted with 15 acres Chardonnay.

NOTES

1 Leon D. Adams, *The Wines of America*, p. 389
2 Kathy Marcks Hardesty, 'Everything's Not Peachy', *New Times*, 1998
3 Gerald Asher, *Vineyard Tales*, pp. 25–30

10

Santa Barbara and the South Coast

Although Santa Barbara County has rapidly developed a fine reputation for its wines, it is a newcomer among California wine regions, while the largely forgotten southern California vineyards around Los Angeles were once more significant economically than those of the North Coast.

As at Paso Robles, Monterey, and Sonoma to the north, the Spanish mission brought viticulture to the county in the 1780s, but by 1810 it had faded out. In 1885 French immigrants planted a 150-acre vineyard on Santa Cruz Island off the coast near Santa Barbara, but with Prohibition that too went into terminal decline. Then in the 1960s the professors of UC Davis identified Santa Barbara as a viticultural region of fine potential. Growers and winemakers driven out of Santa Clara by inexorable urban expansion or unable to afford vineyards in Napa and Sonoma, looked southwards instead. Pierre Lafond began his Santa Barbara Winery in 1972 and Uriel Nielsen planted a vineyard in Santa Maria Valley. In 1969 there were a mere 11 acres under vine in the county, but soon, in the early 1970s, such wineries as Zaca Mesa, Firestone, and Rancho Sisquoc were setting up in Santa Maria and Santa Ynez valleys. For the most part these were large-scale farming operations rather than boutique wineries. As in Monterey, some of the largest vineyards were established as tax loopholes. Santa Barbara County was still ranching country, and viticulture, for all the Davis assurances, was an unknown quantity.

Inevitably many wrong choices were made. Few of those original plantings from the 1970s survived once growers realized the errors of their ways. At Zaca Mesa almost all the original vines were grafted over to other varieties, most recently the Rhône varieties that seem to do well here. In the 1980s and 1990s large players such as Mondavi and Kendall-Jackson bought up some of the largest vineyards, which may have been bad news for some of the small wineries that could no longer obtain grapes from them, but it did help raise the reputation and credibility of the region as a whole. Beringer/Meridian now own over 3,000 acres, Kendall-Jackson 2,515, and Mondavi 1,709 acres. Not surprisingly, small wineries were none too pleased when vineyards such as Sierra Madre, which had formerly sold them grapes on a regular basis, cut back heavily on such external sales. The very large vineyards have focused on Chardonnay, which certainly does well in Santa Barbara (by 1995 prices per ton were higher in Santa Barbara than in Sonoma), but 55 per cent of those grapes go to wineries based further north, leaving locally based wineries to concentrate on finely tuned expressions of such tricky grapes as Arneis, Marsanne, Pinot Noir or whatever else takes their fancy. Average yields are 4.4 tons per acre.

Almost all vineyards were planted on their own roots, which means that the vines have few defences against the threat of phylloxera, which became apparent in 1992. Subsequent plantings have, of course, been on resistant rootstocks. Growers have also taken advantage of up-to-date thinking on close spacing, with vines planted at 1,200 stocks per acre, which, it is hoped, will give greater intensity. By 1998 almost 11,000 acres had been planted in the county, mostly in the Santa Maria and Santa Ynez valleys. Chardonnay is planted on 7,000 acres, Pinot Noir on 1,200, with Cabernet Sauvignon and Merlot level at about 500 each. There are about forty wineries in operation, most of them in SantaYnez Valley. White varieties account for three-quarters of the plantings. In general the climate has proved too cool for Cabernet Sauvignon, which easily develops a herbaceous quality. Pinot Noir performs much better, and wineries such as Au Bon Climat, Sanford, and Byron have enjoyed tremendous success with their bottlings. The secret of Santa Barbara's success would appear to lie in the fruit's admirable structure. There is no difficulty, in general, in obtaining very ripe fruit, yet at the same time acidities remain very high, while pH is low, often registering 3.0 to 3.2.

The climate is very distinctive. Winters tend to be mild, even warm; springs more so. Bud-break is very early, at least a month earlier than other cool-climate regions such as Carneros and Russian River Valley. Rainfall is minimal, at about 12 inches annually, so irrigation is essential. During the summer months, fog rolls in from the Pacific through the east-west valleys in which the vines are planted and it tends to swathe the vineyards until mid-morning. Although this cools down the vineyards, it also brings a risk of mildew. Summer afternoons can be very hot, yet harvesting is relatively late, giving a very long growing season that brings the fruit to complete maturity without plummeting acidity.

Those who have committed themselves to the region, such as Jim Clendenen of Au Bon Climat, are convinced that the best is yet to come. The early vineyards were not always well laid out, and with exposure to the sun blocked by sprawling canopies, wines often turned out green and vegetal. That lesson has been learnt. Equally important, those developing vineyards in the 1990s are much more aware of the different clones available and their individual qualities. In the 1970s growers simply planted what was on offer from UC Davis. 'That plant material,' Clendenen told me, 'tended to be boring and over-productive. Some growers admit they don't even know what clones they planted twenty years ago. It wasn't that much of an issue. This is true of Chardonnay as well as Pinot Noir. What amazes me is that even with such mediocre material we were still able to make some very good wines – thanks to the astonishing climate of Santa Barbara. Nowadays we are planting on hillside sites with much more attention to spacing and canopy and clones and irrigation, so I'm convinced that the wines we'll be producing in a few years' time will be fabulous.'

Santa Maria Valley

Just south of the county line that separates San Luis Obispo County from Santa Barbara County to the south is the town of Santa Maria. To the east of town lies the Santa Maria Valley AVA, which was approved in 1981. This is usually the coolest of the Santa Barbara wine regions. The region is blocked to the northeast by the Santa Maria Bench, which forms part of the foothills of the Sierra Madre, and the best vineyards tend to be located along these once grassy benchlands, facing southwest. Many are planted at an elevation of between 300 feet, the height of the valley floor, and 800 feet. The valley runs from east to west and is thus open to maritime influences, especially during the afternoon, since the Pacific lies about ten miles west of the town. Rainfall is sparse, averaging about 15 inches. Spring frosts can be a problem. Irrigation is essential, given the absence of summer rains. Not all the valley is Region I. Some of the more easterly parts are slightly warmer, but overall the average temperature during the growing season is a very moderate 74 degrees.[1] The soils are of marine origin, with much sandy loam and clay loam, the proportion of sand diminishing inland. Sand in the soil can retain heat well, which can be an advantage when the maritime influence threatens to become excessive. Drainage is good.

The first vineyards in modern times were those planted in 1964 by Uriel Nielsen, who sold much of his Riesling, Chardonnay and Cabernet Sauvignon to Christian Brothers in Napa Valley. Before Nielsen came along, the advice from UC Davis was that Santa Maria Valley was too cool for grape production. But he planted the Wente clone of Chardonnay and enjoyed considerable success with his fruit. Many of the subsequent vineyards, planned as large-scale commercial enterprises that would appeal to a northern market that proved somewhat fickle, experienced financial difficulties in the 1980s, and some were repossessed by the banks. This gave some northern wineries an ideal opportunity to purchase vineyards which by that time had an impressive track record. There are some very large vineyards here, such as Tepusquet and Camelot and White Hills, which appealed to large out-of-county wineries such as Mondavi, Beringer, and Kendall-Jackson, who are now the major proprietors in the valley. Kendall-Jackson are particularly proud of the Tepusquet Vineyard, which they have described as 'the filet mignon of Chardonnay'. In all, there are some 7,500 acres in production in Santa Maria Valley.

Not everyone admires the fruit quality from Santa Maria. The Chardonnay can certainly have a tropical-fruit character, familiar to devotees of Australian Chardonnay. But at its best, as from Byron, this exotic hallmark is kept in check by a lively acidity and fresh mouthfeel. Sometimes there is a touch of botrytis, as the valley occasionally experiences autumnal storms that can provoke noble rot. Nonetheless, that is rare, and it is unusual to find the viscosity of some Edna Valley Chardonnays in the same variety from the Santa Maria Valley. It is also possible, again in certain vintages only, to detect a slightly vegetal quality in the Pinot Noir, which Steve Test, formerly of Stonestreet winery and not an admirer of the variety here, describes as a stewed tomato flavour.

In my experience, this is becoming increasingly rare, thankfully, now that growers have learnt how to ripen this exceptionally tricky variety. It is unlikely that the Rhône varieties will ever supplant the ever-popular Chardonnay, but there is no doubt by now that Santa Maria is very well suited to such varieties as Syrah, Viognier, and Marsanne, as wineries such as Qupé have amply demonstrated.

Santa Ynez Valley

Like the Santa Maria Valley, the Santa Ynez was developed in the early 1970s, and acquired its AVA in 1983, by which time 1,200 acres had been planted. For some years the valley has accommodated ranch retreats belonging to the likes of Michael Jackson, and tacky tourist development has seen farm towns such as Solvang distorted into undignified but no doubt profitable theme parks. But Santa Ynez is large enough to handle such incursions without losing its rural character. Today there are about 1,500 acres under vine. The valley is separated from the Santa Maria Valley to the north by the San Rafael Mountains. It is quite a large region, beginning just east of Lomboc, and fanning eastwards for some twenty miles or so, embracing the course of the Santa Ynez River and encompassing the towns of Solvang and Buellton, as well as Santa Ynez itself. The eastern boundary of the region is Lake Cachuma. Richard Sanford, one of the most experienced growers of the region, says that as a rule of thumb you lose a degree of average temperature per mile as you move westwards from Santa Ynez.

As a whole, Santa Ynez Valley is mostly a cool Region II, although the most westerly vineyards, between Buellton and Lomboc, can be distinctly cold. However, unlike parts of the Santa Maria Valley, spring frost is not a danger here. Rain tends to fall from December to May, and the annual average is 18 inches. Fog can penetrate quite a long way to the east, acting as a powerful moderating influence, especially during the summer months. When it persists into the autumn, it can bring mildew and botrytis to the ripening vines. Many of the best-known vineyards lie north of Santa Ynez, where it can become quite warm. This is an exceptionally pretty part of the county, and in its undulating hills there is a seamless blend of ranching and vineyard land. The soils are very varied clay loams and shaly clay loams, although mostly of marine origin. Drainage is uniformly excellent. Elevation varies, from 200 feet close to the river to as high as 1,500 feet up in the San Rafael Mountains.

Although white grapes such as Chardonnay, Sauvignon Blanc, and Riesling thrive best here, there have always been red grapes, especially in the eastern and northeastern sections of the valley. But it's not easy to grow the Bordeaux varieties here, in particular Cabernet Sauvignon, and Pinot Noir tends to be more successful; the Sanford & Benedict Vineyard has an outstanding and richly deserved reputation for this variety. Not surprisingly, the early plantings throughout the valley were hit and miss, especially given the wide variety of microclimates. I recall tasting many Sauvignon Blanc and Cabernet Franc wines in the late 1980s and early 1990s that were distinctly vegetal, but growers such as Frederic Brander assure me that this was a question of viticulture rather than climate, and considerable efforts have been made to correct this character. Yields vary greatly, and although in some locations the soil and spacing keep yields admirably low – Richard Sanford records about 2.5 tons per acre for his Pinot Noir – it is not unusual for Chardonnay to be cropped at 6 tons, and Cabernet Sauvignon at 4–6 tons.

Los Alamos Valley

A less conspicuous player in Santa Barbara County compared to the Santa Maria and Santa Ynez valleys which lie, respectively, to its north and south, Los Alamos has nonetheless acquired a reputation for Pinot Noir of high quality and for Chardonnay with high acidity. It is almost as cool as Santa Maria Valley, and with over 3,000 acres under vine, is more significant in terms of production than Santa Ynez. The reason for its obscurity is its lack of an AVA, so that its wines have to be sold under the plain Santa Barbara County appellation. Chardonnay is the dominant variety, and thousands of acres were planted in the late 1990s. Meridian is the major proprietor, with 2,300 acres at White Hills Vineyard, and Kendall-Jackson cultivates 1,300 acres, of which 700 are now in production.

In 1998 the BATF invited views on the possible creation of a further AVA to be called Santa Rita Hills in the western part of

Santa Ynez Valley; it would include 500 acres of vineyard and plantable land.

SOUTH COAST

The missionaries were the first wine producers in Los Angeles County, establishing wineries at their outposts at San Gabriel and San Fernando. Private producers followed, notably Jean Louis Vignes and then Andrew Boyle, after whom Boyle Heights is named. The first mayor of Los Angeles, Benjamin Davis Wilson, owned a substantial vineyard in the 1850s. Los Angeles County soon became one of the nineteenth-century heartlands of wine production, and fifty years ago there were still about fifty wineries in operation. Most of them produced the sweet and fortified wines that dominated the market before World War II. There were also extensive vineyards near Anaheim, a town founded by Utopian German settlers who planted vines. Pierce's Disease wiped out these vines in 1884, and nowadays there are neither vines nor oranges in Anaheim, which is now associated more with Disney than with agriculture. Even further south, in San Diego County, there were vineyards too, and a small AVA survives at San Pasqual.

By 1910 there were 37,000 acres of vineyards throughout southern California, and by 1939 5,000 acres were still in production within Los Angeles County alone.[2] Today the total acreage for the South Coast is just over 3,000 acres, with Chardonnay dominating. Despite the climate, which is a warm Region III, less than 20 per cent of the acreage is planted with red varieties. Northwest of Los Angeles, Ventura County has a few acres of vines divided between Ojai and Leeward wineries.[3] Avocados now grow where vines used to thrive. Due east of Los Angeles lies San Bernardino County, which also used to be a large wine-producing area centred on Cucamonga. The first vineyards were established in this hot region in 1838. Zinfandel was widely planted here in the 1880s, and by the time Prohibition was enacted there were 20,000 acres of vines in San Bernardino County, exceeding those of either Napa or Sonoma. In the 1920s Secundo Guasti planted a 6,000-acre vineyard which was at that time the largest in the world. However the region is in decline, thanks to unsuccessful efforts to compete with cheap mass-production wines from the San

Joaquin Valley as well as to suburban expansion, and Joseph Filippi is the only winery still operating in the county, mopping up about half the region's grape production. Cucamonga became an AVA in 1985.

If I were inventing a vineyard for purposes of parody, I would probably locate it in Bel-Air, a suburb of Los Angeles even more exclusive than Beverley Hills. Property prices are so high here – about $7 million per acre – that even a modest villa will cost a few million dollars. Moreover, the precipitous canyon terrain seems far from ideal for viticulture. Nonetheless Tom Jones, who acquired his house and land in Bel-Air before prices went through the roof, has planted a 15-acre Bordeaux red-variety vineyard here. His estate, Moraga, has an exceptional microclimate and has produced some superb Cabernets, which sell for impressive prices.

San Pasqual

Created in 1991, this small AVA about ten miles from the Pacific has a mere 75 acres of vines. Not surprisingly, given its southern location, this is a warm region. No winery exists within the region.

Temecula

A hot AVA, verging on Region IV, Temecula, which lies within Riverside County roughly midway between Los Angeles and San Diego to the south, is differentiated from the baking climate of the Central Valley by elevation, as the vineyards are planted at 1,500 feet, and by some marine influence from the Pacific Ocean some twenty miles to the west, and indeed from cool air descending at night from the nearby Santa Ana Mountains. The days are very warm indeed, but the breeze fans through during the afternoon, and at night the temperature can plummet by 40 degrees or more. Ely Callaway of the eponymous winery was convinced that slotting Temecula into a Region III or IV was misleading, as there were microclimatic influences which increased the area's suitability for viticulture. The AVA was approved in 1984.

Rainfall is sparse, with an average of 16 inches annually, most of it falling between December and May. The soils, which are of decomposed granite, are well drained. But erosion has always been a major headache, especially when a storm deposits a slick of water on the land in a short time. There were vineyards here in the nineteenth century, but the major development in the twentieth was the establishment of Rancho California by the land developer Kaiser-Aetna in the mid-1960s. Prohibition had disposed of the existing vineyards, so Rancho California had to make a fresh start, creating a vast 90,000-acre property development that included housing, farms, and a man-made lake. Five-hundred-foot wells were sunk to provide the water for all this development. The vineyards were planted in blocks and then sold by the corporation to wineries and potential wineries. This is where the well-known Callaway winery is based, having been founded here in 1969. Chardonnay is the dominant variety here, giving broad rich wines that can lack the acidity encountered in the variety when grown in Santa Barbara. Sauvignon Blanc and Riesling are also produced, and there is a growing proportion of red wines such as Cabernet and Syrah. Humidity is quite high, and botrytis not uncommon.

Callaway was convinced that the maturation of the grapes in Temecula was significantly slowed down by the maritime breezes and by the strength of the winds. In addition the vineyards were often coated in a blanket of coastal mist which moderated the sun's radiation. He observed that in 1975 they picked their Cabernet on November 18 and 19, and could afford to prolong the hang-time because it hardly ever rained at harvest time.[4]

Framed by the vast conurbations of southern California, Temecula and its wineries are sustained by tourist traffic, and some of its wineries are well equipped to profit from it. Many of the wines contain a dollop of sweetness, which no doubt increases their superficial appeal. In the long term it seems likely that Mediterranean varieties will do better in Temecula than the traditional French varieties. Some 7,000 acres of land planted with citrus fruit, as well as 2,500 acres of vineyards, have been set aside as a kind of agricultural preserve. A vote in 2005 will decide whether that land will remain agricultural or be turned over to the ever hungry property developers.

VINEYARDS

Los Alamos. Los Alamos Hills. Owned by Kendall-Jackson. 532 acres (430 Chardonnay, 77 Syrah, 15 Pinot Noir, 10 Merlot).

Bien Nacido. Santa Maria. Owned by Thornhill Ranches. 900 acres mostly planted from 1973 on the north side of the valley. Planted with Chardonnay (300 acres), Pinot Noir (200), Riesling, Pinot Blanc, Cabernet Sauvignon, Merlot, and Syrah. Sells to many wineries, including Au Bon Climat, Byron, Foxen, Fess Parker, Santa Barbara Winery, Whitcraft, Bonny Doon, Gary Farrell, Fetzer, Lane Tanner, Hess, Qupé, Steele, Ojai, Page Mill, Testarossa, Wild Horse, Villa Mt Eden, and Bernardus.

Buttonwood Farm. Santa Ynez. Owned by Betty Williams. 39 acres planted in the mid-1980s north of Solvang. Varieties include Cabernet Sauvignon, Cabernet Franc, Merlot, Sauvignon Blanc, and Sémillon. Grapes sold to Babcock, Gainey, Ojai, Wild Horse and others.

Camelot. Santa Maria. 206 acres of Chardonnay planted on varied soils in 1970. Owned since 1987 by Kendall-Jackson.

Cat Canyon. Los Alamos. Owned by Beringer/Meridian. 372 acres.

Daly. Santa Ynez. 13 acres of Cabernet Sauvignon and Cabernet Franc.

Gold Coast. Santa Maria. Planted 1993. Sells Chardonnay and Pinot Noir to Au Bon Climat and Costa de Oro.

Huber. Santa Ynez. 14 acres of Chardonnay.

Mission Trails. Los Alamos. Acquired in 1995 by Kendall-Jackson and planted in 1996. Sandy loam soil. 438 acres Chardonnay. 44 acres Pinot Noir.

Mount Carmel. Santa Ynez. Owned by the Carmelite order. 20 acres of Chardonnay and Pinot Noir. Sells to Babcock.

Morehouse. Santa Ynez. Sells Syrah to Foxen.

Nielsen. The oldest vineyard in the county, planted by Uriel Nielsen in 1964. Bought by Byron in 1989.

Fess Parker. Santa Ynez. Owned by Fess Parker winery but also sells Viognier and Syrah to Rosenblum, Jeff Cohn and Villa Mt Eden.

Rancho Dos Mondos. Santa Ynez. Planted in eastern part of the valley with Chardonnay. Grapes sold to Babcock.

Rancho San Antonio. Santa Maria. 2,000 acres, mostly Chardonnay, now owned by Beringer.

Sanford & Benedict. Santa Ynez. Planted in 1971 west of Buellton. 139 acres, with 90 Chardonnay, 40 Pinot Noir, 2 Merlot, and small quantities of Pinot Gris, Nebbiolo, and Viognier. Deep clay loam soil. Density varies from 600 to 1,089 vines per acre. Owned by Richard Sanford, who vinifies much of the crop at his winery (see p. 595) and also sells to Au Bon Climat, Kynsi, Gainey, and Foxen.

Santa Maria. Santa Maria. Planted with Chardonnay and Pinot Noir. Grapes sold to Babcock, Wild Horse, and Sanford.

Sierra Madre. Santa Maria. 640 acres planted from 1979 onwards just east of the town of Santa Maria. Until 1996, when it was acquired by Mondavi, it supplied Chardonnay, Riesling, Sauvignon Blanc, Pinot Noir and Syrah to many wineries, including Lane Tanner, Byron, Sanford, Fiddlehead, John Kerr, Zaca Mesa, Fess Parker, Qupé, and Wild Horse. Now almost all the grapes will be used by Mondavi and Byron.

Stolpman. Santa Ynez. Sells Grenache and Mourvèdre to Jaffurs and Santa Barbara Winery, and Sangiovese and Syrah to Vita Nova.

Sweeney Canyon. Santa Ynez. 18 acres of Chardonnay.

Tepusquet. Santa Maria. Planted 1967. A 4-mile long vineyard of 1,340 acres, mostly Chardonnay, also Syrah, jointly acquired by Kendall-Jackson (1,000 acres) and Mondavi (340 acres). Kendall-Jackson own the rights to the vineyard name.

White Hills. Los Alamos. 2,300 acres due south of Santa Maria. Owned by Beringer/Meridian.

Charlotte Young. Santa Ynez. Close to Los Olivos. Supplies Marsanne to Qupé.

NOTES

1 James Halliday, *Wines Atlas of California*, p. 346
2 Leon D. Adams, *The Wines of America*, pp. 395–8
3 Halliday, p. 368
4 Robert Benson, *Great Winemakers of California*, p. 286

11

The Sierra Foothills and
the Central Valley

This chapter deals with the inland wine regions of California, but it should not be supposed that the Sierra Foothills, with its ancient Zinfandel vineyards, has anything in common with the agribusiness ranches of the Central Valley. They are grouped together here for the practical reason that there is not enough to say about the Central Valley in terms of history, geology or climate to justify a chapter to itself. So I hope the distinguished old Zinfandels will forgive me for putting them in the same pannier as Thompson Seedless.

SIERRA FOOTHILLS

East from the state capital of Sacramento rise the foothills of the mighty Sierra Nevada, which tourists traverse on their way to Lake Tahoe or Yosemite Valley, Reno or Carson City. But in the nineteenth century it was the backdrop for the Gold Rush, which was focused on the so-called 'Mother Lode' in the foothills. The Gold Rush lasted only a few years, so many of those who had come here settled and began farming. Since many of them were Italians, Spanish, or French, it was instinctive for them to plant grapes as well, and viticulture thrived. Driving through the back roads of Shenandoah Valley, I came cross Winzerhof Road, a reminder that German settlers came here too.

Vineyards were established in three counties: Amador, El Dorado, and Calaveras, and in a few outlying areas. In all, the Foothills stretch for over 150 miles from Yuba City down to Sonora. Two northerly extensions of the region are Nevada and North Yuba, the latter an area thus far colonized by a single winery,

Renaissance. Here along the western slopes of the Sierra Nevada the soils are volcanic, with much decomposed granite, and tend to be less fertile than those closer to the coast. Mission was the original grape, and a few patches still survive, but it was soon supplanted by Zinfandel and other robust red varieties. Already in 1860 Shenandoah Valley in Amador County was more significant than Napa Valley in terms of grape production. Expansion was very rapid, and by the 1880s 10,000 acres had been planted, with about 100 small wineries dotting the hills. Much the same was true in El Dorado County, where there were 10,000 acres and sixty operating wineries. Predictably, Prohibition finished off this region as far as wine production was concerned, and only the D'Agostini winery (today the Sobon winery) was still in business after Repeal. By 1965, only 720 acres were still in production.[1] The first new wineries created after Repeal were Monteviña and Boeger in 1972, followed by Stevenot the year after. The acreage has grown to about 3,800, with 2,000 of Zinfandel, and there are about forty wineries.

The Sierra Foothills retain a certain rusticity, which is part of their charm, and the residents of Murphys and Placerville have not been slow to capitalize on their associations with the Gold Rush. Although some of the wineries are off the beaten track, many work hard to attract the traffic going to and from the numerous resorts of the Sierras. The hilly terrain favours small family wineries, which is exactly what one finds. The oldest existing winery here is the former D'Agostini stone winery of 1856 in Shenandoah Valley, which Leon Sobon has converted into a museum and tasting room. Almost as venerable is the former Lombardo Fassati winery of 1860 in El Dorado County, which is now the tasting room of the Boeger winery.

It's a hot region in summer, and the unreliable heat summation system places the Foothills as a whole as a Region III/IV, although given the huge variety of elevations and exposures, it is dangerous to generalize. Dick Bush, the founder of Madroña in El Dorado, gives credit for the revival of viticulture in the Foothills to Dick Bethel, who was the University of California farm adviser in the region, advising growers on what and how to plant. It is a complicated region to understand, with a climate severely moderated by the cold air that flows down from the Sierra at night. The lowest vineyards are at 1,000 feet, and the highest close to 3,000. The

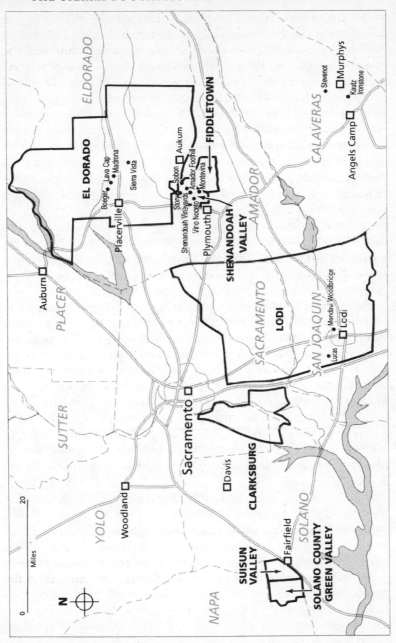

Sierra Foothills

153

winter can be protracted and spring frosts a danger, although some believe the presence of large reservoirs in the hills has a moderating influence on the spring climate. In general the harvest begins about two weeks later than along the North Coast. Although the Foothills are best known for their Zinfandels, other varieties such as Barbera, Sangiovese, Syrah, Merlot, and Cabernet Sauvignon are cultivated with growing success. The soils up here are poor and the vines must struggle to survive, giving the grapes intense flavours. At the same time the substantial rainfall allows for quite good yields even from dry-farmed vineyards at a high elevation. In general, the wineries and their clients seem more open to lesser-known varieties than in Napa or Sonoma. There are also some formidable port-style wines and delicious Muscats.

Zinfandel probably owes its survival in the Sierra Foothills to Darrell Corti. When producers started searching for late harvest Zinfandel grapes, this influential wine merchant pointed the way to Amador County. Bob Trinchero of Sutter Home was one of the Napa producers who, on the basis of a Deaver Vineyard wine made in the mid-1960s by Charles Myers of Harbor Winery in Sacramento, was quick to recognize the quality of old Amador Zinfandel. In 1968 Sutter Home vinified the Deaver grapes for Corti's shop. Sutter Home's Zinfandels were a great success, and led eventually to an explosion in the production of white Zinfandel by this winery; in 1988 Trinchero went so far as to purchase the Monteviña winery.

John Kautz, the owner of Ironstone and one of the major grape growers in California, told me that the Foothills are not suited to the production of inky blockbusters such as one would find in Napa or Sonoma. He sees the future in 'fruit-driven wines' that are ready to drink on release. It is true that the Foothills are full of small family wineries rather than ambitious 'high-end' wineries, but I think Kautz, whose own winery does indeed focus on fruity, easily accessible wines, is playing down the true potential of the region. Wineries such as Madroña and Renwood have for some years been releasing rich, powerfully structured wines that, while far from inaccessible, are by no means lacking in grip and ageing potential.

North Yuba

This AVA, defined in 1988, is synonymous with Renaissance, a magnificent terraced vineyard planted at 1,700 to 2,300 feet. Rainfall is comparable to that of El Dorado County to the south, at 37 inches per year. The soils are rocky and well drained, and seem well adapted to a variety of grapes, notably Sauvignon Blanc and Riesling. There were vineyards in Yuba County in the 1850s, and by 1930 1,000 acres were under vine, but the vineyards were replaced by orchards until 1973 when the Renaissance project brought grapes back to the landscape. Today there are 365 acres under vine, all belonging to Renaissance.

El Dorado

This AVA, created in 1983, is planted with about 1,000 acres and is home to sixteen wineries. All vineyards are above 1,400 feet and most are considerably higher. Most vineyards and wineries lie just east and southeast of Placerville and around Somerset. The Boeger family was responsible for the revival of viticulture here; before the founding of their estate in 1972 there were a mere 12 acres in production. The county was far better known for its Bartlett pears, cherries, apples, and Christmas trees, and still grows them all. The soils are deep, granitic, and well-drained, but erode easily and often require terracing and cover crops to keep them in place. At night the temperature can drop to the forties, even in summer, and the cool mountain air often wraps the slopes until the late morning, although frost is rarely a threat. According to the heat summation system, this is a Region II/III. The coolest, and wettest, vineyards, are the highest, which are those belonging to Madroña at close to 3,000 feet. Thus the grapes retain high acidity, even though there is no problem ripening them. Irrigation is quite common despite the county as a whole enjoying an average rainfall of 36 inches. Zinfandel from El Dorado has a different character to that from Amador, lacking the latter's baked and often raisiny dimension and showing more freshness and elegance. Some growers feel that Merlot rather than Cabernet Sauvignon has a good future here, as do the increasingly fashionable Italian varieties. El Dorado is also a good source of Sauvignon Blanc.

Amador County

This region, though not an AVA, is the heartland of the Sierra Foothills, and the source of its oldest Zinfandel vineyards, some of which were already in existence in the early 1850s, though they have not survived. But centenarian vineyards are by no means rare in Amador, and fortunately they have not yet been attacked by phylloxera. High rainfall allows the vineyards to be dry-farmed. Unlike El Dorado, Amador can be prone to spring frosts, and Zinfandel, which begins its growing season relatively late, is well adapted to such risks, since its buds are less precocious than those of other varieties. The soils, as elsewhere in the Foothills, are of decomposed granite. It can be very hot in Amador County, with temperatures sometimes high enough to push corners of the region into Region IV, which may account for the raisiny, tarry quality of some Amador Zinfandel. On the other hand the cool nights common to the whole of the Sierra Foothills help the grapes retain their acidity. Outstanding years for the county have been 1980, 1984, 1987, 1990, 1993, and 1995.

The region is on a roll. By the mid-1990s there were about 2,000 acres under vine. About 350 more were planted in 1996, and slightly more the following year. Zinfandel is the major variety, followed by Sauvignon Blanc and Barbera. It is widely accepted that Amador is too warm for Chardonnay.

There are two AVAs within Amador County: Shenandoah Valley and Fiddletown (see below). Shenandoah lies in the northwest of the county; Fiddletown borders it to the southeast. In terms of acreage Shenandoah is by far the more significant, with about 1,200 acres planted.

Fiddletown

A high-lying region within Amador County, with vineyards between 1,500 and 2,500 feet. It became an AVA in 1983. Rainfall is also higher than elsewhere, averaging about 40 inches. The Zinfandel is of very good quality, and slightly less robust than from other parts of the county, which may be no bad thing. There were about 300 acres planted in 1998, and given the roughness of most of the terrain, major expansion is unlikely.

Shenandoah Valley

Shenandoah, which became an AVA in 1983 and is partly in El Dorado as well as Amador County, experiences snowy winters, but warm springs help the grapes to evolve steadily, while cool air coming down from the Sierra at night during summer keeps acidity levels high. This is the site of the Foothills' oldest surviving Zinfandel vineyard, the Grandpère, which was planted near Plymouth in the 1860s and is still largely intact. Until the late 1960s the Zinfandel crop from these old vineyards ended up in jug wines, some of which were probably of sensational quality. Then, as we have seen, Darrell Corti and Bob Trinchero rediscovered the intrinsic quality of these old sites, and it wasn't long before other wineries followed their example. Mayacamas, Carneros Creek, and other wineries were soon buying Amador fruit. This encouraged growers to expand their vineyards, and now there are over 1,300 acres planted in the valley. It's not only Zinfandel that thrives here. There are some splendid Muscats, and the Rhône varieties and Sauvignon Blanc also do well. However, Shenandoah does not seem ideal for Bordeaux reds.

Calaveras County

Calaveras County, with about 250 acres of vines, lies just south of Amador County and in terms of climate is slightly cooler, allowing some good-quality whites, mostly Chardonnay and Sauvignon Blanc, to be produced. Nonetheless Calaveras County shouldn't be compared with Monterey – it is still a high Region II. Zinfandel is also grown. The soils are volcanic, although limestone is also encountered. The Stevenot winery began the revival of winemaking here in 1978, although these days it is being outshone by Kautz Ironstone, which is easily the most impressive showcase winery in the Foothills. However, the Kautz family owns thousands of acres in other regions, so only a few of their wines are made from Foothills fruit.

Nevada

No, not the state better known for gambling and brothels, but a small region to the north of Placerville. The 130 acres of vineyards are located at an elevation of 1,500–1,800 feet, and a number of small, family-owned wineries operate in the area. Villa Mount Eden, based in Napa Valley, buy some Syrah from Nevada and speak well of the region. Chardonnay is the dominant variety.

LODI

Properly speaking, Lodi is part of the Central Valley, the town and the vineyards lying south of Sacramento within Sacramento and San Joaquin counties. In recent years it has assumed sufficient importance to be worthy of a detailed entry to itself. It was already an important grape growing region in the 1880s, and remains highly significant, primarily in terms of quantity, but also in terms of the quality of which it is clearly capable. In 1996 Lodi grapes constituted 16 per cent of the entire California crop, including 32 per cent of the state's Zinfandel, 27 per cent of its Cabernet Sauvignon, 25 per cent of its Merlot, 19 per cent of its Sauvignon Blanc, and 16 per cent of its Chardonnay.

In the nineteenth century Lodi was best known for its sweet wines. Captain Charles Weber, who founded the town of Stockton, is believed to have been the first to plant vines in the region, in the early 1850s. Planting expanded quite rapidly, mostly under the aegis of German grape farmers, who set up cooperatives to vinify the production. The principal varieties were Mission, various Muscats, Zinfandel, and the fleshy, red-skinned Flame Tokay, which was primarily grown as a tough-skinned table grape that was easily transported to all parts of the country. It could also be used to produce fortified wines and brandies. By the early years of the twentieth century the Lodi district was responsible for producing one-quarter of California's grapes, both table and wine grapes. A cooperative known as the Woodbridge Vineyard Association handled much of the wine production. Not even Prohibition managed to break Lodi's stride, since the grapes were sold to eager home winemakers, and by 1940 the region was still producing one-fifth of the state's wines, although most of them were fortified.[2] Palomino was the basis of 'sherry', Zinfandel of 'port'.

Unfortunately the viticultural set-up in Lodi was not well adapted to cope with the changes that took place throughout the 1960s, as the overall quality of California's wines began to mount steeply. Although the Lodi vineyards had survived Prohibition, the wineries had not, and Lodi had become little more than a source of inexpensive grapes. Almost all the winemaking there was undertaken by cooperatives. The market for sweet and fortified wines slumped, and the dominant grape varieties, such as Flame Tokay, were no longer in demand. Lodi had become the foremost American producer of sherry-style wines just when such wines fell from fashion. Moreover, as a table grape Flame Tokay had been superseded by the Flame Seedless variety. Many wineries and cooperatives collapsed.

It was the Gallo family that came to Lodi's rescue in the 1960s. Growers stuck with unwanted grape varieties such as Alicante Bouschet, Palomino, Carignane, and Flame Tokay were easily persuaded to plant varieties to which Gallo was committing itself with long-term contracts. Gallo were also prepared to reward growers with bonuses for those who provided fruit of above-average quality. Varieties such as Barbera, Zinfandel, French Colombard, and Chenin Blanc began to replace the old standbys. Nonetheless, as recently as 1985 Flame Tokay still represented an astonishing 41 per cent of the surface under vine.

Gallo was not the only large-scale winery to take a keen interest in Lodi. The Mondavis originated in Lodi, where the young Robert had attended the local high school. As the Napa-based Robert Mondavi contemplated expansion, he returned to his roots in Woodbridge. This was not mere sentiment, as Mondavi knew well that Lodi was capable of producing generous quantities of flavoury fruit that would be ideally suited to the less expensive range of wines that the winery was seeking to launch. In the mid-1970s Robert Mondavi took over the former Woodbridge Cooperative as his winemaking base in the region. This was to become the source of the RM Red and White ranges, and subsequently of the Woodbridge 'fighting varietal' wines, which have become commercially very successful. Sebastiani have also opened a winemaking facility in the region.

Lodi is situated about ninety miles east of San Francisco at the upper end of the San Joaquin Valley. The heavily agricultural region, which once laid claim to be the watermelon capital of the world, lies south of Sacramento and north of Stockton, and includes all of Sacramento County. The neighbouring towns of Lodi and Woodbridge lie in the heart of the AVA, which was created in 1986 on the basis of a petition written by Brad Alderson, the general manager of Mondavi's Woodbridge winery. Lodi as a whole is a low Region III, and its warmth is moderated by the ocean air that is funnelled into the area over the expanses of the San Joaquin Delta. There are occasional summer fogs in the morning, and sea breezes keep the afternoon temperature considerably lower than in the main part of the valley to the south. The maritime influence is greater in the western part of the region, which lies closer to the delta. Rainfall is quite low, averaging about 17 inches per year, and frost is no threat. The soils are mostly deep sandy loams, deposited over time by the rivers Consumnes and Mokelumne, which flow into the Sacramento River and thence into the delta. The soil is also rich in minerals, brought down from the Sierra by the two rivers.

The region is far from uniform. Around the town of Lodi itself, the well-drained loam soils and the steady breezes encourage the growing of lush Chardonnay and Zinfandel. North of the town, in the Borden Ranch area, the soil is red and rocky and the average temperatures slightly warmer, which benefits the Cabernet Sauvignon, Merlot, Zinfandel, Syrah, and Sauvignon Blanc grown there.[3]

Fortunately, the very limited presence of AXR-1 rootstocks and the sandiness of the soil have played their part in fending off phylloxera. The prolific production and overall health of Lodi vines have helped fill the gap in production caused by replanting in parts of the state more badly afflicted by the louse. Drainage is good and if yields can be on the high side, that at least is a factor amenable to human control. One factor accounting for excessive yields in the past was the use of flood irrigation, in which entire furrows alongside the rows of vines were filled with water. Newer vineyards have opted instead for drip irrigation, which is easier to control and manipulate according to the actual needs of the vines. In the past the ready market for Lodi grapes from producers of bland jug wines provided no incentive to growers to focus on quality rather than quantity. Wineries such as Mondavi have special grower relations offices, both to ensure that their contract growers maintain expected quality levels, and also to coordinate the harvesting of the grapes. The quality control demanded by Mondavi and other producers has helped local growers to feel pride in the quality of the grapes they grow, and the proliferation of lots within the Woodbridge winery allows each of the 200 growers they purchase from to follow the development of wines made from their grapes. The system of separate vinifications also, of course, allows the Mondavi winemakers to assess regional variations as well as the typicity of each grower's fruit.

Lodi is still a region of growers rather than wineries. Many growers operate on a small scale, but there are some families, such as Kautz, Ledbetter, and Lange, who own thousands of acres. The overwhelming majority of the 600 growers active in the 45,000-acre region sell their production to the likes of Gallo, Sebastiani, Sutter Home, Fetzer, Phelps, Glen Ellen, Kendall-Jackson, Beringer, Charles Krug, and of course Mondavi. Other wineries, such as Delicato, are developing extensive vineyards of their own. Few use the Lodi appellation, as the wines are often blended and released under the catch-all California appellation.

The Lodi growers have become extremely well organized, which has also proved an important factor in the growing renown of the region. In 1991 the Lodi-Woodbridge Winegrape Commission was founded, both to publicize the merits of the region and to encourage the growers to improve their viticultural practices. Since the region had always been dominated by cooperatives, the growers found nothing objectionable in the notion of concerted action. The Commission has strongly promoted integrated pest management (IPM) programmes that recommend cover crops, the use of compost, and other measures, rather than pesticides and other treatments. Because so many of the growers have agreed to adopt this strategy, it has been possible to rely increasingly on natural predators, and vegetation has been planted to encourage a population of wasps, which devour the grape leaf hopper, and barn owls, which feast off gophers and other rodents. The Commission also encourages producers to indicate on the labels that their wines come from Lodi, to improve consumer recognition of a region still associated with jug-wine quality.

In addition, the Commission was well aware that Lodi's traditional varieties, although modified by the Gallos and Mondavis, were still out of step with commercial requirements. The Flame Tokay vines were rapidly grubbed up to be replaced by more desirable varieties such as Chardonnay, which had scarcely been present until the 1980s, since the official line from the authorities was that Chardonnay would not grow in Lodi. The Kautz family were the first to develop Chardonnay vineyards, having dipped their toe in the waters with 185 acres, and they also planted Cabernet Sauvignon in 1971. The Kautzes had previously grown Bing cherries and vegetables and appreciated the benefits of cool night-time temperatures. They were also among the first to install drip irrigation and to experiment with trellising techniques. 'Growing,' says Steve Kautz, 'is growing, whether it's tomatoes or grapes. It's all to do with fertilization, sunlight, and adaptation to the elements.' Their lengthy experience as farmers gave them a hunch that Chardonnay would work well in Lodi. They were to be proved right on a massive scale.

Nonetheless, by 1985, long after the Kautzes had been planting Chardonnay and Cabernet, those varieties accounted for only 1 and 2 per cent of the crop value respectively, with Sauvignon Blanc slightly higher at 4 per cent.

Today Lodi's 55,000 acres are planted, in the main, with Zinfandel (about 30 per cent), Chardonnay (about 26 per cent), Cabernet Sauvignon (about 18 per cent), and Merlot (5 per cent), in order of importance. By 1995, indeed, Lodi was the state's largest producer of Chardonnay, although the following year it ceded first place to Monterey. However in 1996 Lodi was California's foremost growing region, in terms of tonnage, for Merlot, Cabernet Sauvignon, Zinfandel, and Sauvignon Blanc.

It is risky to generalize, but it is usually fair to say that Lodi fruit is not hugely structured and rarely shows exceptional concentration, probably because yields are still on the generous side. Lance Randolph of Peirano finds fairly low levels of tannin in his grapes, and advises against prolonged cellaring even of wines such as Cabernet Sauvignon and Zinfandel. Charles Spenker agrees, finding that Lodi red wines tend to have a soft finish. Zinfandel from old vines, which remain plentiful, are much sought after, and with good reason. Back in 1968 Ridge Vineyards was probably the first winery to recognize the potential of these old vineyards. However, Paul Draper admits that he deserted Lodi for Amador County because he found the wines rapidly became too soft and broad. Newer plantations of Zinfandel are usually used to slake America's thirst for White Zinfandel. Brad Alderson of Mondavi finds that Lodi Chardonnay has a grapefruit quality that does not benefit from winemaking practices such as skin contact. There is no difficulty in ripening Chardonnay each year, but sometimes the acidity needs to be adjusted. Innovative winemakers such as Jim Clendenen are intrigued by the potential for Barbera in Lodi, which in the mid-1990s was the source of his Il Podere d'Olivos Barbera.

Whatever the potential for quality, the primary attraction of Lodi to large wineries remains the relatively low prices of the grapes, as the following prices per ton of the 1996 crop make clear:[4]

Variety	Sonoma	Napa	Monterey	Lodi
Chardonnay	$1,486	$1,543	$1,420	$773
Chenin Blanc	$577	$661	$731	$362
Sauvignon Blanc	$932	$964	$853	$539
Cabernet Sauvignon	$1,496	$1,804	$1,091	$795
Merlot	$1,660	$1,784	$1,307	$915
Zinfandel	$1,222	$878	$868	$589

Although most Lodi fruit still ends up in blends from the major Californian wineries, there are a handful of growers who are vinifying their own grapes. To date the best seem to be Lucas, Peirano, and St Amant.

CENTRAL VALLEY

The Central Valley is a handy name for a vast region that encompasses the whole of the San Joaquin Valley and, at its northern end, subsidiary regions within the Sacramento Delta such as Suisun Valley, Clarksburg, and Lodi. The San Joaquin Valley itself is about fifty miles wide and 200 miles in length. Although Lodi has been given separate consideration, it is included below in any statistical data cited for the valley as a whole. The Central Valley, including northern counties such as Sacramento and Yolo, accounted for 59 per cent of California's grape production in 1996. Thanks to generous yields, the valley accounts for about 70 per cent of all Californian wine. Apart from a few subregions in the north, the climate is uniformly hot, registering as a Region IV/V. It is fringed to the east by the mighty Sierra Nevada, to the west by lower mountain ranges that block access to maritime influence except at the northern end around the Sacramento Delta.

The valley was first developed as a grape growing region in the 1870s, when the installation of irrigation countered the natural aridity of the area. It appears that the first vineyards were planted near Stockton in San Joaquin County by Captain Charles Weber, who chose Mission vines. Mission grapes were eventually super-seded by Grenache and Carignane and other varieties well suited to the blistering summer heat. There has also been a tendency to plant grapes with naturally high acidity, which is too easily lost in such a climate: Barbera, Chenin Blanc, and that old California warhorse French Colombard. The worst possible choice was Thompson Seedless, which may be an excellent table grape, but is a pitiful wine grape. Its great appeal, commercially, was that it could be sold as a table grape in July or as raisins in August; any surplus could be sold to wineries as a wine grape. Other widely planted varieties such as Flame Tokay also had dual use as table or wine grapes. The factor that unites all Central Valley locations is that sunshine and irrigation ensure regular and generous crops each year. No room for notions of *terroir* here.

However, there is also considerable acreage devoted to the fashionable varieties such as Chardonnay, Zinfandel and Sauvignon Blanc, though these are mostly found in the more northerly, and marginally cooler, areas of the valley. Few of the wines are identified in terms of their origin. The great majority are used for jug wines, which are not necessarily of abysmal quality, or as blending agents by the larger wineries.

From Lodi and Stockton, the Central Valley sprawls southeast-wards past the towns of Modesto (headquarters of Gallo), Livingston, Merced, Madera (headquarters of Heublein), and Fresno, which is home to the state's best known viticultural institute after UC Davis: the department of viticulture and oenology at Fresno State University. Fresno became the heartland of Thompson Seedless in the 1890s, and by 1900 the county contained 70,000 acres of vineyards, though only some of them were destined for wineries. By the early 1990s there were 210,000 acres under vine in Fresno County, of which 160,000 were table grapes.

South of Fresno are the grape growing regions around the towns of Tulare, Delano, and Kern. Here one finds vineyards the size of ranches, corporate agribusiness plantations belonging to wineries or groups whose names are often unknown, even to avid purchasers of wines in gallon jugs. Most of the vineyards in Tulare County are dedicated to raisin and table-grape production. After Repeal the local growers developed cooperatives as the best solution to their problems, and of course Gallo has been a force in the region since 1933. Although nothing can be done to alter the fact that the region is not suited to the production of high-quality wine grapes, technology has come to the aid of the more conscientious producers, and techniques such as night-time harvesting and temperature-controlled fermentation have undoubtedly been of benefit.

Clarksburg and Merritt Island

The Clarksburg AVA, created in 1984, lies southwest of Sacramento, bordered on one side by the Sacramento River and on the other, to the east, by the Lodi region. It is some sixteen miles long and eight miles wide. About 5,500 acres are planted. Within the Clarksburg AVA is a separate AVA known as Merritt Island, in which the Bogle Vineyard winery is the sole producer. Like Lodi, Clarksburg enjoys some maritime influence and is slightly cooler than Lodi, but the soils are quite rich, with peat and clay as well as loams. Merritt Island is technically Region II, has loam soils and is rarely invaded by fog. Although Clarksburg has yet to produce red wines of any distinction other than Petite Sirah, it is the source for some of California's best Chenin Blanc, which is purchased by wineries as distant as Dry Creek in Sonoma. It doesn't have sufficient acidic backbone to age and is best enjoyed in its youth, when it shows melony fruitiness. However, Chenin is steadily being elbowed out by Chardonnay, for which there is greater demand from the large wineries such as Fetzer and Glen Ellen that buy grapes here.

Madera

The region around Madera in the San Joaquin Valley has its own AVA, planted with 38,600 acres of grapes. It is the power base of Almadén. It is also known for its port-style and dessert wines from Ficklin and Quady. The principal grape varieties, in terms of surface planted, are French Colombard (14,700 acres), Chenin Blanc

(5,500), Grenache (4,600), Carignane (2,700), and Barbera (1,914).

Solano County

This county contains two AVAs other than Clarksburg, and they lie between Sacramento and the Bay, just west of the small town of Fairfield. These are Green Valley and Suisun Valley, both approved in 1982 and both situated quite close to Wild Horse Valley, which is part of Napa Valley. In 1983 they were included in the North Coast appellation, rather to the annoyance of some producers who wanted to keep them out. Despite a good deal of coastal influence from breezes coming through the Carquinez Straits, Green Valley is a Region III zone climatically, since the intrusions of fog from Suisun Bay generally prove short-lived. There are 400 acres under vine. The soils are loam over alluvial fans. Chateau de Leu is the principal functioning winery here, and releases wines made from local as well as Napa grapes. In recent years it has been focusing more on Italian varietals.

With 800 acres planted, Suisun Valley has twice the acreage of Green Valley, and has similar clay loam soils. Fog is less frequent than in Green Valley. The Wooden Valley winery, founded here in the 1930s, produces fairly light wines such as Gamay Beaujolais and Riesling.

VINEYARDS

Buley. Shenandoah. Sells Zinfandel to Karly.

Clay Station. Lodi. 1,600 acres. Owned by Delicato.

Deaver Ranch. Amador County. 1,700 feet high, mostly planted with Zinfandel. The vineyard that supplied the grapes to Sutter Home in 1968.

Eschen Ranch. Fiddletown. Owned by Chester Eschen. 40 acres at 1,700 feet in Fiddletown. Zinfandel originally planted in 1924. Grapes sold to Amador Foothill Winery, Easton, and Renwood.

Esola. Amador County. 90 acres at 1,700 feet; 76 acres of Zinfandel were originally planted in 1910. Also Cabernet Sauvignon. Grapes sold to Carneros Creek and Ridge.

Ferrero Ranch. Shenandoah. Owned by John Ferrero. 50 acres planted at 1,600 feet. Zinfandel planted in 1926. Fruit sold to Amador Foothills Winery and, formerly, Monterey Peninsula.

Frank's Vineyard. Amador County. 6 acres planted at 1,700 feet with 7 port varieties. Grapes sold to Quady.

Ghirardelli. Calaveras County. Owned by Alan Ghirardelli. 25 acres of 100-year-old Zinfandel. Sells to Milliaire.

Grandpère. Shenandoah. Owned by Scott Harvey. Ancient 10-acre vineyard originally planted with Zinfandel in 1869 at 1,700 feet. Most of the original vines survive.

Lubenko. Fiddletown. Sells Zinfandel to Sobon.

Miller. El Dorado. Sells Chardonnay to Milliaire.

Potter. Shenandoah. Owned by Don Potter. Sells Zinfandel to Amador Foothills.

Sadie Upton. Zinfandel planted in 1923. Sells to Karly.

Walker Ranch. El Dorado County. Owned by Lloyd Walker. Planted with Zinfandel and Chenin Blanc. Grapes sold to Boeger.

NOTES

1 Leon D. Adams, *The Wines of America*, p. 420
2 Norm Roby, *Decanter*, September 1997
3 Rod Smith, 'Letter from Lodi', *Wine & Spirits*, June 1996
4 Figures from the California Department of Food & Agriculture

Grapes and Wines

12

Growing the Grapes

Perhaps the most important difference between Europe and the so-called New World is that the latter had to develop vineyards on the basis of trial and error rather than long tradition. In Europe there are vineyards that were originally planted at least 1,000 years ago. Indeed, Greeks and Romans made wine and the Romans cultivated vineyards in the Mosel, south of Nîmes, and south of Vienna. The vineyards of Bandol in Provence are believed to have been planted originally by Phoenicians.

There is no merit in antiquity as such. But history brings experience. Any Burgundian grower knows exactly where Pinot Noir will ripen best and where it will perform indifferently. The grape variety blend in any vineyard will not, of course, have remained constant over the centuries, but it's certainly possible to trace the presence of Riesling and Pinot Noir back through the centuries in sites that even today are regarded as those where these varieties show at their best.

For the immigrants who travelled thousands of miles to California, the state was more or less a *tabula rasa*. The friars who planted the earliest vineyards at the Spanish missions were probably motivated by convenience rather than careful site selection. But I don't have the impression that the same was true of those who arrived in the following century and planted the vineyards of Napa, Sonoma, and the Sierra Foothills. Many of them headed for the hills. It would have been easier to plant on the valley floor, but experience from the home country told them that quality derived from vineyards on well-exposed, well-drained slopes. These early growers sacrificed abundant yields for what they perceived as a potential for quality. We don't know what those early wines tasted like, and no doubt many were poor. But the instincts of those early growers were sound. Similarly, Niebaum and others who planted vines on the Rutherford benchland did not, I suspect, choose the location by plunging a pin into a map. The Italian families who opted to plant grapes 2,000 feet up in the Santa Cruz Mountains could not have known for sure that these sites would produce outstanding wine, but they probably had a gut feeling that this was a promising spot to plant vines.

In other respects, the immigrants were on less certain ground. They may have known where to plant, but were restricted in their choice of varieties. The plethora of cuttings imported by Agoston Haraszthy eventually offered growers a wider choice, but it seems probable that growers planted the varieties they were familiar with, and trusted to luck. In time, experience refined those early decisions, and disasters, whether natural or man-made, had the sole benefit of giving those growers who chose to continue as grape farmers the opportunity to think again.

This process is still continuing. Tracts of Sauvignon Blanc and Chardonnay planted on the valley floor in Napa have mostly been replanted, since the outbreak of phylloxera in the 1980s, with other more suitable varieties. Cabernet Sauvignon planted in parts of the Salinas Valley in Monterey has been replaced by varieties more likely to ripen in this cool area. Certain outstanding areas – Carneros, Russian River Valley, Santa Maria Valley – have been identified as being well suited to Pinot Noir. Clarksburg has long been recognized as the source of good Chenin Blanc. The story is far from complete, however. Syrah is a fashionable grape, but there is considerable debate about where it should be planted. Moreover, there can be no doubt that in certain regions, especially those which command high grape prices, varieties are planted more for their commercial value than for their suitability to the location.

In California there has long been a sense that grape growing and winemaking are two different occupations, even though once every year they must join forces. Joe Heitz declared in an interview in 1976: 'I don't waste my time in the vineyard . . . I'm a winemaker; I devote my time to the winery.' That smacks of arrogance, and although I doubt that you would find many winemakers echoing that view today, the underlying assumptions have not necessarily changed that much. It is true that certain wineries have always owned sizeable vineyards, and that trend is certainly continuing. Nonetheless there are numerous wineries that own no or very few vineyards of their own. By means either of long-term contracts or purchases on the spot market or begging and pleading with the best-known growers, they produce their range of wines each year. But there has long been an attitude that it is the job of the grape farmers to grow grapes, and the job of the winemaker to turn them into wine. The winemakers may specify certain targets – sugar, acid, whatever – that they would like the grower to meet, but that is in most cases the limit of their interference. On the vast majority of estates the winemaker and the vineyard manager are not the same person. Much the same would be true of any large estate in Europe, of course, so it is no criticism of the Californian wine industry to note that the two functions are usually separated.

Nonetheless it came as a considerable surprise to learn that at the Peter Michael estate in Knights Valley, Mark Aubert is both winemaker and vineyard manager. Assuming he is competent in both fields, and the quality of the wines suggests that he is, it must be an immense advantage for a winemaker to have an intimate knowledge of the grapes at his disposal.

Winemakers need good-quality grapes, but grape farmers are keen to obtain good crops and good prices. Of course the best growers will be conscientious farmers, applying a blend of technique and instinct to induce their vines to give just the right amount of fruit to provide a balance between good quality and commercial viability. Certain vineyards are known to give outstanding quality. Although vineyard management has to be an important factor, consistently high performance is likely to be the product of that magical combination of soil, microclimate, and exposure that the French call *terroir*.

Yet many Californians are sceptical about the notion of *terroir*, arguing that climate is a far more crucial factor, especially in the North and Central coasts, than nuances of soil structure. However, I would suggest that climate is an intrinsic component of *terroir* and not something apart from it. It is true that, except in the most uniform terrains such as the Central Valley, one plot of vines will differ from another planted alongside. Every sizeable California vineyard is divided into blocks, and every grower knows that Block 1 will give, in most years, fruit that is more precocious/less tannic/deeper coloured/less aromatic – choose your own variables – than the same grape variety grown a hundred yards away in Block 2. We can argue all day long why those differences are perceptible, and that cluster of explanations, which will include climate, soil drainage, wind, and countless other factors, is simply a manifestation of *terroir*.

Growers, even in regions as familiar as Napa Valley, will admit that they have only the faintest notion of how their soils are structured. To be sure, there will be sandy loam here, more gravel there, some shale or clay over there. But nobody pretends to have the exhaustive geological knowledge that is commonplace in Pauillac, Rüdesheim, or Bâtard-Montrachet. This is part of the reason why it has been so difficult to devise uncontroversial geographical appellations within Napa Valley. At what point does Stags Leap, in terms of typicity and consistency, cease to be Stags Leap? In Germany the distinctions between one vineyard in Wehlen and its neighbour have been arrived at after centuries of experience (and a fair amount of political wrangling); newer regions such as Napa or Sonoma cannot expect to have attained that level of understanding. Some producers are certainly making strong efforts to increase their knowledge. Mondavi, for example, has been using spy planes with infra-red cameras to photograph and analyse their vineyards in Carneros; these photos show up variations in temperature of the vegetation and thus variations in maturation.

The sparsity of exact geological and climatic knowledge doesn't necessarily matter that much. Growers still have their hunches, just as their predecessors did a century or more ago, and a hunch is often worth following. It has long been recognized that there are noteworthy differences between individual vineyards. In the 1970s Ridge was bottling Zinfandels and other varieties from a whole range of vineyards, and in 1975 Richard Arrowood produced seven different bottlings of Chardonnay. By then Martha's Vineyard was already a legendary site, and wineries such as DeLoach and Turley take pride in the multiplicity of single-vineyard (or vineyard-designated, to use the California jargon) bottlings they release each year.

However, the truism that one vineyard differs from another is not quite the same as the French notion of *terroir*. When Josh Jensen decided to plant vineyards with Pinot Noir in a remote spot on Mount Harlan south of Hollister, he did so because his instincts and observation told him that this was as Burgundian a *terroir* as one could find in California. Burgundians often attribute the quality of their wines to the presence of limestone in the soil, although it has to be more complicated than that. California is not rich in limestone; indeed, it is rare except in a few outcroppings such as those Jensen stumbled across. However, a Burgundian soil in a Californian climate is not necessarily going to result in a Burgundian-style wine. Excellent though the wines can be from Jensen's Calera estate, I am not sure that they are notably Burgundian. Nor does it matter since they have a style and personality of their own.

If Jensen represented the most Francophile approach one is likely to encounter in California, the genial Bill Jekel, whose own vineyards lay across the mountains in Arroyo Seco in Monterey County, took the contrary view. Soil, he liked to assert, was dirt. It was simply a medium for growing grapes. Obviously there were differences between parcels of vines, but those differences were relatively unimportant. Climate, yield, drainage, and winemaking skills mattered far more. He had the courage to argue his case with such Bordelais luminaries as Bruno Prats of Château Cos d'Estournel. Sadly, Bill Jekel is no longer making the wines that bear his name, but I have fond memories of some of his excellent Rieslings and a few magnificent, brooding Cabernets. He may have been an iconoclast, but he knew how to make good wines. His view was supported by one of America's leading wine historians and connoisseurs, Leon Adams, who wrote in 1984: 'Well-drained, warm soils capable of adequately nourishing the vines are essential for quality and yield. It is not true, as [European producers] would have us believe, that a special soil component climbs up through the vine, enters into the grape and its juice, and gives the wine a distinctive taste.'[1]

Jensen and Jekel take extreme positions but their views are not as opposed as their rhetoric might lead one to think. Jekel wants to downplay a factor that simply has never seemed that important in California. The Mosel has its steep slate slopes, Château Latour its immensely deep gravel soils, Coonawarra its Terra Rossa, Mesnil has its chalk, but California seems largely composed of sandy loam, alluvial fans, and decomposed volcanic soils. Hard indeed to build a sophisticated theory of *terroir* on that lot. The exceptions, such as the three or four very distinctive soil types on Al Brounstein's Diamond Creek estate in Napa Valley, are rare. Josh Jensen, in contrast to Bill Jekel, has latched on to one factor – geology – in his personal pursuit of the vinous holy grail. But surely Jensen would admit that you need more than a bed of limestone and a collection of Pinot Noir cuttings in order to produce a great red wine.

Paul Draper, not surprisingly, believes strongly in *terroir*. 'California winemakers are predisposed to accept the Jekel theory that soil is dirt. They are taught at Davis by professors who are chemists rather than winemakers, and they approach winemaking in much the same way as they would approach any kind of food processing. Given their background, you can't expect teachers at Davis to defend European notions such as *terroir*. In California we are accustomed to buying land with no vines, planting grapes, and hoping for the best. It's the job of winemakers to manipulate the fruit that they obtain to make the best possible wine whatever the quality of the grapes. I definitely feel that in California we need more savvy about *terroir*. Every piece of ground responds differently.'

The late Richard Graff of the Chalone group was another firm advocate of the idea: 'The whole idea of soil versus climate in California was decided in favor of climate many years ago by professors Amerine and Winkler for the simple reason that the factor of climate produces differences in grapes which are measurable in the laboratory. The differences in grapes which are the result of soil are *not* measurable in the laboratory . . . We made Chardonnay at Mt Eden Vineyards for several years – my brother Peter was the winemaker up there – but we used exactly the same methods we use here, harvested at exactly the same maturity, used the same barrels imported from Burgundy, and the areas are very closely equivalent in terms of temperature. The wines are as different as night from day. And that's attributable to the soil.'[2]

Graff's colleague Larry Brooks did attempt to study *terroir* in the laboratory by setting up experiments based on blind tastings that would establish 'descriptors' for distinct wine regions. This research programme was begun in 1987 and focused on Chardonnay and Pinot Noir, and the researchers had greater success with the latter than with Chardonnay. Brooks took a number of wines from the same vintage, the same grape variety, the same region, and invited tasters to come up with descriptors. A clear family resemblance was found within some regions – Central Coast, Carneros, Napa – but not with others, such as Sonoma. Aroma rather than flavour established the 'descriptors'. Among the Chardonnays, Napa showed apple aromas, Carneros citric, and the Central Coast honey and caramel. But only wines of the highest intensity showed these supposed *terroir* characteristics. Does this get one very far? I have my doubts. The three regions which exhibited distinctive character all have distinctive climates, but Napa's soils are so varied that it would be dangerous, if not futile, to build a theory of *terroir* upon them. If one were to attempt a similar experiment with, say, Sauvignon Blanc from the Loire Valley and the same variety from the Graves, I suspect the differences would also be quite marked. But in that case too, I would guess that climate was the determining factor. If anything, Brooks's experiments seem to have confirmed the overpowering influence of climate.

Randall Grahm admits that in California the distinguishing feature is climate rather than soil, but adds that the risk is that the excellence of the climate produces wines of a very consistent quality. Thus too many Napa Chardonnays are indistinguishable. 'You need *terroir* to add interest and character.'

In this chapter I shall look at the choices that confront anyone planting vines in California, and the problems, such as disease. I do not pretend to any great expertise in this subject, and have been relieved to find that nobody else seems to know much either. John Williams of Frog's Leap in Napa admits that knowledge of the thirty-eight different soils of Napa, and anywhere else, is rudimentary; Randy Dunn of Howell Mountain admits nobody can predict how a clone will perform; and it is hard to find any two growers who agree on the merits and drawbacks of high-density spacing in the vineyard. So burdened with uncertainties, we shall take a somewhat tentative look at issues of primary importance in establishing the quality of a wine.

The first decision any grower must make is where to plant the vines. The nineteenth-century immigrants trusted to past experience in Europe and to their instincts. In modern times growers have been guided by such inexact formulae as the heat summation system devised at UC Davis, and we have already seen that costly mistakes were made by relying on that system. Draper has suggested that many growers simply trust to luck. At Sierra Vista in El Dorado County, John MacCready admits that when he cleared his land and planted his vines, he didn't even bother to conduct a soil analysis. I was quite surprised by this but Corky Lovin of the

International Agricultural Visitors Program based at Davis assures me this is quite normal. 'You can tell what the land is like by seeing what's already growing there. Big trees, for example, mean deep soils. There's plenty of information readily available on factors such as pH, so doing an expensive soil analysis probably won't tell you anything you don't already know. And factors such as climate and wind and night temperatures and rainfall are usually more important than geological composition.'

John Parducci admitted to the hit-and-miss approach in an interview conducted in the mid-1970s: 'We were the first to plant fine varietals in Mendocino County in 1964 and we produced wines from those plantings in 1969. How can anyone judge the quality of grapes or wines from an area that has never produced any varietal wine, especially from the largest county in California, with dozens of heat summations and microclimates? It will take a long time for the vines to mature and then to evaluate wines from the different areas. At this point we have no track record to convince us we have the right area or the right variety. In 1964, we planted nine varieties on our Talmage ranch to determine which varieties produced well and made the best wines. We feel that Chenin Blanc, Chardonnay, Cabernet and Sylvaner produce excellent wines, and we've won awards to verify it. However, we're still waiting for the full maturity of our vineyards before we're convinced which varieties do best.'[3]

The next crucial decision will be the choice of grape varieties. I have touched on this earlier, and future chapters will deal with California's grape varieties and where they are grown, so I shall not dwell on it further here.

Row orientation has been the subject of much discussion in recent years, and Dr Richard Smart has summarized the current state of play: 'The differences in sunlight interception due to row alignment occur on the vine sides, and mostly around the mid morning and afternoon. About noon, when the sun is higher in the sky, there is less effect of row direction, as most of the direct sunlight is intercepted by the horizontal top of the vines . . . North-south rows show peaks in midmorning and midafternoon, while for east-west rows the maximum is around midday, and the total sunlight interception less. Computer simulation studies by the author have indicated that there can be a substantial advantage of north-south rows over east-west rows in sunlight interception. For vineyards at latitude 35 degrees and in midsummer, north-south rows intercept 53% of the sunlight (on a daily basis), compared to 36% for east-west rows ... A north-south row orientation is generally preferred due to higher yield and quality potential.'[4]

Rootstocks

Next, the grower must decide on the choice of rootstocks. In some regions, especially those with sandy soils, the vines are planted on their own roots. The majority of California's vines were planted on one of two rootstocks: AXR-1 or St George. Those who chose the former made a fatal mistake, and the history of AXR-1 and its consequences will be recounted in the section on phylloxera. St George has the double advantage of sending roots down deep into the soil, thus minimizing or eliminating the need for irrigation, and it has also proved resistant to phylloxera. The choice of rootstock is extremely important, not only because of its influence on susceptibility to disease, but because it affects the vigour of the vine. Certain rootstocks promote vigour, others curtail it. Professor Carole Meredith of UC Davis observed that 'rootstocks are better understood than clones, and we understand their variations in adaptability. Some reduce vigour by not absorbing water so easily. Others are deep-rooted and better suited to dry sites.'

But Joanne Stimac, Davis-trained and part of the Kendall-Jackson winemaking team until 1997, told me: 'Rootstocks and clones are still a lottery, and I know of a number of vineyards that were planted incorrectly and within two years were dying off. The problem is that rules and experience that are applicable in one region don't necessarily apply to others.' Many of the soils in California are quite rich and if the rootstock chosen is not well adapted to such a soil, it may well encourage over-vigorous growth.

David Ramey, formerly winemaker at Chalk Hill and Dominus, believes that California remains less advanced than Europe in matching rootstocks to specific sites. He reports that there are continued doubts about the resistance of some currently recommended rootstocks to phylloxera. Popular rootstocks such as 3306 seem to be exhibiting previously undetected viral infections, and 5C has come in for some harsh criticism. Even after two centuries of research, planting vineyards still has some elements reminiscent of a lottery. Randy Dunn, like most shrewd growers, has planted a number of different rootstocks as well as clones on his Howell Mountain sites. 'It will take a good deal more time before we can tell what difference they will make. But it makes sense not to plant an entire vineyard with one clone or one rootstock. It's that kind of monoculture which made it so easy for phylloxera to spread in recent years. The aphids don't go round chewing a bit here and a bit there. If they find what they like they stick with it.'

Clones

If it isn't always easy to choose a rootstock, it can be a nightmarish business choosing an appropriate clone. In many European vineyards this is less of an issue, as growers can choose massal selections from existing vineyards of proven quality. Since California is a newer wine region, there is a much greater dependency on clones, which are specially selected and based on genetic subtypes. Clones can be developed to encourage specific qualities – resistance to disease or drought, vigour, size of berries, and so forth – and then propagated so that each cutting is genetically identical to every other from the same source.

The vast majority of clones planted in California have been propagated by UC Davis, and in many cases selected because they gave generous yields and were reliable performers. Some clones were originally transported from Europe, such as the Wente clone of Sauvignon Blanc and the Masson clones of Pinot Noir, and these will be dealt with in more detail in the chapters on grape varieties. A constant lament among some of California's more innovative winemakers is the lack of good-quality clones for some of the new varieties that they are anxious to vinify. This is now being corrected at estates such as Tablas Creek in Paso Robles, where the Perrin family are propagating Rhône and other varietals derived from their own vineyards in southern France; these are now beginning to provide cuttings of excellent quality. Other nurseries have also begun to import top-quality French clones. John Alban believes that the veneration of French clones may be misplaced, since they have been selected to ripen late and lose acidity. Climactic conditions in California require the opposite, and Alban often finds Australian clones more suitable for California than French clones.

For many growers the problem is not so much the lack of clones as the surfeit of them. How are they to choose? Randall

Grahm of Bonny Doon has remarked: 'People still ask "What is the best clone?" as if they were asking "What is the best car?" ' There is no such thing, as any clone must be related to the site on which it is to be cultivated. Since most sites are very different from neighbouring sites, except on large valley floor ranches, the choice of clone is in large part guesswork. Informed guesswork, to be sure, but it is all too easy to make a mistake. Larry Brooks of Acacia believes that it takes twenty years before one can understand the character and quality of any specific clone after its introduction.

Most growers, when planting a new vineyard, select a range of clones. Planting an unknown site with a single clone is, obviously, asking for trouble. When Mondavi were planting Pinot Noir in Carneros, they selected nine different clones, as well as some that were still experimental. As the vines matured, they eliminated those that were proving the least satisfactory. Tim Mondavi tells me that especially with Chardonnay and Pinot Noir there are enormous differences between the various clonal selections available, but that experimentation in recent years has made huge advances in improving the overall quality of Pinot Noir vines in particular.

A few wineries are conducting microvinifications of the clones they have planted. At the Marimar Torres estate in Green Valley, I was able to taste barrel samples of the three Chardonnay clones and the five Pinot Noir clones she has planted. There were indeed striking differences betweeen the wines, but it was hard to be certain that they derived solely from clonal origin: other factors include age of vine, maturity of fruit, and so forth. But it is interesting to note that there are acute differences between clonal selections simply in terms of their aroma and flavour spectrum, quite apart from factors relating to health, resistance to drought, or longevity. Clones do make a difference.

The much maligned UC Davis is fully aware of the importance of judicious clonal selection. Professor Carole Meredith did not dismiss the utility of Torres's microvinifications, but pointed out that such individual initiatives are not undertaken with the scientific rigour that would make their results of more than local application. 'We know of the evaluation trials conducted in France, but they're not relevant to our regions. What we need here are scientifically controlled trials so that we can compare the different clones. In fact we started doing those trials about ten years ago, but it will take more time before we get clear results.' Davis have planted a research vineyard in Oakville with thirty-seven so-called Heritage clones, the idea being to preserve old clones and then make the best of them available commercially to growers.

Spacing

Once the vines and rootstocks have been chosen, it is necessary to plant them. The first question that arises is how densely the vines should be spaced. In French vineyards vines are closely spaced, with up to 10,000 per hectare. Elsewhere in Europe, such as Italy, there are fewer vines per hectare. There is no formula. The traditional density in California was 8x12 feet, which was the equivalent of 454 vines per acre. This meant that the rows were 12 feet apart, and there was a gap of 8 feet between vines. Until the 1940s the density was greater, but from the 1940s onwards UC Davis recommended spacing of 8x12, which was very widely adopted. One theory behind the French preference for denser spacing was that it promoted competition between the vines.

But that, according to English-born winemaker Philip Togni, never seemed relevant to the Californian experience. Vernon Singleton of UC Davis elaborated, when he told me that in his view close planting works where vines are small and the soil infertile; moreover density in the vineyard can offer protection against frost and wind. None of these is a Californian problem. He could not see any fundamental objection to planting vines in fertile soils and was far from convinced that stress is necessarily good for the vine and its fruit.

One reason for leaving 12 feet between rows was to allow easy access to tractors. Indeed, this spacing was often known as 'John Deere planting'. Professor Carole Meredith admits that '8x12 is a remnant of a time when growers had to adapt their farming to the equipment that existed at the time. Tractors and other farm equipment were never designed for grape growers. The French developed machines called *enjambeurs*, which straddled the vines, but such machines did not make an appearance in California until the 1990s, and of course did not exist when the postwar vineyards were laid out.' Other reasons given for recommending 8x12 was that labour costs were lower. It is hard to avoid the conclusion that the overriding justification was economic rather than qualitative. As Patrick Campbell of Laurel Glen in Sonoma put it to me: 'The Davis formula for planting 8x12 was "the fewest vines for the maximum tonnage".'

It is now widely accepted that fruit quality, and in some cases yields, can be improved by replanting with greater density per acre. But by how much? This has become a controversial issue and there is no consensus. In various parts of California I have seen additional vines planted along the rows, giving a density of 4x12 or in some cases 5x10. This more or less doubles the number of vines per acre. For Tony Soter, a well known viticulturalist and winemaker, this is no solution. 'Close spacing by itself doesn't guarantee quality. Placing the vines close together doesn't make any difference in rich deep soils, since the roots simply go down and down. In Europe, where a poor set is routine, it may be the sensible way to ensure a large army of shoots survive. On weak soils you can pack the vines close together, but on richer soils, such as ours in California, you need more space for growth.' His own personal preference is for 6x6, which, he says, is the kind of spacing that would have been common in California before World War II.

Some estates have gone the whole hog and opted for French-style close spacing. At Opus One, Robert Mondavi and Philippe de Rothschild decided to use the 1x1 density (confusing, this: 1 metre by 1 metre, not 1 foot by 1 foot), which gave 2,200 vines per acre, which is 4 times the density of 8x12. Marimar Torres in Sonoma has also gone for close spacing of 2,000 vines per acre. (The record for most vines per acre is currently held by Grace Family Vineyards in Napa, where in 1994 an acre was planted with 3,465 vines.) Although there are many more vines per acre, there are fewer bunches per vine. 'In Bordeaux,' Randy Dunn reflected, 'each vine carries seven or eight clusters only, which most growers in California would regard as a joke.' When one asks the folk at Opus One how this has been working out, it is hard to read between the lines of the reassuring response. Opus reject the suggestion that close spacing can give rise to over-abundant foliage and increase the likelihood of rot. They have used a rootstock that limits vigour, and control the canopy by leaf-thinning several times a year and by hedging the vines. Moreover, in Napa Valley's benign climate rot is far less of a threat than in rainier Bordeaux or Burgundy.

But others who have observed the vineyard out of sheer curiosity are sceptical. One viticulturalist told me that close spacing at Opus

One gave high yields and that the vineyard managers had to remove bunches, as the excessive number of shoots were overburdening the vines. Tony Soter, who has experimented with 1x1 planting, believes it is a disaster, at least in Napa Valley, where the bunches are too close to the ground and the grapes have a tendency to cook. John Williams of Frog's Leap believes that planting in narrow rows is in part a hankering after European practice. 'But in Europe the grapes lack sun, and here the opposite is true. So it's not a clearcut decision.'

Ted Lemon, a winemaker with extensive experience in Burgundy as well as California, quotes Raymond Bernard of Burgundy, who says his heart counsels him to advocate 1x1 planting while his brain tells him to adopt the lyre system of canopy management, which gives more foliage but ensures better exposure to sunlight for each bunch and gives more regular yields. Lemon implies that he takes a similar view. 'My view is that 1x1 is a great victory for treatments salesmen. If you wanted to invent a system designed to promote rot and mildew, it's 1x1. It's still not clear whether Opus devised its system as a response to vineyard conditions or as PR.' Randy Dunn also worries that with 1x1 spacing, the foliage is so close from vine to vine that it's hard for the sun to penetrate. The Opus managers would respond that the answer lies in hedging and good vineyard maintenance, which of course are very costly.

Indeed, Tim Mondavi admits that their own research vineyard behind the Mondavi winery has persuaded them that close spacing is not appropriate to all sites. He believes the fact that growers no longer dominate the vineyards, which are increasingly falling into the hands of wineries, is a positive move in terms of vineyard management. 'A grower might be tempted to plant Merlot because it's fashionable and fetches high prices, but a winery will plant what it needs or what it thinks will succeed on that site. On our own vineyards we gave up planting at 8x12 some time ago. For us 4x4 is the norm, and our lowest density is 6x5. It depends on the site. Indeed, we're also finding that growers have become much more sensitive to site than they used to be.'

A moderate view is taken by Mike Lee of Kenwood, who acknowledges that 8x12 is no longer acceptable, but also feels that a density of 2,000 vines per acre is inappropriate for Californian conditions. At Kenwood he prefers a spacing of 6x8, giving a density of about 1,000 vines per acre. Beringer now plant their vineyards to 1,100 vines per acre, and are wary of closer spacing on the grounds that such vineyards are hard to maintain under Californian conditions, as almost all the vineyard work must be done by hand since conventional tractors can't get through the narrow rows. Kendall-Jackson have also adopted a spacing of 6x8, although some of their vineyards in Santa Maria Valley are more closely planted at 4x6.

Professor Carole Meredith takes a cautious view: 'It really isn't the case that closer spacing has become a general trend, although those who are installing it are receiving a lot of publicity. It's certainly becoming more common in the coastal regions. Slightly closer spacing can certainly give you better quality and productivity, and imported European equipment has made it more feasible. As for 1x1 spacing, I think the results are still inconclusive.'

Australian viticulturalist Dr Richard Smart issues a number of warnings about high-density planting. 'High-density vineyards are expensive to establish and maintain. With grafted vines at $3.50 or more each, the high vine density of 4,000 vines costs $14,000 per acre for vines alone compared to the much lower figure of around $1,500 per acre for 450 vines ... Another disadvantage of high-density vineyards is that they do not reduce vigor in many situations. Rather the opposite seems to be true, and as the vineyards become more vigorous as they become older, yield declines ...

'I believe the answer depends on the site potential. If the soil is shallow and infertile and the vines will be supplied with restricted water amounts (by rainfall or irrigation), then higher vine density is justified. If on the other hand, the site potential is high, the soil is deep, and the vines will be well supplied with water and nutrients, then lower vine density is suggested.' He compares the poor gravel soils of the Médoc, where high density is prevalent, with the heavier-soiled Entre Deux Mers, where wider spacings have long been adopted. In vigorous soils, high-density vines produce too much foliage and declining yields. He argues that the exposure of leaves and fruit to sunlight is of far greater importance than supposed competition between root systems.[5]

For Craig Williams of Phelps, the spacing is related to productivity. 'The idea is to obtain more fruit and not more foliage, and there are two ways to achieve this. One is to adopt closer spacing – say, 1,700 vines per acre rather than Opus's 2,200 – and the other is to divide the canopy or pull leaves.' For him the whole discussion about density is something of a red herring, since the real issue is the number of buds per acre, not per vine. He aims for more vines but fewer buds and vertical trellising, which he believes will both improve the quality and increase the longevity of the vines. He certainly opposes the old style of plantings. 'There is no point devising a huge pumping system into vines treated as trees. What we want is ripening, not growth for its own sake.'

There are conflicting reports about the effect of closer spacing on yields. Marimar Torres says: 'With 8x12 planting you get the most bangs for your buck. With 454 vines per acre, you can crop anything from 4 to 12 tons per acre. When we were thinking about how to space our vines, the people at Davis told us we were crazy to go for 2,000 vines, but we know from our European experience that we would end up with smaller berries and higher quality. I don't believe high density stresses the vines excessively, and the vines seem to live longer. It's an excellent way to lessen the vigour of the vines in Californian conditions.'

Stephen Kistler, in a paper entitled 'Do California Single-Vineyard Chardonnays have "Typicité"?', wrote of experiments that compare 'the wines from vineyards with the same low 2 tons yields, but with different yields per vine, that is 4 pounds per vine (1,800 grapes) for the 5 ft by 8 ft planting, versus 1 pound (450 grapes) for the meter by meter planting. Will the fewer pounds per vine of the meter by meter planting translate into smaller berries, better extract and concentrations and perhaps even a slightly different aromatic expression than those wines grown at 2 tons/acre, but at a wider spacing? If the answer is definitely "yes", then meter by meter planting in California will proceed at an accelerated pace.'

Bo Barrett of Chateau Montelena is convinced that planting 1x1 will lead to rocketing yields in California's climate. 'The Napa water table will support as many vines as you can plant. I'm not convinced that 1x1 is going to work well, as our soils are too rich.' Barrett's fears were confirmed in some respects by some trials that Beringer undertook: closely spaced vines managed to yield 10 tons per acre, which sounds far too high. But in blind tastings no one could discern any difference in quality between wine from the high-yielding vines and wine made from lower-yield fruit. Bernard Portet of Clos du Val, who had to replant most of his vines after phylloxera, did so with closer spacing and finds he can obtain higher yields without any apparent loss in quality; indeed, he finds his Merlots have greater concentration and complexity than before.

The debate is bound to continue, and the most likely outcome is that vineyards will in future be more densely planted, but, most likely, at between 1,100 and 1,700 vines per acre rather than the impressive but potentially troublesome 2,000 or 2,200 favoured by the most European-oriented of growers.

Trellising

Once the decision has been made about how to lay out a vineyard, the grower must turn his attention to how the vines should be trained. This is an equally vexed issue. The decision will affect the ratio of foliage to fruit, the amount of exposure to sunlight the bunches will receive, and the aeration of those bunches. The old view used to be that since California soils, other than some thin-soiled mountain vineyards, are inherently vigorous, it was best to let the vines indulge in typically Californian self-expression. The result was what became known as California sprawl: large chaotic green canopies. After a while it became evident that an awful lot of California wines, red as well as white, were showing vegetal characteristics associated with unripe fruit. The fruit seemed to be ripe at harvest, and the resulting wines certainly didn't lack alcohol, yet the green vegetal flavours were a clear sign that the grapes lacked physiological maturity. What was happening was that the grapes were acquiring the requisite amount of sugar, which could be measured before harvest, but other elements, such as the seeds, were not ripening, giving harsh astringent flavours to the wine.

Many growers, initially puzzled by this phenomenon, decided the solution was to leave the fruit on the vine after it appeared to have reached its usual ripeness. Not surprisingly, the consequence was a lot of overripe, jammy fruit that made powerfully alcoholic wines that even found some acclaim in the 1970s and 1980s, but most of them were poorly balanced and lacked finesse.

Randall Grahm summed up the problem when he told me: 'In California the soil tends to encourage over-abundant foliage, giving the worst possible conditions for the proper maturation of the grapes. We get by because the climate here is so benign. If we could only get our canopy management and other conditions in the vineyard in order, our wines could be second to none. Our wine-making technique is already as good as any in the world, but our vineyards often let us down.'

The problem was that the vines were out of balance, with an over-vigorous canopy blocking the sunlight from the grapes themselves. Such varieties as Sauvignon Blanc and Syrah were notorious for the vigour of their growth. The French were able to hedge their vines, which were in any case far less vigorous than their Californian cousins, and this allowed the sunlight to ripen the grapes properly. Direct or gently dappled sunlight is also required to nourish the buds that would form the crop for the following year, and sprawling canopies tended to conceal those dormant buds. Nonetheless, a canopy remains essential, of course, not simply to protect the grapes from being burnt by the powerful Californian sun, but to perform the photosynthesis that will provide sugar for the grapes. The trick was to achieve the right balance between the natural vigour of the California vine and the need for the bunches to ripen fully.

Various solutions were tried out. One was to train the shoots downwards, which decreased vigour. Or you could train the shoots both upwards and downwards, which would encourage the development of a natural hedge from top to bottom. Some growers adopted the Geneva double curtain, a quadrilateral cordon system developed at Cornell Univeristy in New York State. With this method the vines were trained along two wires six feet off the ground; the canes dangled down from the wires, giving a good crop of fruit. The drawback turned out to be that although the double curtain may have worked well in the New York climate, it proved less satisfactory in California, where the grapes often developed sunburn and the vines tended to overcrop. However, it was better adapted to high-vigour sites than most other systems. Overall it is more appropriate to red varieties than white. High wire systems such as this also had the advantage of being compat-ible with mechanical harvesters. If they were to be hand-picked, you would need, as Doug Meador put it, a harvesting crew of Masai warriors. One of Meador's own solutions was to tighten the spacing between vines to 3.5 feet and train the fruit along unilateral cordons to avoid contact between the bunches. What he was aiming for was light penetration and air movement and the avoidance of a forest of foliage; all these factors would help avoid the vegetal flavours that were the bane of so much fruit from Monterey.

Scott Henry in Oregon devised a system, now named after him, in which vines are trained along two cordons rather than one, with half the shoots trained upwards, the other half downwards. One drawback tended to be that shoots along the lower cordon growing upwards sometimes interfered with bunches growing along the upper. The Scott Henry method is inexpensive to instal, gives good yields, is suited to mechanical harvesting, and thus seems better suited to commercial grape farmers than to those who were adamant about quality, first and foremost.

A more highly regarded option is the quadrilateral cordon, which is most successful on high-vigour soils where the vines have been widely spaced.

In the 1980s the Smart/Dyson system was developed as an elaboration of the Scott Henry system. John Dyson was the owner of the Mistral Vineyard near Gilroy and Dr Richard Smart was an Australian viticulturalist greatly in demand as a consultant throughout the world, including France. Their system of canopy management sought to recognize that in California the vine tended to produce more shoots than were required, simply because the climate and root system encourage vigour. By splitting the canopy, that vigour could be diffused, and at the same time aeration could be greatly improved, thus minimizing the risk of rot. With bunches less hidden by top-heavy foliage it was possible, some vineyard managers estimated, to reduce harvesting costs by 25 per cent. Another powerful argument in favour of Smart/Dyson was that splitting the canopy allowed for more tonnage and thus higher yields. It is also suited to mechanical shoot-positioning and harvesting.

Smart/Dyson was not the only method introduced to control California sprawl. Another was vertical trellising, in which the shoots were trained to grow upwards, exposing the bunches to more sunlight and air. This found particular favour in cooler growing regions, such as the Central Coast, where it lowered the risks of mildew and botrytis infection and, it was thought, gave better aromatic qualities and flavours to the wine. Ray Kaufman of Laurel Glen points out that vertical trellising attracts angular sunlight, while the canopy shades the bunches from the full heat of the afternoon sun. These factors together help promote the full maturation of the fruit. Brad Alderson of Mondavi Woodbridge is another fan of vertical trellising, not only because it permits dappled sunlight to ripen well aerated bunches, but because the buds for the following year are also exposed to sunlight rather than being concealed by a jungle of canopy. Vertical trellising is also well adapted to closely spaced vines, but is far less efficacious in older vineyards with much lower density of vines. It doesn't work equally well in all regions. Richard Sanford in Santa Ynez Valley finds that vertical trellising compacts the leaves too much. Richard Smart believes that vertical trellising is only suitable for low and moderate vigour sites; where the site is too vigorous, the canopy will be shaded, reducing both yields and quality.

Another highly regarded system is lyre trellising, pioneered in France by Professor Alain Carbonneau. It too is a divided canopy system, and thus well adapted to plantings of rows at least 10 feet wide. The drawback is the expense of installation and maintenance, which has to be largely manual. Richard Smart believes that, like vertical trellising, lyre canopies are not appropriate for high-vigour sites.

It should be made clear that canopy management is not just a modish way of increasing the physiological maturation of the grapes. It is also a way to increase the crop without any loss of concentration or ripeness in the fruit. Its advocates point out that one can achieve greater physiological ripeness at *lower* sugar levels. There was no need to leave the grapes unpicked until their sugar levels were so high that the inevitable consequence would be immensely alcoholic wines. Grapes that were perfectly ripe while not excessively sugary would result in wines that were better balanced and more stylish.

Tony Soter has mixed feelings about canopy management, however. 'I see it as essentially remedial work. Much canopy management can be avoided by controlling the growth of your vines so that they stop growing at the right moment. To split the canopy means you haven't controlled the growth. You are fooling the vine. That's not a reason not to do it, but so far as I am concerned this is little more than fine-tuning.'

There is also some debate about the merits of cane pruning as opposed to cordon (or spur) pruning. Cane pruning is more expensive to maintain, and cordon pruning can be more easily mechanized, which reduces costs. Randy Dunn argues that cane pruning can result in poor bunch distribution, with clusters often growing close together and sometimes rubbing up against bunches on the next vine. Cordon pruning, in his view, gives a more even distribution of clusters. Tony Soter prefers cordon pruning for Cabernet Sauvignon, but prefers cane pruning for Pinot Noir. Peter Newton agrees that cordon pruning is well suited to Cabernet Sauvignon and Cabernet Franc, but believes it is less suitable for Merlot. No doubt local microclimatic factors, as well as personal preference, will influence the choices made in this regard.

Luckiest of all were the growers who owned old vineyards planted with varieties such as Zinfandel, Carignane, and Grenache. These tended to be head-pruned vines, that is, vines that required no trellising as they were planted independently and trained as small bushes, without the use of wires or cordons. Head-pruned vines fell out of fashion as soon as mechanical harvesting became feasible, since they had to be picked manually. Now they are back in vogue because the quality of their fruit can be excellent.

Irrigation

Once the vines have been planted a further choice must be made: to dry-farm or to irrigate. It is usually fairly obvious which choice is appropriate. In semi-arid regions such as the Salinas Valley or Santa Maria Valley rainfall is simply insufficient to allow the grapes to ripen. Irrigation is essential. In regions such as the Sierra Foothills and parts of Mendocino, where rainfall is, at least by Californian standards, abundant, dry-farming is perfectly feasible. Elsewhere, there is an element of choice. In Napa and Sonoma there are many water-retentive clay soils, where vines can often get by without irrigation. Although many mountain vineyards are dry-farmed, there is no firm rule. Jeff Patterson at Mount Eden Vineyards, high in the Santa Cruz Mountains, is convinced that his vineyards benefit from irrigation. John Alban in Edna Valley concurs, provided that the irrigation is properly controlled.

Many Californian growers are irritated by European criticisms of their reliance on irrigation, without which grapes simply could not grow in many regions. 'The French don't irrigate,' responds Dick Ward of Saintsbury, 'because in France water falls out of the sky. On the other hand they have no control over how or when. In California we can, in effect, control the rain, we can ensure that fruit and leaves don't get too hot. Nobody sensible overdoes the irrigation, as you don't want it to affect your root structure. But it's typically French to turn necessity into a virtue!'

The original method of irrigation in California was to fill furrows or trenches alongside the rows of vines with water. It is still widely practised in Lodi. The drawback is obvious: it becomes very difficult to control the amount of water each vine receives. The consequence of giving a vine too much water is, of course, to encourage the very growth that most conscientious growers are seeking to diminish. But for those farming grapes as a cash crop, the temptation is keen. Twenty years ago, the Mendocino grower Barney Fetzer deplored the tendency of some farmers 'to flood their vineyards right up to the time of harvest so they can get more weight when they sell by the ton. This makes a very inferior wine.'⁶

The favoured form of irrigation is drip irrigation, by which the farmer can control precisely the location and volume of the watering, as well as its timing. Drip irrigation was an Israeli invention, devised as an aid to growing crops in the Negev Desert. In California, Dick Graff at Chalone claimed to have been one of the first to install the system. A valve releases water, a drip at a time, to the side of each vine. Timing is crucial. If irrigation is practised too early in the growing season, the roots will remain close to the surface. But if the soils are not too sandy and have received sufficient winter rains, then the roots will have been encouraged to forage deep and draw out whatever mineral complexities the soil may have to offer.

It should not be forgotten that irrigation is expensive, especially with water being a scarce resource in the semi-arid regions. So for small-scale growers there is little temptation to turn on the irrigation on a whim. Irrigation systems have also become far more sophisticated in recent years. At Murphy-Goode in Sonoma, the vineyard managers use a neutron probe to monitor the moisture in the ground, and they have installed a form of underground drip irrigation. Growers in the best viticultural regions tend to be more sparing with the water than agribusiness growers. Whereas a Carneros grower will apply 25–125 gallons per vine during the growing season, his counterpart in the Central Valley might use 400–1,000 gallons per vine.

There are also some interesting experiments taking place which show how the timing of drip irrigation can influence the development of phenolics and pigmentation as well as cluster and berry size. Visiting the Columbia Crest winery in Washington State, I participated in a blind tasting of Sauvignon Blancs, all grown and vinified identically, the sole variable between them the degree and timing of irrigation. It was very clear that over-irrigated vines resulted in wines that were flat, dull, and slightly herbaceous. The climate of the Columbia Valley in Washington is very different to that of California, but the principle remains the same.

Leaf-pulling

This inelegant-sounding practice is one more trick in the grape grower's book in order to control that vital balance between foliage and fruit. If canopy management alone doesn't achieve this balance, then remedial action can be taken by simply removing the leaves. This does not have to be labour intensive. Vineyard machinery, originally developed in New Zealand, means that the task can be mechanized. Indeed for some growers leaf-pulling has become an alternative to the far more expensive canopy management.

Doug Meador of Ventana Vineyards counsels caution: 'You have to be very careful about leaf-pulling. Leaves are factories, so you must take care. It's like taking your shirt off on April 1 or August 1 – the timing is crucial.'

Yields

What is the relation between the size of a crop and the quality of the fruit? The question may sound academic, but it generates another of those ferocious debates that enliven the world of wine. It seems only logical that there should be a connection between the two. If the energy generated by photosynthesis has to be shared out among seven clusters on a vine, it seems obvious that it will generate greater concentration and indeed ripeness levels than if that same energy is dissipated among twelve bunches on that same vine. That is the rationale behind European appellation systems that place limits on yields. Overcropping, it is argued, will result in dilute wines that are insufficiently ripe and lack flavour.

Those who believe this is too glib a view like to remind their critics that the much-vaunted low yields of French vineyards a century ago were almost certainly a consequence of high rates of disease and missing vines. If a vineyard is in good health and properly maintained, there should be no contradiction between decent yields and high quality. Naturally there comes a point at which quality will decline, but the threshold, they argue, is considerably higher than the traditionalists would have you believe. They point to exceptionally abundant years in Bordeaux, such as 1986 and 1990, that have at the same time been of superlative quality.

John Williams's instinct at Frog's Leap is to leave nature alone. 'In 1995 we had a low crop because the vines were stressed and wanted to slow down. There's no need to manipulate the vines. Do we know better than nature? I do practise green-harvesting, but as a useful corrective measure.'

We have already seen that modern trellising systems do seem capable of delivering generous crops of very high quality fruit. European orthodoxies are not necessarily applicable in California. Christian Moueix, when he began to cultivate the Napanook vineyard at Dominus, based his viticultural practices on those he was used to at Pétrus; that included keeping yields down to 3 tons per acre. But, reports James Laube, 'he found the wines too austere and tannic. "I crop-thinned too severely," he admitted. By increasing yields to 4 tons, the wines were better balanced.'[7]

In Bordeaux anyone can go to a local town hall and ask to see the *déclaration de récolte,* in which vineyard owners must declare the size of the crop expressed in hectolitres. Divide that figure by the number of hectares owned by the estate and you can calculate the average yield for each and every estate in the commune. In California it is very hard to discover what the yields are for any property. You can ask the winemaker but you have to take the answer on trust. Robert Benson's collection of interviews with *Great Winemakers of California*, published in 1977, deals with this question and the consensus seems to be that yields in those days, according to the owners and winemakers, were between 2 and 5 tons per acre, or approximately 30 to 75 hectolitres per hectare, depending, of course, on grape variety and location. Such yields would be in line with those cropped in other wine regions of the world.

I suspect, but cannot prove, that yields in California are now very much higher. Bob Travers of Mayacamas, whose own mountain vineyards are very low-yielding, believes that yields down on the

Napa Valley floor have increased from 4 to 5 tons per acre to 8 to
10. Some years ago Bill Pease, then winemaker at Clos Pegase, told
me that he was slightly embarrassed when one parcel of Sauvignon
Blanc yielded 9 tons per acre. Although he conceded that this was
excessive, he was convinced that higher yields were compatible
with good quality. Tim Hanni of Beringer admits that yields overall
are higher than ever, but argues that this is the case throughout
the wine world, and it need not lead to more diluted or lower-
quality wines.

Professor Carole Meredith of UC Davis agrees. Many growers,
especially those farming soils that aren't capable of generating high
yields, maintain there is a connection between yields and quality,
but many viticultural researchers now disagree. Growers, she
argues, know that wine writers such as myself revere the notion
that low yields are the best path to high quality, so they reiterate
that view in order to maintain the reputation of their wines. She
believes the key to quality is the ratio of foliage to fruit and the
exposure of the bunches to light. Experiments in Napa have shown
that even Cabernet Sauvignon cropped at 10–12 tons per acre can
be good enough for Reserve-quality wines. With healthier vines
and better understanding of canopy management, Meredith argues,
you can allow the vines to be more productive.

The debate becomes complex because many Californian viticulturalists no longer think we should speak about yields in terms of
tonnage per acre (or hectolitres per hectare). Tim Mondavi told
me that as a grower in Napa Valley, his aim is both low yield and
low vigour of the vine, which is why he believes in close spacing.
But in his view berry size is far more significant than tonnage, since
it influences the ratio of juice to skin and thus the tannic structure
of the wine. Berry size can be controlled by the manipulation of
drip irrigation, by reducing the use of fertilizers, and by using cover
crops to increase competition within the vineyard. Closer spacing
may give more bunches of grapes per acre and higher yields, but
the fruit itself will be of better quality. He also points out that
some years ago there were many more virus-infected vines in Napa
and elsewhere. Those viruses impeded maturation and healthy
yields; yields per acre may have been lower, but that was a consequence of ill health rather than scrupulous viticulture.

James Halliday has thought about this whole issue and notes
that 'the concept of expressing yield in tons/acre has come in for

THE WINES OF CALIFORNIA

increasing criticism in the wake of our greater knowledge of vine training, particularly with the realization that in many high vigor valley floor situations involving widely spaced vines it is almost certain that higher yields of better quality grapes can be obtained by converting the traditional single wire trellis to (say) a quadrilateral cordon. In this circumstance, it is said, yield should be expressed in terms of ounces per inch of fruiting cane or square inches of active foliage. In close-spaced, high density vineyards growers tend to talk of yield in terms of pounds per vine.' However, he goes on to conclude: 'Experience worldwide suggests that the highest quality grapes are obtained from vines which without intervention such as crop thinning, and on the other hand, without undue stress or disease, produce between 2.5 and 3 tons/acre.' [8]

Randall Grahm, so iconoclastic about so many matters, is a traditionalist when it comes to yields. 'High yields can fool most of the people most of the time. Like a film set, you can provide the props that will give the illusion of, say, a Burgundy. The wine won't age, but perhaps that doesn't matter. But I simply don't see how you can have high yields and avoid dilution. In some years California can get higher tonnage than France with good results, but tonnage is bound to be a factor when you're aiming for a specific price bracket. If you're only cropping 3 tons per acre, then you can't charge eight dollars for your wine.'

But Doug Meador of Ventana Vineyards, who prides himself on the ability to deliver high yields without sacrificing quality, is scathing about the equation of high tonnage with low quality. 'Only a bean-counter should pay any attention to hectolitres per hectare or tons per acre. All that matters is the number of grams per 100 square centimetres of exposed leaf surface – in other words, balance. In hot years you should allow the vine's vigour to keep the vine in balance. So there's no magical number for yield. Davis used to advise that Gewürztraminer would give you 2.5 to 3 tons per acre. What they really meant was that one year you'd get 5 tons, the next year none. I had a theory that if you planted the vines at 12x3 and trellised on cross arms – that's to say, with two walls of foliage, giving in effect 6 feet rather than 12 between the rows – then you should be able to end up with 10 tons per acre of better quality fruit. I tried it, got my 10 tons, and all the wines made from that fruit have won gold medals. In fact, one year, 1987, I even got 12.3 tons.

'The way I calculate yields is this. My Chardonnay is planted at 2,000 vines per acre. Each vine has 40 clusters, which equals 10 pounds of fruit. If one pound multiplied by 2,000 comes to one ton, then I'm getting 10 tons to the acre. However, each root system is supporting less weight per vine. Better leaf exposure means that each vine is functioning better, so there is no reason why the fruit shouldn't be of better quality.'

However, Meador does have his detractors. One Napa wine-maker who buys fruit regularly from Meador admires him for having been among the first growers to practise vertical trellising and close spacing. 'But he is also a farmer who likes a big crop. I'm looking for a crop of about 4 to 5 tons on Sauvignon Blanc, but I suspect Meador is getting closer to 6 to 8. So at harvest time I go down to Ventana to ensure that the fruit I buy comes from the block I particularly like, because of the soil, and to make sure that the grapes are picked at ripeness levels that are slightly lower than most of Meador's other clients are looking for.'

One way to control yields is simply to remove bunches: bunch-thinning or green-harvesting. This has now become routine practice throughout Europe. If natural conditions at flowering suggest that the crop is going to be a large one, then the grower removes bunches during the summer so that the surviving bunches will attain better levels of ripeness. It's nothing new. Many of the winemakers interviewed in Robert Benson's book in the mid-1970s, such as David Bruce, mention this as common practice in their vineyards. Given the vigour of vines in California's climate, some growers will remove up to half the bunches in order to increase concentration and ripeness levels.

Maturation and cover crops

The name of the game, whatever one's views on yields, is to achieve the best possible maturation given the climatic conditions of the year. Nobody can make decent wine from unripe fruit, and lack of balance within the grape – such as high sugar levels combined with unripe seeds – can only lead to problems. Of course it is up to each winemaker to determine the desired level of maturation. Some like to pick their Sauvignon or Chardonnay at lower or higher sugar levels than others. There is a vogue, lamentable in my view, to pick Zinfandel at exorbitant sugar levels that will ferment to dryness at about 16 or 17 degrees of alcohol. So winemakers with that kind of vinous aggression in mind will want their fruit picked at different levels of maturity from those, like Doug Nalle or John Williams, who are aiming to produce a Zinfandel that's enjoyable to drink.

For many growers the aim is to curtail the natural tendency of the grape to soar to very high sugar levels. Tony Soter is anxious to have slightly lower sugar levels than most other winemakers, especially for his Pinot Noir. Thus he needs to stop the vines growing at an earlier stage so that they become less efficient sugar producers, while at the same time allowing enough hang-time for the grapes to ripen fully. For Soter and others, the solution lies in planting cover crops. This has the effect of depriving the vines of water because the crops compete with the vine for moisture. The other method of achieving this goal is to leave a larger crop on the vine until veraison, so as to burden the vine, and then thin the bunches.

Mondavi researchers take a similar view, now arguing that 'hang-time' is less important than they used to think. What is important, however, is to push the harvest into the end season. They try to slow down the growth of vines early in the season by planting cover crops, to prevent the vines from becoming overdeveloped and out of balance by the time autumn arrives. They want the growth energy to be directed not towards the vegetation but into the fruit during the final stages of its maturation. It is all part of restoring the natural balance of the vineyards.

Robert Sinskey, with vineyards in Stags Leap and Carneros, reported in a 1996 newsletter that he used to spray with herbicides, but was unhappy with the results and instead planted a cover crop on an experimental block. The effect was that spiders returned to the vineyards and helped control the insect population, including the leaf hoppers that had been attacking his vines. Earthworms also returned to the soil, helping to break it up and increase water absorption. Yields became more consistent and hang-time increased. Sinskey's neighbours, the Shafer family, who own vine-yards in the same districts, are equally keen on cover crops and 'sustainable agriculture'.

Michael Neal of M&L Vineyard Management elaborates: 'Cover crops have several purposes. They (1) consume excess moisture in the upper soil profile in the spring; (2) provide an environment for beneficial insects and earthworms; (3) eliminate soil compaction, allowing oxygen and nutrients to get into the soil; (4) minimize soil loss from dust erosion when cultivation is done; and (5) prevent the development of root pruning and hardpans.'[9] Cover crops also maintain nitrogen levels in the soil, thus reducing or eliminating the need to add nitrogen, which can do long-term damage to the soil structure. Of course, the balance between nice bugs or rodents and pernicious bugs or rodents is hard to maintain. Cover crops also attract gophers, a problem vineyard managers solved by purchasing nesting boxes to attract barn owls, who like to dine off gophers.

The type of cover crop planted is influenced by the age of the vineyard and the soil composition. Philip Togni on Spring Mountain favours barley. Mustard, at least in this location, can grow too high and can hinder vineyard workers, especially in damp weather. He is convinced that in 1988 the presence of barley helped prevent his topsoil from being washed away in the rains, and ten years on he believed his vineyards were in better shape, in this respect, than those of his neighbours. Phil Hurst of Fetzer, with its strong belief in environmentally sound viticulture, notes the advantages of different kinds of cover crop. Clover returns nitrogen to the soil; mustard attracts spiders and aphids; and sunflowers attract ladybirds and wasps, all of which are natural predators.

Organic viticulture

Organic viticulture in California is not as widespread as its practitioners would like us to believe. Only about 5 per cent of vineyards are organically farmed. But it is one thing for a wine to be labelled as made from organically grown grapes, another to declare that the wine itself is organic. To be 'organic', a wine must have been made without the use of sulphur dioxide, which is not the case in Europe. Unfortunately it is extremely difficult to make decent wine without using sulphur dioxide at some stage in the process. There is one organic estate I have sampled extensively, Frey in Mendocino, and it is hard to avoid the conclusion that however virtuous their intentions, the end results in the bottle are far from impressive.

However, there are many estates that seek to minimize the use of pesticides and herbicides, including Gallo Sonoma. The Lodi-

Woodbridge Winegrape Commission has gone to great lengths to encourage its many members to adopt integrated pest management, which may not be strictly organic, but gets as close as most serious grape growers would like to be. The large Monteviña estate in Sierra Foothills also practises IPM, which its brochures summarize as follows: 'The key element in organic farming is the use of Integrated Pest Management. In this system, cover crops such as dill, fennel, daikon, mayweed, mustard, oats, vetch and bell beans are allowed to grow in the vineyard rows. These flowering plants attract vineyard pests such as aphids which in turn attract beneficial insect predators such as wasps, ladybugs, lacewings and pirate bugs. After the predators feast on the aphids, they devour other common vineyard pests, such as mites and leafhoppers ... In addition to providing a habitat for pests and predators, cover crops help invigorate grapevines by translocating nitrogen from the air and releasing it into the soil, reducing the need for fertilization. The cover crops also add organic matter to the soil ... Monteviña vineyard workers dispose of weeds and other undesirable plant material by tilling manually under and around the vine, obviating the need for herbicides.'

The extensive Fetzer vineyards in Mendocino are also organically farmed, although the winemaking is not formally organic. Lolonis, also in Mendocino, created a stir when it became known that they had imported thousands of ladybirds and praying mantises to help keep pests under control. John Williams at Frog's Leap in Napa is also keen on organic farming, planting cover crops and enriching the soil with natural compost rather than fertilizers. Tilling the soil helps it to remain well aerated and healthy. Biodynamic viticulture, so fashionable in France, has been slow to catch on in California, which is curious given the Californians' weakness for new fads. However, up in Mendocino County, Greg Graziano of Domaine Saint Gregory has teamed up with Fetzer to develop a biodynamic vineyard that is supplying grapes for a new range of wines called Fox Creek.

Harvesting

There is nothing peculiarly Californian about most estates' harvesting practices. The majority of quality-conscious estates harvest by hand, especially in mountain vineyards which are in any case unsuited to mechanical harvesting. However, the very large vine-yards laid out in the 1970s and 1980s in the Central Coast, not to mention the Central Valley, were intended from the start to be mechanically harvested. Harvesting machines were introduced in 1968 on a trial basis, and by the mid-1980s were picking about 65 per cent of the crop in California.[10]

The debates about the use of such machines, and whether they are gentler and more efficacious than they used to be when first introduced, are no different from the comparable debates in France and elsewhere. Let me give the last word on the subject of mechanical harvesting to Randall Grahm: 'I have always been opposed to harvesting machines. When I was at Davis they showed us films depicting them. To me they seemed very close to porno movies, with the vines being thrashed to within an inch of their life.' Large commercial growers such as Andy Beckstoffer admit that they can't indulge in selective harvesting, so vintages marked by uneven maturation can present problems.

One example of extreme resourcefulness that I encountered when discussing harvesting practices was related to me by Doug Meador. During the wet 1989 vintage, he staved off rot in his vineyards by blow-drying the grapes by using sprayers without liquid. This seems a budget application of Christian Moueix's expedient of flying helicopters over the vineyards at Pétrus so that the air churned by the blades would dry the grapes.

Phylloxera

It is easy to see how grape growers could have believed themselves safe from phylloxera in the twentieth century. After all, it was American rootstocks that had rescued the world's wine regions in the nineteenth century. The disease had proved enormously destructive in California in the 1890s, as we have seen. Thereafter vines were replanted using the St George rootstock, which proved free of problems – at least as far as phylloxera was concerned.

Then in 1958 Professor Lloyd Lider at UC Davis recommended a rootstock called AXR-1. It was an old creation, a crossing of Aramon with *Vitis rupestris*, generated by a viticulturalist called Victor Ganzin as long ago as 1876. AXR-1 certainly had features to recommend it: it was easy to graft and gave generous crops. In Professor Lider's view it was a perfect choice for new plantings.

What was less well publicized was the fact that AXR-1 had not proved resistant to phylloxera in other parts of the world. It was certainly known that some vineyards planted on AXR-1 in South Africa had succumbed to phylloxera in the 1950s. In 1963 a professor at Montpellier University warned the Californians that AXR-1 spelt trouble, and repeated the warning in 1976. Europeans such as Marimar Torres planting vineyards in California were sufficiently aware of the danger to choose other rootstocks.[11] Nonetheless, in the 1960s and 1970s AXR-1 became widely adopted as the rootstock of choice in California.

It took a while for the dreaded phylloxera louse to pop up. An ailing vineyard near St Helena was diagnosed in 1983 as suffering from a type of phylloxera dubbed Biotype B, which had the unfortunate characteristic of spreading forty times faster than the louse that had ravaged the vineyards a century earlier.[12] At the same time phylloxera was discovered in a Sonoma vineyard. By 1986 flooding in Napa Valley spread phylloxera across the valley floor. One would have thought that some very loud alarm bells would have started ringing at this point, especially since Jeffrey Granett of the Department of Entomology at Davis was already conducting intensive research into the growing problem. However, it was not until 1989 that Davis officially changed its mind and ceased to recommend AXR-1. The consequence was that over half of all the vineyards in Napa and Sonoma became infected and had to be replanted. It wasn't only floodwater that spread the louse through the vineyards, but irrigation systems and farm machinery. The cost of replanting was immense. As Corky Lovin of the International Agricultural Visitors Program put it: 'It was a billion-dollar mistake, but at least some growers got thirty-five great years on AXR-1 before the problems began.'

In 1990 wine industry consultants Motto, Kryla, and Fisher predicted that replanting would cost $250 million in Napa alone. That would prove to be a woeful underestimate.[13] Napa was hit hardest, followed by Sonoma and Monterey. In the decade following the reappearance of phylloxera, at least 35,000 acres have been replanted at an estimated cost of up to $2 billion. In 1994 Mondavi estimated the cost per acre at around $35,000. By 1994 Biotype B was also showing up in Mendocino (where 60 per cent of vines are on AXR-1), Lake, Sacramento, San Joaquin, Alameda, and Santa Clara counties, as well as at some vineyards planted on own roots in San Luis Obispo, Santa Barbara, and the Sierra Foothills. Moreover, another strain of phylloxera was found to be at work, but only vines planted on Harmony rootstocks were affected.[14] Growers such as John Williams in Napa and Paul Dolan, head of the largely organic Fetzer estates in Mendocino, argued that their policy of reducing the use of chemical fertilizers and other treatments helped the vines build up a natural resistance to many predators, including phylloxera, but this may in the long term prove to be wishful thinking.

There were numerous consequences of the enforced replanting. Some were positive. Growers took advantage of the situation to ensure their vineyards were up to date in terms of spacing and trellising, drip irrigation systems, and clonal selections. On the other hand, many commercial growers played safe, favouring best-selling varieties such as Cabernet, Merlot, and Chardonnay over less remunerative varieties such as Riesling or Sauvignon Blanc. There would also be a glut of young vines, although even a staunch European such as Marimar Torres admits she is astonished by the quality of fruit and wine that can be obtained from young vines in California. (Those prize-winning wines from Chateau Montelena and Stag's Leap Wine Cellars in the 1976 Paris tasting were, after all, the products of young vines.)

Experienced vineyard owners such as Peter Newton are not too fazed by phylloxera. 'It's manageable until it starts to give uneven ripeness, and it's at that point that you pull out the affected vines. What we've done with our older Cabernet is to interplant along the rows, so that when the older vines are pulled out, there are younger vines already in place.' Sounds a sensible approach, but one of his neighbours was sceptical, suggesting that the young vines won't necessarily do that well because there will be excessive root competition. Augustin Huneeus of Franciscan is also sceptical, but for different reasons: 'Interplanting is like issuing Nature a challenge to create other and possibly stronger phylloxera mutations. It's just too risky.'[15] However, this method of staggered replanting has also been widely practised in Monterey. Another method of avoiding replanting from scratch is 'in-arch' or 'approach' grafting, whereby the affected vine is linked to a resistant rootstock. A few years later the new rootstock takes charge, and the link with the old one can be severed. The technique was originally developed in Italy for cherry trees. Monticello and

Domaine Carneros report almost complete success with the technique, the only drawback being that you have to retain the vineyard's original spacing, clones, and varieties. However, the cost is only 15 per cent that of replanting the vineyard.

Pierce's Disease

Phylloxera at least is curable, if expensively so. Pierce's Disease is not. This disease is caused by a bacterium known as *Xylella fastidiosa*, which inhabits the water-conducting system within the vine and eventually blocks the movement of water, thus crippling and killing the vine. It is spread by a species of leaf hopper known as blue-green sharpshooters, which feed on infected bushes – they have a passion for blackberry bushes – along riverbanks and then inject the vines. Vineyards close to rivers, landscaped parkland, and lush woodlands are most at risk. The affliction has no effect on the quality of the wine, but it doesn't do much for the lifestyle of the vine. It takes about one year for the disease to take hold, which is much faster than phylloxera.

It destroyed vineyards in the Los Angeles area in 1884 and made a number of appearances in the 1930s and 1940s. It particularly affects young vines, and some varietals seem more susceptible than others. Chardonnay and Pinot Noir are most at risk, while Chenin Blanc, Riesling, Sylvaner, Sauvignon Blanc and Cabernet Sauvignon seem to put up greater resistance. Some researchers speculate that Pierce's Disease may be on the increase because of the many new vineyards planted after phylloxera. The spread has also been blamed on the diminishing use of pesticides and on mild winters.

Its appearance has been sporadic. In Napa Valley, Spring Mountain has probably been worst affected, with some damage done to vineyards at Newton and Togni. Beringer have had to replant some of their vineyards which succumbed. Pierce's Disease has also been encountered in Stags Leap. In Santa Cruz, David Bruce's vineyard suffered badly, with a loss of about 25 acres, and there have been outbreaks in Santa Barbara and Ojai. However, much of Mendocino County is free of the disease, because it cannot survive the cold winter temperatures.

It is particularly troublesome because replanting alone is unlikely to get rid of the problem, since the environmental factors that gave rise to the infection are likely to do so again. Consequently, some growers try to clear vegetation from around their affected vineyards so as to starve the sharpshooters of bacteria. Philip Togni has had to employ vineyard workers to clean out the neighbouring woodlands to prevent further damage. David Bruce has removed certain native plants from his mountain estate, as sharpshooters don't care for evergreens. Very cold winters have been known to kill off the bacteria, and some growers believe that insecticides can be effective. Researchers are also trying out different and stronger rootstocks, which may help to protect the vine but have the side effect of increasing the vine's vigour, which then has to be controlled by other means.

Other afflictions of the vine quite common in California, though hardly unique to this region, include Eutypa and Nematodes. Eutypa is a fungus transmitted through pruning scars. Its effect is to kill off the vine's spurs. Nematodes are insects that feed on plant roots and maim the vine, though vines are rarely killed off by them.

NOTES

1 Leon D. Adams, *The Wines of America*, p. 3
2 Robert Benson, *Great Winemakers of California*, p. 80
3 Ibid., p. 276
4 Richard Smart 'Row orientation of vineyards', *Practical Winery and Vineyard*, July/August 1995
5 Richard Smart 'Tight spacing – the right way to go?', *Practical Winery and Vineyard*, November/December 1996
6 Benson, p. 268
7 James Laube, *Wine Spectator*, 31 July 1998
8 James Halliday, *Wine Atlas of California*, p. 146
9 Cakebread Winery Newsletter, Fall 1997
10 Adams, p. 242
11 Kathryn McWhirter, *Independent on Sunday*, 2 February 1992
12 Halliday, pp. 84–5
13 Frank Prial, *New York Times*, 11 July 1990
14 John De Benedictis, *Phylloxera Phlyer Newsletter*, UC Davis, August 1996
15 Quoted in *Decanter*, May 1993

13

Making the Wine

Once the grapes have been harvested, they have to be processed and made into wine. This chapter will not offer a crash course on winemaking, which does not differ greatly in California from other wine regions of the world. Instead it will focus on aspects of the process that are specific to California.

Pressing

Most Californian wineries are well equipped with up-to-date presses, which in almost all cases means pneumatic or bladder presses. Some smaller wineries still use old hydraulic or vertical presses, which can give exceptionally good musts but are slow and labour-intensive.

Skin contact, which used to be in vogue in the 1980s, is rarely employed these days. It was curious that just when the French, especially in the Graves, were becoming excited about *macération pelliculaire*, the Californians were giving up on the idea and adopting whole-cluster pressing instead. Whole-cluster pressing produces very clear juice, thus eliminating the need for cold-settling (what the French call *débourbage*) or lees filtration, both of which are designed to get rid of the gross lees before fermentation begins. In addition, whole-cluster pressing leaves the seeds unbroken, which means a reduction of potential bitterness in the wine. Winemakers favouring the technique argue that although the procedure is twice as slow (and thus twice as costly) as destemming and pressing (because the stems occupy as much space as the grapes inside the press), the resulting improvement in quality makes it worthwhile.

Yeasts

Yeast provokes the fermentation that converts grape sugar into alcohol. In most small estates in Europe, winemakers rely on natural yeasts that inhabit vineyards and wineries in order to get the fermentation started. Larger wineries, wishing to leave nothing to chance, will employ cultivated yeasts. In California there is a much stronger reliance on cultivated yeasts, although 'natural yeast fermentation' came into fashion in the 1990s.

Those who prefer to use indigenous (or 'natural') yeasts argue that local yeast populations impart their own character to the wine. The use of indigenous yeasts encourages diversity and complexity both of aroma and flavour. It is admitted that some indigenous yeasts can impart unpleasant as well as attractive characteristics to a wine (although this is rare) and that it is more difficult to control the activity of indigenous yeasts. Some work more quickly than others, and it is impossible to predict their speed or efficacy. Patrick Campbell at Laurel Glen finds that natural yeasts give a slower fermentation and that the temperature is less likely to rise sharply. In Europe, where indigenous yeasts are much more firmly established in the local environment, they are more predictable than in California, where many vineyards are too recently planted for a sizeable colony of yeasts to have attached itself to the site.

Cultivated yeasts offer a greater degree of uniformity, and also considerable security. Larger wineries cannot afford to indulge the vagaries of natural yeasts, which go their own way and take their own time. With cultivated yeasts it is easier for winemakers to calculate the amount of time required for each tank to complete its task of fermentation, and thus calculate the management of the harvest in terms of tank space.

UC Davis has always recommended the use of such yeasts, which it cultivated and made available to California wineries. Professor Vernon Singleton couldn't get too excited about the whole issue. 'Yeast is a minor factor,' he told me. 'Alcohol in the wine comes primarily from the ripeness of the grapes rather than from the efficiency of the conversion of grape sugar by the yeasts. We recommend inoculating yeasts for economic reasons, to promote efficiency at the winery. And I'm not convinced that the use of cultivated yeasts has any negative influence on the eventual quality of the wine.'

The principal cultivated yeasts in regular use in California are the following. Montrachet is used for both white and red musts, but is particularly popular with Chardonnay. Its drawback can be slowness and a reluctance to cope with musts rich in sugar. In contrast Champagne yeast works swiftly and has no problems with high must weights. Pasteur is another slow-acting yeast, and Steinberg, originally cultivated at Geisenheim in Germany, has a high tolerance for cold temperatures and is thus well suited to the fermentation of aromatic varieties such as Riesling, Muscat, and Gewürztraminer, which are often fermented at low temperatures. Epernay is another yeast tolerant of cold temperatures. Prise de Mousse is very popular and powerful, and was usually the yeast of choice for Sauvignon Blanc. As for strains best suited to reds, Pasteur Red is a good all-rounder and stuck fermentations are infrequent. There are fewer takers for Assmannshausen, a slow performer; a number of winemakers, such as Tony Soter, are reluctant to use it.[1]

Despite the growing reliance on natural yeast fermentation, it remains a minority pursuit. Bob Travers of Mayacamas stated the case for cultivated yeasts back in the mid-1970s and many winemakers would argue that what he said then still holds true: 'Depending on the type of indigenous yeast, and its population level, there is a good possibility it will affect the flavor of the wine So you're always taking a chance by using wild yeast because you're never sure which of the several wild species on the grape will dominate in fermentation. If you can be reasonably sure which will dominate and you like the flavors it produces, the only disadvantage is it always takes much longer to begin fermentation, increasing the chances of bacterial and oxidative spoilage the longer it sits.'

Ridge Watson of Joullian also uses cultivated yeasts. 'Research seems to show that native yeasts come from the winery rather than the field, and in a new winery such as ours there aren't that many yeasts around.' Doug Nalle in Sonoma notes that with Zinfandel there is a frequent risk of stuck fermentations, so as far as he is concerned it is asking for trouble relying on indigenous yeasts. Moreover there is an impressive range of cultivated yeasts from which to choose. Ric Forman uses Montrachet yeast for his Chardonnay, saying that he wants to avoid the funky flavours that might otherwise mar his 'very expensive juice'.

Nonetheless in an ideal world, many winemakers would agree, natural yeast fermentation would be the method of choice. Indigenous yeasts tend to be slower than cultivated ones, and some would say that slow fermentations give greater complexity and richer texture. Although there is a greater risk of stuck fermentations, leaving unwanted residual sugar in the wine, there is a lower risk of wine with excessive alcohol levels. Time and again in the 1980s, when the use of cultivated yeasts was just about universal in California, a winemaker would apologize when I remarked unfavourably on a wine with a distinct alcohol burn on the palate that 'It turned out to be a killer yeast', meaning the yeast had operated with such vigour and ferocity than the rate of transformation of sugar into alcohol was unusually high. The scientific case in favour of natural yeast fermentation has been made by Dr Mark Herold, a research oenologist who works with Phelps in Napa Valley: 'Low pH and high grape sugar levels limit the selection of yeasts to less than 20 genera. Of these, two main yeast genera have been recognized as main players in natural fermentations: Kloeckera and Saccharomyces ... As a result of the competition for nutrients between Saccharomyces and other wild yeasts during the fermentation, fatty acid esters and other compounds are produced in amount and combination that differ from fermentations inoculated with pure yeast strains. These unique yeast-specific secondary metabolic compounds are important components in the aromatic profile, and ultimate quality of the wine.'

James Hall of Patz & Hall, a high-quality négociant company that occasionally practises natural yeast fermentation, says the whole issue is far less cut and dried than most people suppose. 'The Montrachet yeast has been used for decades in California. After we press the grapes, the cake is usually returned to the vineyards in the form of compost. Some of those yeasts are probably still out there, and have blended into whatever the truly indigenous yeast population may be. And research doesn't support the argument that natural yeasts inhabit the vineyards. Primarily they're on hoses, tanks and other winery equipment. Still, whatever their source, they do give a slower, cooler fermentation, which is why we like to try it from time to time.'

Susan Reed of Matanzas Creek believes there is a discernible difference in a wine made with natural yeasts, but that difference diminishes with time. 'After eight months we can't tell the difference between that wine and another lot from the same vineyard made with cultivated yeasts.'

Extended maceration

Once fermentation begins, other variables come into play: the medium in which the fermentation takes place, the temperature of the fermentation, and its duration. White wines are fermented either in stainless steel tanks or barrels. Varietals such as Riesling or Chenin are invariably fermented in steel at cool temperatures, while Chardonnay is increasingly fermented in barrels. With other varieties, such as Viognier or Sauvignon Blanc, there will be a divergence in view, according to the style of wine the winemaker hopes to achieve. Some Chardonnays are steel-fermented and not aged in oak, and some of them are delicious and appetizing. It used to be quite common for Chardonnay to be fermented in steel (often for practical and economic reasons rather than because of any oenological doctrine) and then aged in oak barrels, but there has been a clear shift to conducting the entire process in wood, on the grounds, which seem demonstrably true, that the oak influence is better integrated into the wine if the must is fermented rather than merely matured in oak.

As for the temperature of fermentation, this is very much up to the winemaker. There are approximate norms for steel-fermented whites, with most winemakers avoiding the very cool temperatures that used to be fashionable, and even more approximate ones for red wines. Much depends on the length of fermentation and on the variety. Most winemakers will try to avoid very high temperatures, except perhaps briefly at the very end of fermentation, for fear of extracting harsh or bitter tannins. With white wines fermented in barrel temperature is rarely an issue, as the small volume of the barrel and the usually cool temperature of the barrel room will prevent the temperature from rising to dangerously high levels.

Once the alcoholic fermentation is completed, which takes roughly 6 to 10 days, the wine is usually left to macerate for some days or weeks 'on the skins'. In other words, the solid matter in the wine, instead of being separated from the juice and pressed, is left in contact with the juice. This is a longstanding practice in Europe, especially Bordeaux, where macerations of 3 or 4 weeks are common in order to increase the gentle extraction of tannin, colour, and other elements. However, over the past decade Californian winemakers have been tempted more and more by what has become known as extended maceration, prolonging the process by anything up to 8 weeks. The theory behind this is that with lengthy macerations, the tannin molecules, instead of becoming over-extracted and bitter as one might suppose, combine to form larger molecules, giving greater viscosity and no bitterness. This process is called polymerization. It is alleged that the larger molecules also give the wine greater stability, which will help it to age after bottling. Some experienced winemakers such as Paul Draper of Ridge are less certain about how stable this molecule bonding really is. Ric Forman is more dismissive: 'Extended maceration is just a buzzword. Macerating red wines for up to three months does give big soft chocolatey wines, but no one really knows how well they will keep or how they will develop.' Randy Ullom, winemaker at Kendall-Jackson, believes extended maceration is risky as there is no carbon dioxide to protect the wine from oxidation or from volatile acidity. It also ties up fermenting tanks for long periods. But he agrees that extended maceration does help polymerize the tannins, and the wines become more lush and free of bitterness.

Christopher Howell of Cain has given the matter a great deal of thought. He acknowledges that high tannin levels can be a problem in 'mountain' grapes such as those he harvests on Spring Mountain. That, after all, was surely the rationale for the blending in of other varieties that is commonplace in Bordeaux: one of the principal functions of Merlot and Cabernet Franc in a claret is to soften up the Cabernet Sauvignon. 'It wasn't until well into the 1980s that Californians began to learn how to control the tannins. Before then most winemakers routinely pumped the *marc* and blended in all or most of the press wine. I believe it was the Mondavis' experience at Opus One that taught them, and then others, what to do, and this gentler handling was also adopted for their Pinot Noir, with brilliant results.

'One way of moderating the tannin is to pick the grapes as late as possible, which is what consultants such as Michel Rolland urge their clients to do. But I have a suspicion this is being taken to an extreme, and the result is wines that are now over-fruity. The other way to control the tannin is to try extended macerations. It is true that polymerization occurs and that the wines are more complete and rounded. But in fact there's no real reduction in tannin – it's just that the tannins you perceive are less painful. With valley floor fruit from Napa I worry that you will end up with flabby wines, and with mountain fruit I worry that you will get greater astringency. It's essential to adapt your maceration system to the fruit or the vineyard.' Patrick Campbell of Laurel Glen confirms these misgivings. He has tried extended maceration with his Sonoma Mountain fruit, but has abandoned it, since he finds it makes wines taste over-extracted and stewed.

Winemakers such as John Williams of Frog's Leap aim to produce wines that are balanced and attractive young. He has no patience with wines that are heavily tannic and harsh in their youth, and sold on the promise that after prolonged bottle ageing they will be magnificent. 'Ugly young, ugly old,' he says cheerfully, adding, 'I've put aside the big powerful highly rated wines of the last fifteen years, waiting for them to open up, and they rarely do.' Chris Howell would not quite agree with Williams's dictum. 'Old-style California Cabernets with high tannins can age very well, just as the best 1975 Bordeaux are ageing well. Wines from Mayacamas and Ridge produced in the 1970s are still superb. However, on the whole I believe our more modern-style wines with their softer tannins do age more rapidly. But everything has to be measured against fruit quality. Spottswoode is the classic example of a balanced Cabernet that ages well. The vineyard has high natural acidity and gives fruit of good colour, and it all comes together and it ages beautifully.'

There is a good deal of experimentation with fermentation issues. A growing number of wineries are trying the Australian method of barrel-fermenting the red wines. Daryl Groom, former winemaker at Penfolds in Australia, brought the technique with him when he came to Geyser Peak. The must is fermented in the usual way and when the sugar level has gone down to about 5 Brix, the wine is taken off the skins and completes its fermentation in barrels. The idea is to achieve better oak integration in the young wine and a silkier texture. Others are toying with Michel Rolland's method of allowing the malolactic fermentation of the reds to take place in barrels rather than in tanks. In both cases the outcome is likely to be soft, more voluptuous, more accessible wines, and also wines that are likely to show their paces better in their infancy than a more traditionally made wine, which is good news when the wine journalists come round to assess the barrel samples. There are sound oenological reasons in favour of the practice: malolactic in barrel gives the wine a degree of protection which means that the addition of sulphur dioxide can be delayed, which aids colour stability.

Malolactic fermentation

Once the alcoholic fermentation is completed, a wine may or may not go through a secondary fermentation, bacterial in nature, that converts malic acid, which gives the wine considerable hardness, into lactic acid. Malolactic fermentation also prompts some changes to the colour and pH, but with white wines in particular it gives a roundness to the wine that Californians gratefully recognize as 'mouthfeel'. Red wines usually go through malolactic of their own accord – a Cabernet Sauvignon bottled without malolactic fermentation would not be pleasant – and the same is sometimes true of white wines. Until 1985 UC Davis was opposed to allowing white wines to go through malolactic. However, some winemakers had long known that Burgundians routinely encouraged malolactic fermentation for both whites and reds. Admittedly acidity levels tend to be considerably higher in Burgundy than in most California wine regions, so there was a greater need for malolactic, but Burgundy-worship compelled some American winemakers to try their hand at it. Richard Graff at Chalone was one of the first, and André Tchelitscheff had long advocated it: 'When I came to California nobody in the industry believed malolactic fermentation, as a phenomenon, even existed . . . They were always talking then about lactic spoilage – an entirely different microbiological phenomenon – but they never considered malolactic fermentation. The first report that was published, in 1947, was my report on malolactic fermentation on red wines in California.' [2]

Winemakers who didn't encourage malolactic fermentation in their red wines often found that nature took its course after bottling. Gus Sebastiani cheerfully explained why he liked to give his red wines two years' bottle age before releasing them: 'We're fortunate in that we get a malolactic fermentation in many of our bottled wines, and this is the difference between a good and a great wine. You can't be sure when you will get it, or even if you will get it. The bottle age we give the wines is good, for many reasons, and one of them is I'd be afraid to release them for fear I'd get a delayed malolactic . . . So we keep it beyond the calculated danger period.' Just the thought of that secondary fermentation fizzing away in the bottle is enough to make any modern winemaker turn pale.

If malolactic fermentation is just about universal for red wines, that is not the case for whites, even in California. A number of the more old-fashioned, but respected, wineries release Chardonnay that has not gone through malolactic. To hell with mouthfeel, they seem to be saying, taste the freshness and acidic zest of this wine. Such wineries include Far Niente, Mayacamas, Forman, and Chateau Montelena. But they are in the minority. 'Full malolactic' has become a code for the rich buttery opulent style of Chardonnay that American winelovers, and many in other countries too, adore. There is a similar disparity when it comes to Sauvignon Blanc. Spottswoode, which makes a delightful version, avoids malolactic fermentation.

Some winemakers aren't greatly bothered either way. When I asked Bill Smith of La Jota about Viognier, his best-known white wine, he replied: 'Usually it happens. But if it doesn't, I won't lose any sleep over it.'

Oak

In ancient times, such as forty years ago, red wines were aged not in small barrels but in redwood tanks, some of which are still in use in more artisanal corners of California such as the Sierra Foothills. There were always small barrels for the finest wines at estates such as Beaulieu, but they were usually made from American oak and were used many times. The cult of new French *barriques* is relatively recent.

Certainly one of the first to purchase French oak was Hanzell, the Sonoma estate of the paper tycoon James Zellerbach. It was his ambition to produce truly Burgundian-style wines. He decided to follow Burgundian methods to the letter and imported traditional *pièce* barrels from France, using them for the first time in the 1956 Chardonnay made by his winemaker Brad Webb. About ten years later, it is claimed, Richard Graff was the first to introduce the idea of barrel-fermenting Chardonnay in oak barrels.

It was, of course, the indefatigable Robert Mondavi who picked up the oak stave and ran with it. In the 1980s he experimented tirelessly with all the variations possible on the theme of oak: different forests, different toasts, different ageing periods, varying proportions of new oak. Tim Mondavi, modest to a fault, told me that he thought his family firm may have overdone the experimentations with oak, 'but at least it prompted everyone to think harder about the purpose of oak ageing. It also improved our knowledge of how to look after barrels, so we at any rate have ended up with less of a reliance on new oak.'

First and foremost oak is a flavour component. Americans love the taste of oak, of vanilla, of coconut, that sweet edge that oak can give. I like it myself, but regret the standardization of wines by a heavy-handed use of young oak. I recall arriving at the old Murphys Hotel in the Sierra Foothills after a long hot day on the road. My host was already waiting in the bar and offered me a refreshing glass of white wine. The wine was clearly Chardonnay but fresh and clean and delicious. It was unoaked, from Kautz Ironstone, and it went down a treat, far more thirst-quenching and zesty than a similar wine smothered in new oak. There should be more room for such wines in the vast marketplace for California whites. There are, I am sure, wine drinkers in America who believe that there is no such thing as an unoaked wine. As Randall Grahm pithily remarked: 'People who think oak is a primary ingredient in wine are the same people who think ketchup is a vegetable.'

Oak barrels are an ideal container for a maturing red wine because of the gentle aeration that they permit. Factors such as the age of the oak and nature of the toasting have an influence on the flavour that is imparted to the wine, but for many winemakers the exchange between the liquid within and the oxygen outside is just as important. Tim Mondavi says that as far as his company is concerned, what oak offers to white wines is yeast contact as much as oak flavour, although winemakers such as Tony Soter use steel drums to allow white wine, especially Sauvignon, to remain in contact with the lees without oak influence.

The war between French and American oak has been waged for decades now, without a clear outcome. There are winemakers who simply do not like the taste of American oak. In the mid-1990s the French cooper Séguin-Moreau put on a blind tasting in London: a number of prestigious wines from Bordeaux, the Rhône, and Burgundy had been aged in different oaks, all supplied by the cooper, and we were invited to taste them. With a few exceptions the tasters, who were overwhelmingly British, preferred the French oak, closely followed by Russian oak, with American oak trailing some way behind. The objection to the American wood, at least from me, was its obviousness, a slight coarseness, a lack of finesse.

Nonetheless there are wineries that swear by it. Paul Draper of Ridge ages the great Monte Bello Cabernet Sauvignon in 85 per cent American oak. He recalls a thesis written by a French acquaintance which unearthed experiments conducted in 1900 in Bordeaux with woods of different origin. Unlike the London experiment in which I participated, this one showed Baltic oak heading the list of favourites, followed by American white oak and Bosnian oak, and the last to cross the finishing line was French oak. Silver Oak, a Napa winery that uses only American oak, has enjoyed great commercial success, despite the high prices charged for the wines. I am not a great fan of Silver Oak's style, but the wines have legions of admirers.

There is no doubt that the quality of American oak barrels has improved enormously over the past decade. Good-quality air-dried French oak barrels are very expensive – David Lucas of Lodi once said to me, 'I just bought some François Frères and Demptos barrels, and I worked out that's the equivalent of sixteen trips to Hawaii' – and wineries are looking for dependable substitutes. There are now six cooperages in California, and four of them are French-owned, applying their native expertise to the crafting of barrels, whatever the origin of the wood. The quality of American oak is now approaching that of French, and its use is likely to increase.

One winemaker is not content to use any old American oak for some of his wines. Jeff Hinchliffe of Gabrielli has aged some of his Zinfandel in barrels made from Mendocino oak, which is the identical species to Oregon white oak, *Quercus garryanna*, and is also encountered in northern Sonoma. The staves are air-dried for two years and coopered in Calistoga. Hinchliffe detects a spicy mineral flavour in this oak.

A few years ago Fetzer became the first Californian winery to have its own cooperage. Fetzer's master cooper, Keith Roberts, did an apprenticeship in Bordeaux, and it was an astute move to hire him to apply his craft in an American setting. The cooperage opened for business in 1993, when they made 4,000 barrels. Three years later they were turning out 16,000 barrels, more enough for the needs of Fetzer and its sister winery Jekel, so they started to sell the excess production to other wineries. They even sold 2,000 barrels of American oak to Bordeaux. Roberts, who has had twenty years' experience in the barrel-making business, has been buying wood from France, but also from Hungary; and he is thinking about setting up a joint venture with Russian suppliers.

One of Roberts's innovations has been to increase very slightly the volume of the barrels he makes for Fetzer. The traditional barrel holds approximately 60 gallons of wine. Roberts has increased the volume to 70 gallons but without increasing the size of the barrel. The 15 per cent additional volume is obtained by pushing out the head staves at either end. The great advantage of the 70-gallon barrel is that it leads to a more economical use of cellar space and doesn't require a larger quantity of wood. When one sees the vast barrel rooms at wineries such as Fetzer, Gallo Sonoma, and Mondavi Woodbridge, it is easy to understand why more economical use of space is a priority.

The Fetzer barrels are made in a thoroughly traditional way. The wood is air-dried for at least twenty-four months. French oak is less dense, so it can sometimes be used after eighteen months, while American oak always requires the full two years. After cutting, the head staves are toasted with gas-fired heaters. Roberts recalls that when he was at Demptos twenty-five years ago there was no toasting as such; the barrels were heated in order to soften them before finishing, but they were not subjected to powerful toasting.

Many winemakers seem to prefer a heavy toast, especially for Pinot Noir. Part of the explanation may be that with a heavy toast the wine requires a shorter period of barrel ageing, which in turn means the barrels can be used more often and are thus more economical. Phil Hurst of Fetzer reports a common belief that using heavily toasted barrels for Chardonnay and Pinot Noir 'protects' the wine against overt oak character and also gives it a deeper colour.

There is little agreement about the ideal proportion of new oak that needs to be used to mature the wine. Jeff Meier of J. Lohr in San Jose suggests that the cooler the region, the more new oak you need, especially to balance the more exotic aromas of the fruit. But perhaps this is mere speculation. New oak is certainly indicative of luxuriousness, and when you are paying $50 for a bottle of red wine, it needs to suggest, on first tasting, that it's worth that kind of money. The first time I tasted Moraga, a pricy Cabernet from Los Angeles, I jotted down on my tasting sheet: 'Smells expensive.'

That is also why, at less exalted levels of winemaking and marketing, there seems to be a trend towards lessening the proportion of new oak. One would have expected middle-of-the-road wineries to replace about 20 to 25 per cent of their barrels each year; now some are opting to change only 10 or 15 per cent. It is impossible to judge whether the reason is primarily economic or whether there is a shift in taste towards a less aggressive expression of oakiness in a wine. Certainly much California Chardonnay is over-oaked, and a diminution in the proportion of new oak used is probably a sign of improvement.

Oak chips and staves are used at some wineries to impart oaky flavours without going to the expense of barrel ageing. Of course the same is true of commercial wineries worldwide.

Treatments

Wandering through California wineries some fifteen years ago, I was struck by the battery of equipment on display at all the larger facilities. Pumps, centrifuges, filters, cold-stabilization tanks – these gleaming steel aids were proudly on show. At the State Domaine in Eltville in the Rheingau at about the same time, the then director Dr Hans Ambrosi showed me a cellar filled with splendid oak oval casks, lovingly polished. Then, opening an unobtrusive door, he said: 'That's for the tourists', and ushered me into a high-tech cellar filled with steel tanks and filtration equipment. The Californians, however, never tried to conceal their love of winemaking technology behind a smokescreen of folklore.

But in recent years there has been a growing recognition that technology, while useful, is not indispensable. The old idea that the winemaker's job is to take hold of whatever fruit comes into the winery and somehow transform it into something drinkable and saleable is on the wane. A system of appellations, whatever its faults, has boosted notions such as *terroir* and made people realize that the winemaker is not a wizard but a medium through whom the specificity of grape and soil are transmuted into wine. As the Californian wine industry as a whole has grown in confidence, there has been a diminishing reliance on technology and a greater trust in a less interventionist style of winemaking.

The winemakers who learnt their craft in the 1970s and 1980s were mostly trained at Davis or Fresno, and, as Tim Mondavi points out, 'The Davis approach to vinification was essentially defensive. You learnt how to avoid having things go wrong, or how to deal with them if they did. The use of sulphur dioxide, filtration, centrifuging, these are all techniques to avoid wine-making faults. That's important, of course, but the emphasis has changed to a celebration of the natural assets that California has to offer. At Mondavi we got away from the "repression of fault" approach when we started to work on Pinot Noir, which doesn't respond well to a lot of manipulation. These days we are placing more emphasis on the vineyards, on achieving low yields, on closer spacing, on working to have smaller berries. These are the things that will have a lasting impact on the quality of our wine and help us to achieve greater elegance and complexity. Not the equipment in our wineries.'

It is fascinating to see what highly respected winemakers had to say about their craft twenty years ago. Joe Heitz had no doubts about his role as winemaker: 'I basically believe Mother Nature is a mean old lady, and mankind has to help make wine . . . I don't waste my time in the vineyard . . . I'm a winemaker; I devote my time to the winery.' Equipment such as the centrifuge was greeted with enthusiasm. Karl Wente declared: 'The principle of centrifuging is just to clean up the lees. It doesn't make the wine brilliant, unless you heavily bentonite it and recentrifuge. In the old days, we used to do four or five rackings to get the wine clear, and every time you do that you stir them up, oxidize them, and kick them around. We've found wine is in better shape if you take it off the fermenter fast with the centrifuge.' When asked whether the lees themselves didn't contribute something positive to the wine, Wente responded unequivocally: 'Not in the case of white wines. The darn thing starts breaking down and pretty soon you've got rotten egg smells. I think trying to get the flavor and aroma of the grape is much more important, so we get our whites real clean real quick.'[3]

Mary Ann Graf, then the winemaker at Simi, agreed with this approach but also admitted to an economic motive for centrifuging, which, she declared, 'is really beneficial to separate the wine from its lees as soon as possible after fermentation. Economically, it frees fermentation tanks for subsequent musts.' Richard Arrowood, then winemaker at Chateau St Jean, pointed out that conventional settling of the must could take from three days to three weeks (thus occupying tanks that could be used for other purposes), whereas centrifuging 'does it right away and does it scientifically and precisely'.[4]

Richard Peterson, who succeeded André Tchelitscheff as winemaker at Beaulieu, was even more emphatic: 'I'll bet 90 per cent of the problems you have later on with a wine can be traced to your failure to get rid of the lees promptly after fermentation. Wineries with centrifuges invariably have cleaner, fruitier white wines than those who don't. Germans have proved that for decades . . . Fining, filtration and centrifuging are *good*, not bad. They're gentle, not harsh. They remove elements from wine that would downgrade the wine if left in – and often would fall out on their own anyway if not removed . . . You know, if you leave the winemaking up to God, he'll make vinegar, not wine.'[5] It's hard to think of a more oenologically incorrect statement in today's non-interventionist climate. And what would today's young winemaker, standing proudly in his or her gravity-fed, pump-free winery make of the breezy view of Don Alexander, winemaker at Mirassou: 'The most we do is centrifuge the wine twice, fine with bentonite, go through a pad filtration, and another filtration before bottling.'[6]

Not all the winemakers interviewed by Benson in 1975 were so in love with their machinery. Mike Grgich wisely pronounced: 'Make it right, and then leave it alone. Many other winemakers are proud of having a centrifuge, having all the filters and machinery, and I'm proud to say that I am making wine with a minimum of machinery. I know how to be a wine chemist, a wine microbiologist, a wine doctor, but I don't want to be a wine doctor; I consider myself a wine-sitter.' [7]

Centrifuges may still be glimpsed, I have no doubt, in some of the largest wineries of California. Those producing millions of bottles a year (or month) need the kind of security that advanced technology can offer. Similarly, many wineries will still give their wines a period of cold stabilization, although this practice also seems in decline. Its purpose is to allow tartaric acid crystals, which are present naturally in the wine, to precipitate out and fall to the bottom of the chilling tank. They are then removed, and the wine can be bottled without fear of crystals developing after bottle ageing. Such crystals used to induce panic attacks in diners and sommeliers unaware that this is a natural and harmless byproduct. Fearing that the crystals were in fact specks of glass, worried customers would return freshly opened bottles or even threaten to sue the winery responsible. Better wine education has made this largely a problem of the past.

A new form of treatment is de-alcoholization. Dick Ward of Saintsbury explains: 'Everyone is picking the grapes later and later to get more richness and colour in the wines. But you also get high alcohol, and with it, heaviness and clumsiness. This you can remove in two ways: by adding water, which is illegal, or by de-alcoholizing with techniques such as spinning cone technology. It's said that adding water will only dilute the wine, but you may end up with a more balanced, fresher, if less intense wine. What happens with de-alcoholizing technology is that it is applied to just part of the wine, which is then blended back in so as to reduce the overall alcohol level. Of course, what's preferable is to make the wine in the vineyard, to obtain the desired amount of extract and ripeness together with the right amount of potential alcohol.' Volatile acidity can be a problem in certain late-harvested wines, such as botrytis wines and late harvest Zinfandels, but this too can now be cured. A company called Vinivation, based in Napa Valley, specializes in removing both volatile acidity and alcohol from afflicted wines.

It is legal to acidify in California. Chaptalization, the adding of sugar during fermentation, is not permitted, however. Of course in California, unlike the classic wine regions of France or Germany, lack of ripeness is rarely a problem, and most winemakers are more concerned by high than low alcohol. The winemakers at Mondavi say there is a case for allowing light chaptalization towards the end of fermentation, not to boost the alcohol level of the wine, but to give a more protracted fermentation.

An even more common treatment is filtration, which is simply a way of removing solid particles, some of which may be very small, before bottling. In the past most wineries filtered their wines routinely as a security measure, but there has been a move away from the procedure. Very thorough filtration can remove not only minute particles but compounds that contribute to the colour and flavour of the wine. Encouraged by Robert Parker, who is adamantly opposed to the severe filtering of fine wines, growers have been moving towards the bottling of wines without filtration. This is certainly feasible with wines that have spent many months or years maturing in casks with frequent rackings. In France producers such as François Faiveley in Burgundy bottle their finest wines directly from the cask without any treatments. The drawback is that with time the wine may throw a deposit and need to be decanted before serving, a ritual that consumers of such wines are tempted to perform in any event. There is also a slight risk that the wine may contain some substances which could in time lead to the development of off-aromas or off-flavours. One assumes that conscientious producers will have the wines analysed before bottling to ensure that the wine is stable and that bacterial or other infection is not present.

The other common procedure is fining, often performed by adding eggwhites or isinglass to the wine. As the fining agent gradually sinks through the wine, any remaining particles will adhere to it and be removed by racking. Fining is both a method of clarifying the wine and of removing tannin.

Some winemakers believe in fining but not filtering; others in filtering but not fining; others don't bother with either operation. Although it is modish to omit filtration, there are strong arguments for the procedure. Randy Dunn argues that since his customers are paying a lot of money for his Cabernets, then he is obliged to filter the wine to ensure its stability. On the other hand, he never fines, which he believes is more damaging to the wine. 'Many winemakers fine their wines to make them softer, to give them better mouthfeel and higher scores from the wine critics when they are released.' Craig Williams of Phelps also believes fining is more damaging than filtration, and even filtration is something he prefers to do with a light hand. Since in his view it is possible to adapt your vinification to ensure moderate tannin levels, then it becomes less necessary to fine. In blind tastings at Phelps they have found that fined reds have less flavour than those left unfined. Tony Soter finds eggwhite fining unsatisfactory. 'It doesn't refine, it's remedial. I think light fining can be justified if it is done to provide clarity, which is a desirable feature in a wine. We prefer to use isinglass in minute quantities rather than eggwhite.' Françoise Peschon, the winemaker at Araujo, agrees that by taking care not to over-extract in the first place, she can usually avoid having to fine. 'Fining,' adds Bo Barrett of Chateau Montelena, 'is an admission that you've done something wrong.' But he does filter: 'Bacteria can be positive in winemaking, but when their work is done it's best to remove them.'

Chris Howell of Cain, who trained in France, is less opposed to fining. While accepting that it is essentially remedial, he also believes it can contribute finesse. Like Randy Dunn, he thinks it is risky to avoid filtration. 'If you don't filter, you can end up with a microbial environment in the bottle that can with time give you gaminess in the wine. There is something of a mystique about that gamy quality in an older red, but as French winemaking technique improves I think that will also diminish.' Tony Soter agrees: 'Filtration has to do with microbiological stability. Most of my wines are aged for a long time in barrel, so they rarely require filtration. I will filter if I consider it necessary. But I use a kind of diatomaceous earth of a pharmaceutical grade as my filtering medium. It costs ten times as much as other kinds of diatomaceous earth, but it's worth it. We know that impurities in diatomaceous earth can add flavours to a wine, so some kinds of filtration can add elements to a wine as well as remove them.'

Filtration is now considered a Bad Thing on the grounds that it 'strips' a wine of flavour. No doubt a brutal forcing through a sterile filtration system will do exactly that, but filtration systems are as varied in their efficiency as laxatives or sleeping pills. It is possible to moderate the dose. There used to be an old dodge in California, which involved centrifuging the wine to 'clean it up' so thoroughly that both fining and filtering became unnecessary. These wines were then labelled 'Unfined and unfiltered', which suggested some delightfully attentive artisanal winemaking of the highest order, when what was actually being presented to the consumer was a wine ruthlessly stripped of much of its flavour. Richard Arrowood admitted as much when interviewed in the 1970s: 'We use [the centrifuge] to clarify the juice before fermentation on almost every white wine. We also use it on some whites after fermentation, and I've experimented with centrifuging reds after fermentation rather than racking, and this has allowed us to market some "unfined and unfiltered" red wines.'[8]

I think it would be a mistake for wine enthusiasts to be swayed one way or the other by professions of adherence to certain wine-making fads. In Burgundy and Bergerac, on various occasions, I have been asked by winemakers to taste side by side the same wine, one bottling filtered and the other not, and express my preference. In all cases I have slightly preferred the unfiltered, and on the theory that it is better to leave something alone than interfere with it, I would support the move to bottle wines without fining or filtration. But these practices, or lack of them, should not be elevated into dogmas. If a good winemaker, with a long track record of superlative wines, decides it is necessary to fine or filter, there is probably a sound reason for it.

NOTES

1 Norman Roby and Charles Olken, *New Connoisseurs' Handbook of California Wines*, pp. 15–16
2 Robert D. Benson, *Great Winemakers of California*, p. 123
3 Ibid., pp. 73–4
4 Ibid., p. 242
5 Ibid., pp. 106–7
6 Ibid., p. 95
7 Ibid., p. 154
8 Ibid., pp. 241–2

14

The Bordeaux Red Varieties

Cabernet Sauvignon

The fascination, not to say obsession, with varietal wines in California is surprisingly recent. Until 1983 a wine with a varietal label was only required to contain a minimum of 51 per cent of wine made from that variety. Even today, in certain appellations the minimum is no more than 75 per cent. For many years wines have been sold under deceptive or meaningless labels such as Chablis or Burgundy or even, as the height of absurdity, Pink Chablis. Varietally labelled Merlot didn't even exist before the late 1960s.

By the 1970s, however, varietal names were becoming marketing tools. The success of Chateau Montelena and Stag's Leap Wine Cellars at the Paris tasting of 1976 not only made those two wineries famous, but reinforced the impression that Cabernet Sauvignon and Chardonnay wines were worth drinking. With no native varieties other than Zinfandel to relish, the Californians looked to Europe for its varietal fads and fashions. They have been numerous. Thus, despite the extraordinary popularity of Chardonnay, varieties such as Sauvignon Blanc have enjoyed a strong following (often among those deterred by the high prices demanded for most Chardonnays), as did Petite Sirah. I have found it instructive to hang around tasting rooms watching the tourists sample a few wines. Very often, the seemingly unsophisticated tourist has much preferred the off-dry Rieslings or Gewürztraminers to the conventionally revered Chardonnays. Often they were right to do so.

Unfortunately the statistics reveal a standardization of varietal choice. Riesling, Gewürztraminer, and Sauvignon Blanc are in decline. The grape grower, especially when replanting vineyards after phylloxera, is unlikely to choose varieties for which the demand is not strong and for which prices are low. Nor will the large winery, with its thousands of acres along the Central Coast, waste its time by planting extensive areas of unfashionable varieties, however excellent their quality, and however well suited the region may be to those varieties. It will be countered that, perhaps as a consequence of the Anything But Chardonnay campaign and the sterling efforts of the Rhône Rangers, there is a greater range of varieties available to California winemakers than ever before. That is undoubtedly true, but the quantities are minuscule. Viognier, Roussanne, and Sangiovese may be in vogue in certain quarters, and some exceedingly fine wines are being made from these varieties, but they are statistically insignificant.

There is no point in faddishness for its own sake, and it would be foolish to deny that California delivers extraordinary results from varieties such as Cabernet Sauvignon and its Bordelais stablemates. Cabernet Sauvignon has been present in Napa Valley and elsewhere for well over a century. It was famous in the nineteenth century and it remains famous today. It probably made its first appearance not in Napa Valley but in Sonoma, at Glen Ellen, where it was planted by J. H. Drummond in 1878. The first Napa planting was probably by H. W. Crabb a couple of years later. Its success as a varietal was soon evident and most growers lost no time in planting not only Cabernet but the other Bordeaux varieties. Each winery would blend the different Bordeaux varieties to produce what was often known as California Médoc.

As has already been related, Prohibition discouraged growers from retaining the Cabernet Sauvignon they had planted. Thicker-skinned varieties were hardier and better suited to being transported across the county to eager home winemakers. After Repeal, fewer than 100 acres remained in Napa Valley, almost all of it at Beaulieu, Beringer, and Inglenook, and total California acreage for Cabernet Sauvignon was a mere 200 acres. Even in 1961 there were only 600 acres planted in all of California, but the surface has risen steadily since then. By 1986 there were 23,149 acres under vine; by 1997, there were 45,307.

Napa Valley, with over 10,000 acres of Cabernet Sauvignon, remains its heartland, but Lodi-Woodbridge and Sonoma County are close behind. There is also significant acreage in San Luis Obispo County, especially within Paso Robles AVA, and in the San

Joaquin Valley. There are some fifteen established clones of Cabernet Sauvignon, so the matter of clonal selection is far less contentious than with Burgundian or Rhône varieties. Gary Eberle has experimented with different Cabernet clones and reports that in blind tastings the BV clone, supposedly introduced to California by Georges de Latour at Beaulieu, has performed particularly well. It is not widely used because it gives a low yield, although he and some of his neighbours in Paso Robles have planted it. Much of the difference between Cabernet clones lies in the size of the berries. Whereas growers such as Tim Mondavi will moderate their viticultural practices on the valley floor of Napa Valley to ensure that the berries remain small, growers at mountain vineyards such as Cain or Hess have often chosen larger-berried clones, on the grounds that given their growing conditions, small-berried Cabernet grapes would result in excessively tannic wines.[1] The significance of berry size lies in the ratio of skins to juice; the lower that ratio the more tannin will be extracted from the skins and pips.

Although few would dispute the fine quality of Cabernet wines from such counties as Sonoma, Mendocino, and San Luis Obispo, the greatest Cabernets do seem to emerge, time and again, from Napa Valley. The explanation seems to be a fortunate alliance of climate and soil. Around Rutherford and Oakville in particular it seems very difficult to produce a mediocre Cabernet. The gravelly loams of the benchlands, warm, well-drained, with both sufficient moisture and sufficient heat, suits Cabernet Sauvignon perfectly. Although wet autumns can diminish the quality of harvest, Napa hardly ever experiences the horrors of 1972 in Bordeaux, when simply everything tasted unripe. There are vintage variations, to be sure, but truly abysmal years are exceedingly infrequent. Cabernet, in short, delivers the goods just about every year.

The climatic and soil variations within the valley simply deliver different styles of Cabernet Sauvignon, although it seems justifiable to claim that Rutherford, Oakville, and Stags Leap generally offer fruit of a quality superior to most other parts of the valley. But the coolness of Napa itself and the warmth of Calistoga offer variations on the overall theme, just as a St Estèphe will have a different structure to a Margaux. Which you prefer is a matter of taste. Clearly the mountain vineyards above Napa Valley, with their sparse volcanic soils and very different climate, will deliver fruit of a very different structure. Again, the choice between a voluptuous Stags Leap wine and a densely structured Howell Mountain wine is a matter of personal taste, not definitive judgment. Where the vines are touched by extreme conditions – excessive tannin or excessive softness – those tendencies can be compensated for by the constantly improving techniques in trellising, spacing, and tannin management.

What should Cabernet Sauvignon taste like? This is not an easy question to answer. The European enthusiast for claret will probably expect aromas of cassis on the nose, moderated as always by the degree of new oak used by the estate, developing with time into a more complex bouquet of cedarwood (sometimes described as cigar-box or lead-pencil). Fruit, while obviously important, is sometimes less often cited than structure, tannin, and secondary aroma and flavour characters. Californian 'descriptors' will suggest a more fruit-driven wine. Norm Roby and Charles Olken list 'the grape's tendencies toward curranty, or sometimes cherryish, fruit, fairly firm structure, and noticeable tannins and astringency'. Other frequently used analogies to Cabernet Sauvignon's varietal character include herbs, green olives, truffles, loam, briar, tobacco leaf, raspberry, violet, mint, tea, cedar, bell pepper, tar, and black cherry'[2] – which adds up to quite a cocktail.

To add further complication to the breadth of this spectrum, Cabernet Sauvignon can be made in many different styles. From Napa Valley there are the lean, tannic, slow-developing examples from Mayacamas, the rich eucalyptus-scented wines from Martha's Vineyard, the graceful balanced Cabernets from Frog's Leap, the lush yet magisterial examples from Chateau Montelena, the intense, opaque wines from Dunn, the soft sweet bottlings from Silver Oak, and so on. I find this diversity positive. The gloss of new oak has given quite a few California Cabernets a certain sameness, but the assertiveness of the Cabernet grape still comes bursting through.

Styles of Cabernet are definitely changing. Some ten years ago I lined up a couple of dozen leading California Cabernets, sheathed the bottles in foil, and invited some fellow wine writers to come and taste. One wine struck most of us as excessively tannic, and even our European palates, nurtured on wines such as 1970 Château Latour, found this wine hard to enjoy or admire. It turned out to be the 1985 from Philip Togni. Philip was none too pleased when, in a tactless moment, I relayed to him our assessment of this wine. Ten years later, over dinner with the Tognis, I tasted some of his subsequent vintages and there was no doubt that although Philip's mountain fruit does give a fairly austere style of Cabernet, these later vintages were far better balanced, truly impressive wines built for the long haul but by no means inaccessible in their adolescence. I find the wine all the better for it. Although my experience of the wine is limited, I discern a similar evolution in Diamond Creek wines, which seem more accessible when young than they used to be.

There undoubtedly were wines in the 1970s and 1980s that were too tannic for their own good; wines reminiscent of the uneven 1975s in Bordeaux. A handful of the latter eventually shook off their iron cloak of tannin to reveal sumptuous fruit beneath – but the majority never did. Yet wine is a mysterious thing, and occasionally stubborn ill-tempered teenagers do evolve into gracious, charming adults. I remember a leading grower in Gevrey-Chambertin singing the praises of the 1957 vintage, not exactly one of the classic Burgundy vintages. 'Of course,' he conceded, 'they were undrinkable for thirty years, but now some of them are coming round beautifully.'

Few of us have the patience to wait decades for a wine to emerge from its shell. Most wine drinkers are tearing off the capsule as they carry a newly bought bottle through the front door. The great majority of California Cabernets are now made to be drinkable when purchased. There are a handful of wines, such as those from Mayacamas and Dunn, that still require five to ten years in bottle to start showing their quality, but they have become rare. It seems to me that this is appropriate for Californian wines. They are not, after all, Bordeaux. That may seem to be stating the obvious, but everything about the Californian climate, not to mention temperament, suggests exuberance, sensuality, lushness, sumptuousness. Bordeaux, with its leaner, tougher, more mineral wines, most of them demanding quite a few years in the cellar to shed their tannins and attain their unmatched elegance, has established a style that California can't really aspire to. Bordeaux wears neck-ties, has impeccable manners, and secures its cuffs with silver links. California Cabernet likes to take its shirt off, head for the beach in a Mercedes convertible, and chase girls. California, despite efforts to emulate Bordeaux, has not moved very far in that direction. Bordeaux, however, has become increasingly Californian: softer, richer, more accessible when young, plumper and more voluptuous.

Agustin Huneeus of Franciscan discerns the opposite trend, arguing that a Napa Cabernet made in 1978 was much more obviously a Napa wine than a similar wine made today. He sees a move towards making more claret-like wines, which he deplores, as he believes Napa Cabernet should have power rather than elegance. He attributes this change in style, which I haven't discerned myself, to the influence of Robert Parker and his love of Bordeaux wines.[3] I believe, however, that Parker's taste in Bordeaux is influenced by his American palate, which places no premium on austerity or discretion and prefers a more voluptuous taste experience.

Because California Cabernet is more enjoyable in its youth than it used to be does not mean that it is not capable of ageing. Many wine connoisseurs define greatness in a wine as its capacity to age and mature and evolve in bottle. Be that as it may, a wine capable of such an evolution does become, at the very least, more *interesting* than a wine that delivers the entire message within a year of bottling. I have absolutely no doubt that California Cabernet, in particular Napa Cabernet, does keep extremely well. David Stare and Larry Levin, respectively owner and winemaker at Dry Creek in Sonoma, suggested, perfectly plausibly, that cooler vintages, in which pH is relatively low, are more likely to deliver age-worthy wines. Long hot harvests may give rich and powerful fruit, but the must is also likely to have high pH, low acidity, and some overripeness. Thus as far as Levin is concerned, the great California Cabernet vintages are years such as 1974, 1980, 1987, 1990, 1991, 1994, and 1995, whereas vintages such as 1975, 1976, and 1982 were probably over the hill. As general advice that seems fair enough, except that there are always exceptions, which is what makes wine such an alluring subject. I have 1982 Sonoma Cabernet and 1976 Napa Cabernet in my cellar that are still going strong. Gary Andrus of Pine Ridge agrees with Levin that cooler vintages usually give longer-lived Cabernet: 'In wines from these vintages, the acidity is high and natural. In warm to hot years the grape skins tend to thick up as a form of protection, but that ultimately gives wines their overly tannic personality. 1986 is a classic example of a hot vintage. Also 1988 was another warm year that does not seem likely to age long. But 1983, which had almost too much acid in the beginning, was always atypical and is only now showing signs of coming into harmony.'[4]

It is interesting that Warren Winiarski has never been interested in his wines' longevity. You want the wine to last, but that's almost a subsidiary issue that is difficult to evaluate and build towards.' Winiarski is right that one shouldn't make a cult of longevity, yet the ability of a wine to keep giving pleasure into its second and third decades is not a negligible characteristic either.

Of course the climate during the harvest makes an essential contribution to the style and longevity of a wine. But maturation and sugar levels at harvesting are no longer the primary issue. Techniques discussed earlier, such as better rootstocks, vertical trellising, better-controlled drip irrigation, and canopy management, are all aiming to provide fruit that is better balanced and riper in flavour, not just richer in sugar. It seems fair to predict that with an increase in fruit of this quality, the outcome is bound to be better wines, above all wines that are better balanced, with acidity and sugar in harmony, and with tannins present but not too assertive. Although one can recall wines from 1974, 1985, and 1991 that were simply wonderful, I believe the overall quality of Napa Cabernets has never been higher. There is still a tendency towards overripe jammy fruit – some Californians, unlike Europeans, think that 'jammy' is a compliment – but I am sure this is less prevalent than it used to be. Ed Sbragia of Beringer is well aware of the danger of overripeness: 'In vintages when the fruit was overripe, the Cabernet Sauvignon may have displayed early appeal, but with time these overripe vintages do not mature as attractively as others.'[5]

Winemaking issues such as tannin management and maceration, fining and filtration, have been discussed in an earlier chapter. Al Brounstein of Diamond Creek has found that Cabernet Sauvignon is the variety least modifiable through winemaking techniques. 'Our winemaking is as simple as could be,' he told me. 'But you have to remember that Cabernet Sauvignon is a doll, a forgiving variety. Make a tiny mistake, like leaving the wine on the skins a touch too long, and it won't make a great difference. It's not like Pinot Noir. With Cabernet Sauvignon, all you have to do is get out of the way.'

Outstanding Cabernet Sauvignon is produced in just about every region within Napa Valley, though I have had few wines from south of Yountville that appealed to me greatly. All hit parades are expressions of personal taste. A list of my own favourite Napa Cabernets would have to include, in no order of preference, Stag's Leap, Dunn, Shafer Hillside Select, Spottswoode, Dalla Valle, Araujo, Phelps Insignia, Forman, Hess, Niebaum-Coppola, Dominus, Togni, Chateau Montelena, Mondavi Reserve, Mondavi Oakville, the newly incarnated Spring Mountain, Opus One, and Beringer Private Reserve. I have never been able to work up the required reverence for Caymus, not even for its Special Selection, and the Silver Oak style is not for me either. I have had wines from Mayacamas, Heitz, and Diamond Creek that have been magnificent, but also some disappointments.

In an earlier chapter I deplored the growing trend, almost entirely limited to Napa, for rich folk to plant an acre or two, hire a superstar winemaker, and release a pitifully small quantity of wine, its outrageous price based as much on 'collectability' as on quality. It's a theme I shall take up again in the concluding chapter. While not denigrating the quality of wines from Staglin, the Grace Family, and other sought-after Cabernets, I have much greater admiration for a Tim Mondavi or an Ed Sbragia of Beringer, either of whom can turn out 10,000 cases or more of outstanding Cabernet – which is far more difficult than making a few barrels of something exceptional. I do not object to a wine being expensive, if, as in the case of *grand cru* Burgundy or Sauternes, the production process is inherently costly. But I do object to wines being exorbitantly priced primarily as a means of attracting attention or jockeying for position in a crowded market.

Away from Napa, Alexander Valley appears to be the best favoured region for Cabernet Sauvignon. Excellent producers throughout Sonoma include Clos du Bois, Chateau St Jean, Peter Michael, Laurel Glen, and Ferrari-Carano. Close on their heels are Kenwood, Hop Kiln, and DeLoach. In Mendocino Greenwood Ridge produces excellent Cabernet. Ridge Montebello and indeed the Santa Cruz Mountains bottling from Ridge are, together with Kathryn Kennedy, the outstanding Santa Cruz Cabernets. In Paso Robles there are some lovely wines from Eberle, Meridian, and Justin. And down in Los Angeles is the luxuriant Cabernet from Moraga.

Paul Draper of Ridge has remarked: 'It seems odd that California should have chosen for its flagship wine Cabernet Sauvignon, one of the toughest and most tannic of all grapes. The French revere Bordeaux but they probably drink more Beaujolais. We actually choose to drink Cabernet Sauvignon.' Fair point: but given how delicious California Cabernet can be, especially from regions such as Paso Robles and Carmel Valley, perhaps the Californian taste isn't as perverse as Draper makes it sound.

Merlot

Merlot has become the *wunderkind* grape of California. This phenomenon is full of paradoxes. Bearing in mind Draper's stricture quoted above, Merlot would seem to be the perfect grape for the American market: supple, lush, quaffable. Generous in its yields, it delivers higher tonnage than Cabernet and can be sold at a reasonable price. At the same time Merlot is the grape of Pétrus, the mouth-filling core of voluptuous Pomerol and, in Tuscany, of Ornellaia's magnificent Massetto.

Yet Merlot is not an easy grape to grow. Its fecundity is part of the problem. If yields are excessive, the resulting wine can be dilute and bland. Yields in Napa Valley seem to range between 4 and 5.5 tons per acre, which is quite a lot of fruit. The vast acreage being planted in the ultra-high-yielding Central Valley suggests that the insatiable market for Merlot will increasingly be fobbed off with nondescript though admittedly inexpensive wines. Merlot is a thin-skinned grape, which means it is prone to rot. It doesn't always get through flowering unscathed either, since its buds open early, which also means it can succumb to frost if planted in the wrong spot. Shatter (or *coulure*) is a common hazard. It must also be picked at right moment, since it can make a rapid transition from greenness to jamminess. The variety also tends to show more variation from vintage to vintage than Cabernet Sauvignon.

Merlot was originally planted as a blending grape that would soften the frequent toughness of Cabernet Sauvignon, just as it does in Bordeaux. In 1982 Roy Andries De Groot could write: 'Unquestionably, Merlot has won its battle on the West Coast as blending wine with Cabernet Sauvignon. What I am concerned with here is Merlot as a wine on its own. In this direction, it has not yet quite fully established itself.' In general, he concluded, Merlot gives 'dry, easy to drink, light, soft, summery, thirst-quenching red wines. They are for drinking down – not for serious and thoughtful sipping.'[6] That was undoubtedly a fair conclusion to reach in 1982. Many of the early plantings of Merlot had been in inappropriate sites and it took a while for the original enthusiasts for Merlot, such as Firestone, Sterling, and Martini, to get that sorted out. UC Davis had never been keen on the variety, for purely practical reasons.

But by the mid-1980s Merlot was being taken far more seriously. Some delicious wines, a few of which have aged very well too, had already emerged from Duckhorn, and Newton would release some impressive versions. Other wineries, such as Matanzas Creek, admit that until the mid-1980s their Merlots were overly tannic and scarcely distinguishable in style from Cabernet Sauvignon; nor did they age well. Just as Merlot had been blended in to Cabernet to add suppleness, so some Cabernet was now being blended in to Merlot to give it more grip and seriousness. Some chose to add a dash of Cabernet Franc for its colour and perfume. This was an approach that Duckhorn, who always stated that he was trying to emulate Pomerol, pursued with great success. He and Ric Forman had been to Pomerol in 1977, but after his return he made a point of buying Merlot grapes not from fertile clay soils but from rocky alluvial soils, reflecting the very different conditions prevailing in California. Even at more modest levels, Merlot had a role to play. It is a good all-rounder food wine, less berry-like and forwardly fruity than Zinfandel, less demanding and tannic than Cabernet Sauvignon, less neurotic than Pinot Noir. It's fine with pasta, but can stand up to red meats. With its supple texture, it offers more guiltless drinking than the more serious California reds.

Although it is undoubtedly true that Merlot in general is more supple than Cabernet, this is not necessarily the case. Hank Wetzel of Alexander Valley Vineyards notes that in certain vintages his Merlot can be more tannic than Cabernet grown in an adjacent vineyard. Moreover, mountain-grown fruit from Napa or Sonoma can also have high tannin levels, just as Cabernet does from similar sites.[7]

The first varietally labelled Merlot was produced as recently as 1969, when Louis Martini made a blend of the 1967 and 1968 vintages, using fruit from their Los Vinedos del Rio Vineyard in Russian River. However, the first vintage-dated varietal Merlot emerged from Ric Forman at Sterling in 1969. The Three Palms

Vineyard, which was to become an important source of Merlot for Duckhorn, was planted in 1968 although Duckhorn's first Merlot wine was made in 1978, and Matanzas Creek planted its Merlot vines in Sonoma in 1974. Stag's Leap Wine Cellars made a Merlot in 1974. Clos du Val followed in 1977. The consensus nowadays is that Merlot thrives in slightly cooler soils than those where Cabernet Sauvignon is grown. Some of the earlier plantings were made on soils that, in retrospect, were a touch too rich for the variety. Moreover, Dan Duckhorn and other early growers of Merlot have conceded with some embarrassment that in many cases what they thought was Merlot (clone 6) when they planted it has turned out to be Cabernet Franc instead. Nothing to be embarrassed about: a lot of Cabernet Sauvignon, Merlot, and Cabernet Franc can taste interchangeable, especially in the warm California climate that tends to smooth out their differences in aroma and flavour. This emerged after clonal trials undertaken jointly in 1995 by Dan Duckhorn and UC Davis in which various clones were matched to various rootstocks. It will take twenty-five years to complete the study.

Growers are now trying to plant Merlot in cooler regions. Whereas Cabernet rarely ripens in Carneros, that region seems quite well suited to Merlot. Some producers, such as Chris Howell at Cain, believe that the Bordeaux model should be followed and that Merlot should be planted on soils with a notable clay content. In practice, however, Merlot is being planted all over the place, and often does well, apart from the viticultural problems attached to the variety just about wherever it is grown, and as long as the vines enjoy good drainage.

Its rise to stardom has been exceedingly swift. In 1972 only four wineries in the whole of the United States were offering Merlot; by 1980 there were sixty-six; by 1991, 225. As recently as 1986 there were only 2,881 acres planted. By 1995 that figure had risen to about 25,000 acres, and in 1998 it had rocketed to just over 38,000. Whereas the average price per ton for Napa grapes rose 52 per cent between 1984 and 1994, the average price for Merlot rose 70 per cent. By the late 1980s Merlot was clearly 'hot'. In 1994 the average price per ton was $1,530 for Napa Merlot, and one lucky grower managed to raise $2,513 for his grapes. By this year Merlot was the most actively planted varietal in Napa after Chardonnay. As with Cabernet Sauvignon, post-phylloxera

plantings have benefited greatly from advances in trellising techniques and understanding of rootstocks and clones. This, says Dan
Duckhorn, 'will lead to a whole new era of vineyard-designated
Merlot. But it will probably take another thirty years before we
have paired up the right clones on the right soils.'[8]

Like Cabernet Sauvignon, Merlot can produce superb results in
Napa Valley. It seems to do particularly well in Oakville and Stags
Leap, where the wines can be luxurious and plummy. Merlot from
Carneros is a touch brighter and brasher. Robert Sinskey points
out that despite the coolness of Merlot, it is still warmer than St
Emilion and Pomerol in Bordeaux in terms of heat summation.
The clay soils, although shallow, are also well suited to Merlot. The
variety also thrives in some mountain sites such as the Bancroft
Vineyard on Howell Mountain and at Newton on Spring Mountain, both generating wines that, unlike many Merlots, age
extremely well. Liparita on Howell Mountain also makes
impressive Merlot. In Sonoma, Alexander Valley gives good results
and quite powerful wines, but the slightly cooler Sonoma and Dry
Creek valleys are also well suited to Merlot. A few producers in
Mendocino, notably Lolonis and Parducci, are having considerable
success with Merlot, and the variety also does well in the warmer
regions of Monterey: in the southern Salinas Valley around King
City, and in Carmel Valley.

Vast quantities of Merlot vines are also being planted in regions
perhaps not so well suited to the variety, and the inevitable consequence will be a great deal of mediocre Merlot coming onto the
market. The greatest vineyard expansion has been in the Central
Valley. Lodi, which admittedly is capable of growing excellent if
not wildly concentrated fruit, now generates 25 per cent of the
state's supply of Merlot. There's plenty more going into the ground
in the Modesto region, in Monterey, in the Central Coast as a
whole. Moreover, about 40 per cent of the total acreage was
planted between 1994 and 1997; these are very young vines. So
long as consumers aren't expecting anything other than a simple,
and possibly weedy, red wine for easy drinking, then it may not
matter. But winelovers in search of California's answer to Pomerol
are going to have to search harder.

The leading Merlot producers in Napa Valley include Duckhorn,
Beringer Bancroft Vineyard, Silverado, Lewis, Cuvaison, Newton,
Franciscan, Pine Ridge, Sterling Winery Lake, Harrison, Markham

Reserve, Cosentino, Whitehall Lane Reserve, and Swanson. In Sonoma Matanzas Creek have a very high reputation for their very expensive and arguably overrated Merlot, and other fine producers include St Francis, Arrowood, Chateau St Jean, Gundlach-Bundschu, and Geyser Peak.

Randall Grahm of Bonny Doon refers scornfully to the mania for Merlot as 'Merlonoma'. That may be an extreme view, since Merlot has the not negligible merit of drinkability. I do recall tasting my way through the range of wines made by John Williams at Frog's Leap. I enjoyed the Merlot and said so, but couldn't help adding that it seemed simple when tasted alongside the Cabernet Sauvignon. John agreed and murmured: 'Sure, the Merlot is nice, but the Cabernet is wine.'

Cabernet Franc

Cabernet Franc was originally planted in California by Gustav Niebaum in the 1880s, but remained insignificant until the 1980s. It bears little relation to the slightly grassy red wine from the Loire Valley. Instead it often shows a distinctive blueberry or blackberry flavour. It has a particularly fragrant aroma, and is often blended into other Bordeaux varietals to contribute some lift and perfume and more overt fruitiness. If Cabernet Franc sometimes lacks character and a recognizable personality, it is probably the conse quence of overcropping, as it's a vigorous variety that can easily develop tartness or vegetal tones, just as it can in the Loire, if the canopy becomes too luxuriant. In general it has a leaner structure than Cabernet Sauvignon, and winemakers worry that while it contributes lovely aromas to a blend, it lacks substance on the middle palate when made as a varietal wine. Much in demand, good Cabernet Franc grapes are now more expensive on average than Cabernet Sauvignon. In 1997 the average price per ton for Cabernet Sauvignon was $1,115; for Cabernet Franc, $1,450.

There are about 2,000 acres planted in California, the great majority planted over the last fifteen years. So most of the vineyards are still young. Some 750 acres are grown in Napa Valley, followed by 500 in Sonoma. Smaller acreage is planted in Santa Barbara and Mendocino. Within Santa Barbara County, the slightly warmer Santa Ynez Valley shows promise. Fred Brander planted the variety in 1990, using spacing of 2,700 vines per acre, and Fess Parker introduced a bottling in 1995. Gainey produce a bottling from Santa Ynez Valley. Perhaps the best of all the Santa Barbara Cabernet Francs is made by Vita Nova. John Kautz is the state's major grower of the variety. It is also grown and vinified by Hahn in the Santa Lucia Highlands in Monterey County.

One of the best varietal Cabernet Francs comes from La Jota on Howell Mountain, and John Skupny's St Helena-based Lang & Reed specializes in the variety. Turnbull's delicious Old Bull Red is mostly made from Cabernet Franc. Other examples come from Jarvis and from Gundlach-Bundschu and Ravenswood in Sonoma. Nelson Estate in Bennett Valley, Sonoma, produce nothing but Cabernet Franc. In Mendocino, Yorkville Cellars produce a successful version.

Malbec and Petit Verdot

No one is trying to produce the Californian equivalent of Cahors. Indeed Malbec is not a popular grape variety, and there are only about 150 acres planted. Low yields make it of no interest as a commercial variety, and Chris Howell, who uses Malbec in Cain Five, reports that it suffers from shatter (*coulure*) almost every year. Some Malbec is planted in Sonoma, and much of it seems to go to Richard Arrowood, who vinifies and ages it as though it were Cabernet Sauvignon.

Petit Verdot is marginally more popular, with about 200 acres planted, almost all in Napa and Sonoma. The variety is well thought of by some growers, as it performs with more regularity in California than in climatically unsettled Bordeaux. Surprisingly, but probably as a consequence of its scarcity, in 1997 it was the varietal commanding the highest average price per ton of any variety grown in Napa: $2,131.

As in Bordeaux, it is used as a blending component, and is only planted in small quantities. There is some planted in the Eisele Vineyard, where it forms part of the Cabernet blend, and there used to be a little in Sterling's Three Palms Vineyard. On Spring Mountain, both Newton and Cain have Petit Verdot. Both Peter Newton and Chris Howell say that it does ripen properly in the Californian climate, and does best on very poor soils. Unfortunately, says Newton, it sets poorly, so crops tend to be irregular. Nonetheless he has stuck with the variety for twenty years and likes to include it in his Cabernet blend. Chris Howell uses Petit Verdot in Cain Five, but confesses to being puzzled by the variety. It has deep colour and high tannins, and ripens fully. Howell handles the grape gently, not macerating it and finishing the fermentation in barrel. But he is uncertain whether it has a great contribution to make to his blend, as it can give an astringent finish to the wine. In Bordeaux both colour and tannin are useful components in certain vintages, but at 2,000 feet up on Spring Mountain he rarely lacks for either in his grapes.

Benziger grow Petit Verdot at their Sonoma Mountain estate and occasionally bottle the wine as a varietal. De Lorimier is another Sonoma winery that offers the wine. Jekel in Monterey also bottle a Petit Verdot.

NOTES

1 James Halliday, *Wine Atlas of California*, p. 121
2 Norman Roby and Charles Olken, *New Connoisseurs' Handbook of California*, p. 40
3 Larry Walker, *Wine* Magazine, March 1997
4 Quoted in *Decanter*, September 1997
5 Ibid.
6 Roy Andries De Groot, *The Wine of California*, pp. 112–5
7 Eleanor and Ray Heald, 'Merlot: Exploring the Diversity', *Practical Vineyard and Winery*, September/October 1995
8 Richard Neill, *Decanter*, September 1997

15

Zinfandel

Zinfandel is California's greatest viticultural treasure. It isn't an indigenous variety, but it comes close. It might have been on its way to extinction by now had it not been, ironically, for the overwhelming popularity of white Zinfandel in the 1980s, which encouraged growers not only to keep their acreage but to plant more. In the early 1980s it had become almost impossible to sell red Zinfandel, so the invention of white Zinfandel certainly contributed to the survival of the variety, although in practice, the precious old head-pruned vineyards were hardly ever used for the blush wine, since they had to be manually harvested and yields were too low to make it economical. Nonetheless the surge in Zinfandel sales throughout the 1980s must have encouraged many growers who might otherwise have been tempted to pull out the vines in favour of more lucrative varieties. Interest in the wines has been ardently promoted by ZAP (Zinfandel Advocates and Producers), an association founded in 1992 by twenty-two wineries as a non-profit organization. By 1998 ZAP represented 151 wineries.

In 1986 there were 25,797 acres planted in California. By 1995 the figure had risen to 43,998, and by 1997 to 50,498. This is great news for unabashed Zinfandel fans, even though most grapes are still destined for white Zinfandel. Though red Zinfandel can rise to great heights, the wine is still slightly undervalued. Prices per ton are about half of those for Cabernet Sauvignon. Consequently prices for Zinfandel, though they have been rising slowly over the past decade, remain reasonable. There are some lamentable exceptions, unfortunately. Kendall-Jackson's 1994 Hartford Court Zinfandel was released at $29. Many of the Turley Zinfandels are between $30 and $40; Cline's Jacuzzi Vineyard from

Contra Costa and a Zinfandel from Martinelli (winemaker: Helen Turley) are both priced at $45. It would be unfair, I think, to place the responsibility solely at the door of greedy producers. Growers have become aware that their vineyards, in the course of a few years, have become a prized asset and that estates keen to produce high-quality Zinfandel are constantly searching for outstanding fruit. This has driven up the price for old-vine Zinfandel. It is now a sellers' market.

The name Zinfandel must surely be derived from the Austrian variety Zierfandler, to which, of course, it is not related. The puzzle about the origin of Zinfandel is that genetically it seems to be identical to the Italian variety Primitivo, but there is no record of Primitivo having been cultivated in America until the 1890s and Zinfandel was known to have been in the United States in the 1830s. Paul Draper speculates that Italian growers may have taken Zinfandel cuttings back to southern Italy from California towards the end of the century, which would explain why the two varieties are apparently identical. Wine historians have pointed to the documented existence of a Black Zinfandal [*sic*] Vineyard on Long Island in 1830, and another vineyard with the same grape in Salem, Massachusetts.[1] Zinfandel's American journey began in Massachusetts where it was grown as a table grape. It was brought to the Bay Area in 1852 by Captain F. W. Macondray and soon after it was introduced to Napa Valley by J. W. Osborne. It rapidly became popular and was widely planted in Napa in the 1860s.[2] Gerald Asher quotes George Husmann, author of a definitive book on winemaking in California published in the 1880s, who declared that he had 'yet to see the red wine of any variety [that he preferred] to the best samples of Zinfandel produced in this state.'[3]

Zinfandel is planted throughout California. The variety is happy with hot daytime temperatures but also seems to thrive best in regions where the nights are cool. The acreage in Napa Valley seems to be shrinking, alas, reflecting the disparity in price per ton of Zinfandel when compared to varieties such as Cabernet Sauvignon and Merlot. Nonetheless some excellent Zinfandels are still produced from Napa fruit. Calistoga Zinfandels can be rich and deep, with a sustaining but not coarse tannic structure. In 1997 Zinfandel from the Black-Sears Vineyard on Howell Mountain was fetching $2,500 per ton, five times as much as the statewide average that year. Gerald Asher, reporting on a large Zinfandel tasting in

which he participated, found Napa Zinfandels to be 'well structured, well-bred, and impeccably straight-backed. Though
vigorous, they are restrained. They have perfect balance: nothing
is to excess . . . Zinfandels from the hillside vineyards above Napa
Valley . . . have characteristically tighter flavors. Closed when the
wine is young and then, as it develops, opening to an unexpected
(sometimes even medicinal) intensity, the flavors are nevertheless
all of a piece with the wines' lean and forthright hillside style.'

Zinfandel does well in almost all of Sonoma, especially Dry
Creek, but also in Russian River, Sonoma, and Alexander valleys.
In some years Russian River Valley is simply too cool and damp
for Zinfandel to ripen properly, but in warm years the variety can
do exceptionally well, showing a vibrant acidity as well as rich
plum and cherry fruit character. Sonoma County is also the source
of some very old vineyards that deliver fruit of intense quality. But
Dry Creek Valley is the heartland of Sonoma Zinfandel, and many
old hillside vineyards have been preserved. The wines are intensely
fruity, enlivened with dashes of pepper, and a dense brambly quality
that can be very satisfying.

With considerable variations in vintage and winemaking style,
it is difficult to generalize about Sonoma Zinfandel, but Gerald
Asher has discerned that 'Zinfandels from Sonoma Valley were the
hardest, the most tannic, and the most astringent. Those with a
bright, crisp style – an edge of acidity, rather than tannin, coupled
with the clear, forward berry-fruit aroma and flavor we most
associate with California Zinfandel – were likely to be from Dry
Creek Valley, Russian River or Lytton Springs region, where the
previous two areas meet. Wines from the upper part of Dry Creek
Valley or from Alexander Valley, across a watershed, were more
mellow, had a more complex – or at least a deeper – flavor, and
were generally more plump.'[4]

Zinfandel was also planted in the Santa Cruz Mountains, of
course. Paul Draper recalls how when his partners at Ridge investi-
gated the vineyards soon after they bought the site, they discovered
some very old Zinfandel vines in place. 'Some years their wines
would be way underripe; other years, too ripe. But when it was
good, the wine was fascinating. Here was a grape that could deliver
the intensity, concentration and complexity of great Cabernet, and
yet in all other areas it was completely different.'[5]

Lodi is awash in Zinfandel, about 14,000 acres of it, but most of it ends up as white Zinfandel. A recurrent problem with Zinfandel is uneven ripening, but Lance Randolph of Peirano in Lodi finds that in this region there are often very hot days at veraison, which allows underripe grapes to make great strides, while the grapes that have already ripened sufficiently shut down, so that the fruit continues evolving towards harvest time with even maturation. Or that's the theory. Randolph admits that raisining can occur in Lodi too, and most growers, himself included, will tolerate about 10 per cent of raisined fruit in the wine. Draper, who made wines from both Lodi and Amador County Zinfandel, stopped doing so because the fruit quality was inconsistent and because the wines did not evolve that well after bottling.

Another excellent region for the grape is Paso Robles, where the wine has charm and roundness rather than great structure or longevity. However, there are considerable differences within the region, depending on whether the grapes are grown on the Estrella Bench plateau east of Highway 101, or in the hills to the west of the highway. Also along the Central Coast, in a remote inland spot in Arroyo Grande, is the fascinating Saucelito Canyon vineyard. Bill Greenough bought the vineyard in 1974. The winery that had existed here until the 1940s was derelict, but he found that the Zinfandel vines, originally planted in 1879, were not actually dead. The vine tops were dead, but not the roots, so Greenough picked out a single shoot from the root crown and then created a new trunk. By this method he resuscitated the ancient head-pruned, dry-farmed vineyard, which is still productive, although supplemented by more recently planted vines. Finally, there are the venerable vineyards of the Sierra Foothills, especially Amador County, and some old vines in Contra Costa County that yield wines with quite an earthy character.

There is no single flavour profile for the variety. From Paso Robles, where some 1,500 acres are planted, you are likely to find a soft, rounded, crushed berry quality, whereas Dry Creek Zinfandel is more likely to be plummy and peppery, with a robustness comparable to a wine from the southern Rhône valley. In the Sierra Foothills, Zinfandel will often display a raisiny, pruny edge, a dried-fruit quality that some find old fashioned but which other winelovers particularly seek out. One enthusiast for this style is Jeff Meyer of Monteviña. In his view, Sonoma Zinfandel can be too jammy (though rarely in my own experience), Napa has more focused berry fruit, while Amador Zinfandel has berry fruit given additional complexity with undertones of brambles and aniseed. Zinfandel made from very old vines tends to have a denser, more peppery and extracted flavour that is distinct from the overtly fruity style offered by the best mass producers such as Fetzer.

Zinfandel is often aged in American oak, which adds a vanilla dimension to the taste spectrum. Although a few producers – such as Joel Peterson of Ravenswood – are adamant that Zinfandel should be aged in French oak, most winemakers find that the variety marries nicely with the sweetness of American oak. The variety is subject to overripeness, either deliberately or accidentally, and this too can give the wine a baked or jammy quality.

There is an enormous difference between old Zinfandel vineyards and those planted more recently. The former were planted with head-pruned vines, and, being elderly, often don't yield more than 2 tons per acre. However, they were able to generate a sizeable second crop if damaged by spring frost, and this was clearly a commercial advantage to growers.[6] Many of them were also field blends, incorporating rows of Carignane, Grenache, Mourvèdre or Petite Sirah vines among the Zinfandel. These field blends can give additional complexity to the resulting wines, and what Joel Peterson of Ravenswood has called 'the element of surprise'.[7] In Anderson Valley, Ted Bennett of Navarro once separated the Petite Sirah in his field blend of grapes destined for their Zinfandel and fermented it separately. Later he blended it back in because he decided it made for a more interesting wine that way.

A few decades ago UC Davis developed clones that are more productive and don't give the ripeness levels of old-vine Zinfandel. These new clones are well adapted to the production of white Zinfandel, but will not give red wine of outstanding quality. Whereas head-pruned vines can be picked at 24 or 25 Brix to give the rich full-bodied reds that Zinfandel enthusiasts look for, the Davis clones rarely ripen to more than 22 Brix. They are also more prone to rot. Their advantage to growers, especially those with large vineyards, is that the vines can be trellis-trained and consequently harvested mechanically, unlike head-pruned vines. However, the viticulturalists at Davis, well aware of the renaissance in red Zinfandel, are developing clones from old vines that will be of much higher quality. The university's vineyard at Oakville has gathered together sixty-three massal selections from Zinfandel vineyards all over the state, and in the future this is likely to be a splendid resource for those keen to plant high-quality vines.

There is a tendency to make a fetish of old, dry-farmed, head-pruned vineyards, but experienced growers such as Dick Bush of Madroña in the Sierra Foothills believe that old-vine Zinfandel can be overrated. 'Young vines can give excellent fruit but the important thing is not to overcrop. Five or 6 tons per acre is all right, and it could be slightly higher if one plants to a higher density – 726 vines per acre rather than 512.' John Williams, of Frog's Leap in Napa Valley, where the growing conditions are different, feels that 4–5 tons per acre is about right for Zinfandel. Doug Nalle, a Zinfandel specialist, believes yield is an essential factor. 'Young Zinfandel vines can easily carry 8 tons per acre, or more. I feel 3 to 4 tons is about right. But I'm not hung up on old vines. You have to remember that around here in Dry Creek, this was bulk wine country. The farmers were poorly paid and didn't take great care. In the 1970s most Zinfandel produced here was not that good, although the grape does well on the benchlands. Its great appeal was its versatility. It could be picked early to make rosé, or late-harvested for sweet wines.

'To grow Zinfandel well, you need to pull leaves selectively. Now that the grape is selling for up to $2,000 per ton, commercial growers are having to do that too. You should irrigate if you have to, remove the second crop, thin the bunches, and keep yields to no more than 5 tons per acre, and 3 to 4 if possible. Don't assume that the old vines were necessarily low-yielding.' Near his winery Nalle showed me a vine planted in the 1930s with eleven spurs, each of which would carry one or two clusters. 'That makes 22 pounds of fruit per vine, which is equivalent to a yield of 8 tons per acre. If we look round we'll probably find some of these old vines pruned with a kicker vine as additional insurance. So if hail or rain or shatter came along and diminished the production on the spurs, there were up to twelve clusters more on the kicker cane, which could always be removed if it proved unnecessary. What would you call this: greed or prudent insurance?'

Devotees of old-vine Zinfandel such as Joel Peterson and Paul Draper observe that the nineteenth-century growers almost always planted on hillside sites where the grapes could soak up the heat, enjoy cool evenings, and retain health and longevity on well-drained soils. It remains true that location as much as antiquity is what makes the old vineyards so alluring. Doug Nalle also points out that the vines in the old sites tend to be virused and their maturation is slower, which is a positive thing. 'These days, with cleaned-up vines from Davis, you can easily slide into high Brix.'

The great problem with Zinfandel is that it ripens very well, but unevenly. Part of the reason is that it blooms unevenly, and in a damp spring flowering takes three weeks. (One solution, of course, though not universally practised, is to eliminate persistently green bunches at veraison.) Visiting one of John Williams's Zinfandel vineyards in Napa during the harvest, he showed me deep blue berries that were fully ripe and ready to be picked, while within the same cluster there were other berries that were already raisining. The ripe berries were being picked at 23 or 24 Brix, while the raisined berries had already reached about 27 Brix. In some years the cluster can also contain pink berries with no more than 20 Brix in sugar content. If you pick too soon, you can end up with underripe fruit in the vat; wait too long, and you will end up with an excess of raisined grapes that will give the wine a porty flavour. Should it rain during harvest, Zinfandel can easily rot, as the bunches are tight, while the skins are thin and liable to split. David Lucas of Lodi says that in his experience it is not always easy to spot unripe Zinfandel grapes on the vine, as they often look quite close in colour to the fully ripe ones.

With the growing popularity of old-vine Zinfandel has come a more attentive approach to winemaking. Zinfandel is sometimes accorded the kind of reverence previously reserved for Pinot Noir. Some estates justify their high prices because their winemaking techniques – fermentation in open-top fermenters with frequent punching down of the cap – are labour-intensive and costly. Assuming the winemaker has managed to make a fruity, well structured and well balanced Zinfandel, it is not easy to decide when to drink it, and considerable debate rages over the suitability of Zinfandel for bottle ageing. There is no doubt that it can age well, but it is not always clear that it gains in complexity or interest by being kept. My own views have moderated, and I no longer keep Zinfandel as long as I used to. It is usually so pleasurable to drink at around five years old that there seems little point hanging on to bottles for any longer. By doing so one sacrifices their freshness and vigour, and it is not clear what is gained in exchange. It is also seems clear that some of the strapping, high-alcohol Zinfandels,

unless exceptionally well balanced, could easily dry out with prolonged bottle age. David Lucas in Lodi told me he used to make
blockbuster Zinfandels but for the most part they did not keep
well.

James Halliday puts a persuasive case for drinking Zinfandel
young: 'The problem which most Zinfandels suffer with age is a
loss of identity, even if they retain vinosity and a certain warmth . . .
Surely the outstanding feature of Zinfandel is its brightness, its
freshness, its silky/satiny texture, and its array of fruit flavors . . .
It is not tannic. It is a wine driven by its exotic perfume and sheer
exuberance of its fruit . . . What is to be gained by cellaring such
a wine? In most cases the loss of fruit freshness and personality
will not be compensated for by a gain in complexity (and softening
of tannins), because neither the tannins nor the latent complexity
are there in the first place. Yet this is a reality which many of the
top makers deny in public.'[8]

Paul Draper believes that Zinfandel is capable of ageing in an
interesting fashion. It depends, of course, on the style of the wine,
and since many Zinfandels are made to be enjoyed young, keeping
them for five years in hopes of seeing some marvellous evolution
is clearly pointless. However, he also believes that in top vintages
it is worth keeping the best wines, as with age they become more
exotic in flavour. Zinfandel's evolution in bottle tends to be curious,
rather like Chenin Blanc from the Loire. Drunk young, it will show
youthful fruitiness and zest. Then after eight or ten years, when it
is losing its primary fruit, it can taste disappointing. 'But keep a
great vintage twelve or fifteen years and the wine can develop
interestingly.' Nonetheless, Draper does not deny that keeping Zinfandel is more likely to result in disappointment than revelation.[9]
I have tasted a range of Zinfandels that were about fifteen years
old, and they were very hit-and-miss, although winemaking,
especially in Amador where some of those wines originated, was
also more rough and ready in those days. Tom Hill, an American
wine writer and Zin fanatic, reports that recent tastings of Ridge
bottlings from 1979 to 1981 and of Edmeades Ciapusci Vineyard
wines made by Jed Steele in 1980 and 1982 showed that the
bottles were still in fine condition and provided further proof that
Zinfandel can age interestingly.[10]

One might not think that so robust a varietal as Zinfandel would
be that susceptible to site variation. Winemakers clearly disagree.

From the start Ridge released a bewildering selection of single-vineyard Zinfandels from various parts of the state, though the list has subsequently been pared down to about four. Turley has made a point of producing about a dozen different Zinfandels, most of them in such minute quantities that they are virtually unobtainable despite their high prices. Kent Rosenblum releases eight or so, from very varied sources. DeLoach in Russian River Valley offers about half a dozen, and so does Ravenswood. Although there are evident differences between many of these single-vineyard bottlings, there is a hint of faddishness about the concept, especially when the vineyards are all in the same region.

There is also much discussion about the style in which the wine should be made in the first place. In the 1970s and early 1980s there were a number of 'killer Zins' on the market, wines with 15 degrees of alcohol or more. I rather liked that combination of richness and power, though far too many examples were coarse and clumsy and too transparently alcoholic in flavour. During the course of the 1980s the best winemakers sought, by picking at the right moment, to produce wines that were better balanced, and that showed elegance and vigour as well as brutal power. Producers such as Frog's Leap, Nalle, and often Ridge, released Zinfandels with 13.5 or 14 degrees that seemed about right. Nalle's wines are invariably delicious, lovely gulpable reds that don't lack structure, finesse, or depth of fruit. However, in the 1990s there was a return to the old blockbuster style, which is now very much in vogue. When *Decanter* Magazine organized a tasting of 1994 and 1995 Zinfandels (Turley's most extreme bottles were not included), the alcohol content of the thirty-five submitted wines was analysed: seven were below 14 degrees, and of the rest six exceeded 15 degrees and six more exceeded 16.

Turley is one of the prime offenders. The winery specializes in small lots – 200 to 500 cases – of *barrique*-aged wines from individual vineyards; few of those wines contain less than 15 degrees of alcohol, and some have 17. Some of them are very good, and seem well balanced despite the terrifying amount of alcohol. Most of them are not and strike me as freaks. Ehren Jordan, the winemaker at Turley, was unrepentant when I politely told him I found some of his wines monstrous. 'We just pick the grapes when they are ripe. You have to look at the total acidity and pH. At 14 degrees you'd have a pH of 2.9 and the wine would be undrinkable.' (Others seems to manage at 14 degrees, however.) 'We find that even with very high sugar content, old-vine Zinfandel retains acidity in a remarkable way, so the wines aren't that heavy despite the alcohol.'

The first late harvest Zinfandel was made by mistake. In 1968 the grapes ripened early, and Bob Travers at Mayacamas asked his Zinfandel grower to delay picking for a few days as the tanks were full of other grapes that had just been delivered. When the grapes eventually arrived at the winery they were clearly raisined, but Travers fermented then anyway and ended up with a dry wine with 17.3 degrees of alcohol. The wine was acclaimed, and Michael Broadbent went so far as to describe it as resembling 'a big young Latour in cask'.[11] Late harvest Zin was born. When conditions were right, Travers deliberately aimed for this style. I bought a few bottles of the 1974, which were magnificent in their early years, but then went into a sudden decline.

At Ridge, Paul Draper was duplicating Travers's feats with what he called Zinfandel Essence. This style was made not from raisined Zinfandel, a flavour Draper never cared for, but from botrytized grapes. To his surprise, Draper found that the wine retained its colour, since one of the consequences of botrytis infection is a loss of colour. Trockenbeerenauslesen from Pinot Noir that I have tasted in Germany are invariably an orangey-pink as a result of botrytis infection. Draper picked these grapes at 40 Brix, and although the five vintages he made were only sold at the winery, he was quite proud of the wines, since they were totally natural sweet red wines made, unlike Recioto in the Veneto, without drying the grapes before pressing. The wine has not been made since 1993. Other celebrated and exceedingly alcoholic late harvest Zinfandels were made in Santa Cruz by David Bruce from 1969 to 1971.

There is no shortage of excellent Zinfandel producers in California. As a varietal wine it doesn't require the emulation of acclaimed European models, so you can style the wine in any way you like. Fine examples from Napa fruit are to be found at Elyse, Storybrook Mountain, Sky, Rosenblum, Newlan, Turley, Fife, Acacia, Burgess, Clos du Val, Robert Biale, Franciscan, Frog's Leap, La Jota, and sometimes at Grgich and Chateau Montelena. I particularly like the wines from Elyse, Frog's Leap, Storybrook Mountain, and Burgess, but that is a personal choice.

In Sonoma, the historic heartland of Zinfandel, one is spoilt for choice. There are the single-vineyard bottlings from Ravenswood, and from Ridge (Geyserville and Lytton Springs), and excellent wines from Limerick Lane, DeLoach, Nalle, Sausal, Rafanelli, Rabbit Ridge, David Coffaro, Quivira, Rosenblum, Farrell, Topolos, Rochioli, Hop Kiln, J. Fritz, Dry Creek, and Kunde. There are also good wines to be found at Chateau Souverain, Mazzocco, Martinelli, Pedroncelli, Pezzi King, Seghesio, Hartford Court, Alderbrook, Rodney Strong, Kenwood, St Francis, and Davis Bynum.

In Mendocino, both Fetzer and Parducci are reliable, but there are more characterful bottlings from smaller producers such as Hidden Cellars, Gabrielli, Steele, Lolonis, Fife, Edmeades Ciapusci Vineyard, Lonetree, Navarro, and Claudia Springs. From the Sierra Foothills, good bottles are to be found at Renwood, Sierra Vista, Amador Foothill Winery, Sobon, Boeger, Sutter Home Reserve, and Easton. From the very old vines in Oakley in Contra Costa County, some fine Zinfandels are produced by Cline, Rosenblum, and Bogle. In Lodi, David Lucas is the top producer, with other good wines from Peirano. From Paso Robles, good Zinfandel is made by Ridge, Eberle, Tobin James, Peachy Canyon, and Castoro. Saucelito Canyon is an exceptional producer in the Arroyo Grande region.

Since Zinfandel is made in so many parts of the state, it is difficult to generalize about vintages, but 1994 was certainly outstanding, although 1993 also produced some very good wines. In 1994 conditions were ideal, with a late, rain-free harvest after a relatively cool growing season. 1995 is also excellent, but 1996 seems to have delivered wines that are less intense and focused. There is every indication that 1997, despite generous yields, will turn out to be outstanding. Kent Rosenblum has gone so far as to declare that it may turn out to be the best Zinfandel vintage of the 1990s. On the other hand, readers will be aware that it is common in all wine-producing regions to talk up the latest vintage. Older vintages which produced exceptional Zinfandels include 1984, 1985, 1986, 1987, and all the vintages of the 1990s with the possible exception of 1996.

White Zinfandel

Various wineries compete for the dubious honour of having been the first to produce a 'blush' wine from Zinfandel. Most people believe it was first created by Sutter Home, but in fact there were earlier versions from David Bruce and others.[12] There is even evidence that it was produced as long ago as the 1860s by George West near Stockton.[13] Zinfandel had also been used for some time to make rosé, and Roy Andries De Groot noted that its character was 'generally quite dry with perhaps a more complex balance of tastes and textures than any other type of rosé', which doesn't sound at all like commercial white Zinfandel. Moreover he thought the 'tangy-tart berry flavor' of the variety came through strongly on the rosé, which is rarely the case with the 'blush' wine.[14] According to De Groot, the best rosé Zinfandels were made by Concannon and Pedroncelli.

However, in 1972 Bob Trinchero of Sutter Home made a small batch of white Zinfandel, which was both dry and oak-aged. In 1975, the Sutter Home winemakers found that the fermentation stuck, leaving some residual sugar in the wine. (A similar story accounts for the creation of the Kendall-Jackson Vintners' Reserve style of sweetish Chardonnay.) The customers seemed to like it, the wine sold well, and white Zinfandel in its modern form had come into existence. Nonetheless it took a while for the style to take off. By 1979 only four wineries were offering it, one of them being Monteviña in Amador County, which Sutter Home would later purchase. DeLoach's production reached 27,000 cases at about this time, but the winery did not continue with the style. Shenandoah also produced one, and still does. Indeed, Shenandoah's white Zinfandel, with its zesty watermelon flavours, is one of the better ones on the market, though its production has dropped dramatically from its maximum of 36,000 cases in 1987. Shenandoah's owner, Leon Sobon, cut production because he could no longer compete in price with the mega-wineries.

Since the early days Sutter Home have certainly cornered the market. By the mid-1990s this Napa-based winery was producing 6 million cases, accounting for about one-quarter of the total market. The demand for the wine meant that Sutter Home and other wineries specializing in this style of wine could not just rely on existing plantations of Zinfandel. Some 3,000 acres of new vineyards were planted to the east, in counties such as Colusa where grape growing had never been a major industry. But given the undemanding nature of the vine and the acceptable climatic conditions in those eastern counties, not to mention the low price of the land, they proved suitable for Zinfandel destined for the 'blush' tanks. Everything is geared to maximum tonnage. Flavour development seems an irrelevancy, since the winemaking is aimed at stripping this variety of any flavour it may have. Some wineries, such as J. Lohr in San Jose, have taken a different route. Lohr purchase their Zinfandel grapes from growers who also grow the variety for red-wine production, and they ensure that the crop levels are kept down to a level where the varietal character is not obliterated. Lohr also blend in a little Riesling, presumably for aromatic complexity.

The white Zinfandel concept really took off in the mid-1980s when major players such as Beringer and Gallo began producing the wine in large quantities. So did Mondavi, and I was quite taken aback when at a major London tasting of Mondavi wines in about 1990, this distinguished winery chose to serve a sweetish white Zinfandel with lunch. The Mondavi people seemed surprised that we did not like it much. By this time white Zinfandel had assumed immense commercial importance, which is presumably why Mondavi wanted to dazzle the British wine press with their version. By 1991 white Zinfandel accounted for 18 per cent of all sales of California wines in the United States.[15] Sales in that year amounted to 15 million cases, compared to a trifling 900,000 cases for red Zinfandel.[16] Like Nouveau wines, it is a technological wine that can be produced rapidly and put on the market shortly after the harvest.

Styles still vary. Shenandoah's white Zinfandel is relatively dry, with only about 10 grams of residual sugar. Another Foothills winery, Renwood, pick the grapes at about 20 Brix, cold-ferment, and balance the wine with 11 degrees of alcohol and 30 grams of sugar, which is more typical of white Zinfandel. In 1996 Turley produced a white Zinfandel from the Smoot-Hawley Vineyard in Napa; it had 11.9% and at $41 must have set a recommended retail price record for a white Zinfandel. I have not tasted the wine. The great majority, unfortunately, are soupy, nondescript, sweetish wines best knocked into submission with a bunch of ice cubes.

NOTES

1 Roy Andries De Groot, *The Wine of California*, p. 160
2 Charles L. Sullivan, *Napa Wine*, p. 135
3 Gerald Asher, *Vineyard Tales*, p. 211
4 Ibid, pp. 213–4
5 Quoted by Richard Neill, *Decanter*, September 1997
6 James Halliday, *Wine Atlas of California*, p. 160
7 Quoted in *Wine Spectator*, October 1992
8 Halliday, pp. 160–61
9 *Wine Spectator*, 15 October 1992
10 Tom Hill, *Tom Hill Wine Tasting Archives*, January 1988
11 *Decanter*, June 1997
12 Michael Broadbent, *The Great Vintage Wine Book*, p. 413
13 Robert Benson, *Great Winemakers of California*, p. 42
14 Sullivan, p. 319
15 De Groot, p. 181
16 Halliday, p. 268

16

Pinot Noir

There can be no doubt that for many winemakers in California, Pinot Noir represents the greatest oenological challenge of them all. It is hard enough to find good Burgundy in Burgundy, so the attempt to produce Pinot Noir outside that very special region can seem well nigh impossible. So many factors, which may not be crucial as far as other varietals are concerned, are absolutely central when it comes to growing and making Pinot Noir: site, clone, climatic conditions, yields, and the finer points of vinification.

Although Pinot Noir is no longer considered well suited to the warm climate of Napa Valley – Carneros excepted – it was planted there in the nineteenth century, both at Inglenook and Charles Krug. Over in Livermore, Carl Wente had Pinot Noir, and so did Paul Masson south of the San Francisco Bay. Phylloxera, of course, spelt the end of those vines and Pinot Noir was not widely replanted. However, Georges de Latour at Beaulieu did replant Pinot Noir in 1902. According to André Tchelitscheff, these vines had come directly from Burgundy and this particular clone was known as Petit Pinot Noirien. Tchelitscheff made a famous wine from these vines, the 1946 Beaulieu Pinot Noir. By that time the vines were already quite old and the yield was pitifully low. These vines no longer exist. However, the clone still seems to be around. Michael Robbins, the former owner and winemaker at Spring Mountain, obtained his cuttings from this clone from Martin Ray. Ray claimed that it originated from the Louis Latour vineyards in Beaune (another, less likely story says the cuttings came from Romanée-Conti), and were given to Paul Masson in 1898.[1]

After Repeal, the clones planted were those recommended by UC Davis, mostly on the basis of resistance to disease and good yields. By the 1970s Pinot had suddenly become popular (or fashionable) and a considerable acreage was planted. Unfortunately much of it was planted in unsuitable places, such as Napa Valley, and the results were discouraging. Winemakers accustomed to rich, gutsy musts from Cabernet Sauvignon and Zinfandel did not know how to handle the more delicate and fragile Pinot Noir. Jammy and unstable wines were all too common. Disillusionment set in, and prices for Pinot Noir grapes tumbled. The variety survived because of the dogged determination of a handful of growers and because the grape was used in sparkling wine. There has been a recovery, but Pinot Noir, for all its cult status, is no best-seller in California, perhaps because the wine, being fickle in the vineyard and hard to vinify, is costly to produce. In 1986 there were 7,667 acres planted; by 1997 that figure had increased to only 11,158. In 1997 the average price per ton was $1,539, although good growers in the most sought-after regions, such as Russian River Valley and Sonoma Coast, were charging and obtaining $2,000–$4,000 per ton. The acreage is fairly evenly divided between Napa (mostly Carneros) and Sonoma (more widely spread within the county), at about 3,000 acres each. There are some 1,400 acres in Monterey, 800 in Santa Barbara, 700 in Mendocino, and about 200 in San Luis Obispo County. Accurate figures are hard to come by, and these may be slight underestimates.

To appreciate how ignorant many Californian producers were about the specific character of Pinot Noir, consider the remarks made in the mid-1970s by the respected winemaker Karl Wente: 'Pinot Noir sometimes has a little of something else in it, like Pinot St George or Petite Sirah. I think even the Burgundians will agree that Pinot Noir needs a little monkeying around, blending here and there.'[2] It is perfectly true that at that time certain Burgundian *négociants* and British importers were not averse to beefing 'Burgundy' with a dash of Algerian red, but nobody argued that this practice should be universally adopted. The American debasing of the name Burgundy didn't help either. In the mid-1970s even a respected producer such as Louis Martini was producing a 'Burgundy' composed of 60 per cent Petite Sirah, plus Gamay and Pinot Noir. Moreover, the style Martini were aiming for was 'a heavy-bodied red wine'. To be fair, that was the common interpretation of the Burgundian style in California at the time.

However, by the mid-1970s there were already a handful of

winemakers who were turning their hand, with some success, to this notoriously difficulty variety. In Sonoma, Hanzell was consciously aping Burgundian methods, and so was Richard Graff at Chalone. Martin Ray was producing some notable wines in the Santa Cruz Mountains, where he planted Pinot Noir in 1942, and Robert Mondavi was turning his prodigiously inventive mind to the problem too. Josh Jensen planted Pinot Noir at Calera in 1974. I have tasted very few of those early efforts, but those who have done so report that the problem remained unsolved, with many of the wines tasting stewed and bitter. Joseph Swan in Russian River Valley did enjoy some success. He had selected a clone of good quality, now known as the Swan clone, and from 1973 he produced a series of acclaimed wines. The precise origin of the Swan clone is unknown. Davis Bynum was another pioneer of Pinot Noir in this region that has subsequently become so celebrated for it.

David Bruce also had a good clone, and claims that Chalone obtained it from his vineyards. Some growers in Anderson Valley told me that some of the Pinot Noir planted there also originated from Bruce's vineyards, but Dr Bruce was unable to confirm this when I asked him about it. Also in the Santa Cruz Mountains, Merry Edwards, later winemaker at Matanzas Creek, made some revered Pinot Noirs at Mount Eden Vineyards.

Mondavi began working with Burgundian methods in the early 1970s, retaining stems during fermentation and macerating at fairly high temperatures, but it would take a decade before the indefatigable Mondavi team mastered the variety, not only by refining their winemaking techniques, but because vastly superior sources of fruit were by then coming on stream from regions such as Carneros. Tim Mondavi also came to realize that Pinot Noir was a variety that resisted 'overprocessing'. The winery stopped fining and filtering their Pinot Noir and kept the use of sulphur to a minimum. Early experiments in retaining stems during fermentation were curtailed. The secret of Pinot Noir was to leave it alone. In the vineyards too Mondavi tried to restrain the high vigour of the vines, and by the mid-1980s the density of plantation had been increased and artificial fertilizers were no longer used.[3]

Ken Volk, who makes good Pinot Noir at Wild Horse in Paso Robles, agrees that the variety is very susceptible to farming practices. 'Change one detail,' he told me, 'and you change its character.' Paul Draper observes that to make good Pinot Noir you need to plant the appropriate clone in an outstanding site. 'It's a very challenging grape, because Pinot Noir is lower in phenolics than most other varieties, which means that as a winemaker you're not playing with a full deck.'

Roy Andries de Groot, writing in the early 1980s, noted that Pinot Noir grapes ripened fast and had a tendency to become overripe unless picked fast, which would explain the jammy character of many Pinot Noirs of that period.[4] However, Mike Lee of Kenwood believed that Pinot Noir was often picked *before* it was fully ripe – no doubt reflecting the old confusion between must weights and physiological ripeness. At Kenwood they used to pick Pinot Noir at 23 Brix, but now aim for 24. Gary Farrell, a leading Pinot Noir specialist, worries about the tendency to pick at even higher ripeness levels, such as 25 Brix. He prefers to pick earlier, to secure fruit with lower pH and, in his view, better balance. He worries that high-alcohol Pinot Noirs may not age well. Richard Sanford in Santa Ynez Valley looks for full ripening with high acidity – which, to be sure, is a nice trick if you know how to achieve it.

Spring frosts and rot can be a major problem with Pinot Noir. It's a thin-skinned variety particularly subject to mildew and rot, which can result in excessive levels of volatile acidity as well as off-flavours. Moreover, dry weather in the autumn is all the more vital because Pinot Noir is not rich in pigments, and growers wish to avoid an even more washed-out colour than normal. Californian winemakers, used to the dark opaque wines easily attained from Cabernet, Petite Sirah, and Zinfandel, may have worried that the more lightly pigmented Pinot Noir needed the maximum extraction in order to achieve an impressive depth of colour which, of course, is not intrinsic to its character.

Clonal selection is a crucial issue, just as in Burgundy itself. This has been recognized for some time. In 1975, Francis Mahoney of Carneros Creek winery planted some twenty clones on 1.75 acres in conjunction with UC Davis on an experimental basis. He and UC Davis vinified each clone's juice separately. From that range he selected a Davis clone, a Hanzell clone, and four different Pommard clones, as well as one derived from a Chambertin vineyard in Burgundy. These were then planted on a 10-acre plot, and today the vineyard is considerably larger. The estate releases three different Pinot Noirs in which the various clones play their part. Thus the Pommard clone has proved ideal for Mahoney's light, easy-drinking Fleur de Carneros.

In Russian River Valley Davis Bynum says that the Martini clone, which was originally developed for sparkling wine, gives bright strawberry fruit. Neither the Martini nor the Pommard clones are very thick-skinned, which may explain why many California Pinot Noirs lack tannin. The Martini clone is not universally admired, but Gary Farrell likes it for blending, and it has been a popular choice in Mendocino, as has the Wadenswil clone. Farrell's favourite clones are the Pommard and Dijon. Marimar Torres chose five clones for her estate: Beringer, Pommard, Dijon, See, and Swan.

A particularly interesting project aimed at improving the range of clones available to Californian winemakers and growers is the collection of so-called Heirloom clones of low-yielding vines that are not in normal commercial use. Tony Soter at Etude has been vinifying some of them and bottling them separately to monitor their character. Most of them are planted in the Hudson and Hyde vineyards in Carneros, and the clones include a so-called Romanée-Conti clone which came from Domaine Chandon (despite its glorious name, it gives generous yields), St Vivant, and Musigny, which gives a tiny crop and seems to be the same as the Hanzell clone. In general these Heirloom clones have clusters about half the size of most clones in regular use, and the yields are often no more than a quarter of those normally encountered from California-grown Pinot Noir. Tasting some of these wines in early 1998, I could discern clear differences between them. A group of selections from Calera, planted at Hyde, did not seem that concentrated despite yields of 2 tons per acre, but had good length. Pommard clones from Hudson Vineyard had a wilder nose of violets, but the wine was slightly jammy on the palate. The yields were a trifling 1 ton per acre, after bunch-thinning. Easily the best wine, to my taste, was a rich, dense, complex and very long example from the Musigny clone. Tony Soter stresses that these are experimental bottlings, but he still knows what he's aiming for. 'I'm for the school of seductive, charming Pinots,' he told me. 'It's lamentable that some well-thought-of Pinots are over-influenced by oak and tannin. Tannin is like a skeleton. You need it, but it shouldn't stick out.'

Everyone agrees that it is very difficult to make Pinot Noir. David Bruce recalls how difficult it was to get the wine to complete its malolactic fermentation – though he need not have worried, since some of the 1996s in Burgundy took almost a year to complete theirs. Martin Ray used to worry about lack of acidity, which, in his experience, could lead to premature browning of the wine. That problem has more or less been solved by planting the vines in cool regions where low acidity is rare. Other problems were encountered by the neo-Burgundians such as Richard Graff and Josh Jensen, who, some critics aver, were simply too dogmatic about such matters as the inclusion of stems during fermentation, a decision that has to be based on the ripeness levels of those stems. Jensen argues that destemming 'bashes up the stems and extracts more astringency than if you leave the bunches alone'.[5] But it cannot be entirely coincidental that the Pinots from both Calera and Chalone, for all their many virtues, can and often do have an austerity that is not always modified by bottle ageing.

Acacia, which under Larry Brooks's direction was a pioneer of Carneros Pinot Noir, promotes a non-interventionist approach. One of its press releases notes that Pinot's 'aroma is heady, like a white wine almost. We've chosen to accentuate that aspect of Pinot Noir. We have tried to let the grapes and the land have their say and to keep our stylistic voice muted. This is sometimes referred to as a transparent style. It is a style that tries not to color or distort the terroir of Carneros.'

Ted Lemon of Littorai takes a Burgundian approach, which is hardly surprising since he spent many years in France, working with Jacques Seysses at Domaine Dujac and as winemaker at Domaine Roulot in Meursault. He believes strongly in low yields and careful clonal selection, in minimal intervention and gentle handling; he avoids the use of pumps and filtration. Lemon is suspicious of what he perceives as the trend towards excessive hang-times, which result in high-alcohol wines and overripe flavours. Instead he aims for finesse and balance. His Pinot is given a short cold soak, a technique that evolved in Burgundy in the 1970s. Fermentation is delayed until a maceration at low temperatures has taken place in order to extract colour and perfume without the need for a prolonged fermentation at high temperatures. The must is fermented by Lemon in open-top tanks, using 15 to 40 per cent whole clusters. No cultivated yeasts are added. During the fermentation the cap is routinely punched down. Malolactic fermentation takes place in barrel and the wine is aged in 30 to 50 per cent new French oak. There is a tendency at many California estates to use high-toast barrels for Pinot Noir; Ted Lemon prefers a range of different toasts, but admits that overall his barrels would be more toasted than those typically employed at most Burgundian estates. Bill Smith of La Jota likes a heavy toast for his Pinot Noir, as it gives more smoke and tar flavours, which he thinks is more Burgundian, though others might differ. Others point out that the full ripeness of Californian Pinot Noir demands heavily toasted oak.

Don Blackburn at Bernardus in Carmel Valley took a different approach, preferring a much shorter fermentation, usually no more than seven days, since he believes longer cuvaisons do not add anything to Pinot Noir. Both the free-run and the press wine will go through their malolactic fermentations in large French oak upright casks, rather than in barrel. There never have been formulae for making Pinot Noir, which demands, perhaps more than any other variety, the quivering antennae of the individual wine-maker to make the important judgments that will determine the wine's quality and character.

Although there is still a tendency at most wineries to use heavily toasted French oak, the ageing period has overall been reduced. From the mid-1980s onwards, Mondavi cut its barrel ageing for Pinot Noir by approximately half, from 20 to 24 months to about 10 months. This would be true of many other wineries too. On the other hand, Mondavi favour a substantial proportion of new oak, especially for the Reserve wines.

As with Zinfandel, there is much discussion about the ageability of Californian Pinot Noir. For that matter, there is considerable debate about the ageability of French Burgundy. There is no more swoon-inducing wine than a superlative 30-year-old red Burgundy, but they are rarely encountered, and tend to be a miraculous combination of great vineyard site, skilled winemaking, and impeccable cellarage. In general, California Pinot Noir has a slighter tannic structure than its French counterpart, so it is not normally advisable to age the wine for decades. Out of curiosity, mine rather than his, Dick Ward pulled out some older vintages from the Saintsbury wine library. I had to agree with him that after about ten years in bottle there seems little to be gained by keeping the wine any longer, even though some wines were clearly capable of an extended life.

Not long ago many of the wines from Williams-Selyem were presented at a vertical tasting that covered vintages from 1984 to 1995. Some of California's most avid Pinot fans were there, and the consensus seems to have been that the wines were holding up better than expected, with very few over the hill. I asked Burt Williams' neighbour Tom Rochioli how his own acclaimed Pinot Noirs had aged. He replied that he made his regular Pinot Noirs to be drunk young, and his clients only cellared the Reserve bottlings. Of these, the 1982 had aged well, the 1983 had collapsed after five years, 1984 and 1985 had aged well, 1987 and 1988 had aged adequately. He added that since he believed he had refined his winemaking techniques in the 1990s, the wines of this decade would probably evolve better than those he made in the 1980s. All this suggests that the longevity of Pinot Noir has as much to do with balance as with tannin and extract.

Over the years the best regions for growing Pinot Noir have become apparent, although their competing claims have not been resolved, and are not likely to be for some time to come. Regions where the variety used to be planted have largely been abandoned. Pinot Noir was rarely successful in Napa Valley, both because it was planted in over-rich soils with excessively warm microclimates and because winemakers in the 1960s and 1970s tended to treat Pinot Noir as though it were Cabernet, going for maximum extraction and failing to realize that the grape's complex of aroma, filigree texture, and flavour required gentle rather than forceful treatment.

A few Pinot enthusiasts went off in search of Burgundian soil types. Unfortunately California is not rich in the limestone subsoil common along the Côte d'Or. Josh Jensen found an outcrop south of Hollister, which is where he planted his vineyards and created his winery. The results have been mixed. On the whole Jensen seems to have succeeded, and I have drunk excellent wines even from unpromising vintages such as 1983. However, the wines are inconsistent, though much the same is true of his beloved Burgundy. Wiry and hard in their youth, they definitely need time to show complexity. Jensen himself is satisfied with his venture: 'I like our Pinot Noirs more than anybody else's in California. We're quite different from the currently fashionable wines from the Russian River and Carneros, which are enjoyable wines, but they don't possess the long-term ageing potential that requires a skeleton, the tannic backbone from low-yielding vines ... My wines require an intellectual commitment to see what they will become.' James Halliday argues, quite persuasively, that Jensen's quest for Burgundian soil was mistaken: 'Soil type does not provide the answer. The limestone soils of Burgundy are not important per se; they are important because they provide particularly good drainage in a region in which rainfall is spread evenly ... throughout the growing season.'[6]

Russian River Valley is in many Pinot lovers' opinion the outstanding region in California for the variety, and I am inclined to agree. Rich Sayre of Rodney Strong believes that 'depending on the clonal selection, red cherries or black cherries are the characteristic [Russian River Valley] fruit in both aroma and flavor.' He adds that they have 'a supple, velvety mouthfeel'. Other winemakers identify the aroma and flavour spectrum as running 'the gamut from fresh, strawberry, plum and dried rose petal to sandalwood, leather, toasty oak, and hints of barnyard.' Tom Rochioli adds, 'Carneros Pinots are very showy, but many lack the concentration and mouthfeel of Russian River Valley [where] we get full, rich, concentrated flavors and supple wines.'[7]

At their best the wines are quite rich and solidly structured, yet they also show considerable finesse. Gary Farrell, whose knowledge of these wines is as intimate as anyone's in the region, finds Russian River Pinot is fleshier yet more elegant and less simple than, say, Carneros fruit. It usually shows a pronounced red-fruit character: strawberry, raspberry, plum. There are years when rain can mar the harvest and cause problems for this most sensitive of red varieties, but overall Russian River Pinot, with its low pH and fine acidity, has a bright fruitiness and a lingering finish as well as a complex flavour spectrum. The wines tend to be medium-bodied and the tannins are discreet, yet good vintages are capable of evolving for a decade or more. There also seems to be an exceptional harmony between Russian River fruit and good-quality French oak. It's a dangerous thing to say, but the fruit quality here seems the most Burgundian, for what it's worth. The outstanding producers here are William-Selyem, Gary Farrell, Davis Bynum, Dehlinger, Torres, Rochioli, and Martinelli.

Naturally, Carneros has its powerful advocates too, and my fellow wine writer (and Burgundy enthusiast) Robert Joseph is convinced that 'the heartland of Pinot Noir-making today has to be Carneros.'[8] Not surprisingly, Dick Ward is another fan, though he points out that 'Carneros Pinot Noir is changing constantly. Ten years ago the wrong clones were often planted in the wrong places. Winemaking was often mediocre. All this gave Pinot Noir a different character. You can characterize Carneros Pinot Noir as fruit-driven, moderate in tannin, with medium colour, red-fruit flavours, a wine that was enjoyable young. Now it's changing to a softer, riper style, with riper tannins, better colour, more concentration, more black-fruit flavours. When young it's easy to confuse some Carneros Pinot Noir with Burgundy; but with age, the *terroir* emerges. In general I'd say we have tighter, harder tannins, and the Burgundians have more purity of fruit because it's cooler. In Carneros the best years are cool, such as 1991, 1994, and 1995, whereas in Burgundy the best years are hot.'

Tony Soter finds Carneros Pinot Noir more supple than the same variety from some other regions. Jim Clendenen, who as a founding father of Central Coast Pinot Noir has certain biases, finds that Carneros Pinot has good fruit but little identity. 'It's clean, fruity, simple.' The leading producers using Carneros fruit include Acacia, Saintsbury, Mondavi, Etude, Kent Rasmussen. Good producers include Bouchaine, Cuvaison, Sterling, Sinskey, Carneros Creek, and ZD.

The distinctly cool Anderson Valley in Mendocino is often mentioned as an excellent Pinot Noir region. Certainly the region is very well suited to the production of Pinot Noir as a base for sparkling wine, and Scharffenberger (now Pacific Echo) and Roederer are well established there. The still wines sometimes seem to have more structure than fruit, and it is probably too early to say whether Anderson Valley should be ranked alongside Carneros and Santa Maria Valley. I have certainly enjoyed good Pinots from Navarro, Edmeades, Handley, Husch, Claudia Springs, and Pepperwood Springs.

A more promising region would seem to be the Central Coast. Monterey County, despite its renowned coolness, has yet to deliver outstanding results, except at the mountain outposts of Calera and Chalone. Santa Barbara, however, has performed extremely well, with superb wines emerging from vineyards such as Bien Nacido in Santa Maria Valley and Sanford & Benedict in Santa Ynez Valley. Jim Clendenen of Au Bon Climat, who has been working with Pinot Noir here for longer than most, describes the character of Santa Maria Valley fruit as spicy and sappy, with notes of wild herbs and flowers, with ample fruit and fine texture derived from its low pH and long hang-time. He adds that Pinot Noir has proved very site-specific in Santa Barbara, so some growers who planted it initially have removed it. Gary Farrel detects a mushroomy, earthy quality in Central Coast Pinot Noir that I do not recognize myself. Instead there can sometimes be a slightly vegetal tone to the fruit, and the small handful of winemakers who do not care for Santa Barbara Pinot Noir, such as Steve Test, also find a stewed-tomato character.

I have found some inconsistency in Santa Barbara Pinot Noir, as well as wines that strike me as confected. But at its best it can be delectable wine, perfumed and pure and seductive. Jim Clendenen points out that the early growers had no idea which clones they were planting and no idea where to plant them. The early mistakes are being rectified, and he is convinced that the future for the region, now that these viticultural questions have been resolved, is very bright. Apart from Calera and Chalone, the outstanding producers here are Au Bon Climat, Sanford, Byron, Cambria, Lane Tanner, Foxen, and Hitching Post. Many wineries outside the region buy fruit from here and produce some fine bottlings: David Bruce (who also buys some grapes from Chalone), Fetzer, and Bernardus.

Slightly to the north, in Paso Robles and Arroyo Grande, there is some exceptional Pinot Noir. Talley in Arroyo Grande is probably the outstanding producer, but Wild Horse is also notable. The quantities are minute but there are some superb Pinot Noirs coming out of Santa Cruz Mountains, from David Bruce and Mount Eden Vineyards.

One other region being spoken of in excited tones in winemaking circles is the Sonoma Coast. I am convinced that some of California's most exciting Pinot Noirs are likely to emerge from here in the years ahead. Sonoma Coast is a vast region, but the prime sites here are high in the hills and close to the ocean. Maritime influence is strong, and the microclimates cool. They must be dangerous areas to cultivate, prone to rot and lack of ripeness, but when all the factors come together the fruit quality is sensational, with flavours of bracing intensity and purity. Kendall-Jackson has not been slow to recognize the potential of the region, but thus far the most exciting Pinots have come from smaller, quality-conscious winemakers such as Steve Kistler and Ted Lemon at Littorai. The wines are very expensive – these must be the most expensive Pinot Noir grapes in the state – as the vineyards are isolated and hard to cultivate, and yields tend to be very low.

Finally, there should be a brief round of applause for Vin Gris. A few growers in Burgundy produce a rosé by the simple expedient of bleeding the fermentation tanks. The idea is to remove excess liquid and thus to increase the ratio of skins to must, with the intention of giving a more concentrated wine. The bled wine, or *saignée*, continues to ferment, and the result is a light-bodied but fresh and charming dry rosé. It is rarely encountered in California, but is the perfect picnic wine. The best examples I have encountered come from Sanford and Saintsbury.

NOTES

1 Robert Benson, *Great Winemakers of California*, p. 145
2 Ibid., 74
3 Terry Robards, *Wine Spectator*, 15 September 1989
4 Roy Andries De Groot, *The Wine of California*, p. 136
5 Marq de Villiers, *The Heartbreak Grape*, p. 128
6 James Halliday, *Wine Atlas of California*, p. 348
7 Eleanor and Ray Heald, 'R. R. V. Pinot Noir', *Practical Winery and Vineyard*, March/April 1995
8 Robert Joseph, *Wine* Magazine, March 1997

17
Other Red Varieties

If the wine-drinking public is, by and large, content with its Cabernets and Merlots, the winemakers are bored. Among red wines, only Cabernet and, increasingly, Merlot can fetch the very high prices that make estate owners salivate. But just as there is an Anything But Chardonnay movement among white wine fanciers, so there is a restlessness among winemakers, and some consumers, when it comes to the annual duplication of Cabernets and Merlots. Some winemakers, notably Randall Grahm, will even argue that California as a whole is far better suited to what he calls the Mediterranean varieties (French, Spanish, Italian) than to northern French varieties such as Cabernet and Pinot Noir. Others, such as the Martin brothers in Paso Robles, are obsessed by Italian varieties and also believe the Californian climate is perfectly suited to growing them. Many wine estates – Martini and Prati, Viansa, Mondavi, and others – were founded by Italian-Americans who know there is still a substantial market for such wines. Yet other estates such as Monteviña have climbed on to a bandwagon that is trundling rather than rolling along.

In general I welcome this search for other varieties. The more diversity the better. The Rhône varietals have, as will become clear, tremendous potential in California. Hugh Thatcher, a wine merchant in California, follows the trends closely. 'Syrah is hot,' he confirmed, 'but Sangiovese has been too pricy and the jury is still out. The trouble is that too many people are planting in the wrong place.'

Even though the commercial success of those venturing into the non-traditional varietal market is still uncertain, one has to applaud their relish and determination. Jim Moore, the winemaker in charge of Italian varieties for Mondavi's La Famiglia range, greeted me with the cry: 'I come from the planet Sangiovese and I have come here to destroy your Cabernet!'

Alicante Bouschet

This variety was created in France in 1866 by crossing Grenache and Petit Bouschet. It attained immense popularity during Prohibition, when its thick skins and deep colour made it an easily transportable grape destined for the tubs and cellars of home winemakers. In those days some 30,000 acres were planted. Most of the surviving 1,300 acres are in the Central Valley, with 450 in Fresno County. In this hot region Alicante used to be a component in jug wines. A handful of varietal wines are occasionally made by Central Valley wineries such as Papagni. In Sonoma varietal Alicantes are made by Topolos at Russian River and Cotturi. In Napa, Kent Rasmussen has toyed with it.

A pure Alicante, grown near Calistoga and vinified by Phelps for its Mistral blend, proved surprisingly rich on the nose and sweet and spicy on the palate; but the finish is short, and the wine lacked structure.

Barbera

The most positive attribute of this celebrated Italian variety, as far as Californian wine producers are concerned, is that it can retain its high acidity even in the baking expanses of the Central Valley. Its popularity among growers has declined slightly, and the low prices obtained for Barbera mean that revival is unlikely. In 1997 the average price per ton was only $304. In 1986 there were 13,417 acres planted, and by 1997 there were 11,137 acres still under vine, almost all in the Central Valley, with 5,756 in Fresno County and 1,914 in Madera County. Until recently growers could plant clones that were supposed to be virus-free but were not; however, a touch of shatter at flowering often improved the quality. Alternatively, they could buy genuinely cleaned-up clones, but their drawback is the size of the berries and consequent dilution of the wine.

A handful of growers and producers in the North Coast and Sierra Foothills take Barbera seriously. Monteviña and Monte Volpe are two of the wineries that specialize in the variety, and

Louis Martini and Sebastiani were long-time supporters. Indeed Sebastiani has been increasing production. A majority of growers believe that trellised training is superior to bush-vine cultivation for Barbera. Yields tend to be modest, at around 4 tons per acre, and thinner, less fertile soils are more favourable to the variety than richer clay soils. Greg Graziano of Monte Volpe, who believes Mendocino Barbera is generally superior to that grown in the Sierra Foothills, feels it should be picked very ripe, at 25 Brix, but Randall Grahm argues that Barbera does best in a relatively cool climate with a long hang-time to moderate the acidity. From a winemaking point of view, the main challenge it poses is its tendency to reduction. 'Just look at Barbera and it starts to stink,' says Grahm. In addition to the producers already mentioned, others include Boeger in El Dorado County, Renwood in the Foothills, and Gallo Sonoma, who are beginning to release Barbera made from their Barrelli Creek Vineyard in Alexander Valley. Benziger also produce a Barbera from Alexander Valley fruit, and Preston make an impeccable version in Dry Creek Valley.

Black Muscat

Also known as Muscat Hamburg, this intriguingly perfumed variety is treasured by the handful of winemakers who use it. Only 63 acres are left. One of the best-known vineyards is that of Don Gallagher in Madera, who has some old vines but has also replanted the variety. Producers include Togni, Shenandoah, Gan Eden, and Rosenblum. For more information, see Chapter 21.

Carignane

If a pollster asked French grape growers to name their least favourite grape variety, they would probably reply: Carignan (which gained an 'e' after it crossed the Atlantic). Even in regions where it does best, such as Corbières, it often yields rather hard wines with little fruit or charm. Some blame the poor showing of Carignan on the use of over-productive rootstocks and insist that if yields are moderate, the results can be surprisingly good. And almost everyone agrees that old-vine Carignan can be exceptional. For all its supposed virtues, the problem, at least in France, is that if you ask a grower whether he would rather plant Syrah or, alternatively, Carignan and wait forty years for it to become interesting, the answer will be obvious.

California has a surprising amount of Carignane. During Prohibition there were about 50,000 acres under vine, and even today about 8,500 remain, about 2,700 in Madera County. Moreover, almost all the Carignane is indisputably old-vine, if only because hardly anybody would think of planting it today. In old vineyards in Sonoma and Mendocino it appears as part of the field blend, and is rarely bottled as a varietal wine, although Husch in Anderson Valley still do so. In Mendocino Fetzer used to make a wine called Mendocino Premium that was pure Carignane, but Fetzer's present-day winemakers, such as Bob Blue, report that although the variety is still abundant, it tends to give simply, cherry-flavoured wines. In Sonoma, Doug Nalle says Carignane's main drawback is its tendency to rot.

Randall Grahm at Bonny Doon has made varietal Carignane from fruit sourced in the Sacramento Delta. When I accused him of sheer perversity in releasing a wine that nobody else wants to make, he beamed. But he is not entirely alone. Pellegrini in Sonoma also make Carignane from Alexander Valley. Amador Foothill Winery also release Carignane. The Cline vineyards in Oakley contain some Carignane, which is mostly used in blends but is also bottled as a varietal wine.

Carnelian

Not exactly a household name, Carnelian is a crossing between Grenache and an existing crossing that had married Cabernet Sauvignon with Carignane in 1936. Introduced in 1973, it was first vinified commercially by Franciscan in 1975 as a light red. It was quite widely planted, and within a couple of years there were 1,600 acres under vine. Its popularity was almost certainly related to its ability to give very generous yields and its alleged similarity to Cabernet Sauvignon. Unfortunately wine made from Carnelian turned out to be light and bland, despite its depth of colour. About 1,000 acres remain in the Central Valley where it was mostly planted, but it seems to have been abandoned as a varietal wine.

Charbono

Qu'est que c'est, Charbono? Good question. Philip Wagner described it as an Italian grape variety, though one with a flavour resembling Côtes du Rhône.[1] Jancis Robinson thinks it is 'probably' the same as the French variety Corbeau, also known as Charbonneau.[2] Since the French variety is extinct, the question has become academic. Others have suggested the variety is related to Dolcetto or to Douce Noire of Savoie.

It is almost extinct in California too, with some 50 acres hanging in there in North Coast vineyards. A large-berried variety, it ripens with difficulty to give dark, tannic wines which some critics have maligned as 'generally lacking in definable or interesting flavors'.[3] It retained some popularity as part of the old Inglenook range. It still has its advocates in California, notably Duxoup in Sonoma, but also Fife and Parducci. Markham's second label Glass Mountain has offered a Charbono. Randall Grahm made a silky, sensual Charbono for the first time in 1993. Greg Graziano of Monte Volpe is not a great fan of a wine that has, in his view, an aroma of bubblegum, but Fife are certainly keen on their own version, describing it as 'sensual, velvety, suffused with blackberries and black pepper. As soft as flannel pajamas ... it just rocks with blackberries and exotic spices. Tannin? Yes, but so ripe and soft, it melts in your mouth.'

Over the top? Indisputably, but Charbono is still worth a try.

Cinsault

Rarely encountered as a varietal wine, but it is produced by the Lake Sonoma Winery in Dry Creek Valley.

Counoise

A relatively rare Rhône variety, Counoise is one of the thirteen grapes permitted to participate in the Châteauneuf-du-Pape blend. There are enthusiasts scattered about: the Domaine du Piaugier in Sablet, one of the Côtes du Rhône Villages, is keen on Counoise. The only varietal example I know of in California comes from Gary Eberle in Paso Robles, and he vinifies it as a rosé.

Dolcetto

In Piedmont, this lovely grape gives deeply coloured, intensely flavoured wines with low acidity that are delicious when drunk young. It is not a wine that responds to small barrels or other fancy vinification. Its simple juiciness and sensible price are its principal attractions. Unfortunately the few examples in California take it all too seriously, as Kent Rasmussen's $20 price tag for his 1994 bottling suggests. Viansa also produce the wine, and so do Bargetto. Greg Graziano is puzzled by Californian Dolcetto, which seems to produce wines that are more inky and tannic than those from Piedmont.

Freisa

This variety is quite rare in its native Piedmont, and is unusual in that it can be made as a light fresh *frizzante* wine or as a dense red. The version from Viansa is neither, having a rather tart cranberry flavour and little concentration.

Gamay Beaujolais

Such a simple grape variety but, in California, such a complicated story. Gamay cuttings first came to the state in quantity after the phylloxera outbreak. It wasn't always clear to the recipients exactly what these cuttings were, but it said 'Gamay Beaujolais' on the box. However, purchasers in Napa Valley received boxes labelled 'Gamay Noir'. After some experience of growing these vines in different parts of the state, it became evident that the Gamay Beaujolais planted south of the San Francisco Bay was not identical to the Gamay Noir in Napa. The Napa vines ripened earlier and were more productive. Some argued that such differences had to do with microclimatic and soil differences, and were not of genetic origin. Nonetheless the Napa growers decided their Gamay should be differentiated, and it became known as Napa Gamay Noir or Napa Gamay.

In time it became clear beyond doubt that the two vines were indeed different. UC Davis's leading authority on grape varieties, Dr Harold Olmo, journeyed to Beaujolais itself and returned with tablets of stone. Napa Gamay, he announced, was the same as the

French Gamay, while the prolific Gamay Beaujolais was a clonal variation, albeit a very pallid variation, of Pinot Noir. (Philip Wagner was sufficiently impressed by the Gamay Beaujolais from the Digardi Vineyard near Martinez to declare that it 'strengthens the belief that the Gamay, *not* the Pinot Noir, offers the best hope for true Burgundy characteristics in California.'[4]) The Napa growers, pleased to have the real thing, changed the name to Napa Gamay of Beaujolais and increased the price per ton to such an extent that at one point it became more expensive even than Pinot Noir. Acreage increased substantially during the 1970s and by the early 1980s there were about 6,000 acres of Napa Gamay planted, as well as 4,500 of Gamay Beaujolais.

In 1971 the Bureau of Alcohol, Tobacco and Firearms stepped in to clarify matters, and issued the following statement: 'Wine made from grapes identified as Napa Gamay may be labeled either as "Napa Gamay" or as "Gamay", and a wine made from grapes identified as Gamay Beaujolais may be labeled as "Gamay Beaujolais" or as "Pinot Noir" [*sic*] . . . The vines which are currently erroneously named Gamay Beaujolais will be replaced, over the years, by new plantings of either Napa Gamay or Pinot Noir. All such new plantings will not be permitted to be titled Gamay Beaujolais and, accordingly, the use of the term Gamay Beaujolais will be entirely terminated with the life of the present plantings.'[5]

Perhaps the BATF thought this would clarify the situation, but confusion remained. The French authorities were certainly unhappy with the decision to retain the use of a name to which they thought they were exclusively entitled. As far as I understand the current situation, the Gamay Beaujolais will cease to exist after the year 2007, and any wine bottled under that name must contain 75 per cent Pinot Noir or Valdiguié. What, you may ask, is Valdigiué? Apparently, it is the correct name for Napa Gamay. In any event, both varieties are in decline. By 1995 there were 1,250 acres of Napa Gamay remaining, and 1,000 of Gamay Beaujolais.

The best known, if rarely available, Gamay Beaujolais was that produced by Martin Ray. More recently, a few wineries have embraced the newly hatched Valdiguié. Gallo Sonoma produce an inoffensive example, and there is another from Hop Kiln. J. Lohr's is unoaked but lacks character. Wineries that used to produce Gamay, but have long ceased to do so, include Mondavi, Stag's Leap Wine Cellars, and Joseph Swan. It seems curious that so much bureaucratic energy should have been expended on such an uninteresting pair of grape varieties.

Grenache

Grenache, the great variety of southern France and Spain, has never been valued in California. Its primary use was as a blending variety in jug wines, and this accounts for the vast acreage in the Central Valley, where 98 per cent is planted. The variety tolerates both hot dry conditions and strong winds, as its stems are sturdy, so it is well suited to the arid Central Valley. Its propensity to attain high degrees of alcohol also makes it a useful corrective when blended with other, more delicate varieties less well endowed in that respect. Grenache enjoyed a new lease of life as a rosé, a perfectly sensible use of a variety that was often light in colour. Almadén was the first producer to market a Grenache rosé, and it was so successful that many other wineries followed suit. Joseph Phelps still produces a pink Grenache, a delicious wine.

In addition a handful of winemakers tried to take Grenache more seriously. David Bruce made some red Grenache at his winery in 1970 and 1971 and pronounced himself pleased with the results. Randall Grahm at Bonny Doon tracked down the source: George Benson outside Gilroy. This became a key component in Grahm's Clos de Gilroy. He was happy with the quality he encountered, since he knew that most Grenache was planted in the wrong places and delivered indifferent and mediocre wine. Probably the finest Grenache from California I have tasted is the 1996 from Alban. When tasted blind against what turned out to be 1996 Château Rayas from Châteauneuf-du-Pape, the latter was instantly recognizable as Grenache, but Alban's wine, although less varietally true, was much richer and denser.

The acreage devoted to Grenache has been gradually slipping. In 1986 there were 14,669 acres under vine; by 1997 the figure had dropped slightly to 11,699, of which 3,700 are in Madera County. The average price per ton was negligible: $242 in 1997.

Grignolino

Joseph Heitz has long had a sentimental liaison with this Piedmontese variety. When he bought his first vineyard in Napa Valley, it was planted with just over 8 acres of Grignolino, which he later expanded to 15. Initially he produced both a red and a rosé from these grapes. The rosé is a good wine, slightly tart but all the more refreshing for it. Heitz also produces a successful 'port' from the variety. It has a sweet spicy nose, and is charming, delicate, and peppery on the palate. It is estimated that only about 50 acres of Grignolino remain in California.

Mission

Mission was the first *Vitis vinifera* grape to be brought to California, where it was planted by Franciscan missionaries as they made their way up the West Coast from Mexico. Some believe it to be related to the Pais of Chile and the Criolla of Argentina. By the mid-nineteenth century it was being replaced at a rapid rate by cuttings of more distinguished varieties imported from Europe, but Mission continued to be planted. Mission's chief virtue, as a commercial variety, was the enormous crop of brownish-red berries it routinely produced. In 1983 there were still about 3,000 acres in existence, mostly in San Bernardino County.[6] Some 900 acres still survive, so it is possible to taste wines made from Mission, as I have done in the Sierra Foothills. As a pallid red wine it seems of negligible interest, but it is not without merit as a sweet wine, although hardly the equal of Riesling or Sauvignon or even Zinfandel.

Mourvèdre

The great grape of Bandol in Provence almost vanished before it was revived by Lucien Peyraud after World War II. Since many of the Mourvèdre vines still growing in California are over 100 years old, it is certain that they are considerably older than any now growing in Bandol. There used to be a good deal planted around Cucamonga in southern California, but now the stronghold for the grape is Contra Costa County, where the centenarian vines are found in the Cline family's vineyard in Oakley. These 220 acres or so are ungrafted vines, planted on sandy soils and dry-farmed, giving very low yields. That also accounts for the superlative quality of much of the Mourvèdre produced in California by Cline,

Jade Mountain, Ridge, Thackrey, and Bonny Doon. Sebastiani also buys its Mourvèdre from Contra Costa County.

Whereas the French Mourvèdre is usually very dense and tannic and requires many years in bottle to soften up and develop its extraordinary aromatic complexity, Mourvèdre in California (where it is often known, as it is in Australia, as Mataro) is a simpler, brighter wine, which appears to be lower in tannin than its French counterpart. Nonetheless good Californian Mourvèdre is a serious wine showing layer upon layer of rich fruit.

Unfortunately the acreage has fallen dramatically to about 370. acres. However, the enthusiasm of the likes of Paul Draper and Randall Grahm for the variety should ensure its survival. In southern France Mourvèdre is said to thrive best in locations which are both very hot and exposed to maritime influence, which is why Bandol has proved ideal for the variety. That also seems to be the case in California, where the proximity of the Oakley vineyards to the Sacramento Delta may be a determining factor in the quality of the fruit.

Apart from the wineries already mentioned, other producers of Mourvèdre include Edmunds St John, Phelps, and Rosenblum. Joseph Swan launched a 1994 Mourvedre made from old vines in Russian River Valley.

Nebbiolo

Since the fashioning of a good Barolo-style Nebbiolo has become a kind of Holy Grail to a few Californian producers, it came as some surprise to learn that it was once quite widely cultivated in the Central Valley. Acreage has fallen, however, and by 1995 only 132 acres were in production, although I suspect that the figure has risen somewhat as driven winemakers continue their quest.

It is a very tricky grape to grow. Greg Graziano of Monte Volpe finds it very frustrating, since it easily overcrops and lacks colour. Fetzer and Beringer have also played with the variety, but they too find it too light. In the Sierra Foothills Jeff Meyers of Monteviña, who must have tried out almost every Italian variety in existence, finds Nebbiolo workable only for rosé wine. Nick Martin in Paso Robles is the leading specialist, but even after a decade of experience it has to be said that his results are not exactly impressive. Nor do his neighbours at Arciero do any better with the variety, although Jim Clendenen seems to think it could do well in Santa Barbara. Viansa in Sonoma have also tried their hand at it, and Kent Rasmussen in Napa produces 200 cases.

For what it's worth, that other testing ground for red grape varieties on the West Coast, Washington state, has had no more success with Nebbiolo. Both Mike Sauer of Red Willow Vineyard and David Gelles of Knipsun Vineyard have planted it and declare themselves unimpressed. Nebbiolo, on present showings, seems to be one Italian variety best left to the Italians.

Négrette

Under the name Pinot St George this was once a common grape variety in California, but it is now very rare. There are some old vines in the Gemelli Vineyard in Cienega Valley, and Wild Horse have recently planted 3 acres which Ken Volk plans to use to make a port-style wine.

The grape's home base is the Frontonnais region of France, and it also contributes to red Gaillac. Although it can make quite a good wine, as many Côtes de Frontonnais demonstrate, the grape is susceptible to grey rot and other maladies. When planted in California it was often vinified in a slightly sweet style, which Volk clearly intends to build upon.

Petite Sirah

In the late 1980s I tasted a Petite Sirah made by Paul Draper in 1971. The colour was an opaque inky-red and it tasted as if it had been made the day before. Its rusticity was mildly troubling, but it was clearly indestructible. I suspect that if I opened another bottle of that wine today, it would taste exactly the same. The point of preserving a bottle of wine is to appreciate its evolution, not to watch it treading water. Nonetheless, that Petite Sirah was undeniably impressive, and so were others I have tasted over the years.

So it is sad to report that it appears to be in decline. In 1978 there were still some 14,000 acres in production, mostly in the Central Valley where it would have given some guts to jug wine blends. But it had also been planted in good locations on the North Coast, including Napa Valley, and here too the acreage was dropping sharply. In 1986 just under 5,000 acres remained and by 1997 there were only 2,692, 350 in Napa. This is curious because the demand for Petite Sirah is quite strong, if its relatively high price per ton in 1997 – $990 – is anything to go by. Only about sixty wineries in California produce bottlings.

But what is Petite Sirah? Roy Andries De Groot, writing in the early 1980s, presented the prevailing view, which was that in the nineteenth century Syrah wines had been shipped to California mixed in with another varietal which mysteriously became 'a new vine with substantially smaller, round, black grapes. They decided to give it a new name, including a French word for prestige, and something a bit easier to spell than Syrah. Both requirements were met calling the new American vine Petite Sirah.' De Groot was clearly no fan: 'It was always powerful and strong, with a deep, almost black colour, but its taste was ordinary and rough, with virtually no interest of bouquet or varietal character.'[7]

The story has proved more complicated than De Groot could have known. The UC Davis vineyards preserved five strains of Petite Sirah, which were recently subjected to a DNA analysis by Professor Carole Meredith. She discovered that three of them were Durif, one was Pinot Noir, and the fifth an obscure French grape called Peloursin. In 1997 Professor Meredith was invited by the Davis farm adviser in Mendocino, Glenn McGourty, to come up to the county and take a look at some plots of old-vine Petite Sirah. Her team sampled sixty vines from twenty-one vineyards. Analysing these vines, she discovered that the official Davis-approved Petite Sirah is identical to Durif, a variety the parents of which are Syrah and Peloursin. It appears that Durif represents about half the 'Petite Sirah' vines encountered in Mendocino, while the remainder are composed of fourteen genetically distinct varietals. One of them has been identified as Aubun, an obscure but frost-resistant French grape from the southern Rhône, apparently not found anywhere else in California. It is believed by authorities as notable as Galet that Aubun is identical to Counoise. There are four other varietals that do not match any of the hundreds of genetic examples filed away at Davis. So the investigation continues, and the mystery of Petite Sirah, although partly solved, has not been fully cleared up.

Since Petite Sirah can give impressive wine, one may well ask why Durif has become of negligible importance in its native France.

The answer seems to be that it is prone to rot, which it resists far more successfully in the warmer, drier climate of California. Dennis Patton of Hidden Cellars, who worked closely with Professor Meredith on these analyses, believes that in California Durif has picked up the physical attributes of Peloursin more than Syrah, and it is very hard to differentiate Peloursin from Durif with the naked eye.

It also appears that some of the complex old vineyards that are identified as Petite Sirah contain some authentic Syrah too. Sean Thackrey, who makes one of California's best Syrahs, believes some cuttings from Hermitage were brought over and subsequently dubbed Petite Sirah.

Petite Sirah does seem to be enjoying a revival of sorts, however. Dennis Patton is keen on the variety (or cluster of varieties) despite its defects, which are very late ripening, high tannins, and a susceptibility to rot. Yields are naturally low, and the average for Sonoma is 1.66 tons/acre, for Mendocino 3.5 tons/acre, and for Napa 2.7. It's important to select from the best sites and preferably from 50-year-old vines. Paul Draper regards it primarily as an excellent blending grape, adding complexity, spice, and tannin to Zinfandel. But it does need to age. Ehren Jordan at Turley also admires Petite Sirah, and points out that in 1997 some growers were charging up to $3,500 per ton for outstanding parcels of the variety.

There seems to have been a change in winemaking styles in the 1990s, with winemakers more confident about how to control the tannins always present in Petite Sirah. Dennis Patton gives the grapes a cold soak before fermentation, and sometimes fines the wine to calm the tannins. When drinking a 1996 Central Coast version made by David Bruce, I was surprised at how voluptuous and accessible the wine was. Paul Draper agrees that while Petite Sirah is naturally tannic, it is possible to deal with those tannins during fermentation, vinifying a wine that is rich and rounded, with remarkable depth of colour and viscosity. Many tasters discern a boysenberry fruit flavour, with spicy tones reminiscent of cloves, and a cedariness that develops with age but which is not derived from barrel ageing. Its character varies from site to site, and so do factors such as pH. Most winemakers favour ageing the wine in American oak.[8]

In the past excellent Petite Sirahs were produced by wineries such as Burgess, Kenwood, Concannon, Cuvaison, Mondavi, and

Freemark Abbey, but most, if not all, have given up on it. Today many of the best examples are emerging from Ukiah and Redwood valleys in Mendocino, where Lolonis, Hidden Cellars, Fife, Edmeades, Fetzer and Parducci all release bottlings. Foppiano is the leading producer in Sonoma, if not California.

Pinot Meunier

There are about 200 acres of this variety, which of course is primarily used for sparkling wines. Almost all of it is planted in the North Coast. Schramsberg, who only use fruit from Napa Valley, have always included it in blends such as their Blanc de Noirs and Rosé. The only still version I have come across is the Pinot Mystere from Handley in Anderson Valley.

Pinot St George

See Négrette (p. 276).

Ruby Cabernet

Ruby Cabernet was developed by UC Davis and launched in 1948, making it the oldest of the crossings created by the university and the ubiquitous Dr Olmo. It is a crossing of Cabernet Sauvignon with Carignane. It proved extremely successful and eventually 18,000 acres were planted, mostly in the Central Valley. Like many crossings, it gives a generous crop of up to 9 tons per acre. Unfortunately it is prone to mildew, and the resulting wines lack distinction and ageability. Although it is principally used for blending, one occasionally sees varietally labelled versions (I seem to recall even Ridge made a Ruby Cabernet) and about ten wineries release such wines. About 6,000 acres remain.

Sangiovese

Whoever decided that it would be a good idea to plant Sangiovese in California (and it seems to have been Robert Pepi in Napa Valley) may not have known what he was letting himself in for. The problem has been twofold: where to plant the variety, and the choice of appropriate rootstocks and clones. Even in Tuscany there has been enormous debate about which selections of Sangiovese give the best fruit, with the vote usually going to Sangiovese Grosso. Italians have no fewer than 200 different clones to choose from, but Sangiovese Grosso was the choice of Pepi, who brought over cuttings from Biondi-Santi in Montalcino, and also of Piero Antinori for his Atlas Peak vineyard, who imported the budwood from his Santa Cristina estate. Gustav Dalla Valle in Napa Valley played safe and planted four different clones. Jeff Hinchcliffe of Gabrielli in Mendocino believes that site is possibly even more important than clones for Sangiovese. Hinchcliffe planted the same clones as those present at the Trentadue Vineyard in Alexander Valley. Trentadue get large clusters, whereas in Redwood Valley he finds that the same clone produces much smaller clusters.

Another problem is excessive yields, so it's essential to plant the vines on low-vigour sites. Moreover, Sangiovese attains higher sugar levels in California than in Tuscany, where in many years it struggles to achieve ripeness. Like Zinfandel, it can be prone to uneven ripening. So there are considerable variations in site type, rootstock, and trellising, as Californian growers learn how to obtain balanced fruit from the grape. Almost all growers find themselves obliged to practise canopy management and bunch-thinning, which makes Sangiovese expensive to cultivate. John Shafer recalls that his first vintage of Sangiovese in Napa Valley overproduced, so the wines were light in colour and needed a good dose of Cabernet Sauvignon to give the wine some structure. Now he bunch-thins and keeps yields down to 4 tons per acre. Recent vintages of his Firebreak wine have had 88 per cent Sangiovese in the blend, and there are no longer problems with colour and structure.

Although some Sangiovese was apparently planted in the 1860s as part of field blends, and a small plot of ancient vines survives at a vineyard in Sonoma now owned by Seghesio, it never became a significant varietal until the late 1980s, since when there has been a steady increase in the area under vine. I believe Pepi's 1988 Sangiovese was the first to be released commercially in California. In 1993 there were 450 acres planted, by 1995 there were 900, and by 1997, 2,498. It has become an expensive variety too, currently priced at about $1,230 per ton. Ferrari-Carano in Sonoma have invested strongly in the variety by planting some 50 acres in various parts of the county. After Robert Pepi, the first estate to take Sangiovese seriously was Atlas Peak. With Piero Antinori as one of the partners, it was to be expected that he would only authorize the planting of outstanding clones. Yet the wines were seriously disappointing, although in recent years the Reserve bottlings have been much more impressive.

Oak ageing of Sangiovese is quite a contentious issue in California, as it is in Italy. Greg Graziano, an enthusiast for Italian varieties, believes that Sangiovese is easily overpowered by new oak: 'It's a mistake to treat Sangiovese as though it were Merlot, as the wines need more acidity.' Sangiovese does seem to soak up oak influence, and many critics initially complained that Atlas Peak Sangiovese was over-oaked. Early vintages were partly aged in new oak, but Atlas Peak has changed its mind, and now uses only one- and two-year-old barrels. Quite a few California winemakers are following the Tuscan example by ageing the wine only in older barrels. Greg Graziano maintains that by using heavily toasted oak, as he does for his Reserve bottlings, he gives the wines a smoky rather than a vanillin edge. Until quite recently many Californian Sangiovese wines, such as that from Monteviña, have been distinctly light. It's true that Sangiovese does not give heavy, full-bodied wines, but good Tuscan examples are complex and packed with flavour, which is more than can be said for many of the weedy offerings that have been emerging from California. It no doubt has something to do with the age of the vines, but also with, in some quarters, a failure to understand the nature of the grape. Moreover, Sangiovese is a naturally high-acid variety, even at full ripeness, which many Californian winemakers and consumers find disconcerting.

Although pure varietal Sangioveses do exist in Italy, notably in Montalcino, it is often blended with other varieties to flesh out the lean, often acidic structure of the wine. Some California growers are following suit. At Staglin in Napa Valley, where the budwood came from Biondi-Santi, 20 per cent Cabernet Sauvignon is blended in, and Shafer do exactly the same with their excellent Firebreak.

For all the problems, Sangiovese is undeniably catching on in California, and in 1997 Atlas Peak played host to the first International Sangiovese Symposium, which was attended by forty-seven Sangiovese producers from California. John Shafer, however, does not predict a huge market for the variety, despite the profusion of Italian restaurants in America. Among the sixty or more wineries producing Sangiovese, some of the better known include, in Napa Valley, Pepi, Shafer, Swanson, Saddleback Cellars, Turnbull, Staglin, Altamura, Luna, and Silverado. One of the best comes from Dalla Valle and is called Pietre Rosse: a bold, ripe, smoky style. Lighter styles from Napa include Mondavi, Beaulieu, Flora Springs, and Clos du Val. In Sonoma, producers include Trentadue, Iron Horse, Seghesio, and Ferrari-Carano; in the Sierra Foothills, Noceto; in Mendocino, Gabrielli, Lonetree, Fetzer Bonterra, and Monte Volpe; from other parts of the state, Bonny Doon's Il Fiasco, Martin, and Mount Palomar. In Sonoma Gallo is also planting Sangiovese, and in Livermore Valley Wente have ambitious plans to produce a top-quality Sangiovese in 2003.

Syrah

If there is one non-traditional red variety that has enormous potential in California, it has to be Syrah. Wineries throughout the state have started releasing some truly succulent and prodigious Syrahs. Tim Spencer in Lodi was perhaps being too self-deprecating when he told me: 'There are three problems with Syrah. We don't know where to grow it, we don't know how to make it, and we don't know whether anyone will want to buy it. Other than that, we're high on it.'

The variety has a very complicated history in California. It appears that J. H. Drummond brought cuttings to Sonoma in 1878 and it was soon taken to Napa by Charles Krug and others. H. W. Crabb in Oakville blended it with Refosco and labelled the resulting wine 'Hermitage'.[9] But since the grape was also referred to as Petite Syrah, we are entitled to be somewhat sceptical when it comes to claims to its authenticity. Moreover, what is almost certainly the oldest surviving Syrah vineyard in California, at McDowell in Mendocino, was originally known as Petite Syrah, and that's how the wine was labelled for many years. The vines date from 1919, 1948, and 1959. At some point UC Davis analysed the vines, which were from an unknown source, and decided they were authentic Syrah. That might have been true of many other older vineyards as well.

In 1936 Davis imported a Syrah clone from Montpellier and called it 'French Petite Sirah'. Over twenty years seem to have gone by before any winery bothered to plant the clone, and when

Christian Brothers eventually did so, they blended the results into other wines. But the vineyard was the source for Phelps's Syrah, which was subsequently expanded to 20 acres. Phelps began releasing the wine in the late 1970s, and I bought and drank a good deal of it. I was impressed, but when I tried it on French oenologists they were less than thrilled. Doug Meador, who worked with the Christian Brothers' Montpellier clone in 1976, told me that nobody was sure what it was, and it wasn't even certain that it was Syrah. However, the Phelps Syrah tasted plausibly like Syrah to me. Gary Eberle shares some of Meador's doubts about the Christian Brothers vines. They were pulled up in the mid-1990s and Phelps now grows Syrah in its own Carneros vineyards.

In 1973 another clone made its appearance; UC Davis imported it from the Rhône valley and it became known as Espiguette after the research station where it originated. When Lou Preston decided to plant Syrah in Dry Creek Valley that year, he selected both the Montpellier and the Espiguette clones.

A short while later, in 1975, Gary Eberle, when establishing the Estrella River vineyards in Paso Robles, planted 30 acres of Syrah from a selection that apparently originated from the Chapoutier vineyards in Hermitage, although Michel Chapoutier has no recollection of any cuttings going to the United States. Eberle's vineyard became the source for other Syrah vineyards established by Ojai and by Sierra Vista in the Foothills, but it succumbed to phylloxera and no longer exists. Eberle first encountered Syrah through Brian Croser, a fellow student at UC Davis. Croser, who was to become the illustrious winemaker at Petaluma in Australia, was of course familiar with the Shiraz of his native land. The Syrah he planted made good wine but proved impossible to sell. Eberle was just about ready to give up on Syrah when along came Randall Grahm and Bob Lindquist looking for Syrah grapes, and Estrella River began propagating budwood for other wineries. The offspring of Eberle's plantings, according to Gary's own calculations, have found their way into 80 per cent of all existing Syrah vineyards in California.

The others came from the Espiguette clone, which was planted at the Bien Nacido Vineyard in Santa Maria Valley and at Ojai. Some growers identify an intense, berry-like, smoky-bacon flavour with this strain. Yet another strain, imported from Australia by Davis and labelled 'Shiraz', went to Shenandoah, Phelps, and R.

H. Phillips.[10] I don't know the origin of the Syrah in the former Schmidt Vineyard in Napa Valley, where Sean Thackrey used to obtain the grapes for his Orion Syrah. Until Thackrey discovered them, these excellent grapes had been sold to Charles Krug for use in jug wines. In 1991 the vineyard was bought by Swanson, who replanted most of it, although the old Syrah has been retained.

Syrah in California is very vigorous, easily delivering 8 tons per acre if uncontrolled, and so it needs to be controlled by using low-vigour rootstocks. Jeff Meier of J. Lohr says that even with bunch-thinning, it can yield 5 tons per acre. Most growers find it a pleasure to cultivate, since the clones planted are for the most part disease-resistant, and the vine is a reliable producer. Another way to control Syrah's vigour is by the use of specific trellising systems. But there is little agreement about which is the most suitable, and clearly there is no single answer. Geyser Peak and Qupé favour a Geneva Double Curtain, McDowell and Meridian plant bush vines, Phelps and Preston use bilateral cordons. Recent plantings have often adopted vertical trellising.[11]

There is much discussion about where Syrah should be planted. Sean Thackrey believes it will do well wherever Cabernet Sauvignon thrives, although it tends to ripen a bit earlier than Cabernet. Doug Meador grows it in Arroyo Seco in Monterey and believes it has great potential there. In Monterey's cool climate it retains its distinctive black-pepper component. Villa Mount Eden, however, like to pick Syrah very ripe indeed at about 25 Brix and don't mind if the berries are beginning to shrivel. Randall Grahm insists, however, that Syrah is a cool-climate grape and finds himself routinely turning down growers' offers of Syrah from sites he considers too warm. 'The vineyard must be in a cool location that receives a tremendous amount of light. It helps to have a well-drained slope with good exposure, but, more importantly, the soil must be very poor. If you can just barely ripen the grapes most years (but ripen them completely) you've found the right spot.'[12] Doug Nalle seems to agree with Grahm, and believes regions such as Dry Creek and Alexander valleys in Sonoma are too warm. Nonetheless it has been growing at Lytton Springs vineyard, and Ridge will make its first Syrah from that fruit. John Alban, who grows Syrah and other Rhône varieties in the cool Edna Valley, points out that the northern Rhône, in Californian terms, is a Region I. The quality of his Syrah wines strengthens the case for a cool-climate location. Geyser Peak, in Sonoma, has bought Syrah from Doug Meador's Ventana Vineyard and has planted 30 acres of the variety in Alexander Valley. There seems to be great potential in Carneros, however, and Dick Ward has described some Carneros Syrahs as 'stunning, rich wines with pure fruit characteristics, softer tannins, almost voluptuous but with good acidity.'[13] Havens, Truchard, and Cline make Syrah from Carneros grapes. Steve Edmunds of Edmunds St John has pointed out that he and Kendall-Jackson buy some of their Syrah from the same Carneros vineyard, yet the wines are totally different, so it's hard to define the regional character of Syrah in different parts of California.[14]

Syrah also does well in the Sierra Foothills, especially at Sierra Vista. John Kautz, however, prefers the black-fruits style he associates with Australian Shiraz rather than French Syrah. In Mendocino there are excellent examples from MacDowell, Fetzer, Lonetree, Navarro, and Gabrielli. In Santa Barbara, Babcock, Foxen, and Zaca Mesa make good versions. Sean Thackrey's Orion, Edmunds St John, Qupé, and Ojai, sourcing grapes from various vineyards, produce some of California's outstanding Syrahs. The grapes formerly used for Orion are now harvested by Swanson for their own excellent bottling. Phelps continues to make good Syrah in Napa, as do Turnbull and Elyse.

The kind of quality already demonstrated by Thackrey, Qupé, Sierra Vista, Bonny Doon, McDowell and others has convinced me of the potential for this variety in California. Fortunately acreage is increasing so perhaps in future the rather high prices demanded for the better Syrahs may start to come down. Randall Grahm is also unhappy about some of the prices being charged for grapes: 'Growers assume that wherever it's cultivated it has to be a "premium variety" for which they can charge $1,800 a ton.' (The average price per ton in 1997 was $1,142.) In 1986 there were only 119 acres in existence, but by 1995 there were 1,331, and by 1997, 4,277.

Steve Edmunds believes that Syrah should not be put into a stylistic straitjacket in California. Stylistic variety is unavoidable but welcome. 'Decisions about how to handle a wine must start with the individual fruit. I get such different Syrah grapes from Durell than from Placerville or any of my other sources. They are completely different animals. There may be places in California that are suitable for producing Syrah in a Beaujolais style, and by the same token, there may be sites capable of producing something more like Côte Rôtie.'[15]

Teroldego

In northern Italy, especially Trentino, Teroldego makes fresh lively reds that have some affinity with Gamay. Few examples exist yet in California, though Sebastiani have taken up the cause with some enthusiasm.

Trousseau

Trousseau is a mystery of the wine world. Even in its native Jura it produces coarse, tannic, ungainly wines that are utterly without charm. Why anyone should have wanted to bring it to California beats me, but there it is, growing happily in the Gemelli Vineyard in Cienega Valley. These vines are believed to be about seventy-five years old. The variety was much touted in the nineteenth century apparently, but, not surprisingly, never caught on with the public. Its sole champion nowadays is Ken Volk of Wild Horse in Paso Robles. No doubt at Volk's instigation, 7 acres have been planted, using cuttings from Gemelli, at the Siletto Ranch Vineyard in San Benito.

NOTES

1 Philip Wagner, *American Wines and Wine-making*, p. 66
2 Jancis Robinson, *Vines, Grapes and Wines*, p. 228
3 Norman Roby and Charles Olken, *New Connoisseurs' Handbook of California Wines*, p. 42
4 Wagner, pp. 63–4
5 Roy Andries De Groot, *The Wine of California*, pp. 106–9
6 Robinson, p. 227
7 De Groot, p. 155
8 Eleanor and Ray Heald, 'Rediscovering Petite Sirah', *Practical Winery and Vineyard*, March/April 1966
9 Charles L. Sullivan, *Napa Wine*, p. 138
10 Steve Heimoff, *Wine Spectator*, 30 June 1990
11 Eleanor and Ray Heald, 'Que Syrah, Shiraz', *Practical Winery and Vineyard*, July/August 1994
12 Steve Pitcher, *Inside Wine*, June 1995

13 Brian St Pierre, *Decanter*, September 1997
14 Heald, op. cit.
15 Ibid.

18

Chardonnay

'California Chardonnay,' writes James Laube, 'with all its diversity and complexity, is the most consistently excellent wine in the world today.'[1] This breathtaking but meaningless statement is the kind of declaration that makes many wine drinkers see red, as it further legitimizes the varietal dictatorship of Chardonnay. But what does 'most consistently excellent' actually mean? How large is this particular category? Does it refer only to varietal wines? Or to regions? Does this make California Chardonnay as a whole more 'excellent' or 'consistent' than, say, Bordeaux? Or Condrieu or Brunello di Montalcino? It would be foolish to deny that there are many superlative Chardonnays coming out of California, but equally foolish to ignore the many more marred by excessive oak or by residual sugar or by dilution from overcropping.

Clearly, a zillion customers can't all be wrong. California Chardonnay has been an astonishing success story. Thirty years ago it was all but unknown as a varietal wine. In 1961 there were no more than 295 acres of Chardonnay throughout the state, and by 1969 only 2,500. That it caught on so slowly is partly explained by the fact that selections then available to growers were very low-yielding. Acreage expanded through the 1970s, when the variety came into vogue. By 1975 there were 4,900 acres under vine, and by the end of the decade about 14,000, an area that steadily increased until in 1986 there were 29,319 acres planted. Throughout this period Chardonnay continued to play second fiddle to the ubiquitous French Colombard, the mainstay of industrial winemaking in California, but in 1991 Chardonnay rose into the lead as the most widely planted white variety, and by 1994 it was even outselling white Zinfandel. By 1995 there were an astonishing 72,624 acres in the ground, many of them newly replanted after the ravages of phylloxera and not yet bearing fruit. By 1997 the figure had risen to 88,517. It is grown throughout the state, almost 13,000 acres in Sonoma and about 10,000 in Napa. There are large plantations in Monterey and Lodi, as well as Santa Barbara. The average statewide price per ton in 1997 was a healthy $1,151.

Despite the relatively recent surge in popularity of Chardonnay, the variety has been around for some time. Nursery lists from Napa in the late nineteenth century refer to varieties such as 'White Pineau-Chaudenay' and 'Pineau Charennay', and Inglenook were cultivating 'White Pinot' in 1899. All of these grapes were probably Chardonnay.[2] In Livermore Charles Wetmore brought in some cuttings from Meursault, and early in the twentieth century his neighbours at Wente were planting Chardonnay cuttings from Montpellier, as well as cuttings descended from Wetmore's original plantings.

A few years earlier, the Burgundian immigrant Paul Masson planted Chardonnay vines at his La Cresta Vineyard in the Santa Cruz Mountains. They were believed to have come directly from Corton in 1896. After Martin Ray bought the property in 1936, he used cuttings from this vineyard to plant at his own vineyard after the sale of Masson in 1942. This is the strain that clings on at Mount Eden Vineyards, a low-yielding and virused selection that nonetheless gives outstanding fruit. Meanwhile, the Wente plantings were scattering their progeny through many new Chardonnay vineyards. Wente claim to have been the first winery to release a varietally labelled Chardonnay, the vintage being 1936. Sterling took its budwood from Wente, and so did Fred McCrea when he planted his Stony Hill vineyard in 1948. McCrea's widow Eleanor recalled that at this time UC Davis was advising growers that Chardonnay was difficult to grow, although the authorities did not dispute that quality could often be high.

The Stony Hill vines then became the source of budwood for Louis Martini and others. Martini reared his vines at the Stanly Ranch in Carneros, where he referred to them as 'Wente clones'. Crucially, it was these vines that were selected by Davis when in 1955 the university decided to make clonal propagations of Chardonnay. As Gerald Asher, to whose essay on the origins of California Chardonnay I am greatly indebted, has pointed out: 'Both this original material from Davis and the mass selections taken directly and indirectly from the original Wente vineyard are all dubbed indiscriminately now with the name "Old Wente clone". Not surprisingly, vines so called vary considerably.'[3] It has been claimed, but I cannot substantiate the claim, that about 80 per cent of all Chardonnay clones planted in California are descended from the Wente clones. The Wente clones supplied by UC Davis in the 1970s and 1980s are known as Clone 4 and Clone 5, and were propagated to produce high yields rather than superior quality. They also have considerable uniformity of flavour.

In the meantime the Mount Eden strain also had its offsprings, and its budwood was used at the Kistler vineyards as well as elsewhere in the Santa Cruz Mountains. This strain, although genetically identical, gives very different fruit quality at the two sites, no doubt reflecting microclimatic and soil differences – *terroir* – as much as winemaking practices.

Although Chardonnay was recognized as a good-quality variety from both the Masson and the Wente vineyards, these two sites did not make its reputation. The estate that secured the renown of Chardonnay was Stony Hill, which many regarded as the greatest white wine of America, renowned for its longevity as well as its intrinsic quality. That enthusiast for all things Burgundian, James Zellerbach at Hanzell, was the next grower to put Chardonnay on the map. He imported barrels from Burgundy, which he used for the first time in 1956. It was a formula that worked astonishingly well and a trend was born: California developed a passion for rich, buttery, oaky Chardonnays, models of succulence and generosity of fruit. Wineries such as Robert Mondavi were soon releasing substantial quantities of Chardonnay of remarkably high quality. In the 1970s and early 1980s quality was equated with power. The richer, riper, and more alcoholic the wine, the happier the consumer appeared to be. Then it occurred to somebody that such wines were not ideal with food, and as California was now developing its own eclectic cuisine, wines were trimmed down to become more food-friendly. As with all reactions, it was taken to extremes, and by the 1990s the big brash style was back.

The phylloxera crisis of the late 1980s and early 1990s prompted a reconsideration of fundamental viticultural issues, including clonal selections. In addition to the Wente and Masson strains, there was a selection known as the Spring Mountain that became popular in Sonoma County. According to Gerald Asher, it has a

Muscat-like aroma. The Rued clone, another aromatic strain, is named after the grower Paul Rued, but he knows little about its origin, other than that it was bought from a Calistoga nursery in 1971. Another well regarded strain, from the Hyde Vineyard in Carneros, traces its ancestry back to Wente via Stony Hill and then Long vineyards. Viticulturalists at UC Davis initiated clonal research in 1984 at the Jaeger vineyards near Napa and at Beringer vineyards near Yountville. Results were significant. While the Martini clone No. 4, for example, had a cluster weight twice as great as that of an Australian clone, yields also varied greatly.[4]

Most growers and wineries planting Chardonnay over the past decade have opted for Clone 108. According to Steve Kistler, this clone 'produces 150–200 gm clusters on most sites and neutral wines with no expression of their place of origin. Its chief advantage has been that it can be planted in areas which are really too warm for Chardonnay, yet still produce grapes with acceptable acidity and pH. Old clones of Chardonnay can have pHs of 0.2–0.3 units higher than clone 108, and are not suited to the warmer parts of Napa and Sonoma.'[5] Many other clones, of French and Italian origin, are pouring on to the market. In 1990 Richard Kunde had nineteen Chardonnay clones in his Sonoma vineyards. By 1995 he was experimenting with ninety-five. Kunde is by no means alone, and many estates, including Saintsbury in Carneros and Torres in Green Valley, have been trying microvinifications of the different clones in their vineyards.[6]

Chardonnay remains a popular choice in Napa Valley, even though there are clearly many spots that are simply too warm and where the soils are too rich. Some wine critics believe that Napa as a whole is unsuitable for Chardonnay, but that is clearly too sweeping. Locations in the southern part of the valley, around Napa itself and Yountville and Coombsville, yield fruit with reasonable levels of acidity. Often Napa Chardonnay is picked overripe, giving wines of high alcohol, which find favour in some quarters and can undeniably make an impression in a blind tasting, but soon become cloying. Carneros, of course, must be considered separately, since it is clear that this cool breezy region is capable of giving very stylish Chardonnay. Some of the finest Napa Chardonnays have emerged from hillside sites on Mount Veeder, Diamond Mountain, and Howell Mountain, wines with good acidity and a hint of mineral character.

Sonoma County, in terms of surface, is more significant for Chardonnay than Napa. It is also very varied, with warmer locations, such as Alexander Valley, giving rich exuberant fruit that may lack finesse. Chardonnay from Russian River Valley can have a more citrussy edge and more robust acidity. Altitude and exposure also play their part. In the hot Knights Valley, very high vineyards planted by the Peter Michael estate are yielding excellent fruit. There is also good Chardonnay emerging from Mendocino, where just under 5,000 acres are planted. Dennis Martin of Fetzer finds that Mendocino Chardonnay has pear and apple flavours that adapt well to barrel-fermenting and malolactic fermentation. The large vineyards in Monterey County often give Chardonnay with a pronounced tropical-fruit dimension, which is also present in fruit grown in Santa Barbara and Edna Valley. Central Coast Chardonnay can develop botrytis during harvest, though even in Burgundy, as in 1995, winemakers don't mind a dash of noble rot to give some additional complexity to a dry Chardonnay. Mount Eden Vineyards produces two Chardonnays, one from its own celebrated vineyards in the Santa Cruz Mountains, the other from Edna Valley. The latter is much more lush, more obvious, more fruit-salady, while the Santa Cruz wine is more restrained, more subtle. Clearly the Santa Cruz Mountains are capable of producing some first-rate Chardonnay, as recent bottlings from Ridge and others have demonstrated. The rocky soils can sometimes give a mineral quality to these wines, and Duane Cronin believes that Santa Cruz Chardonnay has flavours that are not encountered elsewhere in California.

Site is important, of course, but Chardonnay is ideally suited to manipulation. Since the grape is not intrinsically rich in flavour or personality, practices such as malolactic fermentation and oak ageing take on particular significance. Fruit quality is also heavily influenced by what goes on in the vineyard and by clonal selections. That is why it has been relatively easy for wineries to change style according to fashion and consumer demand.

It has become increasingly common for winemakers to opt for whole-cluster pressing. This is an expensive method, because if you retain stems you can load the press with, say, only 1.5 tons of grapes as opposed to 5 tons of crushed and destemmed fruit. This in turn means the presses will be tied up for much longer. There is no uniformity about this. Susan Reed of Matanzas Creek says that if all the fruit is whole-cluster pressed you can end up with thin rather than elegant wines. So Matanzas Creek uses both techniques, and so do Kunde and Iron Horse. Other wineries, such as Sonoma-Cutrer, are completely convinced that whole-cluster pressing is the way to obtain maximum finesse, at least from their grapes.[7]

Except for large-volume, low-priced brands, most Chardonnays will be oak-aged, although some unwooded examples can be delicious as well as inexpensive. Some years ago many wines would have been fermented in temperature-controlled stainless steel tanks and then aged in barrels for a number of months. The thinking behind this was that the primary fermentation was easier to control in tanks, even though the small volume of an oak barrel tended to discourage high temperatures during fermentation. This was the Davis recommendation: to give the grapes some skin contact, and then ferment in steel without letting the wine go through malolactic fermentation. Experience showed, however, that a wine fermented in tank and then aged in oak, especially oak with a high proportion of new barrels, took on a more aggressive oakiness than wines that had been fermented in oak. The explanation for this seems to be that the fermentation process itself allows for a better harmonization of the flavours of the wine and the nuances of vanilla, coconut, smoke and other attributes conferred by the wood.

There has been some fresh thinking about the nature of the fermentation process. As we have seen in the chapter on winemaking, the Californian instinct is to 'clean up' the must to the greatest extent possible, to avoid complications or any risk of off-aromas or flavours. Steve Kistler argues persuasively that 'the challenge for many California Chardonnay producers is to learn to manage the fermentation of nutrient deficient musts, not to correct them.' Those corrections which he deplores are mostly aimed at ensuring a swift clean fermentation that is problem-free. They include oversettling the juice before fermentation begins; fermenting at excessively cool temperatures; adjusting nutrient levels in the wines before fermentation; excessive dependence on cultivated yeasts; and adding bentonite to the must before fermentation. Kistler argues in particular that since almost all wineries are equipped with gentle pneumatic presses that leave fewer solids in the must, there is even less justification for over-settling the juice than there was in earlier times.[8] I imagine Jim Clendenen at Au Bon Climat would echo much of this, as he too steers clear of sulphur dioxide during vinification, doesn't clean up the juice excessively, and leaves the wines on the lees for up to 18 months.

The arguments for and against the use of cultivated yeasts have already been presented. Some wineries such as Franciscan with its Cuvée Sauvage are now distinguishing on the label the wines fermented with natural yeasts. When Helen Turley was the wine-maker at Peter Michael she also experimented with natural-yeast fermentation. In her experience the wines fermented more gradu-ally and exhibited sleeker texture. The winery continues to make natural-yeast Chardonnay under its Cuvée Indigene label. Frog's Leap and Calera are two other wineries that have been experi-menting with natural yeast fermentation for their Chardonnays. Another fashionable winemaking technique for Chardonnay, pion-eered by Zelma Long at Simi, was to allow the juice to oxidize before fermentation, with the aim of promoting complexity rather than primary fruit character.

During the early days of Chardonnay cultivation, malolactic fermentation was rare. It was regarded as appropriate for regions such as Burgundy, where acidity levels tended to be considerably higher than in California. Eleanor McCrea, whose highly acclaimed Stony Hill Chardonnay did not go through malolactic, feared that wines that did could show 'a somewhat bland flavor, less appley and fragrant.'[9] A handful of wineries, including Mayacamas, Far Niente, Flora Springs, Forman, Shafer, Gundlach-Bundschu, Iron Horse, Chateau Woltner, and Chateau Montelena, still seek to block the malolactic fermentation. It seems probable that the lon-gevity of Chardonnays from wineries such as Stony Hill and Mayacamas is partially attributable to their higher acidity. Forrest Tancer of Iron Horse argues that the absence of malolactic fermen-tation allows vineyard character to shine through more clearly.[10]

However, the purpose of malolactic fermentation is not merely to lower high levels of malic acidity by converting them into less fierce lactic acids. Malolactic also gives texture (the beloved Cali-fornian 'mouthfeel') and complexity. It may be true that a wine that does not go through malolactic can be cellared for longer, but few American consumers, or European ones for that matter, believe much is to be gained by keeping Chardonnays for many years in bottle. Since a non-malo Chardonnay can be somewhat hard and austere in its youth, unlike a more buttery, supple, obviously more palatable wine that has completed its malolactic, it is hardly surprising that the overwhelming majority of Californian Chardonnay producers opt for this secondary fermentation. It remains the case that a non-malo Chardonnay can have a greater crispness and vibrancy and a transparency that can allow attributes of *terroir*, if any, to emerge. Equally, many Chardonnays, especially from warm areas, that go through malolactic can be flabby and dull. But neither is necessarily true, and there are some excellent examples of both styles. James Laube, who has tasted more Californian Chardonnays than I have had cups of tea, organized a blind tasting of 1990 and 1991 Chardonnays to see if the non-malolactic wines could be identified, and he concluded that 'the malolactic bottlings showed more of everything and were more impressive than the non-malolactic wines'.[11]

Robert Parker recalls a vertical tasting of Ric Forman's Chardonnays which 'poignantly revealed that (1) they survive as they get older, (2) they become greener and more Sauvignon-like with each additional year of cellaring, and (3) because of the green, tart acidity that develops, they are far less enjoyable after 2–3 years of cellaring than when they are young.'[12]

Unfortunately a fetish has developed about malolactic fermentation. Standing one day in a Sonoma tasting room, I watched two young men wander in and brusquely demand: 'Is your Chardonnay really malo?' 'Well, ours goes through 90 per cent malo,' came the reply. 'In that case,' replied one of the young men, 'start me right in on the Zin.' This is an example of stupidity, not connoisseurship.

Contemporary Californian winemaking orthodoxy would accept that the grapes should rarely receive skin contact, should be barrel fermented, and should go through malolactic fermentation. During the barrel ageing, moreover, the wine should be left on the fine lees, as in Burgundy, and those lees stirred up from time to time. Some believe this gives the wine better texture, greater richness, greater freshness. The quantity of new oak varies according to taste and budget. However, it is generally assumed that a Reserve Chardonnay, usually with a price tag of $25 or more, will have been barrel fermented and aged in new oak, with full malolactic fermentation and stirring (or *batonnage*); sometimes the wine will have been bottled unfiltered for good measure. The trouble is that such practices will often obliterate any local or soil characteristics the wine may ever have exhibited. That is why so many Californian Chardonnays taste the same, and why the initial statement quoted from James Laube must be continuously questioned. Dan Gehrs, until recently winemaker at Zaca Mesa, agreed that many 'top-end' Chardonnays taste identical. 'Focusing on nuances such as toasted heads and which forests the wood came from is silly. It's far more important to explore the *terroir*.' Doug Meador also criticizes the tendency to over-oak Chardonnay: 'Only a termite could love California Chardonnay. People think that if you buy a French barrel, you'll end up with a great wine. But with too much oak, you can't taste the vineyard.'

Steve Kistler is very anxious that soil character should be present in a Chardonnay that has pretensions to outstanding quality. 'My contention,' he has written, 'is that the most complex Chardonnay comes from nutrient-deficient musts which, in turn, come from lighter, less nutritionally rich soils . . . There is a lot of Chardonnay planted in California on soils that are too rich or complete. The fermentation of the juice from these vineyards tends to produce simple fruit aromas and little else.' In the same paper he also inveighed against the use of clones with a powerful Muscat-type aroma, which can also disguise the *terroir* character of the wine.

However, there is an additional factor working against any expression of the soil, and that is the tendency to leave residual sugar in the wine. The most prominent offender has been Kendall-Jackson with its Vintner's Reserve. Apparently the wine was a mistake that had a happy ending. A stuck fermentation occurred leaving residual sugar in the wine. To the delight of the Kendall-Jackson marketing people, this went down a treat with the consumers, so now the wine is deliberately made with some sweetness. Of course this all too common in other parts of the world as well, notably Australia and Chile. Supermarket buyers know that while wine drinkers profess to drink dry wines, what they actually buy under the guise of dry white wine is slightly sweet. Sugar is a popular component in inexpensive wines because it can mask many a fault. The problem is that wines such as the Kendall-Jackson blend mentioned above are far from cheap, and some wines with a healthy dose of residual sugar, such as Mer & Soleil, are very expensive. Although it would be unrealistic to insist upon bone-dry Chardonnays in every case – a dash of botrytis can sometimes leave a little residual sugar in the wine, and sometimes a little may be desirable as a balancing agent if the wine has high acidity – the routine doctoring of a wine to ensure a residual sugar level of around 7 or 8 grams per litre is undesirable, if unstoppable. Why take the trouble to grow high-quality fruit if its nuances are to be slicked over with sugar? There is in any case a natural sweetness to much California Chardonnay, provided not by sugar but by alcohol.

Brian Talley, who produces exceptional Chardonnay in Arroyo Grande, wearily observes that most wineries simply regard Chardonnay as a cash cow, so they focus more on tricks of winemaking than on growing or buying good grapes. Gary Eberle and Mat Garretson, admittedly in a document trumpeting the virtues of Viognier, justly remark: 'In our opinion, most California Chardonnay has fallen victim to the "Carmen Miranda Syndrome". These wines tend to offer up lush, tropical fruit aromas and flavors, fat, creamy mouthfeels, and a good dose of residual sugar. While perhaps a nice aperitif wine, these Chardonnays fail when paired with most foods; not to mention lack the true character of the variety.'

Allied to the Carmen Miranda Syndrome is the tendency to produce Chardonnays with ever-higher degrees of alcohol. Jayson Pahlmeyer, an engaging and enthusiastic proprietor, poured me a Napa Chardonnay with 14.9 degrees of alcohol, made under his label by Helen Turley. The wine was also modishly unfiltered, and hazy. Pahlmeyer was unapologetic: this was the style of Chardonnay he and Turley were aiming for. 'We're looking for fully ripe fruit. We harvest according to taste and flavour, row by row, and we don't care about alcohol. In fact, as Helen says, it's our friend, as it gives richness and viscosity. I admit it, I like our "industrial strength" wines.' I disagree, but most wine writers are fervent admirers of Pahlmeyer and Turley's wines. I have similar problems with, for example, some of the Chardonnays made by Patz & Hall, who in almost every other respect are extremely competent and conscientious winemakers.

I hesitate to list the Chardonnays that in my view reflect California's interpretation of this variety at its best, since, as should by now be obvious, it is such a personal matter. My own taste veers towards elegance and concentration rather than towards fatness, power, and buttery richness – although there are some wines in the latter category that I greatly enjoy.

In Napa I do not share the enthusiasm for Beringer's Private Reserve, which is too oaky and overblown for my taste (unlike their superb Private Reserve Cabernets), but there are excellent wines from Flora Springs, Mondavi, Grgich, Franciscan, Forman, Signorello, and Swanson. From Carneros, there are some very good wines from Saintsbury, Mondavi, Cuvaison, and Acacia.

In Sonoma, Kistler is almost unmatched for the dazzling quality and flair of their Chardonnays. The various cuvées from Peter Michael are immensely impressive. There are also excellent wines from Ferrari-Carano, Landmark, Arrowood, Kunde, J. Fritz, Rochioli, Simi, Chateau St Jean, Matanzas Creek, Dehlinger, Iron Horse, Sonoma-Cutrer, and Torres.

From Mendocino, I admire Chardonnays from Fetzer, Navarro, Steele, and Hidden Cellars. Excellent Central Coast Chardonnays are made by Au Bon Climat, Talley, Byron, Chalone, Estancia, Ojai, Mount Eden, Sanford, Ridge, Gainey, Edna Valley, and Talbott.

Since 1989 there have been no duff vintages of Chardonnay in California, although in some years crops have been quite low. 1994 to 1996 inclusive are of outstanding quality. The 1985 and 1986 vintages were of exceptional quality.

NOTES

1 James Laube, *Wine Spectator*, 31 January 1998
2 Charles L. Sullivan, *Napa Wine*, p. 140
3 Gerald Asher, *Vineyard Tales*, pp. 162–9
4 James Wolpert, Amand Kasimatis, and Ed Weber, 'Field performance of six Chardonnay clonal selections', *Practical Winery and Vineyard*, January/February 1995
5 Stephen Kistler, 'Do California Single-Vineyard Chardonnays Have "Typicité"?'
6 Jeff Morgan, *Wine Spectator*, 31 July 1997
7 Eleanor and Ray Heald, 'Winemakers Discuss Chardonnay Essentials', *Practical Winery and Vineyard*, November/December 1994
8 Kistler, op. cit.
9 McCrae, pp. 243–4
10 Heald, op. cit.
11 James Laube, *Wine Spectator*, 31 July 1997
12 Robert Parker, *Wine Buyer's Guide*, 4th edition p. 883

19

Sauvignon Blanc

———

Sauvignon Blanc has always been a troublesome variety in California. The problem is not that it is difficult to grow, but that no one can decide what to do with the grapes. Some have opted for a vaguely Graves-style wine, generously oak-aged; others have treated it like a grade-two Chardonnay for customers who can't quite afford the real thing; and a few, a very few, have tried to make a wine with strong varietal character, rather like a Sancerre. For some time the variety has been in decline, partly because of the stylistic uncertainty that hovers around it, but also because low prices per ton have deterred growers from retaining or replanting it. In 1986 there were 15,193 acres planted throughout California. The expansion had been rapid: in 1965 there were only 700 acres, but the surface rose steadily through the 1970s, from 3,706 acres in 1976 to 9,000 by 1982. But by 1997 the acreage had declined to 11,312. Average prices per ton in 1997 were $770, although some growers managed to receive prices of up to $1,400. The most substantial plantings are in Napa (about 2,250 acres), Sonoma (1,500), Monterey (1,200), Mendocino (700), Lake County (700), Santa Barbara (200), and a substantial 1,400 in San Joaquin County.

Sauvignon has been in California for a long time. It was brought to Santa Clara by J. B. J. Portal in the 1870s, and by the late 1880s H. W. Crabb and J. II. Drummond in Napa Valley had both Sauvignon and Sémillon in their vineyards.[1] The Wente vineyards in Livermore Valley also planted Sauvignon Blanc in the 1880s and their dry white wine from the variety was greatly admired. In 1934 Wente were the first winery to release a varietally labelled Sauvignon Blanc, which proved a critical and popular success. Wente's attempts to make a Sauternes-style wine called 'Wente

Brothers' Chateau d'Yquem' roused the ire of the French wine authorities, and the name had to be changed to 'Chateau Wente'.[2]

It was Robert Mondavi who turned Sauvignon Blanc into a nationally popular wine, when he released his first Fumé Blanc in 1967. Pouilly-Fumé was quite a well-known name in American wine-drinking circles, so Mondavi exploited its reputation by borrowing the 'Fumé' component. Not that the Mondavi wine bore much resemblance to its model from the Loire. From the beginning the Mondavi wine, unlike all Pouilly-Fumé of that time, was oak-aged, and in the case of the Reserve bottling it was heavily oaked. Mondavi did not disguise the fact that he hoped oak-ageing would tame the widely encountered grassy character of the variety. The wine was a great commercial success, and other wineries rushed to copy the Mondavi example. Fumé Blanc became a nationally recognized synonym for Sauvignon Blanc, even though there was no formal agreement on what style of wine the label was promising. While most Fumés tended to be oaked, there were some that were not. Preston in Dry Creek, for example, used to release two Sauvignons: Cuvée de Fumé, which was briefly oak-aged, and Estate Reserve, a more serious version of the same style. The point remains, however, that the label rarely indicated what kind of wine the consumer would find once the cork was pulled. More recent regulations require wines labelled Fumé Blanc to have the subtext Dry Sauvignon Blanc on the label too.

There were always good and dependable Sauvignons on the market – both Mondavi and Kenwood were reliable – but so many of the wines were dull, and indeed still are. Others developed strong vegetal flavours, as indeed do many Sauvignons from the Loire Valley. Was this a part of the intrinsic varietal character of the grape, or was it a failure of either viticulture or winemaking? For many years nobody seemed to know. There are still growers and producers who don't seem to know. I have tasted more than a few highly touted Sauvignons from New Zealand that have tasted like liquid asparagus. Surely this is not a pure varietal expression of Sauvignon?

By about 1990 the Californians had worked it out. The secret to obtaining non-vegetal Sauvignon Blanc lay in canopy management. Sauvignon vines are very vigorous, especially when planted, as many of them were, on the rich valley soils of Napa. Jungly canopies shaded the bunches, and the absence of direct sunlight on the berries encouraged the development of vegetal tones. Many growers opted for the open-canopy systems developed by Dr Richard Smart, although UC Davis expressed no interest in conducting trials of his trellising system. According to Davis Bynum, it was left to Santa Rosa Junior College's viticultural programme to set up experiments in canopy management at Shone Vineyard in Sonoma, and these trials proved very successful. For some growers, part of the answer lay in planting Sauvignon vines on leaner soils that would discourage excessive vigour. Virus-free rootstocks and clones also seemed to give more generous yields, and some growers clung on to their virused vines because, for all their deficiencies, they gave better-quality fruit.

Robert Pecota pointed the finger at the large plantations in the Salinas Valley, where herbaceous tones seemed most prominent. For Doug Meador, who was growing Sauvignon there, that grassiness was a consequence of the wrong clonal selection. 'All the recommendations made by Davis and other authorities were made on the assumption that California is warm. But that doesn't work in Monterey, which really is cool. So the Wente clone never did well here. Just because it was descended from vines from Yquem didn't mean that it would grow in our vineyards, and in cold areas such as this it gave vegetal flavours.' Meador's answer was to develop a new clone, called the Ventana or Musqué clone. 'Davis had it all along, but under the wrong name of Sauvignon Musqué. Nobody knows where it came from. I tested that clone in 1978 and it became commercially available in 1980 under the name Musqué. But the French ampelographer Pierre Galet confirmed that it was indeed Sauvignon Blanc. It works marvellously in cold climates, giving decent crops of 4 to 8 tons. Because the quality is so good, I can get very good prices for it.' By 1990, 2,000 acres were planted with the Ventana (or Musqué) clone, and it has been selected for outstanding sites such as the Hyde Vineyard in Carneros and the Eisele Vineyard in Calistoga. Duckhorn planted it too. Perhaps the best-known winery to make regular use of Sauvignon from Meador's Ventana Vineyard is Cain in Napa Valley.

Whatever the source of the objectionable grassiness in the wine, the winemakers were confronted with the conundrum of how to deal with it. For some the answer lay in barrel fermentation. Jeff Baker at Carmenet was sure that fermentation in tanks only accentuated whatever herbaceous character was present in the must.

Others reduced skin contact, or blended in some Sémillon. Rick Longoria from Santa Ynez Valley believes lees ageing is a good way to reduce herbaceous character.

It was not clear, either, to what extent the vegetal quality of Sauvignon Blanc was related to yields. Many highly regarded wine-makers were convinced that, despite conventional wisdom in Europe, copious yields did not necessarily induce grassiness. Indeed, one winemaker at Kendall-Jackson insisted to me that with low tonnage, the vines put their energies into leaf production and gave vegetal flavours; but with crops of 8 or 9 tons per acre the vine was better balanced and gave better quality fruit. This sounds hopelessly simplistic, but Craig Williams of Phelps recalled abun-dant years such as 1982 and 1985 when the juice was free of herbaceousness because the vines were in balance; the harmony between the root system and the foliage meant that the vines could focus their energies on bringing the grapes to full ripeness. Some viticulturalists, such as Tony Soter and Susan ffrench of Mondavi pointed to bilateral and quadrilateral cordon systems, which gave good crops without jeopardizing quality. Of course, given the low prices fetched by Sauvignon grapes, growers and wineries needed large crops if their continuing production of the wine was going to be justified. Dan Duckhorn, who has long made a good Sau-vignon, says that 'the problem is that because the grape is low-priced, growers either opt for high tonnage or T-bud the vines over to more profitable varieties. I used to buy from a hillside vineyard that gave very good grapes, but the owner budded it over to Merlot.'

For Mike Lee and Jeff McBride at Kenwood, the vegetal flavours that had once marred so much Sauvignon in California were a thing of the past. 'Growers have solved the problem with canopy management, with better trellising. They've got better exposure on to the grapes, which now ripen earlier. We're keen here on training the vines along wires and leaf-pulling, because that increases exposure and thus aeration, and that means we are less susceptible to mildew and bunch-rot than we used to be. In the 1980s typical Sauvignon yields were around 4 tons. Today you can get 8, even 10, without any loss of quality. With closer spacing we have less fruit per vine, but of course more fruit per acre. Unfortunately just as we've cracked the problem, growers are switching to other varieties after phylloxera.' Kenwood experimented in the mid-

1980s with numerous Sauvignon clones, but came to the conclusion that clonal variation was less significant with Sauvignon Blanc than with varieties such as Pinot Noir. The Ventana clone remains a popular choice, and some Sauvignon specialists such as Jeff Baker believe that it gives leaner and more racy fruit than most other available clones.

Having spent quite a few weeks in 1991 visiting Sauvignon vineyards and producers in California,[3] I am convinced that the overall quality of Californian Sauvignon Blanc improved greatly throughout the 1990s. Truly vegetal Sauvignons are rarely encountered. However, there is no consensus about how the wine should be made. Canny wineries are aware that most consumers don't actually like the taste of authentic Sauvignon Blanc. The racy, grassy, gooseberry-fruited Sauvignons so characteristic of the Loire and New Zealand are not welcome in the United States, where they are condemned as grassy or herbaceous. Instead the Californians like to cosset Sauvignon with oak. Adulatory tasting notes in the American wine press focus on terms of approbation such as 'melons' and 'figs', whereas few Europeans would associate the decadent sweetness of figs with the lean assertive flavours of Sauvignon. Ripe Sauvignon, however, and Sémillon too can have melony flavours. Mineral flavours are notably absent from most California Sauvignon.

Skin contact for Sauvignon, which Professor Denis Dubourdieu popularized in Bordeaux in the 1980s, has never caught on in California. Craig Williams of Phelps noted that skin contact can extract a lot of tannin, which then requires you to fine at a later stage to remove it. Far better, in his view, to grow the fruit in such a way that skin contact becomes superfluous. The academic view, from Professor Vernon Singleton at Davis, was that skin contact could broaden and coarsen the wine, and most winemakers seem to agree with him. As with Chardonnay, whole-cluster pressing seems to be the answer.

Some of the uniformity of so much California Sauvignon may be related to the very widespread use of Prise de Mousse yeast. Natural yeast fermentation does not seem to have become an option for Sauvignon. Another drawback of Prise de Mousse is its high conversion rate, which means that grapes picked at a perfectly reasonable 22.5 Brix can easily ferment to 13 degrees or more. Some producers, such as Kenwood, try to compensate for this by picking early, especially in hot vintages. With barrel fermentation, however, high alcohol is less usual. Before bottling, the wine is usually subjected to a battery of treatments, including cold stabilization for tartrates, fining and filtration, as it needs to be broachable immediately on release.

Two wineries epitomized the different styles of Sauvignon one could encounter in California. The first was Newton. Peter and Su-Hua Newton were unabashed about their determination to make a Graves-style wine, with about 25 per cent Sémillon added to the Sauvignon. Beginning in 1983 they barrel fermented the must and aged it in 50 per cent new *barriques*. Yields were low, at about 3 tons per acre, and the wine was aged on the fine lees for up to 9 months; usually the wines were given a great deal of bottle age before being released. The wine was barrel fermented in up to 50 per cent new oak, but aged in older barrels for about 9 months. After a few years the Newtons gave up. The costs of production were high, but the market would not accept a realistic price for the wine. It was superb – I bought some vintages and have tasted all of them – but it had to be priced at a level lower than most mediocre Chardonnays. American buyers were simply unprepared to pay Chardonnay prices for a Sauvignon. The Newtons understandably tired of losing money on the wine.

Meanwhile Philip Togni on Spring Mountain was producing an unoaked Sauvignon. He admitted that his primary motivation was not commercial, but rather to ensure a supply of wine he could enjoy drinking at home with oysters. His vines were Wente clones, which he picked early, fermented cold, and bottled young. It was as close as California would come to a Sancerre style: bracing, high in acidity, tangy. The price was the highest of any California Sauvignon at the time, but since production was very limited that did not pose a problem. But after the 1994 vintage the vines were grubbed up and this excellent unwooded Sauvignon became history. Until 1992 Flora Springs produced a rich but Loire-style wine in Napa, but disguised it by labelling it Soliloquy without any reference to the grape variety.

Susan Reed and Bill Parker, the winemakers at Matanzas Creek, which developed a fine reputation for Sauvignon Blanc under their predecessors, openly admit that their winemaking techniques for the variety scarcely differ from those they would use for Chardonnay. They have no intention of attempting to produce a

Sauvignon Blanc in the style of Cloudy Bay. They are certainly right from a commercial point of view. As James Halliday has pointed out: 'When makers such as Rochioli produce crisp, unoaked, varietally exact wine with distinct herbaceous characteristics, opinions polarize. It is quite clear that a body of opinion either does not like or does not recognize (or both) the true flavor of Sauvignon Blanc.'[4] Raymond of Napa Valley confirm their customers' prejudice when they note in a release announcing one of their own Sauvignons: 'Flavors and aromas show only the slightest hint of grassiness. Rather, this wine is distinguished by appealing fruit and oaky richness.' Given the commercial imperatives and the absence of an American taste for unoaked Sauvignon, the best one can settle for is a wine that has ample ripe melony fruit, perhaps with a race of grapefruit tanginess to keep the palate tingling, a touch of roundness from oak, and a good positive finish. A seminar on Sauvignon Blanc organized by a professional journal concluded that most California winemakers agreed that ' "Chardonnay-like" is a legitimate goal because it fits a taste and texture pattern that consumers seek, but it comes at them in a different aromatic and flavor profile.' Even participating winemakers who disagreed, such as Nick Goldschmidt of Simi and Ken Deis of Flora Springs, agreed that a Chardonnay-like texture and mouthfeel were desirable.[5]

In November 1997 I tasted a small range of 1996 Sauvignons, mostly from Sonoma. They gave a good cross-section of the county which is probably, overall, producing the best Sauvignons in California. Only one of them was poor, from Canyon Road. It had a California appellation, so the grapes could have come from anywhere, but the fruit was unripe and the wine hard. Geyser Peak was the only 1997 in the line-up, already in bottle; it was a fresh, ripe, simple wine, a touch dilute. DeLoach was better: more austere, bone-dry, yet slightly mineral. Pedroncelli was slightly herbaceous and bitter, but presumably one of the least expensive wines in the range. Dry Creek was dry and bracing but not complex. Kenwood was its usual reliable self: with aromas of melons and pears, and on the palate fresh, well balanced, and long. Murphy-Goode, who release no fewer than three different Sauvignons, offered their Fumé, which I found rich and broad yet a touch flabby. The Reserve, which goes through malolactic fermentation, had a slightly bitter oak finish, and I preferred their barrel-fermented Deuce, which was rich with ample oaky bite, creamy and luxurious. Also excellent was the fresh but full-bodied Kenwood Reserve, with its well-judged oak. The best of these wines were a pleasure to taste and would have been a pleasure to drink, especially since the prices are reasonable. They show that California Sauvignon may not have the pronounced varietal character of its counterparts from the Loire or Marlborough, but can nonetheless be very good wine.

The style of Sauvignon is also influenced by the fact that no one in America would dream of cellaring such a wine. Whereas a fine white Graves, from Haut-Brion or Domaine de Chevalier, can, perhaps should, be cellared for ten years before being drunk, California Sauvignon is bought to be consumed instantly. Some of the more serious wines do age interestingly – that was certainly true of the Newton bottlings – but anyone buying Sauvignon probably has this evening's dinner in mind. St Helena wine merchant Mark Kinley explained that the American palate likes roundness, so winemakers opt for malolactic fermentations and sometimes a touch of residual sugar. Because wineries need to move smoothly from one vintage to the next, they do not want to produce wines that are not ready to drink. Powerful vintage variation is not acceptable in an instantly consumed wine such as Sauvignon Blanc.

In Napa Valley, Sauvignon Blanc tends to be planted on the valley floor, on fairly rich soils that give generous crops. Dan Duckhorn recalls some superb hillside grapes with the small berries that he looks for, but such grapes are hard to find. Mountain soils give low yields, and few growers can justify planting undervalued varieties such as Sauvignon Blanc here. The best producers include: Duckhorn, Spottswoode, Silverado, Cain (using Monterey fruit), Cakebread, Grgich Hills, Mason, Selene, and Mondavi. Honig had a reputation as a Sauvignon specialist, but quality was not outstanding. I particularly like the Frog's Leap Sauvignon, most of which is tank-fermented, then aged in large oak casks; it undergoes partial malolactic yet always has ample acidity.

In Sonoma the following wineries make very good Sauvignon: Murphy-Goode, Kenwood, Dry Creek, Simi, Matanzas Creek, Peter Michael, and Rochioli. Rochioli still has some of the vines it planted in 1959. In Mendocino, the Ukiah and Redwood Valleys tend to give Sauvignon Blancs with that rounded melony character that finds most favour with the American consumer, while the much cooler Anderson Valley grows grapes with a more assertive, grapefruity varietal character. The best producers include Husch, Greenwood Ridge, Parducci, Fetzer, Jepson, and Navarro. Lake County, with little maritime influence but an elevation of around 1,300 feet, is a good source of Sauvignon grapes, and Jed Steele made some good examples when Kendall-Jackson were based here before their imperial expansion.

From Santa Barbara County there are sound versions from Firestone, Santa Barbara Winery, and Babcock. Boeger and Shenandoah are reliable in El Dorado County in the Sierra Foothills.

Although not yet on the endangered species list, Sauvignon Blanc is almost certainly a variety in decline. Acreage may not have dropped much in the last few years, but there is little incentive to plant the grape in most regions, since prices are so much lower than they are for Chardonnay or the fashionable white Rhône varieties. And since most producers have been too afraid of 'grassiness' or high acidity to make a wine quite distinct from Chardonnay, Sauvignon Blanc has failed to establish a firm niche for itself other than as a cheaper substitute for Chardonnay.

NOTES

1 Charles L. Sullivan, *Napa Wine*, pp. 141–2
2 Roy Andries De Groot, *The Wine of California*, p. 189
3 Stephen Brook, *Sauvignon Blanc and Sémillon*, pp. 207–34
4 James Halliday, *Wine Atlas of California*, p. 23
5 Eleanor and Ray Heald, 'Expectations for Reserve-Style Sauvignon Blanc/ Sémillon', *Practical Winery and Vineyard*, September/October 1994

20

Other White Varieties

Arneis

This rather obscure Piedmontese variety does not have much of a following in California. Jim Clendenen has obtained Arneis grapes from a vineyard near Gilroy but is not entirely happy with the quality. He finds that Arneis varies greatly according to the grower, and that it has a shampoo and white peach quality that is hard to define. Seghesio produce Arneis, as do Wild Horse, and a fresh, almondy version has been made by Robert Pepi since 1996. (The best West Coast Arneis I have encountered comes, I regret to say, from Ponzi in Oregon.)

Burger

This high-yielding vine, planted almost exclusively in San Joaquin Valley, generates neutral wine that ended up in gallon jugs and more recently in wine coolers. Some 1,800 acres survived in 1995, despite serious viral infections. In France the variety is known as Monbadon, but is in decline.

Chenin Blanc

Chenin Blanc is very popular in California, but not held in high regard by wine connoisseurs. There is certainly a good deal of it around, although it is in decline. In 1986 just over 40,000 acres were under vine; in 1997 that acreage has dropped to 21,647, of which 85 per cent has since the late 1970s been found in the Central Valley, with 5,500 acres in Madera County alone. The very low average price – $264 per ton in 1997 – understandably discourages vineyards from retaining or replanting the variety.

In California it was originally known as White Pinot, and the correct name did not appear on a wine label until 1955, when Charles Krug released a varietal Chenin. The rapid expansion of the variety in the 1960s may well have been a consequence of technological advances that allowed cold fermentations to release the full fruitiness of Chenin. In the North Coast some excellent dry wines were produced; elsewhere its high yields, as much as 12 tons per acre in the Central Valley, gave characterless wines which Roy Andries De Groot, writing in the early 1980s, described as 'drab in flavor, lackluster in fruity refreshment, with an underlying bitterness and a vague vegetable earthiness.'[1] Its appeal to bulk producers is its floweriness (when not throttled by sulphur or poor winemaking) and high acidity, which can give some zest to an otherwise indifferent white blend.

There is some excellent Chenin Blanc in California, but it does have to be hunted down. A great deal of varietally labelled Chenin is slightly sweet, although such a style will be familiar to admirers of demi-sec Vouvray, which can be a delicious wine. Among dry Chenins, Chalone's, which is oak-aged, is one of the most illustrious examples, coming as it does solely from vines planted in 1919 and 1946. In Napa Valley, Chappellet produce a bracing oak-aged dry Chenin, and Pine Ridge also release examples. Girard (now renamed Rudd) phased out its dry Chenin after 1996. Charles Krug has long been known for the variety and has recently introduced a Reserve Chenin called Pineau, which is barrel-fermented and dry, and aged in *barriques*. Dry Creek Vineyard also produce a first-rate example, but the fruit comes from Clarksburg in the Sacramento Delta, which happens to be the source of some of the best Chenin in the state. I was surprised to come across a splendid Chenin called Pavane from Adelaida in Paso Robles.

The reputation of Chenin is not enhanced by the continuing production of sugary examples that seek to mask the variety's natural acidity. Less structured and acidic than Loire Chenin, the Californian versions can't easily sustain a dose of residual sugar without becoming soft and soupy. In Chenin as in Riesling, some balancing residual sugar can be attractive, but too many wineries overdo it in an attempt, one assumes, to attract buyers with a very sweet tooth. No wonder the market for Chenin is fading away.

Cortese

Mount Palomar in Temecula claims to have been the first winery to have planted Cortese. I have not tasted it or heard of any others.

Emerald Riesling

This Davis crossing, a marriage of Muscadelle and Riesling, was specifically created to give very large yields (up to 12 tons per acre) in very hot conditions, while retaining a good level of acidity. It was developed in the late 1930s but not launched until after World War II. Its thick skins made it eminently suitable to mechanical harvesting and it was also able to withstand long journeys from vineyards to wineries in the Central Valley. Much of the acreage was planted in Kern County, one of the hottest corners of the Valley. When pressed, the thick skins tended to become gelatinous, requiring the juice to be drawn off after pressing as rapidly as possible. Its appeal was a gentle floweriness, but it did not give a wine suitable for bottle ageing. Jancis Robinson found the grape most successful in Monterey, but I have never encountered varietal Emerald Riesling from this county.[2]

The variety appears to be on its way out. In the early 1980s about 3,000 acres were under vine, but by 1995 only about 675 survived. In the few instances when the wine is varietally labelled, it is usually offered in a lightly sweet, inoffensive style.

Fiano

This nutty Italian variety has a small but enthusiastic following in California, personified by Jim Clendenen, who made an excellent version at Au Bon Climat until the late 1990s.

Flora

Flora is a crossing between Gewürztraminer and Sémillon, and it achieved the glimmerings of popularity in the mid-1980s, when about 350 acres were planted. It did not catch on and now the acreage is down to about 50. Its floral character makes it suitable for vinification in a fairly sweet style. John Parducci in Mendocino commented some years ago: 'We have not been able to come up with a great dry Flora, and what I want to do is produce a sweet one, a Sauternes type ... Flora has a tremendous nose, but the finish is always coarse.' A loyal adherent to Flora has been Schramsberg, which uses the variety in its sweet sparkling Cremant.

Folle Blanche

Given that California likes fruit in its wines, it is puzzling that anybody decided to plant Folle Blanche, the grape that used to give the thin wines that were distilled into Cognac and Armagnac and that, under its local name of Gros Plant, produces the tart little numbers best consumed with shellfish on the Brittany coast. In California it was planted in warm San Benito County, presumably to provide a burst of acidity in jug-wine blends, not to mention its very high yields. Its acidity has been useful as a component in some sparkling wines, but the variety appears to be in terminal decline, with just a few vineyards left in Napa and Sonoma. Louis Martini used to produce a highly regarded crisp dry example from his Monte Rosso vineyard in Sonoma.

French Colombard

Until 1991 this was the most widely planted white variety in California, and even in 1996 its tonnage (not acreage) was still higher than that of Chardonnay. Its decline in popularity, despite its ability to retain acidity in very warm conditions, has been gradual. In 1986 there were almost 70,000 acres planted, and by 1997 there were 46,076, of which nearly 15,000 were in Madera County alone. Its high yields – 11.7 tons per acre on average in 1980[3] – make it an economical variety to grow, and its appearances have by no means been restricted to the Central Valley. In the 1970s it was widely planted in Sonoma, where, according to Davis Bynum, it could attain yields as high as 12 tons per acre.[4] It seems that Parducci was the first winery to offer a varietally labelled version. When offered as a varietal wine, it is sometimes vinified dry, sometimes lightly sweet. Carnival, a commercially successful French Colombard produced by the Peju Province winery in Rutherford, has 45 grams of residual sugar.

Furmint

The great grape of the Tokaj region in eastern Hungary doesn't seem to travel that well, but Ted Markoczy has planted a few acres at Limerick Lane in Sonoma. At present he makes a good assertive dry wine from the variety, and is hoping to make a Tokaj-style wine. He has also planted a little Hárslevelű, so, other than botrytis, he already has all he needs.

Gewürztraminer

It seems probable that Gewürztraminer was one of the varieties brought to California by Agoston Haraszthy, but there has never been great enthusiasm for it, even though some very fine wines have been made. In the 1960s it was correctly planted in fairly cool regions, such as Monterey, Sonoma, and Mendocino. By the 1970s there were about 3,000 acres under vine, and by 1978 it was being bottled by over thirty wineries, including some large producers such as Wente and Martini. It was also made by Simi and Stony Hill. Gewürztraminer attained its highest acreage in the mid-1980s, when almost 4,000 acres were planted, but sadly it is now down to 1,715, most of it in Monterey and 500 acres in Sonoma. There must, however, be some demand for the wine for it to sustain a price per ton in 1997 of $950. Some Mendocino growers grumble that, although they have no difficulty selling the wine, they have difficulty obtaining grapes, as growers are replacing it with more profitable varieties such as Pinot Noir. It is also tricky to grow, giving fairly low yields. It can be quite costly to buy, but no winery dares price it above $14.

The variety has always done especially well in Russian River Valley, where the cool climate keeps some freshness and zest in a wine that can be flabby if grown in regions that are too warm. As in Alsace, it is sometimes vinified dry, but quite often a discreet amount of residual sugar is left in the wine to give it greater succulence. Outstanding versions from Russian River have been released by Mark West, Rochioli, Alderbrook, Z. Moore, Martinelli, and DeLoach. The Vinedos del Rio Vineyard here is the source of Louis Martini's Gewürztraminer.

The grape also gives exceptional results in another cool region, Mendocino's Anderson Valley, where Navarro and Lazy Creek

make excellent examples. Elsewhere in Mendocino, Fetzer grow
an Alsatian clone with great success, and have become the nation's
major producer of Gewürztraminer. It can do well in Monterey,
and Fogarty makes a good version from Ventana Vineyard. There
is very little Gewürztraminer in Napa Valley, but Mitch Cosentino
makes a largely barrel-fermented version from Yountville grapes,
and Richard Evensen in Oakville makes a highly regarded dry
version.

Green Hungarian

Of little commercial significance, the 40 or so acres that remain of
Green Hungarian, all in the Central Valley, are usually consigned
to sparkling wine production. Its origins are obscure and its flavour
bland.

Grey Riesling

Grey Riesling has nothing to do with the celebrated German
variety, and is in fact a strange mutation of Trousseau known in
France as Trousseau Gris. The best-known version was made by
Wente, and Herman Wente originally planted the variety in Livermore. It also survives in very small quantities in Napa and
Monterey. The Christian Brothers also made a very popular
version. Today only about 250 acres remain, and Wente's is still
the most widely available bottling. I don't believe I have tasted
Grey Riesling in fifteen years, but Wente versions from the 1980s
were perfectly pleasant, versatile, not enormously characterful but
with ample fresh fruitiness. Martini & Prati disguise their version
under the inappropriately Italian name of Vino Grigio.

Malvasia Bianca

Although the variety is planted in the Central Valley as a workhorse, there are some winemakers who think highly of it. Randall
Grahm uses it as the basis of his Big House White. He buys his
grapes from the vast San Bernabe Vineyard in Salinas Valley, where
it was planted in the 1970s on the instructions of the Gallo family.
There are about 2,300 acres in the Central Valley, about 500 in
Monterey. Unfortunately the vines are seriously diseased, and it

isn't known if the variety will be replanted here. Grahm describes its aroma as one of lychees, and adds: 'It's like Gewürztraminer on acid.'

Ken Volk of Wild Horse wants to get away from the traditional style of Malvasia as a soft, light, sweetish wine. He allows the grapes to reach high levels of ripeness before harvesting, and then ferments to dryness. He ages the wine in older and thus neutral *barriques*, with full malolactic fermentation. It emerges very exotic indeed.

Marsanne

Occasional versions of this northern Rhône variety are released from time to time, but a fresh start is being made. Most of the existing acreage in California is diseased, but the Tablas Creek vineyard and nursery in Paso Robles have healthy material that is now being released to interested vineyards. It is also grown in Sonoma by Cline. Preston, who make some very good Rhône-style wines, can't avoid dullness in the Marsanne. The best I have encountered is from McDowell in Mendocino.

Muscat of Alexandria

This least prestigious Muscat was planted primarily as a raisin grape in the Central Valley. It is also used as a blending grape because of its strong aromas. The acreage is declining quite fast. In 1976 there were 11,500 acres planted, a figure which held steady into the early 1980s. But by 1997 only 5,230 acres remained.

Muscat Canelli

Unlike Muscat of Alexandria, this is a variety that can give delightful wines if carefully vinified. It is also known as Muscat Blanc or Muscat Frontignan, although the latter name is usually reserved for fortified styles. One of the Christian Brothers' best known wines before its demise, Chateau La Salle, was made from this grape. Its superior quality can be gauged from the fact that whereas Muscat of Alexandria in 1997 was fetching an average price of $228 per ton, Muscat Canelli was worth $521. About

1,300 acres are planted, divided between the Central Valley and the coastal wine regions.

Like its Italian original in the Asti region of Piedmont, Muscat Canelli works best as a light, gently sweet wine with a dash of carbon dioxide to give it sparkle and charm. There are also richer, denser, more cloying versions made in a fortified style, but that seems a waste of a particularly charming and delicate variety. Gary Eberle, a fan of Muscat Canelli, comments in one of his newsletters that 'the problem with muscat is that when you try for a "drier" version, you run the risk of making a wine that tastes like diesel fuel.' His approach relies on a very cold fermentation prolonged for up to 2 months, and leaving some carbon dioxide in the filtered wine. 'We aim,' he continues, 'for a wine that highlights the apricot, mandarin orange, and grapefruit aromas and flavors found in great Muscat Canelli. We like a bit of residual sugar, but, twenty seconds after you taste the wine, we want you to experience a clean, crisp, and slightly tart finish that refreshes.' That sounds like a recipe for Muscat Canelli at its best. (See also Chapter 21.)

Pinot Blanc

For a couple of decades now, there has been considerable discussion about what, precisely, Californian Pinot Blanc really is. French ampeleographers have claimed that many Pinot Blanc vines are in fact Melon – in short, the Muscadet variety. Maybe, although I have yet to taste a Californian Pinot Blanc that tastes remotely like Muscadet. The J. Fritz winery in Sonoma bravely releases a wine called Melon rather than Pinot Blanc, and even that, fortunately, doesn't taste like Muscadet.

In 1939 Martin Ray was bottling a Pinot Blanc. What, one wonders, was that? It also appeared at Chalone, where it made a very fine wine, and Heitz used to buy Pinot Blanc grapes from Stony Hill from 1964 until 1971, when the vines were removed. These vines were indeed Melon. Paul Truel, a French viticulturalist, identified some 'Pinot Blanc' in Australia as Melon. The cuttings had come from UC Davis, so when Truel turned up at the California university it became clear that almost all Californian Pinot Blanc, including the venerable vines at Chalone, were Melon de Bourgogne. That has been changing over the past decade, and vineyards such as Saralee Kunde's in Sonoma and Byron in Santa Barbara are now planted with authentic Pinot Blanc.

It would seem that about 1,300 acres are planted, mostly in Monterey. Some of it ends up in sparkling wine blends, and wineries such as Schramsberg in Napa Valley have always used some Pinot Blanc in some of their cuvées. Norm Roby and Charles Olken report, somewhat to my surprise, that 'the number of producers offering it as a varietal wine has dropped from twenty-four to ten in just the last few years.'[5] If that is true, it may well be because Pinot Blanc lacks a strong identity in California.

For instance, Richard Arrowood, a veteran winemaker, declares authoritatively: 'This is what Pinot Blanc should be in California: a rich dense wine with honey and orange aromas bursting with fruit flavours. We always strive to produce Pinot Blancs that showcase the fullest potential of the grape ... with complex oily and butter components and weighty density that sets it apart from Chardonnay.' Sets it *apart*? Arrowood's description sounds exactly like most Californian Chardonnay. And all that oil and butter doesn't sound particularly appetizing to me.

In contrast, the newsletter writers at J. Lohr describe their Arroyo Seco Pinot Blanc as 'rich in floral and citrus descriptors complemented by a moderate acidity. The result is wine less heavy than some of today's fat, almost oily textured Chardonnays, but more complex and satisfying than the typical Sauvignon Blanc.' They add a note of caution: 'Because of its moderate natural acidity, it is susceptible to oxidation and browning.' Lohr's version of Pinot Blanc sounds closer to the European style than Arrowood's concoction. Interestingly, however, Arrowood finds that his Pinot Blanc often ages better than his Chardonnay. I find Pinot Blanc from Alsace or Baden in Germany the perfect model: a delicious wine, crisp but fruity, with body but no undue weight, a wine best drunk young, not complex but invariably balanced and satisfying, and very dependable with a range of foods. Christina Benz of Murphy-Goode defines the variety well: 'Compared to Chardonnay, Pinot Blanc is more neutral and toned down. A grower once said to me Pinot Blanc is to Chardonnay what Merlot is to Cabernet Sauvignon, the kinder, gentler version, and I agree.'[6]

I have come across admirable Californian examples from a range of wineries, including Au Bon Climat, J. Fritz (Melon), Chalone, Etude (the grapes are bought from Shafer's Carneros vineyards), and Benziger. Nils Venge at Saddleback Cellars has been making the wine since 1984, often blending his estate-grown barrel-fermented lots with steel-fermented Pinot Blanc from Carneros. The wine I have enjoyed most came from the little known Paraiso Springs winery in Monterey. It is also grown at Bien Nacido in Santa Maria Valley, which also supplies Pinot Blanc to Villa Mount Eden. Other versions are produced by Byron, Murphy-Goode, Lockwood, Mirassou, and Wild Horse.

The most agreeable feature of most European Pinot Blanc is that it is inexpensive. If only one could say the same for its Californian counterpart.

Pinot Gris

Although Pinot Gris has proved an enormous success in Oregon, it has not made much of an impact in California. Indeed it seems that only about 200 acres are planted. It was first made by Elliston Vineyards in Pleasanton, and subsequent versions have been released by Edmunds St John, Au Bon Climat, Navarro, Long, Chalk Hill, Swan, Luna, and Monte Volpe. In Alsace the variety makes a rich, full-bodied alcoholic wine; in northern Italy it is vinified as a simple, frisky thirst-quencher, and this, for the most part, is the style favoured in California, although the wines tend to have considerably more fruit than their Italian counterparts. The barrel-fermented Pinot Grigio from Viansa is a lovely wine. It is also being planted in the Russian River Valley by Gallo Sonoma, and Greg Graziano of Monte Volpe believes that the variety has good potential in Redwood Valley. Tony Soter at Etude has started dabbling with Pinot Gris. Robert Pepi's Pinot Grigio from Central Coast fruit, introduced in 1996, is clearly intended to be an Italianate expression of the variety, but is rather too plump. Seghesio produce a tank-fermented Pinot Grigio.

Navarro is one of the wineries that seems to have the measure of the variety, making it without barrel and malolactic fermentation, and with limited amounts of new oak. Other wineries do ferment the wine in wood, usually older oak, and employ malolactic fermentation, with varying degrees of success. In Napa, Richard Mendelson uses Pinot Gris as the basis for a 'white port' (see Chapter 21). Oregon is still streets ahead of California.

Riesling

Like Gewürztraminer, Riesling is much enjoyed by a substantial number of wine drinkers but given little value by growers and consequently by wineries. Although much of California is clearly far too warm for Riesling, there are a few areas where it gives good results. Sadly, it is in danger of becoming an endangered species. In 1986 there were 8,449 acres planted; by 1997 the acreage was down to 2,522, of which over half has been planted in Monterey. Kenwood, for instance, used to make Riesling. No more: in 1989 the vines were grafted over to Merlot. Riesling fetches reasonable prices, however. In 1997 the average price per ton was $805.

German immigrants such as Emil Dresel were among the first to bring Riesling vines to California, in his case to the Rhinefarm Vineyard in Sonoma. Agoston Haraszthy also shipped in Riesling and other German vines. They flourished in the cooler areas of Sonoma and Jacob Schram did well with it at his Napa vineyard.[7] During the 1960s, Norm Roby and Charles Olken report, Riesling was often made in a dry style high in alcohol, and occasionally aged in oak, although I have never encountered any of these wines.[8] In the 1970s it was usually made in a slightly sweet style.

There were various techniques for achieving the right balance of alcohol and sweetness in a Riesling. Richard Peterson at The Monterey Vineyard would ferment the wine to dryness and then add grape juice concentrate just before bottling; Stag's Leap Wine Cellars used the same method. Joe Heitz, however, didn't like to use concentrate. Instead he would add a Süssreserve. This was not a method of which Mike Grgich approved. Instead, he explained, 'we chill the wine when the sugar drops to one and two-tenths per cent sugar. That stops fermentation; then I rack or filter out the yeast.' Richard Arrowood, when he was at Chateau St Jean in the late 1970s turning out some superlative sweet Riesling, arrested fermentation by centrifuging and filtration.[9]

Although a very sweet or botrytis Rieslings are occasionally produced in the few areas where noble rot infects the vineyards regularly (see Chapter 21), the majority of Rieslings are medium-bodied with a touch of residual sugar. The major producers are Fetzer and J. Lohr. Chateau Montelena also offers Riesling, a pretty wine made from Potter Valley fruit. Smith-Madrone on Spring

Mountain based its reputation on the quality of its Rieslings. Randall Grahm is a great fan. At a dinner in London in 1998 he sang its praises: 'What is Riesling? A lost cause? A challenge? It is the ugly duckling, the Cinderella of grapes: it should be at the ball wearing the crown, but often ends up taking out the garbage. It's perceived to be a nerdy variety but in fact it's the hippest grape we have.' Unfortunately, Grahm feels obliged to purchase most of his Riesling grapes from Columbia Valley in Washington state.

Rkatsiteli

This fine Georgian grape is said to exist in California, but I have never encountered a bottle. In the 1970s Concannon had an experimental acre planted with cuttings that came from the Vavilov Institute in what was then Leningrad.

Roussanne

This splendid variety from the southern Rhône was first planted at Alban Vineyards in San Luis Obispo County and has also been planted by another Rhône variety specialist, Cline in Carneros. It's a tricky grape to cultivate, being late-ripening and susceptible to mildew and rot, but it can give very complex wine, with gorgeous flowery aromas and a rich palate. It also responds well to new-oak treatment, which is just as well in California. Good versions are made by the two estates mentioned above, who also supply grapes to Qupé, Sean Thackrey, and Sine Qua Non. Zaca Mesa in Santa Barbara have been making very good estate-grown Roussanne since 1995, but it is not aged in new oak. Bonny Doon's is rich, broad, and spicy. Presumably, newly propagated cuttings from French vines at Tablas Creek Vineyards will soon be made available to growers.

Sauvignon Vert

See Tocai Friulano (p. 322).

Scheurebe

A speciality of Phelps in Napa Valley, dating from the days when German-born and trained winemaker Walter Schug was at the helm. In 1974 the winery planted 5 acres of the variety in one of its vineyards near Yountville. The first commercially released vintage was 1979, made in a lightly sweet style. Scheurebe can have a grapefruity flavour when vinified dry or off-dry, but is also capable of making sumptuous sweet wines. Phelps produced a series of late harvest wines, and even though the Scheurebe vines were budded over to another variety, the estate has continued to produce the variety. In 1994 they adopted the technique of freezing the grapes after harvest in order to concentrate the sugars; the result was a rather unsatisfactory wine in an ice-wine style.

Twelve acres of Scheurebe are planted at Balverne in Sonoma.

Sémillon

Sémillon has never caught on California, although there are a few enthusiasts for the variety such as Bernard Portet of Clos du Val. The problem seems to be endowing this prolific grape with personality. In the early 1980s there were about 3,000 acres planted, but by 1997 acreage was down to 1,381. Prices per ton have been modest, standing in 1997 at $569, which means there is virtually no incentive for growers to replant the variety.

It has to be admitted that Sémillon in California seems to give rather dull results. There is no Californian equivalent to the superb dry Sémillons from Hunter Valley in Australia. It is mostly used to blend in with Sauvignon Blanc in Graves-style wines. According to Sauvignon specialist Jeff McBride, it contributes good mouthfeel and roundness to counter the more aggressive character of Sauvignon. As a low-acidity variety, it can calm down the extravagance of high-acidity Sauvignon Blanc. But few winemakers like to work with it. It is a fleshy grape, makes a terrible mess during pressing, and the juice has a high solids content. Craig Williams of Phelps, who produce late harvest Sémillons from time to time, believes that the proliferation in mediocre Sémillon is due to a combination of poor clones planted in the wrong soil in inappropriate climates. Dan Duckhorn agrees. 'Unless you have stressed soils, Sémillon will develop berries as large as watermelons. There's no way you can make great wine from huge berries.'

Jeff Baker of Carmenet, which has long specialized in Sauvignon/Sémillon blends, admits that Californian Sémillon is often neutral in flavour, but believes that if the grapes are of good quality the resulting wine can develop complex honeyed tones after some time in bottle. He finds that North Coast Sémillon can be especially neutral and ripens with difficulty, and he greatly prefers the variety grown in Edna Valley, where it seems to acquire more richness. There used to be a fashion for Sauvignon/Sémillon blends, usually made in a rich oaky style, with names such as Chevrier and Chevrignon, from wineries such as Lyeth, Monticello, Merlion (which closed down in 1993), Kendall-Jackson and Vichon. Although some of these were well made and good value, most of them seem to have been phased out, presumably because of lack of commercial success. Alderbrook in Healdsburg continues to make a blend called Duet; another version, Nuovo Mondo, comes from Canyon Road in Geyserville; and in 1993 Simi bravely launched a new attempt to blend the two called Sendal.

Other winemakers believe Sémillon makes no useful contribution. Forrest Tancer of Iron Horse just can't see the point of Sémillon. 'It adds very little,' he says, 'and it only encourages the wine to fall apart. Bob Pecota in Napa Valley also finds it lacklustre, claiming it can easily be misused to fatten up a white blend to make it more forward and approachable.

Clos du Val is one of the few prestigious wineries to produce a varietal Sémillon. Bernard Portet daringly proclaims: 'I prefer Sémillon to most Chardonnay. Sémillons can be such rich, silky wines, very complex, and they can be consumed so much sooner than most Chardonnays. But the retailers won't sell them ... Ask a restaurateur to put Sémillon on his wine list, and he says he doesn't have room!' He admits that California Sémillon doesn't have the longevity of the variety in Bordeaux or Hunter Valley.[10] Also in Napa Valley, Signorello have had the courage to produce a fairly high-priced Sémillon, using whole-cluster pressing and a sizeable proportion of new oak. In Mendocino, Hidden Cellars make a wine called Alchemy, which is dominated by barrel-fermented Sémillon.

Late harvest wines are still made by Phelps and others, and these are discussed in the following chapter.

Sylvaner

This German variety must have come to California in the mid-nineteenth century, no doubt at the same time as Riesling. Very little is left. In the early 1980s there were about 1,000 acres under vine, but today only about 90 acres remain, most of them in Monterey. In the late 1970s wineries producing the variety included Monterey Vineyard, Charles Krug, Paul Masson and Bargetto. Today the best known producer is probably Rancho Sisquoc in Santa Barbara, with 10 acres dedicated to the variety, which they claim is the last surviving Sylvaner in California.

Symphony

This is one of Dr Harold Olmo's crossings, developed in the 1940s by marrying Muscat of Alexandria with Grenache Gris, although it was only planted in the early 1980s. By 1995 there were 295 acres planted. By far its best-known exponent was Chateau de Baun in Sonoma, which is now a tasting room for Kendall-Jackson. Chateau de Baun made a surprising range of wines from the variety, from dry to sweet to sparkling. Its advantages are that it grows easily and gives good crops, and can be powerfully aromatic, even after rapid fermentation at high temperatures. Now that Chateau de Baun is out of business the major producer is Kautz Ironstone, who label the wine Obsession, which sounds more like a perfume than a wine. Like certain full-bodied and aromatic Alsatian wines, it is said to be a good partner for hot spicy dishes.

Tocai Friulano

This variety has nothing to do with the Hungarian varieties that make up the great sweet wine Tokaj, and seems in fact to be the same as the lowly Sauvignon Vert or Sauvignonasse which is so widely planted in Chile. It has its admirers in California. Jim Clendenen seems to have produced the first varietal Tocai Friulano in 1992, and other fans include Mondavi, Monte Volpe, and Monteviña. Nils Venge at Saddleback Cellars has even contrived to make a late harvest wine from the variety. Very little Sauvignon Vert is planted under that name (about 60 acres), although some planted in 1946 by the Nichelini family in Chiles Valley still survives. However, the winery believes their Sauvignon Vert is identical to Muscadelle!

Trebbiano

Why anyone would want to plant one of the dullest of Italian varieties in California is beyond me, but Viansa produce a wine called Anatra Bianco from Trebbiano, masking its neutrality with a layer of oak. Iván Tamás also make Trebbiano, from low-yielding vines.

Viognier

Viognier has become wildly fashionable in California. It can of course be a stupendous variety, giving magnificent results in Condrieu in the northern Rhône valley and in parts of southern France. In France it tends to be a fragile variety, and its very low yields and susceptibility to crop-reducing maladies accounts for its very high price.

Phil Hurst of Fetzer points out that one of the reasons why Viognier is such a poor producer in Condrieu is that much of it is infected with leaf-roll virus. In California it experiences fewer problems with its health as the Viognier vines planted in California have been cleaned up. Randy Ullom of Kendall-Jackson finds that it can yield up to 5 tons per acre without compromising quality. Nonetheless La Jota on Howell Mountain initially had problems with shatter, and Randall Grahm finds that it ripens unevenly. Bill Smith of La Jota has dealt with potential shatter by means of zinc treatments, and says he gets good yields, up to 4.5 tons per acre, using a Geneva double curtain trellising system.

Viognier was first planted by Josh Jensen of Calera, who got to know the variety when harvesting at Château Grillet in 1970. He started looking for cuttings in the 1970s but none were available in California, as it was not among UC Davis's recommended varieties. He eventually found cuttings in Geneva, New York, which he planted in 1983. 1988 was Calera's first crop. His interest in the variety was shared by La Jota and Ritchie Creek, and they obtained their cuttings from Geneva too. La Jota's first vintage, a mere twenty-five cases, was in 1986. Since then there has a profusion of bottlings, with about forty wineries releasing Viognier in 1996.

Fetzer has access to 100 acres, and Callaway to 23. It has been planted by Fess Parker in Santa Barbara, and by the leading Rhône variety specialist John Alban. The acreage is steadily rising. In 1995 there were 489 acres in California; in 1996, 645, and just a year later 1,117 acres had been planted, if not yet bearing. The largest plantings are in Mendocino, followed by Napa. Given the demand for the variety, it is not surprising that prices are high: in 1997, the average price per ton was $1,400. It is even grown in Madera, where Central Valley grower John Simpson has planted 110 acres.

Quality remains uneven, just as it does in France. It's a variety that only fully ripens at fairly high sugar levels, which means that the wine is invariably high in alcohol. At the same time the charm of Viognier lies largely in its superlative bouquet, which can be compromised if the wine is made in a sledgehammer style. I recently tasted the Phelps version side by side with the costly version from Niebaum-Coppola, and Phelps won hands down. Other fine versions come from Alban, Calera, Cline, Preston, Kunde, and Arrowood, and some very good bottlings from Benziger, La Jota, Fetzer, Kendall-Jackson, and Rosenblum. Some producers use oak; others avoid it, to allow the perfume of Viognier to emerge in all its purity and complexity. La Jota makes Viognier in both styles, so you can choose which you prefer – if you can find the wine in the first place.

Viognier is an expensive wine, and it is too soon to say whether the enthusiasm for the variety will be just a passing fad. I hope not, as some stunning Viogniers are emerging from California. Wineries such as Fetzer that have planted a good deal of Viognier point out that if the wine doesn't catch on, it can always be blended in to the Chardonnay! Gary Eberle, an admirer of Viognier, observes, however: 'Americans can't pronounce the name, it's expensive, and it doesn't age well. So will the trend last?'

NOTES

1 Roy Andries De Groot, *The Wine of California*, p. 48
2 Jancis Robinson, *Vines, Grapes and Wines*, p. 264
3 James Halliday, *Wine Atlas of California*, p. 22
4 Robert Benson, *Great Winemakers of California*, p. 231

5 Norman Roby and Charles Olken, *The New Connoisseurs' Handbook of California Wine*, p. 51

6 Eleanor and Ray Heald, 'Pinot Blanc demands consume attention', *Practical Winery and Vineyard*, January/February 1997

7 Charles L. Sullivan, *Napa Wine*, p. 139

8 Roby and Olken, p. 48

9 Benson, pp. 104, 156, 204, 243

10 Dan Berger and Richard Hinkle, *Beyond the Grapes: An Inside Look at Napa Valley*, p. 52

21

Wine Styles: Rosé, Meritage, Sparkling, Sweet and Fortified Wines, Kosher Wines

Rosé

In California rosé has been made from many different grape varieties. The cheapest brands are made by blending mediocre red wine with poor white wine; the result is execrable rosé. Almadén pioneered the use of Grenache to make rosé of good quality. Phelps still make a very good dry rosé from Grenache grown in Monterey, and McDowell make a refreshing example from Mendocino fruit. In Shendandoah Valley, Leon Sobon makes a slightly sweet Rhône-style rosé from Grenache and Syrah. Preston's Petit Faux is a Provençal-style blend of Cinsault, Mourvedre, and Grenache; John MacCready uses the same blend for his Belle Rose.

Veedercrest and Mirassou used to make some from Petite Sirah which was said to be dry and fruity, and rosés from Pinot Noir have been made by Mayacamas, Husch, David Bruce, Firestone, and Kenwood. It was probably never a good idea to make rosé from a tannic variety such as Cabernet Sauvignon, but it was done in the past, notably by Firestone. Fred Brander in Santa Ynez Valley used to make a Cabernet Blanc 'blush' wine from Cabernet Sauvignon. Simi too makes an off-dry rosé from Cabernet Sauvignon. Amador Foothill Winery and Swanson produce a rosé from Sangiovese, and Pedroncelli in Sonoma make a good dry rosé from Zinfandel. Gamay, Grignolino and Counoise are other grape varieties used to produce rosé. White Zinfandel, the most popular and least distinguished rosé of them all, has been discussed earlier.

Randall Grahm produces Vin Gris from Mourvèdre, and more

conventional Vin Gris, made by 'bleeding' tanks of fermenting Pinot Noir juice in order to concentrate the must, are made by Sanford, Sinskey, and Saintsbury, all of them delectable wines. Sinskey's is mostly fermented in steel tanks to ensure maximum freshness.

Randall Grahm dreams about his ideal rosé: 'It is an uphill battle to make the world safe for pink wine. The difference between Vin Gris and White Zin is that the former is good. I dream of making the world's great pink wine from blend of Bracchetto, Tiburin, Counoise (I love the grape because of the way it sounds, like Marseilles slang for something unspeakable), and a few other obscure varieties. But it will probably sell only four cases a year.' Jim Clendenen at Il Podere dell'Olivos believes he has found his ideal rosé already. Moana Arrossisce is a blend of Aleatico and Barbera, barrel-fermented, no less.

Meritage

Marketing by consensus is probably not the best way to make decisions, but in the 1980s California wine producers had no idea how to label their Bordeaux blends. Fewer pure varietal Cabernets were being released, and producers who kept the maximum contribution of any single variety to below 75 per cent had no label to attach to the wine other than the proprietary name, such as Phelps's Insignia, dreamt up by each winery. So in 1988 an association for American Bordeaux blends was set up to help create an identity for such wines. A contest was held to find A Name, under the chairmanship of the late Richard Graff. Six thousand entries were sent in. The winner was Meritage, which provoked almost as much mirth as some of the rejected entries, such as 'Claret Cake'. The name was officially registered in 1989.

The regulations stipulated that the Red Meritage had to be composed of two or more of the five Bordeaux varieties or St Macaire, Carmenère, and Gros Verdot. The White Meritage had to be a blend of two or more varieties from a pool containing Sauvignon Blanc, Sémillon, and Sauvignon Vert. No single variety could make up more than 90 per cent of either blend. Production had to be limited to fewer than 25,000 cases in any vintage. A Meritage must also be the 'best wine of its type' to be offered by any winery.

Many wineries adopted the new term – Boeger, Carmenet, Cosentino, Franciscan, Geyser Peak, Jekel, Merryvale, among others – but a few other producers such as Madroña declined to use the word Meritage on the grounds that they objected to paying a fee, as regulations required, to use a term that they felt should be in the public domain.

In practice most Meritages, such as Justin's Isosceles, Phelps's Insignia, and Cosentino's The Novelist, are better known by their proprietary names, so one wonders why Graff and his fellow judges spent all that time on an issue that nobody greatly cares about. A number of original members of the Meritage Association – Dominus, Sterling, among others – soon dropped out, and Opus One never bothered to join in the first place.

Sparkling wines

Sparkling wines have had a long history in California, with specialist wineries such as Korbel producing sweetish wines of good basic qualities over many generations. The first sparkling wines were producer in Los Angeles in the 1850s and Agoston Haraszthy was a pioneer of the style in Sonoma. In the first half of the twentieth century Paul Masson was probably the most prominent producer. The cheaper wines have usually been made by the Charmat method, which involves a second fermentation induced in a base wine by simply adding more yeast. The advantage is that it can be made economically in large tanks, which seal in the carbon dioxide induced by the second fermentation. The wine is bottled under pressure to preserve the bubbles. Alternatively, some adopted the transfer method, by which yeast was added to the wine in bottle, but instead of riddling and disgorgement, the wine is poured into tanks for removal of the yeast before re-bottling. In the 1970s an increasing number of producers adopted the champagne method, by which the secondary fermentation takes place in bottle and the wine is aged for some years on the yeast. In 1979 there were thirty-nine wineries offering sparkling wine, but only half of them used the *méthode champenoise*.

When I was living in the United States in the 1970s the quality of sparkling wine I encountered was often dire. The two words 'cold duck' said it all. Of course imported champagne was available, but the quality was irregular. As Eileen Crane, the winemaker at Domaine Carneros, points out: 'In those days there wasn't really a culture of sparkling wine here. A lot of the champagne that reached America arrived in damaged condition, oxidized or yeasty. Often the wines had remained on the dock for weeks in hot weather or been badly stored. American sparkling wine producers thought that this was what champagne was supposed to be like and tried to imitate it.'

The first winery that set out to make a Californian version of *méthode champenoise* of the highest quality was Schramsberg, revived in 1965 by Jack and Jamie Davis, who were inspired by some of the sparkling wines made by Martin Ray from Burgundian varieties. They were followed by Domaine Chandon in 1977. Eileen Crane, who worked at Domaine Chandon before she became wine-maker at Domaine Carneros, recalls that it wasn't easy to make sparkling wine in those days. 'If we ran into technical problems, there was nowhere to go other than France. No one was sure which varieties would work, and wines were being made from Riesling, Chenin Blanc, and Folle Blanche. It really isn't surprising that most of the wines in those days were not very good.'[1]

It soon became clear that, despite these teething problems, the California wineries were capable of turning out sparkling wine of high quality. The pioneering work was done by Schramsberg, Domaine Chandon, and Mumm, and soon the French champagne houses, constrained by the limits set on their vineyards in France, were opening up subsidiaries in California. Roederer and Pommery came to Anderson Valley. Rémy-Cointreau opened Piper-Sonoma, Taittinger constructed Domaine Carneros, Deutz opened up in San Luis Obispo, Laurient Perrier had a flirtation with the long-established Iron Horse winery, and two Spanish cava houses, Codorníu and Freixenet, set up wineries. One or two of the established wineries stuck to their own traditions. Hans Kornell had come to California from Germany in 1940 and in 1958 bought the historic Larkmead winery south of Calistoga. His wines were based on Riesling, and he was best known for his Sehr Trocken. But sales declined, as consumers favoured the French-style wines over Rieslings. In 1990 Kornell changed direction, adding a Brut, a Blanc de Blancs and Blanc de Noirs to the range. It was too late, and in 1992 the winery went out of business.

By and large the French investors in California told the directors of the new wineries to pursue their own ideas and not to think of

THE WINES OF CALIFORNIA

themselves as a cheaper version of champagne. Winemakers such as Eileen Crane and Dawnine Dyer, who has been at Domaine Chandon since 1976 and winemaker since 1981, have been encouraged to develop their own styles. It used to be widely stated that California sparkling wine has more fruit and less finesse than its French model, but I think that is less and less true. I am increasingly impressed by the delicacy achieved by wineries such as Domaine Carneros.

Most growers seem to favour picking at 19 Brix. There is a danger in this. If you do not require wines to attain high must weights, then it is tempting to allow them to overcrop, since even a heavily overcropped Chardonnay vine should make it to 19 Brix without difficulty in California's benign climate. At Roederer, for example, the managers want vines capable of attaining 23 or 24 Brix, even if the grapes are picked at much lower ripeness levels.

Producers have different policies when it comes to malolactic fermentation, just as they do in Champagne. Although one might suppose that acidity levels in California would be lower than in northern France, this is not necessarily the case, so the decision regarding the suitability of malolactic fermentation is essentially a stylistic one. A few producers, such as Iron Horse, make a point of suppressing it.

Acidity levels tends to be quite high because it did not take the best producers long to recognize that the most appropriate fruit would come from the coolest regions. Hence the proliferation of wineries in Carneros and Anderson Valley. Eileen Crane recall that in the late 1970s Domaine Chandon, although based in southern Napa, was well aware of the suitability of Carneros fruit, although they were at that stage unclear about its specific characteristics. There is less microclimatic variation in California than in Champagne, so blending components are based less on *crus* and *terroirs*, as they are in France, and more on clonal differences. At Domaine Carneros, for instance, they have planted six clones of Chardonnay and six of Pinot Noir. These clones are vinified separately. In London recently the winemaker of Veuve Clicquot presented still base wines from six different villages, all *grands crus*, that were likely to be components of the next vintage blend. In California a similar tasting might focus on varietal and clonal components, as well as some individual vineyards.

It has taken a while for the Californians to master their craft.

They have known from the start that whereas their French masters may be able to advise on technical matters, the Champenois have no greater understanding of the Californian fruit character than Californians do. Chardonnay in California, even from cool regions, tends to be a little fatter, even coarser, than its wiry counterpart in Champagne. Picking the grapes early provided the desired acidity, but it also gave some base wines a greenness that no one found attractive. The usual remedy for unripe fruit and the consequent excess of malic acid was to beef up the *dosage*, but this led to unbalanced wines. The alternative strategy of picking fully ripe grapes and acidifying the wine could lead to unbalanced and over-alcoholic wines. By the late 1980s these problems had essentially been solved, and growers were focusing better on achieving the required fruit quality.

Just as Californian houses are beginning to produce some excep-tional wines, the market seems to be slipping away from them. Domaine Carneros now produces still Pinot Noir as well as spark-ling wines. Although Californian sparkling wines are not that costly, they are very expensive to make. For a table wine you need 2.3 pounds of fruit to make a single bottle. For a good-quality bottle of sparkling wine you need 4.2 pounds. Moreover, a bottle of Chardonnay can be sold a year or so after the vintage; sparkling wine needs to be aged, usually up to three years, and that adds to the cost.

So in the early 1990s the market for sparkling wines lost its fizz. By 1995 domestic shipments had fallen by 2.4 per cent, which may not seem a great deal but at the same time Chardonnay sales had grown by 16 per cent. Sales in 1997 (12.8 million cases) were one-third lower than they had been in the mid-1980s. There were some immediate consequences. Some producers – Cordoníu, Gloria Ferrer, Domaine Carneros, S. Anderson – expanded their pro-duction of table wines. The problem, for once, can't be that prices are too high. Now that $20 Chardonnays and $25 Pinots are becoming the norm, American consumers can hardly complain that $12 to $15 for a good-quality *méthode champenoise* or $20 to $25 for a stylish vintage sparkling wine is exorbitant. If anything the problem is that the wines are too cheap when the costs of production are taken into account. At these prices, it is hard for sparkling wine producers to show a profit.

Some wineries have simply closed down, such as Piper-Sonoma

(winery and vineyards were acquired by Jordan in 1996 to produce their 'J' sparkling wine), or, as in the case of Deutz, were rehatched as still wine producers under the name of Laetitia. Others, such as Sebastiani, have closed down their sparkling wine facilities. One beneficial consequence is that a slump in sales makes it more feasible for the wines to spend longer periods on the yeast, which of course is a basic way of improving quality.

By 1998 it seemed that a corner had been turned. Dawnine Dyer told me the worst was over and that sales were increasing. Jean-Claude Rouzaud, the head of Roederer, said that sales had always been steady at the top end of the market. There is still a question mark over the future of some the smaller, quality-conscious houses such as S. Anderson and Schramsberg. They cannot compete on price with the major producers such as Domaine Chandon, Korbel, and Mumm, and although the quality of their wines is extremely high, they are in direct competition with Champagne itself. In Anderson Valley, Milla Handley explained that sparkling wine accounted for one-quarter of her production, but she could no longer afford to continue, as she was so easily undercut in price by the major producers.

One finds the same proliferation of styles in California that one would in Champagne. As in France, Pinot Noir is valued for its contribution of body and flesh, Chardonnay for its elegance, subtlety, and nerve; Pinot gives the wine its immediate appeal, Chardonnay the backbone for ageing. Pinot Noir tends to dominates most blends, although many producers release a Blanc de Blanc or other form of Chardonnay-dominated cuvée. Roederer give the edge to Chardonnay for the regular bottling, even though their Champagne is Pinot-dominated. Possibly Pinot Noir from Anderson Valley doesn't have the weight and body the same variety demonstrates further south.

But there are significant differences between France and California in some styles. An American Blanc de Noirs often resembles a rosé, being pink-tinged. Each house has its own philosophy. At Domaine Chandon, for example, there are no vintage-dated wines. Instead it has followed the Champagne practice of laying down reserve wines for blending purposes. Elsewhere, it is argued that because there is less vintage variation in California, it doesn't make much sense to pursue this costly practice. Handley has gone in the other direction, only producing vintage sparkling wines, making the candid admission that she didn't have sufficient experience to make up consistent blends that would develop in the way she wanted. Mumm are unusual in using quite a lot of Pinot Gris in some of their blends. Iron Horse also emphasize vintage wines, but have established a niche for themselves at the top end of the domestic market. So have Domaine Montreaux in Napa Valley, which is linked to the Monticello estate. Their wines are unusual in having been barrel-fermented and aged on the lees, and then aged a full seven years on the yeast. Another luxurious style is made by Wente, who age their nonvintage Brut Reserve for five years on the yeast, and by Kristone. However, it is worth recalling that one-third of the market share for Californian sparkling wine is occupied by E. & J. Gallo.

Sweet and fortified wines

American wine drinkers have always had a sweet tooth and, as we have already seen, until fairly recently the great majority of wines were made in a sweet, often fortified style. In this section I am not concerned with mass-produced sweet wines, mostly of poor quality, made from a blend of grapes such as Muscat and Malvasia, and sugared up with grape concentrate.

At the tiny tip of this vast iceberg, however, there have long been a handful of conscientiously made sweet wines. In Livermore Valley, Wente made a wine they labelled as their own Château d'Yquem, until wine regulations put a stop to that practice in the 1930s. I have also come across references to a 'Château Yquem' produced by the Shewan-Jones winery in Lodi, also in the 1930s; this was made from Flame Tokay and Burger! After the use of the French name was outlawed, the winery released the wines as 'Chateau Lejon'.

Genuine botrytis wines were unknown in California until the late 1960s, when conditions at various Monterey vineyards planted with Riesling allowed Wente to produce wines in 1969 and 1972 they dubbed Spatlese (the German government soon intervened to put a stop to the use of the term). A few years earlier, in 1967, federal inspectors in Napa Valley had found botrytized Sémillon grapes at the winery of Louis Martini and ordered them to be destroyed as unfit for processing into wine for human consumption. Eventually Martini did receive authorization to vinify the grapes.

Botrytis wines were made in California before the 1960s, but they had been produced after spraying gapes with botrytis spores. This method was pioneered at Cresta Blanca in 1956[1] by Myron and Alice Nightingale with Sémillon (occasionally Sauvignon Blanc) grapes. These wines were released in 1961 as 'Premier Sweet Sémillon', and the last vintage was 1966. The idea, clearly, was to make a Sauternes-style wine without having to await botrytis infection in the vineyard, which was relatively rare in California. So healthy bunches of Sémillon were picked at about 23 Brix, then laid on chicken-wire trays at the winery, and sprayed with the botrytis spores, which had been gathered from France and Germany and suspended in a spray solution until required. The grapes were then wrapped in plastic to maintain very high humidity, and cool and then warm air was wafted over them to simulate field conditions. Amazingly, it worked: the grapes shrivelled in response to the botrytis infection and sugar readings doubled. In fact the proportion of grapes attacked by the botrytis spores was close to 90 per cent, slightly higher than the proportion that ever occurs naturally in the vineyard. The grapes were pressed and the juice fermented, then chilled to arrest the fermentation.

After Nestlé took over Beringer, they were so impressed by the Nightingales' skills that they were hired to produce such wines under their own sub-label. I never much liked the wines, having tasted the 1980, 1982, 1985, 1989, and 1992 vintages. They were certainly rich, but they lacked charm and vigour. Dirk Hampson of Far Niente, which has produced a Sauternes-style wine since 1985, suspects that the chemical reaction of the botrytis spores may be different when it comes into contact with live rather than picked grapes. I much preferred Beringer's Late Harvest Rieslings, which had better acidity.[2]

Other Napa wineries began producing botrytized Sauvignons in the early 1980s. Mondavi made such a wine, but it was somewhat hot and blowsy. Rather better were the lush Chateau M from Monticello Cellars, and the intensely sweet 1982 Rutherford Gold from Cakebread. Almadén used botrytized Sauvignon from Monterey to make some melony but unexciting wines under their Charles Lefranc label in the early 1980s, and Christian Brothers made similar wines, though some of them showed vegetal tendencies that were far from attractive. Jed Steele at Kendall-Jackson produced botrytized Sauvignons in 1983, 1985, and 1989.

Phelps opted for Sémillon rather than Sauvignon Blanc for their late harvest wines in the Sauternes style. They were better known for their German-style late harvest wines, but their barrel-fermented 1985 Late Harvest Sémillon was extremely good. The main drawback of using Sémillon is that it is a loose-clustered variety rarely subjected to rampant attacks of botrytis. Chateau St Jean, which also made some sensational sweet Rieslings in the 1970s, occasionally made a wine called Sémillon d'Or (or Sauvignon d'Or). Later in the decade, in 1986 and again in 1989, Jeff Sowells in Napa Valley made some first-rate Sauternes-style wines under the Topaz label. Chalk Hill produced late harvest Sauvignons and the occasional Sémillon in 1982, 1983, 1985, 1986, and 1994. Ferrari-Carano's Eldorado Gold is a botrytized Sauvignon and Sémillon. One of the best examples of the style is undoubtedly the extremely expensive Dolce from Far Niente, which is luxuriously aged for three years in new *barriques*. Swanson also makes the occasional late harvest Sémillon, which is barrel-fermented and then aged for 27 months in new oak – a process similar to that used at Far Niente. In Paso Robles, Wild Horse make late harvest Sauvignon from time to time.

Many, perhaps most, of these Sauternes-style wines had problems with their balance. Sometimes there was insufficient residual sugar to balance the alcohol; sometimes they lacked acidity; sometimes the alcohol left a hot finish. On balance, the late harvest Rieslings from California were more consistent, better balanced. Freemark Abbey were the pioneers. In 1973 botrytis made a rare appearance in their Rutherford vineyards, and winemaker Jerry Luper was quick to exploit the situation. Beginning in 1973 Freemark Abbey made a series of wines called Edelwein (Beerenauslese style) or Edelwein Gold (Trockenbeerenauslese style). After Luper left the winery, the Edelwein style continued to be made by his successors in vintages such as 1982, 1989, and 1994. These wines were thoroughly Germanic in style, perhaps with slightly higher alcohol and slightly lower acidity than one would find in a Mosel Beerenauslese. Nonetheless they were succulent, concentrated, and cleverly made botrytis wines, lush but not inelegant.

The master of the Germanic style, without question, was Richard Arrowood at Chateau St Jean, who wrote his graduate thesis on botrytis cultures. Most of these wines were made from Riesling, but there were also some memorable Gewürztraminers from the

Belle Terre Vineyard in Alexander Valley. Arrowood never let these wines near an oak barrel, unlike his Sauternes-style wines. Chateau St Jean used a hierarchical system of labelling to indicate the sweetness and concentration level of the wine: Select Late Harvest, Special Select Late Harvest, and Individual Dried Bunch Late Harvest. Select was roughly equivalent to Auslese, Special Select to Beerenauslese, and Individual Dried Bunch Late Harvest to Trockenbeerenauslese (minimum 40 Brix). Statistics citing Brix at harvest, residual sugar, alcohol, and sometimes acidity were printed on a back label so that aficionados could keep a careful check on the structure of successive vintages. Phelps used the same system. Walter Schug began making late harvest wines in 1976 and under Craig Williams Phelps has continued to make them whenever conditions allowed. The best botrytis years of recent vintages have been 1989, 1991, 1993, and 1994. Both Williams and Arrowood relied heavily on modern technology in making these wines: the must was chilled and centrifuged both before fermentation and then later to arrest fermentation; they were also powerfully filtered to ensure no secondary fermentation occurred in bottle. Nonetheless the resulting wines were of very high quality. Perhaps because of slightly lower acidity, they tend not to keep as well as their German counterparts, which can live for decades. Sampling a TBA-style Robert Young Vineyard Riesling from Chateau St Jean about 12 years after bottling, I found the wine already mahogany-brown in colour and treacly-rich; not decaying by any means, but fully evolved and ready to drink.

Walter Schug also made some excellent late harvest Scheurebes. The 1982 was especially brilliant, a viscous wine with aromas of barley sugar and honey. Phelps also makes Eisrebe, an ice-wine style Scheurebe from frozen grapes, but I do not find it attractive.

Many Napa wineries that made late harvest Rieslings, often of very good quality, in the 1980s seem to have given up. I have fond memories of such wines from Raymond, Stags's Leap, and the defunct Christian Brothers, and disappointing notes of wines from Grgich Hills, Mondavi, Caymus, and Franciscan. Chateau Montelena made a late harvest Riesling in 1983 that was, as Bo Barrett cheerfully admitted, a complete disaster, since an aggressive cultivated yeast drove the alcohol up to almost 14 degrees, leaving very little residual sugar. Mike Grgich has also returned to the fray with an intense late harvest Riesling in 1993. Long still produce attractive wines in an Auslese style. Newlan produce a version, but I have never tasted it. I believe that Sonoma wineries such as Mark West (now under new ownership) and Clos du Bois, which used to be produce botrytized Gewürztraminer and Rieslings, no longer do so, and Felton-Empire in Santa Cruz Mountains, which in the 1980s also released excellent Gewürztraminer and Riesling, was sold years ago. Down in Monterey Bill Jekel proved a master of the style, since his Arroyo Seco Riesling vineyards were often invaded by botrytis. He liked to bottle-age the wines for a few years, so they could gain in viscosity. He first made this style in 1978, and repeated it in 1979, 1980, 1981, 1982, and 1985. Further south, in Santa Ynez Valley, Firestone used to make excellent botrytized Rieslings, that, unlike their Napa counterparts, were sold at reasonable prices. Callaway in Temecula have something of a reputation for their botrytized Chenin Blanc, which glories under the tacky name of Sweet Nancy. A curiosity from Livermore Valley is a sweet Chardonnay del Sol from Cedar Mountain Winery; and up in the Sierra Foothills Madroña have occasionally produced a late harvest Chardonnay called Chateau d'Or.

The Italian method of sweet wine production, resulting in *passito* wines, is very rare in California. The idea is to pick very ripe but healthy (that is, not botrytis-infected) grapes, which are then left to dry either in the sun or in trays in well-aerated attics until their sugar content has increased. Stony Hill used to produce tiny quantities of a wine they called Sémillon de Soleil (twenty-two cases in one recent vintage!) using this method. John Alban has made a straw wine from Roussanne, and in 1986 Randall Grahm made one from Muscat Canelli, but it turned out coarse and hot.

Muscats

Muscats come in all shapes and sizes in California, from ultra-delicate to thick and sweet. The best wines are made from Muscat Blanc (also known as Muscat Canelli and Muscat de Frontignan). The more widely planted Muscat of Alexandria, primarily a raisin grape in California, gives rather fat, coarse wines.

The primary appeal of Muscat is its rich grapy, orangey aroma, which seems present even in the most poorly vinified examples. It is far more difficult to produce a well balanced Muscat that isn't overly sweet and cloying. I have never been a fan of Beaulieu's

Muscat de Frontignan, much preferring the (extinct) Chateau La Salle from Christian Brothers. Another good Napa Muscat Canelli comes from Robert Pecota in Calistoga, and a powerful Moscato Frontignan from Teldeschi in Dry Creek Valley, Sonoma. In the Sierra Foothills, Leon Sobon at Shenandoah makes an appealing Orange Muscat and an even better, more peppery Black Muscat. Gary Eberle's Muscat Canelli from Paso Robles is very charming.

Some Muscats are made in an appealing *pétillant* style. Louis Martini built up a tremendous reputation for his Moscato Amabile. Apparently the style was devised by accident, when some Muscat of Alexandria was left undisturbed over the winter and found to be fermenting in barrel in the spring. It was then made commercially by fermenting at very cold temperatures for a very long period, and bottled under pressure as a sweet *frizzante* wine with about 7 degrees of alcohol. As the wine is not properly stabilized it had to be stored under refrigeration. For some years Robert Mondavi made a delicate little number he labelled Moscato d'Oro, in a Moscato d'Asti style without the flair.

From his unlikely base in the Central Valley Andrew Quady has had a tremendous success with his Essensia, made from Orange Muscat grapes, their fermentation arrested by what the French call *mutage*, slinging in some grape spirit which boosts the alcohol and leaves residual sugar in the wine. Quady picks his grapes very early to keep their delicacy of flavour, and fortifies to about 15 degrees. He makes a similar wine called Electra, which is lower in alcohol.

Equally successful has been his Elysium, a purple Black Muscat with the loveliest nose redolent of roses. Philip Togni uses the same grape, which he calls Black Hamburger, to make his intensely aromatic and concentrated Ca' Togni. Other Black Muscats are produced by Gan Eden, whose version is unfortified and thus lower in alcohol; by Topolos at Russian River; and by Rosenblum, which is fortified to 16.8 degrees. The grapes for both Gan Eden and Rosenblum come from the Gallagher Vineyard in Madera.

Late Harvest Zinfandel

The first commercially available late harvest Zinfandel was made by mistake at Mayacamas, as has already been explained in the chapter on Zinfandel. One suspects that late harvest Zinfandels were routinely made by mistake by careless growers, but Bob

Travers was the first winemaker to be brazen enough to bottle it and sell it at a high price. Still, they were wonderful wines, if not as long-lived as first seemed likely. In some ways they were reminiscent of Recioto from Italy, being unfortified yet high in alcohol, and usually balanced with a dash of sweetness. A great Recioto should be elegant as well as concentrated, but elegance is a bit much to ask of Zinfandel, especially when picked at 35 Brix.

There used to be plenty of them around at wineries that no longer produce them. I have sampled late harvest Zinfandels from Calera and Mount Veeder, both of which have retired from that field, but I'm pleased to record that the ultra-refined Paul Draper still produces occasional Zin Essences. The last vintage for this remarkable wine was 1993.

'Sherry'

California is no more capable of producing sherry than any other country where the protective layer of yeast known in Spain as *flor* is incapable of development. But during the decades when fortified wines dominated the domestic market, a good deal of 'sherry' was produced, with Palomino the principal grape for drier styles and Pedro Ximenez the main grape for sweeter styles. Mission used to be used, and even Thompson Seedless. Almost all 'sherries' are produced in the hot Central Valley, and a handful of the better producers employ a solera system, which at least gives the wines a certain consistency. Given the absence of *flor*, dry styles are rare, and the majority of California 'sherries' are modelled on Cream sherries. Artificial yeast induction can be used to imitate the flavour of *flor*. In order to simulate the oxidation and 'nuttiness' of authentic sherry, the newly made wine is heated to 100–140F (38–60C) for three to twelve months. Heating coils are the most common way of maintaining the temperature. This method is, of course, more akin to Madeira than to sherry production. Producers include Louis Martini, Gallo, Papagni and Sebastiani.

'Ports'

Most so-called ports produced in California are simply sweet red jug wines of no distinction. However, a handful of wineries have made serious attempts to emulate the authentic style of a port wine. A number of winemakers, especially in the Sierra Foothills, have had reasonable success with Zinfandel ports, but port-style wines made from Portuguese grape varieties are rare. Some of the very best come from Ficklin in the Central Valley. The 40 acres of vines were planted in 1946 with cuttings of Tinta Madeira, Touriga, Tinta Cão, and Souzao. Fermentation is arrested with grape brandy and the wine is aged in American oak. The nonvintage style is made in a solera system, and in 1995 Ficklin released a good 10-year-old tawny, also aged in American oak. Ficklin's pride and joy is the vintage wine, made mostly from Tinta Madeira, and produced in roughly one year out of three.

Andrew Quady also makes port-style wines, but his grapes come from Frank's Vineyard in Amador County. These wines are made from Portuguese varieties planted in 1978, although Quady also makes 'port' from Zinfandel. The vintage and the Late Bottled Vintage style usually come from Frank's Vineyard. The bottling known as Starboard – Batch 88 is made mostly from Tinta Roriz, but also from Tinta Cão and Amarela. Quady's ports can be delicious but taste sweeter than the Ficklin range and seem to have less tannin and extract.

In Lodi Tim Spencer of St Amant releases a range of 'ports' to rival Ficklin's. Spencer has been growing Portuguese varieties since the 1970s, but has recently had to replant the vineyards after phylloxera. He is also working on a 10-year tawny from 60 per cent Bastardo, with a strong fruit character and a spirity finish; but it lacks tawny character. Spencer also makes a vintage 'port' from Amador County grapes, and a less impressive Late Bottled Vintage.

The vast Mondavi winery at Woodbridge produces 'ports' made from the mostly Portuguese varieties that were planted for this purpose in 1988. The first vintage was 1993, and the wine was aged in French and American oak for two years, then aged a further year in bottle before being released. Heitz has planted some port varieties on Howell Mountain and makes an impressive vintage-dated wine, lush and peppery. He also makes a lighter, more delicate style from Grignolino, which is surprisingly successful.

Leon Sobon at Shenandoah is more eclectic when it comes to blending his 'ports'. In 1979 they were pure Zinfandel, but nowadays they are likely to include Cabernet Sauvignon or Tinta Cão as well. His favoured style is a crusting 'port' that is quite intense if not very complex, and the version bottled in 1996 was made from Zinfandel, Tinta Cão, Souzao, Cabernet Sauvignon, and Touriga, aged in mostly American oak. Renwood age their excellent 'port', made from Portuguese varieties, in *barriques* for 26 months. The Sonora Winery & Port Works uses only Portuguese varieties.

Very little port-style wine is made in the more prestigious wine regions, but Clos Pegase in Calistoga produces small quantities from fifty-year-old Petite Sirah vines. In Sonoma, J. W. Morris has long specialized in port-style wines, and Trentadue make port from both Petite Sirah and, surprisingly, Merlot. In 1996 Richard Mendelson made a 'white port' from late-harvested Pinot Gris, fermented to 16 degrees before the addition of brandy, and aged in *barriques*; production is tiny.

Kosher wines

Kosher wines used to be ultra-sweet treacly blends that were scarcely drinkable. Since the early 1980s excellent kosher table wines have been available from a handful of specialist wineries in California. The pioneer was Ernie Weir of Hagafen Cellars, which he established in Napa in 1979. It specializes in Riesling, a white Pinot Noir, and two blends, red and white, called Harmonia. The large St Supéry winery in Napa, which is owned by the Skalli family from southern France, also has a range of kosher wines, a Cabernet Sauvignon and a Chardonnay. Robert Weinstock founded Weinstock Cellars in the mid-1980s, and the most highly reputed of all the kosher wineries is Gan Eden in Sonoma).

NOTES

1 Leon Adams, *Wines of America*, p. 351
2 Stephen Brook, *Liquid Gold*, pp. 296–319

Gazetteer

Within this capacious gazetteer, the amount of space and attention devoted to a winery is not necessarily an indication of merit. Some wineries are simply more interesting than others. I have deliberately made this a personal account, and as a consequence some injustices may have been done, especially to wineries that have been given shorter shrift than they deserved. Nonetheless I hope the following listing will be of use and interest. I have deliberately eschewed tasting notes and scores. Those who want to find precise assessments of individual wines can easily turn to the hundreds of pages consecrated to this pursuit by James Laube, Robert Parker, and innumerable American-based wine magazines.

The reader is reminded that Napa and Sonoma have two sections each. Inclusion in the first section of each simply means that I wish, for a variety of reasons, to give more detailed treatment to a particular winery. This should not be regarded as an A list and a B list; the reader will find some first-rate wineries discussed in the short-entry section.

22

Napa Valley 1

Araujo
155 Pickett Rd., Calistoga, CA 94515. Tel: 707 942 6061[1]. Fax: 942 6471. Production: 4,000 cases.

This is not so much a winery as a vineyard, made famous for its Cabernet Sauvignon by Ridge and Phelps. There is evidence that grapes have been growing here for a century or more. The soil is rocky and well-drained. Cabernet was planted here in 1964, and, along with Montebello and Martha's Vineyard, it was one of the first vineyards to be identified on the label. Before the vineyard was bought by Milt and Barbara Eisele in 1969, its grapes were sold to the local cooperative, which meant they ended up in one of Gallo's jug blends. However, Ridge bought the grapes in 1971 and made a wine that is still drinking well. In 1972 and 1973 the grapes were sold to Mondavi, but presumably blended into its Cabernet releases. In 1975 the Eiseles entered into a long-term arrangement with Phelps, who used the grapes for their Insignia and for their Eisele Vineyard Cabernet.

In 1989 the Eiseles sold the estate for almost $3 million, and the following year it was sold again to Bart and Daphne Araujo. The dapper Bart Araujo was in the house-building business until he caught the wine bug. Initially the Araujos only wanted to grow grapes and sell them, but in 1991 they both sold their last crop to Phelps and produced their first wine. They hired David Abreu to care for the vineyards and Tony Soter to act as consultant winemaker. Since 1996 the wine has been made by Soter's protégée Françoise Peschon.

Soter and Abreu made some changes in the vineyard, adding Cabernet Franc and Petit Verdot, and Sauvignon Blanc (Musqué clone), Viognier, and Syrah were also planted. Twenty-four acres of the 36-acre estate were replanted with Cabernet in the early 1990s, using close spacing.

The estate practises severe selection. There is no second label, but one-third of the wine is sold off in bulk each year to ensure exceptional quality and judicious balance in the final blend. The barrels are French, from a variety of coopers, and 80 per cent new. The superb 1994 was aged for

345

22 months, and bottled without fining. It is of quite exceptional quality, beautifully textured, and with powerful tones of chocolate and black olives. The 1995 is equally fine.

The brambly 1994 Syrah, blended with a little Viognier and aged in 60 per cent new oak, has won enormous acclaim, but I find the wine over-oaked and almost cloying, unlike the Cabernet. The 1995, however, is magnificent.

Like the Spottswoode Sauvignon Blanc, the melony Eisele version is mostly fermented and aged in steel drums, with only 20 per cent fermented in new *barriques*. There is no malolactic fermentation. The 1997 Viognier, not available commercially, lacked aroma and was rather heavy.

In 1995 Araujo produced 2,700 cases of Cabernet and 350 of Syrah, and the following year the production of Sauvignon was 550 cases. Bart Araujo believes the estate's maximum production will be 4,000 cases. Prices for the Cabernet are high at $60, but the wine is eagerly sought after and very hard to find.

Beringer

2000 Main Street, St Helena, CA 94574. Tel: 963 7115. Fax: 963 1735. Production: 3.6 million cases.

Founded in the 1870s by the German-born Beringer brothers, the property remained in the hands of the family until the 1970s, and it is the oldest winery in Napa to be in continuous operation since its first vintage. It survived Prohibition by producing sacramental wines, but by the 1960s it was turning out mediocre wines without vintage dates, as well as jug wines. In 1971 it was acquired by Nestlé, who hired Myron Nightingale as winemaker. His first task was to clean up the wineries and the wines, which were prone to bacterial infection. He and his wife Alice pioneered the production of artificially induced botrytis wines, which are still made from time to time at Beringer. They were celebrated wines, though I usually preferred the racy late harvest Rieslings. In 1984 the present winemaker Ed Sbragia, who began as Nightingale's assistant, became chief winemaker and is still very much at the helm, aided by the longstanding vineyard manager Bob Steinhauer. Sbragia has maintained a high quality of wine-making, and created a top layer of outstanding Private Reserves.

In the 1990s the estate was bought by a partnership headed by Beringer's former president, Michael Moone. Now named Beringer Estates, the company also owns Meridian, St Andrews, Chateau St Jean and other prestigious properties. The vineyard holdings are colossal, and Beringer owns 1,782 acres in Napa, 596 in Knights Valley, and 122 in Carneros. Large vineyards elsewhere in the state brings the company's holdings up to 8,500 acres.

In 1985 Beringer excited considerable controversy when they created a subsidiary winery called Napa Ridge. Although the name encourages the belief that the wines under this label are from Napa fruit, the grapes come from all over the place and are vinified in Sonoma. Production is well over 1 million cases.

The range is vast. Beringer produce enormous quantities of Chenin Blanc and White Zinfandel. The better whites include a Fumé Blanc, which is mostly barrel-fermented, and a Sauvignon Blanc from Napa and Knights Valley fruit. The Napa Chardonnay is subjected to full malolactic fermentation. All these wines, with county or North Coast appellations, have recently been re-packaged as the Appellation Collection. There is a Graves-style Meritage called Alluvium, aged in 40 per cent new Nevers *barriques*; dashes of Chardonnay and Viognier are added to the blend. The standard Chardonnay is fermented in 20 per cent new *barriques*, and the fruit often comes from Oakville vineyards. Beringer's best-known white is the Private Reserve Chardonnay. The sourcing of the grapes varies from year to year; in 1995 45 per cent of the fruit came from Yountville vineyards. The must is fermented in mostly new Nevers barrels and is aged for about 9 months. It is made in a full-blown Californian style and exhibits rich oak influence, but I can't help finding it often tastes obvious and flat-footed. Of similar quality is the powerful Chardonnay labelled as Sbragia Limited Release.

Beringer produce three Cabernets: one from Knights Valley fruit, and another from Napa Valley. The Private Reserve, surely the best and most consistent wine in the Beringer range, draws its grapes from a number of sources: State Lane Vineyard near Yountville, the estate's home ranch low on Spring Mountain and near the winery, the Chabot Vineyard off Silverado Trail, and the Bancroft Ranch on Howell Mountain. First made in 1977, it was revamped in 1985, since when the wine has been aged entirely in new oak. The greatest vintages include 1980, 1982, 1984, 1985, 1987, 1991, and 1994. The Bancroft Ranch is also the source for the superb Howell Mountain Merlot.

The very reliable Zinfandel is aged for about 18 months in American and French oak. There is also a silky, sensuous red Meritage, Alluvium, made from Knights Valley fruit and aged for two years in mostly Nevers barriques. It has been a long time since Beringer produced Pinot Noir, but it returned to the fray in 1996 with a bottling from Stanly Ranch in Carneros.

The most basic, large-volume wines are bottled under the California appellation.

Cain

3800 Langtry Rd., St Helena, CA 94574. Tel: 963 1616. Fax: 963 7952. Production: 20,000 cases.

There are few more spectacular sites in California than these magnificent terraced vineyards 2,000 feet up on Spring Mountain. The estate was created by Jerry Cain in 1980 on the site of the former McCormick Ranch, and the winery was constructed in 1985, but in 1991 he was bought out by his partners Jim and Nancy Meadlock, who own a computer company. The winemaker, Christopher Howell, was trained at Montpellier, worked at Mouton-Rothschild, Clos Pegase, and Peter Michael, and is one of the most thoughtful and experienced of Napa winemakers. He has been in charge here since 1990.

The 84 acres up here are planted with the five Bordeaux red varieties, which make up the principal wine Cain Five, first made in 1985. The different exposures of the terraced vineyards mean that there is considerable variation between parcels. Soils are thin, mostly weathered sandstone and shale, and drainage is excellent. Pesticides and herbicides are kept to an absolute minimum. Howell is not entirely happy with the original layout and is introducing some modifications which he hopes will further improve the fruit quality. A little Sauvignon Blanc and Syrah have also been planted.

Each of the five Bordeaux varieties is vinified separately, and after a long maceration, the wines are aged in *barriques* for 3 months before the final blend is made up. Malolactic fermentation takes place in barrel. The 1994 vintage was aged for 22 months in 75 per cent new *barriques*. This wine is composed of 64 per cent Cabernet, 24 per cent Merlot, 6 per cent Cabernet Franc, 4 per cent Malbec, and 1 per cent Petit Verdot. It's concentrated, chocolatey, and powerfully structured.

Up to half the wine is eliminated from the final blend, and this is the basis of the second label Cain Cuvée, which was introduced in 1991. Howell insists that this is not a dumping ground for greener, meaner wines, but a wine that offers a softer and more accessible style than Cain Five. Grapes destined from the start for the Cuvée are given a shorter maceration and barrel ageing than those likely to be included in Cain Five.

The estate's Merlot and Chardonnay were phased out in 1991, but Howell continues to produce Cain Musqué, a plump, barrel-fermented Sauvignon made from fruit purchased from the Ventana Vineyard in Monterey.

Chateau Montelena

1429 Tubbs Lane, Calistoga, CA 94515. Tel: 942 5105. Fax: 942 4221. Production: 35,000 cases.

This long-established Calistoga estate was founded in 1882 by Alfred Tubbs, a rope merchant from San Francisco. First he planted the vineyards, then constructed the winery with its mostly underground cellars. The first winemaker, Jerome Bardot, came from France, and under Tubbs and Bardot the winery became one of the most important in Napa Valley.

Prohibition brought an end to winemaking here, and in 1958 the Tubbs family sold the estate to Yort Frank. He and his wife Jeannie used the chateau as a retirement home, and they were responsible for the landscaping of the grounds. In 1968 Leland Paschich bought the estate and brought in partners, including a lawyer called James Barrett.

The vineyards were replanted and the winery restored, and the first vintage was the 1972, made from purchased grapes. Chateau Montelena had a succession of celebrated winemakers, including Mike Grgich, who made the Chardonnay that dazzled the Paris tasters in 1976, Jerry Luper, and since 1981, James Barrett's son Bo. When I first met Bo Barrett in the mid-1980s he looked like a beach bum, but he was making some delicious wines. 'My dad was a lawyer, I was a surfer,' he admitted.

Some 81 acres of the property's vineyards are planted with Cabernet Sauvignon, half of them on alluvial gravel beds, as well as some Zinfandel and Cabernet Franc. There are two clones of Chardonnay planted, the familiar 108 and the Stony Hill clone. There used to be two Chardonnays here, but in 1990 the one from Alexander Valley fruit was phased out. The Chardonnay has always been made in a fairly lean style. There is no skin contact, and the juice is fermented in steel without malolactic fermentation before being aged in *barriques* for 6 to 12 months. Only 10 per cent of the wood is new, as Barrett doesn't want strong oak influence, preferring the wine to retain its crispness. After the heavy-handedness of so much California Chardonnay, I find the style refreshing.

But it's the Cabernet Sauvignon that is the great wine of Montelena. Yields here are low at 3 tons per acre, and fruit from different blocks of the vineyard is vinified separately. No press wine is used. The malolactic takes place in larger oak vats, and then the wine is aged in *barriques* for up to 2 years. Only about 20 per cent new oak is used. The wine is bottle-aged for one and a half years before release, which usually takes place some four years after the vintage. It's a sumptuous wine, dark and brooding, and in good vintages capable of evolving for twenty years or more. Among older vintages I have tasted, 1974, 1976, and 1980 were all great.

Since the Cabernet is relatively expensive ($40 from the winery), although a snip compared to the prices of some Napa Cabernets, Chateau Montelena has had the good idea of offering a wine known as Calistoga Cuvée, which is made from purchased Calistoga fruit, mostly Cabernet Sauvignon. Bo Barrett explains that a local cooperative went out of business in 1991, so the cuvée was devised to use some of their excellent grapes. The blend is aged for up to 16 months in oak.

Chateau Montelena also produces Zinfandel, very good at its best but not always consistent, and in 1990 planted some low-yield Sangiovese. The range is completed with a little Riesling from Potter Valley fruit.

Although demand exceeds supply, Barrett has no intention of increasing production.

Clos Pegase
1060 Dunweal Lane, Calistoga, CA 94515. Tel: 942 4981. Fax: 942 4993. Production: 50,000 cases.

Clos Pegase is not just a winery; it's a phenomenon. It was founded by Jan Shrem, who was born in Colombia in 1930 and raised in Jerusalem. After the war he came to the United States, began by selling encyclopedias, and eventually became a publisher, moving to Japan where he made his fortune selling technical books in English. With his Japanese wife he moved to France, where he began collecting modern art. Interested in wine, he went to Bordeaux to study oenology, but gave up on the idea of finding an estate in Bordeaux, and was put in touch with André Tchelitscheff. In 1983 he bought an estate near Calistoga, which appealed to him as it was possible to build a wine cave into an adjacent knoll (and subsequently to build a luxurious modern house on top of the knoll).

Shrem had always been keen on modern architecture, so he decided to launch an architectural competition for his new winery. There were ninety-six entries and the winning one came from Princeton architect Michael Graves. As the mighty buildings rose from their foundations, some of the neighbours looked on with horror. Built in a style that seems partly Minoan, partly Egyptian, with stumpy earth-coloured columns forming the porticoes to the peach-hued building, it was certainly distinctive. To this day it divides visitors. I love Clos Pegase; others compare it to a waste disposal unit. One neighbour even began a law suit, which delayed completion of the buildings. Finally, in 1987, they were ready. Shrem filled the winery and his offices with his outstanding collection of modern art, and scattered his modern sculpture collection on the lawns around the winery. The building cost a fortune to construct, but Shrem ensured its running costs were low.

Shrem had his winery, but didn't have much wine. Tchelitscheff was the consultant during the mid-1980s and counselled Shrem to focus on lean, elegant wines rather than Calistoga blockbusters. They hired the laconic Bill Pease as winemaker. Early Chardonnays were fermented in steel tanks, a method later abandoned. Two Sauvignon wines were made in the 1980s, but when phylloxera struck the vineyards, the variety was given up and not replanted. Shrem, and his current winemaker Stephen Rogstad, now focus on Cabernet Sauvignon, Merlot, and Chardonnay.

In addition to the 47 acres of vines around the winery, there are 42 acres planted at the Pallisades Vineyard in Calistoga and the 365-acre Mitsuko's Vineyard in Carneros. By 1997 the estate was growing all the fruit it needed and was selling the surplus to other wineries. Current

Chardonnays are made with whole-cluster pressing, barrel fermentation, often with natural yeasts, and full malolactic fermentation. The wine is aged on the fine lees for 10 months in 90 per cent French oak. The Cabernet Sauvignon comes from Mitsuko's Vineyard and from Pallisades Vineyard, and is aged in oak for up to 20 months. The top wine is the Hommage Artist series, in effect a Reserve Cabernet aged for 2 years in *barriques*. A tiny quantity of port is made from Petite Sirah.

The wines of the 1990s are far superior to the rather hollow ones made during the first vintages. There is a sense that Jan Shrem, who is extremely sure-footed when it comes to art and architecture, not to mention publishing, is still not entirely clear about the direction in which he wants to take his winery. The choices he has made have been sound but less adventurous and courageous than his taste in architecture.

Diamond Creek

1500 Diamond Mountain Rd., Calistoga, CA 94515. Tel: 942 6926. Fax: 942 6936. Production: 3,000 cases.

Great wines are often made by accident. Al Brounstein became interested in wine when working as a sales representative for Sebastiani. He started looking for land in Napa on which to plant Cabernet Sauvignon. He talked to experts such as Jack Davies, André Tchelitscheff and Dick Steltzner. He found this steep hillside property and his advisers were sure it had the potential to make very good wine. Brounstein bought it in 1968 and cleared the land. It was only then that he noticed that there seemed to be three distinct soil types, reflected in the names he gave these parcels: Volcanic Hill, Red Rock Terrace, and Gravelly Meadow. The budwood he planted came directly from Bordeaux. 'I had my own plane at the time, and used to fly my girlfriends down to Tijuana from time to time. The customs people thought I was just a roué out for a good time, which is what I wanted them to think. But for me the flights were strictly business.' So somehow the budwood made its way from Bordeaux to Diamond Creek. Fortunately the vineyards have remained healthy, so no damage was done by illegally importing his vines.

Jerry Luper was hired as winemaker, and kept an eye on twenty successive vintages, beginning in 1972. The wines were well thought of, but it took Al Brounstein fifteen years to show a profit.

Al Brounstein is a compulsive landscaper, and although now in his late seventies and afflicted with Parkinson's disease, he is still planning and building. His latest project is a pump-operated waterfall. From the fish pond in the heart of the estate one can see all the vineyards: the 8 acres of Volcanic Hill, the 7 of Red Rock Terrace, and 5 of Gravelly Meadow, and the 0.75 acre of the rarest *cru* of them all, Lake. These vineyards have very different elevations and exposures, and Brounstein captures their different personalities by harvesting row by row over a period that can last up to two months. The vines – 88 per cent Cabernet, 8 per cent Merlot, 4 per cent Cabernet Franc, and recently a little Petit Verdot to disturb these proportions – are planted on St George rootstocks, so phylloxera hasn't proved a problem; yields average 3 tons per acre.

Red Rock Terrace is steep and north-facing, with the most significant iron content; it gives comparatively forward, fruity, and elegant wines. Volcanic Hill faces south, has volcanic ash in the soil, is well drained, and often gives the most dense and powerful wines. Gravelly Meadow faces east, has rockier soil, and often gives harder, earthier wines that are long-lived. Sometimes the creek floods and deposits more gravel on the soil. There's a perceptible afternoon breeze coursing over Lake Vineyard, and there are years when the grapes don't ripen properly; in such vintages the wine is blended in with Gravelly Meadow. The Lake berries are the smallest, and when they ripen they give the finest wine of all, with very intense flavours. Quantities from Lake Vineyard are minuscule: no more than 150 cases, which explains the price tag of $300, whereas the other bottlings are a mere $75. Occasionally, Brounstein will subdivide the property into even smaller units, bottling separately what he calls Microclimate wines, as he did in 1991 and 1994.

The winemaking is rudimentary. Diamond Creek still uses an old hydraulic (or vertical) press and the juice is fermented in small open wood fermenters. Al Brounstein says the indigenous yeasts here are unpredictable, so they do inoculate. The cap is punched down by hand, and the wine is aged 18 to 22 months in *barriques*, mostly from Nevers. New oak is kept to a maximum of 50 per cent. Fining and filtration are rare. All four *crus* are made in the same way.

These have always been burly tannic wines of great intensity, and Brounstein admits that early vintages needed twenty years to come round. The 1990s, in my limited experience, are fleshier and more accessible, and none the worse for it. Brounstein insists that the winemaking hasn't changed; it's just that the vines are older. Some of the wines from the 1970s are still going strong, notably 1974 and 1978; there were some leaner, slightly herbaceous wines in the 1980s, but the 1990s seem to have lifted the overall quality to a new plane of excellence and complexity.

Dominus

PO Box 3327, Yountville, CA 94599. Tel: 944 8954. Fax: 944 0547. Production: 10,000 cases.

What happens when Mr Pomerol comes to Napa Valley? Like Philippe de Rothschild, Christian Moueix was intrigued by the challenge of California, well aware of its extraordinary potential but not quite sure how to exploit it. The heart of the Dominus wine is the fruit from the famous Napanook

Vineyard. This had long been part of the Inglenook estate, but had been retained by John Daniel, and then inherited by his daughters Robin Lail and Marcia Smith, after the sale of the estate. It was Robert Mondavi who put the daughters in touch with Christian Moueix, who came to Yountville to inspect the vineyard in 1981. In 1982 they set up a partner-ship, until in 1995 the Daniel daughters sold their shares to Moueix, who is now sole proprietor.

Of course Moueix knew full well that the 108-acre Napanook was nothing like Pétrus, or anywhere in Pomerol for that matter. The soil was gravelly clay loam, remote from the heavy clay soil of Pétrus. Nor was Merlot the dominant variety. Napanook was 75 per cent Cabernet Sauvignon, now decreased to about 60 per cent. There was Chardonnay too, but that was sold off and eventually removed and replaced by red varieties. St George rootstocks had ensured that the vines survived phyl-loxera. The soil is vigorous and although at first Moueix tried to curtail yields drastically, he later realized that fighting the vines wasn't getting the results he wanted, so he now accepts slightly higher yields. He has adopted a split canopy and avoids irrigating the vineyard.

The wine is aged in one-third new oak, as well as old barrels from illustrious châteaux such as Cheval Blanc, Trotanoy, and Pétrus itself. After 15 months the wine is fined and sometimes filtered. 1983 was the first vintage made solely from Napanook grapes.

The first vintages of Dominus were distinctly tough, even hard. But there was a breakthrough with the 1991 vintage, which was superb. At last the intensity of fruit, the curranty richness, the harmonious oak, were all present in the wine, which lacked the astringency of some earlier vintages. The 1993 was declassified by Moueix, but the 1994 was on a par with the 1991, and although 1995 was a shade light, 1996 and 1997 are apparently back on form. In my view, of the two great Bordelais wines in Napa, Opus One was the clear leader in the 1980s, but with the 1990s I am no longer so sure, and it seems that Dominus is at last emerging as the more complex of the two. Not as sleek, perhaps, but with a massive richness that seems truly Californian. It will be fascinating to see the future vintages that will emerge from the remarkable new winery that was built behind the vineyard in 1997 by the Swiss architects Jacques Herzog and Pierre de Meuron.

Dunn

805 White Cottage Rd., Angwin, CA 94508. Tel: 965 3642. Fax: 965 3805. Production: 4,000 cases.

Angwin on Howell Mountain is home to a community of Seventh Day Adventists. What they make of all that pernicious winemaking activity all around them I cannot imagine. Randy Dunn, for many years the winemaker at Caymus, set up his own winery at his rural home. When I first met him, he was standing alongside a mobile bottling line, keeping an eye on his precious Howell Mountain Cabernet as it made the journey from blending tank to bottle. With his beard and twangy voice, he looked more like a woodsman than one of Napa's most skilled winemakers. Ten years later he looked much the same, only his hair had whitened and the beard had gone. A wine tunnel had been built in 1989 for his barrels. With its constant temperature of 57 degrees and natural humidity, the wine tunnel is his pride and joy.

His first vintage was 1979, and yielded 500 cases. He has gradually expanded his vineyard holdings, and has bought the Park Muscadine Vineyard, which Ridge used to lease. He sells some of his grapes and buys in others, ensuring he has the right kind of fruit for his two wines, the Napa Cabernet and the Howell Mountain Cabernet. He attributes the special quality of the latter to the special quality of the fruit up here, high above the fog line. He is happy with his spacing of 1,000 vines per acre, and has average yields of 2.5 tons per acre, although he feels he could accept 4 tons without any loss of quality. He has deliberately planted a range of rootstocks and clones, as a kind of insurance policy.

The winemaking is straightforward. Dunn destems and crushes, then inoculates yeasts. He is not a believer in extended maceration precisely because he doesn't want a wine that's too soft and accessible in its youth; he also lacks the tank space. The wine is aged two and a half years in French oak, of which about 40 per cent is new. He filters but never fines. There is more Howell Mountain fruit in the Napa bottling these days, so there is less difference between the two Cabernets than there used to be. They are wines for the patient, and although the massive dense fruitiness of a young Dunn Cabernet is a wonderful taste sensation, the wine is even better after ten years, when it has acquired magisterial complexity. Although demand is substantial, Dunn refuses to expand, as he and his wife Lori want to retain control over every aspect of the winemaking process. The wine is expensive – about $45 for the Howell Mountain – but Dunn has an enviable track record for these hugely concentrated wines and his legions of admirers are never disappointed.

Forman

1501 Big Rock Rd., St Helena, CA 94574. Tel: 963 0234. Fax: 963 5384. Production: 4,000 cases.

Ric Forman is a courteous, studious man without the boisterousness and rough edges of so many Californian winemakers. He looks too young to be one of the most experienced men of wine in America. He worked harvests at Stony Hill, and became winemaker at Sterling in 1969. He then went into business with Peter Newton on Spring Mountain, but the two men seem to have had a falling out. In 1983 Forman went off to start up his own winery. Its aims, like those of Dunn, have always been modest: to produce a small quantity of excellent wine to the most exacting standards. Forman only makes Chardonnay and Cabernet Sauvignon.

His 65 acres of vineyards are on the lower slopes of Howell Mountain at about 1,400 feet as well as elsewhere in Napa. Much of the fruit is sold to other wineries. Replanting after phylloxera, he opted for very tight spacing of the Bordeaux varieties. His first plantings of Chardonnay were of a large-clustered clone that he always knew was far from ideal; it is being replaced with small-clustered Dijon clone. Forman marvels at the soil here, which he describes as bottomless gravel. These Howell Mountain sites are dry-farmed. Forman's Cabernet is among the most Bordeaux-like in Napa, and I suspect he would attribute this to the soil rather than to any winemaking techniques.

Along with Richard Graff of Chalone, Ric Forman was a pioneer of barrel fermentation for Chardonnay in California. He inoculates with Montrachet yeast and blocks the malolactic fermentation, as he says it doesn't seem appropriate for his fruit. The wine is aged for 9 months in Burgundian oak, 50 per cent new, and the lees are stirred. Forman's is not a Chardonnay for immediate consumption; it is best broached after about 3 years in bottle. Forman is an admirer of Meursault, but the wine's restraint and elegance is sometimes more reminiscent of Chablis.

In the claret-like Cabernet, Forman quite likes the occasional herbaceousness of the Merlot he blends in, and the peppery tannin of the Petit Verdot, which he planted in 1988. The wine is aged in his humid wine tunnel for about 20 months in 80 per cent new oak. This is always an elegant wine, understated, shapely, discreet.

Some years ago I asked Forman why he stuck to just two grape varieties. He replied that if he were to make Zinfandel, for example, the costs of production would be equally high, but he could never demand the price for a Zinfandel or a Rhône varietal that he can get for Chardonnay or Cabernet. With yields rarely exceeding 3 tons per acre, he needs to price his wines expensively just to break even. He could produce more, but that would mean relinquishing his self-reliance, which he values. Visiting him again eight years later, nothing had changed. Ric Forman is certainly true to himself.

Frog's Leap
8815 Conn Creek Rd., Rutherford, CA 94573. Tel: 963 4704. Fax: 963 0242. Production: 50,000 cases.

John Williams arrived in Napa Valley as a young man and, unable to afford the two dollars needed to camp in the nearest state park, pitched a tent on land that turned out to belong to a doctor called Larry Turley.

They shared a bottle of Zinfandel that John happened to have with him, and the two men became firm friends. They made the ultimate sacrifice, selling their motorbikes in order to raise the money to start a winery together. That original winery was attached to Larry's home, and as it had been a frog-raising farm in the nineteenth century (price: 33 cents per dozen), it wasn't difficult for the partners to choose a name for their venture. Their first release was in 1981. The cramped winery became a favourite port of call for wine insiders, thanks to the relaxed atmosphere that prevailed there. But it was also obvious that the winery was turning out some delicious wines. By 1988 the farming practices were virtually organic, which, John is convinced, help their vines to resist phylloxera; fertilizers encourage the root to remain closer to the surface of the soil, where they are more susceptible to phylloxera attacks. Organic farming also helps prolong the active life of the vines.

By 1994 the winery was outgrowing the space available. John and Larry decided to go their separate ways and split the company between them. Turley set up his eponymous winery, initially assisted by his sister Helen, and John acquired the Red Barn in Rutherford, the site of the Adamson Winery in the late nineteenth century. Here at last Frog's Leap has the space it needs. There are 34 acres of vineyards around the barn, and 35 more on the Rutherford Bench planted with Cabernet Sauvignon and Zinfandel. But most of the fruit is purchased.

John Williams does not share the fetish for mountain fruit. He admits that he is trying to make wines that are supple and harmonious. When he is criticized for his 'drinkable' style, he responds with mock astonishment that it hadn't occurred to him that wines were meant to be drunk. Nonetheless his wines are usually so well balanced that they age perfectly well, although 1984 proved a disappointment over the long term. Indeed, this stylistic preference on John's part was one of the reasons why the partnership was dissolved. Larry Turley, as his own wines have demonstrated, likes a powerful burly style quite different from John's.

The whites are whole-cluster pressed and no cultivated yeasts are used. The Sauvignon Blanc, which accounts for a substantial part of the production, is mostly tank-fermented and goes through partial malolactic, whereas the Chardonnay is fully malolactic. The Chardonnay is fermented in Burgundian oak for about 10 months with just a little lees-stirring.

John Williams favours long macerations for his reds, which may account for their accessibility when young. The Cabernet is aged in *barriques* for about 20 months, and Zinfandel for about a year in American as well as French oak. He is still fine-tuning the ageing of the Merlot. New oak comprises about one-third of the barrels and there is no filtration. All three wines are delicious, though if I had to ditch one, it would be the

Merlot, which Frog's Leap introduced only in 1990, using fruit from Carneros and Napa.

Williams and Turley had fun in 1986, when there was botrytis on Sauvignon and Sémillon. They picked the grapes at 39 Brix and barrel-fermented the juice. Unfortunately there was too much alcohol (16.5%!) and insufficient residual sugar, so they adjusted the wine by adding Sémillon Süssreserve. Somehow it worked, though it lacked some concentration. The wine, called Late Leap, was made again in 1989 and 1993. The label, with its crowned leaping frog, pays homage to Yquem, which fortunately is too grand to sue. In 1997 a new wine was launched: Liebfrögsmilch. It carried an old-style Germanic label and was a blend of Chenin Blanc and Riesling.

Frog's Leap may not be among the very greatest California wineries, but what it does, it does supremely well. It offers stylish wines and abundant fruit and charm, and doesn't overcharge for the pleasure. John and Julie Williams admit that they have to walk a tightrope in marketing terms, since they wish to maintain the popular, unstuffy image of the winery and keep their prices fair, while at the same time they have to keep quality high, which doesn't come cheap.

Heitz

500 Taplin Rd., St Helena, CA 94574. Tel: 963 3542. Fax: 963 7454. Tasting room at 436 St Helena Highway. Production: 40,000 cases.

Joe Heitz was already making wines in Napa Valley before Robert Mondavi set up his operation in Oakville. Whereas Mondavi and others have evolved, trying out new styles of wines, and fine-tuning incessantly in search of some unattainable perfection, Heitz found his style decades ago and has simply stuck with it. Why change a winning formula? Yet there is a troubling sense in which Heitz has stood still while others have moved on. I doubt that this troubles the Heitzes greatly, but it helps explain why their wines are no longer regarded with the same awe as twenty years ago.

Joe was born in Illinois and came out to California while in the air force. After World War II ended he took courses at UC Davis, and then work for Gallo and with Tchelitscheff at Beaulieu, thus acquainting himself with the extremes of the industry. Although he taught winemaking at Fresno State, he had always longed to find a property in Napa Valley. Eventually he bought the Leon Brendel property along the highway, close to where the tasting room now stands. It was only 8.5 acres and it was planted with the little-known Grignolino grape, but it was a start. In 1964 he bought an old stone winery off Taplin Road, and the ranch became his winery and home.

A stroke in 1996 left Joe Heitz frail, but he certainly had his wits about him when I visited him about a year later, and his tongue was as sharp as ever. His first move as a winemaker, he told me, was to pay growers what their grapes were worth, which, he implied, others were not doing. 'That caught on fast!' The high prices he was paying encouraged the growers to grow the best fruit they could. In those days there was little knowledge of such things as *barrique*-ageing, despite early experiments at Chalone and Hanzell. 'In the beginning we used what we had, and it worked. We haven't gone over to ageing all our wines in French oak, because why should we change just because other people are sheep?'

Heitz's great breakthrough was his cornering of the grapes from Martha's Vineyard. He started buying its grapes in 1965, but blended them with other fruit. In 1966 he designated the vineyard on the label for the first time, and the 1968 made the wine and the vineyard truly famous. Many connoisseurs declared it to be the greatest American wine made up to that time. It was aged in 1,000-gallon American oak vats and transferred into Limousin barrels, where it aged for a further 2 years. A total of 8,980 bottles were produced.

Today Heitz still buy grapes from Martha's Vineyard and Bella Oaks Vineyard. They also own 350 acres, including vineyards in Spring Valley planted with Grignolino and Zinfandel; the 'Z' Vineyard south of St Helena, replanted with Chardonnay in 1979 after Pierce's disease killed off the vines; a Chardonnay vineyard near the tasting room, planted in 1978; the 70-acre Trailside Vineyard on Silverado Trail, planted with Cabernet Sauvignon and Chardonnay; and 200 acres of terraced vineyards on Howell Mountain, planted with Cabernet Sauvignon, Merlot, and the port varieties.

The Chardonnay is mostly fermented in tanks, although outstanding lots will be barrel-fermented. The wine is aged in Limousin oak. The Napa Chardonnay is their standard wine, with the Estate Selection produced only in outstanding vintages when certain lots really stand out. The Heitzes admit that this wine was inconsistent in the past, but are sure that it has improved significantly in recent years.

The red wines are fermented in steel tanks, and all the Cabernet is still aged for one year in large American oak casks, before a much longer spell in Limousin barrels. Heitz favoured long ageing as it means the wines were ready to drink on release, and since American oak barrels were of poor quality in the 1960s, he started using Limousin instead. The proportion of new barrels, he admitted, depends on cash flow. Only older barrels are used for Pinot Noir, Zinfandel, and Grignolino.

All the Cabernet is 100 per cent varietal. The basic wine is the Napa bottling. There are three single-vineyard bottlings. Bella Oaks suffered from the vine disease eutypa and had to be replanted, so none was made in 1991 and 1992. It's a lighter wine than Martha's Vineyard, more claret-like, with higher acidity. Martha's Vineyard is dry-farmed and brings in crops of 3 to 5 tons per acre. Because of replanting no wine was released from 1993 to 1995 inclusive, and any wine made was blended in with the Napa bottling. Production varies from 1,000 to 6,000 cases. Trailside Vineyard was introduced in 1989 and comes from their own vineyard. In 1993 3,800 cases were made. It is higher priced than Bella Oaks, but less expensive than Martha's Vineyard, and is aged entirely in new oak.

The other wines are a fairly light Zinfandel, and a charming Grignolino rosé. Grignolino is also the source of a Heitz 'port', and there is also a vintage-dated 'port' from Portuguese varieties, which spends 2 years in oak and is delicious.

There is no doubt that Martha's Vineyard is an American classic, and the 1974 was one of the most memorable Napa wines of the decade. The 1980 was great too. With its distinctive eucalyptus or mint aroma, it has a strong character of its own which most, if not all, admire. Joe Heitz himself dismissed the suggestion that the eucalyptus character has anything to do with the eucalyptus trees planted nearby. Unfortunately the Heitz cellars have had long-term problems with the bacterial infection brettano-myces. This shows up in the wines as a kind of mustiness that doesn't seem derived from mouldy corks or other problems. Heitz is not alone; many Napa wineries have had similar problems, but they seem less per-sistent. James Halliday, tasting all three Cabernets from the 1987 vintage, found them all tainted, and I tasted the 1990 Trailside Vineyard twice in 1998: the first bottle was clearly faulty, the other cleaner but had a pronounced taste of old musty wood. However, the 1992 Cabernets were formidably good.

David Heitz, born in 1950, has been working at the winery for many years and has for some time been the winemaker. Both he and his father must surely recognize the problem, but it remains a delicate subject around the tasting table. Joe Heitz's stubbornness explains why he is one of the great survivors of the Napa wine industry, but it may also be part of the explanation for why the overall quality of the wines has been slipping.

La Jota
1102 Las Posadas Rd., Angwin, CA 94508. Tel: 965 3020. Production: 5,000 cases.

Bill Smith used to be in the oil business and became involved in vineyard ownership in 1974 as it offered a useful tax shelter. He planted vines in 1976 and sold the fruit to other wineries. In 1982 he reactivated the old stone winery of 1898 that stood on the property and released a Cabernet Sauvignon, followed the next year by Zinfandel. Although he established a good reputation for his wines, Smith began budding over the Zinfandel in 1987 to more fashionable varieties such as Cabernet Franc and Viognier, for which, he admits, he could get considerably more money. The estate consists of a 28-acre parcel, mostly Cabernet Sauvignon, but also Marsanne, Roussanne, Merlot, Cabernet Franc, and 3 acres of Viognier. The soil is tufa and volcanic ash, with good drainage; phylloxera has required the replanting of much of the vineyard. In 1997 he bought another 6 acres, and also buys in grapes for some of his wines. Although a pioneer of Viognier in Napa Valley, Smith came late to Chardonnay, making his first one in 1992. The first consultant winemaker here was Randy Dunn, but Helen Turley now occupies that position.

Smith is best known for his Cabernet Sauvignon, which comes in two forms. The Howell Mountain Selection is aged in older barrels, whereas the best lots form the Anniversary Release label, which is aged 21 months in new oak, and is pure Cabernet Sauvignon.

The style of wines here is rich and gutsy. Bill Smith likes his grapes ripe, and never picks below 24 Brix, even for varieties such as Cabernet Franc. But it seems to work. A 1986 Cabernet Franc was remarkably good 10 years after the wine was bottled. A curiosity here is the Pinot Noir, which comes from the Hellental Vineyard in Sonoma Coast. I have only tasted the wine from cask. It is aged in new oak, with a heavy toast, for about 9 months, and even in its extreme youth it tasted wonderful.

Smith is well known for his Viognier, which he began producing in 1986, long before most American wine drinkers had even heard of the variety. Quantities are limited, no more than 700 cases, and the wine comes in two versions: one steel-fermented and unoaked, the other barrel-fermented and aged in mostly older *barriques*. I much prefer the unoaked version, which preserves the aroma and typicity of the variety.

Bill Smith is relaxed and engaging, and in general I like the rich, extracted style of his wines. But they can be inconsistent and lacking in elegance.

Mayacamas
1155 Lokoya Rd., Napa, CA 94558. Tel: 224 4030. Production: 6,000 cases.

In the mid-1980s I sat outside the winery at Mayacamas with the winemaker, and decided I was in one of the loveliest spots on earth. The views from Mount Eden, Cain, and Newton may be more spectacular, but here everything seemed in harmony: the rustling trees beneath a cloudless sky, the sloping vineyards, the crunching of tyres along the track leading to the stone winery. Twelve years later nothing had changed, which I dare say is both a strength and weakness.

The original winery was built here in 1889 by the Fischer family. One wonders what prompted this German family to make their way up through the undergrowth and woodland to the ridge top along the Mayacamas

mountains and decide that this former sheep ranch was the right place for
growing vines. Their instincts were certainly correct. Some wonderful
wines have emerged from these stubborn, low-yielding mountains.
Somehow the Fischers kept the place going through Prohibition. The
property changed hands a few times until it came into the possession of
an Englishman called Jack Taylor in 1941. Until 1946, when they started
up the winery again, the Pinot Noir and Chardonnay grapes were sold off
to other wineries. Under its new name of Mayacamas, the Taylor estate
developed a range of seventeen wines, including sparkling rosé and ver-
mouth. In the late 1950s Philip Togni was the winemaker here, and he
told me the Taylors decided to sell both because they had no successors
and because their wines had been poorly marketed.

They found a buyer in Robert Travers, a youthful banker from San
Francisco, who in his spare time studied winemaking and worked as a
cellar hand at Heitz. When he found Mayacamas in 1968, it was run
down and the 20 acres of vineyards were neglected, but Travers secured
the property for $350,000. Bob Sessions, who later went to Hanzell, joined
Travers as winemaker and stayed until 1972.

Today there are 50 acres of dry-farmed vineyards at a height of between
1,700 and 2,300 feet, all planted on varied volcanic soils. Indeed the vines
in front of the winery are planted inside an extinct volcano. Because of
the sloping hillsides, exposures vary greatly. So do yields, although the
average is a miserly 1.5 tons per acre. Frost is rare, despite the height, and
breezes keep rot at bay. Not far to the west, across the county line, lies
the Monte Rosso Vineyard that belongs to Louis Martini. Bob Travers is
proud of the fact that whereas the vines planted in the rich soils of the
valley floor have a life span of about 30 years, those up here in
the mountains live twice as long. There is still some Chardonnay planted
in the 1940s and Cabernet from the 1960s. The farming is close to organic,
and the estate uses techniques very similar to Integrated Pest Management
to control predators. Sadly about one quarter of the vines are planted on
AXR-1 and are going to have to be replanted. Although Travers used to
have to buy fruit from his neighbours, he is now self-sufficient.

The winemaking hasn't altered much in years. Fermentation takes place
in epoxy-lined cement tanks, and if there are any stainless steel tanks I
didn't spot them. Cabernet spends 2 years in 1,000-gallon casks and then
a year in *barriques*, of which 20 per cent are new but some are up to ten
years old. Pinot Noir spends a year in large casks and a year in barrels;
Zinfandel is aged for 2 years in the large casks. Chardonnay is also aged
in large casks. Most wines are bottle-aged for a year or more before
release.

The Chardonnay is a powerful but austere wine. With its low pH, low
yields, and lack of malolactic fermentation, it needs up to ten years in

bottle to mature. But it doesn't always make it: I recall vintages from the 1970s and 1980s that were austere, hot, and lacking in finesse. What Travers aims for is the pure expression of the grape character, with minimal manipulation. I find the style lush yet mineral, with good length and no alcoholic burn, despite the 14 degrees or more that is customary. The Sauvignon which used to be produced here has been discontinued.

Bob Travers will admit that Pinot Noir is not his signature wine. 'I still regard it as experimental.' With Cabernet Sauvignon, on the other hand, he has defined his style long ago. Bordeaux was his model, which is why he still favours the rather austere tannic style that most winemakers have abandoned for something softer, fleshier, more opulent. Travers is sceptical about claims that the ultra-ripe style in fashion at present will necessarily age better than his overtly tannic wines. He uses both natural and cultivated yeasts, doesn't fine, and only gives the wine the coarsest of filtrations before bottling. The result is a wine that needs about ten years to show its paces. It's no blockbuster, but a lean, elegant, claret-like wine, without any jammy flavours; this is precisely what Travers is aiming for. He argues that his wines should be balanced from the outset. 'Although my wines are intended to be aged, their beauty and potential should be appreciable young, though they will always taste more complex with bottle age. It seems to me that if you have a great *terroir* the ultimate potential of a great wine will never be revealed when it's young.'

Mayacamas is famous for its late harvest Zinfandels, made almost by accident in 1968, as explained in Chapter 15.

Like Heitz, Mayacamas is in a time-warp, although Heitz is marginally more sophisticated in terms of winery equipment. Both Travers and Heitz established their style in the 1970s and haven't really deviated from it since. Certainly Mayacamas made some great wines in the 1970s (the 1974 and 1978 Cabernet were remarkable), but it isn't clear that the quality has been sustained. Perhaps it's just that there is so much more competition than there used to be.

Mondavi

7801 St Helena Highway, Oakville, CA 94562. Tel: 963 9611. Fax: 963 4003. Estimated production: 650,000 cases, excluding those from Lodi-Woodbridge.

As you drive up Highway 29 through Napa Valley you can hardly miss the Mondavi winery, with its lazy arches, its Spanish Colonial styling, and its tall tower. That's the way Robert Mondavi intended it to be. No one in Napa Valley has been more eager to communicate with the public. The man is not only driven as a wine producer, he is also passionate to communicate his enthusiasm to the entire world. The Mondavi winery is also an educational centre, offering excellent tours and other events.

Throughout the world the Mondavis organize tastings and seminars, spreading the word about their experiments, their ideas, their conclusions.

How the Mondavis find time to oversee their winemaking empire is hard to imagine, but they do, and no one disputes that the overall quality is astonishingly high, given the volume of production. Bob Mondavi has never lacked confidence, but his early years as a winemaker were far from easy. At the family winery of Charles Krug, which his father bought in 1943, he shared the responsibilities with his brother Peter. Essentially Robert looked after the management and marketing, while his brother concentrated on the winemaking. In 1962 Robert embarked on a tour of European wine regions that opened his eyes to the overall mediocrity of California wines at this time. He urged Peter to aim for higher quality, but Peter was, according to his brother, content to continue on their existing, commercially successful path. The tension between the brothers increased, and in 1965 Robert was put on six months' paid leave. He decided to leave Krug and found his own ambitious winery, and sued his brother in the process. He did not immediately start up his rival winery. First he bought some vineyards in Oakville, then in 1966 founded Robert Mondavi. Two years later he was out of money. There were tentative negotiations with Suntory and with Nestlé, but in the end he formed a partnership with Washington state brewers Rainier of Seattle. They became the majority shareholders, but left Robert to run the estate. With Rainier's money Mondavi was able to buy the great 500-acre To-Kalon vineyard, which had originally been planted by H. W. Crabb in 1866.

It was the mid-1970s before the lawsuit between Robert and Peter Mondavi was settled. Robert won, and the Charles Krug estate was obliged to hand over many millions to the victor. This was to cripple Krug for some years, and allowed Robert to buy out Rainier for $5 million in 1978. He was now the sole master of his winery. His son Michael was winemaster until 1974, when Michael's brother Tim took over. He is still in charge of winemaking, while Michael focuses more on marketing. In 1991 Robert officially retired and in 1993 the winery went public in order to raise more money, but the family retained 72 per cent ownership. Since 1995, Michael has been chief executive officer, and Tim managing director.

Mondavi buys in over half its grapes from contract growers, but also owns at least 1,200 acres in Napa and 425 in Carneros, which are planted with Chardonnay and Pinot Noir. The Napa holdings include To-Kalon, which has some of the oldest Sauvignon Blanc in California as well as the Cabernet that forms the backbone of the Reserve bottling; the 298-acre Oak Knoll Vineyard along Silverado Trail; and almost 400 acres in Stag's Leap. The purchase and development of vineyards in the Central Coast in 1996 reputedly cost the company $40 million.

During his European tour in the early 1960s Robert Mondavi went to

Burgundy and saw for himself that oak barrels had an enormous influence over the aroma, flavour, and structure of a wine. He started to import barrels from everywhere, including Yugoslavia, Limousin, Nevers and from within the United States. The experimentation was incessant. To his eternal credit, Mondavi was happy to share the results with anyone who was interested. In many ways he was responsible for improving the overall quality of Napa wine in the 1960s and 1970s as well for setting his own high standards. He also turned his attention to the vineyards, trying out different trellising systems and, notoriously in some eyes, adopting close French-style spacing for the vineyards he planted for the joint venture at Opus One.

Until the mid-1980s Mondavi was keen on winemaking technology. Chatting to members of their winemaking team at that time, I was dazzled with explanations of centrifuging and other techniques. If the effect of barrel ageing and toasting could be monitored in a scientific fashion, it was not surprising that other aspects of the winemaking process should be pursued with scientific rigour. But at that time a sea change was already apparent. The Mondavi team was focusing more and more on the vineyards, on typicity. It had already realized that Pinot Noir, for instance, could not be manipulated and cajoled in the way that the Bordeaux varieties could; fruit quality was supremely important, and so was the gentlest of handling. The series of Reserve Pinot Noirs released from the late 1980s onwards showed just how well Mondavi had come to grips with this most neurotic of varieties.

While maintaining a strong range of basic varietal wines, Mondavi began branching out with appellation cuvées: Pinot Noir and Chardonnay from Carneros, where Mondavi had built a special press-house in the 1990s; Cabernet Sauvignon from Oakville and Stags Leap; a Stags Leap District Fumé Blanc and sometimes tiny quantities of To-Kalon Reserve Fumé Blanc; and in 1994, a new line of less expensive Coastal wines from their estates in the Central Valley. In 1995 the La Famiglia range of Italian varietals was added. In addition there were new acquisitions, such as Vichon and Byron.

The grapes for the Fumé Blanc come from To-Kalon and from Oak Knoll, the latter being close to Stags Leap and exhibiting more citric aromas than To-Kalon. The oldest vines tend to be used for the Reserve wine. A good proportion of the grapes are whole-cluster pressed, especially lots destined for the Reserve. About 60 per cent of the Sauvignon is barrel-fermented, and almost all the wine is aged for 6 months in *barriques*. Almost all the Reserve is barrel-fermented and aged in *barriques* that are one or 2 years old. There is no malolactic fermentation, and the wine is aged on the lees for 9 months. Although Mondavi use natural yeasts for much of their red wines, they still inoculate the Sauvignon Blanc.

About half the Chardonnay is whole-cluster pressed, and it is all barrel-fermented. Mondavi favour a 70 per cent malolactic fermentation, though I dare say it's not a hard and fast rule. Special bottlings, such as the Carneros Chardonnay, have a higher proportion of whole-cluster pressed grapes, some natural-yeast fermentation, complete malolactic fermentation, ageing in one-third new oak, and bottling without filtration. The Reserve is also barrel-fermented, with a substantial percentage of the wine undergoing malolactic fermentation, and ageing for about 12 months in 50 per cent new oak. Mondavi use less new oak than they used to. The 1989 Reserve Chardonnay had 70 per cent, now reduced to 50.

Cabernet Sauvignon in general receives a long fermentation and is aged in *barriques* for some 21 months. Some Merlot and Cabernet Franc are blended in. In the 1990s Mondavi started to use wood rather than stainless steel fermenters for their red wines, because of their excellent heat retention and the possibility of thus extending the maceration period. The Reserve Cabernet is always aged in about 80 per cent new oak, and constitutes no more than 10 per cent of the total Cabernet production. The Cabernets are usually unfiltered.

The Napa Merlot uses fruit from Oakville and Stags Leap, and is aged about 20 months in *barriques*, of which 20 per cent are new.

For Pinot Noir, Mondavi use a lot of Carneros fruit, and try to keep yields to about 2.5 tons per acre. Only indigenous yeasts are used for fermentation, and the maceration period is about 15 days. Tim Mondavi now favours malolactic fermentation in barrels, to bring the wine into harmony with the wood faster. Racking is kept to the minimum to avoid oxidizing the wine. The wine is aged in barrels for about 10 months, and the Reserve is aged in 40 per cent new oak.

Old standbys such as Chenin Blanc, Riesling, and Moscato d'Oro seem to have disappeared from the Mondavi range, and the late harvest Sauvignons and Rieslings of the 1970s and early 1980s are also, it seems, no longer made. Instead there is a new excitement about the Italian varietal range, which is being produced at the winery by Jim Moore. Although some of the grapes are estate-grown – there are 16 acres of Sangiovese planted at Oakville, for example – the wines bear the California appellation, allowing Moore to source fruit from the most appropriate locations. The 1995s I tasted were a mixed bag: a confected Refosco, a ripe and vivacious Tocai, a spicy but light Nebbiolo, a medium-bodied but essentially simple Sangiovese. But these are early days.

If there is a danger that Mondavi, with its vast acreage in Santa Barbara and its colossal winery in Lodi in addition to its already complex Oakville operation, might be spreading itself too thin, it really is not apparent in the wines, which remain of excellent quality. It is reassuring that the company does not seem to be resting on its richly deserved laurels.

Newton

2555 Madroña Avenue, St Helena, CA 94574. Tel: 963 9000. Fax: 963 5408. Production: Newton won't say, but it's estimated to be between 30,000 and 50,000 cases.

Newton's vineyards are not open to the public, which is a great shame since these are arguably the most beautiful in all of California. Peter Newton's wife Su Hua is Chinese, and the terraced vineyards are reminiscent of Chinese landscape paintings, the whole effect enhanced with red-lacquer gateways, wooden pagodas, and other Chinese ornaments. Newton was one of the founders of Sterling in 1964, and after the sale of Sterling to Coca-Cola, he used some of the proceeds to start up his own estate on Spring Mountain, planting vineyards at between 500 and 1,600 feet. This was one of the first estates in Napa to plant Merlot, and the first release of the estate's excellent Merlot was 1979. Ric Forman, who had been the winemaker at Sterling, was Newton's partner at first, but there was a falling out, and Forman left. He was replaced by John Kongsgaard, who left in 1996. In 1998 Peter Newton told me that Su Hua is now the winemaker, even though she also pursues a separate career in San Francisco. It's perfectly conceivable that this immensely dynamic and talented woman does indeed make the wines. She has been a model, a scientist, designed much of the vineyard and winery buildings, and has formidable expertise as a wine marketer. There is a mysterious personage at Newton called Luc Morlet; he is the director of oenology, but I have never met him and don't know what he does. The team is completed by the consulting services of Michel Rolland, who only advises on his special subject: Merlot.

The 100 acres of vineyards are planted on a great range of exposures and soil types, but the underlying soil is deep, well-drained and volcanic. There are patches of clay soil, where the Merlot has mostly been planted. There's Petit Verdot too. It doesn't always deliver much crop but when it does it contributes its perfume to the reds. Yields vary from 1.25 to 3.25 tons per acre. Vineyard maintenance costs a fortune, but Newton seem to think it's worthwhile, given the quality of fruit. The must is fermented in a specially designed octagonal tank room, and cellars tunnelled into rock provide perfect conditions for ageing the wines in barrels, all of which are shipped from France. *Barriques* filled with Cabernet Sauvignon slumber 110 feet below the surface.

For a few years in the mid-1980s Newton made some outstanding Graves-style whites from Sauvignon and Sémillon. But the expense of canopy management and new oak, in which one-third of the wine was fermented, made it impossible to continue with the wine in a market that refuses to believe Sauvignon can be the equal of Chardonnay. Today most of those Sauvignon vines have been budded over to Merlot and Cabernet Franc.

The principal Cabernet Sauvignon is the Red Label, and there is also an expensive unfiltered estate wine called Le Puzzle, aged in 50 per cent new oak. The Merlot is delicious, and is blended with 15 per cent Cabernet Franc. With time the wine develops some unusual gamy flavours. Like the Cabernet, the Merlot is remarkably consistent, and only the 1989 was a dud. Indeed, I have never encountered a mediocre Newton Cabernet, though I am less keen on the Meritage awkwardly named Cabernets.

No Chardonnay is grown here, so the Red Label Chardonnay is made from grapes purchased from valley-floor vineyards in Napa and Sonoma. It is fermented with natural yeasts. The top wine is the Unfiltered Reserve, which spends 2 years in oak. It's a sumptuous wine, of course, but it can lack vigour. There is an occasional Viognier, but Peter Newton admits it doesn't always work out as they would like.

Niebaum-Coppola

1991 St Helena Highway, Rutherford, CA 94573. Tel: 963 9099. Fax: 967 4178. Production: 30,000 cases.

This is the reborn Inglenook estate of Gustav Niebaum. When Francis Ford Coppola bought a vineyard here in 1975, it was in need of replanting. By 1997, the vineyard consisted of 125 acres, of which 94 were bearing fruit. However, a substantial addition of 70 acres was made in 1995, when Coppola expended $10 million dollars on the Inglenook 'chateau' and the Home Vineyard of the property, of which 35 acres are in production. I wandered through the vast stone winery shortly after it was purchased, eerily empty after years of use as a tasting and selling room for the mediocre wines produced under the Inglenook label in recent years. But there in the cellars were the old vintages of Inglenook wines, all recorked, but still in place. The temptation to lock myself in with a corkscrew and discover what century-old Napa wines tasted like was hard to resist. But the then general manager of the property, John Skupny, was keeping an eye on me. Coppola plans to convert the chateau into a winery for his Rubicon wine, and a museum chronicling both the estate's history and Coppola's career as movie director. Up on the slopes behind the winery is the white house that used to be the Niebaum residence and is now Coppola's vineyard home.

The viticulture is essentially organic, and most of the vineyards are dry-farmed. When the replanting is completed, the vineyards will be 60 per cent planted to Cabernet Sauvignon, then Cabernet Franc, Merlot, and Zinfandel. There are also experimental lots, including some Italian varieties to which Coppola has a sentimental attachment: Dolcetto, Malvasia

Bianco, Primitivo, as well as a little Chardonnay and Viognier. The replanted vines are closely spaced with 1,200–1,300 vines per acre.

The estate's best known wine is Rubicon, which was first made in 1978 as a blend of Cabernet Sauvignon, Cabernet Franc, and Merlot. Maceration periods vary, but have been as long as 3 months; and the wine is aged in 50 per cent new oak, with the lesser varieties blended in later; this final blend is aged for a further year in oak, making a total of 24 months. The wine was formerly aged for 3 years in bottle before release. Rubicon used to be a very dense tannic wine, impressive but far from accessible. The style has changed in recent years, and this may well be due to the hiring of Tony Soter as a consultant in 1990 and of Scott McLeod as winemaker since 1992. Although the concentration is as formidable as before, the tannins are far more supple, and it is now possible to drink the wine on release, although it will undoubtedly age well. Production of the 1994 Rubicon was almost 3,500 cases.

Other wines are sold under the Family Wines label, such as a minute production of rather heavy Viognier in 1995. There is also a Zinfandel under the Edizione Pennino label; this comes from head-pruned vines and is aged in French-coopered American oak. A cheaper range has been sold since 1997 under the Francis Coppola Presents label. Thus far there is a Rosso from Zinfandel, Syrah and Petite Sirah; and a Bianco from Chardonnay, Riesling, and Muscat.

With the various changes now taking place after the acquisition of the Inglenook property in 1995, it is hard to discern the new direction the winery will take. Rubicon will clearly remain its flagship, and there may well be some interesting additional wines under the Family Wines label.

Opus One

7900 St Helena Highway, Oakville, CA 94562. Tel: 944 9442. Fax: 944 2753. Production: 30,000 cases.

The wine world, both in California and Europe, followed the long soap operatic story of the development of Opus One. It began with an agreement between a baron of Bordeaux, Philippe de Rothschild, and a baron of Napa, Robert Mondavi. They would create a wine together. Rothschild would put up the cash, Mondavi would provide the grapes and vinify them. The baron would pay for the barrels, a new set each year. The baron's winemaker would descend on Napa from time to time to make sure Mondavi was conducting the vinification properly. The costs of building the winery and any profits from the venture would be split between them.[2] Patrick Léon of Mouton-Rothschild and Tim Mondavi were the joint winemakers.

Scott Johnson of Los Angeles was the chosen architect for the splendid building that rose above a mound just across from the Mondavi winery. Beneath the mound were the magnificent cellars of Opus One, in which 1,000 barrels are lined in curved rows without stacking. Unfortunately, as the architects were beginning the excavation, they discovered subterranean hot springs that would heat the cellars, so the whole structure had to be insulated. The cost of construction was estimated at $20 million. A lot of wine would need to be sold.

Planting began in 1981 on 108 acres, mostly in three adjoining parcels. However, 25 per cent of the winery's needs still has to be purchased. The vines were famously planted to tight spacing, which required a great deal of costly hedging to keep the air moving through the foliage. One would suppose that Opus One would be in competition with Mondavi's Reserve Cabernet for the estate's best grapes, but the wines are made in different styles. Opus is supposed to be more restrained, less powerful than the Reserve, although when I blind tasted the early vintages of each, I often preferred the Reserve wine to Opus One. In those days the grapes came from the Mondavi vineyards, and it was not until 1988 that the Opus vineyards were sufficiently mature to be used for the new wine. The quantities produced have been rising steadily. In 1990 10,000 cases were made; today almost three times as much is produced.

The wine is, of course, a Bordeaux blend, but Cabernet Sauvignon makes up 85 to 90 per cent of the volume. Malbec was first included in the 1994 vintage. The grapes are carefully sorted on arrival at the winery, destemmed, retaining about 5 per cent whole berries, which descend by gravity into the fermentation tanks. Both cultivated and natural yeasts are used. The maceration continues for about 45 days, considerably longer than at either Mondavi or Mouton, and longer than it used to be in the early days at Opus. The malolactic fermentation begins in the steel tanks but is completed in barrel. The fruit is handled very gently, and the winery was designed so that, for example, the hydraulic presses can be wheeled next to the tanks so as to avoid pumping the must. The wine is aged 18 months in new *barriques* from seven different coopers. After the first of six rackings the final blend is made up. Opus is fined before bottling.

Although in its generosity of fruit Opus One is a Napa Valley wine, it is also one of the most claret-like of Californian Cabernets, with the emphasis on elegance, balance and length of flavour rather than sheer power and richness of fruit. The wine is expensive at $100 for the 1995 vintage, but the quality is unquestionably high. Unfortunately Opus takes itself far too seriously and often suffers from a humour deficiency. When the inventive Austrian winemaker Willi Opitz named a sweet wine Opitz One, more in homage and wit than in exploitation of a revered name, he was threatened with legal action (which, of course, drew plenty of attention to Opitz that he might not otherwise have received). And when the

369

cigar manufacturers Carlos Fuente produced a cigar called Opus X, Opus One took them to court, and although Fuente won the case, the cigar company was saddled with about $2 million in costs. No doubt the Catholic organization Opus Dei and any contemporary composer embarking on his first composition should beware of the Opus One lawyers.

Pahlmeyer

PO Box 2410, Napa, CA 94558. Tel: 255 2321. Fax: 255 6786. Production: 5,000 cases.

Jayson Pahlmeyer is a lawyer who became obsessed with wine. Even his dogs are called Lafite, Mouton, and Latour. Privileged visitors are welcomed to his large hi-tech house on a hillside overlooking the valley. Pahlmeyer, tall and lantern-jawed and enthusiastic, is genuinely welcoming and clearly takes pleasure from pouring his wines for those who might be expected to appreciate them. One look at the fashionably dressed Pahlmeyer and his imaginatively designed modern house is enough to tell one that this is a man keen on style.

Pahlmeyer buys his grapes from a variety of hillside sources throughout Napa and Carneros. By far the most important is the 25-acre Caldwell Vineyard in Coombsville, which was planted in 1980. The Cabernet Sauvignon, Cabernet Franc, and Merlot here are closely spaced. This is the source for the Pahlmeyer Red. A new vineyard is being developed on Atlas Peak, the Waters Ranch, which will be planted in 1999 with all the Bordeaux varieties, white as well as red, as Pahlmeyer has ambitions to make a white modelled on Château Haut-Brion. A further 70 acres has been purchased along the Sonoma Coast, which will presumably be planted with Chardonnay and Pinot Noir.

The first vintage at Pahlmeyer was 1986. Randy Dunn was the winemaker. In 1990 Dunn decided he needed more time to devote to his own winery, and Helen Turley was brought in. At first the two winemakers collaborated, but since 1993 she has had the sole responsibility. The wine is actually vinified in rented facilities in Oakville.

The Chardonnay fruit comes mostly from the very cool Berlenbach Vineyard in Coombsville. The wine is barrel-fermented in new Burgundian barrels and aged on the lees for 12 months. Usually it is bottled without fining or filtration. I find the 1996 over-blown and over-alcoholic at 14.9 degrees. The wine was also hazy. Pahlmeyer and Turley are unapologetic: this is the style they want, very ripe and rich and powerful. High alcohol gives richness and viscosity, which they both like. They are about to experiment with leaving the wine on the lees for 2 years at cold temperatures in an effort to extract even more flavour. I much preferred the 1991

Chardonnay, which was made by Bob Levy of Merryvale. The wine is much better balanced and holding up well.

If I have reservations about the Chardonnay, I am far more enthusiastic about the powerful and complex reds. The Merlot comes from the Caldwell Vineyard and is aged in 80 per cent new oak. The proprietaty red, from the same source, is fermented on the native yeasts with small lots of whole berry fermentation. Like the Merlot, it remains in oak for over 2 years. No fining or filtration for either wine. Both are wines of real splendour.

Joseph Phelps

200 Taplin Rd., St Helena, CA 94574. Tel: 963 2745. Fax: 963 4831. Production: 100,000 cases.

Joseph Phelps ran a construction company in Colorado before coming out to California to invest in some vineyards. He bought what was then a cattle ranch in Spring Valley in 1972 and began to plant vines. Today Phelps owns the 160-acre Home Vineyard; the 35-acre Banca Dorada on the Rutherford Bench (planted with Cabernet Sauvignon); the 40-acre Los Carneros Negros, planted with Chardonnay, Merlot, Syrah, and Viognier; the 7-acre Backus Vineyard in Oakville; the 40-acre Las Rocas in Stags Leap, planted with Cabernet and Merlot; the 50-acre Renacimiento in Oak Knoll, with the same varieties as Carneros Negros; and vineyards in Monterey near King City, where varieties such as Syrah and Grenache have been planted.

The first winemaker was German-born Walter Schug, who now has his own winery in Carneros. Not surprisingly Schug did what he understood best, planting and vinifying German varieties, notably Riesling and Scheurebe, which at first came from a vineyard close to Yountville and have been sourced more recently from Anderson Valley. Schug was most successful working with late harvest fruit, including Sémillon as well as the two German varieties. The very expensive Delices de Sémillon was barrel-fermented and aged for 12 to 18 months in mostly new oak. The botrytized Sémillon is blended with about 20 per cent Sauvignon Blanc which is picked very ripe, at 25 Brix, but without noble rot, the idea being to inject some acidity into a wine that would otherwise lack it. The 1985 Delices was splendidly lush and toasty.

Craig Williams, who took over from Schug in 1983 and is still the winemaker, has introduced a new sweet wine, Eisrebe, first made in 1994. Scheurebe grapes are frozen after harvest, then pressed to give wines in an ice-wine style. However the grapes are picked at normal ripeness levels, about 23 Brix, and the wine is not especially intense.

There is also a dry Sauvignon, made almost entirely from grapes grown on the Home Vineyard. Only a small proportion of the must is barrel-fermented. There are two Chardonnays. Los Carneros is barrel-fermented, undergoes malolactic fermentation and is then aged in one-third new oak. The more expensive Ovation Chardonnay comes from cool Napa vineyards planted with clones known for their small clusters. It is barrel-fermented using natural yeasts and aged a long time on the fine lees. The winery also makes an off-dry Gewürztraminer from grapes purchased in Anderson Valley.

Phelps has always made first-rate Cabernets. Their Napa bottling uses fruit from their Stags Leap and Rutherford vineyards, and is aged 22 months in barrels, of which one-quarter are American oak. There is also a single-vineyard Cabernet from Backus Vineyard, which has been produced since 1977. Their famous Eisele Vineyard ceased production in 1991, as the grapes are now used by the new owner of the vineyard, Bert Araujo, for his own winery.

In 1974 Phelps were one of the first wineries to produce a Bordeaux blend, which they called Insignia. Its components vary greatly, but in recent years it has been dominated by Cabernet Sauvignon from Stags Leap and Rutherford, with about 10 per cent Merlot, and a small quantity of Cabernet Franc from Rutherford. Williams is not very keen on their Cabernet Franc, which he finds rather lean. The vines are low-yielding, rarely exceeding 3 tons per acre. There has been a slight change in style in this long-lived blend. Since 1990 there has been both a higher proportion of new oak, and an attempt to pick fruit at greater ripeness, even though this means that the alcohol level of the finished wine is at least 14 degrees. The maximum production of Insignia is 12,000 cases and the current price $70.

One of the first Napa Syrahs was produced by Phelps. If there was magnificent wildness and rusticity in some of the early vintages, the current releases are more refined. The 1994 vintage uses fruit from Stags Leap, Carneros, and Yountville, and was aged for 18 months in French and American oak. Merlot was added to the Phelps range in 1986, and is often aged in American oak.

Craig Williams has taken Schug's initial interest in Syrah a few steps further by producing a range of Rhône-style wines. The estate first made Viognier in 1989 from grapes grown here in Spring Valley, as well as Carneros and Yountville. Although barrel-fermented, it only spends 7 months on the fine lees. It is one of the best of California Viogniers. There is also a very attractive dry rosé from Grenache, and Williams, who is keen on the variety, is going to try making a fortified Grenache in the style of a Roussillon *vin doux naturel*. Le Mistral is a Rhône-style blend: with 30 per cent each Mourvèdre and Grenache, plus Napa Syrah and Petite Sirah, Alicante Bouschet and Carignane. I am not the first person to point out that Le Mistral is essentially a well-made jug-wine blend at a fairly high price. The wine is aged 18 months in French and American oak.

The basic Phelps wines are good though not very exciting, but some of the special bottlings, such as the late harvest wines, Backus Cabernet, Insignia, and the Viognier, are first-rate. Unlike most Napa wineries, Phelps under Walter Schug and now Craig Williams has not been afraid to diversify and experiment.

Spottswoode

1902 Madroña Ave., St Helena, CA 94574. Tel: 963 0134. Fax: 963 2886. Production: 9,000 cases.

This long-established estate, based in St Helena itself, was founded in 1882 and bought by Jack and Mary Novak in 1972. They replanted the vineyards the following year. Dr Novak died young in 1977, and for the next few years the grapes were sold to Duckhorn, Spring Mountain, and Shafer. It was obvious to their grateful clients that the fruit was of excellent quality, so in 1982 Mary Novak decided that Spottswoode should make its own wine.

She hired the best talent around: David Abreu to keep an eye on the vineyards, and Tony Soter and his assistant Mia Klein to look after both viticulture and winemaking. Soter remains a consultant here, but since 1997 the winemaker has been Rosemary Cakebread, whose husband Bruce makes the wine that bears his name. Throughout the 1980s the wines were made at other facilities, although there was enough space at Spottswoode to age the wines in the cellars of the house. In 1990 Mary Novak and her daughter Beth Novak Milliken bought an old winery nearby: the Kraft Winery of 1883.

The vineyards lie in a single parcel of 36 acres behind the fine Victorian mansion which is still Mary Novak's home. Phylloxera required the replanting in 1991 of most of the vineyard, and much of the Sauvignon Blanc and Sémillon was replaced by Cabernet Sauvignon. This vineyard has been cultivated organically since 1985. Unfortunately only a handful of the vines from the 1970s survive, and the rest of the vineyards are still very young.

The Sauvignon Blanc, which contains about 20 per cent Sémillon, is fermented partly in new *barriques*, and partly in the steel drums to which Soter is partial. The idea of the steel drums is to allow prolonged lees contact without oak influence. There is no malolactic fermentation, and the wine is bottled young. Soter has always been adamant that he is not trying to imitate Chardonnay, but to produce a wine of distinctive delicacy and freshness. Here he succeeds. Since 1990 some Sauvignon Blanc has been purchased from Musqué clone vines from Hyde Vineyard in Carneros.

Spottswoode is of course famous for its Cabernet Sauvignon, blended with a little Cabernet Franc that seems to impart a whiff of violets. Rosemary Cakebread has no formula for vinification, as it depends on the fruit. Sometimes the must will be macerated for up to six weeks, but not necessarily. Malolactic fermentation takes place in barrel, where the wine remains for 22 months. Spottswoode use mostly Nevers, and half the barrels are new. This is always one of Napa's most stylish Cabernets: not the most extracted or powerful, but unfailingly elegant and balanced, its fruit given zip by the frequent high acidity. The wine is not fined, but is always filtered.

Stag's Leap Wine Cellars

5766 Silverado Trail, Napa, CA 94558. Tel: 944 2020. Fax: 257 7501. Production: 60,000 cases.

In 1970 Warren Winiarski changed gear. Until then a political science lecturer in Chicago, he went out to California and bought land in what would become the Stags Leap District. He planted 33 acres of Cabernet Sauvignon and 4.5 of Merlot. He learnt winemaking the practical way, working as a cellar hand at Souverain and Mondavi. In 1986 he bought the neighbouring Fay Vineyard, which had previously supplied excellent grapes to Heitz and other wineries. It has been mostly replanted with 62 acres of Cabernet Sauvignon, 7 of Merlot, and 1 of Petit Verdot, although some vines from 1961 survive. The first vintage of Fay Vineyard under its new label was 1990. All the estate vineyards are dry-farmed. The grapes for the white wines are purchased.

The estate is best known for its Cabernets, which come in various forms. There is a Napa bottling, then two estate bottlings (SLV or Stag's Leap Vineyards, and Fay), and Cask 23, which is a barrel selection. They share a common style, which Winiarski has long defined as an iron fist in a velvet glove. He doesn't try to make wines that will become museum pieces by enduring forever (although I have drunk older vintages with great pleasure) but seeks balance as well as tannin. The SLV has a good deal of clay in the soil, and the upper slopes, which give the best fruit, are usually the source of lots chosen for Cask 23. The soil at Fay is sandier, with less clay but with more volcanic rock. Daniel Schuster, the vineyard consultant here, finds that Fay gives wines that are more perfumed and less tannic than SLV; they have more charm and, in his view, will eventually producer greater wine than SLV. Cask 23, first made in 1974, is not produced every year, and is usually restricted to about 1,000 cases. It is sold for $120, over twice the price of the single-vineyard wines. Winiarski himself identifies his greatest vintages as 1977, 1978, 1985, 1990, and 1994. I have also enjoyed excellent Cabernets from less fashionable vintages such as 1979 and 1983.

There are two Chardonnays, one from the Beckstoffer Ranch and the other a Napa Reserve. They are not among the most appealing of Napa Chardonnays. Stag's Leap makes an attractive Riesling, which usually comes the Birkmeyer Vineyard. These wines are unoaked, and occasionally show a hint of botrytis.

Sauvignon Blanc was first produced here in 1981, but John Gibson, who was the winemaker here in the 1980s, was never impressed by the early efforts. Later vintages were more crisp and lively, but this has never been among Stag's Leap's finest bottlings.

Warren Winiarski is very proud of the Hawk Crest range, in effect his second label, produced from purchased grapes. The wines are simple but well-made, with limited oak-ageing for the whites, and while the prices of Stag's Leap wines have risen, Hawk Crest has remained excellent value.

Stag's Leap Cabernet has been criticized for inconsistency in recent years, but in my experience the wines remain excellent. If they do not shine out as clearly as they did ten or fifteen years ago, that may be because so many other wineries are now producing Cabernet of comparable quality.

Philip Togni

3780 Spring Mountain Rd., St Helena, CA 94574. Tel: 963 3731. Fax: 963 9186. Production: 2,500 cases.

Although he has lived in California for forty years, Philip Togni has preserved his English accent intact. His has been an extraordinary career. He studied at Montpellier and Bordeaux, worked in Chile as a young man, then made the wine at Château Lascombes in St Julien in 1956. In 1958 he was hired by the Taylor family at Mayacamas to make their wide range of wines, and since then he has also been the winemaker at Chalone and Cuvaison. He founded his own small winery high up on Spring Mountain in 1983. There had been a vineyard here since 1883, and Philip claims that a single old Cinsault vine survives from that time. The vineyard was abandoned from 1915 to 1975, which is when the Tognis bought the property. Most of the vineyard was replanted in 1981 with Cabernet Sauvignon, Merlot, and a little Cabernet Franc and Petit Verdot, as well as his speciality of Black Hamburg. Phylloxera has required much of the vineyard to be replanted, and Pierce's disease has also proved a nuisance. Despite the elevation of 2,000 feet, the soils here are quite vigorous, although dry-farmed. Togni has called in Dr Richard Smart to assist with the canopy management, and green cover of barley is planted between the rows.

After decades of working for other wineries and proprietors, Togni is clearly happy to be doing exactly as he pleases at his mountain vineyard. His Sauvignon, now discontinued, was for many years one of the most distinctive, and expensive, in California. It was always whole-cluster pressed, never saw oak, and was bottled a few months after the vintage, then bottle-aged for a year. The idea was to provide a perfect complement to oysters. The Sauvignon was high in acidity and sometimes a touch green, but it made a refreshing change from the dull, vaguely oaky Sauvignons so common at other California wineries. 1994 was the last vintage, and the vines have been replaced by red Bordeaux varieties.

The Togni Cabernet Sauvignon is a formidable wine, which needs a few years in bottle to become harmonious. The wine is aged in one-third new *barriques* for some 20 months. The press wine is aged separately and only before bottling does Philip decide how much to blend in. Some of the earlier vintages were too tannic and aggressive, but by the late 1980s the style had softened slightly, without losing any of the power, richness, and complexity of the wine. The 1990 beat some of the Bordeaux first growths in a Belgian blind tasting held in 1996, a result which the Tognis find gratifying. Certainly the 1990 and 1991 are both magnificent wines, with none of the harshness that marred some earlier vintages.

Philip planted Black Hamburg for the very good reason that he liked the grape. In 1985 he began to sell it commercially, and it soon won the approval of Robert Parker. Up went the price and now, Togni complains, even he can't afford to drink it. The grapes are picked very late in semi-raisined condition, then pressed and fermented in oak barrels and aged for a year; a little brandy is added before bottling. I used to think it was capable of ageing, but having tried a few older vintages, I am sure now that, like most Muscats, it is a wine to be enjoyed in its flowery, grapy youth. I fear that this wine, known as Ca' Togni, may go the way of the Sauvignon Blanc, as the vines have been badly affected by Pierce's disease.

NOTES

1 The area code throughout Napa Valley is 707, which is omitted from the listings that follow
2 James Conaway, *Napa*, p. 247

23
Napa Valley II

Altamura
1700 Wooden Valley Rd., Napa, CA 94558. Tel: 253 2000. Fax: 255 3937. Production: 3,000 cases.

Founded by Frank and Karen Altamura in 1985. Their 35 acres off Silverado Trail and in Wooden Valley are planted with Chardonnay, Cabernet Sauvignon, Merlot, and Cabernet Franc. The initial releases were of full-powered Chardonnay, later supplemented by Cabernet after long ageing in *barriques*. Recent releases of Sangiovese have been well received.

S. Anderson
1473 Yountville Crossroad, Yountville, CA 94599. Tel: 944 8542. Fax: 944 8020. Production: 14,000 cases.

In 1973 dentist Stan Anderson, who died in 1994, planted vineyards in Stags Leap District with 32 acres of Chardonnay, later supplemented with more acreage in Carneros as well as near the winery. Although a little table wine is produced, notably plump, toasty Chardonnay and a Chambers Vineyard Cabernet Sauvignon, Anderson specialize in full-bodied sparkling wines, all vintage-dated, all aged on the yeast for at least 4 years. The range includes Blanc de Noirs, Blanc de Blancs, rosé, Brut (mostly Pinot Noir), a stylish Brut Reserve (mostly Chardonnay), Tivoli (first pressing only), and Diva, a luxury cuvée in magnums released after 8 years on the yeast. The winemaker is Daniel DeSante.

Anderson's Conn Valley Vineyards
680 Ross Rd., St Helena, CA 94574. Tel: 963 8600. Production: 5,000 cases.

The 28 acres of vineyards were planted just east of Napa Valley, and Gus Anderson's first release was a 1987 Cabernet Sauvignon. The winery specializes in small lots of Cabernet, Pinot Noir, and Chardonnay. In my limited experience, the Cabernet is better than its reputation.

Atlas Peak

3700 Soda Canyon Rd., Napa, CA 94581. Tel: 252 7971. Fax: 252 7974. Production: 25,000 cases.

This immensely ambitious project was created by vineyard developer William Hill, who sold it to the British brewers Whitbread in 1984. Other partners were brought in, and in 1993, one of them, the Tuscan estate of Antinori, became sole owner. The 465 acres of vineyards planted at a height of 1,450–1,800 feet included 150 acres of Sangiovese, as well as some other Italian varieties. The first vintage was 1989. Other than 1990, initial releases were disappointing, but recent vintages have been of better quality, especially the tight, seamless 1995 Reserve. The regular Sangiovese is aged for 12 months in casks of various sizes, while the Reserve is aged in *barriques* and oak puncheons, and bottled without fining. New oak, used at first, is no longer employed. The blend called Consenso is a Cabernet Sauvignon with 16 per cent Sangiovese, aged in oak for 2 years. The winery also produces Chardonnay, Cabernet Sauvignon, and barrel-fermented Chardonnay. The winemaker is John Falcone.

Bancroft

1000 Las Posadas Rd., Angwin, CA 94508. Tel: 965 3080. Production: 1,500 cases.

Jim Bancroft's vineyards on Howell Mountain have long supplied grapes to Stony Hill, Beringer, and other wineries, but since 1988 a small amount of Chardonnay has also been produced under the vineyard label.

Barnett

4070 Spring Mountain Rd., St Helena, CA 94574. Tel: 963 7075. Production: 3,000 cases.

The 14-acre terraced vineyards were planted in 1984 to produce small quantities of Chardonnay, Cabernet Sauvignon, and Merlot, as well as Pinot Noir from Talbott vineyards in the Santa Lucia Highlands. Kent Rasmussen made the wines until Charles Hendricks took over.

Beaulieu

19860 St Helena Highway, Rutherford, CA 94573. Tel: 967 5200. Production: 650,000 cases.

The early history of this illustrious estate has been given elsewhere in this book. In 1969 it was bought by Heublein. Production grew rapidly, from 150,000 cases before the purchase to 450,000 cases in the 1980s. The current owner of the estate is the drinks complex IDV. Beaulieu currently owns 383 acres planted with Cabernet in Napa Valley, as well as 350 acres in Carneros, planted with Chardonnay and Pinot Noir. In all, Beaulieu now owns or leases 1,500 acres. In 1973 the moderately priced Beautour range was introduced, and in 1998 the range was repackaged as BV Coastal.

In the 1990s the entire range was revamped. Cabernet Sauvignon remained the top wine, still made in limited quantities (about 11,000 cases) as Private Reserve, continuing the tradition of the top-quality Cabernet aged mostly in American oak inaugurated by André Tchelitscheff in the 1930s. There was also a Rutherford bottling, which often offers exceptionally good value, and the Beautour. BV also offers the Napa Series, which consists of barrel-fermented Sauvignon Blanc, Zinfandel, Carneros Pinot Noir, Carneros Chardonnay, and Merlot aged in French and American oak.

Limited-production wines are released as the Signet Collection series, introduced in 1994. The range includes a Rhône variety blend called Ensemble, a Zinfandel from Spring Mountain, Sangiovese blended with some Cabernet Sauvignon, barrel-fermented Viognier, San Benito County Grenache, Syrah, and Petite Sirah.

In addition to the Private Reserve Cabernet, there are other reserve wines: Carneros Chardonnay, Carneros Pinot Noir, and a Meritage called Tapestry. The Cabernet remains a very good wine, but I have been deeply disappointed by certain vintages, such as 1983 and 1989. From 1990 the style changed when French as well as American oak was used, and some Merlot was blended into a wine formerly pure Cabernet. It is clearly not at quite the same quality level as its obvious competitors such as Beringer Private Reserve and Mondavi Reserve Cabernet. The efforts made to improve the overall quality have been only patchily successful. Forty per cent of sales are still taken up by white Zinfandel. The winemaker since 1985 has been Joel Aiken.

Robert Biale Vineyards
2040 Brown St., Napa, CA 94559. Tel: 257 7555. Fax: 257 0105. Production: 3,000 cases.

The Biales have been growing grapes for over 40 years, and in 1991 began to produce wines from both their own and from purchased fruit. The Zinfandels, from a number of sources including Monte Rosso in Sonoma, are the best wines. There are plans to produce some Italian varieties too.

Bryant Family Vineyard
PO Box 332, Calistoga, CA 94515. Production: 1,800 cases.

Only Cabernet Sauvignon is grown on these 10 rocky acres of north-facing slopes in the eastern hills of Napa Valley near Pritchard Hill. Yields are low, at about 2 tons per acre. The owners are Don and Barbara Bryant and the winemaker Helen Turley, who since 1993 has employed her usual techniques of a 5-day cold soak before fermentation, natural yeast fermentation, and no filtration. In 1995 replanting diminished production to a mere 700 cases of very ripe Cabernet priced at $100 – per bottle.

Buehler
820 Greenfield Road, St Helena, CA 94574. Tel: 963 2155. Production: 35,000 cases.

John Buehler Sr was a senior executive with the Bechtel corporation when he bought this 63-acre estate near Lake Hennessey as a tax shelter in 1972. Initially the vineyard was planted with Zinfandel, Cabernet Sauvignon, and Pinot Blanc (which was grubbed up in 1990 after phylloxera arrived in the vineyard). Grapes were also purchased. Heidi Peterson Barrett was the winemaker here in the mid-1980s. The estate is best known for its intense Zinfandels and Cabernets.

Burgess
1108 Deer Park Road, St Helena, CA 94574. Tel: 963 4766. Fax: 963 8774. Production: 30,000 cases.

Tom Burgess, a former pilot, founded the estate in 1972. The winery attained early renown as the old Souverain Winery run by the legendary Lee Stewart, who bought the property in 1943. The 70 acres of Cabernet Sauvignon, Merlot, and Cabernet Franc are located at a height of 1,000 feet. In addition Chardonnay is grown on their 50-acre Triere Vineyard near Yountville. Additional Zinfandel is planted at another Burgess-owned site on Howell Mountain. Riesling and Chenin Blanc used to be made but were phased out some time ago. Most of the fruit is dry-farmed. Bill Sorenson has been making the wines since the outset.

The Chardonnay is a full-malolactic wine, as is the Triere Reserve Chardonnay, which is fermented in new Vosges oak. A Merlot aged in French oak has been added to the range, and the Cabernet sees a good proportion of new oak. There were some superb if tannic Cabernets in the 1970s. A favourite wine, which has often triumphed in blind tastings in which I have participated, has been the superb Zinfandel, which is aged in French and American oak.

The estate's second label is Bell Canyon.

Cafaro
1591 Dean York Lane, St Helena, CA. Tel: 963 7181. Production: 2,000 cases.

The well-known winemaker Joe Cafaro, who has worked for Chappellet, Keenan, Acacia, and Sinskey, has planted 14 acres in Stags Leap District, focusing on Cabernet and Merlot. He also buys fruit from Hess and Spottswoode. Quality is good.

Cakebread

8300 St Helena Highway, Rutherford, CA 94573. Tel: 963 5221. Fax: 963 1034. Production: 50,000 cases.

Jack Cakebread bought 20 acres along the highway in 1971, and built a winery two years later. A 1973 Chardonnay was his first release, followed by a 1974 Cabernet Sauvignon. Zinfandel and Sauvignon Blanc were added to the range in 1976. Today there are 75 acres under vine, and the entire vineyard was replanted after phylloxera in the early 1990s. This vineyard is insufficient for the winery's requirements, so they buy in 75 per cent of their needs.

Cakebread have always made a good Sauvignon, and experimented with trellising in the late 1980s. Blind tastings, in which I participated, did show a distinct if subtle difference in quality between the trellising systems employed. The wine is aged about 7 months in *barriques*. The burly Chardonnay comes from southern Napa and Carneros, and the Reserve Chardonnay is fermented in new *barriques*, with 50 per cent malolactic fermentation.

The 1994 Cabernet Sauvignon was a blend of fruit from Rutherford, Oakville, and Stags Leap, which was aged 2 years in *barrique*. Their top Cabernet, the Rutherford Reserve, comes from older vines and is aged 31 months in *barriques* and bottle-aged for 2 years before release. In 1995 there were two cuvées, Three Sisters and the leaner Benchland Select. There is also a Zinfandel from Howell Mountain fruit, and unfiltered Merlot from Oakville and Carneros grapes. Rubaiyat is a fairly light blend of mostly Pinot Noir with 20 per cent Cabernet Sauvignon and Zinfandel; it is intended to be drunk young. Overall the wines are good and reliable, but for some reason they have never quite been in the top tier, although prices are far from cheap.

Cakebread remains a family operation, and Bruce Cakebread has been the winemaker since 1979.

Caymus

8700 Conn Creek Rd., Rutherford, CA 94573. Tel: 963 4204. Fax: 963 5958. Production: 55,000 cases.

The Wagner family bought an old prune and walnut farm here in 1941, but not until the 1960s did Charles Wagner begin to plant the land with Riesling, Pinot Noir, and Cabernet Sauvignon. The Pinot Noir and Riesling were pulled out in the 1970s. From 1972 onwards Caymus became well known for its Cabernet Sauvignon. There are 62 acres of vineyards in production. George Deuer, formerly of Inglenook, was the initial wine-maker, and from the late 1970s Randy Dunn was in charge of making the wines, staying with Caymus until 1986, long after he had started his own winery. Charles Wagner's son Chuck is now the chief winemaker, while Jon Bolta looks after white wine production.

Caymus also owns a Monterey estate from which they produce a fruit-salady, sweetish Chardonnay called Mer & Soleil. They are also developing a Sonoma Coast winery. The Liberty School range, a kind of second label of good-value wines, has been discontinued, and the label sold to Treana in Paso Robles. Zinfandel and Pinot Noir are made from purchased grapes.

The white wines include a Napa Sauvignon, which is barrel-fermented in 75 per cent new oak, and blended with 10 per cent Chardonnay. To my taste, it lacks typicity. Conundrum is a blend of Sauvignon, Chardonnay, Viognier from Monterey, Sémillon, and Muscat Canelli (being diminished in volume in favour of Viognier). Most of the wine is barrel-fermented. It has received critical acclaim, but the wine contains at least 5 grams of residual sugar and I find it undrinkable and overpriced at $20 for a very commercial blend.

It is of course the Cabernet Sauvignon for which Caymus is most famous. In 1984 they launched a Napa Valley Cuvée from purchased grapes. In 1987 this was combined with estate-grown Cabernet. This wine is aged for up to 27 months in American and French oak barrels, of which up to 30 per cent are new. Sometimes a little Cabernet Franc is blended in. There was some discontent when the 1995 was released at $65, compared to $36 for the 1994. Wagner explained that he needed to continue to secure the grapes which were sought after by other producers too; and in addition, he wanted to 'secure our position as a top California producer.'[1]

The Special Selection Cabernet, first made in 1975, is produced entirely from a 14-acre parcel of estate-grown Rutherford grapes. The soil is a rich gravelly loam. Randy Dunn explained that the cuvée began as a parcel simply left in wood for an additional year. Today it receives special treatment. It is often a blend of up to five lots, which are kept separate until shortly before bottling. The wine is aged for up to 4 years in new and old *barriques*, although two and half years is more usual. Since the wine goes in and out of *barriques*, it is very hard to determine the nature of the oak component of the final blend. The wine is bottled without fining or filtration.

I may be lynched for saying so, but the Special Selection, acclaimed by some as the greatest California red of them all, is a wine that has always left me cold. The long barrel-ageing does not seem designed to assist the structure of the wine but to make it accessible and drinkable on release, which, Chuck Wagner openly admits, is the intention. Unlike, say, Ridge Montebello, it is not at all evident that the wine evolves well with age. The fruit is forward and often jammy, the wine is not especially concentrated or dense, and I find it lacks finesse. Nor do I perceive an enormous difference in quality between the Napa Cuvée and the Special Selection, and since the latter is released at $100, I would rather spend my money, if at all, on three bottles of the lesser wine.

As for the white wines, I find both the Sauvignon and Conundrum hard to take, and the same goes for Mer & Soleil. The sweetness that mars these wines may have commercial appeal, but I am puzzled that palates as acute as James Halliday's can find them so exceptional. When I tentatively mentioned my lack of enthusiasm for the Caymus range to a New York wine merchant who specializes in high-priced offerings from California, he muttered: 'Everything Caymus does is sugar-coated.' So perhaps I am not entirely alone.

Domaine Chandon

1 California Drive, Yountville, CA 94599. Tel: 944 8844. Fax: 944 1123. Production: 500,000 cases.

It took a few years for Moet & Chandon to decide whether or not to set up a sparkling wine facility in Napa Valley. In 1973 their master wine-maker Edmund Maudière produced an experimental vintage at Trefethen winery, and after much reflection decided that the varietal base for the new sparkling wine should be Chardonnay, Pinot Noir, and, to a lesser extent, Pinot Blanc and Pinot Meunier. The winery was built in 1977, making it the first French-owned sparkling wine facility in California. The estate is now the owner of 1,600 acres throughout the North Coast, and the second largest grower in Carneros, where it controls some 500 acres. Domaine Chandon was the first sparkling wine producer in California to use Pinot Meunier in the blend, and has long planted its vineyards with closer spacing, again reflecting French influence.

The operation is technically sophisticated. Much of the fruit is picked by machine at night, and gyro-palettes are employed at the winery. All the cuvées are non-vintage, but include up to 30 per cent reserve wines. The range includes Brut Cuvée (a blend of Napa and Sonoma fruit, with 60 per cent Pinot Noir; aged 24 months on the yeast), Blanc de Noirs (sold as Shadow Creek in export markets, from 80 per cent Pinot Noir and 20 per cent Pinot Meunier, aged 30 months on the yeast), and Reserve Cuvée (66 per cent Pinot Noir, aged 4 years on the yeast). In contrast Etoile, launched in 1992 as a blend of older vintages, is mostly Chardonnay, aged 3 years on the yeast; there is also a rosé version. Overall quality is good, though rarely outstanding. The absence of vintage cuvées means that there is no opportunity for an outstanding lot to shine out. Moreover the style used to be broad and rather heavy, though recent bottlings have shown much greater freshness.

Dawnine Sample Dyer has been in charge of the winemaking here since 1981.

Chappellet

1581 Sage Canyon Rd., St Helena, CA 94574. Tel: 963 7136. Fax: 963 7445. Production: 25,000 cases.

Donn Chappellet's winery was only the second to be constructed in Napa after Prohibition. There was already a vineyard in place when Chappellet acquired the property, and he planted more vines in 1967 on Pritchard Hill at a height of 1,500–1,700 feet. Today there are 120 acres in production, almost half them on terraces. The soils are stony, and the wines tend to be lean and angular, although recent modifications, such as the suppression of press wine from the final blend, have led to a slightly more approachable style.

Riesling is no longer produced, but Chappellet's Chenin is one of the best in California, made in both a dry and sweet style. The dry wine comes in two versions, a crisp fresh mineral version, and the Old Vine Cuvée, which is barrel-fermented, with 50 per cent malolactic fermentation. The late-harvested wine is released in half bottles. The Chardonnay is barrel-fermented but only half the wine goes through malolactic fermentation. The Cabernet Sauvignon is made in an austere tannic style, and the wine needs a lot of bottle age. The top bottling is called Signature.

Cathy Corison was the winemaker here throughout the 1980s, and was replaced in 1991 by Phillip Corallo-Titus. The wines are priced fairly, making it scarcely necessary to buy the second label, Pritchard Hill.

Chateau Potelle

3875 Mount Veeder Road, Napa, CA 94558. Tel: 255 9440. Fax: 255 9444. Production: 30,000 cases.

Jean-Noel and Marketta Fourmeaux du Sartel came to the West Coast on behalf of the French government, their mission being to study the Californian wine industry. They liked what they found so much that they bought part of it, settling on a Mount Veeder estate founded by Hamilton Vose and which they purchased in 1988. They now cultivate 100 acres around the winery, one-third planted with Chardonnay, the remainder with red grapes. The soil up on Mount Veeder is volcanic shale and the grapes ripen three weeks later than on the valley floor. In addition they own a 90-acre vineyard off Silverado Trail planted with the Bordeaux red varieties, and a further 90 acres in Paso Robles planted with Zinfandel and Syrah. More grapes are bought in: Sauvignon Blanc from Pope Valley, Chardonnay from Carneros, Cabernet Sauvignon from Alexander Valley.

The Sauvignon Blanc is partly barrel-fermented, and some Sémillon is blended in before it is aged in *barriques*, with the lees stirred from time to time. There's a curious wine called Epice, a blend of Gewürztraminer, Viognier, and Chardonnay; despite the presence of these aromatic varieties that wine is curiously bland and flat on the palate. The Mount Veeder

Chardonnay can sometimes be hollow and lacking in fruit; it is supplemented with a barrel-fermented Central Coast Chardonnay; American as well as French oak is used. The Reserve lines are labelled VGS, and come from estate-grown Mount Veeder fruit. The Chardonnay comes from low-yielding vines and is aged in mostly new *barriques*.

The Zinfandel comes from head-pruned vines in Stags Leap District cropped at 3 tons per acre, and aged for 18 months in mostly American oak. The only vintage I have tasted was rather hard and baked. The pricy VGS Zinfandel, assertive and peppery, is cropped at 2 tons per acre, given a long maceration, and aged for 18 months in mostly French oak. The VGS Cabernet Sauvignon is aged in new *barriques* for up to 20 months.

The winemaker is Steve Hall, and I imagine he has a hard time working with so many varieties from so many sources. Although Chateau Potelle has won much praise in recent vintages, I find the wines very inconsistent.

Chateau Woltner

3500 Silverado Trail, St Helena, CA 94574. Tel: 963 1744. Fax: 963 8135. Production: 20,000 cases.

The Woltner family must have experienced considerable culture shock, when after years as majority shareholders in Château La Mission Haut-Brion, they sold their interest and moved to California. There one would have expected them to focus their energies on Cabernet Sauvignon, but instead they did the unthinkable. They went Burgundian and cultivated nothing but Chardonnay, pointing out that Cabernet Sauvignon would never ripen in their mountain vineyards. They maintained continuity by finding an old stone winery founded in 1886 on Howell Mountain by two Bordelais, Jean Adolphe Brun and Jean Chaix. This pair of Frenchmen had made wines that were highly regarded in the nineteenth century. The winery was abandoned after Prohibition, and Francis and Françoise DeWavrin Woltner had to spend a fortune restoring the property after they acquired it in 1983.

They made the curious decision to plant their 55 acres with a single rootstock and a single clone of Chardonnay. Their first harvest was in 1985, when the wines were made by Ted Lemon, who had considerable experience making wine in Burgundy. Another renowned winemaker, Ric Forman, was hired as consultant. The winemaking has been meticulous, without cultivated yeasts, and with fermentation (partial only for their basic Howell Mountain Chardonnay) and ageing in Burgundian oak. The Woltners have been wary of new oak, and kept it to a maximum of 35 per cent. There is no malolactic fermentation, but instead prolonged lees contact in the barrels.

The Woltners seem to have taken a leaf out of Al Brounstein's book at Diamond Creek Vineyard by bottling separately the production from different parcels, which they have named St Thomas, Titus, and Frederique. Production of the last two is tiny (fewer than 200 cases of each) and prices correspondingly high.

I confess that the wines puzzle me. They are certainly hard to appreciate when young, and seem to lack fruit. The Woltners would undoubtedly point out that these wines are made from low-yielding mountain grapes and that, like fine white Burgundy, they demand patience. Perhaps with time they will develop complexity in bottle and the portfolio of 1990s was very impressive. In the meantime it seems audacious to charge very high prices for wines on the basis that they may eventually turn out well.

Chimney Rock

5350 Silverado Trail, Napa, CA 94558. Tel: 257 2641. Fax: 257 2036. Production: 22,000 cases.

Since 1980 this estate has belonged to Sheldon 'Hack' Wilson, a former Pepsi executive and hotelier. Between 1980 and 1982 75 acres of Cabernet Sauvignon, Chardonnay and Sauvignon Blanc were planted on a former golf course; the winery was not built until 1989, by which time phylloxera had obliged Wilson to replant the vineyard. He did so with high spacing. Today the winery focuses on Cabernet Sauvignon, Merlot, Cabernet Franc, and an unoaked Fumé Blanc. The long-term intention is to phase out Chardonnay and replace it with a Merlot-based Meritage called Elevage. The winemaker is Doug Fletcher. Until quite recently the winery had a dim reputation, but from the early 1990s onwards it began to be taken very seriously, and there have been some impressive reds, especially Cabernet.

Clos du Val

5330 Silverado Trail, Napa, CA 94558. Tel: 259 2200. Fax: 252 6125. Production: 65,000 cases.

One of the earliest wineries in Stags Leap District, it was established in 1972 by the Bordeaux merchant John Goelet and Bernard Portet, whose father had been the manager at Château Lafite, where he and his brother Dominique (who owns Taltarni in Australia) were raised. The estate has grown considerably over the years, and since 1986 has been self-sufficient in terms of grape supply. The 265 acres are divided between Stags Leap District and Carneros, as well as some acreage in Yountville. Most of the vineyards had to be replanted after phylloxera, and Bernard Portet believes that with closer spacing, both yields and quality have greatly improved.

Clos du Val offers a full range of varietal wines, a Carneros Chardonnay that is barrel-fermented and aged in *barriques* for 9 months; a good Sémillon, from Stags Leap fruit; Carneros Pinot Noir, aged for 12 months in *barriques*; a Stags Leap Merlot, first produced in 1977; a full-bodied Zinfandel; a pricy Sangiovese, first made in 1994; and a very good Cab-

ernet Sauvignon. The Reserve Cabernet is macerated for a long period
and also aged longer in oak, most of which is new.

With Portet at the helm, it is not surprising that there is a French
approach to styling the wine, which is reticent in its youth but ages very
well. There was a bad patch during the late 1980s, when many wines
seemed mean and charmless, but in recent vintages they have returned to
their former high standard. The second label is 'Le Clos', mostly made
from purchased fruit.

Colgin-Schrader Cellars
7830 St Helena Highway, Oakville, CA 94562. Tel: 524 4445. Production:
700 cases.

Another ultra-fashionable winery, based around the steep and rocky 7-
acre Herb Lamb Vineyard at the foot of Howell Mountain. A smaller
vineyard is being developed near Grace Family Vineyards. Ann Colgin and
Fred Schrader, art dealers from Florida, are the owners, and Helen Turley
the winemaker. Ann Colgin is now head of Sotheby's wine department in
Los Angeles. The first release was in 1992, to rave reviews, and the only
wine is Cabernet Sauvignon, which is priced at $90, but fetches consider-
ably more at auction.

Conn Creek
See Villa Mount Eden (p. 438).

The estate was founded in 1974 by Kathy and Bill Collins, and their early
Cabernets were very successful, even though the winery was not completed
until 1979. Quality faltered in the 1980s and in 1986 the property was
acquired by Stimson Lane, who also own Villa Mount Eden as well as the
Chateau St Michelle and Columbia Crest wineries in Washington state.
Stimson Lane have focused on a few wines: Cabernet Sauvignon, and a
fleshy, luxurious Meritage called Anthology, which in 1994 was 50 per
cent Merlot, 36 per cent Cabernet Sauvignon, and 14 per cent Cabernet
Franc. This wine is aged for 18 months in *barriques* and bottled without
filtration.

Corison
PO Box 344, Oakville, CA 94562. Tel: 963 7357. Fax: 963 5776. Production: 2,500 cases.

Cathy Corison established a fine reputation as a winemaker throughout
the 1980s, working for Freemark Abbey, Chappellet and other wineries.
In 1987 she set up her own label and rented winemaking facilities at
Sinskey. Buying fruit from good benchland sites throughout Napa Valley,
she produces only Cabernet Sauvignon, which is aged in 50 per cent new
barriques. Initial releases were very well received.

Cornerstone

Tel: 255 6884. Production: 2,300 cases.

Bruce Scotland, a former wine merchant, specializes in producing small lots of mostly Cabernet Sauvignon and Zinfandel from outstanding vineyards from Howell Mountain, Carneros, and elsewhere. He has also produced a proprietary red called Tay, blending Cabernet with Merlot from Carneros.

Cosentino

7415 St Helena Highway, Yountville, CA 94599. Tel: 944 1220. Fax: 944 1254. Production: 18,000 cases.

Mitch Cosentino began his winemaking career as a hobby winemaker, producing such delicacies as sparkling pink Carignane. He bought land in Napa Valley in 1986 and opened his winery in 1990. Cosentino produces a wide range of wines, often in small lots. His favourite winemaking technique is punching down the cap during fermentation, as the labels remind customers. The winery owns only a few acres in Napa, so grapes are bought from various locations in North Coast counties.

Current releases include a Yountville Gewürztraminer, mostly barrel-fermented; a white Meritage called The Novelist that sees a good deal of new oak; three different Chardonnays, of which his top example is called The Sculptor and uses Yountville grapes.

There is a Napa Cabernet and a Reserve Cabernet, and a Meritage called M.COZ (48 per cent Cabernet, 26 per cent Merlot, 21 per cent Cabernet Franc, and 5 per cent Petit Verdot) to the immense annoyance of Château Cos d'Estournel in the Médoc. A second Meritage is known as 'The Poet'; made mostly from Cabernet, it is aged for 25 months in oak. His Oakville Merlot and Reserve Merlot have been well received. There are Pinot Noirs from Napa, Carneros, and Russian River, a Cabernet Franc from St Helena fruit, and Zinfandels blended from various sources.

My acquaintance with these wines is limited, but reports suggest that quality is wildly inconsistent.

Costello Vineyards Winery

1200 Orchard Ave., Napa, CA 94558. Tel: 252 8483. Production: 20,000 cases.

John Costello founded this property in 1982 and some of the wines emerged from his own 40 acres planted with Chardonnay, Sauvignon Blanc, and Gewürztraminer. There were some good-quality Gewürztraminers in the 1980s, but now the focus has shifted to Chardonnay.

Robert Craig Cellars

Tel: 252 2250. Production: 3,000 cases.

Robert Craig was general manager at Hess before setting up on his own. The first vintage here was 1992. This estate produces Cabernet Sauvignons from Howell Mountain and Mount Veeder, and a stylish proprietary red called Affinity and composed of Cabernet Sauvignon, Merlot, and a little Cabernet Franc, all from Craig's vineyards in Coombsville. Quality is high.

Crichton Hall

1150 Darms Lane, Napa, CA 94558. Tel: 224 4200. Fax: 224 4218. Production: 6,000 cases.

This estate is named after its owners, British banker Robert Crichton and his American wife Judith Hall. They own some Chardonnay vineyards close to Trefethen in southern Napa. Their 1995 Chardonnay was barrel-fermented in 25 per cent new *barriques*, and after partial malolactic fermentation was aged 10 months. Their Merlot blends Carneros and Yountville fruit, and the Pinot Noir is made from Carneros fruit. Some early vintages were of a high standard, but recent vintages have been less impressive.

Cuvaison Vineyards

4550 Silverado Trail, Calistoga, CA 94515. Tel: 942 6266. Fax: 942 5732. Production: 63,000 cases

This well-established estate has been through many changes of ownership, but has been fortunate in retaining the services of its winemaker John Thacher since 1982. The property was founded in 1969 by Silicon Valley engineers, then bought in 1974 by Oakleigh Thorne, who appointed Philip Togni as winemaker. In those days the range of wines was eclectic, including Chenin and Gamay. In 1979 Cuvaison was bought by the very rich Schmidheiny family of Switzerland, who own the world's largest cement company. After they installed Manfred Esser as export manager in 1986 – he subsequently became president – Cuvaison won a fine reputation for its Chardonnays, which easily dominate production, and Merlots. More recently the celebrated French winemaker Michel Rolland, a Merlot specialist, has been taken on as consultant.

Cuvaison's vineyard holdings include 400 acres in Carneros, which account for the great majority of the grapes used at the winery. The estate releases a number of different Chardonnays. The Reserve bottling was introduced in 1986, and is given the full-throttle California treatment, including 95 per cent new oak.

In the early years Cuvaison produced some blockbuster reds, but Thacher has refined the style, making the wines more supple and approachable. Most of the Cabernet fruit comes from Oakville and Rutherford. There are two Pinot Noirs. The Carneros is the top bottling, but the Eris, made in a more forward style, can be delicious too. The Merlot has long been exceptional, and is aged in 65 per cent new oak. The range is completed with Zinfandel. The ATS range consists of small lots of reserve wines.

Production has grown considerably, and some of the basic bottlings have been disappointing, especially Chardonnay, although at its best Cuvaison still produces some impeccable wines.

Dalla Valle

7776 Silverado Trail, Yountville, CA 94562. Tel: 944 2676. Fax: 944 8411. Production: 5,000 cases.

An elderly Italian-born scuba-gear tycoon, Gustav Dalla Valle (who died in 1995), arrived in Napa Valley in 1982, planted 26 acres of Bordeaux red varieties, and in 1986 built a winery. The core of the estate is a 6-acre vineyard on eastern slopes of Oakville which give some intense Cabernet Sauvignon. The other Bordeaux-style wine is Maya, which in 1994 was a blend of 55 per cent Cabernet and 45 per cent Cabernet Franc. The range is rounded off with a rich, forceful Sangiovese called Pietre Rosse.

From 1987 to 1995 Heidi Peterson Barrett was the winemaker, crafting dense tannic wines that seemed curiously old-fashioned in their structure. She was particularly keen on the 1990, 1992, and the spectacular and highly complex 1994. The 1995 is of comparable stratospheric splendour. They are definitely wines for cellaring, but how long will it be before the wine becomes enjoyable as well as admirable? Maya, however, is more accessible, thanks to its generous infusion of Cabernet Franc, but at twice the price of the Cabernet ($80 for the 1994), it certainly needs to be of exemplary quality.

Deer Park

1000 Deer Park Rd., Deer Park, CA 94576. Tel: 963 5411. Production: 3,000 cases.

Fairly low down on Howell Mountain stands this stone winery, founded in 1891 by John and Jacob Sutter. It closed at Prohibition and was bought in 1978 by the Clark and Knapp families. David Clark is the winemaker. The dry-farmed vineyards, steep and rocky, are planted with Chardonnay and Sauvignon Blanc. Zinfandel is often purchased from Beatty ranch. The wines are burly rather than elegant.

Duckhorn

3027 Silverado Trail, St Helena, CA 94574. Tel: 963 7108. Fax: 963 7595. Production: 70,000 cases.

Duckhorn is perhaps best known as the winery that made superb Merlots long before it became fashionable, and immensely profitable, to do so. Dan Duckhorn, a former banker, bought the winery in 1976. His first vintage was 1978, and his first winemaker, Tom Rinaldi, is still with him. At first almost all their grapes were bought in, but over the years the estate has grown to 318 acres, of which 162 are at six locations in Napa Valley, including 80 acres on Howell Mountain. A recent expansion has been into Anderson Valley, where Duckhorn has purchased 85 acres near Philo, and is planning to produce a top-quality Pinot Noir called Goldeneye.

Merlot was first produced in 1978, and there were separate bottlings from Three Palms Vineyard. In 1989 Duckhorn introduced a Howell Mountain bottling, which is in effect a Meritage with a slight dominance of Merlot. Three Palms Vineyard has been hurt by phylloxera, but replanting will bring it back into full production by the year 2000. In the meantime Duckhorn have added a Vine Hill Merlot and, since 1995, an Estate Grown Merlot. These rich concentrated wines, with none of the shallowness that afflicts cheap commercial Merlots, are aged in *barriques*, of which 50 to 75 per cent are new.

The Napa Cabernet comes mostly from Yountville fruit, but eight other vineyards make their contribution. In 1995 it was aged in one-third new *barriques* for 16 months. Although Duckhorn has made its reputation with Merlot, the Cabernet can be equally good. In 1994 a new wine was introduced: Paraduxx, a blend of Zinfandel, Merlot, Cabernet Sauvignon, and (in some vintages) Petite Sirah, aged in 50 per cent new oak for 17 months.

Since 1982 Duckhorn have made a good Sauvignon Blanc, into which 25 per cent Sémillon was usually blended. Surplus Sémillon was released under the Decoy label. The Sauvignon was only partly barrel-fermented, but that portion was aged in a sizeable proportion of new oak. It has always been quite a rich style. Dan Duckhorn insisted he was looking for viscosity, not for a light shellfish wine.

Dan Duckhorn is not a man to rest on his laurels. He has been planting Pinot Blanc, Viognier, and the Musqué clone of Sauvignon Blanc. It will be fascinating to see what he makes of the fruit, and whether he can produce a world-class Pinot Noir from Anderson Valley.

El Molino

PO Box 306, St Helena, CA 94574. Tel: 963 3632. Production: 1,200 cases.

Reg Oliver's winery dates from 1871, although it was closed down in 1920. Only two wines are produced, a Carneros Pinot Noir, aged in new *barriques*, and a Rutherford Chardonnay. The wines enjoy an avid following among mail-order clients.

Elyse

2100 Hoffman Lane, Napa, CA 94558. Tel: 963 5496. Production: 5,000 cases.

Ray Courson, who used to make the wine at Whitehall Lane, is the perfect example of the laid-back Californian winemaker. He doesn't give the impression of being a stickler for detail, and admits that he has been accused of 'making wine by neglect'. Indeed, there are occasional disappointments from Elyse, but also some wonderful wines. He owns only 4 acres of vineyards, Cabernet Sauvignon planted between Yountville and Napa, so most of the fruit is bought in.

Ray specializes in Zinfandel, either from Howell Mountain or from the Morisoli Vineyard in Rutherford. The wine is aged for a year in American oak. It ages well for a Zinfandel, and only the 1988 is showing signs of decline. The Howell Mountain Zinfandel comes from the Black-Sears and Park Muscadine vineyards. It is blended with 14 per cent Petite Sirah and a dash of Gamay. Ray says he has to be careful to keep the alcohol level under control. In addition there is Nero Misto, a blend of Petite Sirah, Zinfandel, Alicante Bouschet, and other old-fashioned varieties, sourced from three old vineyards. The Napa Zinfandel called Coeur du Val comes from eight vineyards.

There are other wines too. A Syrah and a Cabernet from Tietjen Vineyard which is aged in mostly American oak, but this will be changed in future vintages. A Morisoli Vineyard Cabernet is aged in *barriques*, of which half are new. In 1989 Elyse made a barrel-fermented dry Riesling, but, not surprisingly, nobody wanted to buy it.

Etude

PO Box 3382, Napa, CA 94558. Tel: 257 5300. Fax: 287 6022. Production: 8,000 cases.

As well as acting as a consultant winemaker to some of California's top estates (Araujo, Moraga, Niebaum-Coppola, Spottswoode, Viader, and Dalla Valle), Tony Soter has since 1985 operated his own winery, specializing in the great challenge of Pinot Noir. Soter was a philosophy student, and he takes a considered, scientific view of the viticultural and winemaking problems he encounters in the course of his work. He is one of those rare men who is as comfortable and expert in the vineyard as in the winery. He has always worked as closely as possible with growers to ensure that he gets the quality and structure of fruit he wants, and he even compensates growers for natural disasters such as hail, so that the costs of such catastrophes are not borne solely by the farmer. For Etude he deliberately buys more fruit than he needs, and sells off about 20 per cent, as there is no second label.

Soter often sees his wines as practice pieces, rather than definitive expressions of a variety or vineyard. With Pinot Noir, he likes a cold soak before fermentation, preferably with natural yeasts, in low squat tanks, so that no pumping is needed. He wants extraction without manipulation. Of course the cap is routinely punched down. The wine is aged for at least 14 months in 50 per cent new *barriques*. Batches are kept separate, and there can be as many as twenty-five different lots in the blend. Etude Pinot Noir is best drunk fairly young.

Soter also makes Cabernet from the Madroña Vineyard in St Helena and from Vine Hill Ranch in Oakville. These are less consistent than the Pinot Noirs, and occasionally show slight toughness and coarseness. As for white wines, Soter makes Pinot Blanc from Carneros fruit, using minimal oak and avoiding malolactic fermentation.

Far Niente
1 Acacia Dr., Oakville, CA 94562. Tel: 944 2861. Fax: 944 2312. Production: 45,000 cases.

Oklahoma nurseryman and antique car collector Gil Nickel bought the old Benson winery in 1979 for $500,000 and spent a further $2 million restoring it. It's a handsome old stone gravity-fed winery founded in 1885 but abandoned at Prohibition. When the restorers were at work they found the Italian phrase 'Far Niente' ('without a care') chiselled into the walls, so Nickel adopted the name for his new estate.

It was an ambitious project from the start. The first vintages of Far Niente were made at Markham and other wineries, yet the opening vintage of Chardonnay in 1979 was priced at $15, slightly higher than the well-established Chalone. Far Niente wines have always been expensive ($70 for Cabernet, $40 for Chardonnay, $55 for a half-bottle of Dolce). No doubt even a rich man such as Nickel needs to recoup his investments.

Far Niente owns or co-owns vineyards in Oakville, Carneros, and Coombsville, many of which had to be replanted after phylloxera. In recent years the estate has grown all its own grapes. The best Cabernet vines are alongside Martha's Vineyard and the Mondavi Reserve parcels. Chardonnay is planted in Oakville and Coombsville. Only four wines are made: Cabernet, Chardonnay, a very little Merlot, and the Sauternes-style Dolce, which was introduced in 1985. Dolce now has its own winemaker, Ashley Heisey, who used to work at Opus One. There are no second labels, so any wine not deemed good enough for the blend is sold off.

Like a handful of other estates – such as Cuvaison and Duckhorn – Far Niente has had the same winemaker for most of its existence. Chuck Ortman started Nickel off, but in 1983 26-year-old Dirk Hampson took over and has been there ever since. With experience at Schloss Vollrads, Mouton-Rothschild, and Phelps, the youthful Hampson was no novice.

The Chardonnay is made in a style that now seems old-fashioned, but none the worse for that. It is fermented in tanks, then aged in mostly new *barriques*, but does not go through malolactic fermentation. The wine is intended to be consumed up to six years after the vintage. My problem with the Chardonnay is its lack of stylistic consistency. For his Cabernet, Hampson wants finesse rather than power, though the vintages of the 1980s were very tannic. Nowadays the Cabernet gets a long maceration to soften the tannins, and it is aged for 20 months in new *barriques*.

Dolce is not made every year, since it relies on the timely arrival of botrytis. Like Château d'Yquem, the wine is aged in new oak for 3 years; Hampson insists that he is not trying to emulate Yquem, but he does want to produce a wine of comparable excitement. The grapes, largely Sémillon, come from Napa, particularly Coombsville. The 1985 was surprisingly citric and lacked intensity, though there was certainly ample botrytis in the wine.

Far Niente has attracted a good deal of criticism, but I have usually enjoyed the wines, although they often seem overpriced for the quality. The Chardonnay in particular can easily appear over-oaked.

Flora Springs

1978 W. Zinfandel Lane, St Helena, CA 94574. Tel: 963 5711. Fax: 963 7518. Production: 35,000 cases.

In 1977 Jerome Komes, a former president of the Bechtel corporation, bought land and a ghost winery in St Helena. At first he planned simply to grow grapes, but like so many other gentleman farmers in Napa, he turned to winemaking too, although three-quarters of the crop is still sold to other wineries. Today the Komes, and the next generation (Julie and Pat Garvey), own 450 acres in seven locations in Napa, planted with the Bordeaux varieties as well as Chardonnay, Pinot Blanc, and Sangiovese. The winemaker is Ken Deis.

There are two Chardonnays, which begin their fermentation in steel and complete it in varying proportions of new *barriques*. Malolactic fermentation is usually discouraged. Soliloquy is pure Sauvignon Blanc from a 34-year-old vineyard in Oakville. The succulent Cabernet comes from the Rutherford vineyard, and is aged for 2 years in *barriques*. The Reserve is a selection from the best block of the vineyard. There is also a Merlot. Perhaps the best wine is Trilogy, first made in 1984, and a blend of one-third each Cabernet Sauvignon, Cabernet Franc, and Merlot. In 1989 Flora Springs planted the Sangiovese Grosso clone in their Cypress Vineyard in Pope Valley, and this wine is aged in Burgundian oak. It has yet to find a consistent style. None of the red wines is fined or filtered.

Over the last ten years Flora Springs has established a fine record for its rich elegant wines. This is an often underrated property.

Folie à Deux
3070 St Helena Highway, St Helena, CA 94574. Tel: 963 1160. Fax: 963 9223. Production: 10,000 cases.

Walk into the tasting room at this unpretentious estate and it soon becomes obvious that the folks here do not take themselves too seriously, as their name promises. The property was acquired by the Dizmang family and by Gary Mills, a psychologist, in 1974. There were 21 acres here, and they acquired 15 more in Yountville. Rick Tracy was the winemaker until 1995, when the estate was sold to a consortium that included Richard Peterson, the former winemaker at Beaulieu and the founder of Monterey Vineyard. Since 1996 the winemaker has been Scott Harvey. Since he is the owner of the venerable Grandpère vineyard of Zinfandel in Amador County, this is bad news for Renwood, who used to buy the grapes.

The 1996 Chardonnay mostly comes from Nevada County, the remainder from Monterey; it has a dab of residual sugar. The Reserve Chardonnay is fermented in new oak. Fantasie is a sparkling wine made from Chardonnay and Muscat Canelli, and aged one year on the yeasts. The Cabernet Sauvignon is better, and the chewy Reserve is aged in new oak. Recent changes at Folie à Deux have made it hard to gain a clear picture of its activities. Prices are reasonable.

Franciscan
1178 Galleron Rd., Rutherford, CA 94573. Tel: 963 7111. Fax: 963 7867. Production: 60,000 cases.

Franciscan had a chequered early history. It was established by a consortium from San Francisco and its first vintage was 1973. After the group went bankrupt, it was bought in 1975 by an oilman from Colorado, Ray Duncan, and Justin Meyer, who had been a senior winemaker at Christian Brothers. A few years later, in 1979, it was sold to the German firm of Peter Eckes, who arranged a 50-50 partnership with the Huneeus family of Chile. Since then Agustin Huneeus has been running this very enterprising estate. In 1998 Larry Levin, for many years winemaker at Dry Creek Vineyards, was appointed to that post here. Under Huneeus's management there has also been considerable vineyard expansion, with 620 acres in Rutherford and Oakville. The company has also opened the Estancia winery in Monterey and another site in Rutherford specifically for the Quintessa [q.v.] wine, a Meritage. In addition, Franciscan has bought the old Mount Veeder winery.

There are two Chardonnays. The basic Napa Chardonnay is aged in one-third new *barriques* and goes through malolactic fermentation. The second Chardonnay, the vigorous, individual Cuvée Sauvage, is fermented with natural yeasts and aged for 15 months in mostly new oak.

The Cabernet and Merlot are aged in American as well as French oak, and the Zinfandel is entirely aged in American oak, which only accentuates its jamminess. Between 25 and 35 per cent new oak is used for these wines. Franciscan's top red is the sumptuous Meritage called Magnificat, which is essentially Cabernet with 25 per cent Merlot blended in. It is aged for 20 months in 40 per cent new *barriques*.

Franus

2055 Hoffman Lane, Yountville, CA 94599. Tel: 945 0542. Production: 2,000 cases.

Peter Franus was the winemaker at Mount Veeder winery until 1993. Now, at his own small winery, he specializes in single-vineyard Zinfandels from Mount Veeder vineyards and a very little Cabernet Sauvignon. The 1996 Brandlin Zinfandel was rich and flamboyant.

Freemark Abbey

3022 St Helena Highway, St Helena, CA 94574. Tel: 963 9694. Fax: 963 0554. Production: 38,000 cases.

There were vineyards here in the 1870s, planted by William Sayward. A winery was built in 1886 and passed through various hands until 1939, when it was acquired by the Ahern family, who devised the present name. There have never been any ecclesiastical associations with the property. The old stone winery was reactivated in 1967 by seven partners, most of whom were prominent grape farmers in Napa Valley. They included Charles Carpy, the managing partner who died recently, Bill Jaeger, and winemaker Brad Webb. The partners control about 300 acres of fine Napa vineyards.

Under Webb, Freemark Abbey was one of the first Napa wineries to age its Chardonnays in French *barriques*. There is a separate barrel-fermented Chardonnay from the Carpy Ranch. He also produced some exceptional Cabernets. In addition to the regular Napa Cabernet, there were special bottlings from the Sycamore Vineyard, which belonged to partner John Bryan, and from the Bosché Vineyard. These were excellent wines and were given a long ageing in good-quality *barriques*. Merlot, which had been used as a blending component from the beginning, was released separately in the 1990s, presumably in response to the Merlot craze.

Perhaps Freemark Abbey's most notable achievement was to create Edelwein, the first authentic Beerenauslese-style wine from naturally botrytized Riesling grapes (see Chapter 21). Edelwein Gold is their TBA-style wine, most recently made in 1989 and 1994.

For many years Freemark Abbey set high standards and although the wines are still reliable and sensibly priced for the quality offered, they seem to lack a little excitement, as though the winery is resting on its laurels.

Galleron
Production: 300 cases.

Gary Galleron, the winemaker at Whitehall Lane who also used to make the wines from Grace Family Vineyards, has set up his own boutique winery, at present featuring only Rutherford Cabernet Sauvignon. The first vintage was 1993.

Girard
See Rudd.

Goosecross Cellars
1119 State Lane, Yountville, CA 94599. Tel: 944 1986. Fax: 944 2762. Production: 6,000 cases.

Ray Gorsuch established his 10-acre Chardonnay vineyard in 1978, selling grapes to Far Niente and others. In 1988 he set up his own winery. The property was acquired in 1993 by his son Geoff Gorsuch and David Topper. In 1996, after Bernard Pradel left California in bizarre circumstances, Goosecross acquired his inventory and label rights and contracted to buy his Howell Mountain grapes. This has enabled them to supplement their range of Chardonnay, Sauvignon Blanc and Syrah with Cabernet Sauvignon. Since Goosecross do not submit their wines to press tastings and since I have never managed to visit the estate, I have not tasted the wines.

Grace Family Vineyard
1210 Rockland Rd., St Helena, CA 94574. Tel: 963 0808. Production: 400 cases.

This tiny, organically farmed estate was planted by Dick and Ann Grace with the Bosché clone of Cabernet Sauvignon in 1976, and the first vintage was 1978. The first few vintages were made at Caymus, and the first vintage released under the family label was 1983. At this time the vineyard consisted of a single acre, which yielded 150 cases, but a second was planted in 1985. The winemaker was Gary Galleron, who was succeeded in 1995 by Heidi Peterson Barrett. The wine achieved its glowing reputation as a consequence of the very high prices it attained at charity auctions. In 1995 an acre was replanted, which would be of little consequence anywhere else, but meant here a hefty cut in production, especially since yields are usually as low as 2 tons per acre despite very close spacing.

The wine is punched down rather than pumped over, for a more gentle extraction, and aged in 100 per cent new oak from Séguin-Moreau. The wines, which are pure Cabernet, are renowned for their consistency, with the 1985, 1987, 1990, 1994, and 1995 particularly magnificent. The wines are sold to a mailing list of 480 at $75 per bottle, and there is a waiting list of 1,200 to join the mailing list.

Green & Red

3208 Chiles-Pope Valley Rd., St Helena, CA 94574. Tel: 965 2346. Production: 5,000 cases.

In 1972 Jay Heminway planted 16 acres at an elevation of 900 to 1,500 feet. He chose Zinfandel and Chardonnay, supple wines for relatively early drinking. There was a change of direction in 1991, when Helen Turley was hired as a consultant to move the wines up a notch or two.

Grgich Hills

1829 St Helena Highway, Rutherford, CA 94573. Tel: 963 2784. Fax: 963 8725. Production: 60,000 cases.

Mike Grgich is a legend in Napa Valley. Born and trained in Croatia, he came to the United States in 1958. He worked with the likes of Lee Stewart at Souverain and André Tchelitscheff at Beaulieu. In 1968 he joined Mondavi, then Chateau Montelena, where he made some stupendous wines, including the famous 1973 Chardonnay that triumphed at the Paris tasting in 1976.

Backed by coffee tycoon Austin Hill, he opened his own winery in 1977. They have Chardonnay vineyards in Rutherford, Cabernet Sauvignon at Yountville adjoining Napanook, and more Chardonnay near Saintsbury in Carneros. They are also planting 50 acres of Sauvignon Blanc in the cool American Canyon in southern Napa. Formerly the Sauvignon came from Pope Valley, where the fruit had good acidity. The Zinfandel often comes from old vines at Sausal in Sonoma.

There is quite a large range of wines. The powerful Chardonnay can be outstanding, and Grgich often blocks the malolactic fermentation. There is also an opulent Carneros Selection Chardonnay. The Fumé Blanc is tank-fermented, then aged in older *barriques*. In the 1980s Grgich used a good deal of Limousin oak, which gave very assertive, toasty wines. The tannic Cabernet Sauvignon has since 1991 been supplemented by a Yountville Selection. Grgich likes Nevers barrels, but also uses some American oak. The reds are bold wines, rich and full-flavoured. Occasionally, as in 1993, Grgich makes a late harvest Riesling.

In the 1980s I would wander into the tasting room along the highway, and quite often Mike Grgich, beret on head, would be there, dispensing advice and even pouring wine. Now the headquarters are altogether more swish, but I miss catching Mike Grgich and his fund of Croatian sayings: 'Where I come from we say old chickens make the best soup. The same applies to old vines.'

Groth
750 Oakville Cross Rd., Oakville, CA 94562. Tel: 944 0290. Fax: 944 8932. Production: 40,000 cases.

First prize for the ugliest new winery in Napa surely goes to Groth's bizarre Spanish Colonial structure, better suited to some of the more garish suburbs of Los Angeles than Napa Valley. Dennis Groth, an executive with Atari, bought vineyards here in the early 1980s. His first vintage, with Nils Venge as winemaker, was 1982. Until the Groth winery was complete, the wines were made at Bouchaine. In 1994 Venge left to develop his own Saddleback Cellars, and was replaced as winemaker by Michael Weis.

Almost all the grapes are estate-grown from their 39-acre Hillview Vineyard at Yountville, and the slightly warmer 100-acre Oakcross Vineyard, which is planted with Chardonnay, Cabernet Sauvignon, and Merlot.

The Sauvignon Blanc, which is mostly barrel-fermented, draws on fruit from Napa and San Luis Obispo. Since 1996 this wine and the Chardonnay have been made by whole-cluster pressing. Merlot was added to the range in 1990. The best wine is the Cabernet Reserve, declared perfect by Robert Parker in 1985. It is aged for 23 months in new *barriques*, and some Merlot is blended in shortly before bottling. I find the wines good but not as good as the estate's reputation suggests.

Harlan
PO Box 352, Oakville, CA 94562. Tel: 944 1441. Fax: 944 1444. Production: 2,000 cases.

Bill Harlan, among his numerous careers, transformed the run-down Meadowood country club into a fashionable resort. He also established Merryvale winery. His 26-acre estate, set among the western hills of Oakville not far from Martha's Vineyard, was planted in the mid-1980s with Cabernet Sauvignon, Merlot, Cabernet Franc, and Petit Verdot. Close spacing was adopted, and so was vertical trellising. Yields are very low.

The first wines were made in 1987, but it was the 1990 vintage that made people sit up and take notice. Bob Levy makes the wines, with consultant murmurs from Michel Rolland, and takes a non-interventionist approach. No press wine is used, and the blend is aged for up to 3 years in new *barriques*, and bottled without fining or filtration. The Cabernet is currently priced at $100, and the Merlot has fetched considerably more at auction. The 1994 proprietary red is surely one of the top wines of a great vintage.

Harrison

1527 Sage Canyon Rd., St Helena, CA 94574. Tel: 963 8271. Production: 2,000 cases.

The Harrisons own 17 acres on Pritchard Hill. The first vintage was 1989, vinified at the Pecota winery, as the Harrison winery was not completed until 1994. The Chardonnay is barrel-fermented, rejoices in full malolactic fermentation, and is aged for 6 months on the fine lees. The Cabernet Sauvignon is aged for 2 years in *barriques*. Since 1992 Helen Turley has been the consultant winemaker here.

Hartwell

5795 Silverado Trail, Napa, CA 94558. Tel: 255 4269. Production: 1,000 cases.

Bob Hartwell's micro-estate of a single acre is located on a 400-foot-high slope opposite Stag's Leap Wine Cellars. Replanting in 1996 means there is no Hartwell Cabernet from 1996 or 1997, although the Hartwells also own the 20-acre Sunshine Vineyard. The cuttings came from the Bosché clone planted at the Grace Family Vineyards, where the wines are vinified by Heidi Peterson Barrett and aged in new *barriques* for 21 months. All this adds up to a very fashionable and expensive wine.

Havens

3234 Old Sonoma Rd., Napa, CA 94559. Tel: 253 7153. Production: 6,000 cases.

Michael Havens started up this operation in 1984, renting winery space at Truchard until his own winery was ready in 1989. Havens buys in all his grapes. Truchard Vineyard is the source of much of his Merlot, a variety in which he specializes. There is also a Syrah sourced from the Hudson Vineyard in Carneros. The range is completed with a Chardonnay and a Sauvignon Blanc often made with Calistoga fruit. The Reserve Merlot and the Syrah have been superb.

Hess Collection Winery

4411 Redwood Rd., Napa, CA 94558. Tel: 255 1144. Production: 300,000 cases.

If these wines are often sighted on Swiss wine lists, it's because the Hess family are well-known brewers and mineral water purveyors in Switzerland. Donald Hess came to California in 1978 and bought the former Veedercrest estate on Mount Veeder and leased a stone winery that began life in 1903 as the Theodore Gier winery and continued as the Christian Brothers' Mont La Salle. This gave Hess more space than he actually needed for wine production and storage, so part of the building became a gallery exhibiting his extensive art collection, which helps make the winery a major tourist attraction. Hess planted 285 acres of Chardonnay, Cabernet Sauvignon, Cabernet Franc, and Merlot, and sold much of the fruit to other wineries until his own first vintage in 1983. More recently Hess has bought 350 acres near Soledad in Monterey and 250 in American Canyon as well as 300 acres in Pope Valley where he plans to plant red varieties for his second label, Hess Select. His best wines are bottled under the Hess Collection label. Hess Select wine, which is very good value, often bears the California appellation, allowing Hess to blend wines from all parts of the state. But there are also occasional single-vineyard wines, such as the 1994 Bien Nacido Pinot Noir at a bargain price.

The Chardonnay is 85 per cent barrel-fermented, good wine, but over-shadowed by the sumptuous Cabernet Sauvignon, which is usually aged for 2 years in barrels. Randle Johnson has been the winemaker here from the outset, and quality has been consistent. He very successfully pre-serves the power of mountain fruit while at the same extending maceration to ensure that the tannins are supple and thoroughly integrated into the wine.

William Hill
1761 Atlas Peak Rd., Napa, CA 94558. Tel: 224 5424. Fax: 224 4484. Production: 120,000 cases.

William Hill is a major developer of vineyards in Napa Valley. In the early 1970s he developed steep land on Diamond Mountain which was sold to Sterling as Diamond Mountain Ranch; the Veedercrest vineyards which now belong to Donald Hess; then the Atlas Peak vineyards, now owned by Antinori. Hill founded his own winery in 1974, and the first releases were 1976 Chardonnay and Cabernet Sauvignon. There are two ranges: Napa wines and Reserve wines, the latter being estate grown. The Cabernet usually employs fruit from Mount Veeder.

In 1992 Hill sold the winery to Allied Lyons, now Allied Domecq, also known as The Wine Alliance. Quality was never at the highest level. Allied Domecq hired winemaker Jill Davis, who fine-tuned the Chardonnay, which is mostly barrel-fermented, by blending in some Sauvignon Blanc. A little American oak is being used for the ageing of the Cabernet Sauvignon, but the Merlot is aged in *barriques*.

Honig
850 Rutherford Rd., Rutherford, CA 94573. Tel: 963 5618. Production: 20,000 cases.

In 1966 Louis Honig of San Francisco bought 68 acres from the Wagner family of Caymus. He planted 55 acres with Sauvignon Blanc, Cabernet Sauvignon, and Chardonnay, and sold the grapes to other wineries until his death in 1976. His children took over running the property. With a slump in the grape market in the late 1970s, the manager Rick Tracy persuaded the family to let him vinify the wine. At first Honig specialized in Sauvignon Blanc, and in 1987 added Chardonnay and Cabernet Sauvignon to the range.

There have been many changes at Honig. Rick Tracy left in 1986 to be replaced by James Hall, who in turn left in 1998 to concentrate his efforts on his own growing *négociant* business, Patz & Hall. In 1998 Kristin Belair took over. The estate was best known in the past for its Sauvignon, but replanting after phylloxera switched the emphasis to Cabernet Sauvignon.

Howell Mountain Vineyard
Tel: 963 2915. Production: 1,500 cases.

Mike Beatty and Joyce and Jerre Sears (of respectively the Beatty Ranch and Black-Sears Vineyard, both on Howell Mountain) have begun producing small quantities of wine under this label, beginning with the 1994 vintage and focusing on single-vineyard Zinfandels derived in equal parts from the two vineyards. The winemaker is Ted Lemon, a specialist in Burgundian styles. All wines receive a cold soak before fermentation using natural yeasts. Zinfandel is aged in 35 per cent new oak for up to 18 months, Cabernet Sauvignon in new oak only. The wines are unfiltered.

Jarvis
2970 Monticello Rd., Napa, CA 94558. Tel: 255 5280. Production: 5,000 cases.

In 1985 electronics tycoon William Jarvis began planting his 37-acre vineyard at an elevation of 1,000 feet with Chardonnay, Cabernet Sauvignon, Cabernet Franc, and Merlot. The investment was enormous, estimated at $20 million, both in the vineyards and in the modern underground winery complete with subterranean stream; this is where Dmitri Tchelitscheff takes care of the winemaking. The Chardonnay is barrel-fermented in new *barriques*, and usually bottled without fining or filtration. Unfortunately the wines are very expensive, surely reflecting, as so often in Napa, the need to recoup heavy expenditure. Thus the 1993 Cabernet Sauvignon was released at $55, and even the Cabernet Franc is $40. There is also a proprietary red called Lake William that blends the two Cabernets.

Judd's Hill
PO Box 415, St Helena, CA 94574. Tel: 963 9093. Production: 2,000 cases.

After Art and Bunnie Finkelstein sold Whitehall Lane winery in 1988, they set up this small operation based on 7 acres of terraced vineyards east of St Helena. Their first release was a Bordeaux blend in 1989, aged 2 years in oak.

Robert Keenan
3660 Spring Mountain Rd., St Helena, CA 94574. Tel: 963 9177. Fax: 963 8209. Production: 10,000 cases.

In 1974 insurance man Robert Keenan bought 175 acres on Spring Mountain at 1,700 feet. There had been vines here in the nineteenth century, when the property was known as the Peter Conradi winery. The stone winery from 1904 is still standing. Keenan began making wine here in 1977. Today there are 62 acres planted with Cabernet Sauvignon, Cabernet Franc, and Merlot. Merlot, blended with Cabernet Franc, is the basis of the estate's reputation. The Cabernet Sauvignon is blended with Cabernet Franc and Merlot, and there is also a Napa Chardonnay. The overall style of the wines is lean, sometimes astringent. Joe Cafaro was the original winemaker here, and since 1991 winemaking operations have been in the hands of Matt Cookson.

Kongsgaard Wines
PO Box 349, Oakville, CA 94562. Tel: 963 1391. Fax: 963 4512. Production: 1,200 cases.

The Kongsgaards have been grape growers in Napa Valley for many years, and John Kongsgaard is also a respected winemaker, having worked at Stony Hill, Newton, and Livingston. He also produces small quantities of wine from 7 acres of Chardonnay planted on rocky slopes east of Napa. The budwood came from Stony Hill, and gives small berries. The wine is made with natural yeasts and is aged on the lees for almost 2 years. Some Syrah is bought from the Hudson Vineyard in Carneros. Production so far is tiny and prices high. I have never come across the wines.

Charles Krug
2800 Main St., St Helena, CA 94574. Tel: 967 2200. Fax: 967 2291. Production: 600,000 cases.

This venerable estate was founded by Karl Krug, who was born in Prussia in 1825 and, after he came to America, married a woman whose dowry included a substantial acreage in St Helena. A winery was built in 1861 and Krug was soon a leading figure in Napa Valley, training budding winemakers who would soon become as renowned as he was. Phylloxera destroyed the vineyards and Krug died in the middle of the outbreak in 1892. A banker called James Moffitt bought the estate but it was closed at Prohibition.

The modern history of Charles Krug begins in 1943, when Cesare

Mondavi of Lodi bought the property for $75,000. His son Robert was appointed general manager, his other son Peter was the winemaker. After Cesare died in 1959, tension between the brothers, with their mother Rosa uneasily in the middle, led to Robert's departure in 1965, at which point Peter Mondavi became president of Krug.

No one questioned Peter's ability as a winemaker. He was one of the pioneers of cold fermentation at the family's other winery of Sunny St Helena, initiating the technique in 1937 and greatly improving the overall quality of all the white wines. Other technical innovations included sterile bottling and vacuum corking. Vintage-dating was also introduced from the start at Charles Krug. Peter also created the very impressive Vintage Selection Cabernet Sauvignon. Yet once Robert had left, some of the dynamism left with him. Charles Krug has remained in the Mondavi family, and Peter's two sons have been involved in the estate. But quality rarely reached great heights, and marketing was uninspired. There were improvements in quality in the late 1980s, but Charles Krug has yet to recover its reputation.

The estate's 1,200 acres include vineyards in Carneros and Yolo County. In Napa Valley there is a home ranch in St Helena, planted with Merlot, Sangiovese, Sauvignon Blanc, and Riesling; the 100-acre Lincoln Ranch in Oakville; and vineyards in Yountville. The range of wines is extensive. Much of the Chardonnay and Pinot Noir comes from the winery's Willow Lake Vineyard in Carneros. In addition to the classic varieties, Krug is known for its Chenin Blanc and for a Meritage called Generations, which is about 50 per cent Cabernet Sauvignon, plus Merlot and Cabernet Franc. The winery has also introduced a Sangiovese, made from the Grosso clone; the Reserve is aged one year in barrels.

The wines are better than their reputation, and prices are very reasonable. Quality is not always consistent, but anyone stopping at their spacious tasting room will find some pleasant surprises.

Lail Vineyards
Tel: 967 0707. Production: 1,000 cases.

The daughter of the late John Daniel of Inglenook, Robin Lail has sold her share in Dominus and Merryvale to set up her own winery, drawing on fruit from Yountville and Howell Mountain. Philippe Melka is the wine-maker. The 1995 blend of Merlot and Cabernet Sauvignon, called J. Daniels, was released at $60. The fruit came from Rutherford.

Lamborn Family Vineyards
2075 Summit Lake Dr., Angwin, CA 94508. Tel: 415 547 4643. Production: 2,200 cases.

Bob Lamborn is self-taught as grape grower and as winemaker. In 1973 he bought 25 acres of land as a vacation retreat, then in 1979 he planted 9 acres of Zinfandel, which is dry-farmed but gives good yields. His best known wine is Howell Mountain Zinfandel, which is aged in oak for about 18 months. There is also a Zinfandel 'port'.

Lang & Reed
PO Box 662, St Helena, CA 94574. Tel: 963 3758. Production: 3,000 cases.

John Skupny used to manage the Niebaum-Coppola estate and since 1993 has been producing some wine on his own account, advised by John Kongsgaard and Tony Soter. He has been specializing in Cabernet Franc, one of the very few winemakers to do so.

Lewis Cellars
Tel: 415 342 8017. Production: 5,000 cases.

As the former owners of Oakville Ranch Vineyard, Randy and Debbie Lewis have supplied much of the fruit for this new winery from that site, although other sources are also being explored. The best and richest wines are their highly regarded Reserve wines from Chardonnay, Cabernet Sauvignon, and Merlot. Joe Cafaro is the winemaker.

Liparita Cellars
200 Las Posadas Rd., Angwin, CA 94508. Tel: 965 2720. Fax: 963 2776. Production: 4,000 cases.

This Howell Mountain estate, owned since 1983 by Bob and Fern Burrows, consists of 80 acres planted at 1,650 to 1,800 feet. The Chardonnay grown here used to be sold to Chateau Montelena and Grgich Hills, and Sauvignon Blanc found its way to Peter Michael, Duckhorn, and Spottswoode, but since 1987 Liparita has been producing its own wines, all with the Howell Mountain appellation. Merry Edwards was the first winemaker. Cabernet Sauvignon has been very impressive, as has the Merlot, which was first made in 1990; the range is completed with Chardonnay and Sauvignon Blanc.

Livingston
1895 Cabernet Lane, St Helena, CA 94574. Tel: 963 2120. Production: 5,000 cases.

John and Diane Livingston own 10 acres on the western edge of the Rutherford bench. The dry-farmed vineyard, originally known as the Moffett Vineyard, was planted with Cabernet Sauvignon in 1969 and sold grapes to wineries such as Chappellet, Spring Mountain, and Burgess, until in 1984 the Livingstons began vinifying their own grapes. Cabernet Franc and Merlot were also planted. The range was expanded in 1989 with a wine made from purchased fruit and called Stanley's Selection. A single-vineyard wine, from the Gonser Vineyard, was added to the range in 1993, but quantities are tiny. In 1996 a Sangiovese was added to the list. Randy Dunn made the wines here from 1984 to 1990; he was followed by Greg Graham, and in 1996 John Kongsgaard, former winemaker at Newton, became the winemaker.

Lokoya

7525 St Helena Highway, Oakville, CA 94562. Tel: 944 2807.

This label is part of the Kendall-Jackson empire, and specializes in Cabernet Sauvignon from Napa's mountain vineyards. The first releases were 1994 Cabernet Sauvignons from Oakville and Mount Veeder. The latter was rich, soft, and forward. In 1998 Marco DiGiulio became winemaker.

The 1995 bottlings of Cabernet Sauvignon from Rutherford, Mount Veeder and Diamond Mountain were each released at $100 per bottle.

Long

1533 Sage Canyon Rd., St Helena, CA 94574. Tel: 963 2496. Production: 3,500 cases.

The father of Bob Long, the present owner, bought this hillside estate on Pritchard Hill as a weekend retreat in 1965. It's an unpretentious estate, with views from the house on to the vines which are planted on a kind of amphitheatre at a height of 700 to 1,200 feet. Bob Long planted Riesling and Chardonnay, selling their fruit to other wineries. Their own winery opened in 1978, with Sandi Belcher as the winemaker. Zelma Long of Simi also contributes to the winemaking, although she and Bob divorced some years ago.

Despite drip irrigation, the 18-acre vineyards are very low-yielding, and the climate is considerably cooler than on the valley floor. Long hesitated for many years about Cabernet Sauvignon, and finally planted one acre. The winery has also been trying Pinot Gris. Another novelty is the Sangiovese made from fruit bought from Seghesio in Sonoma. The Chardonnay is quite distinctive, and often has a Muscatty aroma; this distinguished wine is barrel-fermented in 50 per cent new oak. Sauvignon is made from bought-in fruit. At first the grapes came from Chalk Hill, and since 1989 from the Hyde Vineyard in Carneros. An unusual feature of the Sauvignon is that it is always blended with up to 20 per cent barrel-fermented Chardonnay. The Riesling is often made in a late harvest style akin to a German Auslese.

Markham

2812 St Helena Highway, St Helena, CA 94574. Tel: 963 5292. Fax: 963 4616. Production: 150,000 cases.

After a career in advertising, Bruce Markham renovated the former St Helena cooperative winery in 1978. With early releases from Gamay Beaujolais Blanc and Muscat and other unfashionable varieties, Markham never developed much of a reputation, until Merlot came into fashion. Markham has been producing Merlot since 1980 and is now releasing about 50,000 cases annually. The estate owns about 140 acres of the variety in Calistoga, Yountville, and Napa, and has contracts with growers for 50 more. In 1988 the winery was sold to Sanraku of Japan. By 1997 the range had been refined to Merlot, Cabernet Sauvignon, Chardonnay, Sauvignon Blanc, old-vine Zinfandel, Petite Sirah, and a Meritage. Bob Foley was the winemaker here until he left to work for Pride Mountain, and his Merlot and Chardonnay were very reliable. The second label is Glass Mountain, introduced in 1991.

Louis Martini

254 St Helena Highway, St Helena, CA 94574. Tel: 963 2736. Fax: 963 8750. Production: 200,000 cases.

The young Louis Martini, whose father Agostino emigrated to San Francisco, studied winemaking in Genoa before returning to California in 1911. His first venture as a wine producer ended in failure, but he started up again in San Joaquin Valley in 1922. After Repeal he moved operations to Napa Valley. Gradually he built a fine portfolio of vineyards, such as La Loma and Las Amigas in Carneros (200 acres), Los Vinedos del Rio in Russian River; Perini Springs Vineyard in Lake County; and Monte Rosso in Sonoma (250 acres).There are now 550 acres in production, and 440 available for planting.

Louis Martini retired in 1959 and was succeeded by his son Louis Peter Martini. He was one of the pioneers of mechanical harvesting. In 1977 he passed the reins to his son Michael and his daughter Carolyn, and died in 1998. Over the years the winery was responsible for a number of innovations. They invented the Moscato Amabile style (see Chapter 21), made the first Carneros Pinot Noir, and the first varietal Merlot. Martini became one of the leading producers of Barbera, drawing its grapes mostly from Perini Springs and blending it with Petite Sirah. Some outstanding wines were made under the Special Selection label in the 1950s and 1960s, especially Cabernet Sauvignon that was lighter and less intense than its rivals from Beaulieu or Inglenook yet had an unexpected capacity to age in bottle. The 1974 and 1975 were both excellent.

Martini still produce a large range of wines, with their most interesting offerings under the Heritage label. Many of the wines carry a California appellation, but there is a good range of Napa and single-vineyard wines too. In general the wines are sound but not very exciting, and some of the reds are quite light. Well aware that they were falling behind in terms of winemaking sophistication, the winery has been making changes over the past decade, such as introducing ageing in small barrels, which had rarely been done in the past. The range still offers good value, and the Barbera is still reliable.

Merryvale

1000 Main St., St Helena, CA 94574. Tel: 963 2225. Fax: 963 1949. Production: 30,000 cases.

This winery started life as the Sunny St Helena Winery built shortly after Repeal. In 1937 it was acquired by Cesari Mondavi of Lodi, but he sold it in 1943 when he bought the Charles Krug winery. In the 1960s the winery served as a cooperative, then was used for storage by Christian Brothers. In 1983 William Harlan and his partners reactivated the estate, renovating the winery a couple of years later. In 1992 Jack Schlatter of Switzerland bought a 50 per cent interest in the property. Merryvale still has no vineyards of its own, so it buys its fruit from Spottswoode and elsewhere. Bob Levy was the winemaker until 1998, when Steve Test of Stonestreet took over. Michel Rolland of Pomerol acts as a consultant.

Initial releases were a Bordeaux blend and a barrel-fermented Napa Chardonnay. The Reserve Chardonnay is aged in new oak. The Meritage is known as Profile, a wine aged nearly 2 years in new *barriques*. There's a fine white Meritage too, which is usually about two-thirds Sauvignon Blanc; it is fermented in new *barriques* and aged for 5 months in oak. The Napa and Hillside Cabernets and the Merlot are powerful and robust, and the Chardonnay, after a dull start, is improving.

As there are three tiers of wine released by Merryvale – Merryvale Vineyards being the middle range, and Sunny St Helena the bargain range – the winery can ensure that only the best wine ends up under the Merryvale label itself. Overall quality is very high.

Monticello

4242 Big Ranch Rd., Napa, CA 94558. Tel: 253 2802. Fax: 253 1019. Production: 20,000 cases.

Monticello had its origins as a farm planted mostly with Chardonnay and Pinot Noir in about 1970. In 1980 the owner, Jay Corley, built a winery. The estate takes its name, and borrows its architecture, from the home of Thomas Jefferson, for whom Corley has a deep regard. The first vintage was 1982. Some Gewürztraminer, Sauvignon Blanc and Sémillon were produced in the 1980s, including a splendid botrytized Sauvignon in 1982, but these wines have been dropped. As for Chardonnay, Monticello favoured a less full blown, less oaky style than most emerging from Napa in the 1980s, but today the Reserve bottlings are made very much in the modern style, being barrel-fermented with a substantial proportion of natural yeasts, and aged on the lees, which are regularly stirred. About one-third new oak is used, but only about one-third of the wine goes through malolactic fermentation. Some vintages have been clumsily made.

There are two Cabernets on offer. The lighter, with a higher presence of Merlot, is the Jefferson Cuvée, which is aged 2 years in *barriques*. The weightier wine is the Corley Reserve. Both are good, but made in different styles, since Monticello sources its Cabernet grapes from all over Napa Valley. There is also a Reserve Merlot, aged 18 months in Nevers barrels. The Pinot Noir is less impressive.

Allied to Monticello are the sparkling wines produced under the name Domaine Montreaux. The winemaker for both labels is Geoff Murray. He barrel-ferments the base wines, which is unusual in California, and the wine spends a further 10 months on the lees. Once bottled, it spends 7 years on the yeast. In 1998 the current release was the 1988. Production is limited to 2,000 cases.

Mount Veeder
1999 Mount Veeder Rd., Napa, CA 94558. See Franciscan (p. 395). Production: 8,000 cases.

The vineyards used to be a cow pasture until Mike Bernstein planted the first vines in 1965. The elevation is between 1,000 and 1,600 feet, and the soil is decomposed shale, clay, and some volcanic ash. The winery was completed in 1973. At first it produced a range of wines, including Chardonnay (from Long vineyards), Zinfandel, barrel-fermented Chenin, and Cabernet Sauvignon. In 1982 the estate was bought by Henry Matheson. Peter Franus was the winemaker in those days and there were some powerful Cabernets produced here; he claimed to be one of the first winemakers in California to make a blend from the five Bordeaux red varieties. In 1989 the estate was sold again, this time to Franciscan for $3 million.

Franciscan planted an additional 17 acres, bringing the total to 57. Much of the original vineyard had to be replanted after phylloxera. Under Franciscan, most of the reds are aged in American as well as French oak. In addition to the Cabernet, Zinfandel, and Merlot, the reborn Mount Veeder winery is best known for its fine Reserve, which in 1994 was composed of 57 per cent Cabernet Sauvignon, 12 per cent Merlot, 28 per cent Cabernet Franc, 2 per cent Petit Verdot, 1 per cent Malbec. It is aged 21 months in barrels, of which 15 per cent are American oak.

Mumm
8445 Silverado Trail, Rutherford, CA 94573. Tel: 942 3400. Fax: 942 3469. Production: 230,000 cases.

As part of the Seagram group, Mumm was able to make its first wines at the Sterling facilities until its own winery was completed in 1988. It was lucky to have the services of Greg Fowler, who had previously worked at Schramsberg and is one of California's top sparkling winemakers. In 1997 Rob McNeill took over. Quality remains high.

The grapes are sourced from some fifty vineyards, including Winery Lake in Carneros. Indeed, about half the fruit comes from Carneros. Some 30 per cent of the grapes are now estate-grown. Fowler liked to pick at around 19.5 Brix, which means that the grapes are slightly riper than they would be in Champagne.

The range consists of the very successful Cuvée Napa; Brut Prestige (60 per cent Pinot Noir, aged 26 months on the yeast); a nonvintage Blanc de Noirs first made in 1990; the Vintage Reserve (60 per cent Pinot Noir, 40 per cent Chardonnay, with 36 months on the yeast); a vintage bottling from Winery Lake (80 per cent Pinot Noir, 20 per cent Chardonnay); and a Blanc de Blancs (60 per cent Chardonnay, 40 per cent Pinot Gris). In 1991 Mumm introduced a new wine called DVX, a high-priced vintage wine with a 15 per cent barrel-fermented component; it is half Pinot Noir, half Chardonnay, and is aged 4 years on the yeast.

Newlan

5225 St Helena Highway, Napa, CA 94558. Tel: 257 2399. Fax: 252 6510. Production: 10,000 cases.

Bruce Newlan defied conventional wisdom in 1967 when he planted Cabernet Sauvignon in an area south of Yountville that most people considered too cool for the variety. But the soil was an alluvial fan, and the vines did well. He has also planted various clones of Pinot Noir, and at present there are 30 acres under vine. His own winery started up in 1981. In addition to his own Cabernet Sauvignon and Pinot Noir, he makes a field blend from Spring Mountain called Century Selection, which includes Zinfandel, Petite Sirah, Carignane, Grand Noir, and Alicante Bouschet. There are two Pinot Noirs, one from estate fruit; the other, lower priced, is made from Paso Robles fruit. Newlan avoids fining and, usually, filtration for his red wines. The only dry white is a Chardonnay mostly made from Carneros fruit and aged 12 months in French oak. The range is completed with a small quantity of intense late harvest Riesling.

Nichelini

2950 Sage Canyon Rd., St Helena, CA 94574. Tel: 963 0717. Fax: 963 3262. Production: 2,500 cases.

A small operation up in Chiles Valley, but one of the oldest in Napa. It was founded in 1890 by Swiss-born Anton Nichelini. It passed through to his grandson Jim, who died in 1985. Other family members took over the property in 1988. One of them is Greg Boeger, who in addition to running his own winery in El Dorado County, makes the wines here. The wines produced here are Riesling, Sauvignon Vert, Zinfandel, Cabernet Sauvignon, Merlot, and Petit Sirah. Although some of the vines are very old, quality has been modest, even rustic.

Oakville Ranch Vineyards
7781 Silverado Trail, Napa, CA 94558. Tel: 415 284 1620. Production: 4,000 cases.

Bob Miner, who owns 50 acres of mountain vineyards, teamed up with a former racing driver, Randy Lewis, to create this label. Bob Miner died in 1994, Randy Lewis left to form his own winery, and now Oakville Ranch is run by Miner's nephew David. Joe Cafaro makes the wines, which include a robust Cabernet Sauvignon.

Paloma
Tel: 963 7504. Production: 1,000 cases.

Jim and Barbara Richards bought this Spring Mountain property in 1983 and for many years sold Merlot to Conn Creek, Newton, and other wineries. The vines are planted at a height of 2,200 feet on 15 acres of terraced vineyards. In 1993 the Richardses decided to produce their own Merlots, and arranged for Bob Foley to make the wine for them at nearby Pride Mountain. The 1995 and 1996 releases were well received. Production will expand as sales of grapes to other wineries are curtailed.

Paradigm
683 Dwyer Rd., Oakville, CA 94562. Tel: 944 1683. Production: 3,000 cases.

This small 55-acre estate has been owned since 1991 by Ren and Marilyn Harris, who have been grape growers since 1964. The varieties, which were planted here in 1975, are 32 acres of Cabernet Sauvignon, 18 of Merlot, 2 of Cabernet Franc, and 1 of Zinfandel. They opened their own winery in 1991, but only use 20 per cent of their crop themselves. The first releases were 1991 Zinfandel and Cabernet. Their principal wine is an acclaimed Cabernet Sauvignon currently priced at $50, blended with Merlot and Cabernet Franc, and the first Merlot was made in 1994. The winemaker is Heidi Peterson Barrett.

Robert Pecota
3299 Bennett Lane, Calistoga, CA 94515. Tel: 942 6625. Fax: 942 6671. Production: 20,000 cases.

Robert Pecota's first experience in the wine business was as a grape buyer for Beringer in the 1970s. In 1973 he bought 28 acres of land, which in 1978 he planted with Sauvignon Blanc and Cabernet Sauvignon. In the same year he built his own winery. The vineyards have now been expanded to 20 acres, and he also buys some Sauvignon Blanc from Monterey. He has always been known for his Sauvignon and the style has changed over the years. In the 1980s he used techniques such as skin contact and sought out ultra-ripe grapes. During the following decade he abandoned skin contact and allows more than half the wine to go through malolactic fermentation; alcohol has been reduced by picking a bit earlier. Although Pecota is aiming for a Graves-style, I find it a typically ripe, rounded Napa Sauvignon.

The two principal reds are Merlot, first made in 1989; it is aged in heavily toasted barrels. The other is Kara's Vineyard Cabernet Sauvignon, an unfiltered and muscular wine.

Pecota is also known for his good Muscat Canelli, here called Moscato d'Andrea, and produced from estate grapes. In 1997 he added to the range a Chenin Blanc from Monterey fruit.

Peju Province
8466 St Helena Highway, Rutherford, CA 94573. Tel: 963 3600. Fax: 963 8680. Production: 10,000 cases.

Tony Peju bought a 20-acre vineyard in Rutherford in 1982, which he planted with Cabernet Sauvignon, Petit Verdot, and Chardonnay. Unfortunately the authorities were unwilling to allow him to build his winery along the highway, and it took until 1991 before it finally opened. He produces a large range of wines, of which his sweet French Colombard called Carnival is the best-seller. In addition there are two Cabernets, an Estate Merlot, and Cabernet Franc, all aged between 14 and 18 months in oak. His first Estate Chardonnay was produced in 1992, and is aged for 6 months in oak; the wine is marred by its residual sugar, but this seems to appeal to Peju's clientele. From time to time Sauvignon Blanc and late harvest wines are also produced. Although a fairly commercial establishment appealing to passing trade, prices are far from cheap.

Robert Pepi
7585 St Helena Highway, Oakville, CA 94562. Tel: 544 4000. Fax: 544 4013.

The Pepi family, formerly furriers in San Francisco, came to Oakville in 1966, bought 70 acres of land and planted vineyards. They produced Cabernet Sauvignon, a Sauvignon and Sémillon blend, and various other wines. In 1983 the Pepis had planted some Sangiovese Grosso that had come from Biondi-Santi in Montalcino, and in 1988 they had produced the first Sangiovese in California, Collini di Sassi. It took a few years before the wine was really worthy of attention, as it was in 1991. However in 1995 the estate was bought by Kendall-Jackson, who are developing the property as a source of Italian varietals. The huge new winery on the site will produce not only the Pepi range but also the high-priced Cardinale wine, for which Ed Farver is the winemaker. Cardinale is made principally from Cabernet Sauvignon grown on mountain vineyards along the Napa/Sonoma boundary. Marco DiGiulio was the winemaker for the Pepi wines until transferred to Lokoya in 1998.

The range includes a rather plump Pinot Grigio from Central Coast fruit, and a fresh, almondy Arneis. Both wines were first made in 1996. 1995 saw the first vintage of the revamped Sangiovese known as Two-Heart Canopy, a jammy but very peppery style, and the best wine so far is the Due Baci, a blend of two-thirds Cabernet with one-third estate-grown Sangiovese.

Mario Perelli-Minetti

1443 Silverado Trail, St Helena, CA 94573. Tel: 963 8762. Production: 5,000 cases.

This family were major producers of wine in the Central Valley. However, it began to founder commercially, and in 1988 Mario Perelli-Minetti moved to Napa to cultivate 8 acres of vineyards and make a little wine. The estate specializes in Chardonnay and a rich but chunky Cabernet Sauvignon.

Pine Ridge

5901 Silverado Trail, Napa, CA 94558. Tel: 253 7500. Fax: 253 1493. Production: 100,000 cases.

Gary and Nancy Andrus founded this estate in 1978. His background was not propitious: a Mormon by upbringing and an Olympic team skier in 1967. He gained a degree in chemistry and worked a good deal in Bordeaux before using the profits from the ski academy he and Nancy ran in Colorado to purchase Pine Ridge for $300,000.

Today the estate has 328 acres which supply almost all of their needs. Their main vineyards are in Stags Leap, Oak Knoll, Oakville, Rutherford Bench, and Carneros. Andrus's enthusiasm for the wines of Bordeaux led him to plant all five Bordeaux red varieties. He was one of the first growers to adopt closer spacing, beginning in 1985. Today the vines are planted at a density of 1,800–2,400 vines per acre. However, in the late 1980s Gary Andrus ran into financial difficulties. He had been unhappy with the 1988 and 1989 vintages and declassified the wines. This seemed to make matters worse, and his venture was saved by a partnership with Leucadia Cellars, an investment firm from the East which sank $8 million into the winery. The Andruses have also bought 110 acres in Oregon, where they make some high-priced Pinot Noir at Archery Summit. In Napa, Gary Andrus is assisted by winemaker Stacy Clark.

The most impressive feature of Pine Ridge is the series of Cabernets with different Napa appellations. The Rutherford bottling is estate-grown, and aged in 40 per cent new oak for up to 18 months. The Howell Mountain bottling is made from fruit grown at 2,000 feet. The must receives a slightly longer maceration than the Rutherford cuvée; malolactic fermentation takes place in barrel, and the wine is aged 19 months in new, heavy-toast *barriques*. The Stags Leap cuvée also comes from their own vineyards, and is aged for about 15 months in new, heavy-toast *barriques*. There is also the Andrus Reserve, a Bordeaux blend from Rutherford fruit made only in outstanding vintages such as 1980, 1985, 1986, 1990, and 1991. The vinification is similar to that for the Howell Mountain bottling. There are also two Merlot cuvées: one from Carneros fruit, the other called Crimson Creek being made solely from Napa fruit. Since 1992 none of the reds has been filtered, and in some cases there is no fining either.

Although these reds are very impressive, I have been less taken with the whites, especially the Chardonnay. A 1992 Knollside Cuvée was exotic and distinctly sweet. Perhaps it was atypical. Since then, Pine Ridge has introduced a Stags Leap Chardonnay and a special bottling using only Dijon clones. Andrus is one of the few prominent Napa winemakers to produce Chenin Blanc in substantial quantities. The off-dry California cuvée blends fruit from Yountville and Clarksburg. In 1992 Andrus introduced La Petite Vigne, which is bone-dry and includes 15 per cent Viognier. Late harvest Chenin has only been made in suitable vintages such as 1988, 1989, 1992, and 1994; quantities are minuscule.

Plumpjack
620 Oakville Cross Rd., Napa, CA 94558. Tel: 945 1220. Fax: 944 0744. Production: 10,000 cases.

A newcomer to Napa Valley, the winery is located in the former Villa Mount Eden facility, and 1997 was the first vintage vinified there, although the first releases were from the 1995 vintage. Nils Venge is the consultant winemaker. The estate has 53 acres on gravelly soil and a rocky knoll planted with Cabernet Sauvignon, but also relies on purchased fruit. One of Andy Beckstoffer's sons is director of the winery, so Merlot comes from the Beckstoffer vineyards. The winery is focusing on Chardonnay, Merlot, and Cabernet Sauvignon, with Reserve bottlings for all three. The Reserves will have a higher proportion of new oak and longer barrel-ageing, up to 26 months in the case of Cabernet. Despite its recent arrival on the scene, Plumpjack has the confidence to pitch its wine prices high.

Pride Mountain
Spring Mountain Rd., St Helena, CA 94574. Tel: 963 4949. Production: 10,000 cases.

This 70-acre estate on Spring Mountain was founded by Jim Pride, a dentist, and his wife Carolyn in 1989; the first vintage was 1991. The vineyards, 2,000 feet high, are on the site of the former Summit Ranch, and yields are low, no more than 2 tons per acre. At present the wines are being made at Chappellet by Bob Foley, formerly of Markham, but the Prides are constructing their own winery. The range consists of Cabernet Sauvignon, Merlot, Chardonnay, and Viognier. The Reserve Claret, which is their top Cabernet, is made in tiny quantities but has won great acclaim.

Quintessa
1178 Galleron Rd., Rutherford, CA 94573. Tel: 963 7111. Fax: 963 7867. Production: 20,000 cases.

This is the 180-acre estate from which the Franciscan group are producing a top Meritage red. It consists of five different vineyards on varied soils, mostly alluvial, as well as volcanic ash, loam, and gravel. Cabernet Sauvignon, Merlot, and Cabernet Franc are planted here, and the first vintage was 1993, which was aged 22 months in French oak. The winemaker is Alan Tenscher, and the release price $70.

Raymond
849 Zinfandel Lane, St Helena, CA 94574. Tel: 963 3141. Fax: 963 8498. Production: 200,000 cases.

Roy Raymond Sr went to work for Beringer in 1933, when Prohibition was repealed. There he was fortunate enough to marry a Beringer daughter and was soon running the winery. In the early 1970s he set up his own winery with his sons Roy Junior and Walter. Walter was the winemaker from the outset, assisted by Kenn Vigoda. In 1989 the Japanese brewery Kirin became the majority shareholder. Roy Senior died in 1998.

Over the years Raymond has grown considerably, and its identity is less clear than it used to be. The winery owns 450 acres in Monterey as well as Napa. Their original vineyard is near the winery along Zinfandel Lane and was planted in 1972. In the early 1990s they acquired a vineyard in very cool part of southern Napa in Jamieson Canyon. South of Gonzalez are 300 acres of Chardonnay planted in 1990. Chardonnay dominates production.

The problem with Raymond is that there have been reorganizations of the labelling and structure, which can be confusing. The basic range is now called Amberhill, which bears a California appellation. No doubt a good deal of Raymond's Monterey fruit ends up here. The next tier up is Raymond Estate, although the wines are not necessarily derived from the family's vineyards. What used to be Raymond Private Reserve is now called Raymond Generations, although the Meritage is still labelled as Private Reserve.

An attractive Sauvignon Blanc is made, with only partial barrel fermentation to preserve the wine's freshness; the Reserve is aged for 3 months in *barriques*. As for Chardonnay, the 1995 Estates wine is Monterey fruit aged for 4 months in oak. The Napa Chardonnay blends grapes from various sources, and is aged for 6 months in *barriques*, as is the Napa Reserve Chardonnay. The 1996 Generations is aged longer, for 9 months.

The Cabernets, which are probably Raymond's best wines, are aged for 16 to 24 months in *barriques*. There is also a Napa Reserve Merlot and Napa Reserve Pinot Noir.

Raymond used to be a source of attractive late harvest Rieslings, but the variety was grafted over to Chardonnay some time ago. However in 1989 they did release a late harvest Sémillon.

Reverie

1520 Diamond Mountain Rd., Calistoga, CA 94515. Tel: 942 6800. Production: 2,000 cases.

Norman Kiken came to Diamond Mountain in 1994. The 27-acre estate vineyard has been planted with Cabernet Sauvignon, Cabernet Franc, and Merlot, and small parcels of Tempranillo and Barbera.

Ritchie Creek

4024 Spring Mountain Rd., St Helena, CA 94574. Tel: 963 4661. Production: 1,200 cases.

In the late 1960s Peter Minor, a dentist from Santa Rosa, planted a few acres of Cabernet Sauvignon and Merlot on Spring Mountain at an elevation of 2,000 feet. The winery was constructed in 1974, and some more vines were planted; 3 acres of Chardonnay and 1 of Viognier. These two white varieties were added to the range in 1986. But up here in the mountains Viognier does not always ripen fully, so much of it has been taken out. The Cabernet, which is planted on a north-facing slope and retains good acidity, is made in an elegant, lean style.

Rocking Horse

1001 Franklin St., Napa, CA 94559. Tel: 255 5555. Production: 2,000 cases.

This small winery, established by Jeff Doran and Brian Zealear in 1989, uses the facilities at Honig. There are no vineyards, so fruit is purchased: Zinfandel from Lamborn Vineyard on Howell Mountain, and Cabernet Sauvignon from two Napa vineyards, one in Stags Leap District, the other in Rutherford. There is also a distinctive wine called Old Paint, a blend of Zinfandel, Petite Sirah, and Carignane from very old vines. James Hall has been the winemaker and quality has been impressive.

Rombauer

3522 Silverado Trail, St Helena, CA 94574. Tel: 963 5170. Fax: 963 5752. Production; 15,000 cases.

Koerner Rombauer, a pilot, bought some woodland in Napa Valley in 1972, but ten years went by before the family decided to plant vineyards here. Rombauer was a partner in Conn Creek Winery before selling his share in 1980. The winery opened here in 1982, and has produced wines for many other estates on a custom-crush basis. The winemaker is Greg Graham. In 1994 they bought the ailing sparkling wine house of Kornell, but its future is uncertain.

The range of wines includes a barrel-fermented Carneros Chardonnay, Napa Cabernet, Napa Merlot, Estate Zinfandel which is aged 12 to 14 months in oak, and two top wines. The first is a Special Selection Cabernet from Diamond Mountain. The other is called Meilleur du Chai, and blends 40 per cent Cabernet Franc, with 30 per cent each of Cabernet Sauvignon and Merlot.

Rudd

7717 Silverado Trail, Oakville, CA 94562. Tel: 944 8577. Fax: 944 7823. Production: 15,000 cases.

In 1974 Steve Girard, a senior executive at Kaiser Industries, bought a 44-acre plot in Oakville, and Chardonnay, Sauvignon, and Chenin vines were planted in 1980. In 1992 the Girards bought the 40-acre Viridian Vineyard behind Napanook. The Sauvignon was phased out after 1985 and the Chenin after 1996, after the sale of the winery. The purchaser was Leslie Rudd, who renamed the winery after himself. Visitors to St Helena can hardly help noticing the immense new delicatessen erected by Dean & Deluca, of which Rudd is the proprietor. Rudd's great coup in 1998 was to lure David Ramey away from Dominus to be his winemaker.

Although the vineyards were not susceptible to phylloxera, they were substantially replanted with closer spacing after Rudd took over. Leslie Rudd plans to produce mostly Cabernet Sauvignon, with about 20 per cent Chardonnay. It seems clear at this early stage that Rudd plans to go into competition with the top wineries of Napa Valley. Under Steve Girard, the winery produced good barrel-fermented Chardonnay, made with natural yeasts; the Reserve Chardonnay was only made in top vintages and was entirely aged in new oak. Viridian Chardonnay was made from the Rued clone only and was fermented with natural yeasts. Viridian was also the source of the Reserve Cabernet, which was aged for 2 years in oak. It will be fascinating to see what direction the winery will take under Rudd and Ramey.

Rutherford Hill
200 Rutherford Hill Rd., St Helena, CA 94573. Tel: 963 3187. Fax: 963 1904. Production: 110,000 cases.

Rutherford Hill used to be a name to be reckoned with. It was founded in its present form by some of the growers who set up Freemark Abbey. This was a way of expanding Freemark's range without overloading the original winery's facilities. This was formerly one of the wineries known as Souverain and owned by Pillsbury. In the 1980s, when Jerry Luper was winemaker, the winery had a great reputation for Merlot, and I recall excellent Cabernet Sauvignon from the late 1970s and early 1980s. The wines were aged in caves tunnelled half a mile into the cliffs; at the time they were the largest in California.

Some poor vintages and vineyards devastated by phylloxera dragged down the quality at Rutherford Hill, and it does not seem to have recovered. In 1996 the winery was bought by Paterno Imports of Chicago, who culled the inventory to weed out poor bottles and wines, but it seems there is a long way to go before Rutherford Hill recovers its reputation.

Saddleback Cellars
7802 Money Rd., Oakville, CA 94562. Tel: 944 1305. Fax: 944 1325. Production: 4,000 cases.

Nils Venge, who made the Groth Cabernet Sauvignon in 1985 to which Robert Parker gave a perfect score, has his own winery, which he established in 1983. The vineyards here consist of 17 acres planted with Cabernet Sauvignon, Chardonnay, and Pinot Blanc in 1994. Much of the vineyard had to be replanted in 1995 and 1996.

As well as Chardonnay and Cabernet Sauvignon, the winery produces Sangiovese blended with some Bordeaux varieties. It is aged in older *barriques*. Since 1984 Saddleback has been releasing Pinot Blanc, a blend of estate-grown grapes which have been barrel-fermented, and purchased grapes from Carneros, which are fermented in stainless steel. The result is a medium-bodied but toasty style.

Zinfandel is aged in new American oak, and is usually a hefty wine. Small quantities of Merlot are made in a full-throttle style. The top Cabernet is the very ripe and concentrated Family Reserve, which comes from the same parcel each year, and is aged in French and American oak, of which 70 per cent are new.

A curiosity is a late harvest Sauvignon Vert, which doesn't sound very promising. But I haven't tasted it.

St Andrew's Winery
2921 Silverado Trail, Napa, CA 94558. Tel: 252 6748. Fax: 252 0220. Production: 18,000 cases.

In 1972 Imre Vizkelety, who, despite his Hungarian name, was Swiss-born, planted 82 acres of Chardonnay here in southern Napa. At first the fruit was sold to Domaine Chandon, but in 1980 Chuck Ortman, one of Napa Valley's most renowned winemakers, was hired to look after the vinification. Over the years the winery developed a good reputation for Chardonnay. It also produced Sauvignon Blanc until 1988, when the variety was discontinued. In 1989 it was acquired by Clos du Val, which installed Daryl Eklund as winemaker. Then a few years later it was bought by Michael Moone of Beringer, and it was his plan to replant the estate to Italian varieties, especially Sangiovese and Pinot Grigio.

St Clement

2867 St Helena Highway, St Helena, CA 94574. Tel: 967 3033. Fax: 963 9174. Production: 20,000 cases.

This charming Victorian mansion was built in 1878 by a San Francisco merchant. In the late 1960s it was bought by Michael Robbins, who named the estate Spring Mountain. Then in 1975 he sold it to Dr William Casey, an eye surgeon, who renamed it St Clement and hired Chuck Ortman as winemaker. The winery was constructed in 1979 and in 1980 Dennis Johns became the winemaker, earning a good reputation for Cabernet Sauvignon and Sauvignon Blanc. In 1987 the Japanese Sapporo Corporation bought the property for $5 million, but retained Dennis Johns. Sapporo invested further in the estate by buying the 20-acre Abbott's Vineyard in Carneros, which supplied St Clement with Merlot and Chardonnay.

The wines here are made with a light touch and are far from the customary Napa blockbusters. There's a delicate Sauvignon Blanc, using Pope Valley and Napa Valley fruit, and a barrel-fermented Chardonnay from Abbott's Vineyard. In addition to the regular Cabernet, there is an occasional Howell Mountain bottling. There is also a Merlot and a complex Bordeaux blend called Oroppas. The reds are all given a fairly short maceration, at least by Napa standards, as Johns doesn't look for heavy extraction and tannin.

St Supéry

8440 St Helena Highway, Rutherford, CA 94573. Tel: 963 4507. Fax: 963 4526. Production: 100,000 cases.

The Skalli family of southern France, who produce the widely distributed Fortant wines, bought this property in 1986 and the first vintage here was 1988. The estate dates back to 1881, and the house built at that time is now used as the visitors' centre. St Supéry offers one of the best educational tours in the wine country. The winemaker is Australian, Michael Scholz, and he can take advice from the winery's consultant, Michel Rolland.

For its grapes, St Supéry can draw on the huge resources of its 450-acre Dollarhide Ranch in Pope Valley, and the vineyard is well suited to mechanical harvesting. The wines in general are supple, fresh, medium-bodied, drinkable young, and offer good value. They don't have much excitement or personality, but given their undemanding style, they are well made. The range includes an unoaked Sauvignon Blanc, Chardonnay fermented both in oak and in tanks, a juicy Merlot, a very good Cabernet Sauvignon, and a red and white Meritage. The white is unusual in that it contains more Sémillon than Sauvignon Blanc; the Sémillon, unlike the Sauvignon, is barrel-fermented.

V. Sattui

11 White Lane, St Helena, CA 94574. Tel: 963 7774. Fax: 963 4324. Production: 40,000 cases.

Vittorio Sattui opened a winery in San Francisco in 1885, but Prohibition finished it off. The wine bug was transmitted through the generations to Vittorio's great-grandson Daryl. In 1975 he started buying bulk wines and blending and bottling them. Through the 1980s the operation expanded, and the winery produced some good Cabernet Sauvignon, Zinfandel, and Riesling. About half the wines are estate-grown on the 60-acre Sattui vineyards near Yountville. With its tasting room on the main highway through the valley, Sattui has always attracted a large number of passing tourists, who also take advantage of the house delicatessen and the adjoining picnic site. The wines themselves are made in an upfront commercial style, but there are some serious wines too, such as the Howell Mountain Zinfandel.

Schramsberg

1400 Schramsberg Rd., Calistoga, CA 94515. Tel: 942 4558. Fax: 942 5943. Production: 40,000 cases.

The original winery on the site was built by Jacob Schram in 1862, and its most intriguing feature was the caves tunnelled into the hills by Chinese labourers, which provide perfect conditions for ageing the wines. After Jacob's death in 1905, the estate passed through various hands, but nobody had any commercial success with it. By 1965 the estate had become derelict, but it was bought by Jack and Jamie Davies on the recommendation of Fred McCrea of Stony Hill.

To make wine for the reborn estate's first vintage, 1966, Davies bought some Riesling grapes and then exchanged them for Chardonnay grapes from Mondavi. Slowly the estate expanded and its reputation grew. From the start the idea was to make sparkling wines of the highest quality, and most of the wines were aged from 4 to 5 years on the yeast. In 1970 the production was still only 1,000 cases, but by 1980 it had grown to 20,000 cases. In 1985 the Davieses acquired the neighbouring McEachran estate, which gave them 60 acres of vineyards in all. They supplemented this supply by buying in other fruit from Napa. Schramsberg had a series of excellent winemakers, including Greg Fowler and Alan Tenscher, and the present incumbent is Mike Reynolds.

The range is quite large. There's a Blanc de Noirs; a Blanc de Blancs made from Pinot Blanc as well as Chardonnay; a Brut Rosé; a Reserve from Pinot Noir, Pinot Meunier, and Chardonnay, aged up to 5 years on the yeasts; and their biscuity prestige blend, J. Schram, which was first made in 1987. Only Chardonnay and Pinot Noir are used, and some of the base wine is fermented in cask. Production is limited to about 1,000 cases. A curiosity here is the Cremant, bottled at half the usual pressure. It is made from a crossing called Flora and is aged for only 2 years. There seems to be no dogma at Schramsberg. In 1996, for example, there were eighty lots of base wine, some fermented in wood, others in steel; some had gone through malolactic fermentation, others had not. The art is in the blending.

All the sparkling wines are vintage-dated except for the less expensive Mirabelle range. Not even the prestigious Schramsberg winery could avoid the slump in sparkling wine consumption of the early 1990s, and in 1997 they produced red table wines for the first time.

Jack Davies died at the age of 75 in 1998. He was genuinely missed in Napa Valley, as he had done much to ensure that Napa escaped the uncontrolled urban expansion that dealt a death blow to the vineyards of Santa Clara and Santa Cruz.

Screaming Eagle
Oakville. Tel: 944 0749. Fax: 944 9271. Production: 550 cases.

This dot on the map is the property of Jean Phillips, an estate agent in Napa, and Tony Bowden. They own some 50 acres of vineyards but sell most of their grapes to other wineries; Screaming Eagle is produced from 2.2 acres. Given that the production of Cabernet Sauvignon (the only wine) was a trifling 135 cases in 1993, it is not surprising that the wine has become a cult collector's item. At an auction in 1998 the 1994 vintage was selling for $700 per bottle. The wine, which is made by Heidi Peterson Barrett, is no doubt of high quality, but the proliferation of such collectors' wines in Napa Valley is a deplorable trend.

Seavey
1310 Conn Valley Rd., St Helena, CA 94574. Tel: 963 8339. Production: 2,000 cases.

Since 1990 William and Mary Seavey, and winemaker Gary Galleron, have produced sound Cabernet Sauvignon and Chardonnay from their own 33-acre vineyards in Conn Valley. The Chardonnay does not go through malolactic fermentation, and is made in a sleek elegant style.

Selene Wines
Tel: 258 8119. Production: 1,200 cases.

This small wine company belongs to Mia Klein, who assisted Tony Soter in his consultancy work for many years, and her husband Ed Powers. The only wine I have encountered from here was a well judged Carneros Hyde Vineyard Sauvignon Blanc from the Musqué clone, but a Caldwell Vineyard Merlot is also produced.

Sequoia Grove
8338 St Helena Highway, Napa, CA 94558. Tel: 944 2945. Fax: 983 9411. Production: 20,000 cases.

In 1978 James and Steve Allen bought 25 acres of vineyard in Rutherford, and founded their winery two years later. They later sold Sequoia Grove to Kobrand Corporation, and James Allen became the winemaker. They have expanded their vineyard holdings, acquiring 138 acres in Carneros, which was later bought by Domaine Carneros. However, Sequoia Grove still have access to the vineyard's Chardonnay. Recent plantings have been on vertical trellising and have used closer spacing. No insecticides or herbicides are used.

There are two Chardonnays, neither of which goes through malolactic fermentation. The Carneros Chardonnay is fermented in steel and in oak; the Napa Chardonnay is barrel-fermented in 25 per cent new *barriques*. There can be as many as three Cabernet Sauvignons in some vintages. The basic wine is, unusually, aged for 6 months in large wooden casks before continuing the process in *barriques* for up to 14 months. In some years a powerful, meaty Estate bottling is produced from Rutherford fruit; vinification and ageing are similar. The Reserve bottling, first produced in 1985, is aged in *barriques* for 22 months. In general the very good Cabernets are more reliable and successful than the Chardonnays.

Shafer
6154 Silverado Trail, Napa, CA 94558. Tel: 944 2877. Fax: 944 9454. Production: 30,000 cases.

John Shafer was a textbook executive from Illinois, and in his late forties decided to move his family out to California. In 1972 he bought a 30-acre vineyard, which was promptly replanted and expanded to 50 acres. The estate's first vintage was 1978. Shafer employed as consultants Chuck Ortman and Tony Soter at various times, but today the wines are made by his son Doug and by Elias Fernandez.

The Shafers cultivate 170 acres: 50 acres near the winery planted on terraces with Cabernet Sauvignon, Merlot, Cabernet Franc, and Chardonnay; 25 acres in Oak Knoll, where Syrah has been planted; and, since 1990, 75 acres of Chardonnay and Merlot in Carneros. The Shafers have taken advantage of the replanting required after phylloxera to make certain changes: Zinfandel was grafted over to Merlot in the mid-1980s, and Chardonnay in Stags Leap is being replaced with more Cabernet. They have also planted some Syrah. The Shafers are keen on 'sustainable agriculture', employing cover crops and using natural predators.

Shafer is best known for its red wines, but the Chardonnay can be good too. Their top Chardonnay comes from Red Shoulder Ranch in Carneros: the grapes are whole-cluster pressed and fermented with natural yeasts. There is no malolactic fermentation, but instead there is long contact with the fine lees for 15 months. 'We have low-yielding clones,' John Shafer explained, 'so we get very ripe grapes at 3.5 tons per acre. So with great richness and high alcohol, we block malolactic to retain freshness in the wine.'

The basic Cabernet Sauvignon is aged for 22 months in half American, half French oak. It has long been an excellent wine, reflecting the sleek elegance of Stags Leap District fruit, but is surpassed by the more structured Hillside Select, a pure Cabernet produced only from estate-grown grapes; in recent vintages it has been aged for up to 34 months in new *barriques*.

Merlot, not a patch on the Cabernet, is made in a fruitier style, with a relatively brief maceration; the wine is aged for 18 months in French oak. Firebreak, first made in 1991, is Sangiovese with a dash of Cabernet Sauvignon. The grapes, planted in 1989, come from Stags Leap and Oak Knoll, and the wine is aged for 14 months in *barriques* of which one-third are new. Shafer admits that the model for this wine is Antinori's Tignanello, which impressed him greatly in Tuscany in the 1980s.

There are few estates in Napa that maintain such consistency and such a high level of quality across the range.

Signorello

4500 Silverado Trail, Napa, CA 94558. Tel: 255 5990. Fax: 415 392 4040. Production: 7,500 cases

The Signorello family have been farming grapes in Oak Knoll since 1977. They now cultivate about 100 acres, some of which are planted with varieties such as Viognier, Mourvèdre, Nebbiolo, and Sangiovese. The red grapes are planted using vertical trellising at a density of 1,200 vines per acre. Yields are kept to below 3 tons per acre.

Before beginning to produce their own wines in 1985, the Signorellos sold their grapes to Caymus, Cakebread, Cuvaison, and others. Their first wine was a Chardonnay, followed by Cabernet Sauvignon and Pinot Noir in 1988. In 1991 their winery was built. Until 1992 they purchased their Cabernet fruit, and they still buy Pinot Noir from Russian River Valley and Carneros. Wines such as Sauvignon Blanc, Petite Sirah, and Merlot are no longer produced, and today the range consists of Pinot Noir, Chardonnay, Cabernet, and, unusually, Sémillon.

The Chardonnay and Sémillon are whole-cluster pressed, and fermented mostly with natural yeasts in *barriques*, of which half are new. The barrels are quite heavily toasted. With the Sémillon, malolactic fermentation is kept to only 30 per cent. The Sémillon is aged for 11 months, the Chardonnay for a few months longer. In addition to the Estate Chardonnay, there is a pricy but inelegant Founder's Reserve, which is a barrel selection of the best wines.

The reds are made with extravagant care. Some 20 to 30 per cent of the berries are left whole and fermentation, using natural yeasts, takes place in open-top fermenters, which are punched down by hand regularly. The must is macerated for 20 to 30 days. The Pinot Noir is aged for 17 months, the Cabernet for 22. Neither wine is fined or filtered.

There are in fact three different Pinot Noirs: one from Martinelli Vineyard in Russian River Valley, one from Los Amigas in Carneros, and a blend under the North Coast appellation.

The other reds are the Estate Cabernet, which is aged in one-third new *barriques*. There is also an oaky Founder's Reserve. There have also been Zinfandels from Howell Mountain, and Sangiovese from Atlas Peak.

Considering the estate's fastidious winemaking practices and sophisticated packaging it will come as no surprise that the wines are very expensive.

Silver Oak
915 Oakville Cross Rd., Oakville, CA 94562. Tel: 944 8808. Fax: 944 2817. Production: 60,000 cases.

The co-founder, Justin Meyer, used to be a monk, but the kind of monk who had made wine at Christian Brothers. After he left the priesthood he helped found Franciscan before setting up Silver Oak in partnership with Colorado oilman Raymond Duncan. Until 1979 all the grapes came from a vineyard in Alexander Valley which the winery bought in 1988. Then a Napa Cabernet was added to the range, as well as a single-vineyard wine named after Meyer's wife Bonny. The thinking behind Silver Oak was simplicity itself. There would be one varietal: pure Cabernet Sauvignon, and it would all be aged in American oak. Meyer experimented with many different American oaks, and eventually settled on a cooper in Missouri who produced barrels that he liked.

The vineyards were largely planted on AXR-1 so have had to be replanted. Bonny's Vineyard is near the winery and consists of 4 acres on gravelly soil. The wine was discontinued after 1992. It had by no means been evident that the single vineyard gave superior wines to the other Silver Oak blends – indeed, some critics detected a disturbing vegetal tone in some of the Bonny's Vineyard offerings – so that realization may have contributed to its elimination. It had also been higher priced than the other two wines and usually failed to deliver anything extra.

Meyer is keen on roto-fermenters, and Mondavi uses them too for some of its wines. He is not looking for extended maceration but a fairly rapid extraction. The wines are aged up to 32 months in oak and 12 months in bottle. With most of his bottles going to restaurants, Meyer wants to release wines that are ready to drink. He insists, however, that they are perfectly capable of ageing, which does indeed seem to be the case.

These are wines that divide those who taste them. Those who like them adore their svelte texture, elegance, and sheer drinkability. Those who dislike them, and I confess to being in the second camp, find them too slick, too sweet and smooth, lacking in virility despite their concentration of flavour. I have marginally preferred the Napa bottling to the Sonoma one, but both are very well made. By far the largest quantity comes from Alexander Valley. What Meyer has achieved is two distinctly Californian styles of Cabernet. He has never set foot in Bordeaux and has no interest in making monuments to Cabernet. He wants fruit, accessibility, immediate sensual pleasure, and a natural balance that will allow those who like aged wines to cellar them without risk.

Silverado Vineyards
6121 Silverado Trail, Napa, CA 94558. Tel: 257 1770. Production: 90,000 cases.

Although this estate was founded by the widow of Walt Disney, there is nothing Mickey Mouse about the operation. This is a large, well-run estate that has always delivered very good wines at fair prices. Lillian Disney bought a lot of acreage in Stags Leap in 1976 and started farming grapes; the winery followed in 1981. She hired Jack Stuart as winemaker, and he is still there. She, however, died in 1998 at the age of 97. Her daughter Diane and Diane's husband Ron Miller now run the property.

The estate now consists of 350 acres, mostly in Stags Leap District. There are parcels of Sauvignon Blanc and Chardonnay in Yountville, and 168 acres in Coombsville, planted with Mourvedre, Sangiovese, Merlot, and Cabernet Franc. Jack Stuart has high hopes for their 19 acres of Sangiovese, which he considers an ideal variety for Napa Valley. There are also 43 acres in Carneros.

The Chardonnay is barrel-fermented in Burgundian oak, and about half the wine goes through malolactic fermentation. The result is a refined elegant wine, far removed from some Napa Valley blockbusters and all the better for it. The Sauvignon is delicious too, consistently one of the best from Napa. But even better are the Cabernet Sauvignons, which have been excellent from the start, a fruity accessible wine with a light underlay of tannin and very well balanced. The Merlot is also sound.

Sinskey

6320 Silverado Trail, Napa, CA 94558. Tel: 944 9090. Fax: 944 9092. Production: 12,000 cases.

Robert Sinskey was an eye surgeon and partner in Acacia until its purchase by the Chalone group. Then in 1982 he started buying vineyards in Carneros and Stags Leap District, and now has 150 acres in all. His first winemaker, in the late 1980s, was Joe Cafaro, so it is not surprising that the initial releases were of high quality. The present winemaker, Jeff Virnig, seems to be maintaining those standards.

The winery has always shown a keen interest in Pinot Noir, which is planted in a number of its vineyards. The simplest Pinot is called Aries, mostly made from grapes purchased from Mendocino; the wine is aged about 9 months in medium-toast *barriques*, and is intended to be enjoyed young. The more serious version is from Carneros, fermented largely in open vats, and aged for 10 months in *barriques*. The Reserve is also from Carneros, and is aged for 14 months in 50 per cent new *barriques*. Sinskey is one of the few wineries to make a Vin Gris from Pinot juice drawn off during fermentation (see Chapter 21).

The Merlot, also made with Carneros fruit, is good. I have also drunk a delicious Cabernet Franc from Carneros. The estate's Meritage is called RSV and is a Cabernet-dominated Bordeaux blend aged for 20 months in *barriques*.

Visitors to Napa wisely travelling up the Silverado Trail rather than Highway 29 often overlook Sinskey, but it is worth a visit, both for the qualities of the wine and for the usefulness of the delicatessen adjoining the tasting room.

La Sirena

Tel: 942 1105. Production: 400 cases.

Heidi Peterson Barrett spends so much of her time making extravagantly praised and highly priced wines for other proprietors that it must be a relief to produce small quantities of wine for which she is accountable only to herself. La Sirena is her own label. Thus far she has only released Sangiovese, grown in Pope Valley.

Sky

1500 Lokoya Rd., Napa, CA 94558. Tel: 935 1391. Production: 2,000 cases.

I first met the co-owner of Sky, Linn Briner, at Mayacamas, where she was then assistant winemaker. Here she and Lore Olds make nothing but Zinfandel, 14 dry-farmed acres of which are planted 2,100 feet up on Mount Veeder. The volcanic hillsides are steep and airy, the drainage excellent. The wine is aged for a year in *barriques*, and aged for a further year before release. The one vintage I have drunk was very good.

Smith-Madrone

4022 Spring Mountain Rd., St Helena, CA 94574. Tel: 963 2283. Fax: 963 1265. Production: 5,000 cases.

In 1971 Stu Smith cleared 200 acres of wooded land 1,600 feet high on Spring Mountain above Stony Hill. It appears that there was a vineyard here in the nineteenth century, but it had long vanished. There have been a number of changes in the dry-farmed vineyards, planted on red volcanic soil, over the years, and Pinot Noir was phased out in 1989. The current plantings are of Chardonnay, Cabernet Sauvignon, Riesling, and a little Cabernet Franc and Merlot which were added in 1990. Smith-Madrone has always had a reputation for its dry Riesling, and for lean Chardonnay and Cabernet.

Spring Mountain

2805 Spring Mountain Rd., St Helena, CA 94574. Tel: 963 5233. Fax: 963 2753. Production: making its way towards 35,000 cases.

This property has a somewhat complicated history. In 1968 Michael Robbins founded a winery with this name; today it is known as St Clement. In 1974 Robbins moved operations to Spring Mountain's present home, a fine Victorian mansion built in 1885 by a man with the splendid name of Tiburcio Parrott. The house was known as Miravalle, but countless Americans know it as Falcon Crest, since a famous television soap series of that name was filmed here. Robbins expanded the estate until 150 acres had been planted. In 1990, however, he filed for bankruptcy. Two years later the estate was bought for $5.5 million by a group headed by Tom Ferrell, former president of Sterling and Franciscan.

   The new owners have reconstituted the vineyards. They have replanted the Miravalle Vineyard originally planted by Parrott; the varieties are Cabernet Sauvignon, Petit Verdot, and Merlot. In addition there is the 55-acre Chateau Chevalier vineyard planted with Merlot and Cabernet, and a small parcel called Alba. This amounts to about 100 acres, much of it close-spaced. The yields are between 2 and 3.5 ton per acre. The first releases under the new regime were the 1990, 1991, and 1992, none of which had of course been vinified by the Ferrell team. The first wine made by Craig MacLean, the new winemaker, is the 1993, a blend of 76 per cent Cabernet Sauvignon, 13 per cent Merlot, 11 per cent Cabernet Franc. The wine is aged in new *barriques* for 22 months and bottled without fining. The wine is very impressive and clearly structured for long ageing.

Since 1994 Spring Mountain have also produced a Sauvignon Blanc, given some floweriness with a small addition of Muscat. Half the wine is fermented in barrels, of which one-quarter are new, and aged for 6 months.

Staglin

1570 Bella Oaks Lane, Rutherford, CA 94573. Tel: 963 1749. Fax: 963 8784. Production: 5,250 cases.

My first visit to Staglin was not a success. Having driven all the way from Sonoma for my appointment, I found myself taken for a courier collecting bottles for a tasting. When Mrs Staglin made an appearance, she announced breathlessly that she was on her way out. With apologies, I was granted a two-minute chat before she flew out of the door. I have decided to forgive the Staglins, as their wine is very good. So it should be, as the vineyards are on the Rutherford bench, and were originally planted in 1965 under the direction of André Tchelitscheff. The grapes were used by Beaulieu for its Private Reserve. When the Staglins bought the property in 1985 they replanted the vineyard, using various trellising systems on the advice of David Abreu. The 50-acre vineyards are cultivated without pesticides and herbicides and are planted with Cabernet Sauvignon, Chardonnay, Cabernet Franc, and Sangiovese. The Staglins wanted to build a winery nearby, but this is some of the most precious land in Napa Valley, and permission was denied. They sold their grapes to other wineries for many years until they started producing their own wines in rented facilities. Cathy Corison has been the consultant here since 1990, and the winemaker is Celia Masyczek, who used to work at Pepi.

The Cabernet Sauvignon contains a dash of Cabernet Franc but no Merlot. It is aged for 21 months in 40 per cent new oak. It's a rich earthy Rutherford wine of excellent quality. The Sangiovese is produced from the Biondi-Santi selection, and has been blended with 25 per cent Cabernet Sauvignon. Chardonnay is produced but has not yet been released. The Cabernet is currently priced at $43, which is not too brazen for a Rutherford wine of this quality, but the Sangiovese carries a $33 tag, which seems a bit steep for a wine that strikes me as over-extracted.

Stags Leap Winery

6150 Silverado Trail, Napa, CA 94558. Tel: 944 1303. Production: 50,000 cases.

In 1970 a restaurateur named Carl Doumani bought a few acres in the Stags Leap District, including the nineteenth-century Chase house, which had been empty for two decades and was in a derelict condition. The house was named after a Chicago businessman called Horace Chase, who also established a medium-sized winery on the property. In 1920 the house, then known as the Manor, became a hotel until it was closed in 1953.

When Carl Doumani named his own winery Stags Leap, he was sued by his neighbour Warren Winiarski of Stag's Leap Wine Cellars. Since it seems that the name Stag's Leap was first devised and used by Horace Chase, it was not surprising that Doumani wished to revive it. However, Winiarski wished to avoid confusion with his own winery. The case rumbled on for a long time, with appeals and counter-appeals. When the state supreme court decided not to take on the case, the two men came to an agreement which depended on the use of an apostrophe. Winiarski's Stag was singular, Doumani's plural. And that was that, except that confusion persists, as I have witnessed at first hand when visiting these wineries. To complicate matters the appellation Stags Leap has no apostrophe at all.

Doumani's first vintage was in 1979. By this time the vineyards consisted of 121 acres: 56 of Cabernet Sauvignon, 42 of Merlot, 4 of Cabernet Franc, some Petit Verdot and Malbec, and 19 acres of Petite Sirah, of which 5 date from the 1930s and gave fruit of high quality. The winery also produced Chardonnay, from purchased grapes. The winery never developed much of a reputation, except for its Petite Sirah. After Robert Brittan became winemaker in 1989, quality improved, but just after the promising 1994 wines were released, the property was sold to the Beringer group in 1997.

Steltzner

5998 Silverado Trail, Napa, CA 94558. Tel: 252 7272. Fax: 252 2079. Production: 12,000 cases.

Dick Steltzner was a well-known figure in the development of Napa Valley that took place in the 1960s. He had planted vineyards for a number of famous wineries, and planted his own vineyards along the Silverado Trail. In Stags Leap he has 44 acres of Cabernet Sauvignon, 5 each of Merlot and Cabernet Franc. In Oakville he has 20 acres planted with white varieties. The range includes Sauvignon Blanc, Chardonnay, a Claret, Merlot, and Cabernet Sauvignon. The Claret contains 62 per cent Cabernet Sauvignon, the rest being Cabernet Franc. Prices are low but quality is surprisingly nondescript given Steltzner's intimate knowledge of the Napa Valley.

Sterling

1111 Dunaweal Lane, Calistoga, CA 94515. Tel: 942 3400. Fax: 942 3466. Production: 300,000 cases.

In 1964 some paper company executives, including former *Financial Times* journalist Peter Newton, bought some land in northern Napa, and in 1967 acquired the knoll on which this distinctive winery was later built. Ric Forman, only 24 but already one of the top winemakers at Mondavi, knew that the family structure of that company would limit his progress. So he moved to Sterling, which made its first wines in 1969. The modern winery was built in 1973 to a striking design by Martin Waterfield. Forman was one of the pioneers of barrel fermentation for Chardonnay and also tried his hand at extended maceration, a technique that would become popular twenty years later.

In 1977 Sterling was bought by Coca-Cola for about $8 million. They made various changes. The range of wines was narrowed down to Cabernet Sauvignon, Merlot, Sauvignon Blanc, and Chardonnay. Some excellent vineyards were acquired, Winery Lake in Carneros, and Diamond Mountain Ranch, which had been developed by William Hill. Then in 1983 Coca-Cola decided it had had enough of the wine business and sold the property to Seagram, to which it still belongs. When Peter Newton decided to establish his own winery on Spring Mountain, Ric Forman went with him. For most of the 1980s the winemaker at Sterling was Bill Dyer, who was succeeded in 1997 by Greg Fowler, who took on responsibility for the winemaking at the Seagram properties in California, which included Mumm. Rob Hunter has specific responsibility for Sterling.

Today Sterling owns 1,200 acres of vineyards. Many were badly affected by phylloxera and have been replanted. During the replanting of Diamond Mountain Ranch, Chardonnay is being replaced by red varieties. The most basic range of wines are the Napa varietals. Then there are vineyard-designated wines, such as Pinot Noir, Chardonnay, and Merlot from Winery Lake, and Cabernet Sauvignon and Merlot from Diamond Mountain Ranch, and Merlot from Three Palms Vineyard. There is also a Bordeaux blend called Sterling Reserve.

The Napa Sauvignon Blanc is made in a fresh style, with only 10 per cent fermented in new oak, the rest in steel. There is also a cheaper North Coast Sauvignon Blanc, which is made only in steel tanks. Sometimes Sterling produce a Graves-style Sémillon as well. The Napa Chardonnay is barrel-fermented and aged for 7 months in 50 per cent new American oak. The Winery Lake Chardonnay is fermented with natural yeasts.

The Napa Cabernet Sauvignon and the Napa Merlot are aged 18 months in *barriques*. The sometimes dour Diamond Mountain Cabernet contains about 20 per cent Cabernet Franc, and is fermented using natural yeasts; it is aged for 22 months in French and American oak. Three Palms Merlot also contains Cabernet Franc and is aged in 55 per cent new French oak, and bottled without fining or filtration.

The Winery Lake Pinot Noir, a wine that's not always convincing, is given a short cold soak before fermentation using natural yeasts. Malolactic fermentation takes place in barrel, and over 60 per cent new oak is used to age the wine over a 10-month period. Other wines include Zinfandel from old vines planted in Calistoga; and a Sangiovese from Atlas Peak.

The Sterling style has softened up since the early days. Most of the wines are made in substantial quantities and are made to be drunk fairly young, though many of the reds are perfectly capable of ageing well. By the late 1980s and early 1990s a certain blandness was becoming apparent. The Cabernet and Merlot and the Sterling Reserve were all good wines, but there was a heavy dependency on American oak and some of the wines lacked concentration. It seems that the new team is aware of these problems and is keen to twist Sterling's reputation up a few notches.

Stonegate
1183 Dunaweal Lane, Calistoga, CA 94515. Tel: 942 6500. Fax: 942 9721. Production: 10,000 cases.

The winery was founded in 1973 by James and Barbara Spaulding, whose son David has been the winemaker since 1985. However, after the Spauldings divorced, the winery was bought by Bandiera of Sonoma. The first wines here were made from purchased grapes, but the Spauldings also developed 32 acres of vineyards of their own, including a ranch in Calistoga and some mountain vineyards on Diamond Mountain and elsewhere. The range includes a Cabernet Sauvignon from Chiles Valley, a white Meritage called Felicity, a red Meritage Reserve made from Cabernet and Merlot, and from time to time late harvest Sauvignon Blancs. The wines have had a spotty reputation and it will be interesting to see whether the new owners will make improvements.

Stony Hill
Bale Grist Mill State Park Rd., St Helena, CA 94574. Tel: 963 2636. Production: 5,000 cases.

This legendary estate was founded by advertising executive Fred McCrea in 1943, when he paid $7,500 for 160 acres on Spring Mountain. He wasn't planning to grow grapes, but like so many who have followed him to Napa Valley, he was persuaded to do so. In 1946 he planted his Chardonnay vines, with assistance from André Tchelitscheff, who apparently had some doubts about the whole enterprise. The grapes were at first sold to other wineries and the first vintage was 1953. McCrea knew his Chardonnay grapes were of high quality and after a while couldn't bear to see them disappearing into the crushers at Charles Krug alongside mediocre grapes from less scrupulous growers. In those days it wasn't easy even to acquire such elementary materials as yeast and barrels, all of which had to be shipped in from afar. Other wineries also helped out, by supplying McCrae with cuttings. Fred McCrae made wines here with Mike Chelini until his death in 1977 at the age of 80. Thereafter the estate was run by his gracious and humorous widow Eleanor. She admitted to me that much of the mystique of Stony Hill was connected to the fact that the wines are so difficult to obtain. After her death in 1991, her son Peter took over the estate.

The 40 acres are planted at an elevation ranging from 800 to 1,200 feet. The Chardonnay is the Wente clone, and is supplemented by smaller quantities of Riesling, Sémillon, and Gewürztraminer. Unfortunately Pierce's disease has taken its toll here, and the vineyards were mostly replanted in the 1990s. Eleanor McCrea told me that apart from grapes, their main crop is rocks, and the soil is indeed volcanic and stony. The vineyards are dry-farmed and yields rarely exceed 2 tons per acre.

The wine that made Stony Hill famous was its Chardonnay. Of course in the 1950s and 1960s there was not a great deal of Chardonnay around for American admirers of the white Burgundy style. At Stony Hill the grapes were fermented in large 160-gallon casks, malolactic fermentation was blocked, and the wine was aged in barrels of various sizes and ages. There was never much new oak in use. It was a lean, citric wine that always needed a few years in bottle to develop complexity. Those fortunate enough to taste older vintages confirm that the wine was of superb quality, but my own few experiences of it were less exciting. There used to be a second label called SHV which was used for some purchased Chardonnay from Howell Mountain, but this fruit is now blended in with the estate wine, which some claim has changed its character.

The 1.5 acres of Sémillon have been used since 1969 to produce a *passito* wine, an Italian style made by picking the grapes very ripe and then drying them in the sun in order to concentrate their sugar content even further by a kind of raisining. Production was always minimal, and the vines are now on their last legs. Some full-bodied Riesling and Gewürztraminer are also produced, but the Pinot Blanc which was grown from 1964 and sold to Heitz was replaced with Chardonnay in 1971.

The wines are still sold mostly to a loyal mailing list.

Storybrook Mountain
3835 Highway 128, Calistoga, CA 94515. Tel: 942 5310. Fax: 942 5334. Production: 8,500 cases.

There is no doubt that Calistoga is a good region in which to grow Zinfandel, which relishes the heat and coolish nights here. The Grimm

winery was established at this northernmost of Napa properties and operated until Prohibition. Attached to the winery were caves in which the
barrels were stored. When history professor Jerry Seps bought the property
in 1976 it was in a poor state, having been completely abandoned 15
years earlier. In 1977 he planted 36 acres of Zinfandel, the only wine he
produces. The first vintage was 1983. The grapes come from his estate,
but also from other sources such as the Mayacamas Mountains and from
Howell Mountain (this is known as his Eastern Exposures bottling). All
the wines are of high quality and age well.

Summit Lake Vineyard
2000 Summit Lake Dr., Angwin, CA 94508. Tel: 965 2488. Production:
2,000 cases.

A former nineteenth-century 21-acre vineyard, in which some old Zinfandel vines survive, was bought by Bob Brakesman, who also makes the
wine, in 1971. Eleven more acres of Zinfandel and two of Cabernet
Sauvignon have also been planted. The first vintage was 1978. The wines
are aged in oak for up to 3 years. The only wine I have tasted, the 1993
Zinfandel, was porty and over-extracted.

Sutter Home
100 St Helena Highway, St Helena, CA 94574. Tel: 963 3104. Fax: 963
7217. Production: 7.5 million cases.

This property, which had flourished in the nineteenth century, was bought
by John and Mario Trinchero in 1947. In the 1960s the winery expanded
and produced a huge range of wines, many of them fortified. Sutter Home
would be a winery of little significance were it not for the discovery of
the market potential of white Zinfandel by Bob Trinchero in 1972. He
may not have been the first to produce a 'blush' wine from Zinfandel
grapes, but he set the trend that others have followed. In 1972 he made
only 200 cases, and even in 1975 only 700 cases were produced. However
by 1980 the production had risen to 25,000 cases, and two years later to
85,000 cases. By the mid-1980s Sutter Home was the largest winery in
Napa Valley, generating 1.4 million cases of white Zinfandel alone. Sutter
Home have planted 3,100 acres of vineyards, many of them in inland
regions east of Lake County and not well known for grape production.
Much of the viticulture is along organic lines.

   It would be 1989 before Sutter Home launched their first Chardonnay
vintage, a trifling 360,000 cases. In 1991 Merlot was added to the range,
which already include Sauvignon Blanc and Cabernet Sauvignon. Their
best wine is the red Zinfandel, largely sourced from Amador County,
which is also where their good Reserve Zinfandel is grown. Almost all the
wines are released under the California appellation, allowing the wine-

THE WINES OF CALIFORNIA

maker, Steve Bertolucci, to blend wines from all over the state in order to achieve the quality and volume he requires.

In 1996 Sutter Home introduced a new range of higher quality wines under the M. Trinchero label. At present these consist of Chardonnay, Cabernet Sauvignon, and red and white Meritage. This range has its own winemaker, Derek Holstein. It is estimated that the maximum production for the M. Trinchero wines will be 10,000 cases, a drop in the ocean compared to Sutter Home's total production.

Swanson

1271 Manley Lane, Rutherford, CA 94573. Tel: 944 1642. Fax: 944 0955. Production: 20,000 cases.

In 1985 another rich man arrived in Napa with ambitions to own a wine estate. This was W. Clarke Swanson, the owner of Averys of Bristol and other companies. Initially he bought 80 acres in the heart of Oakville, where he planted Merlot, an unusual choice in those days. He later added a further 60, also spending a great deal of money on replanting and vineyard management. In 1991 he acquired the Schmidt Ranch in Oakville, which included some very old Syrah vines that had previously been sold to Sean Thackrey for his acclaimed Orion. Swanson replanted much of the vineyard but left the old Syrah vines in place. Much of the fruit is sold to other wineries. The first vintage was 1987, a Cabernet Sauvignon; Chardonnay followed in 1988. Since then the range has expanded to include Merlot, Syrah, Sangiovese, and late harvest Sémillon.

Swanson has been moving towards full natural-yeast fermentation for his Carneros Chardonnay, a barrel-fermented wine from purchased grapes that sees a good proportion of new oak. There is also a Reserve Chardonnay made in small quantities.

The Cabernet Sauvignon is put into barrel for its malolactic fermentation (a practice winemaker Marco Cappelli has adopted for all the Swanson reds), and aged for 19 months in one-third new French oak. The Estate Merlot is made in a similar way, but not aged quite as long, and American rather than French oak is used. There is also a proprietary red called Alexis, which is a blend of Cabernet Sauvignon, Merlot and Syrah. The wine is aged mostly in French oak for 20 months, and half the barrels are new.

There are 10 acres of Sangiovese planted in the Oakville vineyards, and this is aged for a year in 1- and 2-year-old barrels. Swanson is also one of the few producers to make a rosé from Sangiovese.

Syrah was first made in 1994 from the Schmidt Ranch. It is given an extended maceration of 32 days and aged for 20 months in new oak, of which 25 per cent is American. Production is limited and the price is high, but the quality is excellent.

434

A curiosity here is the late harvest Sémillon, made in 1988 and 1991. This is barrel-fermented and aged for 27 months in new oak – clearly a rival to Far Niente's Dolce.

When I have participated in blind tastings of California wines, Swanson have often emerged among the top wines. They can epitomize the generosity of flavour of the best California wines, but also have a stylishness that is harder to find. The wines are exceedingly well made, and although Swanson and Cappelli are not shy to use a lot of new oak, the wines rarely seem over-oaked, thanks to their richness of fruit. Since 1992 Helen Turley has been a consultant to the winery.

The Terraces
PO Box 511, Rutherford, CA 94573. Production: 1,000 cases.

Wayne Hogue bought a small hillside property off Silverado Trail in 1977, and planted 5 acres of Cabernet Sauvignon and Zinfandel in 1981. Until 1992 the wines were made for Hogue by Chuck Wagner at Caymus, and thereafter at the estate's completed winery. Like the Caymus Cabernet, The Terraces spends many years in oak.

Topaz
3291 St Helena Highway, St Helena, CA 94574. Tel: 963 1123. Production: 500 cases.

Jeff Sowells is an itinerant winemaker with an obsession about botrytis wines, which he makes with great skill. Never having had his own winery, he uses rented space at other wineries. He had made a sweet Sauvignon Blanc in 1985 but was unhappy with it, as it lacked botrytis. The next year, however, he found some very rich and heavily botrytized Sauvignon, which he blended with 40 per cent Sémillon from Yountville, which had been less completely infected. The wine was fermented in mostly new French oak for 5 weeks, and then aged for 18 months. The original idea was to release the wine under the name of Macauley, a winery owned by Ann Watson, who had provided the Sauvignon grapes. Unfortunately she was killed in a car crash, so Sowells released the wine under his own label of Topaz.

In 1989 Sowells made another Topaz, acquiring the fruit from Monticello's vineyards near Yountville. Another followed in 1991 and 1994. These are splendid wines, rich and unctuous, if a touch weighty from all that botrytis. They are made very much in the Sauternes style, though they are a touch sweeter than a typical Sauternes. Topaz also produces a Meritage called Rouge de Trois, a blend of finished wines assembled by Sowells.

Trefethen

1160 Oak Knoll Ave., Napa, CA 94558. Tel: 255 7700. Fax: 225 0793. Production: 100,000 cases.

The Eshcol Ranch was founded in 1886 in southern Napa by two local bankers, James and George Goodman. They only produced bulk wines, as did their successor, J. Clark Fawver, who bought the estate in 1904. Fawver died in 1940 and the vineyards were leased to Beringer until 1968, when they were bought by Gene Trefethen, an industrialist. For some years his son John, and John's energetic wife Janet, have run the estate. They replanted the vineyard and restored the gravity-flow winery. The first vintage was 1973.

This is surely the largest single vineyard in Napa Valley, consisting of 600 acres, and the Trefethens own a further 50 acres of Cabernet Sauvignon and Merlot in the Mayacamas foothills. Not surprisingly, they sell off half their crop to wineries such as Domaine Chandon and Schramsberg. The soil is loam with clay and silt, and some parcels have a high clay content.

The wines are made in a discreet style – some would say over-discreet. Oak-ageing is used with discretion, only some of the Chardonnay goes through malolactic fermentation, and there is no lees contact; only half the wine is barrel-aged and only for a few months. The wine is consequently lean, even a touch hard, but does benefit from some bottle-age. In recent vintages the style has been slightly modified, with a little barrel-fermentation.

Trefethen also produce a fairly dry Riesling, as well as Merlot and Cabernet Sauvignon, which also comes in a Reserve bottling. I find the style of the Cabernet too grassy and lean for my taste.

There is a second label of wines, Eshcol, that is good value.

Tudal

1015 Big Tree Rd., St Helena, CA 94574. Tel: 963 3947. Production: 2,000 cases.

Radish farmer Arnold Tudal planted 10 acres of Cabernet Sauvignon in Napa Valley, and began producing wine in 1979. He uses an old hydraulic press. I have never tasted the wines, but opinions are sharply divided as to their merits.

Tulocay

1426 Coombsville Rd, Napa, CA 94559. Tel: 255 4064. Fax: 963 1007. Production: 2,000 cases.

Bill and Barbara Cadman own no vineyards but buy in grapes from vineyards in southern Napa, from which they have been producing Pinot

Noir and Cabernet Sauvignon since 1975. The wines are inconsistent in quality.

Turley Wine Cellars
3358 St Helena Highway, St Helena, CA 94574. Tel: 963 0940. Fax: 963 8683. Production: 10,000 cases.

After John Williams and Larry Turley dissolved their partnership at Frog's Leap, Turley set up his own winery, located in the expanded original winery where he and Williams had made their wines before moving to the Red Barn in Rutherford. The first vintage was 1993.

In the section on Zinfandel I expressed my views on the wines for which Turley is most renowned. At present the range consists of 12 single-vineyard Zinfandels and two Petite Sirahs. The wines are made in small quantities and very high prices are charged for them. They are collectors' items, but does anybody drink them with pleasure? Very extracted, sometimes bitter, and very high in alcohol, they are mightily impressive, but so huge and powerful that they obliterate anything that comes in their path, such as food.

Until 1995 the wines were made by Helen Turley, who is Larry's sister. Ehren Jordan has now taken over. They are fermented with natural yeasts, many whole berries are retained, and malolactic fermentation takes place in barrel. The proportion of new oak ranges from none to 40 per cent; American as well as French oak is used. The wines are neither fined nor filtered. Most are fermented to dryness, but occasionally residual sugar is left in the wine, which is all for the good.

As I struggled my way through the complete tasting Jordan had generously laid on, he joked: 'If you can't finish the bottle, you can always paint your house with it.'

Turnbull Wine Cellars
8210 St Helena Highway, St Helena, CA 94562. Tel: 963 5839. Fax: 963 4407. Production: 10,000 cases.

Strategically located along the main highway, this estate, which used to be known as Johnson Turnbull, was founded in 1979 by lawyer Reverdy Johnson and architect William Turnbull. There was a vineyard here when they bought the land, but it was run-down and much was replanted, and further replanting was required in 1932 after phylloxera. In 1993 the property was bought by Patrick O'Dell. Kristin Belair was the winemaker from 1988 to 1998.

Today there are 145 acres dispersed among four sites. The Turnbull Vineyard consists of 17 acres near the winery, planted on clay and clay loam soils with Cabernet Sauvignon, Merlot, Sauvignon Blanc, Barbera, Petite Sirah, Malbec, and Malvasia Bianca. Fortuna Vineyard is 53 acres on the west side of Silverado Trail, planted with white and red Bordeaux varieties, as well as Syrah and Sangiovese. The Weitz Vineyard consists of 33 acres higher up above Silverado Trail, planted with a broad selection of French and Italian varieties. Finally, Skellinger Vineyard is 42 acres along the Napa River, a heavy soil that will soon be planted with Cabernet Sauvignon and Merlot.

I was greatly impressed by the wines when I tasted them in late 1997. The 1995 Syrah (the first release of the variety), the 1995 Sangiovese, the Cabernet, Merlot and Zinfandel, and the Old Bull Red (a blend of 95 per cent Cabernet Franc and 5 per cent Syrah) were excellent and stylish.

Viader

1120 Deer Park Rd., Deer Park, CA 94576. Tel: 963 3816. Fax: 963 3817. Production: 4,000 cases.

Dr Delia Viader comes from Argentina, and bought 18 acres on a rocky slope 1,100 feet up on Howell Mountain. Although there was hardly any top soil, the volcanic soils offered excellent drainage. The vertically trellised vines are closely spaced to 2,000 vines per acre, and organically farmed. Yields are very low at 2 tons per acre.

Viader has decided to concentrate her efforts on a single wine, which is a blend of 60 per cent Cabernet Sauvignon and 40 per cent Cabernet Franc, as she likes the way in which the elegance of the latter tempers the tannins of the former.

Tony Soter is the consultant winemaker, and the first vintage was 1989. The wines seem to be improving with each vintage, as Viader and Soter get to grips with the fruit from these mountain vineyards. The wine undergoes malolactic fermentation in barrel, and is aged in 60 per cent new oak, both French and Russian, for 21 months. The wine is unfiltered. Quality is very high, and the wines are sufficiently structured to age well.

Vichon

1595 Oakville Grade, Oakville, CA 94562. Tel: 944 2811.

Founded in 1980 by a consortium, Vichon made some interesting wines in the early 1980s, such as the Sauvignon/Sémillon blend called Chevrignon. After the partners fell out, the estate was bought by Mondavi in 1985. Mondavi produced some decent wines here, and by the mid-1990s production had reached 50,000 cases. Then in 1997 Mondavi decided to use the Vichon label solely for French and Mediterranean wines, and to use the winery itself to vinify the La Famiglia range of Italian varietals.

Villa Mount Eden

8711 Silverado Trail, St Helena, CA 94574. Tel: 963 9100. Fax: 944 9657. Production: 300,000 cases.

The original winery, founded in 1881, is now occupied by Plumpjack winery. After various changes in ownership, it was bought in 1969 by Anne and Jim McWilliams, and they planted 80 acres. At first they sold fruit to other wineries such as Heitz, and their own first vintage was 1974. Under the winemaker Nils Venge they developed a reputation for pure Cabernet. In 1986 the estate was bought by Stimson Lane, the owners of Chateau Ste Michelle in Washington state, and in 1994 the winery was disposed of and winemaking operations were transferred to Conn Creek winery, which was also under Stimson Lane ownership. Since 1982 the winemaker has been Mike McGrath, and since 1992 Jed Steele has been a consultant.

The winery owns and leases extensive vineyards, of which few are in Napa, although they do lease 231 acres in Yountville which formerly belonged to Beaulieu and are being replanted to Bordeaux red varieties as well as to Pinot Noir. They also lease 196 acres in Monterey near Arroyo Seco, recently planted with Chardonnay, Pinot Noir, Pinot Gris, and Pinot Blanc. There are a further 560 acres in Paso Robles, which will be planted with red varieties.

There are various categories of wines. The basic range may carry a California or a regional appellation. The next tier is Grande Reserve, which often comes from single vineyards. Even more starry is the Signature Series, with the label 'signed' by McGrath and Steele. These too tend to be small lots of single vineyard wines.

Quality is mixed. I didn't care for the 1996 Pinot Blanc from Bien Nacido, drenched in new oak. But there are many more wines I do like. There's a splendid Grand Reserve Zinfandel from Monte Rosso, Grand Reserve Pinot Noir from Bien Nacido, a Grand Reserve Syrah from Fess Parker vineyards in Santa Barbara blended with fruit from Nevada county. With his enthusiasm for Mendocino fruit, it is not surprising that Steele selected Cabernet Sauvignon from Greenwood Ridge for his 1994 Signature Series Cabernet. Given the large quantities of wine produced here, quality is gratifyingly high, and prices are very fair.

Vine Cliff
7400 Silverado Trail, Napa, CA 94558. Tel: 944 1364. Production: 3,500 cases.

This was the site of the largest winery in Napa Valley in the 1880s, but it ceased production when phylloxera wrecked the terraced vineyards in 1901; the winery was burnt down in mysterious circumstances. The site was bought by hoteliers Nell and Charles Sweeney in 1984. They replanted the 22 acres of terraced vineyards and built a new gravity-flow winery in time for the 1995 harvest, though wines had been produced since 1993. The viticulture is essentially organic. Under winemaker John Gibson, who use to work at Stag's Leap Wine Cellars, the estate has focused on barrel-fermented Chardonnay, Merlot, Cabernet Sauvignon, and Meritage. Prices as well as quality are quite high.

Vineyard 29
2929 Highway 29, St Helena, CA 94574. Production: 750 cases.

Created by Teresa Norton and Tom Paine, this tiny estate consists of 3.5 acres of densely spaced Cabernet Sauvignon, planted in 1990 and 1993 using budwood from the nearby Grace Family Vineyard, which is where the wine is made by Heidi Peterson Barrett. The first vintage was 1992 and the wine is aged in 100 per cent new oak.

Von Strasser
1510 Diamond Mountain Rd., Calistoga, CA 94515. Tel: 942 0930. Production: 2,000 cases.

If you struggle through the undergrowth around the Diamond Creek vineyards, you will come across this newcomer to Diamond Mountain. The vineyard was originally planted in 1970 with 8 acres of Cabernet Sauvignon. From 1970 to 1984 it was run as Roddis Cellars. Then in 1985 it was acquired by the Gilbey family, and became the source of the Diamond Mountain bottlings from Pine Ridge in the late 1980s. Then Rudy von Strasser, a Davis-trained winemaker who had worked at Trefethen and Newton, bought the property, and made significant changes to the vineyard, doubling the density, introducing vertical trellising and organic viticulture. In 1998 von Strasser also planted 5 more acres of Bordeaux red varieties. The Chardonnay comes from a different vineyard on Diamond Mountain. Von Strasser also produces a range of Napa wines called Freestone. These are intended for earlier drinking and are cheaper than the von Strasser wines. The present range is Sauvignon Blanc, Chardonnay, Merlot, and Cabernet Sauvignon.

The first vintage of von Strasser was 1990, and this little winery is going from strength to strength. The 1995 was a quintessential Diamond Creek Cabernet. Von Strasser likes a good dose of new oak in his Chardonnay and Cabernet Sauvignon, but the wines have sufficient richness to absorb it. In 1995 he introduced a Reserve blend, made from Cabernet Sauvignon, Merlot, and Petit Verdot, but quantities were tiny. This is clearly an estate to watch.

Whitehall Lane
1563 St Helena Highway, St Helena, CA 94574. Tel: 963 9454. Fax: 963 7035. Production: 15,000 cases.

This estate was founded in 1979 by Art and Bunnie Finkelstein and by Alan Steen. They replanted the existing 25 acres of vineyards with

Chardonnay, Sauvignon Blanc, and Merlot. In 1988 they sold the property to a Japanese investor, Hideaki Ando, for $4.2 million. It was sold again five years later to Tom Leonardini. He brought in Gary Galleron as winemaker, but in 1998 he was replaced by Dean Sylvester.

Vineyard production is supplemented by purchased grapes from Napa and from Knights Valley, and its best-known wine has been the Merlot. After some indifferent years, quality seems to be rising again.

White Rock
1115 Loma Vista Dr., Napa, CA 94558. Tel: 257 7922. Production: 3,000 cases.

In 1977 Claire and Henri Vandendriessche began to restore a vineyard and winery that had been established in 1870 in the southern part of Stags Leap. They planted 35 acres of Chardonnay, Cabernet Sauvignon, and other Bordeaux varieties. White Rock was the first vineyard to plant the Cabernet clone that was later chosen for the Opus One vineyards. The site is steeply terraced and the vines closely spaced. No pesticides or herbicides are used. At first fruit was sold to other wineries, until the winery was completed in 1988, and Douglas Danielak of Jade Mountain was hired as winemaker. The Chardonnay is whole-cluster pressed, then barrel-fermented in new French oak and aged on the fine lees. The Cabernet is aged for 24 months and blended with other Bordeaux varieties.

Wing Canyon
Production: 1,000 cases.

A small 12-acre property on Mount Veeder, owned by Bill Jenkins and organically farmed. Jenkins only grows Bordeaux varieties and purchases his Chardonnay grapes. The first vintage was 1991. The wines are well thought of, but I found the 1992 Cabernet Sauvignon weedy and unbalanced.

ZD
8383 Silverado Trail, Napa, Ca 94558. Tel: 963 5188. Fax: 963 2640. Production: 25,000 cases.

This often underrated estate was originally located in Sonoma, but its owners, Gino Zepponi and Norman de Leuze, moved the winery to Napa Valley in 1979. Gino Zepponi was killed in a car accident in 1985, but the de Leuze family still own the winery; indeed the winemaker for the past fifteen years has been Norman's son Robert. ZD own a few acres of Cabernet Sauvignon close to the winery, but more significant are their holdings in Carneros, where they own about 40 acres of Chardonnay and Pinot Noir. ZD used to produce a wide range of wines, including Gewürztraminer, but has simplified the list.

At least half the production is of Chardonnay, which they ferment in American oak. Much of their Chardonnay is labelled under the California appellation, as it is a blend of North and Central Coast fruit.

There are two Pinot Noirs. The Rosa Lee Pinot Noir is too light to make much impact, but the regular bottling is much better. Merlot comes from Atlas Peak, and is aged up to 24 months in oak. The Napa Cabernet comes mostly from mountain sites, and is aged for 22 months in American oak; the Reserve Cabernet receives additional ageing of up to 34 months. The red wines are good, if rather expensive, but the Chardonnay is still ZD's most reliable wine.

NOTE

1 *Wine Spectator*, 15 September 1998

24

Sonoma I

Arrowood

14347 Sonoma Highway, Glen Ellen, CA 95442. Tel: 938 5170.[1] Fax: 938 1543. Production: 27,000 cases.

Richard Arrowood was for many years the brilliant winemaker at Chateau St Jean, turning out a series of remarkably rich and powerful Chardonnays and Fumé Blancs from some of the finest vineyards in Sonoma. He started up his own winery in 1986, four years before he left Chateau St Jean. He owns 25 acres, but also buys in grapes from fine vineyards all over Sonoma. Michel Berthoud is the winemaker, although no doubt Arrowood keeps a close eye on winery operations.

The style of the wines is not as sumptuous as those that emerged from Chateau St Jean. They may be less rich, but they are certainly more elegant. There are two Chardonnays, one a rather heavy Sonoma County blend, almost entirely barrel-fermented and put through full malolactic fermentation; while the second, the Reserve Speciale, is similar, but a barrel selection that receives 15 months rather than 10 months of ageing. There is also an overripe-tasting Pinot Blanc made in a full-throttle style and aged in 50 per cent new *barriques*.

Arrowood began making Viognier here in 1991. Often the grapes come, as they do for the Pinot Blanc, from Saralee's Vineyard. One-third of the Viognier is fermented in steel, the rest in older oak. In some vintages there are also Late Harvest Viogniers, often botrytis-affected. The 1995 is a lovely, floral honeyed wine. Of course Richard Arrowood has continued to make botrytis-affected Rieslings, the style of wine he perfected at Chateau St Jean. Thus in 1995 he produced a TBA-style wine with 218 grams of residual sugar, and made more late harvest Rieslings in 1997.

The reds are made in a lean intense style. The Cabernet Sauvignon fruit comes from various parts of Sonoma, and is aged in French and American oak for 22 months. The Reserve Speciale is aged only in French oak, and for an additional 5 months. The lush Merlot is made in the same way, as

443

is an Arrowood speciality, Malbec. There is also a Syrah, aged in older *barriques*. These wines are hardly ever fined or filtered.

The estate's second label is Domaine du Grand Archer.

Davis Bynum
8075 Westside Rd., Healdsburg, CA 95448. Tel: 433 5852. Fax: 433 4309. Production: 18,000 cases.

Davis Bynum used to work for the *San Francisco Examiner*, with a sideline as a hobby winemaker. He inherited his father's keen interest in wine, an interest transmitted to Davis's own son Hampton, who made the wines at this estate during the 1970s. In 1965 Bynum became a full-time wine producer, buying in wines and blending them at his winery in Albany, near Berkeley. His best-known wine was a blend he called Barefoot Bynum. It was a great success, but Bynum sold the rights to the name in 1979 when he decided to focus on the wines from Russian River Valley. He had already bought an 83-acre ranch there in 1973, and planted 25 acres of vines on hillside sites with Merlot, Cabernet Sauvignon, and Pinot Noir. The viticultural practices here are close to organic.

Davis Bynum may not be the most prestigious estate in Russian River Valley, but Bynum really was the pioneer, although he is too modest to claim much credit for the renown that came to the region. Nonetheless in 1973 he was the first to make Pinot Noir from locally grown grapes. His associations with such prestigious growers as the Rochioli family go back to the days when, Bynum admits, there was hardly anybody else around who was growing good grapes. In 1978 Gary Farrell became the wine-maker, a job he still performs although he also has his own label. Farrell believes in minimal handling of the fruit, especially a delicate variety such as Pinot Noir, and he aims to make a restrained silky style of wine. Pinot is given a cold soak and the bunches are destemmed before fermentation.

A number of different Pinot Noirs are made. The basic wine is the Russian River Valley, a blend from four sites and made to be drunk young. The Limited Edition is also a blend, but includes fruit from well-known vineyards such as Allen. Le Pinot is only made in top vintages and is made from either Allen or Rochioli vineyard fruit, or a blend of the two. Quantities are minimal.

There is also a finely balanced Cabernet Sauvignon, a robust estate-grown Merlot, a succulent Bordeaux blend called Eclipse, and an attractive Old Vin Zinfandel.

The whites are good if not exceptional. The Sauvignon Blanc is made from Shone Vineyard, where Richard Smart carried out his experiments in open canopy management to reduce the variety's vegetal tendencies. Oak influence has been steadily reduced, and the wine is fresh and attractive. There are a number of single-vineyard Chardonnays, mostly barrel-fermented; these are produced in small quantities.

Davis Bynum Pinot Noirs are rarely as dazzling as the best from Williams-Selyem or Rochioli, but they are in the same style and of very good quality. Moreover they are reasonably priced and, unlike the more starry names, they rarely sell out ten minutes after release.

Clos du Bois

19410 Geyserville Ave., Geyserville, CA 95441. Tel: 857 3100. Fax: 857 3229. Production: 800,000 cases.

Clos du Bois originated in 1970 when Frank Woods and his partners planted 100 acres of vineyards in Alexander and Dry Creek valleys. The first releases were in 1976. The estate expanded quite rapidly, and by 1980 they owned almost 600 acres. For many years they operated out of a ramshackle facility in downtown Healdsburg, but in 1995 they moved to an immense new winery near Highway 101. By then they had been bought by Hiram Walker, who were merged into Allied Domecq. Throughout the 1980s the winemaker was John Hawley, and in 1990 he was succeeded by Margaret Davenport. The current vineyard holdings are 540 acres in Alexander Valley and 100 in Dry Creek Valley.

The wines have long been of very good quality, even the basic ranges of the major varietals. Far more interesting are their single-vineyard bottlings. There are two Chardonnays. Calcaire is a single block of gravelly loam in their Alexander Valley vineyard, on which the vines were planted in 1965; its characteristic flavours are citric and vanillin. Flintwood is a parcel on volcanic soils in Dry Creek, and the must is fermented in heavily toasted *barriques* to give a less lush but firmer style than Calcaire.

The regular Cabernet Sauvignon is aged 18 months in oak and is a good wine. It is regularly outshone by Briarcrest and Marlstone. Briarcrest is grown on heavily silty clay loam, and the vines are head-pruned. This wine is aged 2 years in *barriques*. Marlstone, first made in 1978, comes from Alexander Valley, grown on silty loam with a clay subsoil. Whereas Briarcrest is pure Cabernet, Marlstone is a blend of all five Bordeaux varieties, aged for up to 30 months in *barriques*. It is a wine I have always enjoyed hugely.

The other reds are the Merlot, a blend of Alexander Valley and Dry Creek Valley fruit; it is aged in American as well as French oak, as is the Zinfandel. The Pinot Noir comes from Carneros.

Clos du Bois has never disguised the fact that it is a large commercial winery, and perhaps that is why it has lacked the recognition of some of its smaller and more chic neighbours. Yet large-volume production has never resulted in lean or dilute wines, and the general quality level is also an implicit reminder of how very good Alexander Valley fruit can be.

Dehlinger

6300 Guerneville Rd., Sebastopol, CA 95472. Tel: 823 2378. Production: 9,000 cases.

One of the oldest properties in Russian River Valley, this former orchard was bought in 1973 by Dr Klaus Dehlinger of Berkeley, who planted vines in 1975 and built a winery the following year. The wines are all estate-grown; the 50 acres of vineyards are composed of Pinot Noir, Chardonnay, Cabernet Sauvignon, and Merlot. Tom Dehlinger has been making the wines for some years, and is intrigued by the clear differences in soil and fruit quality between different parcels within the vineyards. He has mapped them closely, so that he can be very selective when deciding when to pick each block and how his blends should be made up.

Dehlinger defies conventional wisdom by fermenting and ageing his Chardonnay in 130-gallon puncheons rather than 60-gallon barrels. The amount of malolactic fermentation varies according to the character of the fruit, and ranges from 60 to 100 per cent. It is relatively lean and capable of ageing in bottle.

Although Dehlinger made a robust Cabernet Sauvignon (now phased out) and a little Syrah, he is best known for his Pinot Noirs. Another Pinot Noir specialist told me Tom Dehlinger was the only winemaker able to make good-quality Pinot from relatively high yields, but whether this was meant as a criticism or a compliment I am not sure. There can be up to five different cuvées of Pinot, as there were in 1994. Like the Chardonnay, they are often aged in puncheons and since the volume is larger the wine spends longer in oak, about 20 months, than if it were ageing in *barriques*. They are at the fleshy end of the flavour and texture spectrum, but are not jammy, over-extracted, or over-oaked in the way that old-fashioned Napa Pinots used to be.

Dry Creek Vineyards

770 Lambert Bridge Rd., Healdsburg, CA 95448. Tel: 433 1000. Fax: 433 5329. Production: 120,000 cases.

In 1972 David Stare came here from Boston and opened the first winery in Dry Creek Valley since Prohibition. Both he and the winery are still going strong. Stare now owns some 100 acres in Dry Creek and Alexander Valley, both on benchlands and more fertile river-level soils. But two-thirds of the winery's requirements are purchased. They used to include Riesling and Gewürztraminer, but these varietals are no longer produced, and Petite Sirah, which used to be estate-grown, is now bought from the Kunde vineyards. A recent change has been the departure of Larry Levin, wine-maker here from 1981 to 1998. His place has been taken by Jeff McBride, formerly of Kenwood.

The Sauvignon Blanc has always been a great success here. It comes in two forms, both pure Sauvignon. The Fumé is fermented in steel tanks without malolactic fermentation, and aged in *barriques*. It gives a grassy vibrant style which I like. The Reserve is barrel-fermented and does go through malolactic fermentation. The Chardonnay, a blend from various parts of Sonoma, is less distinctive. It is aged in American and French oak, while the Reserve is aged only in French oak. Another Dry Creek classic is the unoaked Chenin Blanc, made from Clarksburg fruit; the seven grams of residual sugar are not obtrusive and the wine is well balanced.

The reds – Cabernet, Merlot, Old Vine Zinfandel, and Meritage – are not given extended maceration, and American oak is lavishly employed, although Dry Creek does not go in for prolonged barrel ageing either. The Reserves are very good.

Gary Farrell

PO Box 342, Forestville, CA 95436. Tel: 433 6616. Fax: 433 9060. Production: 8,000 cases.

As well as making the wines for Davis Bynum and, during the mid-1980s, for Rochioli, Gary Farrell has had his own label since 1982. Since all the grapes are purchased in small lots from individual vineyards, the range changes from year to year. His best-value wine is the Russian River Valley Pinot Noir, which blends fruit from Rochioli and Moshin vineyards. Gary Farrell is tall and bearded and rather reserved, and one has the impression he prefers to let the wines speak for themselves, which they do, most eloquently.

Farrell's Pinot Noirs are vinified in small fermenters, with about 50 per cent whole clusters. The grapes are given a cold soak, fermented for about 12 days and punched down by hand. Farrell does use natural yeasts, but not dogmatically, as he has had poor as well as excellent results from them. The vinification is essentially the same for all the Pinot Noir bottlings, but the single-vineyard wines such as Allen or Rochioli Vineyard are aged in a high proportion of new oak, varying from 50 to 100 per cent. Farrell also uses grapes from Bien Nacido. These Pinots are elegant yet do not lack fruit and charm; but they are discreet wines rather than show-stoppers, which is why I like them.

His other wines are good too, and I was struck by the grandeur of the 1994 Collins Vineyard Zinfandel. Bien Nacido in Santa Barbara also supplies the grapes for one of his Chardonnays, but his finest example of this variety is probably the Allen Vineyard.

Since the wines are made at Davis Bynum there is no question of conflict of interest, although there must be a sense in which the two wineries, both using grapes from the same vineyards, are in competition with each other. Farrell likes having his own label as he can control the grape quality more closely than he can at Davis Bynum, where Hampton Bynum is in charge of dealing with growers. As for Davis Bynum, he feels that Farrell's skill clearly benefits his own wines.

Ferrari-Carano

8761 Dry Creek Rd., Healdsburg, CA 95448. Tel: 433 6700. Fax: 431 1742. Production: 100,000 cases.

What happens when the owner of hotels and casinos in Reno, Nevada, comes to Sonoma to make some wine to supply his restaurants? The answer is Ferrari-Carano and the Villa Fiore, a hideous neo-Palladian 'hospitality centre' surrounded by showy gardens. Don and Rhonda Carano came to Dry Creek in 1978, looking for property. Gradually it accumulated: a house, some vineyards, a winery, and more vineyards. But if the facilities are flash, even vulgar, the wines are certainly not.

There are a number of reasons why the wines are excellent here. The first is that the estate now owns 600 acres of vineyards dispersed around seventeen sites all the way from Carneros to Alexander Valley. A number of different clones are planted, some of which will be vinified separately as blending components. Another reason is the presence of George Bursick, who has been the winemaker since 1985 and helped design the winery to his own specifications. The winery has magnificent underground cellars, paved with cobblestones that are moistened to increase the natural humidity. The vineyard manager, Barney Fernandez, has been with the estate for almost as long as Bursick, and the two men work closely together.

The first wine made here was the 1985 Chardonnay, and now there are three Chardonnays. The first is a complex blend of Alexander Valley fruit, entirely barrel-fermented and aged in *barriques* for 10 months. Tre Terre Chardonnay is a selection from three vineyards in Alexander Valley and only new oak is used. The toasty Reserve blends Alexander Valley and Carneros fruit and goes through full malolactic fermentation.

The Fumé Blanc has always been outstanding, pure Sauvignon from various parts of Sonoma, partly barrel-fermented and aged on the lees in *barriques*. The Reserve is the stereo version, barrel-fermented in new oak, with 75 per cent malolactic fermentation. Occasionally the estate produces a wine called Eldorado Gold, a ritzy name for a late harvest and botrytized Sauvignon and Sémillon.

The Cabernet Sauvignon is in fact a blend of all five Bordeaux varieties, all grown on benchland or hillside sites in Alexander Valley. Long barrel ageing, about 27 months, means that it is accessible young. The rounded Merlot blends grapes from various parts of Sonoma. The Zinfandel is aged in American as well as French oak, which is unusual at this winery, and the Reserve Red is Cabernet-dominated, using only the finest hillside grapes. A new addition to the range in 1991 was Siena, a Sangiovese blended with Cabernet and Merlot, and aged 15 months in oak.

For wines as luscious and pleasurable as these I can forgive the Villa Fiore's faux-marble columns, pastel-coloured cherubs, and the faery lights in Don Carano's private tasting room.

Gallo Sonoma

2777 Cleveland Ave., Santa Rosa, CA 95403. Tel: 526 1293. Fax: 526 9199.

My requests to visit the virtually impregnable Fortress Gallo in Modesto have always been met with silence, but the family were keen for me to see their operations in Sonoma. The Gallos have had a foothold in Sonoma since 1977, when they bought the former Frei Ranch, which had been in existence since the 1880s, and in 1984 they renamed it Gallo Sonoma. It was not until 1993 that they began launching a series of 1991 wines from their Sonoma vineyards. They were varietal wines – Cabernet Sauvignon, Chardonnay, Zinfandel – and they were given an enthusiastic reception, especially the Zinfandels. The wines were also good value.

I don't know what goes through the minds of those participating in Gallo board meetings, but no doubt somebody in the 1980s came to realize that Gallo was stuck at the lower end of the market, and that there was good money to be made from sensibly priced wines of quality and character. So Gallo began accumulating land in Sonoma, some 3,500 acres of it. Caroline Bailey, a family member with the splendid title of International Fine Wine Manager, told me: 'We invested here because quality lands give quality wine. Sonoma has many different microclimates, so it offers a great tool for the winemaker.' Vineyards have been handled differently; thus the Stefani Vineyard is planted to a much higher density than most of the others, and trellising systems vary too. Some of the vineyards are farmed organically, and the Gallos are keen on integrated pest management programmes.

The Gallos have done a good job of landscaping, and claim that for every plot they developed as vineyards, they retained a plot of equal size as undeveloped land, including woodland that attracts wildlife, which in turn can act as natural predators on insects and other vine pests. Hills were flattened and re-contoured, topsoil was replaced, reservoirs created. Despite all these efforts, some of the old-time growers, in a region characterized by a multiplicity of small vineyards, were unhappy about the sheer scale of the Gallo plantings.

The Gallos had been buying grapes from the Frei Ranch since 1934, and since 1947 had bought the entire crop each year. When they bought the ranch in 1977, it consisted of 200 acres, but it has now been expanded to 700. The region is a gravelly clay loam and it is classified as warm

Region II. So it has been planted with Cabernet Sauvignon, Zinfandel, Chardonnay, Cabernet Franc, and Merlot. There are some dry-farmed blocks but most of the vines are drip-irrigated. The excellent Frei Zinfandel is aged in new French oak for 13 months; in some years the alcohol can be very high – 15.1 degrees in 1994 – yet it never seems obtrusive. The first-rate Frei Cabernet Sauvignon is aged for 25 months in French and American oak, and is neither fined nor filtered. The Merlot is good too.

Laguna Ranch, in the much cooler Russian River Valley, consists of 1350 acres close to the Dehlinger vineyards. This former orchard was bought by the Gallos in 1977 and planted in 1980 with Chardonnay and a test block of Pinot Noir. The Laguna Chardonnay, which is a bit plump and cloying for my taste, is barrel-fermented using mostly natural yeast, and aged in new *barriques* for 10 months.

The 625-acre Asti vineyard, originally part of the Italian-Swiss Colony estate, was bought in 1989, replanted from 1991 onwards, and was renamed Barrelli Creek Vineyard. Being in Alexander Valley, the climate is warm, a Region III, and the varieties planted are Cabernet Sauvignon, Merlot, Cabernet Franc, Zinfandel, Napa Gamay, Petite Sirah, Barbera, Sangiovese, Sauvignon Blanc and Chardonnay.

Chiotti Vineyard is in Dry Creek, 100 acres bought by Gallo in 1990 and replanted from 1992 onwards with Chardonnay and Zinfandel.

Stefani Vineyard, also in Dry Creek, was bought in 1988 and replanted the following year. There are 50 acres planted on gravelly clay soil, whereas most of the other vineyards are on gravelly clay loam. Chardonnay, Cabernet Sauvignon and Zinfandel are the varieties planted here. The sweetish Chardonnay is whole-cluster pressed, partly fermented with natural yeasts, and fermented and aged in new *barriques*.

Other vineyards will soon be providing more fruit, once the vines are mature. Twin Valley Ranch, the former cattle ranch belonging to Fred McMurray, is being planted with 500 acres of Pinot Noir, Sauvignon Blanc, and Pinot Gris. Stony Point Vineyard, in the Sonoma Coast appellation, is also being developed.

These vast quantities of grapes are transformed into different ranges of wines. The basic range is bottled under the Sonoma County appellation. Far more interesting are the vineyard designated wines, and at the top of the tree is the range of Estate wines bearing the North Sonoma appellation, which is a selection of the best parcels from each vineyard. The middle tier offers the best value, except for the cloying Chardonnays. The Estate wines are very good, but the price tag of three times the price of the single-vineyard wines is hardly justified, and one suspects marketing considerations played a greater part in the decision to launch them.

The Sonoma vineyards are managed by Matt Gallo, and the winemaker for the series is Marcello Monticelli, assisted by Gina Gallo. A stupendously hideous winery has been built at the Frei Vineyard to process all this fruit. The Gallos have piously preserved the old wooden winery of 1885, but it is completely hemmed in by modern installations. The vast underground cellars here accommodate 50,000 barrels.

Iron Horse
9786 Ross Station Rd., Sebastopol, CA 95472. Tel: 887 1507. Fax: 887 1337. Production: 40,000 cases.

This estate takes its name from the logging train that used to traverse this part of Green Valley. There were vines here in the 1870s, but over time they disappeared, until in 1971 Forrest Tancer planted a vineyard here on behalf of Rodney Strong. Before long Strong found himself in financial difficulties and sold the vineyards to an international lawyer called Barry Sterling and his wife Audrey. They retained Forrest Tancer to produce the wines, and in 1979 he became a partner in the business. The Sterlings threw themselves heart and soul into Iron Horse. Their daughter Joy, a television reporter, became involved in publicizing the wines, and in 1990 she married Tancer. Her brother Laurence is director of public affairs.

The estate is quite a large one, with 250 acres under vine. The original plantings by Tancer were of 55 acres each of Pinot Noir and Chardonnay, and another 70 or more acres have been added in the 1980s and early 1990s. In addition, Tancer owns his own TbarT Vineyard in Alexander Valley. Whereas the Green Valley fruit is typically cool-climate in its structure and acidity, Tancer's vineyards, being much warmer, are better suited to varieties such as Sauvignon Blanc, Cabernet Sauvignon, Merlot, Viognier, and Sangiovese. Phylloxera forced the replanting of much of the vineyards, but they have profited from the disaster to tighten the spacing.

Tancer has made some very good Fumé Blancs over the years. Since 1985 they have all been barrel-fermented. Although Alexander Valley is far from cool, he likes the quality of the Sauvignon Blanc he has planted there. He describes his style of Sauvignon as having the structure of the Loire but the body of California, which is a useful way of putting it. In the 1990s they began adding Viognier to the wine, sometimes as much as 25 per cent.

The Chardonnay has always emerged in a lean elegant style, a consequence of the cool climate here. David Munksgard, the winemaker since 1996, employs whole-cluster pressing and favours a reductive style of winemaking.

The Pinot Noir is a touch disappointing, probably because the best fruit goes into the sparkling wine for which Iron Horse is justly celebrated. Young vines from the warmest sites are made into the still wine. Techniques such as cold-soaking, pumping over rather than punching down, and completion of fermentation in barrel, seem to combine to give a fairly soft, rounded style. The Cabernet Sauvignon is usually blended with Cabernet Franc to give a wine they simply call Cabernets, which can be delicious in a brambly style. But there is also a pure varietal Cabernet Sauvignon. Sangiovese, which I only tasted in barrel, looks promising.

Whether a parcel of vines will be dedicated to still or sparkling wine is not pre-determined. It all depends on the quality and character of the fruit. 'What I like to do,' explains Laurence Sterling, 'is make a commercial analysis about how the fruit should be used in any new vintage. Forrest takes a look at it every year, and always throws it away. I recall one block of vines which has different exposures. One side was used for still Pinot Noir, the other side for the sparkling wine, and that meant picking the one parcel at different times.'

Iron Horse employ Rafael Brisbois to look after the sparkling wine production. These bottles are all vintage-dated, on the grounds that abysmal vintages, all too common in Champagne, are very rare in California, even in Green Valley. Only estate-grown grapes are used for these wines. They are made without malolactic fermentation. Riddling is mechanized, except for rosé, which has higher solid content and needs a good shake by hand. The style they look for is a wine with good acidity but also forward fruit, this being California not Reims, and they want sufficient complexity to permit the wines to be aged.

The range consists of the bracing Classic Brut (70 per cent Pinot Noir, 30 per cent Chardonnay), aged 4 years on the yeast; the powerful nutty Blanc de Blanc Late Disgorged, aged 6 years; the slightly heavy Wedding Cuvée, a Blanc de Noirs; Brut LD (60 per cent Pinot Noir, 40 per cent Chardonnay), aged over 5 years on the yeast; Brut Rosé; and Russian Cuvée, a fruity demi-sec with a dosage of 20 grams per litre. These are serious wines, with a great deal of elegance.

Iron Horse's second label is self-deprecatingly named Tin Pony.

Kenwood

9592 Sonoma Highway, Kenwood, CA 95452. Tel: 833 5891. Fax: 833 1146. Production: 300,000 cases.

The Pagani winery had been making jug wines in Kenwood since 1906 when a small consortium, dominated by the Lee family, bought the property in 1970. It remains a family operation, although one of the partners, Gary Heck, became the majority shareholder in 1998. Mike Lee has been winemaker since 1981, assisted until 1998 by Jeff McBride.

Kenwood own 350 acres, of which 200 are cultivated organically. They lease a further 250 acres, and purchase grapes from some 65 different growers in Sonoma, with a preference for mountain vineyards. Their pride and joy is the Jack London Vineyard on the western slopes of Sonoma Valley.

Sauvignon Blanc has always been one of Kenwood's strengths and in terms of volume is one of their most important wines. The fruit usually comes from either Carneros or Russian River. It is fermented in stainless steel, and only about half is barrel-aged for some 6 months; the remainder stays in tank or goes into large oak casks until the wine is bottled. There is no malolactic fermentation, so the wine has a freshness and vigour not always encountered in California Sauvignon Blanc. In 1994 a Reserve was introduced, a barrel-fermented wine from two Sonoma Valley sites.

Kenwood make a lot of different series of wines, which can be a bit confusing. Their White Label range consists of soundly made varietals, including Sonoma Valley Cabernet Sauvignon, Sonoma County Merlot (made from ex-Riesling vines grafted over in 1989), Sonoma Valley Zinfandel, Russian River Pinot Noir, Sonoma County Chardonnay, and the above-mentioned Sonoma County Sauvignon Blanc. Although these are made in large quantities, quality is good, and no shortcuts are taken. These are wines intended to be drunk on or soon after release.

The Jack London range comes from a vineyard which is not owned by Kenwood but since 1976 has been managed and marketed by Kenwood on an exclusive basis. The wines are a Cabernet Sauvignon aged for almost 2 years in oak, Zinfandel, and Pinot Noir aged for at least 12 months in new *barriques*.

The Reserve wines include the Artists Series Cabernet Sauvignon, first made in 1975, when a nude drawn for the label by David Goines was ruled obscene by the BATF, which must have seemed a heaven-sent publicity coup. Different artists are commissioned to decorate the label of each new vintage. The wine can be a bit of a bruiser, but it has been showing more elegance in recent years. There are also a number of single-vineyard wines. These include Zinfandels from Mazzoni, Barricia, and Nun's Canyon vineyards, variously aged in French and American oak. An Olivet Lane Pinot Noir is aged for 12 months in mostly new *barriques*. It is rare to find a winery that performs equally well with large-volume wines and with 500-case lots of single-vineyard wines.

Kistler

4707 Vine Hill Rd., Sebastopol, CA 95472. Tel: 823 5603. Fax: 823 6709. Production: 15,000 cases.

When the Kistler winery was located among its estate vineyards, a visit to the property involved one of those long, winding drives up into the mountains that are calculated to defeat all but the most intrepid. In 1992 Steve Kistler and Mark Bixler moved their winery to a new, less remote location, but now it is celebrity rather than distance that makes it difficult to track this pair down.

I have been less than enthusiastic about many California Chardonnays that others rave about. But I have yet to meet a Kistler Chardonnay that has failed to bowl me over.

The two men met at Fresno State College wine tasting groups. Kistler went on to study at Davis and then to work at Ridge; Bixler taught chemistry at college. In the mid-1970s they started hunting for vineyards each weekend, and finally found what they were looking for on the Sonoma side of the Mayacamas range. It was a 280-acre pig farm. They bought it, cleared and terraced the land and planted 30 acres: 18 Chardonnay and 12 Cabernet Sauvignon. Their first vintage, 1979, was made from purchased grapes. Indeed, the estate vineyard has never been that significant, and most of the fruit comes from growers with whom they have established long-term contracts. They look for vineyards with low-yielding clones averaging 2.5 tons per acre.

They knew from the start that they wanted to make Chardonnay, Cabernet, and Pinot Noir. What's more, they were determined to use Burgundian techniques, with full malolactic fermentation and only French oak. New oak is confined to around 40 per cent. Steve is the winemaker; Mark, the chemist, keeps an eye on the vineyards, takes care of some lab work, and markets the wines.

As has already been explained in the chapter on Chardonnay, Steve Kistler has very firm ideas about how the variety should be vinified in order to allow the *terroir* to express itself in the most complex way possible. Certainly, when tasting the 1995 Chardonnays side by side, it was possible to detect distinct differences between them. But what was equally remarkable is that they also shared characteristics: aromatic richness, amazingly vibrant fruit, power without blowsiness, astonishing length of flavour. Kistler uses up to ten different sources for its Chardonnays. I was able to taste and compare the Dutton Ranch, Vine Hill, Hudson, and Cuvée Cathleen; all different, all brilliant.

Although Kistler is not so well known for its Pinot Noirs, they can be on the same stupendous level. They are all fermented with natural yeasts and are hardly ever fined or filtered. Poured a tasting sample of the 1995 Hirsch Sonoma Coast Pinot, I was so overwhelmed by its aroma that I filled the glass and nursed it, quietly sniffing and sipping, for the best part of an hour. I hope my hosts have forgiven my undiplomatic burst of enthusiasm for another producer's wine. Other bottlings come from McCrae, the estate vineyard, Cuvée Cathleen, and Camp Meeting Ridge in Sonoma Coast. I have never been that excited by the Cabernet Sauvignon from Kistler.

Laurel Glen

6611 Sonoma Mountain Rd., Glen Ellen, CA 95442. Tel: 526 3914. Fax: 526 9801. Production: 5,000 cases.

Patrick Campbell was probably not destined from birth to be a winemaker. He studied philosophy at Harvard, was a professional musician for a while, and, in accordance with the hippie modes of the times, entered a Zen monastery on Sonoma Mountain, where he was appointed farming manager. He left the monastery and started his own small vineyard nearby. Gradually he expanded the vineyards, selling the crop to wineries such as Kenwood and Chateau St Jean, and in 1981 produced his first commercial wine. He is assisted by Ray Kaufman.

Laurel Glen consists of 25 acres, and Campbell leases 12 more. The vines are planted above the fog line at 800 feet, and they enjoy an eastern exposure, so that they catch the early morning sun. This is a slightly marginal area for Cabernet Sauvignon, but the area enjoys abundant direct sunlight and warm evenings, and has a narrow range of temperatures, giving a more even maturation than elsewhere. The soil is essentially volcanic.

Patrick is clearly fascinated by the vineyard itself, with its different soils and exposures and particularities. As blocks are replanted he has tightened the spacing, and the newest parcels are planted at 2,000 vines per acre. He has been trying vertical trellising as a means of attracting the angular sunlight that falls into his vineyards. He has also planted a little Syrah, Sangiovese, Mourvèdre, and Tempranillo, mostly, it seems, for the fun of it. Yields are low, between 2 and 3 tons per acre, and harvesting even such a small vineyard can take up to two weeks, so varied are the microclimates.

Some vintages can be very tannic here, so Campbell punches down the cap by hand as his contribution to tannin management. In the early 1990s he tried two new techniques: cold-soaking the grapes before fermentation, and using natural yeasts, which, he finds, give a slower fermentation without sharp rises in temperature. Kaufman and Campbell agree that extended maceration doesn't work with their fruit, as it tends to give over-extracted and stewed wines. After pressing, the wine is put into barrels to go through its malolactic fermentation. Sixty per cent of the barrels are new, and about a dozen lots are kept separate until blending. At the blending stage, about half the wine is consigned to the second label, Counterpoint, after blind tastings. The wine ages for up to 20 months in *barriques*. They try to avoid fining and filtration, but are not dogmatic about it.

The problem at Laurel Glen is that the vines don't always ripen properly. This happened in 1997 and high acidities were troubling Campbell while the wines were in barrel. Hot years tend to produce better wines, as there is a higher ripeness level. Patrick Campbell knows his vineyards are marginal, but that, I assume, is the challenge of making wine here. In cool years the wines can be astringent or tough, but in a rich ripe year such as 1994 the results can be superb.

Since the production of Laurel Glen and Counterpoint is so limited, Campbell supplements those prestigious wines with an inexpensive, high-volume wine called Terra Rosa, made from purchased North Coast fruit and, from 1996, from Chilean wines. Reds is an even cheaper wine, blended from Rhône varieties and Zinfandel from all over the state. But the glory of the estate remains Laurel Glen in a great vintage.

Matanzas Creek

6097 Bennett Valley Rd., Santa Rosa, CA 95404. Tel: 528 6464. Fax: 571 0156. Production: 40,000 cases.

Sandra MacIver, as the descendant of the family that founded Sears-Roebuck, was in a position to invest in some acreage in the rural Bennett Valley, and began planting vines from 1975 onwards. The first vintage was 1978, and a new winery was completed in 1984. By this time Sandra was married to Bill MacIver, and the two work closely together to promote the estate and its wines. Matanzas Creek was fortunate to have the services of two outstanding winemakers: Merry Edwards and David Ramey, followed in 1990 by Susan Reed and cellarmaster Bill Parker.

At present the vineyards consist of 70 acres, but 30 more were purchased in 1994. Some replanting will be inescapable, as many of the vines were planted originally on AXR-1. New plantings will be more closely spaced. This is quite a cool area, and thus good for Chardonnay and Merlot, in which the winery specializes. Bill Parker says it can be as cool here as in Carneros, though less windy, which is why they have never planted Sauvignon. Their Sauvignon and Sémillon are bought in from various parts of Sonoma and also from Redwood Valley in Mendocino. Quality is excellent.

Whole-cluster pressing is employed for the white wines. Half the Sauvignon is barrel-fermented, but all the wine is aged on its fine lees and stirred monthly. It has always been exceptionally well-balanced.

Estate-grown Chardonnay accounts for about one-third of production, and the rest comes from various growers in southern Sonoma, including Sangiacomo Vineyard in Carneros. Their own Chardonnay consists of various clones, notably Rued, Spring Mountain, and Mount Eden. All the Chardonnay is barrel-fermented and since 1987 it has gone through full malolactic fermentation. The wine is aged for some 8 months in 40 per cent new French oak, with the lees stirred regularly.

In exceptional vintages a special Chardonnay is produced: Journey. Bill Parker and Susan Reed may select some particularly fine lots that are ageing in new oak barrels, and will set them aside for an additional 4 months' ageing; then the wine will go into older barrels for 9 months before a final selection is made. Roughly half these barrels will be omitted from the final blend, and the criteria for selection are finesse, delicacy, and strength.

Matanzas Creek was producing delicious Merlot before the variety became fashionable. Ten acres of Merlot vines, their clonal origin unknown, were planted in 1975, as well as a little Cabernet Sauvignon that is blended in. Other grapes are bought from the Sangiacomo Vineyard. The wine macerates for about 3 weeks, and is aged for 18 months in 65 per cent new oak, and bottled with minimal, if any, fining and filtration. The 1992 is sumptuous and opulent. There is also an Estate Merlot. Journey Merlot was first made in 1992 and again in 1994. It is produced only from estate grapes and aged for an extra year in barrels.

I have often visited Matanzas Creek and tasted their wines with pleasure and enjoyment. However, my latest visit in early 1998 proved a bitter disappointment, which was shared by the other tasters present, who, excited by the reputation of the estate, had come with high expectations which were not realized. Perhaps we were jaded by then, perhaps Matanzas Creek really is going through a weak patch. But it was impossible to see how the wines could justify their extravagant price tags. Already in 1991 the Merlot was the most expensive in California at $27.50. By 1998, the basic Chardonnay was priced at $30, the Merlot at $43, the Estate Merlot and Journey Chardonnay at $75; and the Journey Merlot at $125. Such pricing strategies may attract useful attention from the wine press, but they smack of greed.

Peter Michael

12400 Ida Clayton Rd., Calistoga, CA 95415. Tel: 942 4459. Fax: 942 0209. Production: 12,000 cases.

Sir Peter Michael is an electronics and media tycoon with a longstanding interest in wine that was nurtured both in France and during some years spent working in San Francisco. In 1976 he started searching for a suitable site for vineyards and a winery, and looked at forty ranches before finding what he wanted in Knights Valley in 1981. In 1982 he started planting vineyards here. There wasn't a great deal going on, viticulturally, in Knights Valley, apart from the large Beringer vineyards. Sir Peter ignored the valley floor and planted only on hillsides, on soils of volcanic origin that were rocky and well drained. The red varieties were planted at a height of about 1,000 feet, the whites at closer to 1,800 feet, and the vines matured about 3 or 4 weeks later than those on the valley floor.

The first vintage was 1987, and Helen Turley was the initial winemaker, until in 1991 she was replaced by Mark Aubert, who is one of the few winemakers in California who is also the vineyard manager, taking an equal interest in the two indispensable components of a great wine.

The first-rate Sauvignon Blanc, called Après-Midi, used to be made from

Howell Mountain fruit, but that vineyard has been sold, and in future the wine will be made from estate grapes grown at 1,600–1,800 feet. The wine is barrel-fermented and aged in *barriques*, with very little new oak.

There are a number of different Chardonnays. All grapes are hand-sorted and whole-cluster pressed, and none of them is fined, cold-stabilized, or, since 1992, filtered. Mon Plaisir comes from the former Gauer Ranch in Alexander Valley. The vines are being replanted after phylloxera to 2,000 per acre. It is aged in *barriques*, heavily toasted and 60 per cent new, for up to a year. Clos du Ciel comes from Liparita Vineyard on Howell Mountain; it goes through full malolactic fermentation and is aged for 11 months in 50 per cent new *barriques*. Belle Cote, first made in 1994, is made from estate grapes grown at 1850 feet. Cuvée Indigene is a barrel selection of wines made using natural yeasts (as are 70 per cent of all the Chardonnay lots) and aged only in new oak. The top Chardonnay is Point Rouge, priced at an alarming $85, and made from Gauer Ranch fruit and aged for 14 months in new oak with weekly stirring of the lees. Yet another bottling is in the works: La Carrière, from an exceptionally steep estate vineyard planted at 2,000 feet in 1995 with three Dijon clones; the first release will be 1999.

The Cabernet Sauvignon is called Les Pavots, the name of a 47-acre vineyard at an elevation of 1,500 feet below Mount St Helena. The cuttings came from Martha's Vineyard. Merlot and Cabernet Franc are also planted here, all small-cluster clones. Before 1992 it was pure Cabernet and rather tough, but Aubert has been making it as a Bordeaux blend, with about 70 per cent Cabernet, and later vintages have been softer and richer. Cultivated yeasts are used for Les Pavots, and malolactic fermentation takes place in barrel after a 14-day maceration. The wine is aged for 22 months in 50 per cent new Nevers *barriques*, and lightly fined and filtered before bottling.

Peter Michael's top red is Point Blanc, a Bordeaux blend with only 17 per cent or so of Cabernet Sauvignon and 45 per cent of Merlot. It is aged 21 months in new oak, and bottle-aged for 2 years before release.

The winery is also developing a Green Valley vineyard for Pinot Noir, which will be released under the Sonoma Coast appellation. Aubert is convinced that the potential of Green Valley for Pinot Noir is even greater than Carneros.

There seems little doubt that Peter Michael in now in the top rank of Chardonnay producers. There are occasional vintages when some of the wines seem a touch flabby, but in fine years such as 1995 the wines are a triumph, rich and concentrated. They are expensive, but they are hand-crafted and made with the most scrupulous care.

Nalle

2383 Dry Creek Rd., Healdsburg, CA 95488. Tel: 433 1040. Fax: 433 6062. Production: 2,500 cases.

Like John Williams at Frog's Leap, Doug Nalle doesn't take himself too seriously, as the cartoons on his labels make abundantly clear. But also like John Williams, he makes extremely good wines in an undemonstrative style. Nalle made wine at Jordan and Quivira before starting his own label in 1984. He made the wine at other local wineries until his own facilities, beneath a hideous concrete hangar, were ready in 1991.

His grapes come from four growers with vines that were mostly planted between 1880 and 1910. His sceptical view about old vines and yields are given in detail in the chapter on Zinfandel. He is not dogmatic about irrigation, either, and he believes there are instances when drip-irrigated vines can give better quality fruit than dry-farmed sites. The grapes are hand-picked and sorted at the winery, then vinified in open-top fermenters. Nalle favours cultivated yeasts because there is a high risk of stuck fermentations with natural yeasts. He likes a gentle pumping over, to give good colour extraction 'without beating the fruit up'. Malolactic fermentation takes place in barrels, of which 20 per cent are new. Although Nalle quite likes the aromas of American oak when used to age Zinfandel, he sometimes detects a bitterness that doesn't occur with French oak, so he only uses *barriques*.

Nalle wants balance and fruit, and maintains that his wines are best enjoyed at up to six years old. He doesn't want high alcohol – 14 degrees is ample – nor does he want powerful oak flavours. What he does deliver is stylish fruit and impeccable balance. Nobody ever struggles to finish a bottle of Nalle Zin.

Rafanelli

4685 West Dry Creek Rd., Healdsburg, CA 95448. Tel: 433 1385. Production: 10,000 cases.

For what it's worth, Rafanelli Zinfandel is the wine I probably order more frequently than any other when dining out in the North Coast. It is simply as pure an expression as you can find of Dry Creek Zinfandel. The property was founded in the early years of the century by Alberto Rafanelli, and is still run by his descendants. David Rafanelli has been making the wines since 1987.

Seventy acres were planted in 1962, the varieties being Zinfandel, Gamay Beaujolais, and French Colombard. It was only in 1974 that Rafanelli opened a commercial winery, developing a reputation for its Gamay, Zinfandel, and Cabernet. By the mid-1990s, Rafanelli cultivated 50 acres. The Gamay and Colombard had gone. There is Chardonnay and Merlot too, but the grapes are sold off, allowing Rafanelli to concentrate on what it does best. The Zinfandel and Cabernet are made in a similar way, being fermented in open-top tanks, employing natural yeasts whenever possible, with the cap punched down by hand. The Zinfandel is aged both in oak uprights and in Nevers barrels, while the Cabernet is aged entirely in *barriques* for 21 months. Both are bottled without fining or filtration. Outstanding lots of Cabernet are aged over 3 years and labelled Terrace Select.

The Zinfandel is all it should be: rich and deep and satisfying, and the Cabernet Sauvignon is every bit as good.

Ravenswood

18701 Gehricke Rd., Sonoma, CA 95476. Tel: 938 1960. Fax: 938 9459. Production: 90,000 cases.

Joel Peterson trained as a biochemist and in 1973 decided that winemaking would perfectly combine the artistic and scientific sides of his nature. He worked with Joseph Swan in Russian River Valley before starting up his own winemaking operation, on a very modest scale, in 1976. Production gradually expanded, but Peterson kept up his medical work until 1987. In 1981 he moved to a roadside former garage south of Sonoma. This was a low-tech winery, not a steel tank in sight, nothing but oak fermenters and stacks of barrels. In 1991 Peterson moved to the former Haywood winery near Sonoma, having outgrown the old garage.

Over the years Ravenswood has changed. In the 1980s Peterson specialized in small lots of magnificent old-vine Zinfandels (Dickerson from Napa; Monte Rosso, Old Hill Ranch, Cooke, Wood Road), as well as some impressive Cabernet and Merlot. He had scoured Sonoma and Napa, hunting down old parcels of vines, which were the source of his finest wines. There were also good-value Zinfandels called Vintner's Blend, which often included some fruit from Lodi. In the late 1980s Peterson told me he didn't want his production to expand beyond 15,000 cases – but he is now pushing 100,000 cases.

At the top level, the Ravenswood wines remain excellent, uncompromised by the winery's expansion. The winemaking style is non-interventionist, as Peterson explains: 'Eighty per cent of the job is getting hold of good grapes. My contribution is to extract as much flavour, and to enhance that flavour, but not too much. It's better to husband the wine than to make the wine. The problem with hi-tech winemaking is that it always assumes the patient is sick and must be constantly cosseted and protected.' It was a deliberate strategy to specialize in Zinfandel, as Peterson could be a big fish in a small pond. When he started out, the only serious competition was coming from Swan and Ridge.

When the grapes come in they may or may not be destemmed. The wines are punched down regularly during fermentation, using natural yeasts, and are aged about 18 months in *barriques*, of which between 30 and 100 per cent are new. The wines are bottled without filtration.

Peterson's Merlot comes from numerous sources, including Knights Valley and Sangiacomo in Carneros. It can be a sumptuous wine, sometimes reminiscent of Pomerol. His top Cabernet is the Pickberry blend, which comes from a dry-farmed Sonoma Mountain vineyard; there is also a Gregory Vineyard Cabernet. These are tougher wines than the Merlot, and are often softened with a drop of Merlot or Cabernet Franc, and aged for up to 2 years in *barriques*.

After the move to Sonoma, the range expanded to include a Cabernet Franc, a Petite Sirah from Kunde grapes, and a Chardonnay from Sangiacomo Vineyard. All the wines are well made, but the single-vineyard Zinfandels and the Bordeaux reds remain the best.

Rochioli
6182 Westside Rd., Healdsburg, CA 95448., Tel: 433 2305. Fax: 433 2358. Production: 10,000 cases.

The Rochiolis are farmers first, winemakers second, but equally skilled at both. The family began farming in Russian River Valley in 1938, growing hops and beans as well as grapes, which were sold to the local cooperative. In 1959 Joe Rochioli began planting good-quality varieties such as Sauvignon Blanc and Cabernet Sauvignon, but at first no one wanted them and they ended up in bulk wines for Gallo and others. He and his son Tom aimed for lower yields, as their neighbours were obtaining crops of up to 15 tons per acre with varieties such as Gamay. In 1973 he sold Pinot Noir grapes to Davis Bynum, and this was the beginning of the recognition of Russian River as an outstanding region for the variety.

The Rochiolis farm 105 acres of Sauvignon Blanc, Chardonnay, Pinot Noir, and Cabernet Sauvignon, and they lease the 15-acre Allen Vineyard, selling about half the fruit from both to Williams-Selyem, Davis Bynum, Gary Farrell, and others. In 1983 Tom persuaded Joe Rochioli to start up a winemaking business, and the winery was completed two years later. Also in 1985 they took on Gary Farrell as consultant.

The reason for the outstanding quality of the Rochioli grapes is not only the skilled farming, but also the fact that they planted a tight-berried clone of unknown origin. Phylloxera has obliged the Rochiolis to replant, and they have done so with closer spacing. As for clones, Tom Rochioli has conducted many experiments with clones but has come to no clear conclusion; the most recent plantings have been of a Dijon clone.

Half of the Sauvignon Blanc is barrel-fermented and malolactic fermentation is blocked. It's usually a fine example with a lovely aroma, but in 1997 there was a stuck fermentation, leaving the wine rather sweet. Sometimes there is an old-vine bottling from the vines originally planted in 1959. Gewürztraminer was made until 1996, then phased out.

Chardonnay is barrel-fermented with natural yeasts and goes through full malolactic fermentation. In addition to the regular bottling, there are three single-vineyard wines: Allen Vineyard, River Block, and South River Vineyard, but production of these is limited to between 75 and 230 cases, so these wines are very difficult to find.

Rochioli's best-known wine, the Pinot Noir, is fermented in open-top tanks and punched down; malolactic fermentation takes place in barrel. Some twenty different lots are kept separately and not blended until after the first racking. Then the wine is aged for 15 months in 30 per cent new *barriques*. There is no fining and usually no filtration. As with the Chardonnay, the most celebrated wines are parcel selections, such as West Block, usually of old vines, and aged in up to 100 per cent new oak.

Cabernet Sauvignon comes from old estate vines, but they are unlikely to be replanted, as the site is not ideal for the variety. There is also a Zinfandel from the Sodini Vineyard, which was planted in 1905.

Despite the quality of the Chardonnay and Sauvignon, Rochioli will always be revered for its firm ripe Pinots, mouth-filling but elegant.

Marimar Torres

11400 Graton Rd., Sebastopol, CA. Tel: 823 4365. Fax: 823 4496. Production: 15,000 cases.

There were orchards in this part of Green Valley when Marimar Torres, the sister of the distinguished Catalan wine producer Miguel Torres, first laid eyes on what would become her vineyards. She bought the property in 1983 and, on Miguel's advice, planted her vineyards at 2,000 vines per acre. There are now 81 acres of vines, two-thirds Chardonnay, the remainder Pinot Noir, as well as 0.5 acre of the Spanish variety Parellada. Since Parellada here never ripens beyond 17 Brix, it is blended in with the Chardonnay to give some extra acidity. Marimar has paid great attention to the viticultural details, installing vertical trellising despite its high maintenance costs. She has planted a number of different clones, which are sometimes vinified separately, and selected low-vigour rootstocks. The soil is a sandy loam of volcanic origin on a clay, which apparently gives good drainage as well as water retention. As for yields, Torres aims for about 4 tons per acre for Chardonnay, and 3 for Pinot Noir.

The first vintage was Chardonnay in 1989, but the winery here was not completed until 1992. That was the first vintage for Pinot Noir. The winemaking techniques are classic. The Chardonnay is whole-cluster pressed, barrel-fermented using cultivated yeasts in French oak, one-third new, and then it remains on the lees for 11 months, having gone through full malolactic fermentation. Cool-climate fruit ensures that the wine is never heavy-handed: it has a restraint and elegance that are most attractive. The same is true of the Pinot. About 20 per cent of the grapes enter the fermentation tanks as whole clusters after a cold soak; the cap is punched down thrice daily; malolactic fermentation takes place in *barriques*, of which one-third are new. At present the wines are filtered, but the practice may be discontinued.

In 1998 I tasted all the wines produced in the 1990s. The 1991 Chardonnay was flat and tiring and the 1993 a touch neutral, but 1992, 1994, and 1995 were all excellent. The 1993 Pinot was the only disappointment, with 1995 showing the best long-term promise, and 1994 the greatest opulence. But in general these are lean, shapely wines, not flashy, not the kind of wines that leap from the glass in blind tastings, but at the dinner table they work beautifully – especially when Marimar, a specialist in Catalan cuisine, is at the stove.

NOTE

1 As in Napa, the area code is 707, unless otherwise stated

25

Sonoma II

Adler Fels
5325 Corrick Lane, Santa Rosa, CA 95409. Tel: 539 3123. Fax: 539 3128. Production: 15,000 cases.

This winery, which is not attached to any vineyards, stands on a ridge overlooking the Valley of the Moon. It was founded in 1980 by David Coleman and Ayn Ryan. The best known wine is the Fumé Blanc, made from Russian River fruit in quite a strident vegetal style, but Adler Fels also produces Chardonnay, an off-dry Gewürztraminer, Pinot Noir, Sangiovese, and a sparkling wine called Melange à Deux that blends Riesling and Gewürztraminer.

Alderbrook
2306 Magnolia Dr., Healdsburg, CA 95458. Tel: 433 5987. Fax: 433 1862. Production: 37,000 cases.

The Alderbrook tasting room is on the fringes of Healdsburg, but the 55-acre vineyards are in the southern part of Dry Creek, although quite a lot of grapes are bought in from other Sonoma vineyards. The property was founded by Mark Rafanelli in 1981, and bought by George Gillemot in 1991. The winemaker is Kristi Koford. Since Gillemot acquired Alderbrook, the winery has added Merlot, Pinot Noir, and Viognier to its range.

The Dry Creek Sauvignon Blanc is 40 per cent barrel-fermented and 40 per cent of the wine goes through malolactic fermentation. An equal blend of Sauvignon and Sémillon is labelled Duet, and is barrel-fermented in new French oak. The Chardonnay is 60 per cent barrel-fermented, but there is a version from Dorothy's Vineyard in Dry Creek that is fully barrel-fermented and aged in new French oak. There are also two bottlings of Gewürztraminer.

The Cabernet Sauvignon, which is blended with some Cabernet Franc, is aged in American as well as French oak. Other red wines include a Merlot from Kunde vineyards, old-vine Zinfandel, Russian River Pinot Noir, and Russian River Syrah.

On the two occasions I have visited Alderbrook I have been pleasantly surprised by the sound quality and the fair prices, although the wines lack complexity. The whites have been better than the reds.

Alexander Valley Vineyards

8644 Highway 128, Healdsburg, CA 95448. Tel: 433 7209. Fax: 433 9408. Production: 45,000 cases.

This estate on the lower slopes of Alexander Valley was bought in 1962 by aircraft executive Harry Wetzell. His son Hank went to UC Davis and became the winemaker here. There are now 150 acres under vine: mostly Cabernet Sauvignon, Merlot, and Chardonnay, and smaller quantities of Pinot Noir, rather weak Zinfandel, Chenin Blanc, Riesling, and a pungent Gewürztraminer. The winery also produces a little Syrah. The Cabernet, Merlot, and Zinfandel are all aged in American oak.

These are not complex wines, but they are well made, accessible, with all the succulence of Alexander Valley fruit, and they are attractively priced. The Cabernet Sauvignon is often the best offering.

Bandiera

8860 Sonoma Highway, Kenwood, CA 95452. Tel: 894 4295. Fax: 894 2563. Production: 150,000 cases.

From 1937, when Emil Bandiera founded the winery, until 1980, this was a jug-wine producer. It was then bought by the California Wine Company, who brought in John Merritt as winemaker. The estate consists of 57 acres of Cabernet Sauvignon and 42 acres of Carneros Chardonnay. The wines are modest and fairly inexpensive standard varietals, with a good deal of white Zinfandel. The company also owns the Stonegate winery in Napa Valley.

Benziger

1883 London Ranch Rd., Glen Ellen, CA 95442. Tel: 935 3000. Fax: 935 3016. Production: 150,000 cases.

Bruno Benziger of New York founded this property in 1980, and it was run as a family enterprise. Benziger died in 1989, and the present winemakers are Joe Benziger and Terry Nolan. The Benzigers enjoyed enormous commercial success with their Glen Ellen and M. G. Vallejo brands, which they sold to Heublein in 1993. Now the family concentrates on producing a wide range of wines, at differing prices levels and qualities, at a winery well organized to accommodate the frequent tourists. Some of the wines are made from the 85 acres of vineyards owned by Benziger, but most are made from purchased grapes. The basic wines are the Sonoma County varietals, which tend to be correct but rather dull and dilute. Far more interesting is the Imagery Series, which includes some unusual grape varieties, and the Mountain Estate Wines from their own vineyards.

With so many lots of so many wines, quality is hit and miss, but there are many interesting bottles offered as part of the Imagery Series. It has included piquant Cabernet Franc from Alexander Valley, forthright floral Viognier, Sangiovese from Healdsburg, Barbera, some sleek and concentrated Reserve Cabernet Sauvignon, estate-grown and very tannic Petit Verdot, and Zinfandel port. It seems that the Mountain Estate wines are being replaced by two Meritage blends labelled Tribut, and that formerly available estate bottlings of varieties such as Sémillon and Merlot are being phased out. With so many wines on offer, it is sensible to taste before you buy.

Buena Vista

18000 Old Winery Rd., Sonoma, CA 95476. Tel: 252 7117. Fax: 252 0392. Production: 250,000 cases.

This is of course the famous estate created by Agoston Haraszthy in the 1850s. After phylloxera wrecked the vineyards, the property became neglected and forgotten. In the 1940s a journalist called Frank Bartholomew bought the estate at auction. When the American wine authority Leon Adams was invited to visit the property, he realized that it must be the original Buena Vista. In 1968 the estate was sold to a Los Angeles supermarket chain, which developed 700 acres of vineyards in Carneros. In 1979 Buena Vista was bought by the German company Racke, the present owners. They expanded the Carneros holdings to 935 acres, most of which are organically farmed. Buena Vista does not present itself as anything other than a middle-of-the-road winery, offering straightforward varietal wines at fair prices. In many respects quality has improved. The Sauvignon Blanc, which used to be made with quite a bit of residual sugar, is now made in a more elegant dry style. The top wines are the Grand Reserve range. One curiosity here is Spiceling, a blend of Gewürztraminer and Riesling. The winemaker since 1994 has been Judy Matulich-Weitz.

Canyon Road

19550 Geyserville Ave., Geyserville, CA 95441. Tel: 857 3417. Fax: 867 3545. Production: 100,000 cases.

This is a subsidiary label of Geyser Peak, established in 1990. It draws on the vineyards owned by the Trione family, as well as other sources, but for maximum flexibility the wines carry a California appellation. The unwooded Sauvignon Blanc is disappointing. The Chardonnay, which accounts for about half the production, is fermented in tanks and barrels. Cabernet Sauvignon and Merlot are aged briefly in French and American oak. Quality is adequate; prices are low.

Yet another sub-label is Venezia, which includes a barrel-fermented Russian River Valley Chardonnay, Alexander Valley Cabernet Sauvignon, and a Sangiovese blended with some Shiraz. There is also a barrel-fermented Sauvignon/Sémillon blend called Nuovo Mondo, which also uses Alexander Valley fruit.

Carmenet
1700 Moon Mountain Dr., Sonoma, CA 95476. Tel: 996 5870. Fax: 996 5302. Production: 30,000 cases.

There has been a winery and vineyards at this remote spot since 1980, and in 1984 it was acquired by the Chalone Group. Jeff Baker became the winemaker, and remained until 1998, when he was replaced by Karl Wright. The vines, all Bordeaux red varieties, are planted on decomposed volcanic and clay soil at a height of 1,150 to 1,700 feet. Up here there is excellent sun exposure and spring frosts are almost unknown. Baker is particularly proud of the barrel cellars which are tunnelled into the tufa rock, as they have excellent humidity and a constant temperature. In 1996 a brush fire destroyed 45 of the 67 acres.

In the 1980s Carmenet became well known for its rich, spicy Graves-style blends of Sauvignon Blanc and Sémillon. One came from vineyards throughout Sonoma Valley, and the other came from Paragon Vineyard in Edna Valley. From 1990 onwards the Sonoma blend was dropped and the only white sold by Carmenet was the Paragon Vineyard Meritage.

The red Meritage is a gutsy blend of Cabernet Sauvignon, Cabernet Franc, and Merlot, and in some years Baker produces a Reserve Meritage called Vin de Garde. Dynamite Cabernet, despite its name, is a supple blend for relatively early drinking, and there is also a medium-bodied Cabernet Franc with an attractive cranberry tone.

Cecchetti-Sebastiani
414 First St. East 1, Sonoma, CA 95476. Tel: 996 8463. Fax: 996 0424.

This small operation was founded in 1985 by Roy Cecchetti and his brother-in-law Don Sebastiani. Sebastiani is now devoting more time to running his family winery in Sonoma, but is still involved here. From 1985 to 1992 the wines were made at the Valley of the Moon winery, and thereafter space was leased at St Supéry in Napa Valley. The winemaker is Bob Broman, who used to work at Concannon and Guenoc. The business focuses on Cabernet Sauvignon and Merlot, as well as Pinot Noir from Santa Barbara. The only wine I have tasted is the lush, rich 1992 Merlot, which was aged over 3 years in older *barriques*. The inexpensive second label, Pepperwood Grove, must be good for cash flow, since annual production is now 100,000 cases.

Chalk Hill

10300 Chalk Hill Rd., Healdsburg, CA 95448. Tel: 838 4306. Fax: 838 9687. Production: 60,000 cases

The owner of Chalk Hill is Fred Furth, a lawyer from San Francisco who bought a large ranch in Sonoma and in 1974 began planting a number of varietals, which in the early 1980s were trimmed down to Chardonnay, Sauvignon Blanc, Merlot, and Cabernet Sauvignon. There are some 300 acres of vineyards planted on slopes, and some of the grapes are sold to other wineries such as Kenwood and Simi. Despite the name, there is no limestone at Chalk Hill, and there is a good deal of clay in the soil. Green cover has been employed on some sites to prevent erosion.

Despite the enormous investment made by Furth over the decades the wines were never that exciting. The Sauvignon was rather dull, although some very good late harvest wines were made in various vintages during the 1980s and again in 1994. In 1990 David Ramey was appointed winemaker, and immediately set about implementing changes that did improve quality. For example, skin contact for Sauvignon ceased. At Matanzas Creek, Ramey had made one of Sonoma's outstanding Sauvignons, so he swiftly improved on Chalk Hill's earlier efforts. The Sauvignon is barrel-fermented and goes through full malolactic fermentation. The Chardonnay, easily the estate's most important wine in terms of volume, also improved, and so did the Cabernet, which was transformed into a rich, smoky wine. In 1996 William Knuttel, formerly of Saintsbury, was taken on as winemaker.

Chateau St Jean

8555 Sonoma Highway, Kenwood, CA 94542. Tel: 833 4134. Fax: 833 4700. Production: 215,000 cases.

When I was starting to explore California wines in the early 1980s, Chateau St Jean really stimulated my interest. Its white wines were blockbusters: rich single-vineyard Chardonnays and hefty, oaky Fumé Blancs. And then there were the sensational botrytized Rieslings, Gewürztraminer and Sémillon that may have been equalled since in California but surely have not been surpassed. I would probably be more critical of the dry white wines if they were being made today, but at the time I was simply overwhelmed by their fruit and power. Those were the days when Richard Arrowood was making the wine. Arrowood remained until 1990, when he was replaced by Don Van Staaveren; since 1997 the winemaker has been Steve Reeder. Already in the mid- to late-1980s, there were changes taking place at the property, and the range of wines was slimmed down. In part it may have been a marketing decision, but it was also prompted by the sad fact that some of the single vineyards, such as Forrest Crimmins, had been concreted over to make way for housing developments. No doubt more recent wines are better balanced and don't have the tendency shown by some of the single-vineyard wines to collapse after a couple of years under their own weight.

The estate was created in 1973 by a group of grape farmers from the Central Valley. One of them, Ed Merzoian, had a wife named Jean, who was awarded earthly sainthood when the winery was named. In 1976 the winery was completed. Production grew rapidly to about 100,000 cases by 1982. Two years later the business was sold to Suntory, who invested further in winemaking equipment. In the 1990s Chateau St Jean was sold again, this time to the owners of Beringer.

The portfolio of Fumé Blancs was reduced eventually to two: Sonoma County, which contains some Sémillon, and Petite Etoile, which is a 40-acre vineyard in Windsor which the winery bought in 1989. The main difference between the two is that the Petite Etoile is entirely barrel-fermented, whereas the Sonoma bottling is mostly fermented in tanks and has much less character.

One year Richard Arrowood released seven different Chardonnays. Now there are three to choose from: Sonoma, Robert Young, and Belle Terre. If the whites are less exciting than they used to be, the reds are much better. The basic Cabernet Sauvignon and Merlot can be excellent, and there is also a full-bodied and intense Bordeaux blend called Cinq Cepages, which is aged for 2 years in American and French oak. There are also small lots of Rhône and Italian red varieties.

Chateau Souverain
400 Souverain Rd., Geyserville, CA 95441. Tel: 433 8281. Fax: 433 5174. Production: 145,000 cases.

Souverain was the original winery of Lee Stewart from 1943 onwards, except that it was located in Napa Valley. In 1970 Stewart retired and sold his property, and two wineries took the Souverain name. One was in Rutherford, the other in Alexander Valley. Pillsbury owned them both, until in 1976 the company sold the Rutherford winery to Freemark Abbey, and the Sonoma winery to the California North Coast Grape Growers Association. In short, it became a cooperative. In 1986 Nestlé bought the winery and changed its name to Chateau Souverain. Despite considerable investments aimed at improving the quality, Nestlé sold the winery to the owners of Beringer and Chateau St Jean. From 1984 to 1996 the winemaker was Tom Peterson; since 1996 the wines have been made by Ed Killian.

The estate owns 300 acres of vineyards near Asti, planted with a wide range of varieties, all red except for Sauvignon Blanc. The barrel-fermented Alexander Valley Sauvignon is quite rounded, although it doesn't go through malolactic fermentation. The Chardonnays are barrel-fermented.

The Sonoma County bottling is mostly made from Carneros fruit; the Russian River Winemakers Reserve comes from Rochioli vineyards and is aged in 40 per cent new oak.

Among the reds, the Dry Creek Zinfandel is very reliable, as it contains a fair proportion of old-vine fruit. There is also Cabernet Sauvignon and Merlot from Alexander Valley. All these wines are aged in both American and French oak. The Reserves receive longer ageing, and, in the case of the Russian River Pinot Noir, are aged in 70 per cent new Nevers barrels.

Christopher Creek Winery

641 Limerick Lane, Healdsburg, CA 95448. Tel: 433 2001. Fax: 433 9315. Production: 3,000 cases.

This small winery was founded in 1974 by Bill and Helen Chaikin and named Soyotome. In 1988 it was acquired by John and Susan Mitchell, who renamed it. The 10-acre vineyard was planted by the Chaikins and contains Syrah, Petite Sirah, and Chardonnay, all made as varietals here.

Cline Cellars

24737 Highway 121, Sonoma, CA 95476. Tel: 935 4310. Fax: 935 4319. Production: 50,000 cases.

Fred Cline and his brother Matt, who is the winemaker here, own 350 acres of vineyards in Oakley in Contra Costa County. These vineyards are a place of pilgrimage for Rhône rangers, as they include the oldest surviving Mourvèdre in California, as well as Zinfandel, Carignane, Sémillon, and Alicante Bouschet. The Oakley vineyards were planted by the Cline's grandfather, Valeriano Jacuzzi. The Clines have also planted vineyards close to their winery in southern Sonoma, to which they moved in 1991. Here they farm 20 acres of Syrah, Marsanne, Viognier, and Roussanne, all closely spaced.

Visiting the Cline tasting room is always enjoyable, as you don't have to taste Chardonnay and can concentrate instead on Roussanne or Mourvedre. However, the wines are uneven in quality: the whites are generously fruity and full-flavoured, yet often a bit broad and flabby, while the reds can be a touch stewed and raisiny. I can't help wondering whether there simply aren't too many wines on offer. Thus there are two Mourvèdres, Ancient Vines and the pricier Contra Costa Reserve. It isn't always easy to remember the difference between the meaty Oakley Cuvée (50 per cent Mourvèdre, plus Carignane and Zinfandel) and the rather simple Côtes d'Oakley (60 per cent Carignane, the rest Mourvedre, with a little Zinfandel and Cabernet). There can be as many as five Zinfandels. Some people are awed by the $40 Jacuzzi Family Vineyard bottling, but I find its rubbery, raisiny tones offputting, and often prefer the Ancient Vines or other single-vineyard bottlings. Cline is one of the few wineries to bottle a pure Carignane.

David Coffaro

7485 Dry Creek Rd., Geyserville, CA 95441. Tel: 433 9715. Production: 1,500 cases.

Former financier David Coffaro has been farming grapes on 20 acres in Dry Creek Valley since 1979. He used to sell the grapes to Dry Creek Vineyard and Doug Nalle before beginning to bottle his own wines. So far the range consists of Cabernet Sauvignon and Zinfandel, and the Estate Cuvée, which is blend of Cabernet, Zinfandel, Carignane, and Petite Sirah. The wines have intense fruitiness and are of high quality.

B. R. Cohn

15140 Sonoma Highway, Glen Ellen, CA 95442. Tel: 938 4064. Production: 15,000 cases.

In 1974 a former rock group manager called Bruce Cohn bought the Olive Hill Ranch in the Valley of the Moon and began selling grapes to a variety of wineries including Ravenswood and Kenwood. The winery was not built until 1984, and Helen Turley made the wine here from the outset until 1987. Today the estate has 65 acres of well-drained vineyards and John Speed is the winemaker. The top red wines are the Central Coast Petite Sirah, and the supple Cabernet Sauvignon and Merlot, both estate-grown and aged in *barriques*. Chardonnay is purchased from Carneros vineyards.

H. Cotturi

6725 Enterprise Rd., Glen Ellen, CA 95442. Tel: 996 6247. Production: 3,000 cases.

Harry Cotturi bought this property in 1963 and the winery was founded in 1979. It remains very much a family operation, supplementing its own grape production with purchases from numerous single vineyards. The 10-acre vineyard and the winery are run on strictly organic lines, but since in California that means sulphur dioxide may not be used at any stage, the results are uneven at best. Cotturi produce Zinfandel, Pinot Noir, Cabernet, Merlot, Alicante Bouschet, Chardonnay, and a red blend called Albarrello. Excessive volatile acidity and other winemaking faults are commonly encountered. Nonetheless they have ardent admirers, including Robert Parker.

La Crema

8075 Martinelli Rd., Forestville, CA 95436. Tel: 887 1756. Fax: 544 0156. Production: 50,000 cases.

Founded in 1979 by Rod Berglund, the winery operated for many years out of Petaluma. Berglund specialized in the Burgundian varieties. In 1985 La Crema was bought by a consortium based on the East Coast, but financial problems beset the new proprietors, and the winery had to close. In 1993 it was bought by Kendall-Jackson, and wines under the La Crema label are now produced at the Hartford Court winery. The emphasis remains on Chardonnay and Pinot Noir. The Reserve Pinot Noir has real flair.

DeLoach

1791 Olivet Rd., Santa Rosa, CA 94501. Tel: 526 9111. Fax: 526 4151. Production: 130,000 cases.

Exactly how Cecil DeLoach manages to combine the careers of fireman, anthropologist and winemaker I am not sure, but somehow he has done it, with the assistance of his family, and his sons are now active in the winery. There were some 22 acres of old vines in place when DeLoach bought the ranch in 1969, and they were supplemented by other vine-yards bought or leased in Russian River Valley. DeLoach went off to Davis to study winemaking in 1971. His first vintage here was 1975 and his first wine a Zinfandel. The winery wasn't completed until 1975. DeLoach was one of the first wineries to make white Zinfandel, and by 1979 it was producing about 27,000 cases. Then the winery retreated from the style again. The willowy Randy Ullom was the winemaker here from 1981 to 1993, before going on to greater things at Kendall-Jackson. By 1998 DeLoach owned or controlled about 600 acres of Zinfandel, Pinot Noir, Gewürztraminer and Chardonnay.

The tangy Chardonnay is partly barrel-fermented, and there is also a less expensive Sonoma Cuvée. The Gewürztraminer can be a charmer and the bone-dry Fumé Blanc has a flinty mineral character. Among the red wines, the Cabernet Sauvignon is svelte and rounded for a Russian River wine, and Merlot was added to the range in 1991. Pinot Noir is rarely exceptional here. DeLoach has returned to its early interest in Zinfandel, and now releases about five different single-vineyard bottlings in any vintage, usually from very old vines. As at Turley, there is a tendency to harvest late and reach very high alcohol levels, often over 16 degrees, but vigorous fruit comes shining through. The best wines are labelled O. F. S. (Our Finest Selection).

De Lorimier

2001 Highway 128, Geyserville, CA 95411. Tel: 857 2000. Fax: 857 3262. Production: 12,000 cases.

In the late 1960s Dr Al de Lorimier bought a prune orchard here in Alexander Valley. By the time he finished planting, there were 64 acres of

Cabernet Sauvignon, Merlot, Cabernet Franc, Chardonnay, Sauvignon Blanc, and Sémillon. In 1995 more acreage was acquired, bringing the total to 90 acres; these were planted with Chardonnay and Cabernet Sauvignon. It was only in 1985 that a winery was constructed, and the first vintage was 1986. The winemaker Don Frazer specializes in Meritage-style wines, Spectrum (two-thirds Sauvignon Blanc) and Mosaic (the two Cabernets and Merlot), as well as a Chardonnay called Prism, Sauvignon Blanc, and Merlot. A Petit Verdot was released in 1994.

Duxoup Wine Works
9611 West Dry Creek Rd., Healdsburg, CA 95448. Tel: 433 5195. Production: 1,500 cases.

Wine and whimsy don't often go together happily, but there is a rational explanation for the name of this winery. Andrew Cutter, who with his wife Deborah founded the winery in 1981, had a habit of saying 'It's as easy as duck soup', and it became a catch-phrase. Adapting it for his car's vanity plate, he shortened it to Duxoup. Deborah, heretically, has a degree in brewing.

All grapes are purchased from Dry Creek Valley. The winery is largely technology-free: it runs by gravity flow, there is no pumping, and wines are macerated in open fermenters. Their best-known wine is their juicy, upfront Syrah, aged in 25 per cent new French oak. Their most intriguing wine is made from the Charbono grape, dark and lush but bold. Zinfandel is no longer made, but for some reason Duxoup likes to make Valdiguié, known formerly as Napa Gamay.

Estancia
See Franciscan (p. 395). Production: 150,000 cases.

This range of wines is produced by Franciscan. All the reds come from 325 acres of vineyards in Alexander Valley, planted with Cabernet Sauvignon, Merlot, Cabernet Franc, and Sangiovese. The wines are Merlot, Cabernet Sauvignon, a ripe yet fresh blend of 70 per cent Cabernet and 30 per cent Sangiovese called Duo, and a fine Meritage. All the wines are aged in American as well as French oak, and the proportion of new oak varies from 25 to 65 per cent. The white wines and Pinot Noir bearing the Estancia label are, however, made from Monterey fruit. Estancia wines may be on the slick side, but they are very well made and good value.

Field Stone Winery
10075 Highway 128, Healdsburg, CA 95448. Tel: 433 7266. Fax: 433 2231. Production: 12,000 cases.

When engineer Wallace Johnson bought this property in 1955 it was a cattle ranch, but he gradually planted vines on the land. In 1977 he built a winery, but died two years later. His unlikely successor as director of the estate was Revd John Staten, a Presbyterian theologian. At that time the vineyards consisted of 24 acres of Cabernet Sauvignon and very old Petite Sirah, and some years later another 15 acres of Cabernet and Merlot were added. Today there are 150 acres in production, but half the grapes are sold to other wineries. The present owners are Redwood Ranches, and the winemaker until recently was Mike Duffy. Cabernet Sauvignon is the principal wine, and Petite Sirah the most individual wine. In the 1990s a little Viognier was added to the range. Quality is irregular.

Fisher Vineyards

6200 St Helena Rd., Santa Rosa, CA 95404. Tel: 539 7511. Production: 8,000 cases.

Fred Fisher created this estate in 1974, planting 25 acres of Cabernet Sauvignon and Chardonnay. He had some good sites, such as Whitney's Vineyard up in the Mayacamas Mountains, and Wedding Vineyard, planted with Cabernet. By the 1990s, Fisher owned slightly more acreage in Napa than he did in Sonoma. Winemaker Henryk Gasiewicz has limited the range to Chardonnay, Estate Merlot, and Cabernet Sauvignon. The top wines are released under the Coach Insignia label. Since 1989 all wines have been made using natural yeasts, and they are made in a richer, fruitier style than in the 1980s.

Flowers

28500 Seaview Rd., Cazadero, CA 95421. Tel: 847 3361. Production: 7,000 cases.

Walt and Joan Flowers are the owners of the Camp Meeting Ridge Vineyard, planted at 1,100 to 1,400 feet, which is above the fog line in Sonoma Coast. Although it was only planted in 1989, this cool site has already achieved some renown as the source of one of Kistler's most glittering Chardonnays. Starting in 1994, the Flowers began producing wines of their own, having constructed a gravity-flow winery, where Greg La Follette makes just two wines, Pinot Noir and Chardonnay. In 1998 a new vineyard, the Flowers Ranch, was planted at 1,750 feet with Pinot Noir and Chardonnay, bringing the estate's vineyards to a total of 85 acres.

Foppiano

12707 Old Redwood Highway, Healdsburg, CA 95448. Tel: 433 7272. Fax: 433 0565. Production: 200,000 cases.

Foppiano is a survivor of the old Italian family estates that flourished here in the late nineteenth century. It was founded in 1896 by Giovanni Foppiano, and today the property is run by his descendant Louis Foppiano, although since 1985 the wines have been made by Bill Regan.

There are 200 acres under vine here. They used to be planted with varieties such as Carignane, Petite Sirah and Zinfandel, and these were the source of robust but no doubt perfectly palatable jug wines. Eventually good-quality commercial wineries such as Foppiano could no longer compete with the rock-bottom prices of the Central Valley wineries, so they bravely decided to focus instead on good varietal wines. Fortunately, Petite Sirah has survived and gives a forthright wine which is the best-selling example of the varietal in California.

The Dry Creek Zinfandel is not oak-aged, which these days is unusual, but a perfectly valid way of preserving the fruitiness of the variety. The Merlot, added to the range in 1989, is aged in older American barrels, however.

There are three tiers of wines. Riverside Farms, essentially a 'fighting varietals' range, is the cheapest. In the middle are the Foppiano wines, and the top tier is the Reserve quality Chardonnay and Cabernet Sauvignon released under the Fox Mountain label. These wines are aged in new *barriques*, and quantities are limited to a total of 4,000 cases.

J. Fritz
24691 Dutcher Creek Rd., Cloverdale, CA 95425. Tel: 894 3389. Fax: 894 4781. Production: 18,000 cases.

The estate was founded in 1981 by Arthur Fritz, a businessman from San Francisco. The property consists of 90 acres in Dry Creek Valley and 35 acres leased in Russian River Valley. The winemaker is Rob Lawson and Helen Turley acts as a consultant. The quality of the wines has improved dramatically in recent years. Even varieties that usually put in a sulky performance in California – Sauvignon Blanc and Pinot Blanc (Fritz admits that theirs is in fact Melon) – are delicious here, with all the freshness of Russian River fruit. The Sauvignon is fermented in tanks and aged in oak puncheons for a few months. The Chardonnays come from a number of vineyards, including the Dutton Ranch and Poplar Vineyard, though I find them too lavishly oaked for my taste. They are all whole-cluster pressed and go through malolactic fermentation. The Old Vine Zinfandel, aged in American oak, is chunky and aggressive, but a fine example of a more rustic style.

Gan Eden
4950 Ross Rd., Sebastopol, CA 95472. Tel: 829 5686. Fax: 829 0993. Production: 30,000 cases.

Founded in 1985, this winery specializes in kosher wines. It is run by Craig Winchell and his wife Jennifer. The wines, which are all made from purchased grapes, are far superior to the usual appalling kosher wines produced to supply a fairly limited and undemanding market. Most of the grapes come from Alexander Valley, and the Cabernet Sauvignon is the best wine, supplemented by Chardonnay, Chenin Blanc, and Gewürztraminer.

Geyser Peak
22281 Chianti Rd., Geyserville, CA 95441. Tel: 857 9463. Fax: 857 3545. Production: 400,000 cases.

The property was founded in 1990 by Augustus Quitzow, and passed through various hands until in 1972 it was acquired by the Schlitz Brewery in order to produce bag-in-box wines in industrial quantities under the Summit label. In 1982 the winery was bought by banker Henry Trione, to complement the 500 acres of vines he already owned. In 1989 the Australian wine company Penfolds bought half the company. In late 1991 Penfolds were apparently over-extended, so another share of the ownership reverted to Trione, who built a new winery in 1995. At the instigation of Penfolds, the Australian winemaker Daryl Groom had been installed here in 1991. They wanted him back, but Trione, aware of his skills, hung on to him by giving him a share of the business. In 1998 Henry Trione, whose sons were not interested in running the business, sold Geyser Peak to Fortune Brands, the owner of Jim Beam whiskey. Fortune paid $59 million for the winery and name, $35 million to cover debts, and the remainder for the vineyards close to the winery. Daryl Groom was retained by the new owners.

By the mid-1990s the winery owned 1,200 acres of vineyards, 800 in Alexander Valley and Russian River, as well as 300 acres in Lake County and 130 in Mendocino. Much of the trellising has been changed at the suggestion of Dr Richard Smart. In the 1980s, under Trione's direction, quality improved considerably, but it was Groom, who at Penfolds had been responsible for a number of vintages of Grange Hermitage, and his assistant Mick Schroeter, who really turned things around. Some wines of modest quality were eliminated from the range, but the Australians popularized large-volume wines such as Soft Riesling and Semchard, an Australian-style blend of Livermore Sémillon and Sonoma Chardonnay.

Groom wants to make wines of immediate appeal. He is enthusiastic about his rotary fermenters, an enthusiasm also shared by George Bursick at Ferrari-Carano. This permits for a speedy extraction of colour and flavour, and allows him to complete the fermentation in barrels.

The range includes a crisp Sauvignon Blanc, sweetish Riesling and Gewürztraminer, and two Chardonnays, one from various Sonoma sites, the other, a barrel-fermented Reserve, from Alexander Valley fruit. I usually prefer the more vigorous regular Chardonnay.

The Cabernet Sauvignon is aged in American oak, and there is also a Reserve bottling from Alexander Valley. In addition to Syrah, Groom makes Shiraz using Alexander Valley fruit. Again, American oak contributes its vanillin sweetness to these wines. The Merlot is only fermented for about 5 days (and the other reds for scarcely much longer), using the speedy rotary fermenters, and is then aged in French and American oak. The most serious wine is the intense Reserve Alexandre, which pre-dates the arrival of Daryl Groom. This is a Meritage, not made every year, and is typically contains just over 50 per cent Cabernet Sauvignon, and varying amounts of the other Bordeaux varieties. Unlike the Reserve Cabernet, it is aged in French *barriques*.

The Summit brand was sold off in 1985, and the other Geyser Peak labels are Canyon Road (q.v.) and Venezia.

Gundlach-Bundschu
2000 Denmark St., Sonoma, CA 95476. Tel: 938 5277. Fax: 938 9460. Production: 55,000 cases.

A narrow lane leads to this most charming of old Sonoma wineries. It is, by California standards, a venerable institution, having been founded in 1855 by Jacob Gundlach. Another Bavarian immigrant, Charles Bundschu, teamed up with Gundlach in 1862. The two men planted the Rhinefarm Vineyard. Although very successful at first the enterprise was beset by problems: first phylloxera, then a fire in 1906 that destroyed most of their stock and damaged the winery, then Prohibition, which put a stop to winemaking though not to grape growing. The vineyards were replanted by Jim Bundschu in 1967 and the winery reopened in 1976, although wines had been released from the 1973 vintage onwards. Except for the Chardonnay, all the wines are made from estate-grown fruit. Linda Trotta is the winemaker.

The estate now owns 375 acres, 125 on the site of the original Rhine-farm, which lies within the Carneros Sonoma region. The Germanic heritage of the winery is recognized in their good Riesling, Gewürztram-iner, and Kleinberger (a synonym for Elbling). The basic Chardonnay is a simple wine, the Special Selection a more complex barrel-fermented version. There is also a Chardonnay from Sangiacomo Vineyard, half of which is barrel-fermented. In general, the Chardonnays do not go through malolactic fermentation. The Merlot is attractive here, and is aged in French and American oak. In addition to the underrated Cabernet Sau-vignon, there's a fine Cabernet Franc. The most serious wine is the Vintage Reserve Cabernet Sauvignon, which is aged for a few years in bottle before release.

These are not the most sophisticated of Sonoma wines, but they are flavoursome, sensibly priced, and some reds age surprisingly well.

Hacienda
1000 Vineyard Lane, Sonoma, CA 95476. Tel: 938 3200.

After Frank Bartholomew sold Buena Vista, he started up Hacienda in 1973. He had retained some of the vineyards originally planted by Haraszthy in 1857, and they became the basis for Hacienda. He sold the estate in the late 1970s, and in 1993 it was acquired by J. F. J. Bronco, a large Central Valley brand. It never produced wines of great character, and is unlikely to in the future. The wines are cheap.

Hafner
4280 Pine Flat Rd., Healdsburg, CA 95448. Tel: 433 4675. Production: 10,000 cases.

There was a winery here in 1893, and the Alexander Valley estate was bought in 1967 by Richard Hafner. He became a grape farmer, planting Cabernet in 1969 and white varieties in 1973. The vineyards now total 100 acres, and most of the grapes are sold off. A winery was built in 1982. Most of the production is Chardonnay, but there is also well-made Cabernet Sauvignon, and the occasional late harvest Riesling.

Hamel
PO Box 1355, Healdsburg, CA 95448. Tel: 433 9055. Production: 1,000 cases.

Kevin Hamel is the winemaker at Preston and has set a up small-scale winery of his own. The first vintage was 1994, and Hamel is focusing on Syrah. The 1996 Syrah, ripe and peppery, shows great concentration and promise.

Hanna
5353 Occidental Rd., Santa Rosa, CA 95406. Tel: 575 3371. Fax: 431 4314. Production: 24,000 cases.

Dr Elias Hanna, a heart surgeon, established this winery in 1985. He owns almost 300 acres of vineyards, both in Alexander Valley and elsewhere in Sonoma. Unfortunately the water table is high in some of the estate vineyards, and this has made it difficult to control the vigour of the vines. There have been a number of winemakers during the winery's brief existence, and the latest is Jon Engelskirger. This no doubt helps explain the lack of consistent style. In the early 1990s Stephen Sullivan, who had previously been cellarmaster at Kenwood, focused on Sauvignon Blanc, much of it fermented in new *barriques*. The wines were almost all blends, drawing on fruit from different parts of Sonoma, as well as from estate-grown grapes. Chardonnay tends to come from Carneros and Russian River, and Cabernet and Merlot from Alexander Valley.

Hanzell

18496 Lomita Ave., Sonoma, CA 95476. Tel: 996 3860. Fax: 996 3862. Production: 3,000 cases.

James Zellerbach, paper magnate and ambassador to Italy, was fascinated by the wines of Burgundy and wished to produce wines modelled on the Burgundian classics. Since 1952 he had been planting terraced vineyards on his estate, and in 1957 his winery came into operation. He hired Brad Webb as winemaker, and it was he who explored such techniques as malolactic fermentation and barrel ageing, all of which were novelties in California as far as Chardonnay was concerned. He also experimented with punching down the cap while Pinot Noir was macerating. The wines soon acquired an enthusiastic following. However, in 1963 Zellerbach died. His widow Hana sold off the stock and, for a price, Barney Rhodes acquired the young wines still in barrels, which were bottled by Joe Heitz and sold. No wine was produced at all for two years. Then in 1965 Hana Zellerbach sold the 31-acre estate to Douglas and Mary Day, and in 1976 it was sold again to Barbara de Brye, the Australian-born wife of a Parisian banker. She died in 1991.

The wine continues to be made by Robert Sessions, who has been a long-term fixture at Hanzell. Only slight modifications have been made in the winemaking style. Just 10 per cent of the Chardonnay must is barrel-fermented, and only 25 per cent goes through malolactic fermentation. The Pinot Noir is made in a distinctly meaty yet herbaceous style that is out of step with the best Pinots from Russian River Valley and elsewhere.

Although I have drunk a few older vintages of Hanzell wines (including a remarkable 1981 Cabernet Sauvignon) which certainly gave me pleasure, the estate is no longer in the forefront of Sonoma producers of red wines, although the citrussy Chardonnay remains excellent.

Hartford Court

8075 Martinelli Rd., Forestville, CA 95436. Tel: 887 1532. Production: 1,500 cases.

The former Domaine Laurier, which went bankrupt in 1990, has been bought by Kendall-Jackson as a winery where some of their leading Sonoma wines will be produced. Thus the La Crema range is made here, as well as Hartford Court bottlings, which up till now have focused on high-priced old-vine Zinfandel and Russian River Pinot Noir from single vineyards. The winemaker is Dan Goldfield.

Haywood

In 1974 Peter Haywood began planting 90 acres of vineyards, which produced some good white wines after the winery was built in 1980. In 1991 the estate was sold to Racke, the owners of Buena Vista, and the Haywood winery buildings were leased to Ravenswood. The Haywood wines, which were of indifferent quality during the 1980s, are now made at Buena Vista and are released under the California appellation.

Hop Kiln

6050 Westside Rd., Healdsburg, CA 95448. Tel: 433 6491. Fax: 433 8162. Production: 9,000 cases.

Psychiatrist Dr Martin Griffin established this winery, in a handsome old stone building in the heart of Russian River Valley, in 1975. The estate vineyards now cover 240 acres. The range of wines on offer is eclectic, and includes a sweetish Riesling, Valdiguié, a Reserve Zinfandel called Primitivo, a sparkling Riesling called Verveux, and Marty Griffin's Big Red, a blend of Petite Sirah, Valdiguié, Zinfandel and other varieties. His Primitivo is in fact a Zinfandel made from vines at least 50 years old. The bizarrely named A Thousand Flowers is a blend of mostly Gewürztraminer and a little Riesling. Quality is better than one might expect.

Johnson's Alexander Valley

8333 Highway 128, Healdsburg, CA 95448. Tel: 433 2319. Production: 8,000 cases.

The Johnson family originally planted vines here in 1952, but replanted all 435 acres in the mid-1960s. The winery was only built in 1975. The wines, which include Cabernet Sauvignon, Chardonnay, Zinfandel, and White Zinfandel, are run of the mill and made in a somewhat rustic style.

Jordan

1474 Alexander Valley Rd., Healdsburg, CA 95448. Tel: 431 5250. Fax: 433 0255. Production: 80,000 cases.

Tom Jordan is a reclusive man, a geologist and oilman who came here in 1972 and bought a 1,000-acre estate. It is planted with 275 acres of vineyards – Chardonnay, Cabernet Sauvignon, Merlot, and Cabernet Franc – so that all the wines are made from estate-grown fruit. In 1986 Rob Davis was hired as winemaker and is still there, which does help ensure a consistency of style. André Tchelitscheff was the consultant in the early days, helping Jordan to find a suitable property for his ambitions; the first vintage was 1976. Some new vineyards were added in the early 1990s; these were in Russian River Valley, whereas all the other vineyards were on fairly vigorous sites in Alexander Valley.

It is a characteristic of Jordan's Cabernet Sauvignon that the wines are bottle-aged for 2 years before release. This is to ensure that they are drinkable on release. The Cabernet used to be aged in a good deal of American as well as French oak. The American-oak component has diminished over the years, however.

The style of the Chardonnay, first made in 1982, has changed over the years. The 1992 underwent partial malolactic fermentation and was aged for 5 months in *barriques* on the fine lees, then for a further 5 months in oak uprights. The following year 40 per cent of the grapes came from the new Russian River vineyard.

In the mid-1980s Jordan decided to produce a sparkling wine, and built a winery for that purpose in Russian River. The initial release was the 1987, of which 12,000 cases were produced. The sparkling wine, known simply as J, has its own winemaker, Oded Shakked. The wine is a more or less equal blend of Chardonnay and Pinot Noir and it is aged for 3 years on the yeast. In 1996, Jordan, in expansionist mood, bought the vineyards and winery that had been operated by Piper-Sonoma.

It is hard to get excited by the Jordan wines. Part of the problem is that they have been promoted from the outset as something exceptional, as though they were an instant first growth. A great deal of money may have been spent on the enterprise, but the wines themselves are not exceptional. The medium-bodied Cabernet is agreeable but lacks grip and weight, while the Chardonnay simply lacks vigour and distinction. No doubt the growing inclusion of Russian River fruit will give the Chardonnay more shapeliness and edge. J, however, has been attractive and well made from the start.

Korbel
13250 River Rd., Guerneville, CA 85446. Tel: 887 2294. Fax: 869 2981. Production: 2 million cases.

Korbel is California's largest produce of *méthode champenoise* wine. The Korbel brothers from Bohemia planted vineyards in 1881 and made their first sparkling wine in 1896. The winery was bought by Adolf and Paul Heck in 1954. Gary Heck is the current chief executive. Although Korbel own 600 acres, the company also buys grapes from various parts of the state.

The range includes a Blanc de Blancs, a Blanc de Noirs, Brut Rosé, a sweeter Rosé, a vintage wine, and Le Premier Reserve, which is barrel-fermented and wood-aged. Then there are the large-volume wines such as the nonvintage Natural California, California Brut, and, since 1997, a Chardonnay Champagne. Unlikely experiments are under way to produce a red sparkling wine from Cabernet Sauvignon and Merlot – outlandish for California, less so in Australia. Unfortunately in terms of quality, Korbel has been overtaken by the French and Spanish invaders, who seem to be producing wines of much more finesse. Korbel also produces 350,00 cases of brandy in the Central Valley.

Kunde

10155 Sonoma Highway, Kenwood, CA 95452. Tel: 833 5501. Fax: 833 2204. Production: 100,000 cases.

The Kundes are grape farmers. Louis Kunde came to these Sonoma Valley hillsides in 1904 and now the fourth generation is cultivating the land and, in recent years, marketing the wine, which is made by Davis Noyes, who used to work at Ridge. However, these slopes were green with vines decades before Louis Kunde arrived. James Drummond had planted Cabernet vines here, claiming that his cuttings had come from Châteaux Margaux and Lafite.

The estate grows 26 varieties on 740 acres, much of it red volcanic ash soil. There are plans to plant a further 400. There used to be a winery here, but it closed in 1944. The vineyards were expanded further in the 1960s, and a winery was constructed in 1990. Over 5,000 barrels are stored in wine tunnels burrowed into the hillsides. The principal vineyards are called Wildwood, Bell, and Kinneybrook, and within each of them are blocks that are often treated separately, such as the Zinfandel vines that are 114 years old, and the Drummond Cabernet Sauvignon descended from the original cuttings imported from the Médoc. There is also a block certified by UC Davis and planted with a huge collection of clones. About 40 per cent of the fruit is still sold to other wineries.

Although the winery has not been operating for that long, Kunde offer a large range of wines. The Estate Series consists of an attractive Magnolia Lane Sauvignon Blanc which, like that from Iron Horse, is spruced up with a little Viognier as well as Sémillon; single-vineyard Chardonnays from their own estate; Cabernet, Merlot, and the exceptional Old Vines Zinfandel from the Shaw Vineyard. There's an excellent Viognier, tank-fermented and then aged in barrels for 4 months, and a good Syrah. Both Chardonnay and Cabernet are also made in reserve styles, and there's a dry late harvest Zinfandel.

Quality is very high and prices reasonable.

Lake Sonoma

9990 West Dry Creek Rd., Geyserville, CA 95441. Tel: 431 1550. Fax: 431 8356. Production: 3,000 cases.

The estate was founded in 1977, although the wines were made in Contra Costa County until its winery was built in 1990. The principal wines are Zinfandel, Merlot, and Chardonnay, and it has the apparent distinction of being the first winery in California to bottle a varietal Cinsault, which is still produced. The winery belongs to Korbel and the wines are made by Chris Willis.

Lambert Bridge

4085 West Dry Creek Rd., Healdsburg, CA 95448. Tel: 431 9600. Fax: 433 3215. Production: 20,000 cases.

This welcoming winery has a complicated history. The property was bought by Gerald Lambert in 1969, and he planted 119 acres of vines. The winery followed in 1976. The wines were distributed by Seagram and production rapidly expanded. Sales, however, did not, and after a legal wrangle Lambert and Seagram went their separate ways. Production dwindled, and in 1992 the winery closed. In 1993 it was bought by the present owners, the Chambers family. There are now only 5 acres of vineyards attached to the property, so most fruit is purchased. Since 1993 the winemaker has been Julia Iantosca.

I find these wines very attractive, with a delicious Sauvignon Blanc, a good barrel-fermented Chardonnay, using one-third new oak, an oaky but balanced Merlot aged 16 months in *barriques*, and vigorous Dry Creek Cabernet. Only the Crane Creek Cuvée, a blend of two-thirds Cabernet plus Merlot and Cabernet Franc and aged 20 months in *barriques*, was disappointing.

Landmark Vineyards

101 Adobe Canyon Rd. at Highway 12, Kenwood, CA 95452. Tel: 833 0053. Fax: 833 1164. Production: 20,000 cases.

The Mabry family founded Landmark, but the winery was located in Windsor until the move to Kenwood in 1990. In 1989 one of the partners, Damaris Deere Ethridge, bought out the others. She is a direct descendant of John Deere, the tractor magnate, without whose enterprise many California vineyards could not be harvested.

The winemaker is Eric Stern, but since 1993 the estate has retained Helen Turley as a consultant. Most of the grapes are purchased as Landmark owns only 13 acres of its own. Chardonnay is their speciality, and the basic blend, Overlook, comes from various Sonoma sites. It's a forthright wine, vinified in *barriques* with natural yeasts, given full malolactic fermentation, and aged in 25 per cent new oak. The superb, take-no-prisoners Damaris Reserve uses fruit from Alexander Valley and southern Sonoma and is given extended ageing on the lees. There is also a Pinot Noir called Grand Detour. Members of visiting parties with no interest in wine can take a horse-and-cart tour of the vineyards while the rest crowd into the tasting room.

Limerick Lane

1023 Limerick Lane, Healdsburg, CA 95448. Tel: 433 9211. Fax: 433 1652. Production: 3,500 cases.

I expect Ted Markoczy, a Hungarian emigré and the owner of this estate, would admit that its most distinctive feature is the 30-acre Collins Vineyard, planted with dry-farmed Zinfandel grapes between 1910 and 1930. No pesticides are used, yields are a mere 2.5 tons per acre, and when a vine needs to be replaced, it is propagated from the old clone in the vineyard. And best of all, it gives delicious wine. Limerick Lane use open-top fermenters for their Zinfandel, punching down by hand up to six times a day, and age the wine for 12 months in French and American oak, plus 5 per cent Hungarian oak – no doubt a forgivable reflection of homesickness. The wine is neither fined nor filtered. Without doubt this is one of my favourite Sonoma Zins.

But there is another reason to call at Limerick Lane. Markoczy has planted 3 acres of his country's noblest variety, Furmint, and now produces a wine called Cuvée Blanc de Blancs, which is a blend of Furmint and Hárslevelű. This is barrel-fermented, aged in *barriques*, and unfiltered. It's rich, assertive, full-bodied, and no doubt impossible to sell even at the knockdown price of $11. Markoczy plans to make a Tokaj-style wine in the future, which should be worth keeping an eye on.

Lyeth

24625 Chianti Rd., Geyserville, CA 95441. Tel: 857 3562. Production: 35,000 cases.

Grape-farmer Munro Lyeth (pronounced Leeth) bought this property in 1972 and built a winery in 1982. All he produced were Bordeaux-style blends, red and white. Lyeth died in 1988, and the Vintech company bought the winery, managing to sell off the vineyards to Gallo before declaring bankruptcy. Silver Oak, which has made Alexander Valley Cabernet for years, bought the winery to avoid transporting its grapes to its main winery in Napa. In 1992 the property was acquired by the French *négociant* house of Boisset.

Lynmar

PO Box 742, Sebastopol, CA 95473. Tel: 829 3374. Fax: 829 0902. Production: 5,000 cases.

Lynn and Mara Fritz have owned the Quail Hill Ranch in Russian River Valley since 1982. In 1990 they decided to produce wines as well as grow grapes, and their first releases, of Chardonnay and Pinot Noir, were the 1994 vintage. All fruit is estate-grown in the 50-acre vineyards. Daniel Moore is the winemaker.

Lytton Springs
650 Lytton Springs Rd., Healdsburg, CA 95448. Tel: 433 7721. Fax: 433 7751.

This splendid 150-acre vineyard conserves 50 acres of Zinfandel which were planted in the early 1900s. From 1972 the grapes were sold to Ridge. A winery was founded here by Dick Sherwin and his partners in 1977, who were able to acquire the vineyard because the old lady who owned it thought its yields were far too low. The winemaker was Walt Walters. They made some big gutsy Zinfandels, some of which were distinctly weird, but in 1991 they realized that Paul Draper could make better Zinfandels than they could, and they sold the property to Ridge. The winery is now a tasting room.

McCray Ridge
Tel: 433 2932. Production: 650 cases.

Stan Simpson bought 4 acres of Napa Gamay in a remote vineyard 1,700 feet up in the western reaches of Dry Creek. He gradually replaced the vines with Merlot, which he sold to Ravenswood and Wellington until deciding to produce his own Merlot in 1995. Simpson has also planted 6 acres of Cabernet Sauvignon. That vintage was not a success but the 1996 was well received. Phyllis Zouzounis of Mazzocco is the consultant winemaker.

Marcassin
Tel: 258 3608. Production: 1,200 cases.

The ubiquitous super-consultant Helen Turley also has her own label, often used to produce minute quantities of wine from parcels of fruit that she finds of particular interest or quality. She has no winery of her own, but uses the facilities at Martinelli. After leaving Peter Michael in 1990 she found she had difficulty buying grapes of high quality and managed to produce only 200 cases of wine. It was only when the wines were released some two years later to huge acclaim from Robert Parker that she became sought after as a consultant to some of California's most prestigious estates. She is particularly keen on Chardonnay and Pinot Noir from Hudson Vineyard in Carneros and from Lorenzo Vineyard in the Sonoma Coast, where she also owns 10 acres of vineyards at 1,200 feet. These are being planted to her own specifications, with dense spacing, up to 4,000 vines per acre. I have never tasted the wines but they are reputed to be in the ultra-rich style for which she is celebrated. Readers keen to obtain a bottle should join the 5,000 other names on the waiting list.

Marietta Cellars
22295 Chianti Rd., Geyserville, CA 95441. Tel: 433 2747. Production: 25,000 cases.

Chris Bilbro founded this property in 1980, making his wines from 120 acres of Zinfandel, Syrah, and Cabernet Sauvignon. These are old-fashioned, inky, burly wines. The best value is Old Vine Red, but none of the wines is expensive. There is also an Angeli Cuvée, which blends Zinfandel and Petite Sirah, and it benefits from some bottle age. These are not wines for the faint-hearted.

Martinelli
3360 River Rd., Windsor, CA 95492. Tel: 525 0570. Production: 4,000 cases.
The Martinelli family has been growing grapes and apples here since the 1960s. There was a winery here until 1949, when it shut down. Wine-making was resumed in 1987 when Daniel Moore offered to make the wines for Steve Martinelli in exchange for making his own Z. Moore wines at the facility. But by 1993 Moore found himself over-stretched, and Helen Turley became the consultant winemaker. On her advice, part of the 150-acre vineyard was replanted to closer spacing, and she eliminated filtration and most fining. One of Martinelli's best known wines is the Jackass Zinfandel from a 4-acre vineyard; a special bottling of even older vines from this vineyard is labelled Jackass Hill. There are also small lots of exceptional off-dry Gewürztraminer, Sonoma Coast Chardonnay, Estate Pinot Noir, and other wines. I didn't care for the overblown Charles Ranch Chardonnay I once drank.

Martini & Prati
2191 Laguna Rd., Santa Rosa, CA 95401. Tel: 575 8064. Fax: 829 8662. Production: 100,000 cases.

If anyone wants to see what an old-style Italian winery in Sonoma looks like, then this is the place to come. The winery was founded in 1881 and was bought by Rafaeli Martini at the turn of the century. In 1937 Elmo Martini was running the winery, which he sold to Hiram Walker in 1943. Seven years later it was bought back by Elmo Martini and Enrico Prati; the property is now run by Elmo's sons Tom and Jim and by Pete Prati. In 1995 the family came to an arrangement with the Associated Vintage Group to market the wines, and a new winemaker, Dan Kopache, was installed.

A cheerful deli attached to the winery brings in the tourists, who will also find some interesting wines here. This must be one of the last places in California where you can still buy 3-litre jugs of unfined and unfiltered Zinfandel. The wines are aged in century-old redwood tanks. This is not a place to come for sophisticated wines. Both the Barbera and Sangiovese are distinctly thin, and their bottled Zinfandel comes mostly from Paso Robles rather than from local fruit. Vino Grigio is made from Grey Riesling, and there are a few Muscats on offer. Not great wines by any means, but the winery transmits echoes of an old tradition.

Mazzocco Vineyards
1400 Lytton Springs Rd., Healdsburg, CA 95448. Tel: 433 9035. Fax: 431 2369. Production: 17,000 cases.

Dr Thomas Mazzocco, an eye surgeon, founded this estate in 1984, and his first release was a 1985 Chardonnay. His vineyards are fairly dispersed: 13.5 acres near the winery, 10 acres of Chardonnay in Dry Creek, 18 of Chardonnay in Alexander Valley. In addition he buys in fruit, often from Carneros. In 1990 Mazzocco sold the winery to Vintech, which also owned Lyeth and Jekel, but a short while later Vintech was in deep trouble and Mazzocco bought it back. Phyllis Zouzounis is the winemaker.

The wines are hit and miss. The barrel-fermented Chardonnay, which is aged in 30 per cent new *barriques*, is quite stylish but not exactly concentrated. The 1994 Merlot tasted slightly baked and dry, and the 1993 Cabernet Sauvignon, which had spent 26 months in *barriques*, was better balanced. The 1995 Sonoma County Zinfandel was underpowered and lacking in fruit. The Alexander Valley Old Vines Zinfandel is better, but quantities are very limited. The best wine is Matrix, a Bordeaux blend first made in 1992: 70 per cent Cabernet Sauvignon, plus Malbec, Merlot, and Petit Verdot, and aged for as long as the Cabernet. The result is a concentrated, oaky, and dense wine of considerable power.

Meeker Vineyard
9711 West Dry Creek Rd., Healdsburg, CA 95448. Tel: 431 2148. Fax: 431 2549. Production: 6,000 cases.

From their 115 acres of Chardonnay, Cabernet Sauvignon, and Zinfandel, planted on steep hillsides, Charles and Molly Meeker produce small quantities of estate-grown wines. The Zinfandel has the best reputation.

Melim
15001 Chalk Hill Rd., Healdsburg, CA 95448. Tel: 433 4774. Fax: 431 2314. Production: 10,000 cases.

Cliff Melim has been growing grapes since the 1970s on his 85 acres in Chalk Hill planted with Chardonnay, Cabernet Sauvignon, Merlot, and Cabernet Franc. He began making wines with the 1986 vintage, focusing on Chardonnay and Cabernet Sauvignon.

Merry Vintners

3339 Hartman Rd., Santa Rosa, CA 95401. Tel: 526 4441. Fax: 527 9459.

Meredith 'Merry' Edwards is a highly regarded winemaker who once worked at Matanzas Creek. In 1984 she started up her own winery, using purchased grapes. I was not that keen on the Chardonnays I tasted. Edwards ceased production in 1989 and in 1996 sold the property to DeLoach. However she has recently bought 26 acres in Sebastopol, where she plans to plant Pinot Noir.

Michel-Schlumberger

4155 Wine Creek Rd., Healdsburg, CA 95448. Tel: 433 7427. Fax: 433 0444. Production: 25,000 cases.

This estate, planted from 1979 onwards by a Swiss banker called Jean-Jacques Michel, was bought in 1993 by Jacques Schlumberger. Early vintages of the wine, beginning in 1984, were made at Jordan until the vastly expensive winery was completed in 1986. Michel bought the best advice money could buy: André Tchelitscheff. The estate now consists of 51 acres: 25 Chardonnay, 14 Cabernet Sauvignon, 8 Merlot, and 4 Cabernet Franc. There seems to have been some improvement in quality, especially of the Cabernet, since Schlumberger took over, but the Michel-Schlumberger wines have never been greeted with excitement. Fred Payne is the winemaker.

Mill Creek

1401 Westside Rd., Healdsburg, CA 95448. Tel: 433 5098. Fax: 431 1714. Production: 15,000 cases.

This estate has been around for a long time. Bill and Yvonne Kreck first planted Cabernet vines here in 1965, and the winery followed in 1976. Today the vineyards consist of 75 acres. Their good fortune is to have the trademark to the term 'blush wine', a term coined by American wine writer Jerry Mead after he tasted a Mill Creek Cabernet Blush. The winery produces a broad range of varietals, and much of the production is sold at the tasting room. I was resolutely unimpressed by the Cabernet Sauvignon.

J. W. Morris

101 Grant Ave., Healdsburg, CA 95448. Tel: 431 7015. Production: 70,000 cases.

This winery, originally owned by Jim Olsen, is best known for its 'ports', but also began producing table wines in the late 1970s. The property was bought by Ken Toth in 1983. About 1,000 cases of 'port' are still made each year, as well as estate-grown Chardonnay, Sauvignon Blanc, Cabernet

Sauvignon, Zinfandel and Petite Sirah from Toth's Black Mountain vineyard. Prices are very reasonable.

Robert Mueller Cellars
120 Foss Creek Circle, Healdsburg, CA 95448. Tel: 431 1353. Fax: 431 8365. Production: 2,000 cases.

Mueller's first vintage was 1991, and the range includes Chardonnay from the Alexander and Russian River valleys. Quality is high.

Murphy-Goode
4001 Highway 128, Geyserville, CA 95441. Tel: 431 7644. Fax: 431 8640. Production: 65,000 cases.

Dale Goode and Tim Murphy have been grape farmers since the 1960s, and formed a partnership in 1980 as a means of absorbing excess grape production by turning them into wine themselves. Merry Edwards was one of the early winemakers, and since 1987 the winemaker has been Christina Benz. Naturally Murphy-Goode is able to draw on its substantial vineyards for most of its supply. There are 75 acres of Sauvignon Blanc on sandy loam soil; 50 acres of Chardonnay and 25 of Pinot Blanc; 29 acres of Cabernet and 9 of Merlot. The wines are made in a broad gentle style, typical of Alexander Valley, although some wines, such as the Zinfandel, draw on grapes from other regions, in this case Dry Creek.

Although the wines are very well made, it is quite clear that yields are often too high, as I sense a distinct dilution in many of the wines. The Merlot is excellent, and so too is the range of three Fumé Blancs. The regular bottling is fermented in stainless steel and aged briefly in oak barrels – a simple but satisfying wine. The Reserve Fumé is barrel-fermented and aged in 40 per cent new oak for 9 months; one-third of the wine goes through malolactic. The third wine, unhelpfully named Fumé II: The Deuce, is similar, but goes through full malolactic and is aged only in new French oak. The Deuce has a lovely texture and is one of my favourite California Sauvignons.

Nelson Estate Vineyards
7044 Bennett Valley Rd., Santa Rosa, CA 95404. Tel/fax: 206 241 WINE. Production: 4,000 cases.

David and Holly Nelson have been growing grapes since 1977 on 20 acres planted with Bordeaux varietals. As winemakers they show an unusual degree of specialization, producing mostly Cabernet Franc in a rather tart style.

Optima Wine Cellars

PO Box 1691, Healdsburg, CA 95448. Tel: 431 8222. Fax: 431 7828. Production: 3,000 cases.

Founded in 1984, this small winery is owned by Mike Duffy and Greg Smith, and Duffy makes the wines. These are a barrel-fermented Carneros Chardonnay and an Alexander Valley Cabernet Sauvignon.

Paradise Ridge

4545 Thomas Lake Harris, Fountain Grove, Santa Rosa, CA 95403. Tel: 528 9463. Fax: 528 9481. Production: 500 cases.

Walter Byck grows 18 acres of Chardonnay and Sauvignon Blanc just northeast of Santa Rosa. In 1994 he constructed his winery and began releasing bottlings from the varieties he grows.

Pedroncelli

1220 Canyon Rd., Geyserville, CA 95441. Tel: 857 3531. Fax: 857 3812. Production: 130,000 cases.

There was a winery in this spot in 1905, the former Canata Winery. In 1927 it was bought by John Pedroncelli, and the estate remains in the hands of his descendants, and John A. Pedroncelli is the current winemaker. Until the 1960s Pedroncelli produced jug and bulk wines, but launched varietal bottlings from 1965 onwards. A premium range called Special Vineyard Collection was launched in 1995.

Pedroncelli own 135 acres in Dry Creek, but this is not enough to fulfil their needs. They buy some Chardonnay and Pinot Noir from the Frank Johnson Vineyard. Most of the wines are aged in American oak, but some of the reds, such as Cabernet and Pinot Noir, are aged in a mixture of American and French barrels.

The Zinfandels are probably Pedroncelli's best wines, and there are a number of bottlings. There is a Dry Creek version, a Mother Clone bottling from vines planted in 1905 and 1915, and a bottling from the Pedroni-Bushell Vineyard.

There are also two proprietary blends: Primavera Mista blends Chardonnay, Chenin Blanc, and Sauvignon Blanc; Primo Misto blends Zinfandel, Cabernet Sauvignon, and Napa Gamay. Among the white wines, the slightly grassy Sauvignon Blanc is very good value.

Pedroncelli wines are sound, honestly made, with no frills, and they are fairly priced.

Pellegrini

4055 West Olivet Rd., Santa Rosa, CA 95401. Tel: 415 761 2811. Fax: 415 589 7132. Production: 25,000 cases.

Pellegrini obtain Chardonnay and Pinot Noir from their Olivet Lane vineyard in Russian River Valley, and Cabernet and Merlot from Cloverdale Ranch in Alexander Valley. They also produce limited quantities from Mediterranean varieties, and regional blends are released under the Côtes de Sonoma label. The Carignane can be fresh and spicy. Merry Edwards is the consultant winemaker.

Peterson

1040 Lytton Springs Rd., Healdsburg, CA 05448. Tel: 431 1112. Fax: 431 1064 Production: 10,000 cases.

Fred Peterson owns vineyards in Dry Creek Valley and buys fruit from 530 acres of Sonoma vineyards that belong to former financier William Hambrecht. The wines produced are almost entirely red, and include Cabernet Sauvignon, Zinfandel, Barbera, and a Rhône blend. The 1994 Dry Creek Zinfandel was plump and assertive.

(The winery was better known under its earlier guise of Belvedere, which was founded in 1979 by Peter Friedman before being bought out by Hambrecht, who had been Friedman's partner.)

Pezzi King

3805 Lambert Bridge Rd., Healdsburg, CA 95448. Tel: 431 9388. Fax: 431 9389. Production: 35,000 cases.

Jim and Jane Rowe have been buying up defunct properties: first the former William Wheeler winery in 1993, and then the Robert Stemmler winery, which is now the Pezzi King tasting room. They own 48 acres of red Bordeaux grapes and Zinfandel, planted high in the hills on terraced vineyards, and purchase Chardonnay.

Preston

9282 West Dry Creek Rd., Healdsburg, CA 95448. Tel: 433 3372. Fax: 433 5307. Production: 30,000 cases.

Lou Preston founded this estate in 1973 and the first wines were made in 1975. The 125 acres of vineyards include some 90-year-old Zinfandel and a large assortment of Mediterranean varieties. Not all of them have prospered on the gravelly soil, as some parcels have a high clay content; so there has been some replanting in recent years. Since 1989 organic farming practices have been adopted.

Kevin Hamel has been making the wines here since 1989. Preston has always made attractive Sauvignon Blanc and continues to do so. It used to come in two styles. Cuvée de Fumé was a grassy blend of 75 per cent Sauvignon Blanc with Sémillon and Chenin Blanc. The richer, riper Estate Reserve is 85 per cent Sauvignon, the remainder being Sémillon. After

1990 Hamel dropped the Reserve and has improved the overall quality of the Cuvée.

Syrah was planted here in 1978. The 1995 was a delicious wine with masses of upfront fruit; it was aged for 20 months in *barriques* and bottled unfiltered. The Barbera is one of the best I have tasted from California: lively and vivacious, as Barbera should be. Pity about the price, though. The Viognier is a lovely wine, but the Marsanne is rather dull.

Zinfandel is as good as one expects it to be in Dry Creek. In some years, they also release an Estate Reserve Zinfandel.

Faux is a blend of more or less equal amounts of Carignane, Mourvèdre, Syrah, Cinsault, and Grenache, but it's a wine that needs more concentration; while Petit Faux is a rosé from Cinsault, Mourvèdre, and Grenache.

Not everything that Preston produce succeeds, but at least it tries to divert its customers with a wide range of flavours and styles.

Quivira

4900 West Dry Creek Rd., Healdsburg., CA 95448. Tel: 431 8333. Fax: 431 1664. Production: 20,000 cases.

Industrialist Henry Wendt founded this estate in 1981, although some Zinfandel had already been planted in 1963. There are now 90 acres under vine, farmed without herbicides and hand-picked. The winery was constructed in 1987. The first winemaker was Doug Nalle, and since 1990 Grady Wann, equipped with a doctorate in organic chemistry, has been looking after the winery.

The range includes a pleasant Sauvignon, half of which is barrel-fermented, with a brief ageing in oak. Probably the best red is the delicious Zinfandel, which is aged in *barriques* for 12 months. Quivira no longer produces Cabernet, and in 1989 introduced a wine called Cabernet Cuvée, a roughly equal blend of Cabernet Sauvignon, Merlot, and Cabernet Franc. This stylish, blackcurranty wine spends 20 months in *barriques*. Another blend is the Dry Creek Cuvée, half of which is Grenache, and the rest Mourvedre, Syrah, and Zinfandel; a wine to be drunk young.

Rabbit Ridge

291 Westside Rd., Healdsburg, CA 95448. Tel: 431 7128. Production: 50,000 cases.

Erich Russell, the former winemaker at Belvedere, founded his own estate in 1985 and the wines started appearing from 1989 onwards. Russell has planted thirty grape varieties on 40 acres, but also buys in a good deal of fruit, especially for his second label, Meadow Glen. Chardonnay accounts for most of the production, but, not surprisingly, Zinfandel is the wine for which Rabbit Ridge is best known, though there are numerous other wines, including Nebbiolo, Sangiovese, and Barbera. Russell also has a few blends to offer. Allure combines Syrah, Mourvèdre, Carignane, Grenache and Cinsault; while Montepiano blends Sangiovese, Barbera, Lambrusco, and Cabernet Franc, which sounds like a mopping-up operation in the vineyard. Both blends have the merit of being inexpensive. Russell pulls out all the stops for his limited-production Grande Reserve Cabernet from Russian River Valley.

Rutz Cellars
3637 Frei Rd., Sebastopol, CA 95473. Tel: 823 0373. Fax: 823 4654.

This Russian River Valley winery has been attracting some attention with its Chardonnay and Pinot Noir, often from single-vineyard sites such as Dutton Ranch but also bought in from vineyards in Monterey or Mendocino. I have found the Russian River Valley bottlings disappointing, but some of the single-vineyards versions are better structured. Quality is inconsistent.

St Francis
8450 Sonoma Highway, Kenwood, CA 95442. Tel: 833 4666. Fax: 833 6534. Production: 170,000 cases.

Vineyards were planted here from 1971 by Joseph Martin and Lloyd Canton, and the winery was built in 1979. St Francis is now owned by the large wine company Kobrand, although Joseph Martin is still involved. The estate has built up a fine reputation for Merlot; indeed, the Gewürztraminer, Riesling, and Pinot Noir grapes all planted here in the 1970s have been budded over to Merlot. In 1996 St Francis bought the Nun's Canyon Vineyard, which is planted with 115 acres of vines on well drained rocky soils.

The winemaker since 1983 has been Tom Mackey, and the wines are well made but middle-of-the-road, although the Reserve bottlings can be exceptional. The Chardonnay is barrel-fermented and aged 6 months in oak. It offers very good value, as does the Reserve, made from older estate-grown vines and barrel-fermented in new *barriques*. There are two Zinfandels: an Old Vine bottling, and a Reserve from the Pagani Vineyard. Both are aged in American oak and bottled unfiltered.

Substantial quantities of Merlot are produced. It is mostly aged in American oak. The Reserve, first made in 1984, comes from a specific block in the estate vineyards that produces small berries and is usually picked later. Mackey attributes the fine quality of their Merlot to maritime influence combined with the fact that the vines are planted on fairly heavy alluvial soils that suit the variety. Both are fine wines, but no longer the bargains they used to be before Merlot became so sought after.

Sausal

7370 Highway 128, Healdsburg, CA 95448. Tel: 433 2285. Fax: 433 5136. Production: 10,000 cases.

The Demostene family began planting 125 acres of vines here in Alexander Valley in 1955, although the grapes were used for bulk-wine production. In 1973 David Demostene became the winemaker. Yields here on these dry-farmed benchlands are exceptionally low, and the Zinfandel is often of outstanding quality. The best wines are aged longer than usual and released under the Private Reserve label. The winery also makes White Zinfandel, Chardonnay, and a blend of Chardonnay and French Colombard. At its best the Zinfandel is bold and rich, but I have had disappointing bottles too.

Scherrer

Tel: 823 8980. Production: 1,000 cases.

Like many other top Sonoma growers, Fred Scherrer, who sells grapes to Greenwood Ridge and others, has begun to bottle small quantities of wine, in his case old-vine Zinfandel, from his own vineyard in Alexander Valley.

Sebastiani

389 Fourth St. East, Sonoma, CA 94576. Tel: 938 5532. Fax: 996 3349. Production: 6 million cases.

Samuele Sebastiani from Italy founded this winery in 1904. At first only bulk wines were produced, but after Repeal the winery bottled some of its wines. Samuele died in 1944, but his son Gus had been running the business since 1937. In the 1970s Gus introduced vintage-dated varietal wines, and had particular success with Barbera, Zinfandel, and a wine made in a Beaujolais Nouveau style. Gus also boosted production, but by the time of his death in 1980 quality had begun to slip as Sebastiani failed to keep up with more progressive wineries.

Gus's son Sam tried to improve the quality, but this also entailed reducing volume. Eventually he fell out with his brother Don. So Sam left the family business in 1986 and started Viansa two years later. Although Sam left because he felt his efforts were being thwarted, Don maintained the improvements Sam had initiated and certainly improved the packaging. The winery produces an enormous variety of wines: the inexpensive Oakbrook and Vendanges ranges, the Augustus Sebastiani Proprietor's Wines, the Country Wines, the Sonoma Series, and the Sonoma Cask range. The cheaper wines are now made at their winery in Woodbridge. In 1998 it was announced that some of the cheaper lines, such as Vendange and Talus, would be renamed Turner Road.

Most of the best wines are bottled under the Sonoma Cask range. This includes a good Chardonnay from Carneros and Russian River Valley fruit. There is also a Dutton Ranch Chardonnay. Chardonnay and Merlot are mostly aged in French oak, and other wines are aged in American wood. The Cabernet Sauvignon sometimes includes Cabernet Franc and Mourvèdre, and there is a special bottling called Cherryblock. In addition to Merlot and Syrah from Dry Creek Valley, there is a traditional Barbera and a Mourvèdre derived from the old vines in Contra Costa County. Quality at the higher end of the range is sound rather than exciting, but prices are reasonably low.

Sebastopol Vineyards
8757 Green Valley Rd., Sebastopol, CA 95472. Tel: 829 9463. Fax: 829 5368. Production: 3,000 cases.

Since 1995 the Dutton family of Dutton Ranch vineyards, who mostly sell their grapes to other wineries, have been producing some Chardonnay and Pinot Noir of their own.

Seghesio
14730 Grove St., Healdsburg, CA 95448. Tel: 433 3579. Fax: 433 0545. Production: 150,000 cases.

Italian Edoardo Seghesio founded the winery in 1902, but it only produced bulk wines sold to other wineries, including Gallo. After Gallo acquired the Frei winery, it had no further use for Seghesio wines, so in 1982 the family began marketing its own wines. The winemaker is Ted Seghesio.

The Seghesios own 400 acres of vineyards in Alexander Valley, Dry Creek, and Russian River Valley. Their principal claim to fame is that they have been growing Sangiovese since 1910, and it has mostly been used in a field blend called Chianti Station. In 1992 Seghesio introduced a varietal Sangiovese. Seghesio also make Zinfandel, and the Old Vines Reserve can be a rich chunky wine. I have not been impressed by the Pinot Noir. There is a blend called Omaggio, which consists of Cabernet, Merlot, Sangiovese, and Barbera. They have recently released an Arneis.

Simi
16275 Healdsburg Ave., Healdsburg, CA 95448. Tel: 433 6981. Fax: 433 6253. Production: 150,000 cases.

On the outskirts of Healdsburg stands a stone building by the roadside. Although this is the core of the Simi winery and dates from 1890, it was by no means the original base for Simi. Giuseppe and Pietro Simi began making wine in San Francisco in 1876 and then bought acreage near Healdsburg. The first winery was opened in 1881, but they moved to the present site nine years later. The brothers died in 1904, and Giuseppe's

14-year-old daughter Isabelle took over the company, which she continued to run until 1970. In 1908 she married banker Fred Haigh, who helped her keep the winery going through Prohibition, when they were able to build up large stocks of wine. Haigh died in 1954 and in 1970 Isabelle sold Simi, by then a bulk winery, to a grower called Russell Green. It was then bought by a British brewery, and then by an American wine importer, until finally acquired in 1981 by the French Moet & Hennessy group LVMH. (At time of writing the winery is for sale.)

In the early 1970s Simi employed Mary Ann Graf, one of the first women winemakers, and she was succeeded in 1979 by Zelma Long, who transformed the winery into the prestigious producer it remains to this day. Zelma Long is now president of Simi, and Nick Goldschmidt from New Zealand is the principal winemaker. Michel Rolland acts as a consultant.

Simi has substantial vineyard holdings: 175 acres owned and leased in Alexander Valley, and 240 acres acquired in 1990 in Russian River and planted with Chardonnay. But most of the grapes have to be purchased. Some of the fruit for the Chardonnay Reserves actually came from Mendocino, and the Chalk Hill vineyards supplemented their own grapes as the source for their Sauvignon Blanc.

The Sauvignon is mostly fermented in stainless steel, and aged in older *barriques* for about 4 months. In 1993 a wine called Sendal was launched, blending Sauvignon and Sémillon. This is a richer style than the Sauvignon, as it is almost all barrel-fermented and aged in 40 per cent new *barriques*.

Chardonnay usually contains fruit from Russian River and Carneros, and is 60 per cent barrel-fermented, and then aged for 6 months in *barriques*. The Reserve is a much more serious wine, selected from specific blocks in the vineyards, barrel-fermented in almost all new oak, and aged for 8 months on the fine lees. Chardonnay is Simi's flagship wine, representing half their production.

The full-flavoured Cabernet Sauvignon comes from Alexander Valley and is aged for 12 months in 20 per cent new oak. Goldschmidt has introduced the Antipodean technique of completing the fermentation in barrel. The Reserve is aged in new oak for 15 months. I recall encounters with first-rate Reserves from 1974 onwards, and more recently, from 1984, 1990, and 1991, and 1994. Pinot Noir was introduced only to the range in 1994, and Simi is doing well with a wine called Altaire, a nondescript blend of Pinot Noir, Pinot Meunier, and Cabernet Franc. By the mid-1990s the estate was also considering producing some Italian varietals.

Sonoma-Cutrer

4401 Slusser Rd., Windsor, CA 95492. Tel: 528 1181. Fax: 528 1561. Production: 80,000 cases.

Backed by a team of investors, Brice Cutrer Jones founded the estate in 1973, and intended to grow Pinot Noir rather than Chardonnay. But they had difficulty finding the vines they needed, so half the area was planted with Chardonnay. There are now 400 acres planted in Russian River, as well as some acreage in Carneros; an additional 350 acres are also being developed. In 1999 the property was put on the market and was purchased by Brown Forman for $125 million.

Sonoma-Cutrer created quite a sensation in the 1980s with its single-vineyard bottlings. The main Chardonnay was called Russian River Ranches and came from various vineyards covering 210 acres within that region; despite the large volume of production, it was usually a delicious and stylish wine. In addition there were the vineyards of Les Pierres (115 acres) and Cutrer Vineyard (100 acres), Les Pierres being the more mineral of the two.

No short cuts are taken in the winemaking. The grapes are hand-sorted on arrival at the winery, and whole-cluster pressed. From Les Pierres up to fifteen lots are picked and fermented separately. The must is barrel-fermented in underground cellars and aged on the fine lees for about 6 months, although in recent years the style has been changing as Adams has lengthened the ageing period and introduced more malolactic fermentation. In the 1980s the wines were regarded as among the finest Chardonnays to emerge from California, although I was less excited than most. As production has expanded, quality has slipped a notch or two.

Stonestreet
4611 Thomas Rd., Healdsburg, CA 95448. Tel: 433 9463. Fax: 544 1056. Production: 60,000 cases.

Founded in 1973, this Alexander Valley estate was known as the Stephen Zellerbach Vineyard until its purchase in 1989 by Kendall-Jackson. Steve Test was installed as general manager, and Michael Westrick as winemaker. Janet Pagano took over as general manager in 1998. This is potentially an extremely important estate, as Stonestreet has absorbed the former Gauer Ranch, also bought by Kendall-Jackson and one of the great vineyards of Sonoma. The ranch has been renamed the Alexander Mountain Estate, and by the year 2000 expects to have 1,500 acres in production.

Within the Kendall-Jackson empire, Stonestreet represents the top end of the range. About half its production is Chardonnay, made from fruit purchased from Russian River and Carneros, as Alexander Valley is too hot for Chardonnay. The other wines include Cabernet Sauvignon, Merlot, and a dramatically good Pinot Noir from Russian River fruit. The top wine is a Meritage called Legacy, which is aged in new oak.

Rodney Strong

11455 Old Redwood Highway, Healdsburg, CA 95448. Tel; 431 1533. Fax: 433 0921. Production: 400,000 cases.

Rodney Strong has been involved in numerous projects in Sonoma over the years. In 1962 he took over the Windsor Winery and renamed it Sonoma Vineyards. Production was projected to reach 8 million bottles by 1982, but problems accumulated. New investors were recruited and the name of the winery changed to its present one. Then in 1986 the winery and its 1,200 acres of vineyards were sold to Schenley Industries. Schenley was in turn bought by Guinness, who disposed of the winery and vineyards by selling it in 1989 to Klein Foods, who sold off some of the vineyards.

Rick Sayre has been the winemaker since the mid-1980s. The range of wines is extensive. The Sauvignon Blanc comes from Russian River and has a hint of residual sugar, as do the two Chardonnays, one from Sonoma County, the other from Chalk Hill. The regular Cabernet Sauvignon, the Merlot and the Old Vine Zinfandel are aged mostly in American oak. There are two special bottlings of Cabernet: Alexander's Crown, which is aged 19 months in 45 per cent new oak, and the Reserve, which is aged slightly longer in French oak only. There is also a Pinot Noir from Russian River.

The wines have their admirers, but when I last tasted the complete range at the winery I found them disappointingly light and lacking in personality.

Stuhlmuller Vineyards

Tel: 415 291 0766. Production: 5,000 cases.

Fritz Stuhlmuller runs the 130-acre family vineyards in Alexander Valley and recently decided to start his own winery, which will be located in Healdsburg. His first release was a 1996 Chardonnay and he also plans to produce Cabernet Sauvignon.

Joseph Swan

2916 Laguna Rd., Forestville, CA 95436. Tel: 573 3747. Fax: 575 1605. Production: 4,000 cases.

Joseph Swan was a former pilot who bought land here in Russian River Valley in 1969, planting it principally with Pinot Noir and Chardonnay. Swan was a specialist in *barrique*-aged Zinfandel, and by the time of his death in 1988 had acquired a cult reputation for these wines, and for his Pinot Noir, which received extended macerations but no new oak. Swan's son-in-law Rod Berglund took over the estate and has essentially continued to make wines as Swan would have wanted. There is now a whole range of single-vineyard Zinfandels, often with high alcohol. In

1994 Berglund released a Russian River Valley Mourvedre from old vines. The wines, alas, are very patchy.

F. Teldeschi

3555 Dry Creek Rd., Healdsburg, CA 95448. Tel: 433 6626. Fax: 433 3077. Production: 2,000 cases.

Dan Teldeschi's 80-acre vineyard, founded by his father Frank in 1946, supplied Zinfandel grapes to Swan in the past, and contributed to some of his most celebrated wines. In 1985 Teldeschi decided to produce small quantities of his own wines, and a winery was finally built in 1993. The principal wine is a dense old-vine Zinfandel, unfined and unfiltered. A powerful Moscato Frontignan is also made.

Topolos at Russian River

5700 Gravenstein Highway, Forestville, CA 95436. Tel: 887 1575. Fax: 887 1399. Production: 18,000 cases.

The vineyards here were originally planted in 1964 but changed hands numerous times, before the Topolos family became involved in 1979. They changed the farming into an organic enterprise, and are now engaged in introducing biodynamic practices, which have not caught on in California as much as in France. The estate now consists of 26 acres plus 37 more that are leased. The wines are exceedingly robust. In addition to the Zinfandel assembled from various sources there is an Old Vineyard Reserve that is a blend of Grenache, Mourvèdre, and Alicante Bouschet. In a burst of individualism Topolos bottle a varietal Alicante as well as a Petite Sirah and Black Muscat. These are gutsy wines.

Trentadue

19170 Geyserville Ave., Geyserville, CA 95441. Tel: 433 3104. Fax: 433 5825. Production: 25,000 cases.

The Trentadue family bought this vineyard in 1959 and built a winery ten years later. They own 250 acres in Alexander Valley, planted mostly with Cabernet Sauvignon, Zinfandel, and Nebbiolo. Some of the Zinfandel grapes are sold to Ridge for its famous Geyserville bottling. In 1990 Leo Trentadue renovated the winery, and now produces a wide range of wines – Chardonnay, Zinfandel, Petite Sirah, Merlot, Sangiovese, ports, and a field blend called Old Patch Road – from his tasting room.

Valley of the Moon

777 Madrone Rd., Glen Ellen, CA 95442. Tel: 996 6941. Production: 10,000 cases.

This winery produced jug wines until the mid-1970s. In 1996 Kenwood bought the winery, as well as the 60 acres of vineyards attached to it, and have spent a fortune renovating the property. Retaining the splendid name of the estate, Kenwood plan to produce varieties such as Sangiovese, Pinot Blanc, and Syrah here. In time production will rise to a maximum of 30,000 cases.

Viansa
25200 Highway 121, Sonoma, CA 95476. Tel: 935 4700. Fax: 996 4632. Production: 30,000 cases.

Walk into Viansa and you could be forgiven for thinking you were at an Italian delicatessen that sells wine as a sideline. But although Viansa sells a huge range of Italian foodstuffs and advertises itself as a 'Tuscan-inspired oasis', that would be an unfair impression. After Sam Sebastiani left the eponymous winery following a row with his brother Don, he set up Viansa in 1988.

Since 1998 Sam's son Michael Sebastiani has been making the wines, using grapes from their 25 acres of vineyards, supplemented by purchased fruit from Napa as well as Sonoma. Their own vineyards are planted with Italian varieties such as Nebbiolo, Vernaccia, Primitivo, and Malvasia.

The range of wines is impressive. You can find the usual Chardonnay and Cabernet Sauvignon, but the Italian wines are more worthwhile. More interesting than the Sauvignon Blanc is the delicious barrel-fermented Pinot Grigio. By barrel-fermenting 65 per cent of the must of their Trebbiano, Viansa manage to make this insipid variety smell like Chardonnay, but the oak crushes the flavour.

The reds include Dolcetto, cranberry-flavoured but thin Freisa, Nebbiolo, a light Sangiovese, and a blend called Prindelo, which consists of 65 per cent Zinfandel, 20 per cent Charbono, 15 per cent Primitivo, and 5 per cent Teroldego.

The wines are certainly of mixed quality, but they have zest and originality and are a welcome addition to the southern Sonoma landscape.

Wellington Vineyards
11600 Dunbar Rd., Glen Ellen, CA 95442. Tel: 939 0708. Fax: 939 0378. Production: 7,000 cases.

Peter Wellington's first vintage was 1989 and he has concentrated on old-vine Zinfandel as well as Syrah and Cabernet Sauvignon, and Chardonnay from Russian River Valley. His own vineyard is an old field blend, and there is more acreage on the hillsides, giving 22 in all. The winery was built in 1989. One curiosity here is the occasional estate-grown Criolla, which is blended with Alicante Bouschet.

Mark West
7010 Trenton-Healdsburg Rd., Forestville, CA 95436. Tel: 544 4813. Fax:
836 0147. Production: 25,000 cases.

In 1974 Bob and Joan Ellis planted vineyards here, making their first
wines in 1978. They produced some fine old-vine Zinfandels and some
of Sonoma's best Gewürztraminers, including the occasional late harvest
version. But in the early 1990s the property was bought by the Associated
Vintage Group. Some additional vineyards were planted on an estate that
was by now farmed organically, and there are now 65 acres of Chardonnay, Gewürztraminer, Pinot Noir, and Merlot. The wines consist of
inexpensive varietals, cleanly made.

White Oak Vineyards
7505 Highway 128, Healdsburg, CA 95448. Tel: 433 8429. Fax: 433
8446. Production: 15,000 cases.

Bill Myers owns only a few acres of vineyards, so most of his grapes are
purchased. Since the early 1980s he and his winemaker Paul Brasset
have specialized in Chardonnay, Chenin Blanc, Sauvignon Blanc, Cabernet
Sauvignon, and Zinfandel. Formerly located in downtown Healdsburg,
White Oak moved to a new winery in 1997. The wines are cleanly made
in a rather acidic style.

Wild Hog Vineyards
PO Box 189, Cazadero, CA 95421. Tel: 847 3687. Production: 1,500
cases.

This family-operated Sonoma Coast winery, owned by the Schoenfield
family since 1990, draws on its organic vineyards to produce a small range
of red wines: Pinot Noir, Zinfandel, and Cabernet Sauvignon.

Williams-Selyem
6575 Westside Rd., Healdsburg, CA 95448. Tel: 433 6425. Production:
7,000 cases.

This winery has become as celebrated for its cheerfully artisanal approach
as for the quality of its wines. In the early 1980s Burt Williams, a typesetter,
and Ed Selyem, a wine buyer, formed a partnership and made their first
commercial wine in 1981. From 1983 to 1989 they famously operated
out of a garage on River Road, fermenting the Pinot Noir for which they
were celebrated in milk tanks, shallow enough for the winemakers to
clamber in and tread the grapes in order to punch down the cap during
fermentation. A new winery opened in 1990 close to the Allen Vineyard,
from which they obtained some of their best fruit. In 1998 the partners
sold the business to John Dyson, a grape grower best known for his

contribution to the Smart-Dyson trellising system. To ensure continuity Burt Williams agreed to stay on for two years as winemaker, with an option for remaining for a further three.

The winery specializes in hand-made Pinot Noir. They buy fruit from Rochioli, Allen, Olivet Lane, Hirsch, and Summa vineyards, all in Sonoma, and from Ferrington Vineyard in Anderson Valley. The grapes are hand-sorted, destemmed but not crushed, and fermented with manual punching down (plus feet if necessary); the grapes are pressed in a basket press, and racking is done by gravity flow. Then the wines are aged in heavily toasted barrels for up to 18 months.

In a way Williams-Selyem were latecomers, following in the pioneering footsteps of Davis Bynum and Gary Farrell. The first Allen Vineyard bottling was in 1987. More recently the pair were focusing on the increasingly esteemed Sonoma Coast vineyards such as Summa and Hirsch. Despite its homespun image, Williams-Selyem is an expert producer, skilled at extracting the most fruit and elegance from the grapes.

26

Carneros

Acacia

2750 Las Amigas Rd., Napa, CA 94559. Tel: 226 9991. Fax: 226 1685.
Production: 50,000 cases.

This property was founded in 1979 by Mike Richmond and Jerry
Goldstein, with the aim of producing top-quality Pinot Noir and Chardonnay, and the winery was completed in 1981. Their best-known
vineyard was the Marina Vineyard. Larry Brooks became the winemaker,
subsequently assisted by David Lattin. In 1986 Acacia was bought by the
Chalone group. In the 1980s Acacia had developed a reputation for wines
made from single vineyards in Carneros, but since 1993 Acacia has been
phasing them out, partly because phylloxera has damaged some, in favour
of regular and Reserve bottlings.

As far as Pinot Noir was concerned, Acacia wanted ripe but not raisined
fruit, and often blended underripe and overripe fruit to achieve the balance
of richness and freshness they sought. Most or all of the grapes were
destemmed, then given a cold soak of 2 to 4 days; after fermentation, a
slow malolactic fermentation was encouraged, and the lots were blended
in the spring. About one-third new oak would be typical, except for the
Reserve, a barrel selection which is half aged in new barrels. Fining and
filtration are avoided if possible. Brooks aims for a purity of style, with
expressive Pinot aromas.

The Chardonnay is mostly barrel-fermented – Acacia also likes the
aromatic freshness that tank fermentation preserves – with a mixture of
indigenous and cultivated yeasts. The wine is aged for up to 9 months in
35 per cent new oak, although there is no exact formula. Nor is there any
strict adherence to such procedures as malolactic fermentation and lees-
stirring – it all depends on the wine. There used to be a less expensive
version called Caviste, which contained only 20 per cent barrel-fermented
wine, but it has been phased out.

Acacia also produces a chunky Zinfandel from old vines in St Helena.
This is aged in *barriques* for up to 18 months.

503

Since 1986 Acacia has made a sparkling wine in a full toasty style, blending 80 per cent Pinot Noir and 20 per cent Chardonnay. The base wine is barrel-fermented and goes through malolactic fermentation, and is aged at least 5 years on the yeast.

It was always a pleasure to taste Acacia wines in the 1980s, especially if one had the chance to compare wines from different vineyards. The Chardonnay remains good, but in the 1990s the Pinot Noirs seemed to lose character. Acacia, in short, seems to be playing it safe.

Bouchaine

1075 Buchli Station Rd., Napa, CA 95449. Tel: 252 9065. Fax: 252 0401. Production: 25,000 cases.

In 1981 some very rich investors from Delaware and Washington took over the former Garetto Winery in Carneros. For the previous thirty years it had been used for storage by Beringer. Jerry Luper was recruited from Chateau Montelena to make the wines, and was succeeded in 1986 by John Montero. Eugenia Keegan was the energetic president of the company, and with her background in vineyard management had a strong influence on the direction Bouchaine took. In 1995 the winery was extensively renovated.

Bouchaine's 38 acres in Carneros, mostly planted with Chardonnay, provide some but by no means all of their requirements, and much fruit is purchased from Carneros growers. John Montero has also been interested in clonal selection, and has taken budwood from many sources, including Hanzell, Chalone, and some Oregon vineyards. He was particularly taken with the Pommard clone. As far as winemaking is concerned, Montero likes to retain one-third whole clusters during fermentation in open-top tanks, and punches down the cap by hand. The wine is aged for about 12 months. The Chardonnay, which can be austere in its youth, is mostly barrel-fermented, goes through partial malolactic fermentation, and is aged on the lees for about 6 months.

The wines have been uneven in quality, with considerable vintage variation. There have been delicious bottlings, and quite a few dull ones too. Bouchaine has had great and deserved success with its inexpensive Pinot Noir for early drinking, released under the Q. C. Fly label.

Carneros Creek

1285 Dealy Lane, Napa, CA 94559. Tel: 253 9463. Fax: 253 9465. Production: 32,000 cases.

Carneros Creek, now well known for its Pinot Noir, was founded in 1972 as the first Carneros winery opened since Prohibition. It originally made its reputation with Cabernet Sauvignon and some hefty Zinfandels from Amador County. In 1973 Mahoney planted a 30-acre vineyard, of which

10 were Pinot Noir, and two years later he collaborated with Dr C. J. Alley of UC Davis in establishing clonal selections trials by planting twenty different clones on just under 2 acres. When the trials and microvinifications were complete, they selected the best clones and planted them more widely. The chosen clones included some from Davis, one from Hanzell, some Pommard clones, and one that apparently came from a vineyard in Chambertin. Since Carneros Creek produces three different Pinots, Mahoney can use the different clonal selections as components in his blends. Today the estate consists of 121 acres of Pinot Noir, 12 of Chardonnay, and 7 of Merlot; 68 more acres were planted in 1998. The wines are made by Francis Mahoney and Melissa Moravec.

The simplest wine is the enjoyable and bargain-priced Fleur de Carneros, which uses the Pommard clone to produce a light upfront style for early drinking. The Blue Label is the standard bottling, and there is also a Signature Reserve. About 20 per cent new oak is used. Despite Mahoney's undoubted expertise in all things concerning Pinot, I often find the wines under-charged and lacking in character, although the Signature Reserve can be excellent.

Codorníu Napa
1345 Henry Rd., Napa, CA 94559. Tel: 224 1668. Fax: 224 1672. Production: 60,000 cases.

The Raventos family, who own this large Spanish-based sparkling wine producer, bought some acreage in Paso Robles in 1982 with a view to starting up a California winery, but it seems that plans were abandoned until they acquired a site in Carneros in 1989. Their stunning new winery, designed by Barcelona architect Domingo Triay, was opened there in 1991. The first winemaker was Janet Pagano, who was succeeded in 1997 by Don Van Staaveren, formerly of Chateau St Jean.

Codorníu has 160 acres of Chardonnay and Pinot Noir planted. The first releases were in 1991. The wines are made by *méthode champenoise*, of course, and riddling is automated. The quality of the initial releases was very good and the wines are reasonably priced.

The basic wine is a nonvintage Napa Brut, half Pinot, half Chardonnay, and aged 3 years on the yeast. The rosé has 15 per cent Chardonnay, and the Blanc de Noirs 25 per cent Chardonnay; both wine are aged 3 years. There are two vintage wines, both aged for 5 years on the yeast. The Carneros Cuvée is made from 75 per cent Pinot Noir, while the Napa Reserve is 75 per cent Chardonnay.

Like some other sparkling wine producers, Codorníu has begun to develop a range of still wines since 1996.

Domaine Carneros
1240 Duhig Rd., Napa, CA 94559. Tel: 257 0101. Fax: 257 3020. Production: 45,000 cases.

I don't know what possessed the Taittinger family to build a hideous replica of their Château de la Marquetterie on a ridgetop in Carneros, at an alleged cost of $17 million, but this monstrous pastiche, completed in 1989, certainly attracts attention.

The 200 acres of vineyards were developed in 1982 by Jim and Steve Allen, the owners of Sequoia Grove in Napa. They originally planted 60 acres of Chardonnay and 40 of Pinot Noir. They subsequently sold the vineyards to Kobrand, who approached Taittinger with the idea of a joint venture. There is also a little Pinot Meunier and Pinot Blanc in the vineyards. Eileen Crane, who has been making the wines here from the beginning, finds Meunier too neutral, but likes Pinot Blanc, which in her view contributes some richness on the middle palate. In 1989 a second vineyard was planted in western Carneros, but phylloxera has necessitated a good deal of replanting.

The grapes are harvested at night, and only the first pressing is used. After inoculation with Prise de Mousse yeast, the must is fermented at 18 degrees Centigrade, then racked and centrifuged. The blends are made up in November. Hardly any of the wine will go through malolactic fermentation. The *dosage* is slightly higher than most French Brut champagnes, but this is a concession to consumers' tastes. For that matter, some of the Taittinger champagnes have a relatively high *dosage* too. Nonetheless the Domaine Carneros sparkling wines are very delicate and transparent. There is nothing broad or heavy-handed about these wines, although I find some of them, notably the Blanc de Blancs, a touch sweet for my taste.

Eileen Crane is not keen on reserve wines, and obtains the complexity of her blends by using wines made from different clones. There is little climatic variation between sites in Carneros, so clones offer different nuances. Crane told me that she would rather age the wines in bottle than introduce aged wines into the blend.

The basic wine is the Vintage Brut, which has 60 per cent Pinot Noir, 35 per cent Chardonnay, and 5 per cent Pinot Blanc. The vintage-dated Blanc de Blancs is aged about 5 years. The nonvintage rosé, sold only at the winery, is rather fruity and obvious. There is also an excellent Late Disgorged wine, which is only released in magnums.

By 1997 Domaine Carneros, like many other sparkling wine producers, was beginning to release some still wines. Taittinger were quite keen on the idea, as it meant they would have a still Pinot Noir to offer to their clients in France. The wine has proved commercially successful and production may be expanded. There are in fact two Pinot Noirs. The simpler of the two is Domaine Carneros; the other, smokier and oakier, is called Famous Gate. Neither receives a cold soak before fermentation, both are made by punching down the cap, and they are aged in one-third new *barriques*.

Gloria Ferrer

23555 Highway 121, Sonoma, CA 95476. Tel: 996 7256. Fax: 996 0720. Production: 45,000 cases.

The owner of Spain's second largest sparkling wine house, Freixenet, is the Ferrer family – hence the name of their California outpost. They launched themselves into this new venture with zest, investing about $11 million in the new winery, which opened in 1988. The initial winemaker was Eileen Crane, now of Domaine Carneros, and since 1987 the winemaker has been Robert Iantosca.

The estate's 195 acres, of which 132 are Pinot Noir, are planted in front of the winery. The range consists of Sonoma Brut (80 per cent Pinot Noir, with 2 years on the yeast), Blanc de Noirs, Rosé (95 per cent Pinot Noir), vintage-dated Royal Cuvée (aged over 5 years on the yeast), and the vintage-dated Late Disgorged. The grapes are picked fairly ripe, so the wines tend to have rather less finesse than, say, those of Domaine Carneros. The problem is accentuated by the heavy domination of Pinot Noir. I find the Brut sound but unexciting, and the Blanc de Noirs too meaty, but the rosé is attractive and so is the lemony, vigorous Royal Cuvée.

The winery seems to have suffered from the slump in sparkling wine sales in the early 1990s, as it is not operating to full capacity, and is now producing about 12,000 cases of still wines from estate-grown fruit; these wines, it is planned, will eventually account for half the production. The 1995 Pinot Noir had a complex nose of coffee and cloves, and tasted lively and subtle on the palate.

MacRostie

17246 Woodland Ave., Sonoma, CA 95476. Tel: 996 4480. Fax: 996 3726. Production: 9,000 cases.

Steve MacRostie made the wines for Hacienda for many years and was the winemaker at Roche until 1998. Since 1987 he has also run a small winery of his own. He specializes in Chardonnay, Pinot Noir, and Merlot, almost all vinified from Carneros fruit.

Mont St John

5400 Old Sonoma Rd., Napa, CA 94559. Tel: 255 8864. Fax: 257 2778. Production: 22,000 cases.

Andrea Bartolucci started up a winery in Oakville as a 'personal use' winery during Prohibition. After Repeal the name Madonna Winery was adopted until the change to the present name after World War II. Much of the wine was sold in bulk to producers such as Rodney Strong in Sonoma. Then in the 1970s the Bartoluccis sold their 300 acres of vineyards to Heublein. Louis Bartolucci, the winemaker at that time, and his son moved to Carneros and planted 140 acres in 1976, farming them organically. Their best-known vineyard is the Madonna Vineyard. By 1997 they owned 160 acres of Pinot Noir, Chardonnay, Cabernet Sauvignon and Riesling.

The winery was completed in 1978 and the present winemaker is Andrea 'Buck' Bartolucci. Unfortunately the wines are far from exciting. The Riesling and Gewürztraminer are made in a sweetish style. The Pinot Noir receives only a short maceration, and is then aged in *barriques* for 12 months.

Kent Rasmussen

2125 Cuttings Wharf Rd., Napa, CA 94559. Tel/fax: 252 4224. Production: 4,000 cases.

Since 1986 this gifted winemaker who used to work for Mondavi has specialized in Pinot Noir and Chardonnay, mostly made from Carneros fruit. Rasmussen is a low-tech winemaker, and his hands-off approach, so daring a decade ago, has now become orthodox in leading Californian winemaking circles. The spicy Pinot Noir can be very good. In addition Rasmussen releases small quantities of Sauvignon Blanc. He also buys in varieties such as Sangiovese, Syrah, Dolcetto, Nebbiolo, and even Alicante Bouschet, much of which is released under a second label, Ramsey.

Roche

28700 Arnold Dr., Sonoma, CA 95476. Tel: 935 7115. Fax: 935 7846. Production: 20,000 cases.

Joe and Genevieve Roche, both doctors, bought this large ranch in 1977, and planted vineyards five years later. By 1990 they had planted 18 acres of Chardonnay, and 10 each of Pinot Noir and Merlot. The winery only opened in 1990, and the winemaker was Steve MacRostie, who was succeeded by John Ferrington in 1998. The Chardonnay is whole-cluster pressed, barrel-fermented, and aged in French and American oak. I found the 1994 somewhat vegetal on the nose, and alcoholic on the palate; the 1995, in contrast, was thin and bland. The Pinot Noir is pleasant but lacks concentration; the Reserve is aged in new oak. Most of the wines are sold either directly from the tasting room or as futures.

Saintsbury
1500 Los Carneros Ave., Napa, CA 94559. Tel: 252 0592. Fax: 252 0595.
Production: 50,000 cases.

Saintsbury, named after the Victorian professor and wine connoisseur, was founded by Richard Ward and David Graves. The men met while studying oenology at UC Davis in 1976. In 1981 they scraped together enough money to make their first wine, which was vinified at Pine Ridge. They then leased a winery in St Helena until the Carneros winery they were building was ready for occupation. At first they planned to limit production to 25,000 cases, but the wines enjoyed such success that they could not resist doubling the production and were obliged to expand the winery in 1988.

In 1986 Ward and Graves planted vineyards, and acquired more in 1992. These supply about 40 per cent of their requirements. However in some vintages, such as 1994, the estate grapes are not necessarily the best, and the Reserve contained only purchased fruit. Ward and Graves are working hard to improve the quality of their fruit. They have planted a number of different clones, and some of the vines are now trained on a costly open-lyre system to assist even ripening.

Although the founders take a close interest in the winemaking, Byron Kosuge is in overall charge of vinification. The Chardonnay is barrel-fermented and aged in oak for 7 months. All the wine goes through malolactic fermentation; the Reserve is a lot selection, and is aged in barrels, of which over half are new, for up to 14 months.

There are three Pinot Noirs. Garnet is the lightest, made from grapes with low tannin levels and bottled earlier. The main bottling is the Carneros, which, like Garnet, is a blend of various lots. There is a cold soak, followed by a fermentation and maceration of up to 15 days. Curiously, Saintsbury do not practise punching down, but prefer to irrigate the cap by pumping over, gently. Malolactic fermentation takes place in barrel. In the 1990s they began using a higher proportion of new oak, and the Reserve, a lot selection, is now aged in two-thirds new oak, mostly with a heavy toast. The Reserve is also aged for about 14 months, 4 more than the Carneros. The wine is fined with bentonite, but there has been no filtration since 1991. In the mid-1990s Saintsbury introduced a Brown Ranch bottling at a very high price. Saintsbury also offer Vincent Van Gris, a charming rosé from Pinot Noir must bled off from the fermentation tanks. (The winery is keen on its puns, and one of its T-shirts has the slogan: Beaune in the USA.)

Although other Napa wineries are making superb wines from Carneros fruit, Saintsbury is surely the best of the Carneros-based wineries. The wines have richness, elegance, and complexity, as well as wonderful perfume. I do not detect any lowering of quality despite the expansion of production.

Schug

602 Bonneau Rd., Sonoma, CA 95476. Tel: 939 9365. Fax: 939 9364. Production: 15,000 cases.

Walter Schug was born in the German wine village of Assmannshausen, locally famous for its Pinot Noir, and after studying at Geisenheim, emigrated to the United States in 1959, working for Gallo and then for Phelps. While at Phelps, from 1973 to 1983, he developed a well deserved reputation for some outstanding wines in a Germanic style. In 1990 he built his own winery in Carneros, and it also shows signs of German architectural influence.

Schug owns 38 acres of vineyards, two-thirds of which are planted with Chardonnay. He favours close spacing. Although Schug is unquestionably a skilled and very experienced winemaker, the wines here have shown great inconsistency. Part of the problem must reside in the fluctuating availability of grapes from his favourite vineyards. He used to buy Pinot Noir from the Heinemann Vineyard on Spring Mountain, but that has now been replanted with Cabernet Sauvignon. The Beckstoffer Vineyard in Carneros also no longer supplies Schug with grapes. Sauvignon Blanc comes from Brutocao in Mendocino, and is blended with Carneros fruit, and the result is a slightly sweet wine. The regular Chardonnay is partially aged in large oval casks, German-fashion, and does not go through malolactic fermentation: the result is predictably lean and steely. But there is also a barrel-fermented Chardonnay. The Pinot Noir is fermented in rotary tanks and is also partly aged in large ovals, although the Reserve is aged in *barriques* for 14 months.

The North Coast Merlot in fact comes from Marin County – it's a good wine. The Cabernet Sauvignon Reserve is released under a Sonoma Valley appellation, and is aged in American oak for 16 months. Schug also tries his hand at a little vintage-dated sparkling wine, Rouge de Noir, which is made solely from Pinot Noir.

With so many vineyard sources and such stylistic variation, it is not surprising that Schug has failed to establish a clear identity for his wines. This may not be his fault, but it is worrying to find such a wide range of styles and qualities emerging from the same winery.

Truchard

3234 Old Sonoma Rd., Napa, CA 94559. Tel: 253 7153. Fax: 253 7234. Production: 10,000 cases.

In 1974 Tony Truchard bought 20 acres in Carneros, convinced by Francis Mahoney of Carneros Creek of the fine potential here. Today the vineyard has grown to 167 acres of Pinot Noir, Cabernet Sauvignon, Chardonnay, Cabernet Franc, Merlot, Zinfandel, and Syrah. The Pinot Noir clones include two Martini clones, the Pommard, and a selection from Swan. Truchard sold grapes to many wineries until deciding in 1989 to make their own wines. At first facilities were rented, and in 1990 a winery was completed. A lot of grapes are still sold off. The winemaker is Salvatore DiIanni.

The wines – Chardonnay, Merlot, Cabernet Sauvignon, Pinot Noir, and Syrah – are aged in one-third new *barriques*. Truchard is probably best known for the quality of its Syrah, not a variety for which Carneros is usually renowned.

27

Mendocino and Lake Counties

Brutocao

1400 Highway 175, Hopland, CA 95449. Tel/fax: 707 744 1066.[1] Tasting room: 7000 Highway 128, Philo, CA 95466. Tel/fax: 895 2152. Production: 15,000 cases.

Leonard and Albert Brutocao became grape farmers in the 1940s, selling their fruit to Gallo, Beringer, Fetzer, and other wineries. After Albert's death in 1989, Leonard decided to build a small winery, which is now run by Steven Brutocao. Fred Nickel is the winemaker.

The vineyards are enormous, with 475 acres under vine. There's Chardonnay, Sauvignon Blanc, Cabernet Sauvignon, Merlot, Zinfandel, and Pinot Noir, but also, more recently, Sangiovese and Barbera. The wine-making can be a trifle eccentric. The Special Reserve Chardonnay is barrel-fermented in neutral *barriques*, and then aged on the fine lees for 24 months. The Hopland Ranch Zinfandel is made by carbonic maceration, and bottled, like many Brutocao wines, without fining or filtration. Their top-of-the-range yet jammy Cabernet, Proprietor's Special Reserve, was in 1991 aged for 33 months in new *barriques*. I prefer the succulent 1995 Merlot.

Claudia Springs

2160 Guntly Rd., Philo, CA 85466. Tel: 895 3926. Production: 2,500 cases.

This property was founded in 1989 by Claudia and Robert Klindt and Claudia and Warren Hein. Robert Klindt is the winemaker. From their 25 acres and from purchased fruit from Redwood Valley, they release Pinot Noir, Chardonnay, Syrah, and Zinfandel. The wines are nondescript, although the 1996 Pinot Noir is an improvement on some previous vintages. Prices are reasonable.

Duncan Peak
14500 Mountain House Rd., Hopland, CA 95449. Tel: 283 5577. Production: 500 cases.

Duncan Peak, Mendocino's smallest winery, was founded in 1987 by Hubert Lenczowksi. The estate consists of 4 hillside acres in Sanel Valley, planted with Cabernet Sauvignon, Merlot, and Cabernet Franc. The 1994 Cabernet Sauvignon is very light.

Edmeades
5500 Highway 128, Philo, CA 95466. Tel: 895 3232. Fax: 895 3316. Production: 18,000 cases.

Dr Donald Edmeades was one of the pioneers of Mendocino, planting 35 acres of vineyards in 1962 and constructing a winery ten years later. He specialized in single-vineyard Zinfandels, and contributed to the survival of many of these ancient vineyards. After his death in the 1960s he was succeeded by his son Darren, who in the early 1970s hired Jed Steele as winemaker. But the estate was poorly run, and in the late 1980s it closed down. Kendall-Jackson bought and revived Edmeades in 1992, installing Van Williamson as winemaker. The existing vineyards are planted at an elevation of 200 to 400 feet on sandy clay loam soils with Chardonnay, Pinot Noir, and a very little Pinot Gris and Sangiovese. In 1998 the estate was expanded when 160 acres were acquired in Anderson Valley, and 70 of those acres will be planted with Pinot Noir.

Van Williamson is a minimalist winemaker, using as little sulphur dioxide as possible, and preferring natural yeasts for fermentation; he also avoids filtration if he can. The full-bodied Chardonnay is whole-cluster pressed, and goes through malolactic fermentation. It is aged for 9 months in French and American oak and bottled unfiltered. The crisp, dry Gewürztraminer, of which only about 250 cases are produced, is made in a similar fashion.

The Pinot Noirs, which can be earthy, are also aged in a small proportion of American oak and are bottled unfined. Edmeades continues to make small lots of single-vineyard Zinfandels, almost all from hillside sites, headpruned and dry-farmed. The wines are punched down by hand during fermentation, which takes place using natural as well as inoculated yeast, but the maceration is relatively brief. The wine is aged in a blend of French and American oak for 9 months. Single-vineyard bottlings include one from Eaglepoint Vineyard (which also yields a rustic Petite Sirah for Edmeades) and another from Ciapusci. These are rich powerful wines with over 15 degrees of alcohol.

It is good to see that after a period in the doldrums, this esteemed property is once again making excellent wines that are fully typical of Mendocino at its best.

513

Elizabeth Vineyards

8591 Colony Dr., Redwood Valley, CA 95470. Tel: 485 0957. Production: 600 cases.

The Foster family founded this estate in Redwood Valley, which now consists of 40 acres. Much of the fruit is sold off to wineries that include Mondavi, Simi, Chateau Souverain and other wineries to the south. The first releases were in 1987, and the varieties bottled were Sauvignon Blanc, Chardonnay, and Zinfandel.

Fetzer

13601 East Side Rd., Hopland, CA 95449. Tel: 744 1250. Fax: 744 9020. Production: 3 million cases.

Like Mondavi and Beringer and a handful of others, Fetzer is one of those California wineries that manages to produce some superlative wines within a total production of millions of cases. Moreover, the overall quality of the simpler, large-volume wines is high too, and such wines invariably offer excellent value within their price range.

Fetzer began as grape growers. In 1958 Barney Fetzer, a former lumber executive, began planting vineyards. In 1992 the Fetzers sold the winery, which made its first wines in 1968, to the Brown Forman corporation. However, there is still a close relationship between the Fetzers and their former winery, although Barney Fetzer himself died in 1981. Fetzer the growers sell the production of 1,200 acres of their vineyards exclusively to Fetzer the winery. The Fetzer family, and the winery in their wake, are strongly committed to organic viticulture, and the aim is to be using solely organic fruit by the year 2000. The winery is very public about its belief in organic farming. At considerable expense, it has planted a 5-acre garden on biodynamic principles next to the winery.

Paul Dolan was the winemaker here, and is now president of the company and married to a Fetzer daughter. The chief winemaker is Dennis Martin, assisted by Phil Hurst, the international winemaker, and Bob Blue. They are responsible for a number of different ranges. Bel Arbor is the inexpensive range of varietal wines, including Sundial Chardonnay, Valley Oaks Cabernet Sauvignon, Eagle Peak Merlot, and Echo Ridge Fumé Blanc. These wines tend to be light and juicy rather than complex and rich, but they are very well made. They draw on fruit from a variety of sources. Thus the 1996 Sundial Chardonnay was comprised of 40 per cent North Coast fruit, and 30 per cent each from Lodi and Monterey; only 20 per cent of the wine was barrel-fermented.

Bob Blue is responsible for the Bonterra range, first launched in 1983. These wines are made exclusively from organic grapes. The Chardonnay is barrel-fermented and aged in 45 per cent new oak. The Bonterra Red is a blend of Petite Sirah, made using carbonic maceration, and Zinfandel, a wine aged in American oak. A recent addition to the range is a barrel-fermented Viognier.

The Barrel Select range is, as the name suggests, all oak-aged. It consists of Cabernet Sauvignon, Chardonnay, Sauvignon Blanc, Merlot (mostly from Napa and Sonoma), Zinfandel, and Pinot Noir. The winemaking is sophisticated despite fairly large volumes. Thus the Pinot is given a cold soak and employs partial whole-cluster fermentation, while the Chardonnay is barrel-fermented and aged in 25 per cent new oak. Fetzer has no difficulty getting its hands on barrels, since it is one of the very few wineries in California that has its own cooperage, producing 12,000 barrels annually from air-dried wood. This means that the cost of a French-oak barrel is more than halved. The cooperage sustains itself by selling to other wineries. The barrel room at Fetzer is an astonishing sight: 45,000 barrels, stacked six high, and containing two vintages, of red wine only – the whites are stored elsewhere!

The most interesting wines are the reserves, which are in fact single-vineyard bottlings from well-known vineyards such as Sangiacomo in Carneros, Bien Nacido in Santa Barbara, and Eaglepoint Ranch in Mendocino. Some of these wines are made in minute quantities – 'just for fun', says Bob Blue – but they also prove that a vast winery such as Fetzer is capable of producing fine wines at the very top of the range. I've enjoyed a superb 1995 Gewürztraminer Reserve from Beckstoffer Vineyard (alas, only 220 cases produced), 1995 Pinot Noir Reserve and Pinot Blanc Reserve, both from Bien Nacido, and a splendidly vibrant 1995 Eaglepoint Ranch Petite Sirah Reserve.

The real strength of Fetzer remains the quality of its less exalted wines. They claim to be America's main producer of Gewürztraminer, and the basic version is indeed very aromatic, thanks, say Fetzer, to the Alsatian clone they have planted. They are also working on varieties such as Viognier (oaked and unoaked) and Sangiovese. Recent bottlings of Syrah have also been very promising.

Fife

3620 Road B, Redwood Valley, CA 95470. Tel: 485 0323. Fax: 485 0832. Production: 3,000 cases.

Dennis Fife spent seventeen years working for Heublein. As his responsibilities included buying grapes and wine for the Inglenook label, he soon came to realize that grapes such as Zinfandel and Petite Sirah could produce wonderful wines in Mendocino. So in 1991 he set up his own Mendocino winery, and he and his winemaker John Buechsenstein source grapes from number of vineyards in Mendocino and Napa. In 1996 Fife bought a vineyard, which he renamed the Redhead Vineyard; planted largely with Zinfandel at 1,200 feet, it is organically farmed.

The blends vary greatly. The 1995 Petite Sirah contains a little Charbono, while the 1995 Zinfandel contains some Petite Sirah. The Reserve Cabernet Sauvignon comes, however, from Spring Mountain, and is aged in 50 per cent new *barriques*. There is also a proprietary red called Max Cuvée, composed, usually, of Petite Sirah, Zinfandel, and Syrah from the Larkmead Vineyard in Napa, and Zinfandel from the Redhead Vineyard.

These are full-bodied wines, powerful and concentrated, even if at present they lack clear regional identity.

Frey Vineyards

14000 Tomki Rd., Redwood Valley, CA 95470. Tel: 485 5177. Fax: 485 7875. Production: 35,000 cases.

Dr Paul Frey began planting vineyards in the mid-1960s and founded his winery in 1980. He died in 1991, but with eight children, there were no problems of succession. The present head of the estate is Jonathon Frey. The 40 acres of vineyards are dry-farmed at an elevation of about 1,000 feet.

Frey vineyards are organic, and so is the winemaking. This is where the problems begin. No sulphites are permitted to be used in the vineyard or winery, and adjustments of acidity are not allowed either. As a consequence many of the wines are flawed, especially the whites, which can scarcely be recommended. The best Frey wine I have come across was a Syrah.

Gabrielli

10950 West Rd., Redwood Valley, CA 95470. Tel: 485 1221. Fax: 485 1225. Production: 8,000 cases.

This excellent estate was founded in 1989 by Sam Gabrielli, and in 1990 he hired Jeff Hinchcliffe as his winemaker. Jeff had previously been the winemaker at Hidden Cellars. The 13 acres of vineyards are about 900 feet high. The winery produces a surprisingly wide range, though many wines are in small lots.

The Reserve Chardonnay comes from Boonville grapes and is barrel-fermented and goes through full malolactic fermentation. The Riesling is dry, and made from whole-cluster pressed grapes, and the wine is aged, rather surprisingly, for 18 months in *barriques*. Another white wine is a blend called Ascenza, which combines Chenin, Riesling, Sémillon, and Gewürztraminer! It sounds like a dog's breakfast, but in fact the bottled wine is oaky, full-bodied and assertive.

There are a number of impressive reds. Pinot Noir comes from the Wente and Pommard clones planted at the Floodgate Vineyard, and this bottling is more impressive than that from the Weir Vineyard in Yorkville Highlands.

The Zinfandel comes from old vines, as indeed it should in Mendocino.

The Reserve, at least in 1993, was leathery, porty, and alcoholic. Hinchcliffe makes a fascinating wine he called Nativo Zinfandel, which is aged in Mendocino oak coopered in Calistoga. Hinchcliffe discerns a spicy, mineral flavour in the wood, which he likes.

Jeff Hinchcliffe succeeds in making excellent Syrah and Sangiovese from Gabrielli's own vineyards, wines with plenty of guts and personality. This is definitely an estate to watch.

Gemello
9200 Highway 128, Philo, CA 95466. Tel: 895 3814.

This winery operated in Santa Clara County before moving to Anderson Valley. It was founded in 1934 by John Gemello, whose granddaughter Sandy Gemello Obester now runs the winery, which specializes in full-bodied Zinfandels.

Goldeneye
9200 Highway 128, Philo, CA 95466. Tel: 895 3814. Production: 300 cases.

This is the former Obester estate, which was founded in 1977, and belonged to Paul Obester (husband of Sandy Gemello Obester of Gemello estate) until in 1997 it was bought by Duckhorn of Napa. By 1998 Duckhorn had planted 21 acres, and planned to plant 40 more. The aim was simply to produce outstanding Pinot Noir. The first vintage, 1996, was released under Duckhorn's Decoy label, and the 1997 yielded 300 cases, but clearly production is set to grow considerably as the vines mature.

Greenwood Ridge
5501 Highway 128, Philo, CA 95466. Tel: 895 2002. Fax: 895 2001. Production: 6,000 cases.

The vineyards here, 1,200 feet up in Anderson Valley, were originally established by Tony Husch in 1972. He planted 8 acres of Riesling, Merlot, and Cabernet Sauvignon. Soon after, Husch found himself over-stretched and sold the vineyard to graphic artist Allan Green. Today there are 16 acres under vine. The first commercial vintage was 1980, and in the late 1980s and early 1990s the winemaker was Van Williamson.

The wines come from a variety of sources. Chardonnay is purchased from Redwood Valley, elegant Zinfandel from the Scherrer Vineyard near Healdsburg in Sonoma, and Pinot Noir also comes from fruit purchased in Mendocino. The Riesling is made in an off-dry style, and occasionally a fine late harvest Riesling is produced, as in 1996. There is a firm barrel-fermented Chardonnay from the DuPratt Vineyard. Greenwood Ridge is best known for wines such as Merlot and Cabernet Sauvignon, which are among the finest produced in Mendocino.

Greenwood Ridge is one of the main beneficiaries of the new Mendocino Ridge appellation, but having spent many years working to have the
quality of Anderson Valley wines recognized, Allan Green has mixed
feelings about relaunching his wines under a new appellation.

Guenoc

21000 Butts Canyon Rd., Middletown, CA 95461. Tel: 987 2385. Fax:
987 2385. Production: 85,000 cases.

Guenoc's chief claim to fame, other than its Lake County wines, is that
Lillie Langtry lived here from 1888 to 1906. The property now belongs
to a former army engineer named Orville Magoon. He farms 340 acres
planted at a height of 1,000–1,500 feet. The principal varieties are Chardonnay (120 acres), Cabernet Sauvignon (70), Sauvignon Blanc (38),
Chenin Blanc, Petite Sirah and Zinfandel. Most of the vines lie within
Lake County, although some Bordeaux varieties are planted within
northern Napa. Traces remain of the nineteenth-century vineyard that
once existed here, and it's said that there are some ancient vines of Syrah,
and possibly Petit Verdot.

Guenoc released its first vintage in 1976, and the winery was completed
in 1980. Derek Holstein was the winemaker here from 1987 to 1995,
when he was succeeded by Malcolm Seibly. The range of wines has often
changed, but the Chardonnays and the red Langtry Meritage are of good
quality.

Handley

3151 Highway 128, Philo, CA 95466. Tel; 895 3876. Fax: 895 2603.
Production: 15,000 cases.

Milla Handley worked at Chateau St Jean and Edmeades before setting
up her own estate in 1982. She has 25 acres of Pinot Noir and Chardonnay
vineyards in Anderson Valley, and her parents own 20 more in Dry Creek
in Sonoma. She produces Chardonnay from both regions, and her Sauvignon Blanc also comes from Dry Creek.

Handley makes a rather bland dry Gewürztraminer, half of which is
barrel-fermented. Her Pinot Noir, introduced to the range in 1989, is made
in a very traditional fashion: fermented in open vats with 25 per cent
whole berries, punched down three times a day, and then aged for 11
months in 20 per cent new French oak. A curiosity here is the Pinot
Mystere, a Pinot Meunier, *barrique*-aged for 8 months.

I do not know if there is any connection, but with two major sparkling
wine producers in Anderson Valley – Pacific Echo and Roederer – it is not
surprising that Milla Handley has been tempted to try her hand too. Both
the Brut and the Brut Rosé are Pinot Noir-dominated, and aged on the

yeast for up to 3 years. There is also Blanc de Blancs. Quality is sound rather than exceptional.

Hidden Cellars

1500 Ruddick-Cunningham Rd., Ukiah, CA 95482. Tel: 462 0301. Fax: 462 8144. Production: 30,000 cases.

In 1983 a whirlwind of a man called Dennis Patton set up Hidden Cellars, in partnership with John Dickerson. From 1990 to 1994 Greg Graziano was the winemaker, though it is hard to imagine that Patton himself did not take a keen interest. At first Hidden Cellars made mostly white wines, but in the early 1990s Patton decided to focus on the great old-vine vineyards in the county. He has declared: 'We believe that hidden away in these mountains is the largest body of unexplored old-vine red vineyards in California capable of making world-class wine.' By 1997 80 per cent of their production was red, and the range consisted of a bewildering ten different Zinfandels and four Petite Sirahs, usually aged in a blend of French and American oak.

There are a few other wines. Riesling comes from Potter Valley. Alchemy is a blend of 20 per cent Sauvignon, and 80 per cent Sémillon, all barrel-fermented, and then stirred on the fine lees for 10 months while ageing in 25 per cent new *barriques*.

Husch

4400 Highway 128. Philo, CA 95466. Tel: 895 3216. Fax: 895 2068. Production: 30,000 cases.

Since the property was founded in 1971 by Tony Husch, this is the oldest winery in Anderson Valley, The original vineyard consisted of 12 acres of Pinot Noir, Gewürztraminer, and Chardonnay, and is supplemented by further 50 acres nearby. The estate now also includes the 110-acre La Ribera Vineyard in Ukiah Valley, which is planted with Cabernet Sauvignon, Sauvignon Blanc, Chenin, and Chardonnay. In 1979 the Husch estate was sold to the Hugo Oswald family, and the winemaker is Fritz Meier.

The wines are variable. I have had good Pinot Noir from here, and the rustic Old Vine Carignane, cropped at 4 tons per acre, is a curiosity. There are two Chardonnays, one from Mendocino and the other from La Ribera, and a Reserve fermented in new *barriques*, with lees-stirring for 6 months, and 14 months of ageing in all. The Cabernet spends 18 months in American oak, the plummy Reserve a touch longer. The other white wines include a barrel-fermented Sauvignon and a full-bodied off-dry Gewürztraminer.

Jepson

10400 South Highway 101, Ukiah, CA 95482. Tel: 468 8936. Fax: 468 0362. Production: 20,000 cases.

Founded as the Baccala estate in 1982, it was acquired in 1986 by the banker Robert Jepson. The estate consists of 110 acres, mostly Chardonnay and Sauvignon Blanc, but some of the grapes are sold to other wineries. The first releases were white, but since the mid-1990s the winery has been producing Pinot Noir and Merlot as well. Sauvignon Blanc is often the best wine.

Konocti

Highway 29 at Thomas Drive, Kelseyville, CA 95451.

This used to be the winery of the Lake County Vintners cooperative that united thirty-eight growers who cultivated over 500 acres. Over the years it turned out some excellent and reasonably priced white wines, but in 1996 the facility was bought by Jed Steele, who used to work down the road at Kendall-Jackson's Lake County winery.

Lazy Creek

4610 Highway 128, Philo, CA 95466. Tel: 895 3623. Production: 5,000 cases.

The vineyards were planted here in 1973 and consist of 20 acres of Gewürztraminer, Pinot Noir, and Chardonnay. The winery opened three years later. The owner and winemaker is Swiss-born Johann Kobler. The partially barrel-fermented Gewürztraminer is plump and mouth-filling, and the 1996 Pinot Noir was fine too.

Lolonis

2901 Road B, Redwood Valley, CA 95470. Tel: 925 938 8066. Fax: 938 8069. Production: 30,000 cases.

The Lolonis family came to America from Greece and in 1921 planted vineyards in Redwood Valley, which have grown to 300 acres, mostly planted on benchlands 1,000 feet high. These dry-farmed vineyards, planted with Cabernet Sauvignon, Merlot, Chardonnay, Sauvignon Blanc, and Zinfandel, are placed on well-drained, gravelly soil, and the grapes are much sought after by other wineries, including Parducci and Fetzer. Back in the 1970s Fetzer began releasing single-vineyard Zinfandels from Lolonis fruit. The Lolonis family began producing wines under their own label in the 1980s, but quality was variable until Jed Steele became the consultant winemaker in 1992; he also buys fruit from Lolonis for his own label. However, the Zinfandel is often made in a jammy style which I find excessive.

All Lolonis wines are estate-grown and made in a big, chunky style. Some of the Reserve wines are impressive. The Reserve Chardonnay is barrel-fermented and aged in 40 per cent new *barriques* for 9 months. The Zinfandel and Cabernet Private Reserves age in a similar proportion of new oak, but for 14 months. There is a proprietary red called Orpheus which blends Petite Sirah and Napa Gamay, and is aged in French and American oak for 14 months.

Lonetree

PO Box 401, Philo, CA 95466. Fax: 888 686 9463. Production: 3,000 cases.

Lonetree was founded by John Scharffenberger in collaboration with Casey Hartlip, and the grapes come from Scharffenberger's outstanding Eaglepoint Ranch, which also supplies grapes to many other wineries. The first releases have been well-received Sangiovese, Zinfandel, and Syrah. The 1995 Syrah is rather extracted and dry.

McDowell Valley Vineyards

3811 Highway 175, Hopland, CA 95449. Tel: 744 1053. Fax: 744 1826. Production: 125,000 cases.

Located up a quiet valley east of Hopland, this is one of the most remarkable estates in Mendocino. The 360 acres of vineyards – planted 1,000 feet up on benchlands of gravelly loam – include 122 acres of Rhône varieties, including some of the oldest Syrah in California, which was mislabelled as Petite Sirah until the early 1980s. There is also some 42-year-old Zinfandel, which is not that unusual in Mendocino, 32-year-old Cabernet Sauvignon, and 53-year-old Petite Sirah. Some of the Syrah and Grenache date back to 1919. Over half the grapes are sold to other wineries.

However, McDowell has been through some troubled times. The owners are Richard and Karen Keehn, who in addition to the splendid vineyards, had ambitious plans for the winery, which was designed to vinify far more wine than ever came through its presses. Overheads built up, and in 1994 the winery was sold to the Associated Vintage Group, and much of the capacity of the winery is used by custom-crushing for other properties. However, McDowell have managed to lease back the winery. William Crawford is the president and winemaker.

In 1996 McDowell took the brave decision to produce only Rhône varietals, as for some years they had been planting a wide range of varietals, including Mourvèdre, Counoise, Cinsault, Marsanne, Roussanne, Viognier, and Grenache. Almost all of these new plantings are organically farmed. The Marsanne, which can be a dull grape, is barrel-fermented and delicious here, and some of it is blended with the Viognier. There's a refreshing dry Grenache rosé and, of course, the excellent Estate Syrah, which is better than the Mendocino Syrah. The Provençal-style blend called Vieux Cepages is no longer made, as the rights to the label were sold off in 1990.

Milano

15494 South Highway 101, Hopland, CA 95449. Tel: 744 1396. Production: 3,000 cases.

This Sanel Valley winery has been run by the Milone family since 1980. They farm 60 acres of vineyards and focus on Chardonnay, Cabernet Sauvignon, and Zinfandel. Quality is modest.

Monte Volpe

4921 East Side Rd., Ukiah, CA 95482. Tel: 463 1532. Fax: 462 8951. Production: 15,000 cases.

Greg Graziano is the proprietor of the grandly named Domaine Saint Gregory (q.v.), and Monte Volpe is a label he uses for an extensive range of Italian varietals, produced in partnership with Lowell Stone, the owner of 70 acres in Ukiah Valley called Fox Hill, which Graziano has translated into Italian. Certain Italian varieties such Barbera and Sangiovese have, says Graziano, always been around in Mendocino, but became neglected as there was no demand for them. Now he and Stone are replanting them, as well as a few non-Italian varieties for good measure. The range includes Arneis, Chardonnay, Moscato, Sangiovese, Nebbiolo, Dolcetto, Tocai, Barbera, Primitivo, Pinot Gris, and Pinot Blanc. Then, for fun, Graziano is also playing around with Corvina, Cortese, Pinotage, and Montepulciano.

Graziano also delights in blends that are impossible to commit to memory. Peppolino blends equal proportions of Barbera, Sangiovese, Primitivo, and Nebbiolo; Tanaro combines Dolcetto, Nebbiolo, and Barbera. For the tart, vivacious Barbera varietal wine Graziano has bought fruit from Lodi, Amador, and Contra Costa, as well as Mendocino. In general the wines are good, certainly well made and lively in their flavours, although the gloss of new oak can be obtrusive in a few of them. I particularly admire the Nebbiolo, Sangiovese, and Tocai. But there is no doubt that Greg Graziano is expanding the limits of what can be done in Mendocino, and that is to be warmly welcomed.

Navarro

5601 Highway 128, Philo, CA 95466. Tel: 895 3686. Production: 30,000 cases.

If one had to select a single winery to visit in Anderson Valley, it would probably be Navarro, both for the warmth of the welcome tourists receive there and for the exuberant quality of the wines. In 1973 Ted Bennett and Deborah Cahn bought a 910-acre sheep farm, and began planting vines. Today they have 85 acres of Gewürztraminer, Pinot Noir, Chardonnay, Pinot Gris, Riesling, and Muscat. Phylloxera has not come to their hillsides yet, but they are planting additional acreage just to ensure that there is no shortfall should the dreaded louse strike. These new plantings are more closely spaced, and they have taken the opportunity to plant commercial quantities of German and Alsatian clones they had previously only planted experimentally. Some Syrah has gone in, and some more Pinot Noir, this time planted at 1,200 feet. It hadn't been their intention to do this, but a site they had intended for Mourvèdre and Syrah proved too cool for those varieties, so Pinot Noir went into the ground instead.

Ted Bennett wisely ages his Gewürztraminer, Pinot Gris, and Riesling in large ovals rather than *barriques*, and these wines are among the best examples of the varieties in California. The Pinot Noir and the Chardonnay, especially the very ripe Premiere Reserve bottling, are excellent too. Botrytis is not uncommon in their vineyards, so there are some stunning sweet Rieslings. Although they are not cheap, Ted laments that it is impossible to make money off such labour-intensive wines. Although Ted and Deborah are veterans of Anderson Valley, they don't seem to have lost that spirit of inquiry that keeps winemaking and indeed wines fresh and interesting.

Pacific Echo

8501 Highway 128, Philo, CA 95466. Tel: 895 2065. Fax: 895 2758. Production: 40,000 cases.

John Scharffenberger worked at Stony Hill before returning to Mendocino to plant 70 acres of Zinfandel and Petite Sirah on land belonging to his family in the 1970s. In 1981 he sold his interest in these vineyards and moved operations to Anderson Valley, where he specialized in sparkling wine. In 1989 Pommery became a majority shareholder, which helped to finance a new winery and the planting of an additional 180 acres. Pommery's share is now owned by the prestigious LVMH group. In 1996 Scharffenberger left the company, which was reorganized. Tex Sawyer became wine-maker and in 1998 the name was changed to Pacific Echo. John Scharffenberger meanwhile had also developed the Lonetree label (q.v.) for still wines from his Eaglepoint Ranch vineyards.

The Scharffenberger range included a nonvintage Brut and Brut Rosé and Cremant, and a vintage-dated Blanc de Blancs. The Brut was a good elegant lemony wine, but I found the Rosé distinctly earthy. The first release under the new label was a Brut, released at a relatively high price for a California sparkling wine. It will be fascinating to see how the new venture develops.

Parducci

501 Parducci Rd., Ukiah, CA 95482. Tel: 462 9463. Fax: 462 7260.
Production: 350,000 cases.

Parducci predates every other winery in Mendocino. Alfredo Parducci
began planting vineyards in 1921 and founded his winery in 1932, at first
producing only bulk wines. By the 1970s the winery was in a rut and was
sold to a consortium that retained the Parduccis to manage the business.
Its wines were resolutely old-fashioned, and not always in the best sense
of the word. For instance, the Parduccis were adamantly opposed to the
use of small oak barrels, which may have been fine for Zinfandel but
perhaps wasn't such a good idea for Cabernet Sauvignon. In 1996 a
revolution took place. A controlling interest in the winery was taken by
a winemaker, William Hill, and by a venture capitalist, Carl Thoma.
They ousted John Parducci as winemaker, and hired Bob Swain, who had
previously worked at Clos du Val. In 1998 John Parducci left to work as
a winemaker with Associated Vintage Group, the owners of, among other
wineries, McDowell.

Parducci is fortunate to have a range of vineyards, 250 acres in all,
planted with Chardonnay, Petite Sirah, Zinfandel, Sémillon, Cabernet Sauvignon, and Merlot, and they also have contracts with various growers.
Bob Swain insists he is not simply interested in volume, but wants to
improve quality. He has succeeded in installing oak barrels at Parducci,
although oak is used with a light touch. Another innovation is the Old
Vines label, which means that the vines from which the wines are made
are between 20 and 60 years old. The varieties are Cabernet, Merlot,
Pinot Noir, Zinfandel, Petite Sirah, Chardonnay (aged in American oak),
Charbono, and Syrah. The wines remain rather light and blunt, but
improvements are evident from 1995 onwards.

Pepperwood Springs

1200 Holmes Ranch Rd., Philo, CA 95466. Tel/fax: 895 2920. Production:
1,000 cases.

This small winery was founded in 1981 by Larry Parsons, but after his
death in a car crash in 1986 the property was bought by Gary and Phyllis
Kaliher. There are only 7 acres of vineyards, planted at 1,500 feet with
Pinot Noir and Chardonnay. The Pinot is usually the better wine. There
is also a decent Sauvignon Blanc from purchased grapes sourced in the
Yorkville Highlands.

Roederer

4501 Highway 128, Philo, CA 95466. Tel: 895 2288. Fax: 895 2120.
Production: 55,000 cases.

Jean-Claude Rouzaud, the head of Roederer in Reims, had a good look round the West Coast before choosing the site for his American winery. He inspected Oregon as well as Carneros and Green Valley, but found that only in Anderson Valley could he plant a large vineyard entirely to his own specifications. With a similar climate to Green Valley, there was no difficulty in ripening Chardonnay to 11 degrees, which was all that was required for sparkling wine. The firm acquired sheep-grazing and orchard land, as well as 80 acres near Boonville that was already planted with vines, although they were grafted over to suit Roederer's purposes. Planting began in 1982.

Dr Michel Salgues, who trained at Montpellier before going to work at Roederer in France, was installed as winemaker. He now has 350 acres in production, spread over three ranches. He finds that the Boonville vineyards are slightly warmer than those in Philo. Phylloxera has attacked their vines, however, so they are leasing other vineyards to see them through the ten or fifteen years until replanting is completed. About two-thirds of the grapes are Chardonnay, although that proportion may diminish slightly after replanting. The vines are trained on an open-lyre trellis system, which gives twice the usual foliage and better exposure to sunlight for the bunches and more regular yields. The spacing is 8x6 and the vines are drip-irrigated. The soils are very acidic.

Salgues says that conditions are completely different from those in Champagne and the fruit must be handled differently. However, some of the same principles which give the French wines such distinction have been adopted by the California team. Up to 20 per cent of the wines are aged in oak casks and then consigned to reserve cellars for up to 3 years before being used for blending. Only the first pressing is used: thus they take 120 gallons per ton yielded by that pressing, and sell off the other 70 gallons. Malolactic fermentation is rare. When it is time to blend the wines, the home team from Reims flies over. Riddling is automated, and after bottling the wines are given 6 months' ageing before release.

The range is limited. The principal wine is the Estate Brut, first made in 1988. The blend is approximately 30 per cent Pinot Noir, 70 per cent Chardonnay. It is aged for two and a half years on the yeast. There is also a Brut Rosé, an equal blend of Chardonnay and Pinot Noir. Rouzaud is particularly proud of this wine. The prestige cuvée is L'Ermitage, a vintage wine, first made in 1989 from 55 per cent Chardonnay, and aged on the yeast for four and a half years.

Rouzaud told me that he had no preconceptions of the style he wanted to achieve in California, but knew there was room for improvement in California sparkling wine quality. In fact the style is the most champagne-like of all the California sparkling wines, possibly because of the use of reserve wines, perhaps because Salgues is French-trained. However the wines have a marked citric edge, which I happen to like, although Rouzaud is thinking of moderating it by inducing more malolactic fermentation in some lots. L'Ermitage could easily be mistaken for champagne and has real depth of flavour, although the regular Brut is not that far behind in quality. The rosé is a lovely fruity delicate wine, with a charming nose of wild strawberries.

Domaine Saint Gregory
4921 East Side Rd., Ukiah, CA 95482. Tel: 463 1532. Fax: 462 8951. Production: 2,500 cases.

Greg Graziano was born in 1954 to a family of grape growers and winemakers who originally came to Mendocino from Piedmont in 1910. After working for other local wineries and for La Crema in Sonoma, he started his own range in 1990, and has been able to draw on the Graziano family vineyards, which amount to 70 acres of Chardonnay (in which Greg has little interest), Primitivo, Pinot Gris, and Carignane. Graziano has another label, Monte Volpe (q.v.) for Italian varietals.

Graziano is keen on Burgundian techniques, often including whole clusters during fermentation, and racks as little as possible. The wines include a fine Pinot Blanc, fermented in 30 per cent new *barriques* and aged on the fine lees for 11 months. Pinot Noir comes from two mountain vineyards in Potter and Anderson valleys, and the wine is aged in 30 per cent new *barriques* for 18 months. Graziano is an accomplished winemaker and the wines are of high quality.

Scharffenberger
See Pacific Echo (p. 523).

Whaler Vineyard
6200 Eastside Rd., Ukiah, CA 95482. Tel: 462 6355. Production: 2,000 cases.

Whaler belongs to the Nyborg family and has been producing wines since 1981. They only produce Zinfandel, which has a good reputation, from their own 24-acre vineyard, which was planted in 1973. Jed Steele has been a winemaking consultant here in recent years.

Wildhurst
111171 Highway 29, Lower Lake, CA. Tel: 994 6525. Production: 12,000 cases.

A Lake County property founded in 1991, Wildhurst draws on 150 acres of estate vineyards. Jed Steele has acted as a consultant. It is best known for its good Sauvignon Blanc. Pinot Noir is bought in from Mendocino.

Christine Woods
3155 Highway 128, Philo, CA 95466. Tel: 895 2115. Production: 2,000 cases.

Vernon Rose owns 20 acres of vineyards, planted in 1982 opposite the Roederer estate. It is planted with Chardonnay and Pinot Noir, and Greg Graziano thinks so highly of the latter that he acts as a consultant here so that he can get his hands on some of that fruit for his own label. There is also a second, higher vineyard, which is planted with Cabernet Sauvignon and Gamay Beaujolais. Quality is modest.

Yorkville Cellars
Milemarker 40.4, Highway 128, Yorkville, CA 95494. Tel: 894 9177. Fax: 894 2426. Production: 1,000 cases.

This small winery in the Yorkville Highlands was founded in 1994, and Greg Graziano somehow finds the time to make the wines. Edward Wallo, the owner, organically farms 30 acres of Bordeaux varieties, including Sauvignon Blanc. The Cabernet Franc can show an exuberant blackberry fruitiness.

NOTE

1 As in Napa and Sonoma, the area code is 707

28

Around the Bay

Ahlgren
20320 Highway 9, Boulder Creek, CA 95006. Tel: 408 338 6071. Fax: 338 9111. Production: 2,500 cases.

Dexter and Valerie Ahlgren were originally home winemakers, and set up their own winery beneath their house in 1976. They own 10 acres of steep vineyards at an elevation of about 1,000 feet, but also buy in grapes from many parts of the state. Their wines include an exotic Chardonnay fermented in American oak, Chenin Blanc, barrel-fermented Santa Cruz Sémillon, Cabernet Sauvignon, Merlot, Cabernet Franc, and often jammy Zinfandel, mostly released in small lots of fewer than 600 cases and sometimes considerably less.

Aptos Vineyard
7278 Mesa Dr., Aptos, CA 95003. Tel: 408 688 3856. Production: 400 cases.

This small, low-yielding Pinot Noir vineyard, planted on deep soil on well-drained hillsides one mile from the Pacific, belongs to John and Patricia Marlo. The wines are made at the Devlin winery. Aptos also buys in Chardonnay from Monterey. The 1992 Pinot Noir was attractive but light.

Bargetto
3535 N. Main St., Soquel, CA 95073. Tel: 831 475 2258. Fax: 475 2664. Production: 35,000 cases.

When this winery was founded on Repeal in 1933 it specialized in fruit wines, but began producing varietal wines from grapes in the 1970s. Paul Wofford is the winemaker. Bargetto own only 20 acres of vineyards in the Santa Cruz Mountains, so most grapes are purchased from vineyards in Santa Cruz and the Central Coast. Their best wines are the Cabernet Sauvignon and Chardonnay from the Santa Cruz Mountains. The dry

Gewürztraminer is attractive, but they also produce some disappointing and expensive Pinot Grigio and Dolcetto from the Central Coast.

Bear Creek Vineyard Company
21428 Bear Creek Rd., Los Gatos, CA 95030. Tel: 408 395 3718. Production: 1,000 cases.

Greg and Pam Stokes founded this mountain winery in 1989. The vineyards are at 2,000 feet overlooking Monterey Bay, and planted with Sémillon, Chardonnay, Petite Sirah, Zinfandel and Carignane.

Bonny Doon
10 Pine Flat Rd., Bonny Doon, CA 95060. Tel: 408 425 3625. Fax: 425 3856. Production: 80,000 cases.

Randall Grahm's celebrated Bonny Doon winery probably makes most of its wines from grapes purchased everywhere except Santa Cruz. Moreover, the winery was planning to move east to Pleasanton in Livermore Valley, although in 1999 Grahm changed his mind. But for over ten years no visit to Santa Cruz has been complete without a visit to Bonny Doon and its resident sage, Randall Grahm. Grahm's acute and often witty observations have dotted earlier sections of this book, precisely because he always has a fresh take on any aspect of the California wine industry that you care to mention.

Grahm began adult life as, in his words, a 'perpetual liberal arts student' but a spell working at a wine shop aroused his curiosity and he went off to Davis to study. After graduating in 1979, he planted some vineyards in 1981 and opened a winery two years later. He knew the area around Bonny Doon, which is why he planted vineyards here, and he also had a hunch that it would be the perfect spot for Pinot Noir, recalling the splendid Pinots that had emerged from the Santa Cruz Mountains in the 1970s. 'I started as a Pinot Noir acolyte, and my heart was broken over and over again. When I tried to make the wine the results were usually unsatisfactory.' The Burgundian clones he had imported turned out to be unsuitable to this region, and despite his efforts to achieve an authentic Burgundian soil – by adding limestone, and by high-density planting – the results were unexciting and he couldn't prevent the vines from growing too vigorously. He was also dejected to discover that most Pinot Noir from Oregon was superior to anything he was making.

Grahm had also planted Chardonnay, and all the Bordeaux red varieties. They were long ago grafted over to Rhône varietals, red and white, as he underwent his conversion experience: his realization that California's Mediterranean-style climate was better suited to Mediterranean varieties than to northern French grapes. He knew from tasting David Bruce's wines that varieties such as Grenache were well suited to California, so he sought out grapes from the same sources in Gilroy. He also found Syrah in Paso Robles, and the wine turned out well. Then in 1984 he started buying Mourvèdre as well, from the old vines in Contra Costa County that are famous now but weren't then. The result was Cigare Volant in 1984 which, when released in 1986, made his name. Although the wine was closer in style to Beaujolais than Châteauneuf-du-Pape, it was still 'shockingly good'.

With red Rhône styles under his belt, he moved on to the whites: Marsanne, Roussanne, and Viognier. Viognier gave him more headaches than the other two. To complicate his life further, he planted test plots of Italian and Spanish varieties in Monterey. They included Barbera, which became the basis of his Big House Red, Sangiovese, Pinot Gris, Malvasia Nera, Canaiolo, Freisa, Tempranillo, Dolcetto, Arneis, Verduzzo, and Moscato Rosa. To Grahm, 'Italianate' is a compliment, and he tries to emulate the high acidity characteristic of many Italian reds.

Grahm emphatically denies that he is an eccentric. 'I'm an empiricist. I want to do what works. If it doesn't work out, like my Pinot Noir, I won't pursue it. I admit I'm making my life even more difficult by planting these grapes in Monterey County, which is not a good region for red grapes. It's too windy and often they don't ripen well. But I think I can turn those conditions to my advantage. I'm not interested in novelty for its own sake. I want people to buy my wines because they like them. I've used domestic varieties such as Clinton and Isabella, but only for eau de vie, because I find them ideally suited. My approach is a pragmatic one. What I'm trying to do is find the right marriage of grape variety and site. I think the grapes I am growing are suited to the region. Certainly I consider that what I am doing is far less eccentric than, say, trying to make champagne-style wines in Napa Valley.'

Wines come and go at Bonny Doon, but some favourites are produced regularly. Cigare Volant is the perky Châteauneuf-style wine; Old Telegram the splendid Mourvèdre; the Grahm Crew Vin Rouge a blend of Grenache and Mourvèdre in a lighter style than the other two wines. Le Sophiste blends Roussanne and, mostly, Marsanne. Syrah, which Grahm buys from Bien Nacido Vineyard and makes superbly, is likely to stay on the menu. The pure Roussanne is concentrated and powerful. If part of Grahm is intellectually restless, another part of him is passionately populist. He wants his wines to be drunk in quantity and enjoyed. Hence the blends, such as the Big House Red; the white Il Pescatore, a blend of Chardonnay, Roussanne, Sauvignon Blanc, and Riesling; and the bright, crisp, cherryish Fiasco, a blend of Sangiovese and Cinsault. I also like the hefty bracing Barbera and the ripe, sensual Charbono.

Despite the rustic informality at Bonny Doon, the winemaking can be quite sophisticated. The Rhône varieties are often fermented as whole clusters, with a preliminary nod in the direction of carbonic maceration. In 1997, if I understood Grahm correctly, he was experimenting with stirring the lees in red wines as well as whites, which is not as daft as it sounds, as I have encountered the same technique in Burgundy. He has pioneered what he calls Glaciere wines, made by freezing whole grapes to double their sugar content, half-thawing them, and then pressing. Bonny Doon is also one of the first California wineries to release grappa, which in the case of the Moscato is intensely aromatic. He has recently fallen in love with Riesling, producing a Pacific Rim bottling that includes grapes from Washington state, and a more serious Critique of Pure Riesling.

Although Randall Grahm is the presiding visionary at Bonny Doon, he is assisted in the winemaking by Dennis Wheeler and Andrew Rich. Grahm is one of the great luminaries of the California wine world, but I am not sure that Bonny Doon is one of the great wineries. There have been some superb bottles, but also some humdrum wines. Nor is there any great consistency. Grahm has little interest in obsessively studying and learning from a particular vineyard; nuances interest him less than the bold statement. Paul Draper of Ridge told me that he admires Randall Grahm even though their ideas are probably diametrically opposed: 'Randall Grahm will try anything and never repeat himself. He has no interest in perfecting anything. He is not interested in *terroir*, while at Ridge we have the privilege of owning great vineyards.' But without the needling and invigorating presence of Randall Grahm, the California wine scene would be a great deal duller.

David Bruce

21439 Bear Creek Rd., Los Gatos, CA 95030. Tel: 405 354 4214. Fax: 395 5478. Production: 35,000 cases.

Dr David Bruce, a dermatologist, came from a teetotal family, but a love of cooking led to an interest in wine. 'One day I bought for seven dollars, a large sum in those days, a bottle of 1954 Richebourg from the Domaine de la Romanée-Conti. It wasn't a great vintage, but drinking that wine persuaded me that I wanted to make Pinot Noir too. I was also inspired by the Pinots Martin Ray was making. Those were ultra-concentrated wines with high acidity.' After a spell as a hobby winemaker, Bruce found 25 acres of vineyards high in the Santa Cruz Mountains and began his new career with the 1964 vintage. The soils up here are sandy loam on a sandstone base; the vines face south and southwest towards Monterey Bay. Rainfall varies from 40 to 80 inches, which by California standards is quite high. Unfortunately his vineyards were badly hit by Pierce's disease, which limited yields drastically for many years. By 1994 he was compelled to replant his vineyards, and the new vines are more closely spaced and new clones have been introduced. Poor corks, notably in the 1987 wines, also caused major problems, and one-third of his bottles had to be withdrawn. Apparently a new winery was built here in 1997, though when I visited later that year it still looked fairly artisanal.

Bruce is best known for the Burgundian varieties. His estate Chardonnay can be excellent in a pungent limey style, though he seems to have abandoned the fondness for new Limousin oak which he experienced during the 1970s.

For Pinot Noir he looks for yields of 2.5 to 3 tons per acre. He retains a much higher percentage of stems than most Pinot producers in California, and ferments in open-top tanks, punching down the cap with bare feet. He unashamedly likes oak, commonly ageing his Pinots for up to 2 years in heavily toasted oak. Some grapes come from his own vineyards (he believes the 30th Anniversary Pinot Noir he made in 1992 is the best wine he has ever made), but he also buys fruit from Russian River, Chalone, and Sonoma County. The 1994 Russian River Reserve was as good as most wines being made in Russian River itself. Yet in Bruce's view the Santa Cruz Mountains give the longest-lived and most complex Pinot Noir in America.

Bruce makes other wines too. I have enjoyed his Paso Robles Zinfandel, and his San Luis Obispo Petite Sirah, which is made in a delightfully fleshy style without the harsh tannins that can mar this variety. Although Cabernet Sauvignon is not usually his best wine, the 1995 from Santa Cruz Mountains was dense and spicy.

There have, however, always been problems with consistency here. David Bruce acknowledges that, like Heitz and other wineries, he has had bacterial problems with brettanomyces in his cellars. Far too many wines have had weird off-flavours and unclean tastes. At other times, especially with Zinfandel, power and over-extraction have resulted in rather brutal wines. He was among the first winemakers to unleash the ultra-ripe, ultra-oaky Chardonnays that were to set the style for the variety through the 1970s, although today they are more restrained. I have been fortunate in my experiences of the Bruce wines. The older vintages I have encountered have been intriguing, and the wines more recently tasted from the 1994 and 1995 vintages have been of the highest quality. Perhaps I have been lucky, or perhaps David Bruce, having beaten off brettanomyces, duff corks, and Pierce's disease, is back on top form.

Burrell School Vineyards
24060 Summit Rd., Los Gatos, CA 95030. Tel/fax: 408 353 6290.

This winery, founded in 1990 and owned by David and Anne Moulton, is located in an 1890 schoolhouse on the site of a vineyard originally cultivated by Lyman Burrell in the 1850s. The 5-acre vineyard, over 1,500 feet up in the mountains, is planted with Chardonnay and Merlot, and in addition Zinfandel is purchased in Sonoma Valley and Amador County. The barrel-fermented Chardonnay is buttery and rich.

Byington
21850 Bear Creek Rd., Los Gatos, CA 95030. Tel: 408 354 1111. Fax: 354 2782. Production: 12,000 cases.

The industrialist Bill Byington founded this estate in 1987. The vineyards, 2,000 feet up in the mountains, consist of eight closely spaced acres of terraced Pinot Noir and Syrah, but most fruit is bought in from various parts of California, and vinified by Steve Devitt. The main focus is on Santa Cruz Mountains Chardonnay, of which there are a number of bottlings, and Cabernet Sauvignon from the same appellation. In addition there is Merlot from Sonoma, Cabernet Sauvignon from Alexander Valley, and Napa Chardonnay. Initial releases were disappointing.

Calle Cielo
Tel: 408 395 1868. Production: 2,000 cases.

Alan Philips, who was formerly responsible for making wine at Monticello, has set up his own small winery at Byington, the first release being a 1996 Santa Cruz Mountains Chardonnay.

Cedar Mountain Winery
7000 Tesla Rd., Livermore, CA 94550. Tel: 925 373 6636. Fax: 373 6694. Production: 1,200 cases.

The winery was founded in 1990 by Linda and Earl Ault, the latter being the winemaker. The Aults also own the 14-acre Blanches Vineyard, from which they produce medium-bodied Chardonnay and Cabernet Sauvignon.

Chaine d'Or
Woodside, CA. Tel: 415 851 8977. Fax: 851 0145.

The vineyards are planted with Chardonnay and Cabernet Sauvignon, and very small quantities are bottled.

Cinnabar Vineyards
23000 Congress Spring Rd., Saratoga, CA 95071. Tel: 408 741 5858. Production: 5,000 cases.

Tom Mudd established this vineyard in 1984, and the first release was from the 1986 vintage. At an elevation of 1,650 feet, Mudd cultivates 30 dry-farmed acres of Chardonnay planted with the Mount Eden clone, and Cabernet Sauvignon. Both wines are of good quality. There is also a Merlot from the Central Coast. The winemaker is George Troquato.

Clos LaChance

21511 Saratoga Heights Dr., Saratoga, CA 95070. Tel: 408 741 1796. Production: 2,000 cases.

Bill and Brenda Murphy produce Chardonnay, Pinot Noir, and Cabernet Sauvignon only from Santa Cruz Mountains fruit. The Chardonnay receives whole-cluster pressing, is barrel-fermented and goes through full malolactic fermentation.

Concannon Vineyard

4590 Tesla Rd., Livermore, CA 94550. Tel: 925 456 2505. Fax: 456 2511. Production: 100,000 cases.

James Concannon, an immigrant from Ireland, founded this well-known estate in 1883, and ran it until his death in 1911. Extremely well connected with the Roman Catholic hierarchy and aware of its urgent need of sacramental wines, the Concannons continued to produce wine through the Prohibition period. By the early 1980s the company was producing about one million bottles per year. Then it was hit by a succession of changes. It was sold first to Agustin Huneeus, then to Deinhard, and most recently to Wente, its neighbour in Livermore Valley. The winemaker since 1992 has been Tom Lane.

Today Concannon cultivates 150 acres of gravelly vineyards in the valley, and its principal wine is Sauvignon Blanc, which is blended with 20 per cent Sémillon. The Chardonnay is made in a commercial style. Concannon's best-known wine has been its Petite Sirah, now a blend of fruit from Livermore and Monterey, and aged in French oak for 12 months. The Reserve wines include a white and red Meritage called Assemblage, and an old-vine Petite Sirah.

Cooper-Garrod Estate Vineyards

22600 Mount Eden Rd., Saratoga, CA 95070. Tel: 408 741 8094. Production: 3,000 cases.

Since 1972 the Cooper family has been farming 21 acres of vineyards planted with Chardonnay (5 acres), Cabernet Sauvignon (11), and Cabernet Franc (5). From 1991 onwards, George Cooper has made and released estate-grown wines, all with the Santa Cruz Mountains appellation.

Thomas Coyne

51 East Valecitos Rd., Livermore, CA 94550. Tel: 925 443 6588. Production: 5,000 cases.

This winery opened in 1994 on the site of Chateau Bellevue, once a well-known Livermore winery that vanished decades ago. It now produces Merlot and a Rhône-style blend.

Crescini Wines

2621 Old San Jose Rd., Soquel, CA 95073. Tel: 408 462 1466. Production: 1,500 cases.

Founded in 1980 by Richard Crescini, this family-run winery in the Soquel highlands specializes in Chardonnay, Cabernet Sauvignon, and Cabernet Franc from both Santa Cruz and Monterey.

Cronin

11 Old La Honda Rd., Woodside, CA 94062. Tel: 415 851 1452. Fax: 851 5696. Production: 2,000 cases.

From the outside the Cronin winery looks like any other suburban house on the hills near Woodside. The plastic-lined tea chests out in the garden turn out to be the fermenting tanks, buckets take the place of pumps, and the barrels are stored in the basement. Duane Cronin, who moved here in 1975, was a hobby winemaker to start with, but by 1980 was producing too much wine for his own use. His first commercial release was a 1980 Chardonnay. Gradually the business expanded, until in 1992 Cronin committed himself to it full-time, and is now assisted in winemaking tasks by Roger Givens.

Cronin has a small vineyard close to his house. It is planted with Cabernet Sauvignon, which doesn't usually ripen properly, and Chardonnay, and he has recently planted 2 acres of Pinot Noir.

Cronin produces a wide range of wines, and the list will vary from year to year depending on his vineyard sources. He is best known for his often superlative Chardonnays. There is often a Santa Cruz Mountains Chardonnay blending fruit from various vineyards, and an Alexander Valley Chardonnay. Chardonnay always goes through malolactic fermentation, as even the fruit from Alexander Valley can be high in acidity. Both these wines are built to last and benefit from bottle-age. Other whites have included a Sauvignon Blanc from Santa Cruz Mountains; however, the vineyard, St Charles, is about to become a golf course, so it's unlikely that that wine will ever be repeated. There has also been Pinot Blanc from Monterey.

Cronin likes to use whole clusters when fermenting his red wines, even Cabernet Sauvignon. Most of the reds are aged in French oak, though American is used for Zinfandel. Cabernet is aged in 50 per cent new oak (Chardonnays usually gets 40 per cent), slightly less for Pinot Noir. Reds are neither fined nor filtered. Zinfandel comes from Livermore, and from a dying vineyard near Gilroy (another wine that won't be repeated). Other than Pinot Noir, probably his best red is the Santa Cruz Mountains Cabernet Sauvignon.

Changing vineyard sources can be a headache for the winemaker and consumer alike. Cronin no longer makes Napa Chardonnay because the vineyards have been replanted to other varieties (Sangiovese, mostly), and even old vineyards can die off. On the other hand new, untried fruit presents him with a succession of challenges, and his loyal clientele has fully justified confidence in his winemaking abilities. At times Cronin is tempted to limit his range to Santa Cruz Mountains Chardonnay and Pinot Noir, because he feels these are the wines he makes best.

Devlin Wine Cellars
3801 Park Ave., Soquel, CA 95073. Tel: 408 476 7288. Fax: 479 9043. Production: 10,000 cases.

Charles Devlin founded this estate in 1978, and although he has some vineyards, most of the grapes are purchased. As well as fine Chardonnay, Cabernet Sauvignon, and Zinfandel from Santa Cruz Mountains, he makes some Chardonnay and Merlot from the Central Coast.

Fellom Ranch Vineyards
17075 Monte Bello Rd., Cupertino, CA 95014. Tel/fax: 408 741 0307. Production: 1,500 cases.

Not far from Monte Bello, Roy Fellom cultivates an old 14-acre vineyard at a height of 2,400 feet; here he has planted Cabernet Sauvignon and a little Merlot. He also produces Cabernet and Zinfandel from Santa Clara County.

Fenestra Winery
83 East Vallecitos Rd., Livermore, CA 94550. Tel: 510 862 2292. Production: 4,000 cases.

Retired chemistry professor Lanny Replogle started up this small winery in the mid-1980s, buying in fruit mostly from Livermore Valley vineyards but also from Monterey. He offers a wide range of wines, including the standard varietals, as well as a lighter blend called True Red, containing Zinfandel, Pinot Noir, and Merlot, Chardonnay fermented in new oak, and Pinot Blanc from Monterey. Semonnay is an Australian-style blend of Sémillon and Chardonnay.

Thomas Fogarty Winery
5937 Alpine Rd., Portola Valley, CA 94028. Tel: 415 851 1946. Production: 10,000 cases.

Dr Thomas Fogarty established these San Mateo vineyards in the late 1970s and the winery was built in 1982. He cultivates 18 acres of Chardonnay and 7 of Pinot Noir at an elevation of 2,000 feet, but most of his grapes are bought in from Carneros, Napa, and the Central Coast. The winemaker from the start has been Michael Martella. He is best known for his toasty estate Chardonnay and Pinot Noir and for the dry Gewürztraminers which come from the Ventana Vineyard in Arroyo Seco.

Fortino

4525 Hecker Pass Highway, Gilroy, CA 95020. Tel: 408 842 3305. Fax: 842 8636. Production: 30,000 cases.

This old-style Italian winery, founded by Italian immigrant Ernest Fortino in 1970, derives its grapes from the 120 acres of vineyard his family owns or leases. Most of the many wines are made in an undemanding style by Gino Fortino.

Emilio Guglielmo

1480 East Main Ave., Morgan Hill, CA 95037. Tel: 405 779 2145. Fax: 779 3166. Production: 100,000 cases under various labels.

An old-style winery, which used to be known for its rustic jug wines, until it began to offer varietal wines in the 1980s. The winery owns a 100-acre vineyard in Santa Clara but a good deal of the fruit, especially from white varieties, is bought from Monterey and Napa.

Jory

3920 Hecker Pass Highway, Gilroy, CA 95020. Tel: 408 847 6306. Production: 3,000 cases.

This winery, founded in 1984 by Dan Lewis and Stillman Brown, the winemaker, produces a variety of whimsical blends from varieties such as Zinfandel, Mourvèdre, Carignane, and Syrah, mostly from Santa Clara and San Ysidro fruit. Some Chardonnay and Pinot Noir are also made. Quality is middling.

Kathryn Kennedy

13180 Pierce Rd., Saratoga, CA 95070. Tel: 408 867 4170. Production: 1,000 cases.

Kathryn Kennedy does one thing and does it very well. When developers seemed ready to pounce on some of her land, Kathryn Kennedy planted 10 acres of dry-farmed Cabernet Sauvignon on it in 1973 and then again in 1988. The soil here is clay with a rocky subsoil, but the low elevation of the vineyard means that the microclimate is a warm one and the resulting wine is rich in style. At first the grapes were sold to other wineries, but in 1979 Kathryn and her son Martin Mathis began making the wine. It's a dense, structured Cabernet with an intense mint and cassis nose, aged mostly in French oak and unfiltered, intended for long-ageing.

Those daunted by its high price can try the winery's Lateral, a Bordeaux blend first made in 1988 and dominated by Merlot and thus more accessible.

Klein Vineyards
Production: 400 cases.

The Swiss banker Arturo Klein farms 3 acres of Cabernet Sauvignon, from which he produces a small quantity of wine.

Livermore Valley Cellars
1508 Wetmore Rd., Livermore, CA 94550. Tel: 925 447 1751. Production: 3,000 cases.

Chris Laggis owns 34 acres of dry-farmed vineyards. At one time he sold the grapes to Wente, but now he produces his own wines from a rather old-fashioned clutch of varieties including Golden Chasselas, Gray Riesling, French Colombard, and Chardonnay.

McHenry Vineyard
330 11th St., Davis, CA 95616. Tel: 916 756 3202. Winery at Bonny Doon Rd. Production: 400 cases.

Dean McHenry founded this small estate in 1980, cultivating 3 acres of Pinot Noir and 1 of Chardonnay. There is also a Carneros Pinot Noir.

Mariani Vineyards
23600 Congress Springs Rd., Saratoga, CA 95070. Tel: 408 741 2930. Fax: 867 4824.

The winery releases Chardonnay, Cabernet Franc, Zinfandel, and Carignane made from estate-grown grapes.

Mount Eden Vineyards
22020 Mount Eden Rd., Saratoga, CA 95070. Tel: 415 867 5832. Production: 12,000 cases.

Tasting and lunching with Jeff Patterson at his remote house among the vineyards, I was surprised by the number of visitors toiling up a private road to a height of 2,000 feet to an estate that is not usually open to the public. For Mount Eden, to devotees of California wine, is a legendary property, and even being denied a tasting by the owner (fair enough on a Saturday lunchtime) is better to some than not laying eyes on the property at all.

The original vineyard here was the 23-acre Martin Ray Vineyard, but Ray's incessant quarrelling, especially with his business partners, led to his losing control of the property in the 1970s. The vineyard was divided. Ray retained the lower portion and Mount Eden kept the upper part.

Today there are 36 acres under vine, and 9 of those are the 40-year-old Pinot Noir vines that yield minute quantities of superlative grapes. Ten of the 36 acres are planted with Chardonnay, and half of those vines are very elderly too. The low crop means that the total production of estate-grown wine is no more than 2,000 cases. It is not only old age that keeps yields so low: there are constant problems with invading deer and with erosion. There has been some replanting, of course, and the new vines are more closely spaced.

The history of the vineyard and its famous clones has been given earlier. Jeff Patterson is convinced that the marked mineral taste of the Chardonnay derives largely from the clone. The winemaking is traditional, with barrel fermentation, and a year of bottle-age before release. The wine is famously long-lived and needs time to shed its initial austerity. Mount Eden fans in a hurry, and with shallower pockets, can buy the winery's second Chardonnay, which used to be called MEV and is now called MacGregor Vineyard. The grapes come from that vineyard in Edna Valley, and the resulting wine is opulent, fruit-salady, and more of a crowd-pleaser than the noble estate wine. With an annual production of 10,000 bottles, this second Chardonnay also provides cash flow to the winery.

The Pinot Noir is not destemmed, and used to be aged entirely in new oak, although Patterson has reduced that amount slightly in recent vintages. Before bottling the wine is lightly fined but not filtered. The dense Cabernet Sauvignon, which comes from a parcel of vines planted lower down the slope at a height of 1,400 feet, is aged for about 18 months. Both are excellent, long-lived wines, though it is an oddity of Mount Eden that the Pinot Noir tends to fade into old age before the Chardonnay.

Murrieta's Well

3005 Mines Rd., Livermore, CA 94550. Tel: 925 456 2390. Fax: 456 2391. Production: 5,000 cases.

Philip Wente has resuscitated the old Louis Mel winery and its 91-acre vineyard, which was originally planted in 1880. Under winemaker Sergio Traverso, this winery focuses on two blends. The red Vendimia is a somewhat neutral Bordeaux blend with some Zinfandel; the confected white consists of Sauvignon Blanc, Sémillon and Muscat Canelli. There is also a small quantity of Zinfandel from the nearby Raboli Vineyard.

Obester Winery

12341 San Mateo Rd., Half Moon Bay, CA 94019. Tel: 415 726 9463.

This winery, one of the most northerly in the Santa Cruz region, is best known for its white wines.

Pacheco Ranch Winery

Ignacio. Production: 750 cases.

One of the few wineries north of San Francisco in Marin County, Pacheco Ranch farms 12 acres of Cabernet Sauvignon and Cabernet Franc, which has been bottled by the owners, the Rowland family, since the late 1970s.

Retzlaff Vineyards

1356 S. Livermore Ave., Livermore, CA 94550. Tel: 925 447 8941. Production: 3,000 cases.

In the mid-1980s Bob Taylor planted 14 acres in Livermore. The range of wines, mostly estate-grown, includes Sauvignon Blanc, Merlot, Chardonnay, and Cabernet Sauvignon.

Ridge Vineyards

17100 Monte Bello Rd., Cupertino, CA 95015. Tel: 408 867 3233. Fax: 867 2986. Production: 60,000 cases.

This celebrated vineyard and winery has ancient roots. In 1885 Osea Perrone planted his Monte Bello vineyard and built a winery. He chose his site well, as there is limestone in the subsoil. Prohibition put an end to the property, until in 1959 a group of scientists from Stanford University bought land here for a holiday home. They found some old Cabernet vines on the land and vinified them. The wines were so intense that the partners, who intended to grow grapes and sell them to local wineries, decided it was worth building a winery. In 1969 they invited Paul Draper to become their winemaker, and he is still there. In 1986 Ridge was acquired by Akihiko Otsuka of Japan.

The first wines had been made in 1964 by the late David Bennion, one of the original partners. Besides the Monte Bello grapes, fruit, mostly Zinfandel, was bought from neighbouring sites as well as from the Dusi Ranch in Paso Robles. Draper continued this policy, seeking out fine parcels of Zinfandel and field blends from various parts of California, and swiftly transforming Monte Bello into one of the state's great Cabernets. At first the Ridge team vinified grapes from thirty-five different Zinfandel vineyards in order to determine which they liked best and which held up best after bottling.

The winemaking style remains non-interventionist, and Zinfandel receives just as much care as the more costly Cabernet. Draper does not use cultivated yeasts and avoids filtration if he possibly can. He compensates for this by running a very sophisticated laboratory at the winery, to ensure that the wines are stable enough to survive a long life in good condition. Draper favours a submerged-cap fermentation, which is gentle and ideal for rich grapes since it does not over-extract. Their lab also allows them to assess tannin levels before vinification commences, so that they can adjust their fermentation techniques accordingly. It is common for quite a large proportion of whole berries to be left in the fermentation tanks.

The Monte Bello vineyard is planted in reddish decomposed rock mixed with clay, with a subsoil of fractured limestone. The average age of the vines is now thirty years. The more recently planted vines are more closely spaced and trained on vertical trellising. At 2,300 feet, the vineyard is well above the fog line, and in some years not all the grapes ripen. The result is a wine that is dense and structured and long-lived, rather than full and fleshy and sensuous. 'We have from time to time tried ten other vineyards for Cabernet, but we have never found anything remotely as good as Monte Bello. It's a wine that makes itself,' remarks Draper.

In 1992 Monte Bello was composed of twenty-two different lots, and there can be as many as thirty. Early vintages were pure Cabernet and could be fairly tough, but in recent years it has been usual to blend in 10 to 15 per cent Merlot, and up to 10 per cent Petit Verdot. Thus in 1996 the wine contained only 68 per cent Cabernet. These decisions are made on the basis of tasting. Most outstanding California Cabernet is aged in French oak, but not Monte Bello, which has always been aged mostly in American oak, entirely new. Draper insists that he is not trying to make imitation claret. About 3,500 cases are produced. Lots rejected from the final blend are often released as Santa Cruz Mountains Cabernet, although Draper insists that barrels are often rejected not because the wine is second-rate but because they do not have the structure or longevity he is looking for with Monte Bello. Ridge used to make a delicious Cabernet from York Creek Vineyard in Napa, but the source began to dry up in the early 1990s as the owner, Fritz Maytag, decided to vinify the grapes himself.

Monte Bello was not produced in 1966, 1979, and 1983. 1964, a pre-Draper wine, is said to have been outstanding, and so are the 1970, 1975, 1981, 1984, 1985, 1988, 1991, and 1995. Because of its microclimate and late ripening, great vintages for Monte Bello do not necessarily coincide with the top Cabernet vintages in Napa or Sonoma.

The crucial decisions about blends, fining, and bottling are made on the basis of taste rather than analysis. The last time I visited Ridge, Paul asked me to join him and his other winemakers in a blind tasting of two blends from Lytton Springs, one with Petite Sirah, the other without. We tasted, scored, discussed. The results confounded our expectation, and Draper decided it would be prudent to run the tasting again later!

There is some Merlot planted in Monte Bello, and since 1985 some of it has been bottled as varietal wine. Vinification is similar to that of the Cabernet, and the wine is aged for 16 months in American oak.

Zinfandel is of course the other great wine, or range of wines, at Ridge. Visiting Ridge in the mid-1980s was an exhilarating if confusing experience, as there was such a profusion of single-vineyard wines to taste. The range has been trimmed down. The most admired and elegant of the Zinfandels, Geyserville, comes from a gravelly loam vineyard farmed by the Trentadue family in Sonoma. Most of the vines are a century old, and there are equally old parcels of Petite Sirah and Carignane, which are blended in to the wine.

Four miles away is Lytton Springs. Ridge have been making wine from here since 1972. The microclimate is slightly hotter than at Geyserville. The wine is aged in American oak, of which 20 per cent is new. The Paso Robles Zinfandel is, I think, slightly underestimated. It is true that it does not age as well as the Sonoma Zinfandels, but it has a charm and seductiveness not present in the other bottlings. The vines are seventy years old and yields are between 1.5 and 2.5 tons per acre; sadly about half the vineyard has now succumbed to phylloxera. There is a further bottling from York Creek in Napa. From time to time, Draper also makes Zinfandel Essences from botrytized grapes; the last vintage for this style was 1993.

Since 1971 Ridge has produced a Petite Sirah from York Creek Vineyard on Spring Mountain in Napa. This used to be an impenetrable wine, and compared to the Zinfandels it is still a tough mouthful. I like the amazing density of the wine, but it is not to everybody's taste.

In 1990 Ridge began producing Mourvèdre wines sourced from the famous old vines in Contra Costa County. Ridge prefers the name Mataro. The wine is aged for 14 months in American oak, and is always an impressive bottle.

The principal white wine from Ridge is the Santa Cruz Mountains Chardonnay, which is grown on the Monte Bello Vineyard. The vines are not that old but yields are low. The wine goes through malolactic fermentation and is aged for about 15 months, on the lees for the first 9 months, in 25 per cent new oak. About half the oak is American. Lesser lots are bottled and released under the California appellation.

Ridge makes superlative wines across the board. I don't believe I have ever had a disappointing bottle, though clearly some wines evolve better than others. Paul Draper says although the early vintages from Ridge were very slow to develop, this is not the style of wine he wants to make now. He looks for wines that are well balanced, that will be approachable in their youth but have sufficient equilibrium to age for ten or twenty years. He believes that all great wines are an expression of *terroir* and have a distinctive individual character. He has been critical of the trend at certain wineries to issue Reserve wines that are blends from various vineyards. For him, great wine is allied to individual vineyards. His winemaking may not be French in style, but his philosophical approach is.

Roudon-Smith Winery
2364 Bean Creek Rd., Santa Cruz, CA 95066. Tel: 831 438 1244. Production: 2,000 cases.

Two families, the Roudons and the Smiths, teamed up in 1972 to buy vineyards and in 1978 they built their own winery. They grow their own Chardonnay on 12 acres of vineyards, but buy in much of their fruit. The wines are made by Bob Roudon. Four of the wines have the Santa Cruz Mountains appellation: Chardonnay, Pinot Noir, Syrah, and Cabernet Sauvignon. There is also Zinfandel, Merlot and Cabernet from San Luis Obispo. The wines lack finesse but are soundly made. Production is tailing off as the families edge into retirement.

Rubissow-Sargent
Alameda. Production: 2,500 cases.

Named after its principals, George Rubissow and Tony Sargent, this small property cultivates 18 acres of Cabernet Sauvignon, Cabernet Franc, and Merlot on Mount Veeder. The wines are vinified in rented facilities in Berkeley. The only wines made are Cabernet Sauvignon, Merlot, and a blend of Cabernet Franc and Merlot known as Les Trompettes.

Salamandre Wine Cellars
108 Don Carlos Dr., Aptos, CA 95003. Tel: 408 685 0321. Production: 2,000 cases.

In a canyon near Aptos Wells, Shoemaker produces small lots of Chardonnay, Pinot Noir, Merlot, and Syrah and Cabernet Sauvignon from vineyards in Santa Cruz Mountains and Arroyo Seco in Monterey.

Santa Cruz Mountain Vineyard
2300 Jarvis Rd., Santa Cruz, CA 95065. Tel: 408 426 6209. Production: 2,500 cases.

Ken Burnap has for many years been sustaining the reputation of wines from the Santa Cruz Mountains. There were vineyards planted here in 1863, and Burnap started the gravity-flow winery in 1974. Today Jeff Emery is the winemaker. There are 13 acres of Pinot Noir here, and a little Chardonnay; yields are minute, and must be supplemented by purchases from other vineyards in the region as well as Merlot and Petite Sirah from outside it. The first release was a Pinot Noir in 1975. Burnap likes to ferment extremely ripe grapes on the natural yeasts, and the style here is powerful and uncompromising. The wines have been quite tannic, although Burnap is using techniques such as whole-cluster fermentation and punching down the cap by hand in order to soften those tannins. Pinot Noir is usually aged for about 14 months, and the Cabernet Sauvignon for

26 months. The Chardonnay is of course barrel-fermented. All wines are aged in bottle for 2 to 3 years before release. As with most artisanal wines, there are failures as well as successes, but overall quality is high, reminding us of the tremendous fruit quality of these shrinking vineyards.

Sarah's Vineyard
4005 Hecker Pass Highway, Gilroy, CA 95020. Tel: 408 842 4278. Fax: 842 3252. Production: 2,000 cases.

John Otteman bought this property in 1977, and the estate is now owned and the wines are made by Marilyn Clark. The first release was from the 1983 vintage. The vineyards consist of 9 acres of Chardonnay, Riesling, and Pinot Noir, and the winery produces a Grenache-dominated blend as well as a Merlot. Prices are high for the quality.

Sherrill Cellars
1185 Skyline Blvd., Palo Alto, CA 94301. Tel: 415 851 1932.

The winery was built here in 1979, and the wines are made by Nathaniel Sherrill. The second label is Skyline.

Silver Mountain Vineyards
Silver Mountain Dr., Santa Cruz, CA 95063. Tel: 408 353 2278. Production: 2,000 cases.

Jerold O'Brien bought 17 acres 2,000 feet up in the mountains in 1979, but has supplemented his own production with purchased fruit from Monterey and Sonoma. The range of wines consists of barrel-fermented Chardonnays, Cabernet Sauvignon, Pinot Noir, and Zinfandel. There was a severe setback in 1989, when an earthquake destroyed the winery, which rose again from the ashes in 1993. Somehow it managed to produce a sweet, minty Merlot in 1991.

Solis
3920 Hecker Pass Rd., Gilroy, CA 95020. Tel: 408 847 6306. Fax: 847 5188. Production: 5,000 cases.

David Vanni bought the former Bertero winery in 1989 and subsequently expanded its 10 acres of vineyards with 5 more acres of Sangiovese and Cabernet Sauvignon. Vanni and his winemaker Corey Wilson purchase fruit from Santa Clara and the Central Coast. Solis has not managed to win a high reputation, but is best known for its Chardonnay and Merlot.

Soquel Vineyards
7880 Glen Haven Rd., Soquel, CA 95073. Tel: 408 462 9045. Production: 2,000 cases.

This estate was known as Grover Gulch until its closure in 1985. In 1987 the Bargetto winery (q.v.) bought it, and the property is run by Peter and Paul Bargetto. The wines come from leased vineyards in the Santa Cruz Mountains and from Stags Leap in Napa, and only Cabernet Sauvignon, Chardonnay, and Pinot Noir are released. Unfortunately, quality has not matched aspirations.

P. & M. Staiger
1300 Hopkins Gulch Rd., Boulder Creek, CA 95006. Tel: 408 338 4346. Production: 500 cases.

Paul and Marjorie Staiger started off as home winemakers in 1973, having acquired the site originally planted in the nineteenth century. The vineyards consist of 5 acres of Chardonnay, Cabernet Sauvignon, and Merlot. The first vintage was 1979.

Stony Ridge
4948 Tesla Rd., Livermore, CA 94550. Tel: 925 449 0458. Fax: 449 0646. Production: 20,000 cases.

Not far from the Livermore giants of Wente and Concannon, a group of investors set up this winery in 1975. Ten years later the name was sold to the Scotto family that had previously operated a winery called Villa Armando in Pleasanton, and in 1992 the Scottos built a new winery for the Stony Ridge range. The wines are cheap and cheerful: white Zinfandel, Chardonnay, Cabernet Sauvignon, and a sparkling Malvasia.

Storrs Winery
303 Petrero St., Santa Cruz, CA 95060. Tel: 408 458 5030. Fax: 458 0464. Production: 4,000 cases.

Stephen and Pamela Storrs founded this winery in 1988. They own no vineyards. They specialize in full-blown Chardonnays from Santa Cruz Mountains vineyards. These are barrel-fermented, go through full malolactic fermentation with prolonged lees contact, and are aged in a high proportion of new oak. They also produce small lots of Riesling, Gewürztraminer, Merlot, Cabernet Sauvignon, and earthy vigorous Zinfandel.

Sunrise Winery
13100 Monte Bello Rd., Cupertino, CA 95014. Tel: 408 741 1310. Fax: 741 5857. Production: 2,500 cases.

This was the site of the historic Picchetti Vineyard and was acquired by Rolayne and Ron Stortz in 1983. They restored the winery and now cultivate 6 acres of Zinfandel, and buy in Chardonnay from mountain vineyards. Rolayne Stortz makes the wines, which include small quantities of Chardonnay, Pinot Blanc, Cabernet Sauvignon, Pinot Noir, and Petite Sirah.

Sycamore Creek Vineyards

12775 Uvas Rd., Morgan Hill, CA 95037. Tel: 408 779 4738. Fax: 779 5873. Production: 3,500 cases.

In 1975 Walter and Mary Parks founded this estate on the site of the former Marchetti winery. They farmed 14 acres of vineyards that include Zinfandel and Carignane planted in 1906. In 1989 the estate was acquired by the Japanese sake producer, Morita. Jeff Runquist is the winemaker. Cabernet Sauvignon is made from Santa Clara fruit, but Chardonnay comes from Sonoma, and Sauvignon Blanc from Monterey.

Iván Tamás

5443 Tesla Rd., Livermore, CA 94550. Tel: 925 456 2380. Fax: 456 2381. Production: 60,000 cases.

In 1984 winemaker Iván Tamás and Steve Mirassou teamed up to produce wines in Napa, but in 1986 they moved to Livermore. They produce some unusual wines, mostly from Livermore fruit, including Sangiovese and possibly the only Trebbiano in California other than Viansa's. There is also a steel-fermented Fumé Blanc, a broadly flavoured Chardonnay, and a firm oaky Cabernet Sauvignon. There are also some reserve wines. Prices are reasonable.

Testarossa Vineyards

1115 Polk Ave., Sunnyvale, CA 94086. Tel: 408 739 5033. Fax: 732 5724. Production: 3,000 cases.

Rob and Diana Jensen's winery released its first wine in 1994. Only Chardonnay, Pinot Noir, and Pinot Blanc are produced and all grapes are purchased from vineyards in Santa Cruz, Monterey, and Santa Barbara. The wines are made at Cinnabar winery by George Troquato, with Michael Michaud, formerly of Chalone, as the consultant winemaker. The white wines are aged in about 40 per cent new oak, except for the steel-fermented Viognier.

Thunder Mountain

Production: 2,000 cases.

Scott Sterling founded this splendid named vineyard in 1995, and Milan Maximovich, the winemaker, has been specializing in Santa Cruz Mountains Chardonnay and Cabernet Sauvignon. The Chardonnay is barrel-fermented in new French oak, and bottled without fining or filtration. The Cabernet receives extended maceration and malolactic fermentation takes place in barrel. The overall style is lush and hefty.

Troquato Vineyards
247 More Ave., Los Gatos, CA 95030. Tel: 408 866 6700. Production:
1,000 cases.

At this family-operated winery, which opened its doors in 1976, George
Troquato makes small quantities of Chardonnay, Cabernet Sauvignon,
and Zinfandel from their 10 acres of vineyards.

Trout Gulch Vineyards
3875 Trout Gulch Rd., Aptos, CA 95003. Tel: 408 688 4380. Production:
1,000 cases.

Only estate-grown mountain grapes from the property's 15 acres are used
to produce Chardonnay and Pinot Noir.

Wente Vineyards
5565 Tesla Rd., Livermore, CA 94550. Tel: 925 456 2300. Fax: 456 2319.
Production: 600,000 cases.

One of the oldest family-owned estates in California, Wente was founded
in 1883 by Carl Wente, who planted 40 acres in the Livermore Valley,
which was considerably more rural then than it is today. For many decades
Wente produced only bulk wines, but after Repeal it began bottling wines
and was one of the first to do so using varietal names. Carl was succeeded
by his sons Herman and Ernest, and then by Ernest's son Karl, who died
suddenly in 1977. His widow Jean took over, and now the business is run
by her three children: Eric, Philip, and Carolyn. Since then the property
has expanded greatly. In 1981 they bought the Cresta Blanca winery site
and replanted what used to be the Charles Wetmore Vineyard, from which
the Wente clones of Sauvignon Blanc and Sémillon were developed. In
1992 they acquired Concannon. In the mid-1990s they became involved
in a joint venture with a wine-producing company in Georgia in the
Caucasus, but it collapsed, no doubt as a consequence of doing any kind
of business in that part of the world. In 1996, taking on board the fact
that Carolyn Wente was no man, the name was changed from Wente
brothers to Wente Vineyards.

Wente now own some 3,000 acres of vineyards. With suburban expansion in Livermore there was no way Wente could add to its 1392 acres
there, so as early as the 1960s it began to purchase land in Monterey,
especially around Arroyo Seco. Chardonnay is the dominant variety they
have planted there, but Riesling is also grown.

The basic range of wines is the Family Selection, consisting of White
Zinfandel, Grey Riesling, Riesling, and a Chenin Blanc called Le Blanc de
Blancs. Most of these wines have quite a lot of residual sugar. There
are sound estate bottlings of Chardonnay, Sauvignon Blanc, Cabernet

Sauvignon and Merlot, and a whole range of single-vineyard bottlings, many of which come from their vineyards in Monterey. The wines are cleanly made and fairly priced, but I find them somewhat anaemic. They are made in a lean style and lack complexity. From time to time Wente make a late harvest Riesling and in 2003 they will release a Sangiovese from a vineyard recently planted in Livermore. Their sparkling wine, a Brut Reserve, is a fine blend of 60 per cent Pinot Noir, 29 per cent Chardonnay, and 11 per cent Pinot Blanc; it is aged for 5 years on the yeast and deserves to be better known.

Woodside Vineyards
340 Kings Mountain Rd., Woodside, CA 94062. Tel: 415 851 3144. Production: 2,000 cases.

This estate, founded in the 1960s by Robert Mullen, farms or leases 40 acres of Pinot Noir and Chardonnay, and also owns the tiny La Questa Vineyard, which was originally planted in 1882 and now grows Cabernet Sauvignon, released at $50 per bottle. The range is quite extensive, but the wines – Zinfandel, Cabernet Sauvignon, Pinot Noir, Chardonnay, dry Gewürztraminer – are mostly made in small lots and often aged in American oak. The winemaker is Brian Caselden.

Zayante
420 Old Mount Rd., Felton, CA 95018. Tel: 408 335 7992. Fax: 335 5770. Production: 1,000 cases.

This 10-acre property, which was planted in 1984 in the Santa Cruz Mountains, is owned by Kathleen Starkey and the winemaker is Gregory Nolten. The first vintage was 1991.

29

Monterey

═══

Bernardus
5 West Carmel Valley Rd., Carmel Valley, CA 93924. Tel: 831 659 1900.
Fax: 549 1676. Production: 45,000 cases.

Bernardus 'Ben' Pon, a Dutch wine merchant with a sideline in driving
racing cars, shrewdly chose Carmel Valley when he set up a vineyard and
winery in 1989. From the outset until late 1998 the winemaker was Don
Blackburn, an engaging eccentric with a tendency to lapse into New Age
jargon and with weird theories about the 'synaesthesia' between wines
and certain pieces of music. However, Don trained at Beaune and Montpellier and helped lay out the vineyard, so he was deeply involved with
the venture from the start. This 120-acre Marinus Vineyard is planted at
a density of up to 1,750 vines per acre. Some Chardonnay and Sauvignon
Blanc were planted initially, but these vines have been grafted over to
Cabernet Sauvignon and Merlot, trained on vertical trellising. Yields are
low, at below 3 tons per acre.

Blackburn liked to 'clean up' his wines early on so that they throw
minimal sediment, and aerates them to help with the polymerization of
the tannins. He is not a believer in extended maceration. The creamy
Sauvignon Blanc comes from the Ventana Vineyard and is two-thirds
barrel-fermented. The buttery Chardonnay is a blend of grapes from
various vineyards, barrel-fermented and aged in one-third new *barriques*.
I find some dilution in the Chardonnay, but the style is crisp, toasty, and
enjoyable.

Pinot Noir is sometimes made from Bien Nacido fruit in Santa Maria
Valley, but the best wine is the estate Meritage called Marinus, dominated
by Cabernet Sauvignon and Merlot. After going through malolactic in
large oak uprights, the wine is aged for 12 months in 50 per cent new
barriques. It's a good wine but can sometimes show a slight astringency.

Don Blackburn was succeeded by Mark Chesebro.

Boyer Winery
PO Box 7267, Spreckles, CA 93962. Tel: 831 674 2987. Fax: 455 8019.
Production: 2,000 cases.

Rick Boyer has made the wines at Ventana and at Jekel, and since 1985 has produced wines under his own name from his 8 acres of Chardonnay and from Ventana Chardonnay. Pinor Noir and Syrah are also made. He studied viticulture rather than winemaking at Davis, and this, together with his long experience in Monterey, should augur well for the future of this little property.

Calera
11300 Cienega Rd., Hollister, CA 95023. Tel: 408 637 9170. Production: 25,000 cases.

Josh Jensen spent some time in Burgundy in the early 1970s, working at various prestigious estates including the Domaine de la Romanée-Conti, and became convinced that *terroir* was the secret of Burgundy's eminence with Pinot Noir. So on his return to California, Jensen embarked on a search for the ideal limestone soil which, he had decided, was the *sine qua non* of great Pinot Noir. He found it 2,200 feet up in the Gavilan Mountains, but had to clear the slopes of pine and oak before he could plant his vines. In 1975 he planted 24 acres in three sites. In 1978 he had his first crop but needed a winery. He found a former rock-crushing plant, which he cunningly converted into a gravity-flow winery. The winery is lower down the slopes than the vineyards, at 1,300 feet.

The yields are very low, rarely exceeding 2 tons per acre. The vines ripen between 2 and 4 weeks later than those down in the valley in San Benito. Jensen now has four vineyards in production. The 5-acre Reed, the 14-acre Jensen, the 5-acre Selleck, and the 11-acre Mills, which only came into production in 1984. Selleck has the most limestone among its decomposed granite and is usually the most reticent and backward of the wines; Reed has deeper, darker soils and evolves more rapidly than the others; Mills has the most widespread exposition. Jensen is often the most complete and complex of the quartet, but there are strong variations according to the vintage. Jensen and Selleck are priced slightly higher than the other two Pinots. In the early 1990s Jensen planted some additional vineyards with Pinot Noir, Chardonnay and Viognier. Today there are 47 acres under vine, and they constitute the entire Mount Harlan AVA.

The grapes are hand-picked, and fermented with whole clusters without destemming, using natural yeasts. Under winemaker Steve Doerner, who was here from 1978 to 1992 (and succeeded by Sara Steiner), the cap was punched down but there was no pumping over. The Pinot Noir spends 15 months in medium-toast French oak, with minimal racking and no filtration. Like the Chardonnay, the wine is aged only in one-third new oak.

The estate Chardonnay is bottled as the Mount Harlan Chardonnay. In addition to the estate wines, there are Central Coast bottlings of Chardonnay and Pinot Noir, which are made in much greater quantities and sell for a considerably lower price. In 1994, for example, Reed yielded only 270 cases and Selleck only 429. There were just over 1,000 cases of Mount Harlan Chardonnay in 1995, compared to 11,400 of the Central Coast bottling.

Jensen knew about Viognier from the time he spent working at Château Grillet in 1970. He found cuttings in New York and planted them on his estate in 1983, first making the wine in 1987. He now has 5 acres of the variety, which yields about 1,000 cases of powerful wine.

Jensen's Pinot Noir has never been a fruit-driven charmer. These are wines of extract and power and density, sometimes too much so for their own good. In top vintages they keep very well, developing considerable complexity in bottle. Some rather good Zinfandels used to be made here, but they have been discontinued. The Chardonnay, which often tastes overripe, is probably the least interesting of the wines, but the Viognier can be exceptional, if a touch heavy.

Chalone

Stonewall Canyon Rd & Highway 146, W. Soledad, CA 93960. Tel: 831 678 1717. Fax: 678 2742. Production: 40,000 cases.

As one drives ever higher into the Gavilan Mountains, way above the Salinas Valley, it is hard to imagine what persuaded a Frenchman, Curtis Tamm, to plant vines at a height of 1,800 to 2,000 feet in 1919, especially since there was no water or power available. But his instincts were sound, and some of those original vines survive: the oldest Chardonnay and Chenin Blanc in Monterey. More vines were planted in 1946, supplementing the existing varieties and adding Pinot Blanc and Pinot Noir. The postwar owner, Will Silvear, sold fruit to Wente until his death in the 1950s. Subsequent owners included a Dr Liska and a Mr Sigman, who sold the grapes to Almadén. The estate started to bottle its own wines only from 1960. They were made by Philip Togni, who also gave the estate its name, which refers to an Indian tribe that lived in these mountains. He recalls making daily trips down the mountainside to Salinas to find ice to cool the vats.

In 1965 a new era began when Chalone was bought by Richard Graff, who planted more vineyards. Graff was attracted by the presence of limestone, which he, like Josh Jensen, perceived as the indispensable condition for the production of Burgundian varieties. The first vintage of reborn Chalone was 1969, made by his brother Peter Graff. Conditions were primitive, with no telephone or adequate water supply installed until 1986. Graff made a number of changes. He was one of the first California growers to install drip irrigation, which, although very costly, helped improve pH, acidity, and flavour. He also introduced barrel fermentation of the whites and put them through malolactic fermentation. Chalone employs integrated pest management techniques, but is often plagued by problems such as powdery mildew.

The late 1990s saw many changes at Chalone, which had for some time been the key player in the diverse Chalone group, which included Carmenet, Acacia, and Edna Valley Vineyard. The group as a whole enjoyed a $3 million cross-investment with the Lafite Rothschild group, and owned 24 per cent of Château Duhart-Milon in Pauillac. In January 1998 Richard Graff was killed in a plane crash, depriving Chalone of its founding father, and later that year the longstanding winemaker, Michael Michaud, left, and was replaced by Dan Karlsen.

Today there are 187 acres under vine, 67 per cent of which is Chardonnay. In 1997 they planted 50 more acres of Pinot Noir and 50 of other varieties. Yields are low: 1.5 tons per acre for the old vines, but averaging 3 throughout the vineyard. Any fog burns off early, and the hot days are mitigated by mists and cool air from the Pacific, which can lead to startling fluctuations in temperature. Despite this, it is consistently warmer than Salinas Valley. Annual rainfall is a mere 12 inches. The soil here is volcanic and well drained: limestone deposits interspersed with decomposed granite and moderate amount of clay. There are places where the topsoil is only one foot deep. The Chalone team attribute the astringency of some of their wines, especially in their youth, to excessive sunlight on the vines.

The white wines are fermented in French oak barrels, of which one-third are new. Since 1994 whole-cluster pressing has been adopted, and in 1996 Michaud also began using natural yeast fermentation for the must. After malolactic fermentation, the wines remain on the lees for up to 7 months with stirring. The Chardonnay can have a strong mineral element that needs a few years to integrate into the wine.

Fifteen per cent of production consists of Pinot Blanc from the 36 acres planted with that variety. Chalone admit that some of the older vines may well be Melon. I have never warmed to its heavy, oily style. There are also 8 acres of Chenin, which is aged in older barrels. Since it is made only from the vines planted in 1919 and 1946, it is always released as a Reserve. It's spicy, austere, and very dry.

Pinot Noir also represents only 15 per cent of production. At first the grapes were routinely destemmed; from 1977 until 1989 they were fermented as whole clusters; and then in 1990 Michaud switched back to near-total destemming. Fermentation relies on natural yeasts, the maceration is not especially protracted, and the wine is aged in 50 per cent new *barriques* for up to 14 months, whereas in the 1980s it was often aged for up to 24. In some vintages the Pinot clearly lacked fruit.

Chalone's Reserve wines are mostly made from the oldest vines. They used to be given different oak treatment, ageing in entirely new wood, but that has been discontinued. Lighter wines from the estate were released under the Gavilan label, but in 1997 this was phased out in favour of the new Echelon brand which will mop up wines from the entire Chalone group. Minute quantities of sparkling wine are produced, with lengthy ageing on the yeast. Prices are, for some reason, astronomical, with the 1988 Rosé selling at $80.

Despite the renown of the estate, the wines have been patchy. There have been some magnificent Chardonnays in recent vintages, and, less regularly, splendid Pinot Noir and Chenin Blanc, but there have also been bad patches, including much of the 1980s, whereas I recall marvellous wines from the late 1970s. With so many changes recently occurring at Chalone, it is hard to say what directions the wines are likely to take in future years.

Chateau Julien

8940 Carmel Valley Rd., Carmel Valley, CA 93923. Tel: 831 624 2600. Fax: 624 6138. Production: 300,000 cases, under various labels.

Bob and Patty Brower founded this estate in 1983, although it is now owned by Great American Wineries. Bill Anderson is the winemaker. The Browers own 170 acres of vineyards but buy in considerable quantities from other vineyards throughout Monterey. There are three ranges: Chateau Julien itself, the 'fighting varietals' under the Garland Ranch label, and the inexpensive Emerald Bay range. The top wines are released as Grand Reserves, and there is also a white Meritage called Platinum. Almost all the wines are aged in a blend of French and American oak. The wines are well made but distinctly commercial. They lack flair and individuality.

Cloninger Cellars

1645 River Rd., Salinas, CA 93902. Tel: 831 675 9463. Fax: 675 1922. Production: 3,000 cases.

This small operation is a joint venture, founded in 1989, between four families based in the Santa Lucia Highlands, where their 51 acres of vineyards are located close to Talbott's Sleepy Hollow Vineyard. They specialize in Chardonnay and Pinot Noir, as well as Cabernet Sauvignon from Carmel Valley. The winemaker is Dave Paige, who used to work at Jekel.

Cobblestone Cellars

Drawer A, Soledad, CA 93960. Tel: 831 758 1686. Fax: 758 9769.

This small Arroyo Seco vineyard specializes in Chardonnay, which is produced at Paraiso Springs winery.

Deer Valley Vineyards

800 South Alta St., Gonzales, CA 93926. Tel: 831 675 2481. Fax: 675 2611.

This property was founded in 1974, and winemaker Ed Filice began working for the estate in 1977. After various changes in ownership, Deer Valley came into the hands of the vast Canandaigua company in 1994. Deer Valley recently planted 1,600 acres in southern Monterey. The wines are fighting varietals, heavily blended. Thus the Chardonnay is blended with Pinot Blanc and Chenin Blanc; the Sauvignon Blanc with Riesling and Gewürztraminer. The style is very commercial, but the 1994 Cabernet Sauvignon is fleshy and attractive.

Durney

Tasting room at 13746 Center St., Carmel Valley, CA 93924. Tel: 831 659 6220. Fax: 659 6226. Production: 15,000 cases.

High up in the hills, at 1,200 to 1,500 feet, lie the beautiful vineyards of Durney, the landscape broken by large oaks and framed by the hills all around. They were originally laid out in 1968 by Bill Durney, who had bought what used to be a cattle ranch. After much trial and error, he settled on Bordeaux varieties, white as well as red. The winery followed in 1977. However, the venture was not commercially successful, and five years after Durney's death in 1989 the property was bought by a group of investors who expanded the vineyards. Today there are 105 acres, planted on sandy and clay soils of varying depths, and organically farmed. Despite the altitude, this is a hot area, free from frost. Most of the vineyards are dry-farmed.

Since 1994 the winemaker has been Miguel Martin, a Spaniard with much international experience of his trade. The occasionally jammy Cabernet Sauvignon is aged in 50 per cent new oak, and sometimes a Private Reserve bottling is released, though I prefer the less extracted regular version.

The plump, exotic, barrel-fermented Chardonnay is stirred on the lees during its 9 months in oak. The Chenin here is distinctly sweet, and Riesling was phased out after the 1994 vintage. Pinot Noir is given extended maceration, and aged for 2 years or more in up to 50 per cent new oak

Durney give all their wines considerable bottle age, so they are usually ready to drink on release. Thus in 1997 the current Chardonnay was the 1992 vintage. The second label is Cachagua.

Estancia
1775 Metz Rd., Soledad, CA 93960. Tel: 831 678 0214. Fax: 678 9368. Production: 100,000 cases.

This label, created by Franciscan in 1988, has a split personality. Some of the wines, notably the reds, come from Alexander Valley in Sonoma, while the whites predominantly come from Monterey, where the extensive vineyard holdings are planted with Chardonnay, Sauvignon Blanc, Sémillon, and Pinot Noir.

The range consists of a Fumé Blanc, 75 per cent barrel-fermented. The stylish Chardonnay is only 40 per cent barrel-fermented and goes through full malolactic fermentation. The Reserve is barrel-fermented with natural yeasts and aged in one-third new *barriques*. Of the two Pinot Noirs, the Reserve spends a few more months in a large proportion of new oak.

Given the scale of production, quality is very good. In 1998 the winemaker, Dan Karlsen, left to join Chalone.

Galante Family Winery
18181 Cachagua Rd., Carmel Valley, CA 93924. Tel: 727 446 8886. Fax: 447 3776. Production: 4,000 cases.

Jack Galante planted 50 acres of hillside vineyards from 1983 onwards, and at first sold grapes to Morgan. For Galante wines, which are all estate-grown and made by Greg Vita, yields are kept as low as 2 tons per acre. It was not until 1994 that a winery was built. Galante focuses principally on Cabernet Sauvignon, and also produces Merlot and Sauvignon Blanc, all aged in new *barriques*.

Georis
2 Pilot Rd., Carmel Valley, CA 93924. Tel: 831 659 1050. Fax: 659 1054. Production: 4,000 cases.

Local restaurateur Walter Georis owns 22 acres in the valley and began making wines in 1986. The only wines produced are Merlot and Cabernet Sauvignon. The Merlot is usually powerful and tannic.

Hahn
See Smith & Hook. Production: 120,000 cases.

This label has been used since 1991 by the Hahn family, who own Smith and Hook, to bottle less expensive wines, including Monterey Chardonnay, Santa Lucia Highlands Merlot, Cabernet Sauvignon and Cabernet Franc.

Jekel

40155 Walnut Ave., Greenfield, CA 93927. Tel: 831 674 5525. Fax: 674 3769. Production: 100,000 cases.

Bill and Gus Jekel founded this Arroyo Seco winery in 1978. Bill achieved controversial renown for his dismissal of the notion of *terroir*. Climate was the determining factor, he argued, and by such simple ideas as sheltering his vineyards from the Monterey winds he was certainly able to increase the quality of his fruit. Whatever his ideas he made some very fine wines, ranging from dense Cabernets to stunning late harvest Rieslings. But in 1992 Bill Jekel retired, went off to Las Vegas, and sold the winery to Brown Forman, who also own Fetzer. The present winemaker is Rick Boyer.

The Jekel vineyard was created in 1972, when it was a mere 140 acres. Today the estate owns a total of 327 acres, roughly split between the Bordeaux red varieties, Riesling, and Chardonnay. The soils, which Jekel was so tempted to discount, are of gravel, sand and rock, topped with sandy loam. Rainfall is a paltry 8 inches, but in the autumn botrytis is not uncommon.

The winery is planning to shift the emphasis away from white varieties in favour of red wines. As well as the usual varietal wines, Jekel produces Petit Verdot and a Meritage called Symmetry, which can be over-assertive and tannic. There is still a tendency to herbaceousness, by no means disagreeable, in some of the reds. The Chardonnay is usually lean, spicy, and pungent.

Joullian

20300 Cachagua Rd., Carmel Valley, CA 93924. Tel: 831 659 2800. Fax: 659 2802. Production: 14,000 cases.

The Sias and Joullian families of Oklahoma came here in 1981 and liked what they saw. They bought 655 acres of hillside and benchland at an elevation of 1,400 feet. The following year they started planting vineyards. The soil, as at Durney, is a very deep gravelly loam with good water retention. There are now 40 acres, two-thirds of which are planted with Bordeaux varieties, as well as some Chardonnay, Zinfandel and Petite Sirah. The first vintage was 1988, and the winemaker is Raymond 'Ridge' Watson. Ridge takes a close interest in the vineyards too, and has tried out the Smart/Dyson trellising system, with which he is pleased. It works especially well, he finds, with Sauvignon Blanc. Vigour can be a problem on these relatively heavy soils.

The Sauvignon is blended with 25 per cent Sémillon. The grapes are whole-cluster pressed. They are picked as ripe as possible to avoid any grassiness or suggestion of cat's pee. Moreover, most of the wine goes through malolactic fermentation. The Sémillon is aged in American oak, the Sauvignon in French. The Reserve bottling is aged in 50 per cent new oak.

The barrel-fermented Chardonnay comes from a variety of vineyards, including their own and Talbott. Most of the wine goes through malolactic fermentation, and is then aged in 30 per cent new *barriques*. For the Family Reserve the proportion of new oak is slightly higher.

The Cabernet Sauvignon is fermented in open-top vats and a proportion of whole berries is retained. The cap is punched down from time to time, and a 30-day maceration is not unusual, as Ridge is keen to avoid astringent tannins. Then the wine is aged for 22 months in French and American oak.

Although I have the feeling that Ridge Watson is still learning to handle his vineyards and grapes, the overall quality of the wines is very high, and is likely to improve further.

Lockwood

59020 Paris Valley Rd., Salinas, CA 93954. Tel: 831 753 1424. Fax: 753 1238. Production: 80,000 cases.

Monterey is a region of vast vineyards, and Lockwood's is no exception. In 1981 a partnership of growers began planting some 1,700 acres: 925 of Chardonnay and 500 of Cabernet Sauvignon, as well as Riesling, Sauvignon Blanc, Sémillon and smaller quantities of other varieties such as Sangiovese, Syrah, and Pinot Gris. For many years the fruit was sold to Mondavi, Estancia, and other wineries. In 1990 a winery was built and winemaker Steve Pessagno has high hopes for Merlot. The general quality is good, and the wines are largely free of herbaceousness.

J. Lohr

1000 Lenzen Ave., San Jose, CA 95126. Tel: 831 288 5057. Fax: 993 2276. Production: 320,000 cases, including Cypress wines.

Although the Lohr winery is located in downtown San Jose, almost all its wines are derived from Monterey vineyards. The company was started by Jerry Lohr, a property developer from South Dakota who first planted grapes in Monterey in 1972, and also developed vineyards in Paso Robles in 1988. The winery was built in 1974 and the winemaker since 1984 has been Jeff Meier.

At first Lohr planted vineyards in Greenfield, trying out a range of varieties, and it was only after a few years that he realized the advice given to him by UC Davis was unsound and it had failed to take into account the strength of the Monterey winds. Only the whites ripened properly. So he budded over the red vines to Chardonnay (especially the Rued clone), Pinot Blanc, and Riesling, and planted a cover crop to keep the dust down. Lohr now owns 450 acres around Greenfield and 600 in

Paso Robles (mostly Cabernet Sauvignon). The grapes are mechanically harvested, usually at night. Crushing takes place in the vineyard, and Meier is keen on whole-cluster pressing.

Their best Chardonnay, Riverstone, comes from Arroyo Seco and is made in a rich toasty style, despite the fact that only 20 per cent of the wine goes through malolactic fermentation. The Pinot Blanc is in a similar style and is aged in 50 per cent new oak. Riesling used to be one of their leading wines, but it is harder and harder to sell. It has about 20 grams of residual sugar but is balanced by good acidity. From time to time they make a late harvest Riesling, as in 1993 and 1995.

The Seven Oaks Cabernet Sauvignon from Paso Robles is made in a soft, charming style entirely appropriate for the quality of the fruit from this region. The Syrah is burlier, and is aged for 19 months in American oak. There is a Valdiguié made partly with carbonic maceration and unoaked.

Because the wines are not extravagantly priced, J. Lohr has often been under-estimated. The wines are very well made, have marked varietal character, and are not dilute. Moreover, they have a great deal of immediate charm. Jeff Meier is planning to produce some single-vineyard wines which are likely to be aged in French oak. The second label is Cypress; most of these wines are made from purchased fruit and released under the California appellation.

Mer & Soleil

See Caymus (p. 381). Production: 3,500 cases.

Chuck Wagner of Caymus planted 3 clones of Chardonnay in Monterey in 1988, and a decade later had 120 acres under vine on the Santa Lucia hillsides at up to 500 feet, facing southeast. Chardonnay is the principal variety, but there are small parcels of Rhône and Italian varieties too. The grapes are hand-picked, whole-cluster pressed, barrel-fermented with partial malolactic fermentation, and then aged in between 75 and 100 per cent new *barriques* for 10 to 17 months.

From the first vintage in 1993, the wine press has raved about these expensive Chardonnays, but I find this sweetish tropical-fruit style cloying.

Michaud

Production: 3,000 cases.

While still winemaker at Chalone, Michael Michaud planted 18 acres in San Benito County with Chardonnay, Viognier, Sangiovese, and Pinot Noir. The first release will be a 1997 Chardonnay. The name Michaud is temporary and may be altered once the wines are released.

Mirassou
3000 Aborn Rd., San Jose, CA 95135. Tel: 408 274 4000. Fax: 270 5881.
Production: 350,000 cases.

Like J. Lohr, Mirassou is based in San Jose but most of its wines have long come from Monterey vineyards. Indeed, Mirassou was one of the Monterey pioneers, planting vineyards many decades ago. The company was founded in 1854 by a French immigrant called Pierre Pellier, whose daughter married Pierre Mirassou, another Frenchman who owned a neighbouring vineyard, in 1881. Charles Wetmore gave Pellier credit for bringing varieties such as Colombard and Folle Blanche to California back in 1859. Until the 1950s Mirassou produced bulk wines. Many of its early excursions into Monterey, beginning in 1961, were unhappy ones: Zinfandels and Cabernets from the 1970s had pronounced vegetal flavours and most of those vines were grafted over to Chardonnay and white varieties long ago. By 1994 Mirassou owned 200 acres in Santa Clara County, and 600 in northern Monterey. Only 20 per cent of production is of red wines, and sparkling wines are also made, but in a different winery.

Their best wines are bottled under the Harvest Reserve or Family Selection labels. The Chardonnay is usually the best wine, but the Mirassou range as a whole is far from exciting.

Monterey Peninsula
PO Box 460, Rutherford, CA 94573. Tel: 707 963 9783. Fax: 963 3593.
Production: 10,000 cases.

This winery was founded by two dentists in 1974, and in 1995 it was bought by Rutherford Benchmarks, who also own Quail Ridge in Napa. I recall many powerful Recioto-like late harvest Amador Zinfandels from the later 1970s. In general those wines showed rustic tendencies. In the 1980s many single-vineyard wines were released. Today the winemaker Anthony Bell concentrates on Monterey Chardonnay and Pinot Blanc and Amador County Zinfandel and other red wines. The second label is Monterey Cellars.

Monterey Vineyard
800 South Alta St., Gonzales, CA 93926. Tel: 831 675 4060. Fax: 675 4019. Production: 750,000 cases.

The founding of this estate was one of the most ambitious ventures of many in Monterey in the 1970s. It was based on a kind of cooperative venture put together by the McFarland brothers and uniting 9,600 acres of vineyards. Richard Peterson, who had been the winemaker at Beaulieu, was brought in to run the operation, and Gerald Asher, now better known as America's most stylish wine writer, was the marketing director. With so many grapes to process, the winery sold off three-quarters of its production. This was just as well, since the McFarland vineyards were no more immune than most others from the vegetal flavours that plagued much Monterey fruit at this time. After a few years, the connection between Monterey Vineyard and the McFarlands was severed, and Peterson obtained his fruit in more manageable quantities from three independent growers. Nonetheless the project collapsed in 1977 and the winery was sold to Coca-Cola. They in turn sold it to Seagram in 1983. In 1986 Phil Franscioni was appointed winemaker.

The current vineyard holdings of the winery include the 1,100-acre Paris Valley Ranch in San Lucas. Monterey Vineyard now focuses on good-value varietal wines. The top range is the Limited Release, followed by the Classic varietal range. The wines are sound but take no risks and are thoroughly commercial and inoffensive. But prices are very reasonable. In 1995 the winery imported and bottled some wines from southern France.

Morgan
590 Brunken Ave., Salinas, CA 93901. Tel: 831 751 7777. Fax: 751 7780. Production: 30,000 cases.

Dan Lee, who was the original winemaker at Jekel, founded this winery in 1982 with the intention of producing only Monterey Chardonnay. The range has expanded to include Zinfandel and Sauvignon Blanc from Sonoma. For many years Morgan owned no vineyards, but in 1997 Lee purchased 60 acres in the Santa Lucia Highlands. The best wines are the toasty Chardonnays, but there is also Pinot Noir with fine varietal typicity, and a creamy Sauvignon Blanc.

Paraiso Springs
38060 Paraiso Springs Rd., Soledad, CA 93960. Tel: 831 678 0300. Fax: 678 2584. Production: 10,000 cases.

Since 1973 Rich and Claudia Smith have been farming 2,800 acres in the Santa Lucia Highlands, selling to wineries such as Mondavi and Fetzer. Four hundred acres are linked to the Paraiso Springs winery, which was set up in 1988. The winemaker is German-trained Philip Zorn. The only wine I have encountered is the 1996 Pinot Blanc, which was delicious if expensive. Other varieties produced are Chardonnay, Pinot Noir, and off-dry Riesling.

Pavona
PO Box 5664, Monterey, CA 93944. Tel: 831 646 1506. Fax: 649 8919. Production: 4,000 cases.

Richard Kanakaris is a marketing man, and it shows in the bright and

colourful labels he has had designed for Pavona, which he founded in
1995. His winemaker is Aaron Mosley. Kanakaris has good contacts with
Paraiso Springs, and buys his Pinot Blanc and Pinot Noir from the vineyard. The latter is light, but the Pinot Blanc was attractive in an oaky
style. Zinfandel comes from Paso Robles and is aged 12 months in
American oak, then bottle-aged for a couple of years before release. These
are early days, but this could be a winery to keep an eye on.

La Reina
PO Box 1344, Carmel, CA 93921. Tel: 408 373 3292. Production: 5,000
cases.

Founded in 1984 by the Chrietzberg family, this winery uses some of the
vineyard's Chardonnay to produce just one wine: a toasty barrel-fermented
Chardonnay.

River Ranch Vineyard
50 La Rancheria Rd., Monterey, CA 93920. Tel: 831 375 2456. Fax: 659
5472.

Proprietor Bill Stahl and his winemaker Sam Baldares only produce Chardonnay and Pinot Noir.

San Saba Vineyard
1075-B South Main St., Salinas, CA 93901. Tel: 831 753 7222. Fax: 753
7727. Production: 4,000 cases.

Dallas plastic surgeon Mark Lemmon founded this property in 1975 when
he planted 75 acres, principally with Cabernet Sauvignon, Merlot and
Cabernet Franc. The first vintage was 1981. There is no winery, and the
vinification takes place at Smith & Hook, where Joel Burnstein makes
the wines. Chardonnay, Cabernet Sauvignon and Merlot, all hand-picked,
are the principal wines, all aged in French oak. Burnstein is a firm believer
in extended maceration for Cabernet.

Scheid
1972 Hobson Ave., Greenfield, CA 93827. Tel: 408 385 4801. Production:
6,000 cases.

The Scheid family have been farming grapes since 1972, when they established vineyards as a tax shelter. In 1988 Alfred Scheid bought out the
other partners, and in 1991 began producing his own wines, using facilities
at Storrs winery. Scheid owns or leases 4,950 acres in Monterey and San
Benito counties, and sells grapes to large wineries such as Glen Ellen,
Beaulieu, Masson, and Almadén. Having tasted the entire range of Scheid
wines, including different vintages, I have to conclude that the wines are
dilute and characterless.

Smith & Hook

37700 Foothill Rd., Soledad, CA 93960. Tel: 831 678 2132. Fax: 678 2005. Production: 20,000 cases.

The winery takes its name from the two ranches that originally comprised the property bought by the Swiss family Hahn in 1974. The original 250 acres of Cabernet Sauvignon and Merlot have been expanded to 1,400 acres, some of them at 1,200 feet in the Santa Lucia Highlands, the rest on the valley floor. The first vintage was 1979. In addition to classic varietals, Smith & Hook also make a steel-fermented Viognier. The estate's top Chardonnay and Cabernet Sauvignon are bottled under the modest name of Masterpiece. The latter is aged in new American oak. Some less expensive wines are bottled under the Hahn label (q.v.).

Talbott

PO Box 776, Gonzales, CA 93926. Tel: 831 675 3000. Fax: 675 3120. Production: 15,000 cases.

The Talbotts are necktie tycoons, who established this estate in 1983. They planted Chardonnay and subsequently Pinot Noir at their Sleepy Hollow Vineyard in the Santa Lucia Highlands. Unsatisfactory first vintages led to the scrapping of an entire year's wine production, and the winemaker of the day was shown the door. The top Chardonnay is the Diamond T Estate bottling from Carmel Valley, and there is also a limited production called Cuvée Sylvia. The white wines tend to be made in a lush Central Coast style invigorated by good acidity. The second label is Logan.

Ventana

2999 Monterey-Salinas Highway 68, CA 93940. Tel: 831 372 7415. Fax: 655 1855. Production: 20,000 cases.

Doug Meador is best known as a pioneering grape grower who claims to have cracked many of the problems that bedevilled Californian viticulture by developing new trellising and spacing systems that permit, in his view, high yields without any loss of quality. He first cleared land here in Arroyo Seco in 1972 and started a winery in 1978. He now farms 300 acres on rocky sandy soils, and although Ventana sells grapes to many well-known wineries throughout the state, Doug still thinks of it as an experimental vineyard. He works closely with winemakers such as Chris Howell of Cain and Daryl Groom of Geyser Peak, who buys most of his Syrah; no doubt the Australian clone appeals to the Australian Groom. Current experiments include planting Sangiovese on different rootstocks; older ones included identifying the Musqué clone of Sauvignon Blanc and producing a botrytized Chardonnay.

Meador admits that Monterey is the botrytis centre of America, and mildew and rot can also be a nuisance. His own winery leads a troubled existence. In 1988 he was producing 40,000 cases. By 1994 production was down to 2,000 and by 1995 to 388 cases! He explains the decline by saying that the cost of converting some of his vineyards required him to sell almost all his grapes rather than vinify them. However, by 1996 he was again producing 20,000 cases. He also uses the J. Douglas label for odds and ends, and I have tasted some delicious 1993 J. Douglas Syrah. It is difficult to generalize about his other wines since production has been so serendipitous.

A large selection of Monterey wines can be tasted and bought at A Taste of Monterey, 400 Cannery Row, Monterey, CA 93940. Tel: 831 646 5446.

30
San Luis Obispo County

Adelaida

5805 Adelaida Rd., Paso Robles, CA 93446. Tel: 805[1] 239 8980. Fax: 239 4671. Production: 12,000 cases.

John Munch, a graduate in Old English, had been making highly regarded wines here since 1981. In 1990 he encountered the Van Steenwyck family, who were manufacturers of navigational equipment and nut farmers. They were keen to expand into wine production, and teamed up with Munch. In 1994 they managed to buy part of the HMR Ranch. This brings Adelaida's vineyard holdings to 75 acres, most of them organically farmed.

All wines are made with indigenous yeasts. The range is mixed in quality, but the best wines are very exciting. The 1993 Cabernet Sauvignon, aged for 24 months in oak, was excellent, and Adelaida make a powerful, waxy Chenin Blanc called Pavanne, barrel-fermented in older barrels and bottled with a terrifying but far from obvious 15.4 degrees of alcohol! Adelaida also produce Zinfandel, Viognier, and rather oaky Sangiovese.

Alban

8575 Orcutt Rd., Arroyo Grande, CA 93420. Tel: 546 0305. Fax: 546 9879. Production: 3,000 cases.

John Alban became a Rhône convert when he first tasted a Condrieu from the Rhône valley. In 1990 he began planting a 33-acre vineyard with nothing but Rhône varieties, including Grenache, Syrah, Viognier, and Roussanne. The Syrah is the oldest in Edna Valley. He applied to study at UC Davis, but his application was refused on the reasonable grounds that he didn't possess a single one of the necessary qualifications. So he went to study in Fresno instead, and then progressed to Davis.

Winemakers who buy from Alban testify to his skill as a grower and the admirably low yields he obtains. His own first release was a Syrah in 1992, followed by Viognier in 1993. Syrah is fermented with natural yeasts, and Alban believes in a short but hot fermentation rather than extended maceration. The wine is aged in older barrels of various sizes for about 18 months and bottled unfiltered. From 1995 he began producing small quantities of a highly concentrated Reserve bottling named after his wife Lorraine and derived from a particular parcel of the vineyard. The superb Grenache is made in much the same way.

John Alban has the good sense to handle Viognier with a light touch: only a third is barrel-fermented and that in older barrels. In 1994 and 1996 he made small quantities in the style of a *vin de paille* from Roussanne, but I haven't tasted it. The regular Roussanne, like the Viognier and Syrah, is in the very top tier of Rhône-variety wines from California. There is also a Central Coast bottling of Viognier, from vineyards not owned by Alban but grafted over to Viognier by him under a twenty-year contract arrangement. The wine is fatter than the more elegant estate bottling. John Alban is collaborating with Alois Kracher of Illmitz, Austria's great master of sweet wine, and has already grown botrytized Viognier.

Arciero
5625 Highway 46 East, Paso Robles, CA 93447. Tel: 239 2562. Fax: 239 2317. Production: 200,000 cases.

Frank and Philip Arciero came to America from Italy as teenagers in 1939 and made a fortune in the construction business. In 1983 they planted vineyards here and founded a winery three years later. They only use half the production of their 700 acres. They use no pesticides or herbicides. The main varieties planted are Chardonnay, Sauvignon Blanc, Sémillon, Zinfandel, Petite Sirah, French Colombard, and Muscat Canelli. Chenin is being grafted over to Merlot. There are also parcels of Nebbiolo and Sangiovese, thus far producing rather simple wines.

The winemaker Stephen Felten has to adjust his winemaking techniques to suit the fruit the vineyards produce. He tries to pick Chardonnay with high acidity and is reducing the proportion of barrel-fermented must to avoid flabbiness in the wine. Like most of the wines here, it is aged in American as well as French oak.

The reds receive a relatively short maceration and are aged in oak for anywhere between 12 and 30 months. The best wine is a plump, concentrated Petite Sirah, the Italian varietals lack depth, and the principal varietals are routine and deficient in excitement and character. There is a charming Muscat Canelli, however, and Felten is experimenting with blends such as Arpeggio, which yokes together three very different varieties, Sangiovese, Nebbiolo, and Zinfandel. Prices are reasonable, but there are many better wines to be found in this region.

Baileyana
5880 Edna Rd., San Luis Obispo, CA 93401. Tel: 781 9463. Production: 2,500 cases.

The Niven family of Paragon Vineyards in Edna Valley are now producing some wines themselves. At present the range made by winemakers Gary Mosby and Bruno d'Alfonso consists of Pinot Noir and Chardonnay, but Syrah and Sauvignon Blanc will be added. In 1999 Christian Roquenant, formerly of Laetitia, took over as winemaker.

Casa de Caballos Vineyards
2225 Raymond Ave., Templeton, CA 93465. Tel: 434 1687. Fax: 434 1560. Production: 300 cases.

Dr Tom Morgan began making wine as a hobby in 1989, and in 1995 started producing wines on a commercial basis. He owns 2.5 acres of vineyards at a height of 1,200 feet. His range consists of Riesling blended with Muscat Canelli, Pinot Noir, Cabernet Sauvignon, and Merlot.

Castoro Cellars
6465 Von Dollen Rd., San Miguel, CA 93451. Tel: 467 2002. Fax: 467 2004. Production: 15,000 cases.

Niels Udsen owns two vineyards, the colourfully named Hog's Heaven and Blind Faith, and also buys in fruit from up to forty others to supply the winery that his family founded in 1983. Quality is variable, but there can be excellent Zinfandel and Cabernet Sauvignon.

Claiborne & Churchill
2467 Carpenter Canyon Rd., San Luis Obispo, CA 93401. Tel: 544 4066. Production: 4,000 cases.

The first vintages of Clay Thompson's Alsatian-inspired wines were vinified at Edna Valley Vineyards, before he moved to rented warehouse space in town. He buys fruit from various sources, including Edna Valley and MacGregor Vineyards and Ventana in Monterey. The wines include dry Riesling, a fair Gewürztraminer, and some Pinot Noir (astringent in 1993) and Chardonnay. They are aged in neutral oak.

Creston
679 Calf Canyon Highway, Creston, CA 93432. Tel: 434 1399. Fax: 238 1496. Production: 45,000 cases.

Creston was founded in 1981 by a Los Angeles consortium; Alex Trebek is now the majority partner. The 155 acres under vine include 95 acres planted at a height of 1,700 feet, and the westside Bailey Vineyard of 25 acres. The winery also purchases grapes. Long-serving Victor Roberts is now assisted by Tim Spear. The range is wide and includes all the major varietals. Quality is quite high.

Dark Star Cellars

2985 Anderson Rd., Paso Robles, CA 93446. Tel: 237 2389. Fax: 237 2589.

An ambitious new winery founded by Norm Benson in 1994, this will focus on hand-crafted Cabernet Sauvignon, Merlot, Zinfandel, and a Meritage called 'Ricordati'.

Maison Deutz

See Laetitia (p. 570).

Domaine Alfred

7525 Orcutt Rd., San Luis Obispo, CA 93401. Tel: 408 764 0615. Production: 3,000 cases.

This winery started its life as an outlet for the fruit of the 57-acre Chamisal Vineyard. The owner is a restaurateur, Norman Goss, and the wines, only Pinot Noir and Chardonnay, are made by Clay Thompson. I have not tasted them.

Dover Canyon

Bethel Rd., Templeton, CA 93465. Tel: 434 0319. Fax: 434 0509.

A new estate with a winery that first opened in 1997. The owner Dan Panico used to work at Eberle. The whites, including Rhône whites, are barrel-fermented.

Dunning

1953 Niderer Rd., Paso Robles, CA 93446. Tel/fax: 238 4763. Production: 2,000 cases.

   This westside vineyard, planted on rocky limestone soil, was established by Robert Dunning in 1991, and a winery followed in 1994. The first releases were of Cabernet Sauvignon, Chardonnay, and Merlot, but there are plans to plant Syrah, Malbec and Zinfandel too.

Eberle

PO Box 2459, Paso Robles, CA 93447. Tel: 238 9607. Fax: 237 0344. Production: 20,000 cases.

Gary Eberle was already working within the region in 1973, planting 500 acres of vineyards and creating Estrella River Winery, which was actually owned at that time by his relative Cliff Giacobine. These vineyards were famous for including Syrah, in those days a rarity in California, although the vines no longer exist. Gary Eberle nurtured Estrella River until it reached a production level of 200,000 cases, then he left to found his own winery. Its first vintage was 1982. Eberle have 40 acres of vineyards, but buy in from various parts of the region.

The large, bearded, opinionated Gary Eberle is a very fine winemaker and not a man to rest on his laurels. His Cabernets, especially the Reserves, are lovely wines that age elegantly for about fifteen years. The 1991 is particularly good. So are the Zinfandels from the Sauret Vineyard. As one of the earliest Rhône Rangers, it is no surprise to find that Eberle makes splendid Syrah. Of the two single-vineyard wines, I prefer the Fralich Vineyard to the Steinbeck. There is also an Australian-style blend of Cabernet and Syrah, and the lively Cotes de Robles, which blends Syrah, Mourvèdre, Counoise, and Grenache. Particularly intriguing is the dry rosé made from Counoise.

The Chardonnay is usually estate-grown, and there is also a Viognier fermented in neutral oak which Eberle is very keen on. A pretty Muscat Canelli adds a little icing to a very varied range of high quality.

Edna Valley Vineyards

2585 Biddle Ranch Rd., San Luis Obispo, CA 93401. Tel: 544 5855. Fax: 544 0112. Production: 90,000 cases.

The immense vineyards, all 716 acres of them, are owned by the Niven family, and supply much of the fruit for this winery, which is owned jointly by the Nivens and, since 1981, the Chalone Group, which is responsible for vinification and marketing. The vines are planted in a former estuary which opens directly on to the ocean, so foggy mornings keep it relatively cool, though warmer than the valleys of Santa Barbara. The soil is essentially sandy loam and clay, and yields range from 3 to 4 tons per acre. Almost 500 acres are planted with Chardonnay; the remainder with Sauvignon Blanc, Cabernet Sauvignon, Pinot Noir, Riesling, and Sémillon. The Sauvignon and Sémillon go to Carmenet, another Chalone Group winery. Pinot Blanc and Syrah are being added to the range.

The winery was built in 1980. Gary Mosby was the first winemaker, and many others followed; since 1997 Clay Brock, formerly of Byron, has been in charge. The Chardonnay is barrel-fermented and quite opulent, and the Reserve can be outstanding. The Pinot Noir is mostly destemmed, and the cap is punched down with a pneumatic device. Brock has plans to produce a late harvest Riesling when conditions permit.

Considering the scale of production, quality is very high, especially of Chardonnay.

Eos Estate Winery

PO Box 1179, Paso Robles, CA 93447. Tel: 888 EOS WNRY. Fax: 805 239 2317. Production: 30,000 cases.

This new winery is the brainchild of drinks wholesaler Vernon Underwood and Kerry Vix, who also is a partner at Arciero. The estate consists of 700 acres, with plans to expand the acreage further. The first release was a 1996 Chardonnay, and Cabernet Sauvignon, Petite Sirah, Sauvignon Blanc, Zinfandel, and late harvest Muscat Canelli will follow in due course. The wines are aged in American as well as French oak. Tom Eddy is the winemaker.

Grey Wolf Cellars
1985 Penman Springs Rd., Paso Robles, CA 93446. Tel: 237 0771. Production: 1,500 cases.

Joe and Shirlene Barton founded this winery in 1994, and vineyards were planted in 1998. The first release was a 1994 Meritage made from purchased grapes. Other wines include Zinfandel, Chardonnay, and Sauvignon Blanc.

Harmony Cellars
3255 Harmony Valley Rd., Harmony, CA 93455. Tel: 927 1625. Fax: 927 0256. Production: 4,000 cases.

Chuck Mulligan created this estate in 1989, and a winery was completed in 1993. Initial releases were of Chardonnay, Cabernet Sauvignon, and Pinot Noir.

Hart's Desire
Tel: 707 579 1687.

John Hart couldn't resist a good pun when he founded this Edna Valley estate in 1990. His Chardonnay grapes come from MacGregor Vineyard, while Zinfandel and Cabernet are bought in from Sonoma and Napa.

Hope Farms Winery
2175 Arbor Rd., Paso Robles, CA 93446. Tel: 238 6979. Fax: 238 4063. Production: 5,000 cases.

The owners have been farming 140 acres of vineyards for some time, and began producing their own wines in 1990. The varieties include Cabernet, Chardonnay, Sauvignon Blanc, Merlot, and Zinfandel.

Tobin James Cellars
8950 Union Rd., Paso Robles, CA 93446. Tel: 239 2204. Fax: 239 4471. Production: 7,500 cases.

The Tobin James tasting room is done up to resemble a Western saloon, and the exuberance of the decor is reflected in the wines. Toby Shumrick worked at Eberle till 1989, and started making wines under his own label in 1987, using the Eberle facilities and then the Peachy Canyon winery until his own winery was completed in 1994. He is developing 40 acres of vineyards but has to buy in many of his grapes. The range includes barrel-fermented Chardonnay, juicy, peppery Syrah, rather simple Sangiovese, simple accessible Cabernet Sauvignon, and a Cabernet Franc subjected to very long barrel ageing. His top wines are the James Gang Reserves of Zinfandel and Cabernet Sauvignon.

Justin

11680 Chimney Rock Rd., Paso Robles, CA 93446. Tel: 238 6932. Fax: 238 7382. Production: 25,000 cases.

The urbane former investment banker Justin Baldwin and his glamorous wife Deborah have thrown themselves wholeheartedly into their new career of running a wine estate and a charming but luxurious little bed and breakfast adjoining the winery. When he bought the westside property in 1981, this was a barley farm. Now the estate consists of 72 acres, between 1,100 and 1,600 feet high, planted with Cabernet Sauvignon, Merlot, Cabernet Franc, and Chardonnay, as well as tiny quantities of Nebbiolo, Orange Muscat, Viognier, Syrah and Sangiovese. This is not easy land to cultivate: frost and fogs are common, and the heavy rainfall promotes vigour in the vines. The soils are varied: red clay and volcanic pumice in the topsoil as well as sandy loam and rocky limestone.

Steve Glossner is the winemaker, and the whole range is estate-grown. The first vintage was 1987, and Glossner is the third winemaker in 10 years, so perhaps it is not surprising that Justin wines reflect some stylistic uncertainty. Nonetheless, they are very good. Natural yeasts are used a good deal, and the Justin wines are strong on fruit and are not over-oaked. In addition to the usual varietals, there is a Cabernet-dominated Bordeaux blend called Isosceles, which is aged for 28 months in *barriques*, of which about one-third are new. Another blend, made in a similar way, is called Justification and blends Cabernet Franc and Merlot in more or less equal measures. An interesting wine is the 'port' made from Cabernet Sauvignon, aged in puncheons, and called, for some reason, Obtuse. The second label is called Epoch.

Kynsi Winery

2212 Corbett Canyon Rd., Arroyo Grande, CA 93420. Tel: 544 6181. Production: 1,500 cases.

This Edna Valley winery was founded by Don Othman. The first release was a pricy 1995 Chardonnay from the Sanford & Benedict Vineyard, followed by Pinot Noir and Syrah from San Luis Obispo.

Laetitia

453 Deutz Ave., Arroyo Grande, CA 93420. Tel: 481 1772. Production: 15,000 cases.

This is the re-born Maison Deutz. The sparkling wine house was a joint venture between Beringer, Champagne Deutz, and others, and 150 acres were planted in 1983. Sales were disappointing, however, and as more and more still wine was being produced, Deutz was closed down and then re-emerged in 1997 as Laetitia. The new label has 187 acres at its disposal, and will be producing Pinot Noir, Pinot Blanc, and Chardonnay from various vineyards. Christian Roguenant was the winemaker at Deutz and remained here until 1999. Shortly before, the property had been bought by Barnwood Vineyards of Santa Barbara County.

Laura's Vineyard
5620 Highway 46 East, Paso Robles, CA 93446. Tel: 238 6300. Production: 2,000 cases.

Patrick O'Dell owns Turnbull in Napa Valley as well as this property, which he bought in 1996, and Kristin Belair is the winemaker at both estates. The vineyard originated as part of the Estrella River vineyards in 1977, but O'Dell has enlarged his estate to 280 acres. A new winery is being constructed and the plan is to focus on Mediterranean varietals.

Laverne Vineyard
3490 Sacramento Dr., San Luis Obispo, CA 93401. Tel: 547 0616.

This estate specializes in Chardonnay and Cabernet Sauvignon.

Live Oak Vineyards
1480 North Bethel Rd., Templeton, CA 93465. Tel: 227 4766. Fax: 227 4968. Production: 2,500 cases.

Bill Alberts planted 13 acres of Chardonnay in 1981 and founded the winery a year later. Now the family cultivates 93 acres, and this new label was established in 1995.

Martin Brothers
Highway 46 East, Paso Robles, CA 93447. Tel: 238 2520. Fax: 238 6041. Production: 18,000 cases.

The Martin family are wild about Italian wines. They began planting vines in 1982, and now have almost 200 acres under vine, planted with Chardonnay, Dolcetto, Sangiovese, Petit Verdot, and who knows what else? Dominic Martin was probably the first person to make varietal Nebbiolo when he produced the wine in 1982, sourcing the grapes not only from their own vineyards but from the Sierra Foothills. Martin admits that some of the purchased grapes are from high-yielding vineyards, so it is not surprising that the Nebbiolo is thin. There is a Riserva, Nebbiolo Vecchio, aged 2 years in oak, and this is certainly a better wine, but a long way from Barolo or Barbaresco.

Another of Martin's claims is that he made America's first 'Supertuscan', called Cabernet Etrusco, a blend of 85 per cent Cabernet and 15 per cent

Sangiovese. Gemelli was an unusual blend of estate Nebbiolo with wine from Franco Fiorina in Piedmont but the joint venture ceased in 1993. The Sangiovese is called Il Palio. The Vin Santo is a misrepresentation, since it is made from dried grapes but is given no barrel-ageing. Since 1995 the winemaker has been Craig Reed.

Despite the best of intentions, Martin Brothers have yet to master the admittedly difficult task of producing complex, complete wines from Italian varieties.

Mastantuono
2720 Oak View Rd., Templeton, CA 93465. Tel: 238 0676. Fax: 238 9257. Production: 11,000 cases.

Pasquale Mastantuono founded this property in 1976 and opened the winery in 1983. He specializes in hefty reds in the traditional Italian-American style, and the range includes a powerful Zinfandel.

Meridian
7000 Highway 46 East, Paso Robles, CA 93447. Tel: 237 6000. Fax: 239 9624. Production: 500,000 cases.

Chuck Ortman, a veteran winemaker with experience at Heitz, Spring Mountain, St Clement, Far Niente, and Shafer, founded this brand in 1984. At that time he used mostly Napa fruit. Meridian was sold to Nestlé in 1988 and is now owned by the Beringer group. It was at Nestlé's instigation that Ortman was encouraged to relocate to the Central Coast; Beringer bought the former Estrella River winery and remodelled it. The vineyard expansion has been colossal; there are now 5,000 acres in production, and plans to plant 2,000 more. Not all are in Paso Robles, and there are substantial holdings in Santa Maria. Much of the fruit feeds other wineries within the Beringer fold.

The wines offered are the standard varietals, some of them with Reserve bottlings. Given the large quantities produced the quality is very high, and the reasonable prices make these some of the best bargains in California. There are some disappointments, such as Gewürztraminer, but with Reserve Chardonnays selling at $16, one can hardly complain. The best wine I recall tasting is the 1995 Pinot Noir Reserve. The Paso Robles Zinfandel is also very attractive.

Midnight Cellars
2867 Township Rd., Paso Robles, CA 93446. Tel: 237 9601. Fax: 237 0383. Production: 4,500 cases.

Founded in 1995 by Robert and Rich Hartenberger, the winery produces Zinfandel, Merlot, Cabernet Sauvignon, and Chardonnay from its 17 acres of vineyards.

Mission View

Wellsona Rd. at Highway 101, San Miguel, CA 93451. Tel: 467 3104. Fax: 467 3719. Production: 5,000 cases.

This property was founded in 1981, when 40 acres were planted, mostly Chardonnay, Zinfandel, and Cabernet Sauvignon, and also some Sauvignon Blanc and Muscat Canelli. Merlot and Cabernet Franc were added in 1990. The whites are barrel-fermented, and the reds are aged in a blend of French and American oak. Paul Ayers is the winemaker.

Norman

7450 Vineyard Dr., Paso Robles, CA 93446. Tel: 237 0138. Fax: 227 6733. Production: 5,000 cases.

Art Norman planted 40 acres in the Adelaida Hills from 1971 onwards: Barbera, Cabernet Sauvignon, Chardonnay, Merlot, and Zinfandel. The winery was built in 1992 and Robert Nadeau makes the wines, of which the best known are Zinfandels called The Monster and The Classic.

Peachy Canyon

4045 Peachy Canyon Rd., Paso Robles, CA 93446. Tel: 237 1577. Fax: 237 2248. Production: 10,000 cases.

Doug Beckett's winery was established in 1988, and produces Zinfandel, Merlot, and Cabernet Sauvignon. Their vineyards consist of 30 acres of Zinfandel and 10 of Chardonnay, which is being grafted over to Zinfandel and Sangiovese. Tom Westberg makes the wines, of which the most celebrated are the Zinfandels, the Westside and the Especial.

Fratelli Perata

1595 Arbor Rd., Paso Robles, CA 93446. Tel/fax: 238 2809. Production: 2,000 cases.

Although it sounds like an old-fashioned place, this winery was only founded in 1987, by Gene Perata. The estate consists of 25 acres planted with Zinfandel, Cabernet Sauvignon, Merlot, and Sangiovese. Chardonnay and Nebbiolo are also produced. The reds are unfiltered and unfined.

Pesenti

2900 Vineyard Dr., Templeton, CA 93465. Tel/fax: 434 1030.

This family winery, now run by Frank Nerelli, was founded in 1934, after Repeal, although its dry-farmed Zinfandel vineyards were planted in 1923, with additional parcels in 1947 and 1965. There are also Cabernet Sauvignon vines dating from 1957. Pesenti offers a wide range of inexpensive wines, from blush wines to French Colombard and Chardonnay to 'cream sherry' and Zinfandel. The best wines are the Zinfandels, but in general quality is mediocre.

Piedra Creek

6238 Orcutt Rd., San Luis Obispo, CA 93401. Tel: 541 1281. Production: 500 cases.

Romeo Zuech comes from Bolzano in northern Italy, and recently retired after a career in California as an aerospace engineer. He amuses himself by running the smallest bonded winery in Edna Valley. He produces only Chardonnay and Zinfandel, and likes to use a great deal of new oak. The Chardonnay comes from the MacGregor Vineyard and is powerful and somewhat blowsy. As Zuech says himself, 'My Chardonnay is no sissy.'

Poalillo

1888 Willow Creek Rd., Paso Robles, CA 93446. Tel: 238 0600. Fax: 466 3671. Production: 1,000 cases.

Charles Poalillo has been growing grapes since 1980, and the first release under his own label was in 1992. He specializes in Zinfandel, Chardonnay, and Cabernet Sauvignon from westside fruit.

Stephen Ross

1819 Osos St., San Luis Obispo, CA 93401. Tel: 546 VINO.

Steve Dooley used to be the winemaker at Edna Valley Vineyard, and now has his own label, specializing in Pinot Noir, Pinot Blanc, Chardonnay, and Sauvignon Blanc.

Santa Rita Creek

2225 Raymond Ave., Templeton, CA 93465. Tel: 434 1687. Fax: 434 1560. Production: 300 cases.

Originating as a hobby winery, Santa Rita is run by Tom Morgan, who farms 3 acres of Pinot Noir, Merlot, Cabernet Sauvignon, and Muscat Canelli.

Saucelito Canyon

1600 Saucelito Canyon Rd., Arroyo Grande, CA 93420. Tel: 489 8762. Fax: 543 2111. Production: 3,000 cases.

It's not easy to get to this remote spot, 800 feet high and tucked behind several ranches and barred gateways. Wild peacocks roam the hillsides. When Bill and Nancy Greenough bought this vineyard in 1974 it was badly neglected. Even today there is no electricity. Bill found to his surprise a few vine roots that were still alive, and was able to resuscitate part of a Zinfandel vineyard that had originally been planted in 1879. There are now 3 acres of ancient vines, although gaps have had to be filled with newer head-pruned vines; 5 more acres were planted in 1976. The Greenoughs built their winery in 1982.

The vineyards are dry-farmed, even though being quite far inland, the climate is very warm and dry, though cooler than much of Paso Robles. Yields are about 3 tons per acre. The harvest is protracted, and Greenough can be picking for as long as four weeks, especially while waiting for the late harvest fruit. Zinfandel here has low acidity, so Greenough picks some grapes at less than optimal ripeness to balance the wine. The wine is fermented in open-top fermenters and aged in both French and American oak.

The late harvest Zinfandel can be hard to ferment. In 1996 the grapes were picked at 42 Brix, fermented in former pickle barrels, and sealed. Sometimes Greenough has to add a little brandy to stabilize the wine. These wines can be rather hot and raisiny, and I prefer the regular Zinfandels. The estate also makes a small quantity of Cabernet Sauvignon.

Seven Peaks
5828 Orcutt Rd., San Luis Obispo, CA 93401. Tel: 408 781 0777. Production: 40,000 cases.

In 1996 the vast Australian wine company Southcorp (which owns Penfolds and Lindemans) set up a partnership with the Niven family, the leading grape farmers of Edna Valley. Southcorp contributes an Australian winemaker, Ian Shepherd, and technology; the Nivens supply grapes from the Paragon Vineyard, and other grapes are bought from various vineyards along the Central Coast. The first releases were the 1996 Chardonnays, under the California appellation, and, for the Reserve, an Edna Valley bottling. Barrel fermentation in American oak gives a lush, forward style. Cabernet Sauvignon, Shiraz, and Merlot are also being produced.

Silver Canyon
11240 Chimney Rock Rd., Paso Robles, CA 93446. Tel: 238 9392. Fax: 238 3975. Production: 3,000 cases.

Gary and Marian Conway, together with a Hollywood producer called Dean Zanetos, began planting Chardonnay, Cabernet Sauvignon, Cabernet Franc and Merlot in the 1980s, on a limestone ridge west of Highway 101. They founded a winery in 1991.

Silver Horse Vineyards
2995 Pleasant Rd., San Miguel, CA 93461. Tel: 467 WINE. Fax: 467 9414. Production: 4,000 cases.

The horse breeder Rich Simons founded this estate in 1989, growing 20 acres of Cabernet Sauvignon and Zinfandel. The first release was in 1990, and the range consists of Cabernet, Zinfandel, Chardonnay, Pinot Noir and Merlot.

Sylvester Winery
5155 Buena Vista Dr., Paso Robles, CA 93447. Tel: 227 4000. Fax: 227 6128. Production: 20,000 cases.

There were vineyards at this property from 1982 onwards, but Sylvester Feichtinger founded a winery only in 1995. The wines – Cabernet Sauvignon, Chardonnay, Merlot – are made by Dominic Martin of Martin Brothers.

Tablas Creek
9339 Adelaida Rd., Paso Robles, CA 93446. Tel: 237 1231. Fax: 237 1314. Production: aiming for 25,000 cases.

The wine importer Robert Haas had long been on friendly terms with the Perrin family of Châteauneuf-du-Pape, and for some time they thought of collaborating on Rhône-style wines in California. In the 1980s they started looking for land that had some resemblance to the southern Rhône. The Sierra Foothills was tried and found wanting, but the westside hills in Paso Robles looked promising. Unfortunately the limestone-based soils were hard to work and water was in short supply. In 1990 they acquired 120 acres of pasture land here at a height of 1,500 feet, and began importing French cuttings and rootstocks, which spent three years in quarantine before being released for planting. In 1992 some American source material was planted in 2-acre parcels, just to give them some experience of Rhône varietals in this soil. The French material was planted in 1995 and found to be greatly superior to the higher-yielding American, which will eventually be converted. Much of Tablas Creek's business derives from the sale of cuttings to other wineries with an interest in Rhône varietals.

The vines have been planted with a density of 1,800 vines per acre, and are all vertically trellised along double cordons, except for Syrah and Viognier. The first wines were made in 1996, though in small quantities, and the first commercial vintage is 1997. The wines are now being aged in older barrels. Wines made from American vines will be labelled Tablas Hills, those from French vines are released as Tablas Creek Vineyard. It seems safe to predict that quality will be high.

Talley
3031 Lopez Dr., Arroyo Grande, CA 93420. Tel: 489 0446. Fax: 489 0996. Production: 11,000 cases.

Since 1948 the Talleys have been vegetable farmers, and in 1982 Dan Talley realized there was a potential for good-quality grape production here, and planted five varieties in test plots. It soon became obvious that Cabernet Sauvignon was not going to work here. In 1984 Talley planted 106 acres with Chardonnay as well as Pinot Noir (Wadenswil clone), Riesling, and Sauvignon Blanc. The first vintage was 1986, and Steve Rasmussen has been the winemaker ever since.

The estate is now managed by Brian Talley. He is anxious to keep yields down to no more than 3.5 tons per acre. The vineyards consist of two hillside sites. Rincon Vineyard has 77 acres, while Rosemary's Vineyard, a mile west of Rincon, has 15 acres, of Chardonnay and Pinot Noir only. Rincon faces south and has shallow loam and clay with a limestone subsoil; Rosemary's is on steeper, well-drained soil and slightly cooler. There is a third vineyard in Edna Valley called Oliver's Vineyard, and these 16.5 acres were planted with Chardonnay only in 1990.

The winery was built in 1991 and operates by gravity flow. Chardonnay is whole-cluster pressed, and is barrel-fermented and goes through full malolactic fermentation. Only French oak is used; one-third new. The Estate Chardonnay spends about 10 months on the lees, the single-vineyard bottlings up to 15 months.

Pinot Noir is usually destemmed, but sometimes a proportion of whole clusters is retained. The must is fermented using native yeasts in open-top tanks after a cold soak, and there is no extended maceration. The wine is aged in 40 per cent new *barriques* for between 15 and 18 months. It is fined but rarely filtered. Brian Talley says they aim for concentration, balance and complexity, and in my view they succeed admirably.

These are among the finest Chardonnays and Pinot Noirs of the Central Coast. The 1996 Rincon Chardonnay was voluptuous on the nose and creamily textured, and the 1996 Rosemary's is more opulent. The Pinot Noirs have elegance as well as pure fruit. It is worth looking out for the occasional bottlings of delicious late harvest Rieslings.

Treana
2175 Arbor Rd., Paso Robles, CA 93446. Tel: 238 6979. Fax: 238 4063. Production: 5,000 cases.

The Hope family, who planted vineyards in 1980, built a winery in 1989 and Chris Phelps, who worked at Dominus, is now the winemaker. Caymus bought fruit from here for its Liberty School label, and in 1996 the Hope family acquired the label for themselves, and will be releasing its wines under the Treana label.

Twin Hills Winery
2025 Lake Nacimento Rd., Paso Robles, CA 93446. Tel: 415 321 6999. Fax: 805 239 3060. Production: 5,000 cases.

Founded in 1982 by Jim Lockshaw, the winery was bought in 1991 by

Caroline Scott and Glenn Reid. The estate consists of 40 acres of Chardonnay, Zinfandel, Palomino, and Cabernet Sauvignon. The winery speciality is 'port', and 'sherry' made by the solera system.

Vista del Rey

7340 Drake Rd., Paso Robles, CA 93446. Tel: 467 2138. Fax: 467 2765.

A new winery, this was founded in 1997 by Dave King, with assistance from the team at Wild Horse. The vineyards – the 8-acre Hacienda and the 18-acre Colina de Roble – are at 900 feet, planted on moderately deep clay loam. The varieties planted are Barbera, Sangiovese, and Zinfandel.

Wild Horse Winery

1437 Wild Horse Winery Court, Templeton, CA 93465. Tel: 434 2541. Fax: 434 3516. Production: 100,000 cases.

If you feel there is more to drinking wine than Chardonnay and Cabernet, then this is the winery for you. Ken Volk founded the property in 1983. There is a 50-acre vineyard, which is relatively cool compared to the Estrella River region, but Volk has ransacked the vineyards of the Central Coast for parcels of bizarre varieties. He is also planting the James Berry Vineyard near Tablas Creek with Chardonnay and Rhône varieties.

The wines are made by Volk and his cellarmaster John Priest. They are keen on open-top fermenters for reds, and punch down the cap by hand. A peculiarity of Wild Horse is the extensive use of Hungarian oak barrels, which may account for the sweetish tone of some of the wines, notably the Pinot Noir.

The range of wines is enormous. The San Luis Obispo Cabernet Sauvignon is a solid blend from various sources. Pinot Noir also comes from various parts of the Central Coast, and is aged in older oak for 10 months. Ken Volk says that he wants fruit in his wine rather than structure and tannins. His best Pinot Noir is called Cheval Sauvage. In 1994 the fruit came from Bien Nacido and Chalone. The Merlot is aged in older *barriques*; the Syrah comes from westside fruit and from Monterey.

The Chardonnay blends fruit from their own vineyards as well as from Edna Valley and Monterey. It is barrel-fermented and aged in 50 per cent new oak. Pinot Blanc, in fact Melon, comes from San Bernabe in Monterey and is whole-cluster pressed and aged for 5 months in older *barriques*. The exotic Malvasia Bianca is made in the same way.

Among the weirder wines are a barrel-fermented Arneis, late harvest Sauvignon Blanc (made in 1991 and 1994), Trousseau, and Négrette, any of which are worth a try if encountered in the Wild Horse tasting room. The principal wine remains the eminently drinkable Pinot Noir, and all the wines are very well made, although it is hard not to wonder why some of them have been made in the first place. Nonetheless the exuberant variety of wines produced here is worth cherishing.

Windemere Wines
3482 Sacramento Dr., San Luis Obispo, CA 93401. Tel: 542 0133. Production: 5,000 cases.

This Edna Valley winery was established in 1985 by Cathy MacGregor-Bryan, the daughter of Andy MacGregor of MacGregor Vineyards. The winery specializes in Edna Valley Chardonnay and Paso Robles Zinfandel.

Windward Vineyard
1380 Live Oak Rd., Paso Robles, CA 93446. Tel: 239 2565. Fax: 239 4005. Production: 1,200 cases.

Founded in 1990 by Marc Goldberg and Maggie D'Ambrosia, this small 10-acre estate in Templeton Gap produces only Pinot Noir, which is made for them by Ken Volk of Wild Horse. The first vintage was 1993.

York Mountain Winery
7505 York Mountain Rd., Templeton, CA 93465. Tel: 238 3925. Fax: 238 0428. Production: 6,000 cases.

This is one of the region's oldest properties, having been founded in 1892 by Andrew York. It remained in the family until 1970, when it was bought by the Goldman family. It was here that the wines from Paderewski's estate were produced, and York Mountain continued to buy his grapes until 1941, when the vines were pulled. Estate-grown grapes include Pinot Noir, Cabernet Sauvignon, Zinfandel, and Chardonnay, and some Central Coast fruit is purchased. The range of wines offered is broad but quality is far from outstanding.

NOTE

1 The area code throughout this region is 805, unless otherwise specified

31

Santa Barbara and the South Coast

Au Bon Climat
Santa Maria Mesa Rd., Santa Maria, CA 93454. Tel: 805 937 9801. Fax: 937 2539. Production: 27,000 cases.

Jim Clendenen and Adam Tolmach set up their winemaking partnership in 1982, and in 1989 they moved their cellars to a hangar in rural Santa Maria Valley. A number of different labels emerged from these facilities, including Vita Nova and Qupé, although it is hard to keep up with the proliferation of labels created by Clendenen. Adam Tolmach is no longer involved in Au Bon Climat, and Clendenen is assisted by Jim Adelman. The idea behind Au Bon Climat was to use Burgundian techniques – Clendenen had worked in Burgundy – such as open-top fermenters and punching down the cap. These are commonplace nowadays in California, but weren't in 1982. All whites were barrel-fermented, and invariably went through malolactic fermentation, as fruit from Santa Barbara can be high in acidity as a consequence of the coolness of the climate.

Both the Pinot Noir and the Chardonnay have been brilliant from the start. Clendenen rejoices in risk-taking and deliberately adopts the artisanal methods prevalent in Burgundy. There have been a number of single-vineyard bottlings, which have varied considerably according to the availability of grapes. The regular Chardonnay sees only a small proportion of new oak, while the Reserve, a vineyard selection, is usually aged on the fine lees in 50 per cent new wood for up to 16 months. In 1995 the Chardonnay releases were the regular (Santa Barbara County), Alban (for the first time), Bien Nacido, Talley, and Sanford & Benedict. There has also been delicious Pinot Blanc from Bien Nacido but the Pinot Gris lacks flair.

The Pinot Noir, which I have found more consistently stylish than the Chardonnay, usually receives a cold soak before fermentation, and is bottled without filtration. In 1995 the releases were the regular from Santa Maria Valley, Mistral, Bien Nacido, Talley, Sanford & Benedict, and a silky super-Reserve called Isabelle. I have yet to record a less than enthusiastic tasting note for ABC Pinot Noir from 1987 to 1995.

Jim Clendenen's mastery of Burgundian techniques is close to complete, and the wines are of exceptional quality, pure in flavour, only occasionally over-oaked, and intense. With excursions into obscure Italian varieties (Il Podere – q.v.) and botrytized Riesling under the Thumbs Up label, and Oregon Pinot Noir under the Ici/La Bas label, there is a danger that he and his wines are being spread too thin. But overall it would be churlish to complain. Moreover, Clendenen is convinced that the best is yet to come. There are new vineyards around the winery, including 39 acres of Pinot Noir on French rootstocks, and he is sure that thanks to the judicious choice of clones and rootstocks – which nobody was concerned about twenty years ago – the quality of the fruit will improve dramatically, and that we can look forward to even more splendid wines from Au Bon Climat in the years ahead.

Austin Cellars
See Los Olivos Vintners (p. 591).

Babcock
5175 Highway 246, Lompoc, CA 93436. Tel: 805 736 1455. Fax: 736 3886. Production: 10,000 cases.

At this estate, founded in 1983, Bryan Babcock cultivates 50 acres of vineyards in the cool western end of Santa Ynez Valley, but supplements those grapes with purchases from warmer sites in the valley. He has planted varieties such as Arneis, Vernaccia, Tempranillo, Albarino, and Pignolo, but is best known for his Chardonnay and Sauvignon Blanc.

There are three ranges: Babcock Vineyards, Eleven Oaks (Sauvignon and Sangiovese), and a cheaper range under the River Break label.

The Sauvignon is barrel-fermented and about 20 per cent of new oak is employed. Some Chardonnay is bought from Talley Vineyard, and the Grand Cuvée Chardonnay is estate-grown. These are hefty but stylish wines, with a substantial proportion of heavily toasted new oak. Much the same is true of the Pinot Noir and Sangiovese. The Gewürztraminer is a celebrated wine, fermented in older barrels to dryness, but it has not met with universal acclaim. I dislike the Riesling. The overall quality of Babcock is impressive, but the wines are in a bold style and expensive.

Baily
33833 Rancho California Rd., Temecula, CA 92592. Tel: 909 676 1895. Production: 2,500 cases.

This estate, which was planted in 1981 with Riesling and Sémillon, was bought by Phillips Baily in 1986. The range includes a white Meritage called Montage, Chardonnay, Cabernet Sauvignon, and a blend of Riesling and Chardonnay.

Ballard Canyon

1825 Ballard Canyon Rd., Solvang, CA 93463. Tel: 805 688 7585. Production: 12,000 cases.

Gene Hallock, a dentist, founded the estate in 1974, planting 50 acres of vines. The range includes Cabernet Sauvignon, Riesling, Chardonnay (sometimes made in a sweet style), and Muscat Canelli.

Barnwood Vineyards

4250 Highway 33, Ventucopa, CA 93252. Tel: 310 275 9889. Fax: 275 9890.

Barnwood is far from the majority of Santa Barbara's vineyards, being located 3,000 feet up in Cuyama Valley. The wines, all from estate-grown fruit from the 40-acre vineyard, include Sauvignon Blanc and barrel-fermented Chardonnay aged in 33 per cent new *barriques*; and Cabernet Sauvignon and Merlot. The wines are usually bottled unfiltered. I have not tasted them.

Beckmen Vineyards

2670 Ontiveros Rd., Los Olivos, CA 93441. Tel: 805 688 8664. Fax: 688 9983.

Produces Sauvignon Blanc, Chardonnay, Cabernet Sauvignon, Grenache and Muscat. I find the wines distinctly light, except for the Sauvignon Blanc, which has the defect of oiliness.

Bedford Thompson Winery and Vineyard

9303 Alison Canyon Rd., Los Alamos, CA 93440. Tel: 805 344 2107. Fax: 344 2047.

The range of wines includes Chardonnay, Riesling, Pinot Noir, Syrah, and Cabernet Franc. Stephan Bedford, formerly of Rancho Sisquoc, is associated with this new venture.

Brander Vineyard

Highway 154 at Roblar Ave., Los Olivos, CA 93441. Tel: 805 688 2455. Fax: 688 8010. Production: 8,000 cases.

Fred Brander has a 43-acre vineyard laid out in a way that reflects his passion for Bordeaux wine. He has adopted very close spacing for varieties such as Cabernet Franc, is a strong believer in the importance of *terroir*, and the soil here is a gravelly sandy loam over a subsoil of gravelly clay.

Brander made his reputation with some characterful Sauvignons. The regular bottling is 50 per cent barrel-fermented, and there is a Cuvée

Nicolas, which is barrel-fermented and aged in 75 per cent new oak for 9 months. This is a wine strictly for devotees of oak. There is also a good Chardonnay, a herb-toned Cabernet Franc, charming Merlot, and very ripe Bordeaux blend called Bouchet.

These wines may not appeal to everyone, but they have a personality all of their own.

Buttonwood Farm Winery

1500 Alamo Pintado Rd., Solvang, CA 93464. Tel: 805 688 3032. Fax: 688 6168. Production: 5,000 cases.

The Williams family planted their organic vineyards in 1983, but the winery did not follow until 1989. They now cultivate 39 acres of red and white Bordeaux varieties as well as Marsanne. The reds are quite herbaceous, the Marsanne heavy. The wines are made by Mike Brown.

Byron

5230 Tepusquet Rd., Santa Maria, CA 934454. Tel: 805 937 7288. Fax: 937 1246. Production: 60,000 cases.

Byron 'Ken' Brown was the winemaker at Zaca Mesa for many years, and began his own winery in 1983. In 1990 Mondavi bought the estate, but Brown remains in charge, sharing the winemaking decisions with Tim Mondavi. The vineyards are very extensive, 641 acres in all, about half of which are Chardonnay. All the Chardonnay and Pinot Noir are planted to a high density on vertical trellising. Brown admits that, like most Santa Barbara vineyards, the original plantings were of the wrong varieties in the wrong places, but this has now, he hopes, been corrected. The oldest part of the vineyard is the Nielsen block, the oldest commercial vineyard in Santa Maria Valley. A 100-acre experimental vineyard was planted in 1991 to explore the possibilities offered by 29 clones of Pinot and Chardonnay planted on 17 rootstocks. In 1996 a new gravity-flow winery was built by Scott Johnson, who also designed Opus One. Sorting tables allow for careful fruit selection immediately after harvesting.

The appley Chardonnay is *barrique*-fermented using a proportion of natural yeasts, and aged on the fine lees for 9 months. Malolactic fermentation is encouraged because of the high acidity of the grapes. The Reserve bottling has a higher proportion of new oak.

The fresh, elegant Pinot Blanc is authentic Pinot Blanc, not Melon. The fermentation begins in steel tanks, but is completed in *barriques*, of which 20 per cent are new. There is also estate-grown Pinot Gris, vinified in a similar way to the Pinot Blanc, but without new oak – a spicy, stylish wine.

Since 1993 some natural yeasts are allowed to work on the Pinot Noir, which receives a cold soak before fermentation and a fairly long maceration. The Reserve is a lot selection fermented entirely with natural yeasts and aged for 16 months in *barriques*, of which 40 per cent are new.

The Byron wines are quite expensive, but they are beautifully made with no trace of blowsiness. The oak is used with discretion and all the wines, especially the recent Pinot Noirs, strike me as being in perfect balance.

Callaway

23720 Rancho California Rd., Temecula, CA 92589. Tel: 909 676 4001. Fax: 676 5209. Production: 250,000 cases.

Ely Callaway of Burlington Industries came to Temecula in 1969 and planted a 105-acre vineyard. The vineyards have now grown to 720 acres of mostly Chardonnay, as well as Pinot Blanc, Chenin Blanc, Sauvignon Blanc, Muscat Canelli, and Cabernet Sauvignon. When Callaway built his winery here in 1974, it was the largest in southern California. Karl Werner of Schloss Vollrads in the Rheingau was the initial winemaker, but since 1983 it has been Dwayne Helmuth. In 1982 the property was sold to Hiram Walker, which is now part of Allied Domecq, and it was under their management that the estate was expanded to its present considerable size. In 1994 these vineyards were sold, but Callaway retains exclusive access to the grapes.

Despite assurances that Temecula is really quite a cool region, Callaway has had to adopt techniques such as fermentation at very low temperatures in order to produce wines with some freshness and vigour. Its best known wine is Calla-Lees, a Chardonnay which is aged in tank rather than barrel, but with lees contact. Sauvignon Blanc is also aged in tanks, and is quite good value. There is also an oak-aged Fumé Blanc and a dry Chenin Blanc. The main red is the Cabernet Sauvignon, which has been produced since 1989.

Another speciality of the winery is late harvest wines. Sweet Nancy is made from Chenin, and there are sometimes late harvest Chardonnays too.

The wines are inexpensive, which has required the winery's owners to compensate by farming for generous yields. Consequently the wines have little weight or structure, but they are soundly made and quite good value. They do not, however, set the pulses racing.

Cambria

5475 Chardonnay Lane, Santa Maria, CA 93454. Tel: 937 8091. Fax: 934 3589. Production: 100,000 cases.

Jess Jackson used to buy grapes from the Tepusquet Vineyard in Santa Maria valley. Then in 1987 he bought a substantial part of this large vineyard and a year later built the Cambria winery. Since 1991 the winemaker has been Dave Guffy. When I first visited Cambria I met someone known as the Flavor Domaine Manager. I found this incomprehensible, until, some time later, I was introduced to the Kendall-Jackson concept of the Flavor Domaine, by which its vineyards are required, or encouraged, to generate a particular flavour component which can be employed in the massive blending operations that result in the Kendall-Jackson range of wines.

The vineyard has certainly been studied to ensure that it provides the required flavours. There are now 1,200 acres in production, and new plantings to come. They include 1,000 acres of Chardonnay, as well as 125 of Pinot Noir, 10 of Syrah, 10 of Viognier, and 6 of Sangiovese. The soils are varied, but there is good drainage throughout. The elevation ranges from 400 to 850 feet. The vineyard managers use more open canopies than formerly, and newer plantings are to a density of roughly 1,000 vines per acre. No herbicides are used. Yields are about 3 tons per acre for the reds, up to 4.5 for the Chardonnay. Despite the size of the vineyard, I am assured the grapes are hand-picked.

Cambria, as well as supplying grapes to the Kendall-Jackson empire, produces some good wines of its own. There are three Chardonnays. The Santa Barbara is partially barrel-fermented, the Katharine's Vineyard fully barrel-fermented. Cambria uses 10 per cent American oak. The Reserve Chardonnay is fermented in 45 per cent new *barriques*, but I find the wine confected and overblown and prefer the more vibrant, appley flavours of the Katherine's Vineyard.

There are two Pinot Noirs, both in a fairly toasty style. The 1996 Julia's Vineyard is an improvement on preceding vintages. The Reserve is aged for 13 months in 50 per cent new *barriques*. The Syrah sees no new oak, is macerated for 4 weeks, and I find it a less interesting wine. The Sangiovese is sappy and fatiguing.

The Cambria wines are well made, but one does have the impression that they are being produced to a formula. In general the simpler bottlings are preferable to the high-priced Reserves.

Carrari Vineyards
PO Box 556, Los Alamos, CA 93440. Tel: 805 334 4000. Production: 4,000 cases.

The Carrari family have long cultivated 125 acres of vineyards, selling their fruit to wineries such as Arciero. Their own wines include Cabernet Sauvignon, Chenin Blanc, Chardonnay, and Muscat Canelli.

Maurice Carrie
34225 Rancho California Rd., Temecula, CA 92592. Tel: 909 676 1711. Fax: 676 8397. Production: 30,000 cases.

Founded in 1986, this winery draws on a vineyard of 100 acres, as well as the same quantity under lease. Their principal wines are Chardonnay, Sauvignon Blanc, Fumé Blanc, White Zinfandel, Riesling, Merlot, and Muscat Canelli from local grapes. Quality is middling at best.

Chimère
547 West Betteravia Rd., Santa Maria, CA 93455. Tel: 805 922 9097. Fax: 922 9143. Production: 2,500 cases.

Gary Mosby, the former winemaker at Edna Valley Vineyard, founded this label in 1989, and produces small lots of Chardonnay, Pinot Blanc, Pinot Noir, Merlot, and Nebbiolo. I find the whites clumsy and unbalanced.

Cilurzo Vineyard and Winery
41220 Calle Contento, Temecula, CA 92592. Tel: 909 676 5250. Production: 10,000 cases.

Vincent Cilurzo farms the oldest vineyard in Temecula, its 40 acres planted in 1968. He also buys in grapes from various sources, and sells a wide range of varietals. The Petite Sirah is probably his best-known wine. Prices are modest, and so is quality.

Cold Heaven
PO Box 717, Solvang, CA 93463. Tel: 805 688 9630. Production: 500 cases.

Morgan Clendenen, the wife of Jim Clendenen of Au Bon Climat, has had her own label since 1996. The first release was a Viognier from Sanford and Benedict vineyard, and Pinot Noir from Bien Nacido. She hopes to produce a style less flamboyant and more delicate than that of her husband. The aim is to increase production to a maximum of 5,000 cases.

Costa de Oro
Santa Maria Valley.

Wines made by Gary Burk, Jim Clendenen's colleague at Au Bon Climat. Initial releases were Pinot Noir and Chardonnay.

Cottonwood Canyon
4330 Santa Fe Rd., San Luis Obispo, CA 93403. Tel: 549 9463. Fax: 546 8031. Production: 4,000 cases.

Norman Beko founded this winery in 1988, drawing on 78 acres of vineyards in Santa Barbara. The main wines are barrel-fermented Chardonnay and Pinot Noir, and Gary Mosby is the consultant winemaker. When I last tasted the wines, in 1995, they were showing signs of overripe fruit and oxidation.

Culbertson
See Thornton.

Curtis Winery
5249 Foxen Canyon Rd., Los Olivos, CA 93441. Tel: 805 686 8999. Fax: 686 1256. Production: 15,000 cases.

This winery was founded as J. Carey Cellars by Dr James Carey in 1978. Since 1987 it has been owned by Firestone and the wines are made by Chuck Carlson. The vineyard was planted in 1973 and produces Cabernet Sauvignon and Sauvignon Blanc. The winery also owns the 12-acre La Cuesta Vineyard, planted with Cabernet and Merlot. Yields are low. The wines include barrel-fermented Chardonnay, Sauvignon Blanc, Pinot Noir, Merlot, Cabernet Sauvignon, Syrah, Muscat Canelli, and a Meritage called Arabesque which has about 70 per cent Cabernet Sauvignon, as well as Merlot and Cabernet Franc. Quality is sound rather than exciting.

Di Bruno
The longstanding winemaker at Sanford, Bruno d'Alfonso, has his own label, which in 1996 released a Pinot Gris from Sanford & Benedict Vineyard.

Fiddlehead Cellars
1667 Oak Ave., Suite B, Davis, CA 95616. Tel: 916 756 4550. Fax: 756 4558. Production: 2,500 cases.

The ebullient Kathy Joseph used to be the winemaker at Robert Pecota, until she left in 1989 to set up her own winery, using facilities at Zaca Mesa. One of her wines, a Pinot Noir, is produced from Oregon grapes, but her other wines, a Sauvignon Blanc from Santa Ynez and a Pinot Noir from Santa Maria, are, of course, from Santa Barbara.

Joseph likes warm-climate Sauvignon because it has peachy flavours that please her. She uses *barriques* more for texture than flavour, and because she believes the oak gives the wine greater length. She experimented with blending in Sémillon but found it diluted the Sauvignon and made the wine flabby. So now 100 per cent Sauvignon grapes are whole-cluster pressed, and aged in oak for 8 months, avoiding malolactic fermentation. The best vintage I have tasted is the assertive 1996.

Joseph used to buy Pinot Noir from Sierra Madre, but with Mondavi's purchase of the vineyard, that supply is drying up, so she, in partnership with Meridian, has purchased 133 acres opposite the Sanford & Benedict Vineyard. This will gradually be planted with 25 acres of Pinot Noir, using 8 clones on 2 rootstocks. It will be some years before those vines are in production. In the meantime, the Santa Maria wines are lovely. They are aged for 12 months in *barriques*, of which 35 to 50 per cent are new.

Filsinger

30905 De Portola Rd., Temecula, CA 92592. Tel: 909 676 4594. Production: 7,000 cases.

Dr William Filsinger founded this estate in 1980, producing wines from 32 acres of Chardonnay, Riesling, Sauvignon Blanc, and Gewürztraminer. The wines are cheap but quality is uninspired.

Firestone

5017 Zaca Station Rd., Los Olivos, CA 93441. Tel: 805 688 3940. Fax: 686 1256. Production: 175,000 cases.

Brooks Firestone, having limited enthusiasm for the tyre business, planted 300 acres in Santa Ynez Valley in 1972 and in 1975 founded the first winery in the valley. The soil is varied and, being deep and porous, is well drained. There are now 540 acres in production, and the winery also buys in fruit from other growers. There have inevitably been changes over the years: much Riesling has been grafted over to Viognier, and Cabernet Franc and Syrah have been added to the varietal selection. Pinot Noir was abandoned in 1993, as other vineyards were by then producing wines of superior quality to the estate plantings. This estate has now been bought by Suntory, although the Firestone family remain fully involved in running it.

Although quality at Firestone has been patchy, I have a lot of respect for the winery. Since 1981, however, Alison Green Doran has been the winemaker, and her down-to-earth personality and style have given the wine great consistency. Some of the wines are delicious. There have been excellent Sauvignon Blancs, fresh and lively and with only the lightest oak influence, and enjoyable Merlots and Rieslings, including splendid late harvest Rieslings. Perhaps the Cabernet Sauvignon has shown signs of underripeness, but their Vintage Reserve, a blend of mostly Cabernet Franc, Merlot and Cabernet Sauvignon, is very good. Best of all, Firestone has always offered excellent value. Adam Firestone, who has been running the property since 1995, tells me that the Merlot-mania of recent years tempted them substantially to increase the prices of their own bottlings of this 'hot' variety, but it was a temptation they resisted.

Foxen

7200 Foxen Canyon Rd., Santa Maria, CA 93454. Tel: 805 937 4251. Fax: 937 0415. Production: 8,500 cases.

Foxen is a partnership between Dick Dore, who comes from a local cattle-ranching family, and winemaker Bill Wathen. It was founded in 1987. As they own only 10 acres of vineyards, they buy in fruit from Bien Nacido and other local vineyards. The range of wines is quite large, including Cabernet Sauvignon, Cabernet Franc, and Chenin Blanc. The Chardonnay can be patchy, but the Pinot Noir has bold, stylish, charm and positive fruit.

Gainey

3950 East Highway 246, Santa Ynez, CA 93460. Tel: 805 688 0558. Fax: 688 5864. Production: 15,000 cases.

Daniel Gainey is an owner of a large ranch east of Solvang, which includes 65 acres of vineyards. The winery was established in 1984 and Rick Longoria was the winemaker from 1985 to 1997. Most fruit is purchased, from Sanford & Benedict and other vineyards. Gainey offers a full range of standard varietals, which are of good quality. I find them straightforward, well balanced, and thoroughly enjoyable.

Daniel Gehrs Wines

77 Ironwood Way, Solvang, CA 93463. Tel/fax: 688 0694. Production: 2,000 cases.

Dan Gehrs was the winemaker for some years at Zaca Mesa, and also used to have his own winery in Felton in Santa Cruz County. He left Zaca Mesa in 1998, but was already producing small quantities of wine under his own label, this time in Solvang. The grapes are all purchased from Monterey and Santa Barbara, and he will specialize in single-vineyard Pinot Noir and other wines.

Hart Winery

1300 Avenida Biona, Temecula, CA 92593. Tel: 909 676 6300. Production: 6,000 cases.

This property dates from the 1970s, when it was developed by Travis and Nancy Hart. The principal varieties produced are Sauvignon and Chardonnay, and, more recently, Syrah, Merlot, and Viognier. A blend called Cuvée du Sud combines Mourvèdre, Grenache and Syrah.

Hartley Ostini

406 East Highway 246, Buellton, CA 93427. Tel: 805 688 0676. Production: 700 cases.

I first met Frank Ostini at a *Paulée* in Meursault in the late 1980s, where by chance we were seated next to each other. By chance we were also the only participants in this Burgundian orgy to bring along California Pinot Noir: I brought a Saintsbury wine, he a wine under his own Hitching Post label. Some years later I was dining at the Hitching Post in Buellton with Brooks Firestone and recognized the chef, who was of course none other than Ostini. Passionate about Pinot Noir, he has been making small quantities of good wines since 1981, mostly Pinot Noir but also a little Zinfandel and Syrah. Today the wines are made jointly by Frank Ostini and Gary

Hartley at the Au Bon Climat winery, hence the name change to Hartley Ostini. Production is limited, quality is high, and the wines are most easily found at the excellent restaurant.

Hitching Post
See Hartley Ostini (p. 589).

Houtz Vineyards
1670 Ontiveros Rd., Los Olivos, CA 93441. Tel: 805 688 8664. Production: 4,000 cases.

The estate consists of 16 acres of Chardonnay, Sauvignon Blanc, and Cabernet Sauvignon, and the wines are made by John Kerr.

Jaffurs
2319 Foothill Lane, Santa Barbara, CA 93105. Tel/fax: 805 962 8043. Production: 2,000 cases.

Craig and Lee Jaffurs specialize in small lots of wines from grapes bought in from a variety of sources. The lush Chardonnay is aged in plenty of new oak, as is the Syrah. In 1996 Jaffurs introduced a Viognier. The other wines include oaky, jammy Syrah, Grenache, and Matilja Cuvée, which is composed of Mourvèdre, Syrah, and Cabernet Franc. A good deal of American oak is used to age the wines.

JK Vineyard
1251 Quail Ridge Rd., Solvang, CA 93463. Tel/fax: 805 686 0015.

JK stands for owner Joe Kalina, whose wines, from a vineyard east of Solvang planted with Chardonnay and Syrah, are made by Lane Tanner. The first release was the 1996 Chardonnay.

Kalyra
PO Box 865, Buellton, CA 93427. Tel: 805 963 0274. Production: 800 cases.

Mike Brown, the owner of Kalyra, is an Australian who is also winemaker at Buttonwood Farm. Under this label he produces wines from Bordeaux varieties and Syrah, as well as 'port' blends.

John Kerr Wines
900 East Stowell Rd., Santa Maria, CA 93456. Tel: 805 688 5337. Production: 1,600 cases.

Kerr, a winemaker with years of experience at Jekel, Byron, and elsewhere, started up his own winery in 1986. Here he focuses on barrel-fermented Chardonnay and Pinot Noir, and the occasional Syrah.

Keyways Winery and Vineyard
37338 De Portola Rd., Temecula, CA 92592. Tel: 909 676 1451.

Founded in 1990, this property produces Chardonnay and Zinfandel, aged in American oak.

LinCourt Vineyards
343 North Refugio Rd., Santa Ynez, CA 93460. Tel: 805 688 8381. Production: 18,000 cases.

This started life in 1976 as Santa Ynez Winery, a joint venture between a number of local families uniting 140 acres of vineyards. In 1988 the winery was bought by Doug Scott, and much of the fruit is bought in. Stephan Bedford, formerly of Rancho Sisquoc, became winemaker in 1996. The Pinot Noir has elegance.

Richard Longoria Wines
2935 Grand Ave., Los Olivos, CA 93441. Tel: 805 688 0305. Production: 3,000 cases.

Rick Longoria has been the winemaker for Carey and Gainey, and left to develop his own label, which he originally created in 1982. The first releases were limited quantities of Pinot Noir, Chardonnay, Merlot, and Cabernet Franc. Longoria will also be producing wines from the 10-acre Rideau Vineyard, planted in 1998 with Rhône varietals.

Los Olivos Vintners
2923 Grand Ave., Los Olivos, CA 93441. Tel: 805 688 9665. Fax: 686 1690. Production: 8,000 cases.

This used to be Austin Cellars, until the company was bought by Hart White in 1992. Tony Austin made the wines at Firestone in the 1970s, and then started his own label in 1981, building a winery in 1984. (Unfortunately in 1998 he received a seven-year jail sentence for running a methamphetamine laboratory on his property.) There are 20 acres of Chardonnay and Cabernet Franc, but most of the grapes are purchased. In addition to standard varietals and Riesling, Austin produced a white Meritage called Cumulus, and a number of late harvest wines. Confusingly, the Austin Cellars name is retained for some of the wines. Quality has been modest, and vegetal flavours are still too common.

Moraga
650 Sepulveda Blvd., Los Angeles, CA 90031. Tel: 310 471 8560. Production: 500 cases.

The canyons of Bel Air are not the place where you would expect to find a vineyard, if only because of the cost of land – about $7 million per acre

– in this most exclusive of California suburbs. Moraga vineyard belongs to Tom Jones, who used to be head of Northrop Aviation. The canyon where he has his house, Moraga Canyon, has a distinctive microclimate, with an average rainfall of 24 inches, considerably higher than elsewhere in Los Angeles. This makes the climate more moderate, says Jones, than Napa Valley. Nonetheless it registers as a Region III in the heat summation system, but warm days are mitigated by cool nights, and twenty days of frost per year are not unusual. The soil is distinctive too, with deep gravel beds in the canyon bottom, and very steep hillsides consisting of a sandstone bed with strata of fossil limestone.

Jones planted some vines here on a trial basis in 1978, with the first wines vinified in 1985. These wines were never sold, but a wine merchant in Westwood heard about them and encouraged Jones to produce wine commercially. Jones began planting a proper vineyard, only to find it partly ravaged by Pierce's disease. Now, however, there are 8 parcels in production, with the vineyard blend composed of 80 per cent Cabernet Sauvignon, 18 per cent Merlot, and 2 per cent Cabernet Franc. The density is up to 2,200 vines per acre.

Roberto Quintana is the vineyard manager, and since 1987 the wines have been made by Tony Soter. The harvest can take as long as four weeks because of the variety of microclimates. The wine is aged in 70 per cent new *barriques* for 24 months. The result is a sumptuous, opulent, oaky wine, powerful and luxurious, splendid in its way if somewhat obvious. Although it sells for $50, it is clearly on the same quality level as many of the more pricy Napa Cabernets.

Mosby Winery

9496 Santa Rosa Rd., Buellton, CA 93427. Tel: 805 688 2415. Fax: 686 4288. Production: 10,000 cases.

A winery owned and operated by Bill Mosby since 1980. He specializes in Chardonnay and Italian varieties, as well as oddities such as barrel-fermented Gewürztraminer and dry Orange Muscat.

Mount Palomar

33820 Ranch California Rd., Temecula, CA 92591. Tel: 909 676 5047. Fax: 694 5688. Production: 30,000 cases.

In 1975 John Poole founded this estate, which now consists of 100 acres of Chardonnay, Sauvignon Blanc, Riesling, Cabernet Sauvignon, and Sangiovese, as well as a little Cortese. The winemaker Etienne Calper makes a range of wines, including 'sherries', in a commercial style.

Andrew Murray
6701 Foxen Canyon Rd., Los Olivos, CA 93441. Tel: 805 686 9604. Fax: 686 9704.

Murray owns 30 acres of Syrah, Grenache, Mourvèdre, Roussanne and Marsanne, which are vinified at his winery near Zaca Mesa. The first releases were from the 1993 vintage. In addition to varietal wines, there is a southern Rhône style blend called Esperance.

Old Creek Ranch Winery
10024 East Old Creek Rd., Ojai, Ventura, CA 93023. Tel: 805 649 4132. Production: 1,200 cases.

This old ranch belongs to the Maitland family and includes 5 acres of Sauvignon Blanc and Chenin Blanc. The range is supplemented by purchased grapes of Chardonnay, Pinot Noir and Riesling.

Orfila Vineyards
13455 San Pasqual Rd., Escondido, CA 92025. Tel: 760 738 6500. Fax: 745 3773. Production: 10,000 cases.

This winery in San Pasqual Valley near San Diego is the former Thomas Jaeger winery, which was bought in 1994 by Alejandro Orfila of Argentina. He is aiming to produce a broad range of classic varietals as well as Muscat and Sangiovese. Prices are quite high.

Fess Parker
6200 Foxen Canyon Rd., Los Olivos, CA 93441. Tel: 805 688 1545. Fax: 686 1130. Production: 35,000 cases.

Before planting vineyards in Santa Ynez and Santa Maria valleys, Fess Parker was an actor, personifying on screen the king of the wild frontier Davy Crockett, so thousands of visitors come to the winery to catch a glimpse of the great man. They are rarely disappointed, and Fess Parker is often in the tasting room, happy to chat or sign autographs.
There is nothing folksy about the winery operation. Fess Parker's son Eli is the winemaker and Jed Steele the consultant winemaker. The wines are made in a no-expense-spared style, with Reserves aged in new oak. A good deal of Chardonnay and Pinot Noir is bought from Bien Nacido and other vineyards. The Parker estate includes some Rhône varietals, and a good Syrah and Syrah Reserve are produced, as well as a Melange du Rhône white from Marsanne and Viognier. In 1995 Cabernet Franc was introduced to the range. The wines are good but no bargains, and I can't work up enthusiasm for the fruit-salady Chardonnays.

Il Podere dell'Olivos

PO Box 958, Los Olivos, CA 93441. Tel: 805 688 6486. Fax: 688 0976.
Production: 4,000 cases.

The tongue-in-cheek name is a front for one of Jim Clendenen's more eccentric enterprises. As the name suggests, all the wines are Italian varietals, sourced from all over the place. The range has included Nebbiolo, Barbera (sometimes from Lodi fruit), creamy Tocai Friulano (from Gilroy and Santa Maria), the strawberry-toned Pronto (an Aleatico blended with Bonny Doon grappa!), excellent full-bodied Fiano, Freisa and Arneis (both phased out now), 'Moanna Arrossisce' (a barrel-fermented rosé from Aleatico and Barbera), juicy if simple Teroldego, 'Ragazzo Legnoso' (a blend of Nebbiolo and Barbera aged in new oak), and a Muscat blend called Arioso. Almost all the wines are barrel-fermented and go through malolactic fermentation. Naturally, some wines are more successful than others, but the main point is that Clendenen is having a lot of fun and giving wine drinkers some unexpected pleasures.

Presidio

133 East De La Guerra, Santa Barbara, CA 93101. Tel: 805 965 9463.
Fax: 965 4644.

Doug Brawn produces Chardonnay, unfiltered Pinot Noir, and Merlot. The 1996 Pinot Noir lacked concentration and personality.

Qupé

4665 Santa Maria Mesa Rd., Santa Maria, CA 93454. Tel: 805 688 2477.
Fax: 686 4470. Production: 20,000 cases.

The label is owned by Bob Lindquist and the wines are produced at the same winery as Au Bon Climat. Qupé has an excellent track record for its Syrah. There are now three different bottlings. The Central Coast is the basic blend (but a very good wine for all that), Los Olivos (blended with 40 per cent Mourvèdre), and Bien Nacido. The earliest vintages, from 1982, were made from Estrella River grapes in Paso Robles. The range is supplemented with Viognier, Marsanne, and Mourvèdre, as well as rich oaky Chardonnays from the nearby Sierra Madre Vineyard. The Syrah and Chardonnay have proved to be the best wines so far, especially the spicy, gamy, long-lived Bien Nacido Hillside Select, but the others are well worth sampling too.

Rancho Sisquoc Winery

6600 Foxen Canyon Rd., Santa Maria, CA 93454. Tel: 805 934 4332.
Fax: 937 6601. Production: 8,000 cases.

Rancher James Flood planted vineyards – now covering 211 acres – from

1968 onwards and the winery followed in 1978. It is located at the end of a long drive that traverses part of the 37,000-acre Flood ranch. Most of the grapes are sold to Mondavi. The winemaker was Stephan Bedford until he left in 1996, to be succeeded by Carol Botright. As well as the usual varietals, Rancho Sisquoc specializes in Riesling and in off-dry Sylvaner, here known as Franken Riesling. The wines are sound, occasionally herbaceous, and not particularly exciting; however, prices are reasonable.

Rosenthal
Tel: 800 814 0733. Production: 5,000 cases.

Malibu Canyon is not the obvious place to grow grapes, but George Rosenthal farms 15 acres of Cabernet Sauvignon, Chardonnay, and Merlot. The first release, a 1991 Cabernet, was well received.

Rusack Vineyards
1825 Ballard Canyon Rd., Solvang, CA 93463. Tel: 805 688 1278. Fax: 686 1508.

Rusack produce Cabernet Sauvignon, Merlot, Chardonnay, Viognier, and Riesling.

Sanford
7520 Santa Rosa Rd., Buellton, CA 93427. Tel: 805 688 3300. Fax: 688 7381. Production: 40,000 cases.

Sanford is closely associated with the Sanford & Benedict Vineyard, with which it has had a long and not always happy relationship. As a Burgundy fan, Richard Sanford decided to plant Pinot Noir in a cool region and selected the Santa Ynez Valley. He and Michael Benedict began planting in 1971. The Sanford & Benedict winery produced its first wines in 1976. However, in 1980 the partners fell out and Richard Sanford founded his own winery in 1981. Then in 1988 an Englishman, Robert Atkin, bought the vineyard and asked Richard Sanford to manage it, as it badly needed attention. Richard Sanford set to work to restore the 131-acre vineyard, and by 1994 it was back on form. It is now planted with 80 acres of Chardonnay, as well as Pinot Noir, Merlot, Pinot Gris, Nebbiolo, and Viognier. Sanford and Atkin have also bought the nearby Santa Rita ranch, an organic vineyard planted with 7 Pinot Noir clones and 5 Chardonnay clones. This will be the site of the new Sanford winery.

Bruno d'Alfonso has been the winemaker here since 1983. The style here used to be very broad and rich, and the whites, which all went through full malolactic fermentation, often struck me as quite confected, although D'Alfonso assured me the wines were fermented to dryness. The Sauvignon Blanc, which is mostly Monterey fruit, shows this character more than the other wines, and I find the Chardonnays of recent vintages much more to my taste.

There are three Sanford Chardonnays. The regular bottling comes from vineyards throughout the county. The more expensive Barrel Selection is a selection of the best lots that are blended and then aged in new oak for 7 months. The Estate Chardonnay is fermented in new *barriques* and does not go through malolactic fermentation. I prefer the leaner Estate to the richer Barrel Selection.

The Pinot Noir is fermented in open-top vats and the cap is punched down. The Barrel Selection bottling is neither fined nor filtered. These are excellent wines, of considerable weight and richness. The Vin Gris made from Pinot Noir is dry and delicious.

In a curious experiment conducted in 1991 and 1992, different wine-makers – Jim Clendenen, Bryan Babcock, Bill Wathen on Foxen, Rick Longoria of Gainey, Lane Tanner, and Sanford himself – each made a single barrel of Pinot Noir from the vineyard, which were then blended as a Signature blend.

Santa Barbara Winery
202 Anacapa St., Santa Barbara, CA 93101. Tel: 805 963 3633. Fax: 962 4981. Production: 30,000 cases.

This was the first winery in the county, founded in 1962 by architect Pierre Lafond. He planted 67 acres of vineyards in Santa Ynez Valley in 1972, and the winery also leases some 45 acres, which supply the bulk of the grapes. The winemaker since 1981 has been Bruce McGuire, and the winery is the only significant one in the city of Santa Barbara itself. The winery has always produced a wide range, including late harvest Zinfandel, Riesling, and Sauvignon Blanc. Chardonnay and Pinot Noir are the mainstay, and are made in a rich, full style, amplified further in the Reserve bottlings. Other wines include Grenache, Syrah, and Cabernet Franc, and barrel-fermented Sauvignon Blanc.

Santa Margarita Winery
33490 Madera de Playa, Temecula, CA 92592. Tel: 909 676 4431.

Founded in 1992, Santa Margarita produces Cabernet Sauvignon and Sauvignon Blanc. The wines are cheap.

Santa Ynez Winery
See LinCourt Vineyards (p. 591).

Sunstone
125 North Refugio Rd., Santa Ynez, CA 93460. Tel: 805 688 WINE. Fax: 686 1771. Production: 6,000 cases.

Fred and Linda Price farm 25 acres of organically cultivated Cabernet Sauvignon, Chardonnay, Merlot, Syrah, Mourvèdre, and Viognier. I like the sweet, generous Merlot, but the Chardonnay can taste overripe. The winemaker is Douglass Braun.

Lane Tanner
Box 144A, Sant Maria, CA 93454. Tel/fax: 805 934 0230. Production: 2,000 cases.

After making wines at Zaca Mesa, Firestone, and elsewhere, Lane Tanner founded her own label in 1989 and specializes in single-vineyard Pinot Noirs that can have remarkable charm. Unlike many Santa Barbara Pinot enthusiasts she goes easy on the new oak, limiting it to 20 per cent. The wines are fermented in small open boxes, the cap is punched down regularly, and the wine is bottled without fining and with what she calls a 'rock and frog' filtration. In 1997 Tanner added Syrah to the range.

Temecula Crest Winery
40620 Calle Contento, Temecula, CA 92592. Tel: 909 676 8231. Fax: 676 8356.

The winery produces Merlot and a blend of Sauvignon Blanc and Riesling called Contento.

Thornton
32575 Rancho California Rd., Temecula, CA 92589. Tel: 909 699 0099. Fax: 699 5536. Production: 50,000 cases.

Culbertson was an initially successful winery founded in 1981 by John Culbertson, but in 1992 it was sold to John Thornton. The winery specializes in sparkling wine from Burgundian varieties, purchased from the Central Coast. The premium wines are released under the Thornton label, the lesser wines under the Culbertson label. Some still wines are made too, with some promising but expensive Mediterranean varietals.

Van Roekel Winery
34567 Rancho California Rd., Temecula, CA 92591. Tel: 909 699 6961. Fax: 699 3213.

This recently established winery produces Chardonnay, Gewürztraminer, and Syrah, in a light style.

Vita Nova
See Au Bon Climat. Production: 3,000 cases.

This label was founded jointly by Jim Clendenen and Bob Lindquist of Qupé. The wines are made in a bold, rich style. Even the Sauvignon Blanc is fermented in new *barriques*, although with limited barrel ageing.

Chardonnay, usually from Rancho Vinedo vineyards, accounts for half the production, and there is an inconsistent Bordeaux blend called Reservatum. My favourite wine is the delicious Cabernet Franc. A Sangiovese/Merlot blend is in the works, and in 1996 a Cabernet/Petit Verdot blend called Acronicus was first produced.

Whitcraft Wines

3022 Lomita Rd., Santa Barbara, CA 93105. Tel: 805 569 9500. Fax: 688 4833. Production: 1,500 cases.

Chris Whitcraft, a former wine merchant, founded this small gravity-flow winery in 1985, specializing in Chardonnay and unfined, unfiltered Pinot Noir. As well as a ripe oaky Bien Nacido bottling of Pinot Noir, there are others made from Russian River and Sonoma Coast fruit.

Zaca Mesa

6905 Foxen Canyon Rd., Los Olivos, CA 93341. Tel: 805 688 9339. Fax: 688 8796. Production: 60,000 cases.

Zaca Mesa was founded in 1972 by an oilman called Louis Ream, who constructed the winery in 1978. But it produced more than it could sell, and in 1986 Ream sold the property to John Cushman, who made his money in commercial real estate. Ken Brown, now of Byron, used to be the winemaker, and Dan Gehrs was in charge from 1993 until 1998, when he was succeeded by his assistant Benjamin Silver. Zaca Mesa had been through rough times in the late 1980s, uncertain of its direction, and Gehrs was instructed to sort things out.

Today there are 207 acres near the winery, and a further 200 in Santa Maria Valley. The Santa Ynez vineyards are among the highest in the county at 1,500 feet. Some of the varieties originally planted soon proved unsuitable. Chenin Blanc, Sémillon, and Petite Sirah were never even vinified at Zaca Mesa. However, planting Syrah in the mid-1980s worked well, and these may be the oldest Syrah vines in the county. By the early 1990s there were further changes, as Cabernet Sauvignon, Pinot Noir, and Zinfandel were given up. Gehrs moved the winery towards Rhône varietals, planting Roussanne, Grenache, Counoise, and Mourvèdre.

The Chardonnay is whole-cluster pressed, but not entirely fermented in barrel. It is not a wholly satisfactory wine. The Reserve can be woody, the regular bottling can lack concentration. Gehrs was not a great fan of malolactic fermentation, preferring to keep the acidity and freshness in the wines. The Roussanne, first made in 1995, is delicious and sees no new oak. Gehrs liked to blend Viognier into the Syrah, but also bottled a small quantity as a varietal wine. In 1995 he also made a delicious late harvest Viognier.

The reds are given a cold soak of up to a week. The Pinot Noir comes from Sierra Madre Vineyard, with punching down of the cap and prolonged ageing in French oak. Gehrs was experimenting with Syrah, blending some Viognier into the main bottling, but also released a pure varietal version aged in American oak. An early-drinking wine is Cuvée Z, a blend of Grenache, Mourvèdre, Cinsault, Counoise, and Syrah, aged for 9 months in *barriques*.

By the time he left to concentrate on his own winery, Gehrs had definitely put Zaca Mesa back on the map with some very distinctive wines, and I hope the groundwork he laid will be built upon.

Many of the small wineries have no tasting rooms, but their wines can be tasted, on a fairly random basis, at 2905 Grand Ave., Los Olivos (805 937 9801) or 2531 Grand Ave., Los Olivos (805 922 9097).

The Sierra Foothills and Central Valley

Amador Foothill Winery

12500 Steiner Rd., Plymouth, CA 95669. Tel: 209 245 6307. Production: 9,000 cases.

Ben Zeitman made wines for a hobby while he was working for NASA, and in the 1980s he bought land in the Foothills, where he and Katie Quinn now cultivate 11 acres of Sangiovese, Sauvignon Blanc, and Sémillon. The two whites are blended to form a Meritage wine. However, Amador Foothill is best known for its Zinfandels, which are bought in from celebrated old vineyards such as Grandpère, Eschen, Esola, Murrill, and Ferrero. Sangiovese was added to the range in 1992, in a red and rosé version. The wines can be quite pruny and raisiny, and don't always match the quality of the vineyards in which the grapes originated. Prices are reasonable.

Black Sheep Vintners

Main St. and Murphys Grade Rd., Murphys CA 95247. Tel: 209 728 2157. Production: 4,000 cases.

The former Chispa Cellars was bought in 1986 by David Olson, who used to make wines at Stevenot. Zinfandel is the principal wine, and Cabernet Sauvignon and Sauvignon Blanc are also released.

Boeger

1709 Carson Rd., Placerville, CA 95667. Tel: 906 622 8094. Fax: 622 8112. Production: 18,000 cases.

Greg Boeger is a descendant of Anton Nichelini, who founded a winery in Napa in 1890 which is still in existence and now looked after by Boeger. His own winery is in El Dorado County and was founded in 1973. The rustic tasting room is located in an old winery dating from the 1870s, and the new winery stands close by. He has planted almost 100 acres of vineyards, some as high as 3,000 feet, with twenty-five varieties, and these grapes furnish almost all his needs. The surplus is sold to other wineries, including Mondavi for its La Famiglia range. The soils are prone to erosion, which is controlled with cover crops and terracing.

Boeger is a great blender, producing innumerable lots after each vintage and then assembling them later. Migliore combines Refosco, Mourvèdre, Zinfandel, Barbera, Grenache, and Petite Sirah; the Spanish-style Milagro blends Tempranillo, Graciano and Grenache; while Majeure is composed of Syrah, Grenache and Mourvèdre. Not to mention the red Meritage, which has a good deal of Cabernet Franc in the blend. Boeger also makes three Zinfandels, including an Estate Zinfandel and a Walker Vineyard bottling, which I prefer. He is best known, however, for his powerful smoky Barbera (the 1994 had 14.4 degrees of alcohol). Merlot can be good too. In general, Boeger's reds are better than his whites, especially the dull Chardonnay and over-sweet Riesling. Although I can't help feeling he produces too many wines to sustain the highest level of quality across the board, you clearly can't keep a good blender down, and the Boeger wines are never lacking in interest and swagger.

Bogle

37783 County Rd. 144, Clarksburg, CA 95612. Tel: 916 744 1139. Fax: 744 1187. Production: 130,000 cases.

The Bogle family planted vineyards in Clarksburg in 1968 and opened their winery in 1979. They now farm over 1,000 acres, including 450 on Merritt Island, and supply other wineries as well as their own. Bogle used to produce a good deal of Chenin Blanc and Grey Riesling, but the scale now tips in favour of more saleable varieties such as Chardonnay, Sauvignon Blanc and Cabernet Sauvignon. Despite the considerable acreage the Bogles own, they also buy in fruit, and their wines are released under the California appellation. Their Petite Sirah and Merlot are particularly admired. Since 1992 the wines, which are inexpensive, have been made by Christopher Smith.

Chateau de Leu

1635 Mason Rd., Green Valley, CA 94585. Tel: 707 864 1517. Fax: 864 2232. Production: 10,000 cases.

Vineyards were originally planted here on alluvial soils in Green Valley in 1882 and some 50-year-old vines survive on the chateau's estate. Ben Volkhardt built the winery in 1980, and in 1989 it was purchased by a Japanese company. The winery specializes in Mediterranean varieties, and bought grapes from Napa and Sonoma form the basis of their Pinot Noir, Cabernet Sauvignon, and Merlot. The second label, Bella Vista, is used for the produce of young vines.

Chatom

1969 Highway 4, Douglas Flat, CA 95229. Tel: 209 736 6500. Fax: 736 6507. Production: 10,000 cases.

Gay Callan began planting vines in 1981 in Esmeralda Valley, initially selling grapes from her 65 acres, until in 1985 she began producing her own wines. Chuck Hovey is the winemaker. It is a winery that has a high opinion of its products, but having tasted all the wines – Chardonnay, Sauvignon Blanc, Zinfandel, Sangiovese, Cabernet Sauvignon – I was disappointed by the bitterness and dilution in most of them. Only the Syrah showed some flair.

Clos du Lac

3151 Highway 88, Ione, CA 95640. Tel: 209 274 2238. Production: 10,000 cases.

This estate was founded in 1980 as the Greenstone estate, with 70 acres of Zinfandel, Sauvignon Blanc, Chenin Blanc, French Colombard, Palamino, and Cabernet Sauvignon. In 1996 it was bought by businessman Tim Evans, who changed the name. The winemaker is François Cordesse, and the Greenstone name will be retained as a second label. The Greenstone wines were unashamedly commercial in style, and it will be interesting to see whether the new owner will try to improve the quality.

Deaver

12455 Steiner Rd., Plymouth, CA 95669. Tel: 209 245 4099. Production: 1,000 cases.

Best known for Zinfandel, Deaver also produce Barbera, Chardonnay, Orange Muscat, and 'port'.

Elliston

463 Kilkare Rd., Sunol, CA 94586. Tel: 510 862 2377. Production: 4,000 cases.

Located south of Pleasanton, this was an important estate in the nineteenth century, with 150 acres under vine by the turn of the century. Prohibition dealt it the usual death blow, and the estate was re-founded in 1983 by the Awtrey family. Then in 1992 it was sold to the Flavetta family. It is one of the few wineries to make use of the Sunol Valley appellation, and was also one of the pioneers of Pinot Gris, although most of the wines are standard varietals.

Ficklin

30246 Avenue 7.5, Madera, CA 93637. Tel: 209 674 4598. Production: 11,000 cases.

Amidst the vast plantations of the Central Valley, a few family wineries dedicated to quality still hang on. Walter Ficklin began planting vineyards for table grapes and raisins in 1911, and in 1946 his sons obtained cuttings of Portuguese varieties and planted 40 acres of them with a view to making 'port'. The winery was founded in 1948 and remains in family hands, with Peter Ficklin the current winemaker. After harvest, the must is fermented for about 3 days before fermentation is stopped by adding grape brandy. The wine is then aged in American oak. A solera system is employed for the nonvintage styles, and in good years – such as 1980, 1983, 1986, and 1988 – they produce a vintage wine from 70 per cent Tinta Madeira. The Ficklins have also been developing a solera for their 'tawny port', which is aged for 10 years in American oak. The vintage 'port' can be of superb quality.

Fitzpatrick Winery
7740 Fairplay Rd., Somerset, CA 95684. Tel: 800 245 9166. Fax: 530 620 6838. Production: 4,500 cases.

Originally known as Somerset Vineyards, this 15-acre property, which is organically farmed, was renamed in 1985. The wines produced include Cabernet Sauvignon, Chardonnay, Sauvignon Blanc, Zinfandel, and a Zinfandel/Petite Sirah blend called King's Red. The style is very commercial.

Gerwer
8221 Stony Creek Rd., Somerset, CA 95684. Tel: 209 245 3467. Production: 8,000 cases.

Vernon Gerwer planted 12 acres in 1979 at a particularly high elevation: up to 2,600 feet. At present he has 20 acres of Petite Sirah, Ruby Cabernet, Sauvignon Blanc, and Sémillon; Zinfandel and Chenin are purchased.

Gold Hill Vineyard
5660 Vineyard Lane, Placerville, CA 95667. Tel: 916 626 6522. Production: 8,000 cases.

Hank Battjes owns 35 acres of Chardonnay, Cabernet Sauvignon, Merlot, Chenin Blanc and Riesling in El Dorado. Chardonnay dominates production.

Granite Springs
6060 Granite Springs Rd., Somerset, CA 95684. Tel: 916 620 6395. Fax: 245 6395. Production: 10,000 cases.

Les Russell founded this winery in 1981. Like many El Dorado estates, its 24 acres are planted at an elevation well above 2,000 feet. The reds do best, and there are some good-quality wines from Zinfandel, Petite Sirah, and Merlot, as well as port-style wines. The Petite Sirah is blended, unusually, with a little Chenin Blanc.

Indian Rock Vineyards
1154 Pennsylvania Gulch Rd., Murphys, CA 95247. Tel: 209 728 2266. Production: 3,000 cases.

This winery produces Chardonnay, Merlot, Cabernet Sauvignon, and Charbono from 50 acres east of Murphys.

Karly
11076 Bell Rd., Plymouth, CA 95669. Tel: 209 245 3922. Production: 11,000 cases.

Lawrence Cobb founded this property in 1980 and named it after his wife. As an engineer he designed his own winery on a gravity-fed basis. The canyon-slope vineyards, mostly planted in 1981 and 1983, are on mineral-rich soil that is well drained. Viticulture is virtually organic, and their own grapes provide 70 per cent of their needs; Karly also buy Zinfandel from neighbouring vineyards. Their top Zinfandel bottling is usually from the Sadie Upton Vineyard. The Sauvignon Blanc is the best white offering, and there is an unusually rich and unctuous Orange Muscat. Their own vineyards contain parcels of white and red Rhône varieties, which now appear on the list.

Kautz Ironstone
1894 Six Mile Rd., Murphys, CA 95247. Tel: 209 728 1251. Fax: 728 1275. Production: 150,000 cases.

John Kautz is a farmer, who started his business in 1948. Today Kautz is the eighth-largest grape grower in California, and his holdings consist of 4,200 acres of vineyards, with a further 1,000 about to come on stream. Only a trifling 70 acres are planted in the Foothills, mostly Chardonnay at 2,400 feet. Most of the other vineyards, all drip-irrigated, are in Lodi or near Folsom, on flat land suitable for mechanical harvesting. The Kautzes make no apology for the fact that they are farming grapes on a large commercial scale, with yields of up to 8 tons per acre, and their fruit is mostly sold to large wineries such as Mondavi, Glen Ellen, Acacia, Wente, Franciscan and Merryvale.

Kautz, and his son Stephen, who is now the president of the company, came late to winemaking, first bottling wines in the late 1980s. The winery did not open until 1994, and when it did it became clear that this was to be the unrivalled showplace of the Foothills. John Kautz wants it to be the most beautiful winery in the world. It isn't, but it's an extraordinary achievement nonetheless, with its own bakery, catering facilities for up to 1,500 people, organic herb gardens, a delicatessen, a computerized organ, and a park traversed by waterways, including a waterfall created when the end of a hill was blasted off. What draws most visitors is the mining museum, which has a quite astonishing 44-pound chunk of crystallized gold, said to be the largest in the world. It was dug up nearby on Christmas Day 1992. The winery itself is located beneath all the public areas, and old mine shafts now house 3,400 oak barrels.

Kautz find time, amidst all this showmanship, to produce wines, under the supervision of the experienced winemaker Steve Millier, who first talked John Kautz into bottling some wines. The wines are, in their way, exemplary. They are not complex or profound, but they are well made and well balanced. I particularly like the Chardonnay, the perfect antidote to heavily oaked, barrel-fermented versions that are now ubiquitous in California. The Library Collection is barrel-fermented, but I'm happy with the simpler wine. A good deal of American oak is used. There's a fresh Cabernet Franc, a peppery Shiraz, and good Merlot and Cabernet Sauvignon. Millier admits that the wines are styled to suit a particular market. Mostly bottled under the California appellation, they express varietal rather than regional character. But I would rather drink honest, inexpensive wines such as these, than overpriced and pretentious bottlings of overblown wines such as one encounters all too often in the coastal regions.

However, I can't share the Kautz enthusiasm for Symphony, a Davis crossing of Muscat of Alexandria and Grenache Gris. Made in an off-dry style, it has a heavy grapefruity bouquet I find offputting. The Kautzes say it is a good match with hot spicy dishes, but I'd rather have a beer. Nor do I care for the overripe, jammy Meritage. Kautz also make a good 'port' from old vines, a sweet, fresh, peppery wine with a dry finish.

Kenworthy Vineyards
10120 Shenandoah Rd., Plymouth, CA 95669. Tel: 209 245 3198. Production: 2,000 cases.

John Kenworthy makes Zinfandel from his own 8-acre vineyard, and buys in Chardonnay and Cabernet Sauvignon from El Dorado sites.

Lang
Production: 500 cases.

Bob Lang is essentially a grape farmer, with 160 acres of Zinfandel and Sauvignon Blanc. He himself produces small quantities of Zinfandel.

Latcham Vineyards
2860 Omo Ranch Rd., Mount Aukum, CA. Tel: 916 620 6834.

This El Dorado estate produces robust Cabernet Sauvignon, Cabernet Franc, Petite Sirah, and Zinfandel.

Latrobe

4861 Memory Lane, Shingle Springs, CA 95682. Tel: 916 676 0108. Fax: 676 5506. Production: 1,000 cases.

Bob Clarke makes his wines, mostly Sauvignon Blanc, at Madroña.

Lava Cap

2221 Fruitridge Rd., Placerville, CA 95667. Tel: 530 621 0175. Fax: 621 4399. Production: 13,000 cases.

In 1981 vineyards were planted on these weathered volcanic soils, previously the site of a pear orchard, at a height of 2,600 feet. The property now consists of 45 acres but expansion is under way, and eventually there will be 130 acres in production. The wines are made by Thomas Jones, who produces slightly confected Chardonnay but elegant Merlot, as well as Zinfandel, burly Petite Sirah, Sauvignon Blanc, and a rustic, bacony Cabernet Sauvignon too. The proprietary red, Lava Cap Red, is a blend of Cabernet and Zinfandel.

Lucas Winery

18196 North Davis Rd., Lodi, CA 95240. Tel: 209 368 2006. Production: 2,000 cases.

David Lucas makes some of the best Zinfandels in Lodi. His day job involves working for the grower relations department of Mondavi Woodbridge, so he is very familiar with the vineyards of the region. Since 1978 he has been cultivating 20 acres of low-yielding vines. He cold-soaks his Zinfandel before fermenting the must in open-top vats. Lucas favours long maceration, and ages the wine in 25 per cent new oak, racking infrequently. Too much American oak can, in his view, be overpowering, so he uses a mixture of French and American. The wine is fined with eggwhites but not filtered. Lucas releases Reserves not as a selection from the entire vintage, but as his sign of approval that the vintage as a whole is a great one. The wines are rich, complex and capable of long evolution in bottle for those with the patience to keep them.

Madroña

PO Box 454, High Hill Rd., Camino, CA 95709. Tel: 916 644 5948. Production: 10,000 cases.

Dick Bush has been around for a long time. He first planted vines in 1973: 35 acres growing at a height of 3,000 feet. What appealed to him about the region was that it permitted great diversity, and it was possible to grow Gewürztraminer and Zinfandel in close proximity. Until his own winery was completed in 1980, the wines were made at Boeger. Today he is assisted by his son Paul, and the very able young winemaker, Hugh Chappelle.

The Bushes grow a wide range of varieties on the clay loam soils here. Only Sauvignon Blanc has proved unsatisfactory and has been grafted over to Syrah and Mourvèdre. Dick Bush admits that in their early years they picked the grapes too soon and some of the wines had a vegetal character, which is now a thing of the past, especially with alterations to their canopy management. By minimizing irrigation they obtain grapes with small berries, which is excellent for quality but can present problems of tannin management. There are constant improvements to the vineyards, and the Wente clones of Chardonnay are now supplemented with Dijon clones, which they are happy with. The 1996 Chardonnay was excellent, aged in 25 per cent new *barriques* with only partial malolactic fermentation. The Riesling and Gewürztraminer are also good, with just a hint of sweetness.

The Zinfandel is excellent, a powerful wine that doesn't show its high alcohol; it is aged in American oak. Madroña like to age their Bordeaux-style reds for up to 2 years in oak, and in outstanding years they release a blend from all five red varieties called Quintet. The 1993 is outstanding. When botrytis swoops on the vineyards, as in 1993 and 1997, they produce late harvest Riesling and even Chardonnay.

Milliare

276 Main St., Murphys. CA. Tel: 209 728 1658. Fax: 728 8774. Production: 2,500 cases.

When he is not making the wines at Kautz, Steve Millier and his wife Liz produce some wine at his own small facility in Murphys. This allows him to employ French oak, rather than the American barrels that dominate at Kautz. The range is wide, with barrel-fermented Gewürztraminer as well as Chardonnay, Zinfandel from the Ghirardelli Vineyard, and Cabernet Sauvignon.

Mondavi Woodbridge

5950 East Woodbridge Rd., Acampo, CA 95258. Tel: 209 369 5861. Fax: 369 1461. Production: 6.5 million cases.

Robert Mondavi went to high school in Lodi and clearly retained a fondness for the area. He must also have retained a memory of how palatable the grapes could be. So in 1979, seeking to expand production with a range of unpretentious and less expensive wines than those being produced at his Napa winery, he bought the former Cherokee cooperative cellars and expanded them. He hasn't stopped expanding them, and the winery is a perpetual building site. There was plenty of decent Sauvignon Blanc and Cabernet Sauvignon available at the time, so Mondavi launched what became known as Bob White and Bob Red. In 1986 the wines were relaunched as the Robert Mondavi Woodbridge California Varietals, and the range consists of Cabernet, Zinfandel, Sauvignon Blanc, Chardonnay, White Zinfandel, and 'port'. There used to be a Chenin, but it proved hard to sell and has been phased out. However, Syrah may be added in due course.

Brad Alderson has been in charge of the winery from the outset, and clearly knows exactly what he is doing. The director of winemaking is David Akiyoshi, and the crucial decisions at Woodbridge are made by a troika of Alderson, Akiyoshi, and Tim Mondavi. Since they buy grapes from as many as 300 growers, most of them local, Mondavi set up a special grower relations department and keep a team monitoring fruit quality in the vineyards all year round. The winery implements strict quality criteria and has no qualms about rejecting substandard fruit. However the point of the grower relations department is to assist conscientious growers in improving the quality of the grapes they grow and deliver. They also advise on replanting and spacing decisions, and have persuaded many growers to adopt vertical trellising. Not all the grapes come from Lodi. Half the Zinfandel destined for white Zinfandel is bought from Monterey and the Central Coast. Chardonnay is 70 per cent from Lodi.

Nonetheless the operation is geared to making inexpensive wines, so all white grapes are machine-picked at night. A little Sémillon and Riesling are blended into the Chardonnay. Only 15 per cent is barrel-fermented, there is no malolactic fermentation, and both Chardonnay and Sauvignon Blanc are aged for 4 months in oak. Unlike many low-priced Chardonnays, the Woodbridge is fermented to dryness.

The reds are macerated for up to 21 days, slightly longer for Zinfandel, then aged for 6 to 12 months in small barrels (there are 48,000 at the winery), followed by 6 months in larger redwood tanks. Old barrels from Opus One and Oakville are kept in use here until they are liquidated at about 10 years old. The reds are centrifuged rather than filtered.

Alderson's pet project is the Portuguese varieties he planted in 1988. The grapes are used for a vintage 'port' called Porto Cinco, which is oak-aged for 2 years, then aged a further year in bottle. The 1993 was promising.

Given the vast quantities of wine produced here, the quality level is remarkably high.

Monteviña
20680 Shenandoah School Rd., Plymouth, CA 95669. Tel: 209 245 6942. Production: 120,000 cases.

One of the largest Sierra Foothills wineries, it was established in 1972 by the Gott family, who planted some 150 acres at a height of 1,600 feet. In

1988 the estate was bought by the Trinchero family of Sutter Home. The Trincheros expanded the vineyard, planting Italian varieties as well as more Zinfandel; Chardonnay, Sauvignon Blanc, and Cabernet Sauvignon are made from purchased grapes from coastal regions. They also converted the vineyards to organic viticulture. They planted forty varieties in all, but not all proved satisfactory, especially Nebbiolo. The winemaker, Jeff Meyers, acknowledges that Italian varieties are very site-sensitive: they can work perfectly well in Italy and fail completely in California, even if climatic conditions seem comparable.

There are three Zinfandels. The lightest is called Brioso; the regular is aged in American oak for 6 months; while the Reserve is a lot selection and aged in a higher proportion of new oak. American oak is also used for the principal Italian varieties such as Barbera and Sangiovese. I have tried these wines on many occasions and always been disappointed. They are light and lack vigour. Meyers says that Monteviña aims to make wines enjoyable young and intended to be drunk with food, but they could still use more weight and flavour.

Nor are the blends much better. Montanaro consists of 80 per cent Barbera and 20 per cent Zinfandel, while Matrimonio blends roughly equal proportions of Nebbiolo, Barbera, Sangiovese, Refosco, and Zinfandel. Their best wines are released under the Terra d'Oro designation and are made from outstanding parcels of fruit. At present these include a Zinfandel and a Barbera. They are good but hardly exceptional.

Nevada City Winery
321 Spring St., Nevada City, CA 95959. Tel: 916 265 9463. Production: 8,000 cases.

This is the most northerly of all the wineries in the Foothills. It was founded in 1980 by Allan Hayley, who produces highly commercial wines, including blush wines and Charbono, but also Pinot Noir, some interesting late harvest bottles, and good Zinfandel.

Oak Ridge Vineyard
PO Box 440, Lodi, CA 95241. Tel: 209 369 4768. Production: 175,000 cases.

This is a cooperative label founded in Lodi in the 1980s and vinifying the production of 3,000 acres of Zinfandel, Chardonnay, and Cabernet Sauvignon. The wines are commercial but inexpensive.

Papagni
31754 Avenue 9, Madera, CA 93637. Tel: 209 485 2760.

The Papagni family planted vines steadily from the 1920s onwards, and some of the old vines still flourish. Now they have about 3,000 acres of vineyards. The winery was built in 1973. The wines are at least typical of this very hot region: Muscats, Barbera, Zinfandel, and some impressively inky Alicante Bouschet for the few devotees of the variety.

Peirano Estate Vineyards

PO Box 1992, Lodi, CA 95241. Tel: 209 367 1305.

Giacomo Peirano came to San Francisco from Genoa in 1879, and after failing to find gold in Calaveras County, came down the foothills to Lodi and began farming. He planted 80 acres of Zinfandel in 1895. Some of those old Zin vines survive and the estate's present owner, Lance Randolph, believes they are the largest such parcel in existence. Randolph farms 300 acres of Cabernet Sauvignon, Merlot, Chardonnay, and Zinfandel, much of which is sold to Ridge, Renwood, Gallo, and other wineries. In 1992, with winemaker Michael Carr, Randolph launched his own winery, using only estate-grown grapes.

Chardonnay was first made in 1995. Although whole-cluster pressed, the must is fermented in stainless steel, half goes through malolactic, and the wine is aged for 7 months in 25 per cent new oak. The delicious, old-vine Zinfandel is aged in much the same way. At present, the production of Cabernet and Merlot is minimal, but Randolph expects to expand. Quality is good. The winery is keen to make progress, and has the motivation to succeed.

Perry Creek Vineyards

7400 Perry Creek Rd., Somerset, CA 95684. Tel: 530 620 5175. Fax: 620 5367. Production: 20,000 cases.

This El Dorado winery was created in 1989 by Alice and Michael Chazen. There are 68 acres planted at a height of 2,500 feet. It is now producing 11 wines, including Chardonnay, Viognier, Riesling, Mourvèdre, Sangiovese, Merlot, Syrah and Zinfandel.

R. H. Phillips

26836 County Road 12A, Esparto, CA 95627. Tel/fax: 916 662 3215. Production: 400,000 cases.

The Giguiere family own this large winery in Yolo County. The property used to be their family sheep ranch, but as it wasn't profitable they planted vines on it, and launched a winery in 1984. Since 1987 a number of Rhône varieties have been planted, and these are the basis of wines that are supplanting the Chenin and French Colombard that used to be the mainstay of this winery. In all there are 1,000 acres under vine. Alliance is a blend of Syrah, Mourvèdre, and Grenache. Rhône varietals appear under the EXP series label. Barrel Cuvée Chardonnay is, despite the name, only 50 per cent barrel-fermented. A more charred style of Chardonnay and Syrah/Cabernet is produced under the Toasted Head designation. In general the wines are very well made and offer excellent value.

Pigeon Creek

Plymouth. Production: 3,000 cases.

This large estate of 350 acres is mostly planted with Zinfandel and Sauvignon Blanc. Almost all the fruit is sold to other wineries.

Quady

13181 Road 24, Madera, CA 93639. Tel: 209 673 8068. Fax: 673 0744. Production: 20,000 cases.

Andrew Quady had an unusual idea, executed it to perfection, and found himself with a unique and winning formula. He had worked for some of the mega-wineries in the Central Valley in the 1970s and made 'port' from Amador County Zinfandel as a hobby. But it wasn't selling, so he took a look at the Orange Muscat grapes all around him and decided to vinify a light dessert wine.

The cheekily named Essensia is made from Muscat that his growers pick at 21 Brix, when, he believes, the flavour is at its peak. Acidity is not a problem: it can always be added later. After some skin contact and some initial fermentation, Quady adds grape spirit to arrest fermentation and preserve the fresh aromas and flavours of the wine.

In 1983 a grower named Don Gallagher offered Quady some Black Muscat. Its rose-like aroma appealed to him, and, vinifying the grapes in much the same way as Essensia, the result was a new wine called Elysium. There was more to come when in 1990 he made a low-alcohol Orange Muscat and sterile-filtered it to prevent re-fermentation. This is the wine he called Electra.

Quady continues to make 'ports'. Some are made from Zinfandel, others from Portuguese varieties planted in Frank's Vineyard in Amador County, which has long been Quady's primary source. The vintage 'port' and LBV usually come from Frank's Vineyard, and there is a nonvintage called Starboard. In general I find Quady's 'ports' too sweet and not sufficiently structured. The Ficklins are preferable, to my taste.

The Muscats are delectable wines. Their lack of complexity is deceptive. These are difficult wines to make well, and Quady has a very sure hand. The fact that all his wines are brilliantly packaged clearly hasn't hindered their commercial success.

Radanovich

Mariposa. Production: 4,000 cases.

This is one of the few wineries in Mariposa County, northeast of Merced. George Radanovich is a congressman as well as a grape farmer and winemaker. In 1986 he founded this 20-acre Foothills estate planted with Zinfandel, Cabernet Sauvignon, and Sauvignon Blanc. The rustic wines are less illustrious than their producer.

Renaissance

12585 Rice's Crossing Rd., Renaissance, CA 95962. Tel: 916 692 2222. Fax: 692 2524. Production: 25,000 cases.

This extraordinary vineyard, with its vast contoured terraces, was planted from 1975 onwards. It is the only vineyard in the North Yuba area. The investment is said to be around $16 million, and the owners are the Fellowship of Friends, an organization inspired by the Russian mystic Ouspensky and based in San Francisco. Not content with establishing a winery, the Fellowship also set up an art museum here. The 365 acres of vineyards are planted at an elevation ranging from 1,700 to 2,300 feet.

It was not until the late 1980s that the first wines were released commercially, although I recall tasting a 1982 late harvest Sauvignon Blanc. They have included some steel-fermented Sauvignon Blanc, some fine Cabernet Sauvignon, and some rather flabby late harvest Rieslings. Other varieties include Merlot, Sangiovese, and Viognier. Gideon Beinstock, the winemaker, uses natural yeasts as a means of controlling any propensity to high alcohol.

Renwood

12225 Steiner Rd., Plymouth, CA 95669. Tel: 209 245 6979. Fax: 245 3732. Production: 65,000 cases.

Renwood was founded by Robert Smerling in 1992, and 3 years later it absorbed the well-established Santino winery, which had been in existence since 1979. Scott Harvey was the original winemaker, who also happened to own the ancient Grandpère Vineyard. Scott Harvey moved to Napa Valley in 1996, where he is the winemaker at Folie à Deux, so presumably the Grandpère grapes, or most of them, will now go to the Napa winery. Since 1995 the winemaker at Renwood has been Gordon Binz, formerly of Ridge.

Renwood produces a wide range of Zinfandels in addition to the powerful Grandpère. The Fiddletown comes from the Eschen Vineyard, and there is an Old Vine bottling from various sites in Amador County. Other wines include a Sémillon, Sangiovese, Syrah, Nebbiolo, and a vigorous spicy Barbera. Satyricon is a blend of Grenache, Mourvèdre, Syrah, Carignane and Cinsault. The most bizarre wine is Amador Ice, an icewine made from Zinfandel grapes. The 'ports' are very impressive, and it is clear that under Scott Harvey this was easily one of the most accomplished and reliable estates in the Foothills. Whether it can retain that eminence remains to be seen.

St Amant

PO Box 4488, Stockton, CA 95204. Tel: 209 477 3066. Production: 3,000 cases.

Genial, relaxed Richard 'Tim' Spencer owns 43 acres between Lodi and the Sierra Foothills, but phylloxera has taken its toll, and much of the vineyard has had to be replanted. Fortunately he is replanting his precious Portuguese varieties – Touriga, Tinta Cão, Souzao, Alvarelhao, and Bastardo – which he first planted in the 1970s, as well as Rhône varieties which are clearly well suited to the region.

His first releases were in 1981, and although production grew to 8,000 cases, phylloxera has brought about a temporary decline. Syrah is purchased from four growers, and is a delicious wine, with a black cherry nose, and great richness and spiciness on the palate. A cask sample of Mourvèdre was impressive too, while the Lodi Cabernet Sauvignon seemed jammy. The most individual wine is Tres Cachos, made from three Portuguese varieties and aged for 3 years in *barriques*.

As for the 'ports', the 10-year-old tawny is a disappointment, having a spiry finish, but the Amador 'vintage port' from Portuguese varieties is fine, and clearly overshadows the LBV bottling.

Shenandoah Vineyards

12300 Steiner Rd., Plymouth, CA 95669. Tel: 209 245 4455. Fax: 245 5156. Production: 15,000 cases.

Leon Sobon releases his best wines under the Sobon label, but his second winery, Shenandoah, is not to be despised. This estate has 35 acres under vine. In the 1980s Sobon was one of the leaders of the white Zinfandel boom, and at one point he was producing 35,000 cases of wine here, but production has been drastically cut back.

The wines are a mixed bunch. Most of the Zinfandels are unexciting, although the top-of-the-range Vintners' Selection, made from very old vines, can be impressive. There is also a blend called Zingiovese, which is self-explanatory. The Sangiovese is usually better than the Barbera. The Cabernet Sauvignon is blended with Cabernet Franc, and there is also an Australian-style Cabernet/Shiraz blend. The Muscats can be very good, especially the Black Muscat, made in a lush peppery style. The 'ports' are made primarily from Zinfandel, with all kinds of other grapes thrown in for good measure.

The Shenandoah range is good value, but there is no doubt that the best wines appear under the Sobon label.

Sierra Vista

4560 Cabernet Way, Placerville, CA 95667. Tel: 916 622 7221. Fax: 622 2413. Production: 10,000 cases.

John MacCready was an electrical engineer when he and his wife, a mathematician, bought this woodland site in 1972, intending to farm and then sell grapes. The soil is sandy rocky loam of volcanic origin, and MacCready says there are thousands of years' deposits of oak leaves in the soil. The estate's name is not fanciful: from this spot 2,500 feet up, the views on to the Crystal Range of the Sierra Nevada are splendid. The first vintage produced, in 1977, was made from purchased grapes. There are now some 40 acres in production. The Cabernet Sauvignon was grafted over to Viognier, and the rest of the vineyard is basically Zinfandel, Sauvignon Blanc, and Rhône varieties. In the long term MacCready hopes to focus on Rhône varieties alone. At present the vines are trained on quadrilateral cordon trellising, but he is planning to try out vertical trellising in due course.

The standard varieties are competently made. There is an unoaked Sauvignon Blanc, an attractive barrel-fermented Chardonnay, and a powerful and chunky Reserve Cabernet Sauvignon. The regular Zinfandel seems a bit underpowered and hollow, and is outgunned by the Reserve, aged entirely in new American oak. But it is with the Rhône wines that Sierra Vista triumphs. The regular Syrah is good, but the Red Rock Ridge bottling is outstanding. There's an attractive, if not complex, Châteauneuf-style blend of Syrah, Grenache, and Mourvèdre, called Fleur de Montagne, and a gorgeous Viognier, aged in old barrels. Prices, for the Foothills, are quite high, but so is quality.

Single Leaf Vineyards
7480 Fairplay Rd., Somerset, CA 95684. Tel: 916 620 3545.

A new El Dorado winery specializing in Zinfandel and 'port' styles.

Smith Vineyard and Winery
13719 Dog Bar Rd., Grass Valley, CA 95949. Tel: 916 273 7032. Production: 2,000 cases.

Sharon and Wayne Smith cultivate a 12-acre organic vineyard in Nevada County, from which they began making wines in 1988. The range includes Chardonnay, Chenin Blanc, and Cabernet Sauvignon.

Sobon Estate
14430 Shenandoah Rd., Plymouth, CA 95669. Tel: 209 245 6554. Production: 20,000 cases.

In 1856 a pioneer winemaker, Adam Uhlinger, created a winery by gouging a space into the hillside. It later became the D'Agostini winery. Even today, although it is no longer in use as a winery, the old casks and uprights remain in place. After Leon Sobon bought the place in 1989, he renamed the property after himself and converted the old winery into a tasting room and museum. The Sobons had been growing grapes in the Foothills since the late 1970s, and their present vineyards, all dry-farmed and organically cultivated, consist of 84 acres near the winery and a further 12 in Fiddletown. Some of the grapes are used for the Sobons' second winery, Shenandoah. Many vines were replanted after phylloxera, and were replaced by Zinfandel, Sangiovese, and other varieties.

The best-known wine is the Zinfandel, made, like the other reds, by punching down the cap in small vats. There are a number of different bottlings. Lubenko Vineyard is a dry-farmed site, yielding 2 tons per acre, with vines dating from 1910. There is a bottling from Fiddletown grapes. Rocky Top and Cougar Hill both come from other old-vine vineyards. The other reds include a Sangiovese from a Brunello clone and a Syrah aged in older *barriques*.

Sobon get a good crop from their Viognier, but I find the wine slightly heavy, and prefer the Roussanne, which is blended with about 25 per cent Viognier. The Sémillon is less interesting, and the Muscat Canelli is nondescript. A curiosity here is Mission del Sol, a *passito* style wine made from dried Mission grapes. The wine, which has 16.4 degrees of alcohol, is unfortified and tastes quite a bit like sherry.

Sonora Winery & Port Works
17500 Route 5 Rd., Sonora, CA 95370. Tel: 209 532 PORT. Fax: 533 4959. Production: 2,500 cases.

Richard Matranga set out in 1986 to focus on the production of Zinfandel and 'ports' made from Portuguese varieties grown in Amador County. I have not tasted the wines. Sonora itself is located just south of Calaveras County.

Spenker
Lodi. Production: 1,200 cases.

Charles Spenker recently started vinifying Zinfandel from his 60 acres of relatively youthful vineyards. In 1994, for some strange reason, the estate chose to make two wines, one early-harvested, and the other picked three weeks later. Unripe Zinfandel is not a pleasant experience, and I found the early-harvested wine thin and acidic. The other wine spent 12 months in mostly new American oak, and it showed. Fortunately in subsequent vintages Charles Spenker has moderated the new oak. The wines are unfined and unfiltered. They have met with great acclaim, but I find them too astringent.

Stevenot Winery
2690 San Domingo Rd., Murphys, CA 95247. Tel: 209 728 3436. Fax: 728 3710. Production: 40,000 cases.

One of the oldest wineries in Calaveras County, this began life as a cattle ranch, bought by Barden Stevenot in 1969. He planted 27 acres a few years later. When the winery began production in 1978, it was the first to do so in the county since Prohibition. Chuck Hovey, the winemaker, focuses on standard varietal wines as well as Zinfandel, Sangiovese, Syrah, and Barbera aged in new American oak. Most of the production is of white Zinfandel.

Stoneridge

13862 Ridge Rd., Sutter Creek, CA 95685. Tel: 209 223 1761. Production: 1,500 cases.

The Porteous family founded this Amador winery in 1975, and it produces Zinfandel and Ruby Cabernet from 6 acres of vines.

Story Winery

10525 Bell Rd., Plymouth, CA 95669. Tel: 209 245 6208. Fax: 245 6619. Production: 7,500 cases.

The late Eugene Story founded this winery in 1973, but the dry-farmed vineyards here are much older, dating from the beginning of the century. The 40 acres are planted at 1,500 feet, and include some 80-year-old Mission vines. I find the Story wines rather odd. There's an off-dry Gewürztraminer, and both Zinfandel and Mission are made in a porty style. Mission does not make an attractive dry wine, but the Estate bottling, with a touch of sweetness, has more than curiosity value, and the nonvintage Mission Gold, aged 2 years in oak, is a sweet wine of considerable character.

Domaine de la Terre Rouge

10801 Dickson, Rd., Plymouth, CA 95669. Tel: 209 245 4277. Production: 3,000 cases.

The fancy French name sounds odd up here in a region that is very much free of Napa-like pretensions. Bill Easton has 8 acres planted with Rhône varieties, and started producing wines in the late 1980s. The range consists of Zinfandel, Barbera, Syrah, and a Rhône blend.

TKC Vineyards

11001 Valley Dr., Plymouth, CA 95669. Tel: 209 245 6428. Fax: 245 4006. Production: 1,500 cases.

Harold Nuffer founded this winery in 1981. The grapes, Cabernet Sauvignon and Zinfandel, are purchased from various sources in the Foothills. The wines are rather clumsy.

Las Viñas Winery
5573 West Woodbridge Rd., Lodi, CA 95242. Tel: 209 334 0445. Production: 15,000 cases.

John Cotta grows 800 acres of grapes in the Lodi area, and produces simple, inexpensive Cabernet Sauvignon and Zinfandel.

Vino Noceto
11011 Shenandoah Rd., Plymouth, CA 95669. Tel: 209 245 6556. Fax: 245 3446. Production: 2,000 cases.

In 1984 Suzy and Jim Gullett bought 21 acres in Shenandoah Valley. A year later a visit to Tuscany stimulated their interest in Sangiovese, and they started to hunt down clones available in America. In 1987 they planted a few, supplemented in 1988 with Sangiovese Grosso and in 1990 with Sangioveto. The wines are vertically trained and can be harvested late, thanks to the long growing season here at an elevation of 1,500 feet. Daytime heat – it can reach 100 degrees Fahrenheit – can cause the vines to shut down, but they can usually pick at 24 Brix. Alcohol can be well over 14 degrees, but the structure of the wine usually supports it.

Their first vintage was 1990. The wine is made with a substantial proportion of whole-berry fermentation, and is aged for 11 months in 20 per cent new oak puncheons as well as 60-gallon barrels. Any finished wines that are unsatisfactory are eliminated from the final blend and sold off. Suzy Gullett says the style they are aiming for is fruity, drinkable, and affordable. Vino Noceto succeeds on all counts. The 1995 vintage was slightly disappointing, but in general this estate offers a characterful, well-made wine at a fair price. There are plans to introduce a Reserve bottling as well as a Muscat Frizzante from purchased grapes.

Wooden Valley Winery
4756 Suisun Valley Rd., Suisun, CA 94585. Tel: 707 864 0730. Production: 20,000 cases.

Farming 300 acres of vineyards in Suisun Valley, this long-established winery produces a very wide range of simple wines, mostly for the local market.

33
Négociant Wineries

The term '*négociant* wineries' is ungainly, but it is hard to think of a better one to include the many wineries that buy grapes from all over the state and have no single regional base. Some of them are enormous brands, others small boutique wineries with no vineyards of their own. However, there are a few *négociant* wineries that are strongly associated with a particular region, even though hardly any of their wines are sourced there, so they have been listed under the appropriate region. Sutter Home, with its tasting room in Napa Valley, is one example.

Almadén Vineyards
12677 Road 24, Madera, CA 93639. Tel: 408 972 9014.

The French immigrant Charles Lefranc founded the estate in 1852, when he planted cuttings he had brought from Burgundy in a vineyard at Los Gatos in Santa Clara County. The name is Moorish, and means 'silver mine'. In 1941 the property was bought by Louis Benoist, and in the 1950s, with the growing suburbanization of Santa Clara, Almadén began buying large tracts of land in Monterey and San Benito counties. In 1967 the company changed hands again, when it was bought by National Distillers. By the 1980s Almadén was producing a range of sixty wines from 7,000 acres of vineyards. Although most of the production was of very commercial wines, often sold in gallon jugs, a few higher-quality wines were released under the Charles Lefranc label, including some late harvest bottlings, but the winery never shook off its image as a jug-wine specialist. By this time Almadén was producing about 12 million cases. In 1987 it was bought by Heublein, and this new owner closed down most of its production facilities, transferring operations to Madera in the Central Valley. Almadén is once again focusing on the lower end of the market. It is now part of the Canandaigua group.

Bayliss & Fortune
A label created by the Australian Mildara Blass group. Most of the grapes
are purchased from Monterey vineyards, although North Coast sources are
also used. The first release will be a 1997 Cabernet Sauvignon.

August Briggs
1191 Emerald Dr., Calistoga, CA 94515. Tel: 942 4912. Production: 1,500
cases.

This small winery was created in 1995 by August 'Joe' Briggs, who uses
the Honig facilities. Zinfandel is purchased from Napa Valley, Chardonnay
from Russian River Valley and Carneros. All wines are made in small lots.

Bronco Wine Company
6342 Bystrum Rd., Ceres, CA 95307. Tel: 209 535 3131. Fax: 538 4634.

This used to be the well-known Franzia winery, until the family of that
name sold it in 1971. It became part of the Coca-Cola group, who renamed
its wine division The Wine Group, which now uses the Franzia name. In
the meantime some cousins of the Franzias set up this new winery, and
by 1992 it was the sixth largest wine producer in the United States. Most
of the wines are produced in bulk, but brands such as JFJ Winery, Forest
Glen, Rutherford Vintners, and Hacienda also belong to Bronco. Production figures are not disclosed.

Caché Cellars
Pedrick Rd., Davis, CA 95616. Tel: 916 756 6068. Production: 5,000
cases.

Founded in 1978 by Charles Lowe, since 1989 this winery has focused
on vinifying organic grapes, mostly purchased in Napa. Lowe releases
standard varietals and a red Meritage.

Canandaigua Brands
300 Willowbrook Office Park, Fairport, NY 14450. Tel: 716 393 4130.
Fax: 394 6017.

Now the second-largest drinks company in the United States, after Gallo,
Canandaigua controls 130 brands and runs ten wineries. Its best-known
wine brands include Inglenook, Almadén, Manischewitz, Paul Masson,
and Dunnewood.

Christian Brothers
This once-famous winery is no longer based in Napa Valley, although
there was a time when it owned 1,600 acres there. This teaching order
originally produced wine in Martinez in the 1880s, moving to Napa Valley
in 1930 and building a monastery and winery called Mont La Salle.

Brother Timothy (Anthony Diener) was the celebrated winemaker, his first vintage being 1935; he retired in the 1980s. He was assisted by another monk, Justin Meyer, who later left the order and founded Silver Oak Cellars.

The Christian Brothers produced a good deal of fortified wine in the Central Valley, including their famous sweet Muscat, Chateau La Salle. Their table wines were nonvintage blends. In the 1980s the Mont La Salle winery was closed and acquired by Donald Hess. In 1989 Heublein bought the brand for $125 million, and winemaking activities were transferred to Madera. Now their wines are scarcely distinguishable from other mass-production ranges such as Almadén.

Clos du Muriel Vineyards and Winery

33419 Rancho California Rd., Temecula, CA 92592. Tel: 909 676 5400. Fax: 676 9606.

This winery produces Sauvignon Blanc, French Colombard, Merlot, and Cabernet Sauvignon, mostly from Napa and Sonoma fruit.

Corbett Canyon

2195 Corbett Canyon Rd., Arroyo Grande, CA 93420. Tel: 805 544 5800. Fax: 544 7205. Production: 500,000 cases.

After it was founded in 1978 by Jim Lawrence, this winery passed through many hands and is now owned by the Wine Group. Fruit is bought in from Santa Barbara, Napa, and Sonoma, as well as from the winery's own vineyards, which include the 350-acre Los Alamos Vineyard in Santa Maria. The two principal ranges are Coastal Classics and a small number of varietal Reserves. The wines, which are made by John Clark, are undemanding and inexpensive.

Delicato Vineyards

12001 South Highway 99, Manteca, CA 95336. Tel: 209 824 3600. Fax: 239 8031. Production: 500,000 cases.

The Delicato family first planted vineyards in 1924, and its holdings have grown enormously to include the colossal 7,500-acre San Bernabe Ranch in Monterey, and 1,600 acres in Lodi, as well as its 120 acres in Manteca. This mostly bulk-wine producer has done well by supplying large quantities of white Zinfandel to Sutter Home and other wineries.

Donatoni

10604 South La Cienega Blvd., Inglewood, CA 90304. Tel: 310 645 5445. Production: 1,000 cases.

Hank Donatoni used leased space in a Los Angeles winery, where he produced Monterey Chardonnay and Cabernet Sauvignon from Paso Robles.

Dunnewood Vineyards
2399 North State St., Ukiah, CA 95482, Tel: 707 462 2985. Production: 150,000 cases.

Originally a cooperative founded in 1941, the Mendocino winery was bought in 1991 by the Canandaigua group. Quality is average, prices modest.

Edmunds St John Winery
4059 Emery St., Emeryville, CA 94608. Tel: 510 654 1230. Production: 5,000 cases.

Steve Edmunds and Cornelia St John are based in Alameda, but buy Zinfandel and Rhône varieties from various parts of California, mostly from old-vine vineyards. They started the operation in 1985. In addition to varietal wines, such as Mourvèdre from Oakley and Grenache from Mendocino, they produce special blends such as Chapparal and Cotes Sauvage (a blend of Syrah, Grenache, and Mourvèdre). They also own 20 acres in El Dorado County, which are planted with Syrah and Grenache. Quality is high, the range eclectic.

Ehlers Grove
3222 Ehlers Lane, St Helena, CA 94574. Tel: 963 3200.

After running the Stratford and Canterbury wineries, Tony Cartlidge and his partners bought the old stone Ehlers Lane winery and set up a new business, concentrating on the major varietals.

Joseph Filippi Vintage Company
12467 Base Line Rd., Rancho Cucamonga, CA 91739. Tel: 909 899 5755. Fax: 428 6264. Production: 100,000 cases.

The Filippi family began planting grapes here in 1922, and by the late 1940s were farming 400 acres. Today the company owns or leases some 320 acres, from which the winemaker Nick Karavidas makes a range of mostly generic and fortified wines. The winery uses a variety of labels, including Reserve, Premium, Chateau Filippi, Filippi Brothers, Guasti, and Thomas Vineyards. Much fruit is purchased from Monterey and Napa. A Filippi speciality is Angelica Elena, a sweet wine made from Palomino and Pedro Ximénez by the solera system.

Ernest and Julio Gallo
600 Yosemite Blvd., Modesto, CA 95354. Tel: 209 579 3054. Production: 80 million cases.

This famous old company is of unimaginable size. Visitors granted admission to its vast plant in Modesto are predictably amazed as they are whizzed through the world's largest wine facility, but this is just one of the Gallo wineries in California. The main winery, built in the 1950s and covering 45 acres, incorporates a bottle-making facility that never closes down and enough storage space for 12 million cases of wine. Astonishingly, Gallo wine isn't even made here in Modesto, but in Livingston, Fresno, Dry Creek, and elsewhere.

The company was established in 1933 after Repeal, but began to sell wines under its own name only in the 1940s. Julio made the wine, and Ernest sold it. Julio was killed in a car crash in 1993, but Ernest, who was born in 1909, is still at the helm. He is an obsessive marketing man. Those rare few honoured with an invitation to his lunch table find the occasion more of an interrogation than a social gathering, as he picks his guests' brains about his own wines and those of his competitors. The wine world is full of anecdotes about the ruthless, even brutal methods of Gallo salesmen as they pressure retailers to stock and display their wines. The Gallos know how to operate in the political world, and made large donations to the campaigns of Democrats such as Senator Alan Cranston and Republicans such as Governor Pete Wilson, and were rewarded for their largesse with tax concessions. Life in the Gallo compound at Modesto must be fraught at times. In 1989, for instance, the youngest Gallo brother, Joe, claimed that Ernest and Julio had denied him his proper share of the inheritance from their parents. After a court battle, Joe lost. Aware that the image of the company is less than avuncular, Gallo in 1998 embarked on an expensive advertising campaign featuring the younger generations of the family, such as Gina Gallo, to project a kindlier, more youthful image.

The company's scale of operations gave it tremendous clout, and throughout the 1950s Gallo bought the entire production of the major cooperative in Napa Valley. Other cooperatives were also in effect agents of the Gallo empire. One wonders what happened to all this wine, which was probably of decent if not outstanding quality. Gallo was best known for its jug wines, and only introduced varietal wines to its range as recently as 1974. The first vintage-dated wine was a 1978 Cabernet Sauvignon. Gallo's genius was to realize that many Americans had no real desire to drink wine, and that their taste lay in the direction of sweet fizzy drinks. So the chemists at the Gallo laboratories in Modesto produced the vinous equivalent, such as Thunderbird, Ripple, and Boone's Farm apple wine. Thunderbird was targeted at the urban poor, with a famous radio jingle that ran: 'What's the word?/Thunderbird./How's it sold?/Good and cold./What's the jive?/Bird's alive./What's the price?/Thirty twice!' As for the jug wines, Hearty Burgundy was in fact Barbera, much of it grown in Mendocino, and the Chablis was French Colombard.

The Gallo people may be cynical but they are not stupid. Although they were latecomers to the idea of varietal and vintage-dated wines, they embraced the concept wholeheartedly, encouraging contract growers and other suppliers to focus on the varietals that were most in demand. In the 1980s the company also realized that it had been neglecting the ever-wealthier group of wine enthusiasts who were handing over millions of dollars to large but quality-conscious producers such as Beringer and Mondavi. It began to develop and purchase vineyard land in Sonoma with a view to produce wines that could compete with other premium brands.

In the 1980s and 1990s Gallo have diversified in a cunning fashion. While I was writing this, the door bell rang and I took in a delivery of some sample bottles of Garnet Point which turns out to be a range of wines developed specifically for export markets. The press release informs me they are 'the first dual varietal labelled wines from a major Californian branded wine producer.' Makes your mouth water. Other invented Gallo brands include the fighting varietal Turning Leaf brand; Anapamu (Monterey Chardonnay and Cabernet Sauvignon, intended to reach a production level of 100,000 cases); Zabaco (Sonoma wines, mostly from Dry Creek and Russian River valleys, and aged in American oak); Marcelina (Napa Chardonnay and Cabernet Sauvignon); Indigo Hills (wines from Mendocino and the North Coast); and of course there is the vast and admittedly impressive range of wines emerging under the Gallo Sonoma (q.v.) label. Gallo have also been buying land in Paso Robles, Lodi, and the Central Valley. All of these brands are outgunned by the White Label range of varietals, which is the Gallo wine most frequently encountered in supermarkets. Gallo also own brands such as Carlo Rossi, William Wycliff, and Livingston Cellars, as well as a colossal brandy distillery. It is hardly surprising that Gallo mops up one-third of the entire wine market in the United States.

Glen Ellen

21468 Eighth St. East, Sonoma, CA 95476. Tel: 707 939 6200. Fax: 938 0892. Production: 3.5 million cases.

Bruno Benziger of Benziger Vineyards in Sonoma founded the brand in 1981 and the production of these well-made, inexpensive, commercial wines, blended from purchased bulk wines, grew to millions of cases within the decade; the winemaking was contracted out to thirteen different wineries. In 1993 the brand was sold to Heublein.

Golden State Vintners

500 Drake's Landing Rd., Greenbrae, CA 949404. Tel: 415 461 4400. Fax: 461 4497.

This company owns 9,600 acres of vineyards in San Joaquin Valley and operates wineries in Fresno and Monterey. Its labels include Edgewood, Summerfield, and Monthaven. It is also a major producer of bulk wines for such wineries as Gallo, Sutter Home, and Sebastiani.

Golden State Vintners International
70 West Madison St., Chicago, IL 60602. Tel: 312 541 0264. Fax: 541 2912.

Another large company producing bulk wines and bottled wines under labels such as Chateau Dalina and Vinterra.

Guimarra Vineyards
11220 Edison Highway, Edison, CA 93220. Tel: 805 395 7079.

Founded in 1946, Guimarra own 10,000 acres of vineyards around Bakersfield but made bulk wines only until 1974. It is still a major producer of bag-in-box wines. Its best bottled wines carry the label Proprietor's Reserve.

Hallcrest
379 Felton Empire Rd., Felton, CA 95018. Tel: 408 335 4441. Fax: 335 4450. Production: 17,000 cases.

Historically, Hallcrest was one of the best-known estates in Santa Cruz. It was originally established in the 1940s by Chaffee Hall and became known for its excellent Cabernet Sauvignon. The winery was closed down in 1969 and the grapes were sold to Wente and Concannon, who maintained the vineyards, but yields were too low to make the vineyard commercially viable. Hall died in 1963. In 1976 Hallcrest reopened under the name of Felton Empire and the ownership of winemaker Leo McCloskey and Jim Beauregard. They produced Chardonnay and some excellent late harvest wines, mostly Riesling from the 50-year-old estate vineyards and from Tepusquet Vineyards in Santa Barbara, until the winery was sold in 1986. It was revived yet again in 1988, when it was bought by John Schumacher, who was allowed to use the Hallcrest label. It now produces Riesling, over-oaked Chardonnay, Sauvignon Blanc from Napa, and Gewürztraminer from Mendocino. Riesling, now as before, is probably the best wine.

A second range of wines is released under the Organic Wine Works label. They tend to be better than most organically made wines from California.

Paul Hobbs Cellars
Tel: 707 431 8303. Production: 5,000 cases.

Producing his wines at the Kunde winery in Sonoma since 1991, Hobbs, who has worked as a winemaker at Opus One and Simi, buys his Burgundian varieties from Carneros, his Cabernet from Howell Mountain, and Chardonnay from Sonoma Mountain. He also makes one of the few Cabernets sourced from Carneros. The only wine I have encountered is the very good 1994 Hyde Vineyard Pinot Noir.

Inglenook

This once great property is now part of the Canandaigua Brands group. During the last years of the Heublein ownership Dennis Fife attempted to improve the quality of the label the company had rushed to degrade, and I did taste some decent wines during the 1980s, some from the replanted Rutherford vineyards. But sales never picked up, and in 1993 Heublein sold the brand to Canandaigua. The historic vineyards and winery were sold to Francis Ford Coppola a year later and production facilities moved to Mendocino.

Jade Mountain

PO Box 596, Angwin, CA 94508. Tel: 965 3084. Production: 4,000 cases.

Douglas Danielak founded this label in 1984 and has long specialized in Rhône varietals. Much of the fruit comes from the Paras Vineyard planted with numerous varieties at 1,200 feet on Mount Veeder, but he also buys in grapes from the Sacramento Delta and other sources. Some of the wines are clearly blended and are released under the California appellation. As well as dense cherryish Mourvèdre, Jade Mountain produces Les Jumeaux, a tannic and leathery blend of Cabernet Sauvignon and 75 per cent Mourvedre, and tannic Sonoma Syrah. La Provençale blends Syrah and Mourvèdre. Cote de Soleil is a blend for earlier drinking. In 1996 Jade Mountain launched a white comprising 70 per cent Marsanne and the rest Viognier.

JC Cellars

Tel: 510 749 9463.

Jeff Cohn works for the Rosenblum winery in Alameda, but also has his own small winery specializing in single-vineyard Zinfandel, Syrah, and Petite Sirah.

Kalin Cellars

61 Galli Dr., Novato, CA 94949. Tel: 415 883 3543. Fax: 925 283 2909. Production: 7,000 cases.

This quirky Marin County winery was founded in 1977 Terry Leighton, a scientist from Berkeley. He buys in fruit from various parts of the state and vinifies the wines as slowly as possible. The Chardonnays are rich and opulent and usually made from Sonoma and Livermore fruit, whereas most of the Pinot Noir is sourced in Mendocino and Sonoma. The red wines are unfined and unfiltered, and a considerable proportion of new oak is used for both red and white. Kalin's strength lies in its Chardonnays, which are very concentrated and long-lived.

Kendall-Jackson

421 Aviation Blvd., Santa Rosa, CA 95403. Tel: 707 544 4000. Fax: 544 4013. Production: 3 million cases.

Jess Jackson was born in 1930 and trained as a lawyer. In 1974 he bought some orchards in Lake County and planted vines. In the early 1980s the grape business was not doing well, so he decided to make his own wines. The first vintage was 1982 and was well received. As the winery grew, Jackson found himself buying fruit from various parts of the state and began using a California appellation. During the 1980s the winery was in Lake County and the winemaker was Jed Steele. After Steele left in 1990, there was a huge row between Jess Jackson and his former winemaker, whom he accused of appropriating trade secrets, which turned out to be no secret at all to anyone who had tasted Kendall-Jackson Vintner's Reserve Chardonnay – namely, that the wine contained residual sugar. Jackson lost, and Steele went off to start his own winery and to act as a consultant for a sheaf of other wineries. His place at Kendall-Jackson was taken by John Hawley, formerly of Clos du Bois, and in 1997 Randy Ullom, formerly of De Loach, became head of winemaking operations. In 1993 the winery moved to much larger premises in Sonoma: the Vinwood winery. Other wineries exist at Cambria in Santa Barbara, Pepi in Napa, as well as Monterey. Ullom is assisted by a team of other winemakers, though there is a worryingly high turnover.

There is no Kendall-Jackson formula but there is a Kendall-Jackson concept. Jackson told me that he seeks a fruit-driven style made only from ripe fruit grown in coastal regions that gives good acidity as well as ripeness. Almost all the Chardonnay and Sauvignon Blanc will go through malolactic fermentation. Reds are always destemmed but not necessarily crushed: it depends on the variety and the quality of the fruit. A brief cold soak for colour extraction is not unusual, and neither are extended macerations. The Kendall-Jackson style requires soft tannins, so that the wines are drinkable on release.

Kendall-Jackson expanded and diversified greatly in the 1990s, but the bulk of its production consists of varietal blends made in the style Jackson outlined. Each of the Kendall-Jackson estates or vineyards is considered as a 'flavor domaine', each flavour being a component in a blend. If the Santa Barbara contribution is a fruit-salady component, then viticulture and winemaking will be adapted to provide that character, which will then be blended with the products of other 'flavor domaines'.

Ullom has been encouraging his winemakers to get to know their vine-yards. It's particularly important to promote even maturation, since with such large sites they have to harvest all at once. They can manipulate and thus even out ripening in different parcels by use of different clones, rootstocks and viticultural practices. Almost all the grapes are picked by hand, except in Monterey, and they have some facilities for crushing the grapes in the field. Ullom insists he has the capacity to vinify very small lots: 'We can separate one ton of grapes for a whole year if we want to.' This does happen in the case of wines destined for the Grand Reserve bottlings, but of course this constitutes a minute proportion of production.

The domaines consist of 11,000 acres, which will all be bearing fruit by the year 2000. If they achieve this goal, then Kendall-Jackson will be 70 per cent self-sufficient in terms of grape supply. There are 1,000 acres in Santa Barbara, as well as the Cambria winery, and 2,500 acres, mostly Chardonnay, in Monterey. The sparkling wine facility responsible for Kristone is also based in Santa Barbara. More recently the winery has acquired 600 acres in the viticulturally marginal Sonoma Coast. In Mendocino they have bought the Edmeades winery. In Sonoma they now own Stonestreet, La Crema, Hartford Court, and the impressive former Gauer Ranch. In Napa Kendall-Jackson own Pepi, Cardinale, and Lokoya. Jackson also owns 1,100 acres in Argentina, and Vina Calina in Chile. In 1992 he bought a French company involved in buying timber for barrel-making, and part-owns a mill in the Vosges where staves can be air-dried to the winery's specifications. The barrels are assembled and toasted in Missouri. Kendall-Jackson require 25,000 new barrels each year. Half are French oak, half American.

The basic range is Vintner's Reserve, which aims for pure varietal expression. The Chardonnay is the best seller, and in 1996 1.2 million cases were produced of this one variety alone. Half the wine is barrel-fermented, but almost all of it spends some time in barrels. It is not a wine I like, as I prefer my Chardonnay sugar-free. The Sauvignon is correct but dilute. The Pinot Noir is *barrique*-aged and pleasant but a touch feeble, at least in 1995. The Cabernet Sauvignon, at least in 1994, was composed principally of Napa and Sonoma fruit, and it was aged in 25 per cent new oak, and half the barrels were American oak. The Merlot is aged for rather longer, about 15 months, in French and American oak. The Vintner's Reserve Zinfandel blends fruit from Amador County, Mendocino, and Sonoma, and is aged, unusually, in *barriques*.

The top range is the Grand Reserve. The whites receive more barrel-fermentation, longer ageing in French oak, and have greater intensity of flavour. The reds also see more new oak, and some of the wines are bottled without filtration. The winemakers look out for lots of wine from sites they expect to be outstanding. Production varies from 1,000 to 6,000 cases. As well as the standard varietals, the range includes a Viognier. As with Vintner's Reserve, the wines are usually a blend from various coastal regions.

There are also single vineyard wines such as Camelot Chardonnay from Santa Barbara and Paradise Vineyard Chardonnay from Arroyo Seco; Buckeye Cabernet Sauvignon from Alexander Valley; and Durell Vineyard Syrah. In 1999 Kendall-Jackson launch yet another range, JSJ Signature Select, produced solely from the company's top vineyard sites and bearing a heavy price-tag.

Overall, the wines that bear the Kendall-Jackson label (as opposed to other K-J wineries such as Edmeades and Stonestreet) are disappointing. The wines are cleanly made and by no means poor, but they are also far from cheap. Thus the Vintner's Reserve Cabernet Sauvignon retails for between $16 and $18, for which one has the right to expect something that is more than merely acceptable.

Kristone

See Kendall-Jackson (p. 626). Production: 4,500 cases.

Kendall-Jackson's Cambria winery also produces the wines for another of the group labels, Kristone. Winemaker Harold Osborne, who used to by Schramsberg's winemaker, produces nothing but high-priced sparkling wines: Blanc de Blancs, Blancs de Noirs, and Rosé. The grapes come from Santa Maria and Anderson valleys, are picked relatively ripe, and partially fermented in barrels with natural yeasts. The first wines were released in 1996 at a preposterous $60. The only wine I have tried, the 1991 Blanc de Blancs, struck me as simple, soft, sweetish, and with only modest length. Hence overpriced. The Blanc de Noirs is considered superior to the Blancs de Blancs.

Leeward

2784 Johnson Dr., Ventura, CA 93001. Tel: 805 656 5054. Fax: 656 5092. Production: 15,000 cases.

Chuck Brigham and Chuck Gardner founded this winery in 1979 and they and their winemaker Brooks Painter buy in fruit from all over California; supplementing it with 4 acres of their own Chardonnay grown in Ventura County. Chardonnay accounts for the major part of the production and is of good quality. Cabernet Sauvignon and Pinot Noir are also offered.

Littorai

1985 Vineyard Ave., St Helena, CA 95474. Tel: 707 963 4762. Fax: 963 7332. Production: 1,500 cases.

Ted Lemon has probably had more experience of Burgundian winemaking than anyone else working at present at a California winery. After graduating from Dijon University in 1981, he worked for Roumier, Dujac, and other leading estates, and was the chief winemaker at Domaine Roulot in Meursault until 1984. Back in California he was the founding winemaker at Chateau Woltner until 1992, when he became a consultant to Clos Pegase, Franciscan, and other wineries. At the same time he and his wife Heidi began producing small lots of wines – between 250 and 400 cases – from outstanding vineyards of Chardonnay and Pinot Noir. The wines are made on Howell Mountain.

The grapes come from a number of sources, but Lemon works closely with the growers, who share his passion for quality. He believes strongly in careful clonal selection and in low yields. As a winemaker, he likes minimal intervention and gentle handling, avoiding pumps and filters whenever possible. Unlike many other Californian winemakers, he is opposed to overripe grapes and very high alcohol in the wines. What he is looking for is finesse and balance, which is exactly what he achieves.

All the Chardonnay is whole-cluster pressed, and barrel-fermented with indigenous yeasts, although he will inoculate if the fermentation looks as if it is going to be problematic. The wines are aged in French oak, one-third new, and the lees are stirred, but only from time to time. Lemon is perfectly happy with a prolonged malolactic fermentation. Where possible, he dispenses with fining and filtration.

As for Pinot Noir, it is given a short cold soak, then fermented in open-top tanks with roughly one-third whole clusters. Natural yeasts are used. The cap is routinely punched down, and malolactic fermentation takes place in oak barrels, of which between 30 and 50 per cent are new.

Lemon has chosen some exceptionally cool sites from which to buy grapes: Hirsch Vineyard in Sonoma Coast, Mays Canyon in Russian River, One Acre and Savoy in Anderson Valley. It shows in the wines: lean, discreet, stylish, understated, intense. Other winemakers in California – Jim Clendenen, Steve Kistler – use Burgundian techniques, yet their wines still show an often welcome Californian flamboyance. Littorai wines could, I think, easily be mistaken for Burgundies.

Paul Masson
Production: 5 million cases.

Paul Masson was the man who planted the vines that became the basis for the Almadén vineyards in 1852. He became the partner of Almadén's founder, Charles Lefranc, and then married his daughter. In 1892 he set up his own wine business, specializing in sparkling wines. In 1936 he sold the business to Martin Ray and died four years later. In 1942 Ray sold the Masson estate and winery to Seagram, which poured its resources into a major expansion of the business, planting thousands of acres in Monterey and achieving sales of 8 million cases during the 1960s. The Masson carafe, a clever marketing idea, became a standard fixture on dining tables all over the world. In 1987 Vintners International bought the company, which henceforth operated out of the Central Valley and Monterey. In 1993 it was sold again, this time to Canandaigua. The new owners relaunched the carafe. Unfortunately the wine inside it has never been much good.

Montpellier Vineyards
A joint venture between the Franzia and Mondavi families. Some 950 acres of vineyards are being developed to focus on low-priced varietal wines. The wines are made at the Bronco facilities.

Mountain View
1766 D Union St., San Francisco, CA 94123. Tel: 415 441 2990. Fax: 441 0703. Production: 100,000 cases.

Founded by Kevin Shannon in 1980, this brand is now owned by Vininformation of San Francisco. Many of the wines came from Mendocino and Monterey fruit. The wines have been inexpensive and very good value if lacking in personality.

Neyers
St Helena, CA 94574. Tel: 707 963 8840. Production: 12,000 cases.

Bruce Neyers, who founded this label in 1980, was not a winemaker but a salesman for Phelps and other wineries. In 1994 he relaunched the label. Although he owns 15 acres of Merlot in Conn Valley, most of the grapes are bought in from various sites in Napa and Sonoma. In 1997 he took on Ehren Jordan, the winemaker at Turley, as his own winemaker and partner. The 1995 Sonoma Chardonnay was somewhat blowsy and outshone by the complex 1997 Carneros Chardonnay; the 1995 Estate Merlot had charred flavours, but the Hudson Vineyard Syrah is powerful and plummy, and the best wine I tasted is the 1995 Napa Cabernet with its rich black-cherry fruit.

Ojai
10540 Encino, Oak View, CA 93022. Tel: 805 649 1674. Production: 4,000 cases.

Adam Tolmach, Jim Clendenen's former associate at Au Bon Climat, founded this label in 1984. The vineyard holdings in Ventura County are a mere 6 acres, so grapes are bought from other vineyards in Paso Robles and Santa Ynez Valley. Tolmach has a sure hand with Sauvignon Blanc and Sémillon, which have appeared both as varietal wines and as blends. There is also a delicate, citric Chardonnay from Talley, excellent Syrah, and Mourvèdre and Viognier.

Page Mill

13686 Page Mill Rd., Los Altos Hills, CA 94022. Tel: 650 948 0958. Production: 3,000 cases.

Like Cronin, this is another basement winery, founded in 1976, and the owner, Richard Stark, owns no vines. Fruit is sourced from a number of fine vineyards in California: barrel-fermented Chardonnay from the Garbett Vineyard in Santa Clara as well as Bien Nacido in Santa Barbara, which also provides Pinot Noir. Zinfandel and Cabernet Sauvignon come from Chiles Valley. Some Zinfandel, Cabernet, and Merlot come from Napa, and Sauvignon Blanc from San Luis Obispo. Dane Stark has been making the wines since 1992.

Patz & Hall

PO Box 418, Rutherford, CA 94573. Tel: 707 963 4142. Fax: 963 9713. Production: 7,000 cases.

The trio behind this label are the genial Donald Patz, who was sales director for Flora Springs until 1996, winemaker James Hall, and oenologist Ann Moses. The winery specializes in Chardonnay and Pinot Noir, all from purchased grapes. By 1997 there were five Chardonnays: Napa, Sonoma Coast, Russian River, Alder Springs (Mendocino), and Hyde (Carneros). And Pinot Noirs from Russian River, Hyde Vineyard, Sonoma County, Alder Springs, and Pisoni (Santa Lucia Highlands). The team started to produce Pinot Noir only in 1995.

The Chardonnays are whole-cluster pressed, go through full malolactic fermentation, and are aged in mostly new oak. The Pinot Noir is given a 3-day cold soak, malolactic fermentation takes place in barrel, and 80 per cent new oak is used. None of the wines is filtered.

There are considerable differences between the wines, both because of the different vineyards, and because the winemaking practices push some of the wines out of balance. For my taste, many of the wines are characterized by excessive oak and excessive alcohol, leaving them with a burn on the finish. Patz & Hall describe their own style as 'very ripe, full blown, highly concentrated, and intended to maximize flavor in the finished wine'. All well and good: but sometimes these characters are achieved at the expense of finesse and complexity. Nonetheless, these are wines of high quality.

Pedrizetti Winery

1645 San Pedro Avenue, Morgan Hill, CA. Tel: 408 779 7389. Fax: 779 9083. Production: 40,000 cases.

This old-style winery was founded before Prohibition, and acquired by the present owners in 1945. It owns no vineyards and winemaker Ed

Pedrizetti produces a range of inexpensive varietals of very modest quality under the California appellation.

Martin Ray

Tel: 510 450 9450. Production: 6,000 cases.

This winery has nothing to do with the famous name it bears, which in 1991 was acquired as a brand by the Codera Wine Group's Courtney Benham. The wines, which are quite expensive, are good-quality blends from all over the state. Initial vintages were produced for Benham by Greg Graziano in Mendocino.

River Run Vintners

65 Rogge Lane, Watsonville, CA 95076. Tel: 408 726 3112. Production: 3,000 cases.

This family-run winery specializes in Chardonnay, Cabernet Sauvignon, Syrah, and Zinfandel. Much of the fruit comes from Ventana Vineyards in Monterey, and many wines carry a California appellation.

Rosenblum

2900 Main Street, Alameda, CA 94501. Tel: 510 865 7007. Fax: 865 9225. Production: 52,000 cases.

Veterinarian Kent Rosenblum shifted his attention from small animals to small plants in 1978, when he and his brother Roger set up this winery. Although they own 52 acres of Merlot and Chardonnay in Russian River Valley, they purchase most of the grapes, drawing on at least thirty different vineyards. They are among the leading Zinfandel specialists in California, releasing no fewer than fifteen bottlings in 1996, sourced from Napa, Sonoma, Paso Robles, Contra Costa, and local vineyards in Alameda. The basic wine is called Vintner's Cuvée. There are other wines produced by the Rosenblums and their winemaker Jeff Cohn: Merlot, Petite Sirah, and a Napa Meritage called Holbrook Mitchell Trio. But it's the panoply of old-vine Zinfandels, with their richness, power, and concentration, that have sustained the Rosenblums' reputation.

San Antonia Winery

737 Lamar St., Los Angeles, CA 90031. Tel: 213 223 1401. Fax: 221 5957. Production: 200,000 cases.

This winery was founded in 1917 by Santo Cambianica and is still owned by his descendants, the Riboli family. The winery kept going through Prohibition thanks to its production of sacramental wines. Dessert wines were the mainstay until 1963, when table wines were also produced. By 1964, this was the last functioning winery in Los Angeles. The Ribolis own vineyards in Napa, Monterey, and Alexander Valley, which are mostly used for their Maddalena label.

Siduri Cellars
980 Airway Court, Santa Rosa, CA 95403. Tel: 707 578 3882. Production: 1,800 cases.

Adam Lee, a wine retailer from Texas, moved to Sonoma in 1993 to start up a small operation modelled on Williams-Selyem or Littorai. The idea was to purchase small lots of outstanding Pinot Noir grapes from the best vineyards. Their first release was in 1994, and the grapes have been sourced from the Hirsch Vineyard in Sonoma Coast, Pisoni in Monterey, and from Anderson Valley and Oregon. The wines are made at Lambert Bridge winery.

Steele
Highway 29 and Thomas Dr., Kelseyville, CA 95451. Tel: 707 994 4709. Production: 15,000 cases.

Jed Steele, who would not look out of place at a truckers' conference, cut his teeth at Edmeades winery in Mendocino until 1983, when he went to work for Kendall-Jackson in Lake County. Here he built up a formidable reputation, and when he left the company in 1990, the repercussions included a bitterly fought legal battle about 'trade secrets'. During the 1990s Steele set up his own business, eventually purchasing the former Konocti winery in Lake County. At the same time he acted as a consultant for numerous wineries such as Villa Mount Eden and Fess Parker.

Although he buys grapes from some of the finest vineyards in the state – Durell, Sangiacomo, Bien Nacido – Steele has remained loyal to the county where he learnt his craft, purchasing from Lolonis, DuPratt and other growers. His range includes stylish and intense Pinot Noir, excellent Zinfandel, Cabernet Sauvignon, and Chardonnay, and he is increasingly interested in Rhône varieties. The winemaking is rooted in his experience at large wineries such as Kendall-Jackson: he prefers very ripe grapes, uses cultivated yeasts, and filters the wines. The second label is Shooting Star.

Taylor California Cellars
800 South Alta St., Gonzales, CA 93926. Tel: 408 675 2481. Production: 2 million cases.

Founded in 1977 by Coca-Cola, Taylor was sold in 1983 to Seagram, and then to Vintners International in 1987, and now belongs to the vast Canandaigua group. The wines are modest at best.

Tessera
Production: 230,000 cases.

Not a winery but a brand, created in 1996 by Seagram and overseen by Greg Fowler. The concept behind Tessera was to produce a consistent, rich style, primarily for restaurant and supermarket consumers. Sensibly priced and attractively packaged, the wines have had considerable success. The wines – Chardonnay, Zinfandel, Merlot, Cabernet Sauvignon – are made in Monterey by Phil Fransconi, who also produces Seagram's Redwood Trail export brand of well-made bargain varietals.

Sean Thackrey
240 Overlook Dr., Bolinas, CA 94924. Tel: 415 868 1781. Production: 3,000 cases.

Walking through the front yard to Thackrey's house, one passes an ancient pickup, a couple of steel tanks, some sheds and what look like barrels under tarpaulin sheets. It looks like a storage area, but turns out to be the winery itself. There is no problem with temperature control at this outdoor winery, as Bolinas is close to the ocean and is usually damp and cool, rather like San Francisco itself. During harvest time, Thackrey drives his 1940s Chevrolet pickup to the vineyards with which he has contracts, and transports the grapes back to his home.

Unlike most winemakers, Thackrey is an aesthete and intellectual, having earned his living mostly as a book and print dealer. He makes wine to please himself, and his T-shirt carries the proud eighteenth-century motto: 'Je ne consulte que mon plaisir.' The winemaking is artisanal, to put it mildly. Thackrey doesn't filter his wines because he doesn't own a filter. He sometimes makes his blends by assembling all the conceivable components of a wine and then eliminating the elements that displease him. He is fanatical about fermentation, however, and wants to ensure that the wine has been vinified to his complete satisfaction before it goes into barrel. He racks infrequently and hardly ever fines.

Thackrey's first commercial release was a 1981 Merlot/Cabernet blend he called Aquila. His best-known wine is Orion, which is mostly Syrah. In 1986 he identified a plot of old Syrah vines in Arthur Schmidt's vineyard near Yountville. He bought the grapes each year until Clarke Swanson, a great admirer of Orion, bought the entire vineyard and used the grapes at his own winery. Thackrey had to look elsewhere, and from 1991 bought grapes from the Andrew Rossi Vineyard. Here he had found an old clone of Syrah, as well as some vines, part of the field blend, that might well have been Petite Sirah. Orion is expensive, but it is a magnificent wine of extraordinary density and richness.

His other wines – and the range can vary from year to year according to grape availability – include Taurus, a Mourvèdre from the Cline Vineyard in Oakley, Sirius, and Pleiades. Sirius is Petite Sirah, and used to be from the Marston Vineyard on Spring Mountain; but Beringer have taken over the vineyard and replanted it. Pleiades is a nonvintage blend which Thackrey intends to be 'complex, interesting delicious, but easy to drink'; it usually contains plenty of Grenache, Syrah, and Zinfandel, from various regions and from different vintages. 'It's like a chef's special,' Thackrey explains. 'You trust the chef, so you're prepared to order the dish of the day.' When preparing the blend, he starts with the sweet ripe elements and adds other lots to give it more structure and balance.

Thackrey 'plays around', as he puts it, with Viognier and Roussanne which he buys from John Alban in San Luis Obispo; this tasted very promising from cask. His great problem is that every time he discovers a vineyard, his admirers get excited about the wine, 'and then someone with clout like Beringer comes in and either beats my price or buys the whole vineyard. So I'm compelled to reinvent the wheel.'

Tria
Tel: 707 253 2292. Production: 2,500 cases.

This label is jointly owned by two winemakers, Philip Zorn of Paraiso Springs and William Knuttel of Chalk Hill. They produce five varietal wines from Napa, Dry Creek, and elsewhere and a 'port' from Portuguese varieties.

Winters
15 Main St., Winters, CA 95694. Tel: 916 795 3201. Fax: 795 1119. Production: 5,000 cases.

Since 1980 Dave Storm has been producing small lots of varietal wines from Napa Valley, as well as Amador County Zinfandel and old-vine Petite Sirah.

34

The Century to Come

California doesn't contemplate the future. It *is* the future, or so it likes to think. No one has ever known what lies around the corner. There is very little reverence for the past. There are no statues in Los Angeles. In Europe, bound by its rules and appellations – by the frowns of the EU bureaucrats and the occasional small-mindedness of the French INAO, by regulations that bring politicization and corruption in their wake – change is slow. In California it can be explosive. Take the viticultural history of Monterey County. Virtually grape-free until the 1960s, it saw an onslaught of vines as tens of thousands of acres were planted, only to see many of them removed a few years later. Indifference followed by over-excitement followed by disillusionment. Now, thirty-five years later, growers are beginning to get the measure of the county. Or take phylloxera: consigned to the history books until the little louse started to crawl around once again, destroying vines as it went. A short-sighted decision about rootstocks entailed the eventual uprooting of tens of thousands of acres and replanting at vast expense. Yet the silver lining was the restructuring of vineyards, by no means in all cases, but in many, and the eventual outcome will be grapes of better quality.

So it's dangerous to look more than ten minutes ahead in California. Few wine regions are so prone to fad and fashion. Wine is bad for you, even wicked, one decade; a few years later, it's good for your health. In the early 1980s lots of new oak was a Good Thing, so that the wine tasted bold and expensive; by the late 1980s it was frowned upon for its incompatibility with exquisitely cooked food; by the mid-1990s it was back, as consumers apparently tired of the blandness of many wines on offer.

And yet it does not require any great gift of prophecy to foresee that the future for California wine is very bright indeed. No one would question that the climate is close to ideal, that winemaking skills are as sophisticated as anywhere else in the wine world, that years of underestimating the nuances of *terroir* and viticulture are at long last over, and that the domestic market is sufficiently enthralled with California wine to ensure that the best estates and the best vineyards can continue to produce wines of the highest quality. There will undoubtedly be adjustments. It's unclear to what extent the market for sparkling wine will recover and blossom. At the cheap and cheerful end of the market, I dream of seeing the soupier white Zinfandels and sugary blends replaced by refreshing inexpensive rosés from Grenache and other varieties.

While some may cringe at the showbiz elements of much winery promotion, especially the ego-boosting charity auction scene, I find any attempt to communicate with the winemaking public admirable. Whereas the French and Italians until recently didn't give a toss about making contact with the general public, the Californians have long gone out of their way to do so. If estates such as L'Hospitalet in La Clape in the Languedoc have begun to expand their winery buildings with museums and restaurants – tourist centres, in short – the inspiration for such a move must surely have been estates such as St Supéry and Mondavi in Napa Valley. From the start Robert Mondavi adopted a kind of holistic cultural view, though he would never have used such words. It was never enough simply to produce and sell wine. It was also essential to educate, to inform, to show. Winery tours and instructive tastings were always part of the agenda at Mondavi, and have become commonplace throughout the wine regions. Some estates, such as Kautz Ironstone, may be stronger on showbiz than on wine education, but no matter: they bring in the crowds and show them, subliminally, that wine is to be associated with the good things of life: fine cooking, a robust sandwich, a tour of a former gold mine, a tranquil picnic by a lake. Despite all the efforts of the neo-Prohibitionists, this remains one of California's great strengths: the American openness, the enthusiasm, the eagerness to share good news. I am no fan of the buy-by-numbers approach fostered, whether deliberately or not, by Robert Parker and by *The Wine Spectator*, but there can be no doubt that they have opened the world of wine to millions of consumers who might otherwise have been deterred by their lack of knowledge of a product sometimes made remote by connoisseurship.

But there are some disheartening tendencies at work, such as the frenzy for ultra-expensive, ultra-rare wines, which is likely to continue until such time as the American economy takes a nose-dive. True, this only affects a small corner of the market for good wine, but it places a premium on snobbery and greed which true winelovers must surely deplore. In February 1998 I wandered into a leading wine shop in St Helena in the company of a winery manager. I spotted a wooden case containing six bottles of different Cabernet Sauvignons, each from a different micro-estate. The asking price was $2,000. The shop owner said this was the last of these half-cases he had left; he'd sold the others to some Japanese collectors. Just as I was about to deliver a lecture on the iniquity of charging such inflated prices, I could hear my friend the winery manager muttering, in all seriousness, 'You know, that's not such a bad price ... You really ought to try some of these ...' I had to drag him away before he did something he and his wife would regret. What is it about the Napa Valley culture that makes someone think that $350 is a reasonable price to pay for a recently released bottle of red? Such madness has not yet come to Sonoma, although Matanzas Creek, with its $125 Merlot, is heading fast in that direction.

There is no virtue in limited production as such. Lafite and Margaux are made in generous quantities and yet maintain impeccable standards. The same is true of some Californian Bordeaux-style wines such as Opus One and Dominus. But there is surely something manipulative in creating wines that are only released in minute quantities, thus guaranteeing, if all the criteria for expensive wine production are met (low yields, fashionable variety, fashionable winemaker, lashings of new oak, no filter in sight, handsome heavy bottle, and so forth), that it can be released at a hefty price and then, if acclaimed by the right wine writers, re-sold at auction for headline-grabbing prices – close to $1,000 per bottle in the case of a handful of Napa Cabernets.

California is far from unique in this respect. The Bordelais have been no slouches when it comes to inventing micro-estates such as Le Pin and Villandraud. Their quality may be excellent, but it is far from evident that the quality is so fabulous that the wines can justify being offered at prices far higher than those of the great majority of their peers. The wines that can justify high price tags are those with an unimpeachable track record. One can be reasonably confident that an Yquem, a Latour, a La Tâche, is likely to be of superlative quality. Occasionally, high prices, especially in Burgundy, can be justified because the historic vineyard is of diminutive size. Demand for the best wines from the prized vineyards will always exceed supply.

What is disturbing about the American craze for rare Napa Cabernets and Sonoma Pinot Noirs is that the frenzy is directed not at well-established estates, nor at rare old wines long acknowledged as superb, but at new vintages of relatively untried estates. I don't dispute that the high-priced Napa Cabernets are of excellent quality, but as newcomers, a little modesty would not go amiss. No doubt the market for such wines has been stirred up by the uninspiring quality of Bordeaux vintages from 1991 to 1994. American consumers (or, worse, 'collectors') with more money than sense had to direct their acquisitiveness at something else.

It is also related to the cult of the winemaker. It has often been observed that the French have no word for 'winemaker'. Neither do the Germans. When I asked Graf Matuschka, the late owner of Schloss Vollrads, for the name of his cellarmaster, who had been with the estate for decades, he knew his surname but not his first name. He was, in other words, an estate worker, a very good one, but part of the team, not a superstar winemaker. Ask even the most ardent winelover who makes the wines at Château Lafite or Romanée-Conti, and I doubt that many would know the answer. Admittedly, that too is beginning to change, even in France, where the director of Margaux, Paul Pontallier, has a high profile, and wine consultants such as Michel Rolland are becoming well-known names. The French or German cellarmaster, of course, is working within known parameters. Grape variety, climate, fermentation techniques, barrel-ageing, and so forth, are all well understood. Fine-tuning will always be required – longer maceration for this tank, lighter fining for these barrels – but for the most part the cellarmaster or estate director knows what needs to be done. The variables are in the quality of fruit each vintage delivers.

It's different in California. Although the estate-grown wine is far from uncommon, many wineries start with something close to a clean slate each year, as they are not entirely sure where their grapes will come from. A vineyard that has supplied fruit for years may be acquired by a Jess Jackson or a Clarke Swanson; the marketing manager might demand less Sauvignon and more Chardonnay; the owner may want a luxury Meritage to impress his business guests – all of which will influence the output of a winery from year to year. So winemaking skills become very important, especially the ability to deal with a series of variables each vintage.

Winemaking skills are important, but that does not mean the winemaker needs to be elevated to the status of a demi-god, a status denied to the patient, scrupulous grape farmers who provide the working materials in the first place. I have no doubt that Heidi Peterson Barrett and Helen Turley, to take the most obvious names, are very good at what they do. Indeed, Ms Turley has been at it for over twenty years, producing wines at Stonegate, B. R. Cohn, Peter Michael, and at other wineries before she was catapulted to star status, no doubt in part by a wine press keen to create personalities that will capture their readers' interest. Robert Parker even dubbed Helen Turley 'a vinous goddess' (one step up on demi-god status), going on to say that her achievement is 'historic – she'll have an incredible legacy' (whatever that means). Her approach is admirable: closer vine spacing, low yields, natural fermentations, no filtration. But this is hardly revolutionary. Many leading growers and winemakers have been practising these methods for years.

Friends in Burgundy have told me how Helen Turley has spent hours studying the top vineyards of that region, in person, in the vineyard, and she prunes her own vineyard and takes risks in her winemaking. She also has a clear style of her own, which she describes as 'power and finesse'. The power is there, all right, but I search hard for the finesse. She admits she doesn't like to pick grapes at under 24 Brix, and doesn't worry about high alcohol. By and large, the American consumer is less interested in the finesse than the power. They like being overwhelmed. Explosive wines score better than delicate ones. High alcohol gives sweetness and richness to a wine that often makes a positive impression on the taster, if not on the drinker. I don't mind this emphasis, indeed I think I applaud it, but this is opulence taken to extremes.

To be fair to Helen Turley, her own wines from Marcassin may be impossible to find, but they are not ludicrously priced on release. Moreover, she shares the Burgundian fascination with individual vineyard sites and characters. I certainly prefer this approach to that of the super-blenders such as Kendall-Jackson with their 'flavor domaines' defined by their ability to combine to produce market-driven blends with no troubling inconsistencies from year to year.

The cult of the winemaker is leading Californians to take themselves far too seriously. An advertisement for Mondavi in *The Wine Spectator* (31 October 1998) has a picture of the great man seated beside Francis Ford Coppola. The caption reads: 'Wine is art. Robert taught me that.' Well, no. Actually, wine is a drink. It takes great skill to make good wine, but 75 centilitres of wine, however delicious, is not a work of art. It is a work of nature assisted, coaxed, even crafted, by man. If winemakers – or wine producers, in this case – want to have an over-inflated view of their role, I can't stop them, but it's an attitude that only reinforces the snobbery, the high prices, the elevation of the 'collectible' over the drinkable, that are among the more deplorable aspects of the California wine industry. A tasting note in the *Wine Spectator* (31 October 1998) refers to a Beaulieu Georges de Latour Reserve as 'this blue-chip collectible' – clearly not something anyone would actually want to drink.

It remains worryingly true that most California wines, especially from Napa Valley, are overpriced. I recall, after a week spent visiting some of Napa's most prestigious estates, remarking in surprise after I asked for the price of one estate's Cabernet: 'It's only forty dollars?' The surprise came from the fact that almost everything else I had been offered was priced at anywhere between $55 and $125. It's important to remember that in California, certainly in its more prestigious wine regions, price is unrelated to quality. In some cases it has to do with scarcity, as we have seen; but more often it has to do with a desperate attempt to recoup investment. The start-up costs of a vineyard and winery are huge, involving constructing and equipping a building, hiring vineyard managers and winery workers as well as a winemaker, importing costly French barrels, and hiring a marketing manager to fight for a place on restaurant and merchants' wine lists without giving everything away in discounts. All this means that as a rule of thumb, the new proprietor must count on losing money for ten years or so.

Josh Jensen conjures up a vision of Dr Joe, a typical 'lifestyle' winery owner, a city doctor with dreams of the rural idyll. He buys a vineyard, and at first he sells his grapes to other wineries, until he is persuaded that his profits would be far larger if he made, bottled, and marketed his own wine. So he invests. 'Suddenly he finds himself in a position where he's losing money every year, year in and year out, a hundred thousand in a good year, two hundred thousand in a bad year. And his problems are structural and unfix-able. It's a crowded marketplace and Joe can't just raise his prices. He's got boxes stacking up in the goddamn warehouse, so he's got to cut and discount and deal. Soon he tries to sell the winery, but who wants a losing winery making mediocre Chardonnay? So his arcadian dream has led to bankruptcy. And Ernest and Julio buy the winery. They only want it for its vineyards and they get it practically for nothing.'[1]

In the late 1990s there have been few bankruptcies. The American economy is booming and wine sales are buoyant. People with more money than sense are still paying absurd prices for 'collectible' wines, spurred on by the over-excited American wine press. It is unlikely to continue forever. No doubt there are some winery owners who have inexhaustible cash reserves to sustain their adventure; others base their claim to greatness on rarity and have minimal overheads. But the majority of people in the wine business need, at some point, to make a profit, and, as a few dark clouds begin to gather over the world economy, it is not fanciful to imagine that before long a few more bank managers will be placing a few more disconcerting phone calls to proprietors.

High prices also mean that California can compete only to a limited extent on export markets, which may not matter now, but may come to matter in the future. Writing from a British perspec-tive, I see on our shelves some of the great wines of California (but at unaffordable prices) and a good deal of mediocre juice indistinguishable from cheaper bottles from Chile or the Lang-uedoc. There are exceptions, but not many. The upshot is that the regular wine drinker with limited means comes to believe that California is the source either of cheap undistinguished blends or of £25 Chardonnays or £40 Cabernets.

Overpriced wines also mean that innovation, the mainstay of the California wine industry, will be reined in. If it now costs $80,000 to buy and develop an acre of vineyard in Napa Valley, it is unlikely that you will plant anything other than the most fashionable varieties. It's true that there are patches of great and less familiar varieties such as Sangiovese and Viognier in some of the costlier parts of California, but the proportions are tiny. But if

Napa growers are mostly required to play safe, then it does give greater opportunities to growers in the Central Coast or Mendocino or the Sierra Foothills, where land is less expensive and a winery with marketing skills can persuade its customers to give its Gewürztraminer or Grenache a whirl. Randall Grahm at Bonny Doon, who probably hasn't laid eyes on a Cabernet vine in decades, shows that it can be done, although it does help to be a marketing genius. Similarly Greg Graziano and Ken Volk, in Mendocino and Paso Robles respectively, show an unbridled enthusiasm for the obscure and strange and tasty.

I would be quite content to see a somewhat polarized Californian wine industry, with Napa and, increasingly, Sonoma, committed, for financial as well as climatic reasons, to the production of costly Cabernet and Chardonnay, with the occasional Syrah or Zinfandel thrown in for good measure, while in the lesser-known regions more enterprising growers and winemakers focus increasingly on the Mediterranean varieties. While I have enormous admiration for the likes of Ted Lemon, who are looking for ever greater finesse in their wines, usually from Burgundian varieties, I can't help feeling that California's forte does not lie in the exquisite and refined. I have little doubt that in the next decade we will be seeing marvellous wines emerging from cool regions such as the Sonoma Coast and Russian River Valley, but quantities will always be limited. California's strength lies, as I suggested at the very beginning of this long book, in the generous and forthright. The vigour of most California soils and the clemency of the California climate mean that rich, powerful, vigorous, full-flavoured wines will always come more naturally than the pared down, the exquisite, the shapely. We want both of course, but if California's eventual legacy lies in exuberance at the expense of elegance, then that is no cause for disapproval or even regret. California has much to learn from Europe, just as Europe increasingly has much to learn from California, but California must in the long term play to its strengths. No doubt it will do so without any further advice and admonitions from me.

NOTE

1 Marq de Villiers, *The Heartbreak Grape*, p. 113

APPENDIX I

California Vintages

─────

These vintage notes apply only to Napa Valley, unless otherwise stated. In practice, climatic conditions affecting Napa usually have a similar influence over other North Coast regions. It should be borne in mind that there are innumerable subtle variations between vineyards, growing practices, harvesting practices, and microclimates, so that there are some excellent wines from vintages often regarded as mediocre, and poor wines from vintages acclaimed as great. It is always better to trust taste buds rather than vintage charts.

1869   A small crop with mildew.

1873   Very good reds.

1878   Outstanding.

1879   Excellent.

1880   Second crop grapes after May freeze, so rather light. Medium quality.

1881   High quality.

1884   A huge crop but inadequate sugar levels.

1885   Hot at harvest, leading to stuck fermentations.

1886   High quality.

1887   Drought and frost reduced yields to 2 tons/acre. Medium quality.

1888   Average quality.

1889   Storms interrupted harvest but some outstanding wines.

1890   September rain harmed Zinfandel, but the Indian summer gave rich reds.

1891   Many stuck fermentations. October rain reduced the crop size.

1892   Medium quality.

1893   Late September rains damaged Zinfandel. But overall a good vintage.

1894   Hot August but some overcropping.

1895   Small crop but good quality.

1896   Smallest crop since 1876 and not very good.

1897   Mixed quality.

1899   A small but outstanding crop.

1900   Outstanding, with rich and powerful reds.

1901   High quality.

1902   Superlative quality.

1903   High quality.

1905   Rather ordinary, with much overcropping, but some marvellous reds.

1906   Average quality.

1907   Best of the decade, especially for reds.

1908   A dry year, with excellent long-lived reds.

1909   Low yields, giving high quality.

1910   Small crop, of excellent quality.

1911   Very low yields, but the cool summer gave low sugar levels.

1916   Excellent quality.

1918   Ordinary quality after a cool, wet autumn.

1926   Good small crop.

1931   Very low yields after drought.

1933   Famous for an exceptional Cabernet Sauvignon from Inglenook.

1934   Good quality.

1935   Small crop. Some outstanding Cabernet.

1936   Best known for the first, and long-lived, Beaulieu Private Reserve Cabernet.

1937   Very good.

1940 Excellent.

1941 Some great wines, notably Inglenook Cabernet.

1942 Very good.

1945 Rain damaged the harvest

1946 Excellent quality at best, but erratic.

1947 Exceptional Cabernet Sauvignon in Napa.

1948 Mediocre.

1949 Exceptional Cabernet Sauvignon in Napa.

1950 Excellent.

1951 Excellent Cabernet Sauvignon in Napa, ripe and long-lived.

1952 In Napa, many excellent wines, powerfully concentrated, despite some very cold spells.

1953 Satisfactory quality in Napa, but a very small crop after devastating spring frosts.

1954 Exceptional Cabernet Sauvignon in Napa, but rain in August damaged Zinfandel.

1955 In Napa, particularly successful whites.

1956 In Napa, higher prices led to overcropping. Later ripening varieties did well. October rain lowered quality and the wines did not age well.

1957 In Napa, very promising until heavy rain in late September, with more in October. Not very successful for Cabernet Sauvignon.

1958 Exceptional Cabernet Sauvignon in Napa, very long-lived.

1959 Very hot in Napa, but some memorable Cabernets.

1960 In Napa hot summer led to an early harvest. Concentrated wines, with delicious Cabernet Sauvignon from Krug and others.

1961 In Napa spring frosts were followed by a June heatwave. Good whites and Zinfandels, with low yields.

1962 In Napa a large crop. Spring frost, autumn rain, and a cool October almost ruined the crop. Weather improved in late October. Mostly mediocre.

1963 A wet winter in Napa, then frost and a cool summer. A cool, foggy September followed by October rain. Some good wines from hillside vineyards, but overall quality was poor.

1964 In Napa a hot September and a late harvest. Spring frost damage led to low yields. Excellent Chardonnay and Cabernet Sauvignon.

1965 In Napa a big crop. Cool wet August, and a late vintage. Above average quality but not long-lived.

1966 No frost in Napa. Very warm growing season. Harvest began in mid-September, then hot winds dehydrated some grapes. Good overall quality. Very good to exceptional and long-lived Cabernet.

1967 Wet winter and a cool rainy spring in Napa, followed by a warm summer. A late vintage in warm conditions. Good quality overall, but Zinfandel did not fare well. Not for long keeping.

1968 A warm, dry winter in Napa, with light April frosts, followed by a warm growing season. Hot spells caused accelerated ripening and some heat damage. A prolonged vintage. On the whole, the fruit was clean, intense and well balanced, although there was some raisining. Cabernet Sauvignon proved of excellent quality, rich and tannic, arguably the best vintage since 1947, in Santa Cruz as well as Napa. Beaulieu's Private Reserve, Ridge Monte Bello, and Martha's Vineyard exceptional.

1969 No frost in Napa, but some early mildew during a hot summer. Vintage started in late August, then a stampede, and October rains provoked some problems with late-ripening varieties. In general, clean balanced fruit and wines of very good quality. Most wines are now past their best.

1970 A warm March in Napa was followed by severe spring frosts, and half the crop was lost. The growing season was warm with several hot spells, and there was some heat damage. The harvest of fully ripe fruit began in late August, and second-crop bunches after frost damage required selective picking. Some overripeness. Low yields of excellent Cabernet Sauvignon and Zinfandel. The best wines are still drinking well.

1971 A cool spring and bud-break in Napa, and a long, cool growing season with some mildew. There was some rain during the harvesting in warm conditions; the fruit was not badly tainted by rot but there was uneven ripening. The harvest extended into a cool October. Fair quality wines, with a handful of exceptions such as Ridge Monte Bello and Beaulieu's Reserve Cabernet.

1972 The year got off to a poor start with severe spring frosts. July was exceptionally hot, which blocked maturation, but there was rain during the September and October harvest, so rot was widespread. The resulting wines ranged from underripe and poor to soft and simple and were short-lived. But there were some good wines from Santa Cruz and attractive Chardonnays. Short-lived wines.

1973 After a damp, cool winter, spring was warm. The summer was relatively cool and the prolonged growing season delivered a huge crop of fine quality and healthy grapes, especially Cabernet and Zinfandel. The wines proved well structured, elegant, and quite tannic, but most of them may now be past their best.

1974 The spring was cool but frost on May 19 reduced the crop in Napa. The summer was fairly cool, but the autumn months were warm and grapes were picked in ideal conditions. The harvest began in early September but continued into October. The outcome was one of the great postwar vintages, delivering generous quantities of superlative and intense red wines, although some have not aged as well as was initially predicted. Some wines were over-tannic, but Ridge Monte Bello and Heitz's Martha's Vineyard are still in splendid condition, despite some bottle variation. There were also some very good Zinfandels.

1975 The growing season began with a cool spring, frost, and a good deal of rain. The summer was cool, except during July, and some rain marred the harvest in October, which was relatively late. The Napa Cabernets tended to be slightly underripe, giving wines that were medium-bodied and elegant, with ample fruit, best consumed fairly young before their fruit faded. There was also some very fine Chardonnay and Sauvignon Blanc.

1976 In Napa, the winter and spring were dry, and flowering was uneven and yields were low. The dry weather continued through the summer, stressing the vines and thickening the skins, although there was some rain during harvest. The best Cabernets were concentrated and tannic, although many were over-tannic and unbalanced and did not age well. There were some outstanding Zinfandels. Among whites, Sauvignon Blanc often fared better than Chardonnay.

1977 This was another drought year, although the growing season was a little cooler than 1976. Rain interrupted the harvest on 20 September, but it probably proved beneficial to grapes stressed by drought. Picking continued into November in Napa. The Cabernets and Zinfandels were well balanced and supple, showing attractive fruit from the outset. Chardonnay was also very good.

1978 The year began with heavy winter rains, and spring was free from frost. The growing season as a whole was warm, with many hot spells, especially just before and during the harvest, which began in late August in Napa but continued into a warm November. Yields were quite high.

Cabernet in Napa ripened well, but there was also some overripeness which led to stuck fermentations at some wineries. The wines were rich, alcoholic, and concentrated, and the best have aged well.

1979 The year began well, but was marred by an unsettled May and June, which resulted in uneven flowering, especially for Cabernet Sauvignon. The growing season was fairly cool, although it culminated in some hot spells. There was some rain during harvest, which began in early September, and estates that picked before the October rains often produced cleaner, better balanced wines. Other wines showed dilution and low acidity. Overall quality was patchy, and the better wines were good but not outstanding. Most wines evolved quite quickly. Whites, which were mostly picked before the rain, were excellent.

1980 The year got off to a discouraging start, with heavy rain over the mild winter, a wet spring and early summer, and then the coolest growing season ever recorded up to that time. However, despite a chilly August, by harvest time the weather was distinctly warm, especially in October, and the red grapes came in with excellent sugar levels while retaining good acidity. These conditions benefited most regions and varieties, with some superb Cabernet Sauvignon and very good Chardonnays on the North Coast, and some rich Zinfandels too. In general, this has been an underrated vintage, and those who gave the reds some bottle age will have had some very pleasant surprises. However, 1980 does not have the uniform ripeness that is one of the hallmarks of a truly great vintage, and quite a few wines were unbalanced. A large crop.

1981 This atypical year was marked by a very hot, dry summer, with some extremely high temperatures in June. There were signs of uneven ripening. The harvest was unusually early, and the year became noted for its boldly flavoured Chardonnays more than for its sound, lightish, but unspectacular reds, most of which were marked by fairly low acidity and were best drunk young. Zinfandel was uneven.

1982 The year began with a wet winter and a warm spring; thereafter the summer was warm. Yields were very high and some estates prudently bunch-thinned to reduce the crop. Storms in mid- to late September disturbed the harvest, and the late-ripening varieties fared better than others. The damp weather encouraged the development of botrytis, which was occasionally turned to advantage, and some good late harvest Riesling was produced. Cabernets from Napa and Sonoma were very good, and there were some fine whites from Monterey and elsewhere. The best reds, including Zinfandel, were plump and full-flavoured, but sometimes lacked tannic structure, balance, and depth. Chardonnay often proved disappointing, as rot attacked many vineyards in Sonoma before harvesting.

Chardonnay and Pinot Noir picked before the rains in Sonoma were often of fine quality; others were clearly underripe.

1983   Very heavy winter rains were followed by a damp spring. It was indeed a wet year overall, and rot was widespread. Rain in August was particularly unwelcome. Picking began in early September and was interrupted by rain in late September and early October. One unexpected benefit of the awful weather was the production of some good late harvest wines. Yet overall the wines have turned out better than expected. There were some fine, surprisingly rich Chardonnays, especially in Sonoma, although others were tainted by rot and lacked finesse. Cabernets that were awkward and angular in their youth have evolved into firm and flavoury wines. The best Cabernets tended to come from Napa hillsides, while the least impressive were marked by dilution. There were fine Zinfandels from Sonoma. This may well have been the first vintage in which Merlot showed what it was capable of in California. Carneros and the Central Coast were relatively successful. All in all, 1983 turned out better than the climatic data would lead one to imagine.

1984   The spring was exceptionally warm and bud-break early, so the vines were about two weeks ahead of their usual ripeness levels by the summer, which was also warm and dry. Some vines suffered from drought stress but fruit was clean and healthy. In Napa Valley harvesting teams were already at work by mid-August after the shortest growing season on record. The weather was even hotter in September. This caused considerable difficulties, since many varieties ripened simultaneously, and wineries were under pressure for tank space and time. Delay in picking could lead to overripeness, yet surprisingly few wines showed much sign of this. Most red wines turned out to be fleshy and attractive, approachable young yet capable of prolonged ageing in bottle. Some, relying on first impressions, damned the youthful reds as too jammy and lacking in acidity, but the best Cabernets and Merlots are thoroughly concentrated and still going strong. They were probably the best reds since 1978. Sonoma was also successful, with many splendid Zinfandels, and there were good wines from Carneros that have also aged better than expected. Mendocino delivered less impressive results than most other regions. The vintage did not suit white varieties that well, and some Chardonnays were clumsy, although Central Coast vineyards, delivering better acidities, fared better. The Central Coast also began producing some high-quality Pinot Noirs.

1985   This was a dream of a year, with a fairly dry winter, warm dry spring, early bud-break, even flowering, and a relatively cool growing season, followed by an Indian summer that allowed a prolonged harvest in good conditions, marred only by some rain after the first week of September. Picking started during the last week of August, but slow ripening meant that the harvest was far less hectic than that of the previous year. There was some late rain, but much of the fruit had been picked before the downpours, and Monterey escaped altogether. The outcome was the finest vintage for Napa and Sonoma Cabernet and Merlot since 1974, with excellent results from other regions such as Santa Cruz and Mendocino, too. It was not a vintage marked by excessively high sugar levels, so the reds show a great deal of finesse and balance. They are ageing very well. Pinot Noir was very successful in Carneros and Zinfandel did well everywhere. Chardonnays had good firm acidity but are now past their best. Some experienced tasters such as James Laube find that the Cabernets are already fully mature, but I have encountered wines that are showing no signs of tiring.

1986 The year got off to a very wet start, with extensive but essentially harmless flooding in Napa and Sonoma in February, followed by frost and mildew. Bud-break was early, and the spring was warm. The vintage was saved by a sunny August and a fairly cool and prolonged growing season overall. Rain did fall in mid-September, causing some mildew, but much of the harvest was already in. Both Napa and Sonoma produced very good full-bodied and well-structured reds and rich, fat Chardonnays that are now past their peak. Despite generous yields for Cabernet Sauvignon, overall quality is very good, although the vintage as a whole has been overshadowed by 1985. The long growing season also benefited Pinot Noir, which performed especially well in Carneros. Zinfandel yielded very good results throughout the North Coast.

1987 After a very dry winter, spring was mild but flowering was nonethe-less early, although an unusually hot May led to poor fruit-set for Cabernet Sauvignon in Napa. The growing season was cool and low rainfall resulted in small berries that led to great intensity of flavour in the grapes. This applies to Zinfandel in the North Coast and Sierra Foothills, as well as to Cabernet and Merlot. The harvest was precocious, as in 1984, and was under way by mid-August in hot conditions. Yields were low throughout the North Coast, after the shatter provoked by the unseasonably warm May, and this was the smallest crop in five years. Rain began to fall in late October, but by then the harvest was almost over. The grapes were clean and healthy. The outcome was a large selection of rich, succulent, concentrated Cabernet and Merlot and powerful and aromatic whites. Although only a few Bordeaux-style wines were in the same league as 1985 or even 1986, overall quality was very good. Quality was also high in the Central Coast. There were a handful of underperformers, such as Carneros Pinot Noir, which suffered from heat stress, although quality was certainly acceptable. Chardonnays showed relative tartness and aus-terity, and were less immediately appealing than the 1986s.

1988 The winter months were dry and quite warm, and the dry conditions continued until the end of April. May was marked by stormy conditions. June was wet and cool, so flowering was prolonged and erratic, especially for the Bordeaux varieties. In Napa, poor flowering conditions reduced the Merlot crop by half but, if anything, this only helped to improve quality. The summer was bizarre, with great variations in June and July and very hot conditions in August and early September. The harvest began early, with Chardonnay being picked in late August, and continued in good conditions, and the fruit was healthy, though some grapes had low acidity and lower than usual ripeness levels. Yields were low and in many vineyards berries were small. Many growers practised selective harvesting to compensate for uneven ripening. Rain fell in Napa in mid-October, but by then all the Cabernet and other late varieties had been picked. This was a year in which the Central Coast made its mark with a good crop of fine grapes. In the North Coast Cabernet and Merlot were good, sound lean wines, but not of outstanding quality, especially when compared to the trio of preceding vintages. Low acidity, moreover, meant that many wines were not well suited to lengthy cellaring. Merlot, with its severely reduced crop, ripened earlier and was often of excellent quality. Much the same is true of Zinfandel. The major successes lay among the Burgundian varieties, which were rich and well-structured. Many Chardonnays were boldly flavoured and vigorous and best drunk young, and small berries gave some intensely flavoured Pinot Noir.

1989 The spring was fine, flowering took place in excellent conditions, and the summer was cool, which meant that there was little chance of an early harvest. Picking began on average two weeks later than in 1988. Thus, when heavy rain fell in Napa and Sonoma from 16 to 19 September and again towards the end of the month, at least half the crop was still on the vine. Many estates were faced with the uncomfortable choice of picking unripe grapes before rot destroyed them or waiting to pick grapes that might never shake off the side effects of dilution and rot provoked by the rain. Newton believed this to be the most difficult vintage since 1972. Yields were high, so the heavily loaded vines were even more susceptible to rot and growers who had bunch-thinned stood a better chance of ripening their grapes. Botrytis set in rapidly, especially in Carneros and Russian River Valley, and while this may have opened up the possibility for some outstanding sweet wines, it played havoc with the bulk of the crop destined for white wine production.

Growers of Cabernet Sauvignon often sat tight hoping that the return of warmer, drier weather would allow them to make some decent red wines, and the harvest continued through a warm early October and on, sporadically, into November. Some vineyards recovered; others, especially with Cabernet Sauvignon and Cabernet Franc, suffered from underripeness and/or rot. Merlot and Zinfandel were particularly badly hit. The resulting wines were simple and attractive but lacked structure and vigour. In the case of white varieties, late-picked grapes were not necessarily of good quality. Robert Pecota characterized most Napa Chardonnay in 1989 as 'rubbish'. Sauvignon Blanc, picked mostly before the rain, was of better quality. Much of the Pinot Noir from Sonoma and Carneros was also picked before the rain, and the wines turned out to be of average quality. Large quantities of grapes and wines were sold off to wholesalers. However, it was a different story further south, and in San Luis Obispo County there was no rain and the vintage was unproblematic; it was also an outstanding year in the Sierra Foothills.

1990 It rained heavily in May, and this had the consequence in Napa and Sonoma of reducing the size of the crop at flowering, especially for Cabernet Sauvignon and Sauvignon Blanc, which were down by about 25 per cent. However, the summer was warm, and quite hot in early August, which meant that ripening was uniform and the fruit was harvested in excellent conditions. The fruit in Napa was fully mature and acidity levels were good if not exceptional. When light rain finally fell over the North Coast regions in late September, almost all the grapes had been picked. Pinot Noir from Carneros was exceptional, yielding ripe concentrated wines of classic structure. Cabernet Sauvignon was outstanding, and in the opinion of some, such as Tim Mondavi, will age better than those from 1991. With a somewhat reduced crop and dry conditions, the grapes were tannic and solidly structured, and thus built to last. Indeed, it became essential, especially at wineries using mountain fruit, to moderate the tannins in the course of vinification.

Conditions were different in Central Coast regions, where heavy rain fell during harvest, especially in Santa Maria Valley; this affected the quality of the Pinot Noir more than the Chardonnay. In the Sierra Foothills the wines turned out to be lacklustre. Overall, however, and especially in the North Coast, this was arguably the finest vintage since 1985. Chardonnay was impeccable, fruity and exuberant, and there were excellent results from the Central Coast as well as from the northern counties. Zinfandel was outstanding, especially from Dry Creek, and the relatively cool conditions during harvesting meant that raisining and over-alcoholic wines were rare. The crop throughout California was enormous.

1991 After a cold, dry winter, heavy rain fell over the North Coast in March, but during flowering the conditions were ideal, promising a large crop of evenly maturing grapes. The actual growing season was cool, despite a hot spell in early July, but there was perfect weather during harvesting. Some growers thinned the crop to boost maturation, since the cool summer meant that it would be a very late harvest; at Clos du Val

Cabernet was being picked on 25 October, shortly before the rain finally arrived. If anything, it was too warm, and some Chardonnay was low in acidity. Despite the bunch-thinning, the overall crop was enormous, the most abundant since 1982. Climatic conditions were fairly even throughout the state and if some of the red grapes were not immensely ripe, they made up in finesse for what they lost in richness. The result was wines of classic structure and fine acidity. In Carneros this proved another exceptional vintage for Pinot Noir, while some argued that this was the best vintage for Napa Cabernet since 1985; others preferred 1990. Doubts were raised by the fact that in cooler areas, some Cabernet and Merlot simply didn't ripen fully, giving a slight herbaceousness to some wines. But this proved to be the exception rather than the rule.

There was some late rain in the Central Coast, and some outbreaks of botrytis. Nonetheless Santa Barbara Pinot Noir, as well as Carneros Pinot, was of excellent quality, with small berries giving wines of concentration and richness. Zinfandel thrived with the late harvest, and splendid wines emerged from the North Coast and from the Sierra Foothills.

1992   After ample winter rains, a cool frost-free spring, hot May but rainy June meant that flowering was prolonged, with an uneven fruit-set. However, the summer was warm and dry, and hot temperatures in the late summer led to an early harvest in Napa. In fact, picking of some varieties, such as Sauvignon Blanc, began in early August. The harvest all along the North Coast continued in very good conditions, with cool nights, morning fogs, and warm days allowing it to proceed at a leisurely and unforced pace. Thus varieties such as Cabernet Sauvignon were able to ripen fully, although some growers expressed concern that the flavour development of some varieties was less complete than they would have wished. In general, both quality and quantity were high, although the size of the crop led to some dilution in certain vineyards. Carneros once again had an excellent crop of Pinot Noir, which by and large was slightly superior to the Chardonnay. The hot summer meant that alcohol levels in Chardonnays throughout the North Coast were quite high.

The harvest was early in Sonoma too, and Chardonnay did exceptionally well overall. The hot weather kept the berries small, and in general the Cabernet Sauvignon was even more structured than in the two preceding years. There was some overripeness among the Zinfandel, and Paul Draper of Ridge preferred the quality of the 1993 wines. Mendocino experienced very hot weather and here too grapes were picked earlier than usual.

Although the bare facts suggest that 1992 should be an excellent vintage, it is widely agreed that the wines overall are less successful than in 1990 and 1991, although there are bound to be exceptions. Certainly in their youth, the big tannic Cabernets were more closed and less opulent than the wines of most previous vintages. The best wines would evolve splendidly; others might never lose their tannic edge. Merlot, however, ripened earlier than Cabernet and gave softer, more lush wines. Zinfandel gave more mixed results, and many wines were on the light side and lacked acidity.

1993   The spring was warm in the North Coast, but ended with spells of rain and wind in late May and early June, which had a negative effect on the flowering. As a consequence the crop was reduced by about 20 per cent. The growing season overall was quite cool, but there were significant peaks of hot weather in August and September as well as cooler spells. Some bunches experienced sunburn and raisining. In Napa it became important not to pick too early, to allow a longer hang-time to bring the red grapes to full phenolic ripeness. As in 1992, there were problems when grapes reached high sugar levels without attaining that phenolic ripeness. Picking began in late August and continued for just over a month. In retrospect it can be said that many growers picked too early, as much Cabernet was not fully ripe until mid-October. A handful of growers continued picking well into October, when the weather was cooler. However, a number of estates expressed dissatisfaction with the fruit quality and low acidity of the Cabernet grapes, and neither Caymus Special Selection nor Dominus was produced in 1993, but overall it was a vintage of easy-drinking reds for medium-term consumption. The concentration required of a great vintage is simply lacking, though, as always, there were exceptions. Pinot Noir, Merlot, and Chardonnay were also of good quality, charming wines for early drinking; and Zinfandels, which ripened well, turned out better than expected.

In Sonoma too, the crop was reduced at flowering, but the grapes ripened well and there was no rush to pick them. The wines, like those from Napa, are relatively forward and probably best enjoyed young. There were some excellent wines from the Central Coast, especially Chardonnay and Pinot Noir. The Sierra Foothills also enjoyed good harvesting conditions and quality was quite high.

1994   After light winter rainfall, March was dry and sunny, but the rest of the spring was cool and windy. Rain in May caused some problems at flowering, but the crop was nonetheless quite generous, although the yields for Merlot and Pinot Noir were about 10 per cent lower than normal. However, berry and cluster sizes were small, aiding concentration. The growing season in Napa and Sonoma as a whole proved mild and prolonged, offering excellent conditions for perfect maturation. The hottest period was the first half of August; otherwise temperatures were moderate. Grapes ripened properly after lengthy hang-time without losing acidity, and tannins were ripe too. The harvest itself went without a hitch in Napa and Sonoma. It was a late harvest, and Mondavi was not the only

APPENDIX I

estate to complete picking in early November. Cabernet Sauvignon and
Merlot were of superb quality throughout the North Coast, with intense
varietal character; the wines are as good, if not better, than 1991. Tim
Mondavi proclaimed it the best of the decade. The wines were riper and
less tannic than 1992 and 1993, but the coolish weather meant that
overripeness, high tannin, and excessive alcohol were uncommon. In Carneros and Sonoma, Pinot Noir was of equal excellence. It was not all
perfection, however, and Chardonnay was subject to some rot in Carneros
as well as in the Central Coast. There was also some rain in Mendocino,
but it did little damage. Zinfandel quality was high, but yields were down
after uneven flowering, which probably acted as a boost to quality and
fruit intensity. Some examples show signs of overripeness and raisining.

The Central Coast had more climatic problems, with heavy rain in
September provoking outbreaks of rot in Paso Robles, Edna Valley, and
Santa Barbara. Monterey got off more lightly than other southern regions.
This affected Chardonnay and Merlot in particular. Nonetheless, despite
the incidence of rot among some Chardonnay throughout the state, even-
tual quality was very high.

1995   In Napa the winter was wet and the spring damp and cool. Mendocino experienced very wet weather in May and June. Continuing cool
weather at flowering led to uneven fruit-set throughout the North Coast.
These conditions meant that the growing season began later than usual,
leading to a late harvest. The summer was warm, and continuing dry,
warm weather throughout September resulted in some dehydration of the
grapes. The Indian summer gave the fruit extended hang-time, which
assisted maturation. The somewhat reduced crop and small berry size
resulted in elegant white wines with good acidity, and in rich, soft reds.

There were serious problems in the Central Coast, and in Monterey the
crop was only one-quarter of the usual size. Poor flowering also severely
reduced yields in Santa Barbara, and the average yield for Pinot Noir was
less than one ton per acre. In Santa Cruz, winter was stormy and spring
cool and wet; there were problems with mildew and poor flowering.
Although the summer was warm, it was cooler than elsewhere in California. September was cool and temperatures remained moderate until
harvesting was completed. Here too, the crop was small. However, this
turned out to be a first-rate vintage in the Sierra Foothills.

Despite climatic problems that had a drastic effect on crop size, the
quality of the wine eventually made was high, and many 1995s were just
as good as the wines of the previous vintage. Pinot Noir was a touch
lighter, but very elegant. Zinfandel was outstanding. Merlot proved problematic, with many wines showing high tannin levels and astringency.

1996   The winter was warm and there was ample rain, up to 40 inches in parts of Napa Valley. The spring was cool and rain in May caused some problems at flowering, as did a very hot spell in late May. Overall the crop in the North Coast was down by about 20 per cent, and considerably more in some areas. June was cool, but then it warmed up, and ripening was swift. Fortunately, it was slowed down by cooler weather in late August and early September, which prolonged the hang-time and gave better phenolic ripeness. The harvest took place in very good conditions and was fairly rapid. In Sonoma the harvest was relatively early. Pinot Noir from Russian River Valley and Sonoma Coast emerged in a more austere style than some preceding vintages, yet do not seem to have the stuffing to be worth cellaring for many years. Zinfandel from Napa and Sonoma tended to ripen unevenly, and the result was a somewhat lighter wine overall than in preceding vintages, although raisining also led to high alcohol levels in some wines – levels not always balanced by rich fruit. In Mendocino the harvest began as early as mid-August after a summer hotter than 1994 or 1995; here the crop was down by about 15 to 20 per cent.

Central Coast vineyards survived the climatic vagaries of the year better than the North Coast, and crop levels were higher. Paso Robles experienced some exceedingly hot temperatures during the summer months, but conditions further south in Santa Barbara were more temperate. The harvest was swift. The hot summer benefited the growing acreage of Rhône varieties in the Central Coast vineyards. In the Santa Cruz Mountains there was also uneven flowering and the berries were very small, giving powerful tannic reds after a very warm summer.

Initial tastings of the 1996 reds, especially Merlot and Zinfandel, proved disappointingly light. Chardonnays, however, were just as good as those from the two preceding vintages, and some Cabernet turned out to be of high quality.

1997 This was a precocious year, with an early spring culminating in an early harvest. Perfect flowering conditions in June suggested that crop levels would be enormous. The summer was not especially hot. There was some rain in the North Coast in mid-August, and the humid weather that followed provoked rot in some vineyards, especially in Carneros and Sonoma, where Chardonnay and Zinfandel suffered more damage than Pinot Noir. More rain in mid-September didn't help, especially in Sonoma. Well-managed vineyards, without excessive foliage, survived the humidity better than others. Rot-affected grapes often led to stuck fermentations, as fungicides on the bunches killed off some yeasts. The harvest was exceptionally early, and Kendall-Jackson were already picking some grapes in late July. Fruit destined for sparkling wine was also picked very early. Although red grapes were being picked in the North Coast from late August onwards, the harvest was quite protracted and continued into

October, delivering late-ripening varieties, such as Cabernet Sauvignon, of high quality. Most growers thinned bunches to reduce the crop and improve maturation, but the grapes compensated by forming quite large clusters. Maturation was also assisted by very warm weather in September.

In San Luis Obispo County the spring was unusually warm, and flowering again suggested a very large crop would develop. Bunch-thinning was common. The rain that troubled parts of the North Coast in August did not materialize in the Central Coast, except for a little light rain in Santa Barbara. Here the problems were different: the warm days and, equally important, warm nights, led to speedy ripening, and much of the crop had to be picked very fast. (Byron in Santa Maria Valley, however, said they had a long growing season and normal yields.) Nonetheless quality was impressive. The Sierra Foothills also escaped most of the rain, and some estates claimed this was the best vintage of the decade. Dry-farmed vineyards had normal yields, encouraged by very dry weather.

Despite the huge crop – an increase of 32 per cent on the previous year – almost everyone reported that the wines were of high quality. Estates that thinned the crop reported superlative results, although early tastings suggested that there were some mediocre Merlots and Chardonnays to be found. High yields affected Chardonnay in particular, and there was some dilution; yields were only slightly higher for Bordeaux red varietals in North Coast mountain vineyards and for low-yielding Pinot Noir vineyards in Sonoma, where growers such as Rochioli reported that although Pinot Noir grapes were very ripe, they retained good acidity levels, which was very promising. Much the same was true of the Burgundian varieties in Carneros. Despite rot in some areas, Zinfandel looked promising and certainly superior to 1996; some specialist producers such as Rosenblum predicted that this could be the best Zinfandel vintage of the decade.

1998 This was the year of El Niño. To describe the spring as wet would be an understatement: it was sopping wet, torrentially wet. Flowering was exceptionally late and uneven, with a great deal of shatter provoked by the persistent rain. Crop levels were down between 15 and 50 per cent, specially among the Burgundian varieties. The North Coast was worst hit by the unprecedented weather conditions, but some Central Coast areas such as Monterey were relatively unscathed. In the North it remained wet and cool throughout the spring; in July the weather cleared but a series of heat spikes caused further problems. However, those heat spikes were absent in the Central Coast, where the summer proved perfect and grapes were picked in ideal conditions, though growers who overcropped were punished with underripe grapes. Jim Clendenen believes 1998 will be the finest vintage ever experienced in Santa Barbara.

Very warm temperatures in late August and early September gave the North Coast vines a much-needed boost. Some growers bunch-thinned, hoping to speed up maturation in expectation of a late harvest in deteriorating weather. The harvest began at the end of August, when grapes destined for sparkling wine were picked, but for most North Coast growers picking took place in late September and well into October. There was rain in Napa in late September, prompting some growers to panic and pick too early. Those with patience were rewarded with a fine October and excellent ripening. Small berries and the prolonged hangtime led to excellent grapes in Napa. In Sonoma prolonged fog and cool damp weather frustrated many growers, but again the patient were rewarded. At the time of writing, the quality of the vintage was uncertain, but growers were by no means in despair. The prolonged growing season and small crop might yet turn out to produce wines of great intensity. In Napa, some producers predicted a vintage of a quality comparable to 1993 or 1996. And, clearly, this will prove an excellent year for the Central Coast. Overall quantities are about 17 per cent down on 1997, but still more abundant than 1992–6.

APPENDIX 2

Brix, Baumé, and Alcohol

Californian grape growers measure sugar levels in terms of Brix, which is the term used throughout this book. However, other systems of measurement, such as the French Baumé or potential alcohol, may be more familiar to many readers, so a table of comparisons is presented below.

BRIX	BAUMÉ	POTENTIAL ALCOHOL
15.8	8.8	8.1
17.0	9.4	8.8
18.1	10.1	9.4
19.3	10.7	10.0
20.4	11.3	10.6
21.5	11.9	11.3
22.6	12.5	11.9
23.7	13.1	12.5
24.8	13.7	13.1
25.8	14.3	13.8
26.9	14.9	14.4
28.0	15.5	15.0
29.1	16.1	15.6
30.2	16.7	16.2
31.2	17.3	16.8
32.3	17.9	17.5
33.4	18.7	18.1
34.5	19.3	18.7

Bibliography

━━━━━

Adams, Leon D. *The Wines of America.* 3rd edition. London: Sidgwick & Jackson, 1984.

Asher, Gerald. *Vineyard Tales.* San Francisco: Chronicle Books, 1996.

Benson, Robert. *Great Winemakers of California.* Santa Barbara: Capra Press, 1977.

Berger, Dan, and Hinkle, Richard. *Beyond the Grapes: An Inside Look at Napa Valley.* Wilmington, Delaware: Atomium Books, 1991.

Ibid. *Beyond the Grapes: An Inside Look at Sonoma County.* Wilmington, Delaware: Atomium Books, 1991.

Broadbent, Michael. *The Great Vintage Wine Book.* London: Mitchell Beazley, 1980.

Brook, Stephen. *Liquid Gold: Dessert Wines of the World.* London: Constable, 1987.

Brook, Stephen. *Sauvignon Blanc and Sémillon.* London and New York: Viking, 1992.

Carosso, V. P. *The California Wine Industry 1830–1895.* Berkeley: University of California Press, 1951.

Clarke, Oz. *New Classic Wines.* London: Webster's/Mitchell Beazley, 1991.

Conaway, James. *Napa.* Boston: Houghton Mifflin, 1990.

De Groot, Roy Andries. *The Wine of California, the Pacific Northwest and New York.* New York: Summit, 1982.

De Villiers, Marq. *The Heartbreak Grape: A California Winemaker's Search for the Perfect Pinot Noir.* New York: HarperCollins West, 1994.

Halliday, James. *Wine Atlas of California.* New York: Viking, 1993.

Haraszthy, Agoston. *Grape Culture, Wines, and Wine-Making.* New York: Harper, 1862.

Johnson, Hugh. *The Story of Wine.* London: Mitchell Beazley, 1989.

Lapsley, James T. *Bottled Poetry: Napa Winemaking from Prohibition to the Modern Era.* Berkeley: University of California Press, 1996.

Laube, James. *California Wine.* New York: Wine Spectator Press, 1995.

BIBLIOGRAPHY

Mondavi, Robert. *Harvests of Joy*. New York: Harcourt Brace, 1998.

Muscatine, D., Thompson, B. and Amerine, M.A., eds. *Book of California Wine*. Berkeley, Ca.: University of California Press, 1984.

Parker, Robert. *The Wine Buyer's Guide*. 4th edition. London: Dorling Kindersley, 1996.

Pinney, Thomas. *A History of Wine in America*. 1989.

Robinson, Jancis. *Vines, Grapes and Wines*. London: Mitchell Beazley, 1986.

Roby, Norman S., and Charles E. Olken. *The New Connoisseurs' Handbook of California Wines*. 3rd edition. New York: Knopf, 1995.

Schoenman, Theodore. *Father of California Wine: Agoston Haraszthy*. Santa Barbara: Capra Press, 1979.

Sullivan, Charles L. *Companion to California Wine*. Berkely, Ca.: University of California Press, 1998

Sullivan, Charles L. *Napa Wine: A History from Mission Days to Present*. San Francisco: Wine Appreciation Guild, 1994.

Thompson, Bob. *The Wine Atlas of California*. London: Mitchell Beazley, 1993.

Wagner, Philip. *American Wines and Wine-Making*. New York: Knopf, 1956.

Index

Many entries have been grouped within categories. Some are very large, such as 'grape varieties' 'wine regions' or 'wineries'. Others, such as 'viticulture', 'vinification', or 'sweet wines' are considerably smaller. On some occasions it is not self-evident where an entry belongs. Thus Paul Draper of Ridge Vineyards is listed within 'winemaker', whereas Jan Shrem of Clos Pegase, being the proprietor and not the winemaker, is listed under his own name. Some difficult choices have been made; thus Michael Mondavi is listed under his name, his brother Tim under 'winemaker'.